A HISTORY
OF
THE GAMBIA

J. M. GRAY

Judge of the Supreme Court of the Gambia

A HISTORY

OF

THE GAMBIA

With a Foreword by

SIR THOMAS SOUTHORN

Governor of the Gambia

CAMBRIDGE
AT THE UNIVERSITY PRESS
1940

CAMBRIDGE
UNIVERSITY PRESS

University Printing House, Cambridge CB2 8BS, United Kingdom

Cambridge University Press is part of the University of Cambridge.

It furthers the University's mission by disseminating knowledge in the pursuit of education, learning and research at the highest international levels of excellence.

www.cambridge.org
Information on this title: www.cambridge.org/9781107511965

© Cambridge University Press 1940

First published 1940
First paperback edition 2015

A catalogue record for this publication is available from the British Library

ISBN 978-1-107-51196-5 Paperback

Foreword

The scholarly work of His Honour Mr Justice Gray fills a long-felt want in the history of the British connection with the West Coast of Africa. The river Gambia, with its fabulous hinterland of untold wealth, was a magnet which drew adventurers from Europe from the fifteenth century onwards. It was the first point of contact between England and West Africa and from the days of Queen Elizabeth there has been an almost unbroken link between the Gambia and the British Isles.

But until now there has been no authoritative work covering the whole period of the British connection, although, from a historical point of view, the Gambia possesses an interest far surpassing that of any other British settlement in West Africa. Those who wished to know something of the history of the Gambia had to fall back on the Official Handbook of Mr F. Bisset Archer published in 1905, on Mr H. E. Reeve's book The Gambia of 1912 and on Mr W. T. Hamlyn's Short History of the Gambia of 1931, together with such of the many references to the Gambia in books of travel as might happen to be available to them. Mr Bisset Archer's book is too much an official record of contemporary conditions with a historical introduction; Mr Reeve is chiefly concerned in describing the life and scenery of the great river; Mr Hamlyn's Short History is admittedly a school-book which compresses the history of two thousand years into fifty pages.

These three books are interesting and valuable so far as they go, but the authors had no knowledge of the mass of valuable material which lay hidden in the archives of the Public Record Office. These archives and every known reference to the Gambia in literature have been examined by Mr Justice Gray in his exhaustive search for an authoritative record of this oldest British settlement in West Africa. The result is a history which, in its earlier pages, records the romantic story of the struggles and difficulties of the merchant " Adventurers " and early settlers, with a wealth of interesting detail for which Mr Justice Gray quotes his authority with true legal accuracy. In its later pages Mr Justice Gray traces the gradual process of settlement whereby the internecine and *hitherto interminable tribal wars have been brought to an end and, for the first time in its long history, the territory has enjoyed within the last fifty years the blessings of peace.*

A true history such as Mr Justice Gray has set out to write cannot be written without exposing the faults as well as recording the virtues of the people whose actions are brought under review. There have been episodes in the history of European penetration in West Africa which no one would now condone and of these the slave trade reveals the darkest story. Many of these episodes are recorded by Mr Justice Gray but they must be viewed in their true historical perspective with due regard to the state of civilization and the standard of morals then existing. It can at least be put to the credit of the British Administration that the principal object in the foundation of Bathurst was the suppression of the slave trade. The gradual growth of humanism has now reached the stage when the highest ethical conduct is demanded of the individual and when British Colonial Administration devotes its whole endeavour to fulfil the high ideal of trusteeship for the indigenous populations.

We must not think too hardly of the pioneers. Frayed nerves are not unknown in the Tropics even to-day when medical science and inventive genius have done so much to ameliorate the hardships of tropical life. One can still visit James Island and see, in their restricted setting, the narrow confines of a small ruined fort; this fort was once the home for long periods of the soldiers and merchants who live again in Mr Justice Gray's pages and one can only marvel at the courage with which they endured conditions that we should now regard as intolerable.

The late Lord Reading once said that it is never good to look back save to learn a lesson for the future. There are lessons to be learned from the history of the Gambia, and those who look back for them in the pages of Mr Justice Gray's book will find them set out in a story of absorbing interest.

W. T. SOUTHORN

Bathurst
  Gambia
    26 April 1938

Preface

At the end of my labours I am fully conscious of the fact that a colonial official, whose occupation takes him many hundreds of miles from the nearest reference library, is hardly the right person to write a history of the oldest British possession in West Africa. My excuses are that nobody more competent than myself has ventured on the task and that I share with many of my brother officers a deep interest in the history of the country with which our lot has been cast. Realising that there must necessarily be many defects in a work such as this, I would offer the same apologia as did Francis Moore, an earlier writer on the Gambia.

It is the Business of every one, who gives a Book to the Publick, to make it as agreeable as he can to the Reader. For this Purpose Invention, Stile, Learning, and the Ornaments of Eloquence, are employed by those, who are the Masters of them, for setting off their Compositions. As I cannot pretend to any of those Accomplishments, and can value myself upon nothing but Truth, it is not the Manner of writing, but the Subject, that is to say, the Description of a Country, much talk'd of, and little known, which must please in the following relation...I have not attempted to embellish the Work, since I am persuaded that Readers... will rather chuse to read real Facts, told in the plainest way, than beautiful Works of Imagination.... If I had had the Conveniency of Books in Africa, they would have taught me to have made such Enquiries as would have enabled me to give a much better Account than I can now possibly do.

I cannot let this book go to the press without expressing my indebtedness to many people. I am under a great obligation to Mr F. McD. C. Turner of Magdalene College, Cambridge, for enabling me to consult the manuscripts of the Pepysian Library. I also owe a like debt to the officials of the British Museum, the Public Record Office, the Bodleian Library, and the Cambridge University Library. The Reverend G. S. Treleaven of the Methodist Mission in the Gambia has allowed me to consult the interesting local records of his Society. Mrs Treleaven has very kindly undertaken the labour of reading the proofs. I also owe a great debt to Sir Thomas Southorn, Governor of the Gambia, for reading the manuscript of the work, for his very helpful criticism, and, lastly but by no means least of all, for writing a foreword to this book. Finally, I am truly grateful to the Syndics of the Cambridge University Press and to the Government of the Gambia, whose generous grants have alone enabled me to produce this work.

J. M. G.

CAPE ST MARY
  BATHURST
    GAMBIA
      JANUARY 1939

Contents

ix

*Available for download from www.cambridge.org/9781107511965

I : Introduction

The history of the territory, which is now known as the Gambia Colony and Protectorate, has necessarily centred round the river from which that territory has acquired its name. Its climate and its geographical position have in all centuries had a considerable influence upon its history.

The River Gambia rises in the Futa Jallon plateau about twelve miles from the town of Labe in what is now French Guinea. From its source the river finds its way down the side of the plateau, following a general course a little west of north for about one hundred miles in a direct line, though the distance by the actual river is probably near two hundred miles. Very few tributaries feed the Upper Gambia. The last and most important is the Niokolokoba, which flows in from the east. After receiving the waters of the Niokolokoba the Gambia changes its general direction to the north-west for a distance of about seventy miles in a direct line. At the end of this distance the Neriko joins the main stream. The country between the Niokolokoba and Neriko is known as Tenda. In the higher reaches of the Gambia towns and villages are few and far between and a succession of shallow rapids and pools makes navigation in a boat of any size impossible. Though the Tenda country is by no means thickly populated to-day, there was a time when its towns stood upon the trade route from the interior of Africa and were flourishing markets.

Though there are one or two obstructions to navigation below Tenda, after it has been joined by the Neriko the Gambia is navigable for boats of shallow draught. After receiving the waters of the Neriko the river makes a sharp turn and follows a westerly course for about thirty miles. It then turns in a south-westerly direction for some thirty miles more. About sixty miles below its confluence with the Neriko it is joined by the Grey River and then takes a north-westerly course for another eighty miles to the so-called Barrakunda Falls. These falls are in reality a number of ledges of laterite rocks, which form a barrier extending from one bank to within about twenty feet of the other bank. They form a serious impediment to navigation but are very far from being a complete obstacle thereto. Vessels of five to six tons burden and drawing two to three feet can pass the barrier at high water at all seasons of the

year. When the river is in flood, vessels of deeper draught can do
likewise.

The Gambia becomes a tidal river after the Barrakunda Falls.
It meanders considerably in its course but its general direction may
be said to be due west. Its width just below the Falls is about
200 yards. So far the river has flowed through French territory.
Koina, about seven miles below the Barrakunda Falls, is the first
port in British territory. The banks at this point are high, standing
some twenty-five to thirty feet above water level in the dry season.
At some past period the water covered a much larger area of ground
and lapped the ironstone cliffs, which now stand back several miles
from the river. At various places spurs from these cliffs and an
occasional solitary outcrop of ironstone jut out into the valley and
the river has to make a circuit to get round them.

Some 100 miles below the Barrakunda Falls there is a somewhat
similar barrage known as Buruko rocks. It runs across the river nearly
at right angles to its course, but leaves a passage about thirty yards
wide with a channel deep enough to take a large vessel. It presents
no difficulties to steam vessels, but sailing vessels have some difficulty in beating through the passage when the wind and tide are
against them. This barrage serves to hold up the level of the river
above it and acts as a kind of natural sluice. One of the effects of
this natural lock is to increase the speed of the current and consequently to bring down large quantities of silt and sand, which have
formed a succession of islands in the lower reaches of the river. The
first of these islands is known to-day as MacCarthy Island, but its
earlier name was Lemain Island.

After MacCarthy Island the ironstone cliffs recede farther from
the river banks and passing Kai-ai and Baboon Islands the river
gradually becomes wider in the vicinity of Gassan. This in the days
of sail was reckoned the limit of navigation for ocean-going vessels,
as the narrowing of the river above this point hindered tacking
against the prevailing wind. With the advent of steam ocean-going
vessels of 1500 tons burden make their way up to MacCarthy
Island.

Leaving Gassan and the modern Kuntaur, which has replaced
Gassan as a port for ocean-going vessels, the river continues its
meandering course past a succession of islands, which are only just
high enough to remain uncovered at full tide and are more or less
waterlogged when the river is in flood. The last of these islands is

known as Elephant Island about 100 miles from the sea. Below this island the river is a mile wide and has a depth of some five fathoms and increases in width as it approaches the Atlantic Ocean. It is now clear of islands for the rest of its course with the exception of James Island, which lies twenty-five miles above the river mouth, Dog or Charles Island, which lies off the north bank and is eight miles lower down, and St Mary's Island or Banjol, which with a number of sandbanks serve to form a small delta on the south bank of the river about seven miles from its mouth. The actual mouth of the river may be said to lie between Cape St Mary on the south bank and Jinnak Creek twelve miles away on the opposite shore.

The Gambia enters the Atlantic Ocean in latitude 13° 30' north of the equator. The prevailing ocean winds are the north-east trades, which blow with varying degrees of force throughout the year. The Canary current flows immediately off the mouth of the river, whilst farther out to sea the north equatorial current drifts in a westerly direction towards the American continent. The combination of these winds and currents had at one time an important influence on the history of the regions of the Gambia. In the days before steam it made the voyage from the Atlantic coast of Europe to the river and from the river to the West Indies a comparatively easy matter, but the voyage in the reverse direction was more lengthy and a matter of some difficulty. Furthermore the prevalence of the doldrums to the south of the river made communication to the south with the Gulf of Guinea more difficult. The voyage in the reverse direction was further hampered by the fact that it had to be made against the Guinea current. Shipping and trade therefore naturally tended to find its way from Europe to the regions of the Gambia and thence to the West Indies and not to the Gulf of Guinea or the regions farther to the south. The so-called "neighbouring" coasts of West Africa were therefore in many respects far less in touch with the regions of the Gambia than Europe and the West Indies.

The annual rainfall of the Gambia regions is by no means heavy for the tropics, and it is confined to a period of about four months in the year. Past records suggest that the wet period of the year has been slightly different to what it is now, but at the present time the rain begins to fall as a general rule in June and is heaviest in July and August. There are lighter falls of rain in September and October. During the wet season communication by land becomes difficult. At the present time the period is marked by a lull in com-

mercial enterprise. In bygone years it marked a cessation of inter-
tribal warfare.

I propose to leave for a later chapter some account of the races
which at the present time are settled on the banks of the river, but
I shall not attempt to deal at any length with their past history,
traditions, beliefs and customs. In so doing I do not seek in any way
to belittle the interest or importance of these matters—and in particular the importance of tribal tradition, but the object of this book
is to describe the history and fortunes of the regions of the Gambia
since it first came in contact with modern European races. The subjects which I have mentioned are, however, to a large extent outside the scope of this book.[1] For the same reason I omit all reference
to the megalithic remains which are to be found on the north bank
of the river,[2] and shall not attempt to consider the extent to which
the regions of the Gambia were known before the Christian era to
Carthaginian voyagers or at the close of the Middle Ages to Arab
cartographers. The prehistory and the traditional tribal history of
the regions of the Gambia are undoubtedly fascinating subjects and
open a wide field for interesting research, but they do not impinge
to any large extent upon the modern history of those regions.

[1] A summary of the history of the Joloff and Mandingo tribes is to be found
in W. T. Hamlyn, *A Short History of the Gambia*, pp. 1–20.

[2] These remains are described and their origin discussed in *Bulletin d'Études
Historiques et Scientifiques de l'Afrique Occidentale Française*, (1918) No. 1,
p. 57, (1920) No. 3, p. 1, (1921) No. 3, p. 371, (1923) No. 4, p. 563, (1924) No. 1,
p. 31, (1925) p. 105; H. Parker, "Stone Circles in Gambia" (*J.R.A.I.* vol.
LIII, January–June, 1923); Duchemin, *Les Tumulus de la Gambie* (Mémoire de
la Société d'Anthropologie de Paris, 1906); Sir H. R. Palmer, *The Carthaginian
Voyage to West Africa*, pp. 50, 51.

II : The Portuguese in the Gambia, 1455–1588

The age of European discovery began in the early years of the fifteenth century, when Henry the Navigator, son of John I of Portugal and Philippa, daughter of our English John of Gaunt, started his observatory and school for navigators at Sagres. It was at his instigation and by his direct encouragement that Portuguese and other mariners made their way south in the Atlantic Ocean into regions hitherto unknown. Arab geographers and cartographers had previously obtained a certain amount of information regarding the reputed wealth of Africa, and Henry's thoughts were directed towards the discovery of these regions. Madeira was discovered in 1418. Cape Bojador was reached fifteen years later. In 1440 Cape Blanco was reached and six years later Nuno Tristão doubled Cape Verde ninety miles to the north of the mouth of the River Gambia.

Nuno got into touch with the inhabitants at Cape Verde and made a treaty of friendship and commerce with them. Thereafter ships were sent from Portugal every year to trade with them.[1] Nuno himself led an expedition in 1447 to explore the coast to the south of Cape Verde. He stood out to sea from that point and consequently failed to discover the mouth of the River Gambia. Eventually he reached the Rio Grande, which lies about ninety miles to the south of Cape St Mary. Whilst in that river his party was attacked by the natives and he himself was killed.

As a result of the trade between the inhabitants of Cape Verde and the Portuguese, information soon reached Henry the Navigator regarding the River Gambia. According to this report the country on the banks of the river yielded large quantities of gold, much of which found its way overland into Spain.[2] In 1455, therefore, Prince Henry induced a Venetian named Luiz de Cadamosto to undertake with a single ship of ninety tons burden an expedition in search of this river.[3] Later in the same year he despatched a Genoese named Antoniotto Usodimare with two ships on the same quest.[4] The two explorers joined forces near Cape Verde and, keeping close to the coast, had no difficulty in descrying the mouth of the Gambia. After

---

[1] *Navegações de Luiz de Cadamosto*, p. 27.   [2] *Ibid.* p. 49.
[3] *Ibid.* pp. 5–7.   [4] *Ibid.* p. 49.

having sent the smallest of their ships and armed boats to take soundings and to make a preliminary reconnaissance, the other two ships entered the river and proceeded up about four miles. They then met a number of native canoes. Each party was strongly suspicious of the other and eventually the natives attacked the three ships with arrows. The Europeans retaliated with cross bows and cannon shot and the canoes were driven off. Cadamosto and Usodimare proposed to proceed farther upstream in the hope of finding more friendly people, but their crews declared that they would proceed no farther. In the face of this opposition the leaders of the expedition decided to return home.[1]

Cadamosto and Usodimare were, however, not to be deterred from further discovery by either hostile inhabitants or mutinous crews. In 1456 they fitted out two ships to repeat the voyage. On hearing of their enterprise Prince Henry added another ship to the expedition. They reached the river's mouth in May of that year and were able to make their way without opposition some twenty miles upstream. On a Sunday they reached a small island lying in midstream, which Cadamosto describes as being shaped like a smoothing iron. Here one of the sailors, named Andrew, died of a fever. He was buried on the island with full Christian rites and his burial-place was named St Andrew's Island. Many another European was thereafter to be laid to rest on this island, round which the history of the Gambia was mainly to centre for some three centuries.[2]

Leaving St Andrew's Island, Cadamosto proceeded farther upstream. Some native canoes followed him and he managed to get into communication with them. The natives promised to take him to one of their principal chiefs, whom Cadamosto calls Battimansa and who, to judge from this name, was probably the Mandingo ruler of the district of Baddibu on the north bank of the river.[3] Battimansa lived some sixty miles up the river. He gave the Europeans a friendly reception and concluded a treaty of friendship with them. Presents were exchanged and a little trade done. European goods were bartered for a few slaves and a small quantity of gold, but the reputed wealth of the country did not fulfil expectations. During his stay with Battimansa Cadamosto was visited by another chief, who lived near the mouth of the river, who was called Guumimansa and was no doubt the ruler of the Niumi (Barra) district on the north

---

[1] *Navegações de Luiz de Cadamosto*, pp. 48–58.   [2] *Ibid.* pp. 59–62.
[3] "Mansa" in Mandingo means "chief".

bank of the river. After spending eleven days with Battimansa the ships weighed anchor and, returning down stream without incident, made their way to the River Casamance and thence back to Europe.[1]

In 1458 Prince Henry fitted out another expedition of three caravels and placed Diogo Gomez in command. These three vessels proceeded in the first instance past the mouth of the Gambia to the Rio Grande, where they encountered such strong ocean currents that Gomez was forced to put back at the entreaty of his officers and men. On the return voyage they made the mouth of the Gambia and decided to explore the river. Wind and tide being favourable, they anchored the first night off the island where was the freshly dug grave of Cadamosto's sailor Andrew. On the following day they rounded Sikka Point, and got into communication with a chief on the north bank named Frangazick, who gave them a friendly reception and bartered 180 pounds of gold dust for some European goods. Gomez found there a negro, named Buckor, who offered to take him to Kantora. Leaving one caravel at Nomimansa,[2] Gomez proceeded with the two other vessels fifty leagues up the river to a place called Ollimansa.[3] One of the caravels remained here whilst the other went on to Kantora, which Gomez described as a large town on the river bank. The Portuguese found a Moorish trader at this place and also received from the inhabitants very circumstantial accounts of the fabulous gold mines in the interior. The thick growth of trees on either bank of the river made further navigation in the caravel impossible and, as his crew were worn out by the heat, Gomez decided to return.

On his way down the river Gomez got into communication with Battimansa, who promised a safe conduct to all Europeans who passed through his country, and also gave Gomez three slaves in exchange for some wine, biscuits, and other presents. It was decided to test the sincerity of Battimansa's protestations of friendship by landing an Indian interpreter named Jacob with instructions to explore and report on the Joloff country. Jacob was able to carry on his mission unmolested and in due course returned to the

[1] *Navegações de Luiz de Cadamosto*, pp. 63–68.

[2] Apparently Niumi-mansa and the same district as Cadamosto's Guumi-mansa.

[3] Probably the modern district of Wuli. The mileages given in the early accounts of exploration are never very reliable.

ship with a present of ivory and four slaves from the principal chief.[1]

Gomez also got into touch with Nomimansa. His conversation with this chief appears to have been very largely upon religious topics. A Mohammedan priest was living with the chief and Gomez entered into a theological disputation with him. According to Gomez his opponent was so worsted in the argument that the chief peremptorily ordered him to leave the country within three days. Nomimansa and his leading men professed their great desire to become Christians and begged Gomez to baptise them forthwith. As he was a layman and as he did not carry a chaplain on board any of his ships, Gomez declined to perform the rite, but promised that he would on his return to Portugal endeavour to persuade Prince Henry to send out a priest. A few days later he sailed from the Gambia amidst many protestations of friendship.[2]

After some little delay Prince Henry sent out the Abbot of Soto de Cassa and a young man of his household, named John Delgado, to instruct Nomimansa in the Christian faith. History is silent as to the results of this missionary enterprise, but it is just possible that these two missionaries built the Portuguese church at Juffure, which was known as San Domingo and was situated on the north bank of the river opposite to St Andrew's Island.[3] Subsequent history suggests, however, that in the interval between the departure of Gomez and the arrival of the abbot the enthusiasm of Nomimansa and his people had waned. Certain it is that neither at this nor at any later date did Portuguese missionaries make any large number of converts.

Gomez himself returned to West Africa after Prince Henry's death in 1460, but did not proceed any farther south than the Joloff

[1] The printed accounts of both Cadamosto and Gomez say Battimansa lived on the south bank of the river. If this statement is correct, the conjecture that this chief ruled the district of Baddibu on the northern bank must be wrong. But there is reason to believe that both these writers have been incorrectly transcribed by the printers of their narratives. The Joloff country lay to the north of the River Gambia and Gomez was not likely to have landed Jacob on the south bank of the river, if he desired him to explore territory on the opposite shore. This fact suggests that the etymological conjecture that Battimansa ruled over Baddibu is correct. In Mandingo the termination "bu" denotes "country".

[2] R. H. Major, *The Life of Prince Henry of Portugal*, pp. 289–295.

[3] Major, *op. cit.* p. 296; Francis Moore, *Travels into the Inland Parts of Africa*, pp. 51, 55.

country in the region of Cape Verde. He learnt, however, that since his visit a number of Andalusian vessels had entered the Gambia and carried on a more or less successful trade. One of these adventurers was a Spaniard known as De Prado, who appears to have been an unprincipled person and to have supplemented more or less legitimate forms of commerce by selling arms to the Moors for use against the Portuguese. Gomez caused his ship to be intercepted off Cape Verde and carried De Prado a prisoner to Portugal, where he was burnt as a heretic.[1]

In 1475 three Spanish caravels entered the Gambia and kidnapped a local "king" and over one hundred of his subjects. The king was subsequently released by order of Ferdinand V, but the rest of the captives were detained and sold as slaves in Andalusia.[2] In 1484 Diogo Caõ took charge of an expedition, which eventually reached the Congo. On its way this expedition arrived off the mouth of the Gambia, but does not appear to have entered the river. All that Diogo Caõ's cartographer, Martin von Behaim, had to record regarding the visit was that they "came to the kingdom of Gambia, where the malaguetta (pepper) grows",[3] but this one brief sentence conveys a great deal. The Gambia was no longer a country of gold, ivory, and other precious things. Other explorers had by this time found these commodities in greater abundance on the Gold Coast and other lands, where they were also more easily obtainable. More alluring lands had drawn attention away from the Gambia and there was no great colonising or commercial activity in the river. None the less, the stories of the reputed wealth of the countries at the headwaters of the river were not entirely forgotten in Lisbon.

John II, who succeeded to the Portuguese throne in 1481, took an active interest in this part of Africa. The year after his succession he gave orders for the completion of a fort at Arguin, which lay just to the south of Cape Blanco and had been begun by Alfonso V in 1455. With Arguin as a base the Portuguese endeavoured to extend their influence in the countries to the south. A dispute as to the succession to the Joloff throne gave them the opportunity to try to gain a footing in the regions of the River Senegal. Gonçalo Coelho was sent to assist a certain Bemoi, whose claim to the throne was disputed by his brother Sibetah. One of the terms, upon which this aid was granted, was that Bemoi should embrace Christianity. As

---

[1] Blake, *European Beginnings in West Africa*, pp. 18, 23, 24, 38.
[2] Blake, *op. cit.* p. 44.   [3] Major, *op. cit.* p. 330.

he was reluctant to take this step, Coelho withdrew his men. Bemoi then changed his mind and in 1487 arrived in Lisbon to announce his strong desire to accept the faith of his allies. He was accordingly baptised in the name of John and did homage to the King of Portugal for all the lands he possessed. He was then sent back to the Senegal with twenty ships under the command of Pedro Vaz da Cunha. The Portuguese erected a fort at the mouth of the river, but in a short time dissensions arose between them and their ally. Bemoi was murdered at the instigation of da Cunha and the Portuguese returned to their own country. None the less, this expedition led to further communication with the rulers of the adjacent territories. Embassies were sent to Timbuktu and to African chiefs in the interior. In 1491 Rodrigo Rebello and seven others were sent to Mandimansa, the Mandingo ruler of Kantora. Friendly relations were established with this chief and thereafter Portuguese ships did a certain amount of trade in gold with Kantora.[1]

Following upon the opening up of this intercourse a number of Portuguese settled on the banks of the River Gambia and missionaries endeavoured to plant the Christian faith in these regions. In 1520 a proposal was mooted to blow up the rocks at the Barrakunda Falls so as to make the upper reaches of the river navigable, but the project came to nothing.[2] Portuguese historians have, however, very little to record regarding the activities of either missionaries or other pioneers. In accordance with its policy in other parts of the Portuguese empire, the government let out the monopoly of trade in Africa to farmers. In about 1466 the inhabitants of the Cape Verde Islands were granted the privilege to trade between Senegal and Sierra Leone. This strip of the coast came to be known as Guinea of Cape Verde and was for long virtually a dependency of the islands.[3] In 1588 private adventurers were reported to "have a place limited how farre they must go to trade within the river of Gambra; and farther they may not go upon paine of confiscation of their goods, and losse of life; for that the renters themselves send at certaine times their owne barks within the river to such places, where they have great store of golde".[4]

---

[1] De Barros, *Decadas na India*, I, Book III, Chapters 8–12; P. Chagas, *Os Portuguezes na Africa*, I, 46 seq.

[2] Marmol, *Afrique*, III, 74.

[3] Blake, *op. cit.* pp. 6, 31–33.

[4] Hakluyt, *The Principall Navigations of the English Nation*, IV, 52.

The reputed mineral wealth of the river proved, however, to be greatly exaggerated. Some gold was exported as well as hides and ivory, but the principal trade of the river appears to have been slaves, who were purchased for five crusados apiece and exported to the Spanish West Indies.[1] But the more easily available resources of the Gulf of Guinea proved a greater attraction to traders and settlers than those of the fever-ridden banks of the Gambia, where the trade largely depended upon the goodwill and the sufferance of native chiefs, who acted as middlemen. Those settlers, who survived the rigours of the climate, married into the local tribes and the pure European blood rapidly became diluted.

Except in Angola and the regions of the Rio Grande, Portuguese missionaries were not able to achieve much in West Africa despite the labours of a number of men imbued with a real enthusiasm for and devotion to their labours. Portuguese writers have nothing to say of even transient successes in the Gambia. When Cadamosto arrived in the river, he found that there were a number of Mahommedan traders in Battimansa's country, who were slowly but surely planting the seeds of their faith[2] and Christian missionaries found it hard to fight against the rising tide of Islam. None the less, though converts were few and probably very nominal in the profession of their newly acquired faith, the Church did not entirely neglect those Portuguese who settled on the river banks or their descendants. Churches were built in several places. One, which was built on the north bank of the river opposite to St Andrew's Island, was given the name of San Domingo. Another was built a little farther up the river on the opposite bank at Tankular. A third was built some twenty miles up the Bintang Creek close to the modern village of Kansala. The village, which clustered round this church, acquired the name of Geregia, which was a corruption of the Portuguese word "igereja" meaning "church". They were served from time to time by visiting priests from the Cape Verde Islands.[3]

---

[1] Hakluyt, op. cit. IV, 52; Alvares d'Almada, Tratado breve dos Rios de Guiné do Cabo-Verde, p. 36.

[2] Navegações de Luiz de Cadamosto, p. 65.

[3] Moore, op. cit. v, pp. 51, 55; Father Jean Labat states there was also a church at Bintang, but there are reasons for doubting the accuracy of his information, cf. P. Cultru, Le Premier Voyage du Sieur de la Courbe, p. vii seq. Bintang Creek itself was also known as the River Sangrugo, which may be a corruption of the Portuguese San Gregorio. An establishment of twelve friars was maintained in the Cape Verde Islands at the expense of the Queen of

Each of these churches betokened the presence in its vicinity of a population of Portuguese origin. As late as the beginning of the eighteenth century there were more or less substantial houses at Bintang, Geregia and Joar (near Kau-ur) which were built in imitation of the Portuguese style of architecture.[1] At the latter end of the seventeenth century there was still a village near Dog Island Point, which the local inhabitants called "Povoaçao de Brancos", or "the town of the white men".[2] In the early seventeenth century there was a Portuguese settlement over 100 miles up the river at Gassan and another near Kau-ur, which is called on a contemporary map "Casa Diego Gratie". Portuguese traders also used to go at certain seasons of the year to Setuko, which lies a few miles below the Barrakunda Falls, to purchase gold and other commodities from the interior.[3] The inhabitants of these towns affected European dress and spoke a language "called Creole Portuguese, a bastard sort of Portuguese, scarce understood in Lisbon".[4] They were for the most part the descendants of settlers from Portugal, who had married or cohabited with the women of the local tribes. In the early seventeenth century an English traveller described them as follows:

They call themselves Portingales, and some few seeme the same; others of them are Molatoes, betweene black and white, but the most parte as blacke as the naturall inhabitants: they are scattered, some two or three dwellers in a place, and are all married, or rather keepe with them the countrey blackewomen, of whome they beget children, howbeit they have amongst them neither Church nor Friar, nor any other religious order. It doth manifestly appeare that they are suche as have beene banished or fled away from either of Portingall or the isles belonging unto that government. They doe generally imploy themselves in

Portugal to supply missionaries for the adjacent coast of Africa. This establishment was still maintained in the eighteenth century, when "as they diminished, the remaining received the allowance for the twelve, till they were detected, and a reduction made in their pensions, as their numbers decreased", *Report on Slave Trade*, Part vi, p. 2.

[1] Cultru, *op. cit.* p. 202; Moore, *op. cit.* pp. 52, 74, 106.

[2] Barbot, *Description of the Coasts of North and South Guinea*, p. 25. This village is apparently to be identified with that marked on a map in the archives at Mitau as "Tuab Colon" and on modern maps as "Tubab Kolon", *sc.* "white man's well".

[3] Hakluyt, *op. cit.* v, 51; Douilly, "La Rivière Gambia et la Ville de Cassan en Afrique", Add. MS. 16,731 n.; Jobson, *The Golden Trade*, pp. 36, 38, 55.

[4] Moore, *op. cit.* p. 39; Cultru, *op. cit.* p. 192.

buying such commodities the countrey affords, wherein especially they covet the country people, who . . . are bought away by their own nation, and by them either carried or solde unto the Spaniard, for him to carry either into the West Indies to remaine as slaves, either in their Mines, or in any other servile uses they in those countries put them to. . . .

The conditions they live subject unto, under the blacke kings, makes it appeare they have little comfort in a Christian countrey, or else they themselves are very carelesse what becometh of their posteritie; for whensoever the husband, father or maister of the familie dies, if hee be of any worth, the king seizeth upon what hee hath, without respect either to wife, children, or servant, except they have warning to provide before, or are capable of themselves, to looke out for the future time; whereby we find in some those few places we trade with them poore distressed children left, who, as it were exposed to the charitie of the country, become in a manner naturalized, and as they grow up, apply themselves to sell one thing for another as the whole country doth, still reserving carefully the use of the Portingall tongue and, with a kinde of affectionate zeale, the name of Christians, taking in great disdaine, be they never so blacke, to be called a Negro.[1]

A Spaniard, who was living at Geregia in 1686, alleged that most of the original Portuguese settlers were the descendants of Jews, who had either been banished from Portugal or fled to these remote regions to avoid the attentions of the Inquisition and that they took no notice of his proposal to procure the services of a priest for themselves.[2] An earlier visitor said they were " banished men or fugitives, for committing most heinous and incestuous acts, their life and conversation being agreeable; and they are of the basest behaviour that ever we have seene of these nations in any other countrye ".[3] Whatever their origin, their descendants for many years made pathetic attempts to preserve their nationality. They affected European dress and carried swords and muskets.[4] An occasional priest from

[1] Jobson, *op. cit.* pp. 35–37.
[2] Cultru, *op. cit.* p. 208; Labat, *Nouvelle Relation de l'Afrique Occidentale,* v, 22.
[3] Hakluyt, *op. cit.* IV, 52.
[4] Cultru, *op. cit.* p. 193. Individual Portuguese emigrants continued to settle in the Gambia up to the end of the seventeenth century. For instance, when writing on 8 March 1704–1705 to the Royal African Company, Antonio Deagujar said "I am besides a native of Portugall, and married here before the Governor Cleeve, and have been concerned with the Company these twenty yeares", P.R.O., T. 70/52.

Portugal, or the Cape Verde Islands, or the convent at Cachau on the Rio Grande brought them once more into touch with Europe and Christianity.[1] But visiting priests and new settlers eventually became rare. Her conquests in Brazil and Asia drained Portugal of her man power and she had too many other commitments to be able to colonise effectively the unhealthy banks of a tropical river, which yielded but little wealth in comparison with the riches of America and the East Indies. Portuguese blood in the Gambia soon became greatly diluted by that of the surrounding African races. The descendants of the settlers clung to their chaplets of beads, but in course of time a French traveller found that "the greater part of them said neither prayers nor the sala, and some of them say both; for, when they are with the negroes, they say the sala, and when they are with white men, they take their beads and do as they do".[2] In 1635 a French Capuchin, who visited Rufisque near Cape Verde, reported that no priest had celebrated mass between the Rivers Gambia and Senegal for the past eight years.[3] The weakest went to the wall and were enslaved by the local chiefs.[4] The stronger and more capable managed to preserve their liberty and even to acquire some local influence in the country by marrying into the families of the ruling chiefs and raising up large families of children and slaves.[5] But even this patriarchal influence ceased as years went by. A French visitor commented on their debauchery and improvidence.[6] Later

[1] Wilkinson, *Systema Africanum*, p. 4. In 1678 the British Ambassador at Lisbon perused some letters, "which are basely writ by a simple friar that went from hence to Gambia and thence by land to a place called Cacheu on the River Santo Domingo", Sir Robert Southwell to Sir William Bridgeman, 5 November 1678, *C.S.P. Domestic*, 1678, p. 505. Father Palmyra from the convent at Cachau was entertained at James Island in May 1733, Accounts of Fort James, P.R.O., T. 70/1451. Another "Portuguese Padre" received a present in 1735, *ibid.* P.R.O., T. 70/1452. In 1736 the "King" of Geregia seized another Portuguese priest as a prisoner and the Royal African Company sent a present to procure his release, *ibid.* P.R.O., T. 70/1452.

[2] Cultru, *op. cit.* pp. 192, 193.

[3] Saint Lo, *Relation du Voyage au Cap-Vert*, 1637.

[4] The accounts of Fort James include a payment in 1733 to "Diogo Gomez of Essew, the late king of Barrah's head slave" and to Antonio Gomez, a castle slave, to buy medicine, P.R.O., T. 70/1451.

[5] Moore, *op. cit.* p. 94, refers to "Tomba Mendez, son to the late King of Barsally by a Portuguese woman". Antonio Vos, "a noted black Portuguese", whose household is described on p. 49 of the same work, was related to the ruling chief of Foni. Minutes of the Council of James Fort, 22 October 1722, Rawlinson MS. C. 747.   [6] Cultru, *op. cit.* p. 193.

generations lost their wealth and with it their prestige. Their children either emigrated to the banks of the Rio Grande or, definitely throwing in their lot with the peoples of the neighbouring tribes, ceased to make any pretensions whatever to European nationality. Though as late as 1786 there was still a so-called Portuguese settlement at Bintang,[1] the Portuguese, black and white, disappeared during the course of the tribal warfare in the latter part of the eighteenth century and ceased to exist in the Gambia as a separate race.

The hold of the Portuguese on the Gambia was slender at any time. As subsequent pages will show, it required very little effort on the part of later European arrivals to supplant them in the river. But despite the feebleness of their authority they left their mark on the Gambia. Perhaps the most noticeable relic of their bygone supremacy is to be found in a number of words, which have crept into the Mandingo language and that curious jargon known as trade or pidgin English. But their enterprise conferred other more lasting benefits on the country. The coast native learnt a great deal of boat craft and seamanship from a race which once provided the leading navigators of the world. The inhabitants also acquired a number of weapons and domestic instruments from them. Though, like the Dutch, French, and English after them, they exploited the overseas traffic in slaves, the verdict of history must be that the Portuguese conferred some lasting advantages on the country. They imported many useful economic crops into the land, including the orange, the lime, and the papaw from Brazil. Lastly and by no means least, it is to them that the Gambia owes the first introduction of what at the present day is its most staple product and its principal source of revenue, namely, the groundnut.

[1] Durand, *Voyage au Sénégal*, p. 86.

III: The arrival of the English in the Gambia, 1588–1622

It was more or less inevitable that in course of time other European nations should follow the Portuguese into the regions which they had first discovered. It was equally inevitable that the first comers should resent the intrusion of these later arrivals. The papal division in 1493 of the newly discovered world between Spain and Portugal relieved the latter country for the time being of any anxiety from her most formidable rival. But other countries were becoming rising maritime powers and they were not likely to accept without demur a partition of the world in which they obtained no share. Fortunately for Portugal political considerations, which need not be discussed here, induced for a time both France and England to refrain from contesting Portuguese claims in West Africa. In the late fifteenth and early sixteenth centuries the rulers of both these countries definitely forbade their subjects to trade in these regions. In 1483, for instance, Edward IV of England stopped two English merchants from sailing for Guinea.[1] As late as 1562 two English ships, which were equipped under royal patronage for a voyage to the coast of Africa, were directed to confine their venture to places where the King of Portugal "hath not presentlie dominion, obedience, and tribute".[2] French kings were somewhat more slow to interdict their subjects. Though French claims to the discovery of the Guinea coast in the fourteenth century must be dismissed for lack of necessary evidence in support, French sailors had got as far as the Cape Verde Islands in 1483 and French corsairs captured Portuguese shipping off the Azores in 1492. But in 1529, at the Peace of Cambrai, Francis I promised to prevent his subjects from sailing to Guinea and for a year or two the Admiral of France was active in stopping Norman ships from sailing to those parts.[3]

But this attitude was destined to change in the course of a few years. In 1541 and 1559 French ships were once more bound for Cape Verde, Sierra Leone, and the Guinea coast.[4] In 1553 a Portu-

[1] Hakluyt, *The Principall Navigations of the English Nation*, IV, 21.
[2] *C.S.P. Domestic, 1547–1580*, XXVI, 44.
[3] Cultru, *Le Premier Voyage du Sieur de la Courbe*, pp. x, xi.
[4] *Ibid.* pp. xi *seq.*

guese refugee piloted two English ships to the River Sestos. During the next few years both nations were actively engaged in trading ventures to the west coast of Africa. French vessels visited the River Senegal and Cape Verde as well as the Guinea coast, but the English confined their attentions to the last mentioned regions. By 1560 the merchants of Dieppe had established regular communication with Senegal and Cape Verde.[1] Both nations tried to trade in a peaceable way, endeavouring to give the natives of Africa a fairer treatment than they received at the hands of the Portuguese and, being traders, tried to avoid disputes with anybody, white or black. None the less peaceful penetration was not always possible. The Portuguese were determined to exclude the newcomers at all costs and more than once shots were exchanged off the Gold Coast between the Portuguese and English and French interlopers. When the first French trading vessel ventured in about 1570 into the River Gambia, two Portuguese vessels swooped down upon it and drove it away with a loss of thirty of the crew.[2]

As long as Portugal had the sea power, foreign interlopers had a difficult time. But as the sixteenth century drew to its close, affairs both at home and abroad took a disastrous turn. The climax was reached in 1578 when the country suffered an overwhelming calamity in the defeat and death of their king Sebastian in Morocco. Sebastian was succeeded by his uncle, the insane Cardinal Henry, who reigned for only two years. After his death there was no legitimate member of the house of Aviz to fill the throne. Philip II of Spain took advantage of a claim through the female line and the confusion and disaffection following the death of the Cardinal to march with an armed force into the country and have himself crowned king. For the next sixty years Portugal remained under the sway of Spain and thus became involved in her wars with England, France, the Netherlands and Germany. One of Philip II's rival claimants to the throne of Portugal was Antonio, Prior of Crato, who was the illegitimate son of one of the last princes of the Portuguese royal family. He made a bid for the throne as the nationalist claimant, but few people of influence championed his claims. Supported only by the peasantry, he was easily defeated by the Spanish and fled to France and thence to England. He carried the crown jewels with him to England and these soon found their way into Elizabeth's treasury

[1] Hakluyt, *op. cit.* IV, 39 *seq.*, V, 45.
[2] Blake, *European Beginnings in West Africa*, p. 182.

in exchange for a half-hearted promise of support from the English government. Whilst she was only too willing to take any indirect measures, which might impair the strength of Spain, Elizabeth was not yet prepared to commit herself definitely to open war with Philip II. Antonio's cause was therefore alternately supported and dropped according as it suited English policy. Such support as was given was insufficient to set him on the throne and in a few years' time he found himself heavily in debt in the land of his exile.

In order to raise funds for himself and his cause and to liquidate his debts, Antonio took to granting trading concessions in the overseas dominions, which he claimed. In 1587 a Portuguese refugee, named Francisco Ferreira, piloted two English ships to the Gambia. They returned in 1588 with a good cargo of hides and ivory.[1] After this in consideration of a payment of £400 and a promise to pay 5 per cent on all merchandise which they brought back, and a fourth share in all prizes which they might capture, Antonio granted to Antony Dassell, a Barbary merchant, and certain other merchants of London, Exeter, Barnstaple and Colyton the exclusive right to trade between England and the Rivers Senegal and Gambia. As Antonio was in debt to the tune of £4000, he assigned his share of the profits to Roderigo Lopez, physician to Queen Elizabeth. The Privy Council directed that the grantees should pay Lopez only and instructed Lopez to do his utmost to recover all moneys due from them and to pay the same over to Antonio's creditors. On 3 May 1588 Queen Elizabeth by letters patent confirmed Antonio's grant to the English merchants for the space of ten years, at the same time forbidding any others of her subjects to trade to those parts except the grantees.[2]

Following upon this contract the merchants fitted out three ships to go to the River Gambia.[3] Other expeditions were fitted out in succeeding years, but none of the ships actually reached the Gambia. They confined their activities to Rufisque, Portudal and Joal, ports lying between Cape Verde and the Gambia. In all these places they encountered considerable hostility from the local Portuguese, who

[1] Advices from London, 11 March 1588, *C.S.P. Spanish*, 1587–1603, p. 229; Hakluyt, *op. cit.* IV, 286.

[2] *Acts of the Privy Council*, 1588–1589, pp. 264, 265; *C.S.P. Spanish*, 1587–1603, p. 355; *C.S.P. Domestic*, 1598–1601, p. 16; Hakluyt, *op. cit.* IV, 285.

[3] Antonio de Vega to Philip II, 29 July 1588, *C.S.P. Spanish*, 1587–1603, p. 355.

would have none of Antonio's infringement of their monopoly. Furthermore, the Portuguese servants of Antonio, who accompanied these ventures, were guilty of double dealing and of spreading false reports amongst the natives regarding the English. As a result forty of the English were massacred at Portudal and Joal in 1589. Hearing of the fate of the French vessel, which had ventured into the Gambia, the English left the river alone, returning home to report that it was "a river of secret trade and riches concealed by the Portugals".[1]

The adventurers found, however, that they had to contend not only with active Portuguese hostility and native suspicion fostered by Portuguese propaganda but also with French commercial rivalry. In 1594 Alvares d'Almada complained that French and English competition was ruining the trade of the river and causing serious unrest amongst the natives,[2] but, whilst Portuguese trade declined, it is evident that English trade did not make any corresponding increase. The adventurers did not follow up their earlier enterprises with any great vigour and did not make any serious attempt to obtain a renewal of their letters patent, when the period of ten years expired. In January, 1598, the exclusive right to trade to the River Gambia was granted by Elizabeth to Charles, Earl of Nottingham, and Sir John Stanhope, Treasurer of the Chamber.[3] A year before this grant Bacon in his essay *On Plantations* had recommended that those to whom ventures such as this should be entrusted should "be rather noblemen and gentlemen, than merchants; for they look ever to the present gain". But the history of this new grant hardly supported this view. Elizabethan noblemen proved just as chary as Elizabethan merchants of hazarding their money in speculative trading voyages. There are fewer records of the activities of the new grantees than there are of those of their predecessors. English ships traded at Joal,[4] but there is no record of any of their vessels having entered the River Gambia. At the beginning of the seventeenth century Portuguese opposition had become less openly aggressive, but English traders found themselves confronted by other commercial rivals besides the French and Portuguese. The Netherlands had shaken off the yoke of Spain, and Dutch merchants were

---

[1] Hakluyt, *op. cit.* IV, pp. 44–53.
[2] Alvares d'Almada, *Tratado breve dos Rios de Guiné*, p. 36.
[3] *C.S.P. Domestic*, 1598–1601, p. 16.
[4] Astley, *A New General Collection of Voyages and Travels*, II, 247.

beginning to come to the African coast. Their example was followed by North German traders from the Baltic ports.

Though the holders of Elizabeth's second letters patent took no interest in the River Gambia, the merchants of Rouen believed that it had great possibilities both as a settlement and as a port of call for French ships on the way to the East Indies. Accordingly in 1612 the Chevalier de Briqueville was sent to the Gambia with a number of ships to erect a fort on the river banks and to establish a colony. Though the expedition was thoroughly well equipped, it came to nothing. Briqueville reached the Gambia during the rainy season. A large number of his people succumbed to sickness and the survivors returned to France.[1]

Though at this date European seamen bent on legitimate trade did not flourish, other seamen with a more questionable occupation appear to have found the Gambia a very useful base for their operations. At the close of the Spanish wars a large number of adventurers took to piracy. In 1617 there were some twenty-two ships commanded by English, French, Dutch, and other captains roaming the Atlantic Ocean and preying upon commerce. The River Gambia formed an ideal base for their operations. One of their number was a Frenchman of noble birth, Jean, Vicomte de Lormes. In 1617 he approached the French Government on behalf of his companions, who desired to take service under a Catholic ruler. The King of France was prepared to listen to this proposal and de Lormes returned to Africa to get in touch with his fellow-rovers. After he had arrived in the Gambia, the crew of his ship mutinied and put him ashore. He was subsequently picked up by another ship of his squadron and returned to France, where he subsequently found the chief mutineer and killed him.[2]

In 1619 English interest in West Africa was revived by the grant of a patent by James I to a number of persons for the exclusive right of trade to Guinea and Binney (Benin). One of the servants of these patentees subsequently classified them as "gentlemen" and "merchants", but not a few of those of knightly rank were gentlemen, who had at one time or other dabbled in trade. Sir William St John was the first named of the patentees and was given the title of

[1] *Mémoire du Voyage aux Indes Orientales du Général Beaulieu* in Thevenot's *Collection de Voyages*, p. 128.

[2] Cristofforo Surian to Doge of Venice, 16 June 1620, *C.S.P. Venetian*, 1619–1621, p. 281.

Governor of Guinea and Binney. Sir Thomas Button had seen service at sea both in the Atlantic and in the Mediterranean. So had Sir Ferdinando Gorges, who was also destined to take an active part in the colonisation of America. Sir Giles Mompesson was a member of parliament who had closely associated himself with a number of commercial undertakings in England. Others, like Sir Allen Apsley, were no doubt ruined gamesters, who hoped to retrieve their fortunes by the discovery of an Eldorado, but the great majority of the thirty-two patentees were shrewd men of business, whose past records inspired confidence in the undertaking.[1]

One of the first steps taken by the new patentees was to equip a ship for a trading voyage to the River Gambia. The vessel was the *Catherine* of 120 tons, Samuel Lambert, master. She was supplied with a cargo to the value of £1856. 19s. 2d. George Thompson, who had lived for many years in Morocco, was sent out as supercargo. The ship sailed in September 1618, one month after the granting of the patent. It reached the River Gambia without any untoward incident and sailed upstream as far as Gassan. Thompson left the *Catherine* there and proceeded farther upstream in some shallops with a few men. During his absence a number of Portuguese and half castes, at the instigation of a certain Hector Nunez, surprised the ship whilst many of the men were on shore and the few left on board were sick. All the Englishmen at Gassan were murdered. In ignorance of this disaster Thompson sent back some of his party. On their arrival at Gassan they were befriended by the local natives, who had taken no part in the massacre and had gone so far as to expel the perpetrators from the district. With their assistance and under their guidance and safe conduct this party made its way to Cape Verde, whence a French ship carried them to Europe.[2]

When the party reached England, they brought such promising reports from Thompson that, undeterred by the disaster to the *Catherine*, the Guinea Company equipped a pinnace of fifty tons called the *St John* (Thomas Cope, master) and supplied her with a cargo up to the value of £876. 2s. for a voyage to the Gambia. The ship arrived during the rainy season and a number of her crew succumbed to the climate. A small quantity of hides were obtained in

---

[1] *Commons' Journals*, i, 710, 794.

[2] Jobson, *The Golden Trade*, pp. 5, 6, 38, 39, 55; "Account of three several voyages sett forth for the River Gambra", P.R.O., S.P. 1/124, f. 115; Purchas, *His Pilgrimes*, ii, Part vii, p. 922.

exchange for the goods brought out from England, but it was found impossible to obtain any of the gold, ivory, or other valuable commodities, in which the country was said to abound. Thompson none the less was still full of optimism. He believed that if he proceeded far enough up river, he would discover either goldfields or else the markets to which the gold from the interior was brought. He therefore decided to remain behind with seven other men so as to explore the upper reaches of the river. He sent the *St John* back with a request to his employers to send a ship and a pinnace out the following year with a cargo of goods, which he believed would prove useful for the purchase of the commodities which he hoped to discover.[1]

After the departure of the *St John*, Thompson and his seven companions proceeded up the river. He proceeded as far as the Barrakunda Falls, where he got into friendly relations with the local chief, whom he called Ferambra. This chief in fact proved so firm a friend that, when the chief of Nyani, at the instigation of the Portuguese, sent a body of men to attack the English, he mustered all his subjects in their defence and conveyed them to the other side of the river for their better safety. The English established themselves at a place called Oranto on the north bank. As a result of their sojourn there the place acquired the name of Tobabkunda (dwelling-place of the Europeans). After some stay Thompson took a boat with a pair of oars and proceeded with only two of his company above the Falls to within a few miles of Tenda, which place he reached by proceeding overland. He had been informed that he was likely to meet an African merchant named Buckor Sano there and with his assistance to get in touch with the trade of the interior. On his arrival, however, he found that Buckor Sano was away on a journey. Thompson apparently wanted to press on, but his companions opposed him. A violent quarrel arose, which ended in a tragedy. Finding that Thompson was growing "more peremptory than he was wont, and seeming to govern with more contempt", one of his companions killed him. His murder was doubly disastrous. Not only was the party deprived of their leader, but Thompson had committed none of his discoveries or his information to paper. Consequently all the fruits of the expedition were lost.[2] The two survivors

---

[1] Jobson, *op. cit.* pp. 7, 162, 163; "Account of three several voyages sett forth for the River Gambra", P.R.O., S.P. 1/124, f. 115.

[2] Jobson, *op. cit.* pp. 7, 8, 107; Purchas, *op. cit.* II, Part VII, p. 922.

rejoined their five companions at Oranto. During their absence a Portuguese bark had arrived on its way to Fattatenda, sixteen leagues farther up the river. Fearing more treachery, the Englishmen stood to arms and the local natives mustered in force to support them, if they were attacked. Despite the vehement entreaties of their allies, the English refused to attack unless they themselves were attacked, whereupon the natives adopted towards the Portuguese "a kind of sullen and insolent behaviour", which induced the Portuguese to pass on without molesting the five Englishmen.[1]

In the meantime, in ignorance of the tragedy which had taken place in the river, the Guinea Company equipped the *Syon* of 200 tons and the *St John* for a third voyage to the Gambia. The expedition left Dartmouth on 25 October 1620. The *Syon* was commanded by Robert Melhugger and the *St John* by Hugh Musqueate. Richard Jobson and a certain Henry Lowe were the supercargoes. The two vessels were stocked with goods to the value of nearly £2000. The expedition began by practising reprisals on the Portuguese for the massacre of the *Catherine's* crew. Certain of the Portuguese, whom they found on the coast, expressed their detestation of this crime and were left alone, but Jobson learnt that Hector Nunez, the principal offender, had some effects in the River Salum. These he promptly seized. He stayed in this river to build a shallop and finally entered the Gambia on 22 February 1621. On arrival at Tendeba they were informed by a Portuguese settler of Thompson's murder. Leaving the *Syon* with twenty-five men and boys at Tendeba, the *St John* and two shallops proceeded up river to Mangegar where the local king visited them "and dranke himselfe with his consortes so drunke that the customs were deferred till next day". Here they hired a house for a factory and left three men in charge of it. Leaving the *St John* at Gassan, Jobson and Lowe proceeded to Jarakunda, where they discovered that the chief was "a perpetual drunkard". Here they met two of Thompson's party, who had come overland from Oranto. On 17 December Jobson's party reached Oranto, where they found all the Englishmen in good health, and made the acquaintance of Suma Tumba, the local chief, who "made hast to drown his wits in the aquavitee and good liquor we brought him".

Jobson and Lowe had some differences whilst at Oranto. The former afterwards reported that "Lowe's emulation hindred us with

---

[1] Jobson, *op. cit.* p. 40.

delayes, both now and before". Eventually it was agreed that the
St John should proceed no further and that Jobson with nine
Europeans and four Africans should proceed in a boat to Tenda.
Jobson afterwards complained that he had to "take such men as
were given me, not such as I desired", but he appears to have been
a good leader of men, who combined tact with firmness, and to have
treated his men fairly. He insisted on "a loving and orderly course
of diet, wherein everie man had his equall share" and limited the
hours of travel to four in the morning and four in the evening. He
also was able to boast that "our Sabbath day was observed, onely
two houres in the evening, whereas my men earnestly entreated to
be going". The result was that he reached his goal after eleven days
of arduous labour almost without any friction at all. Just at the
end of the journey, when plans seemed momentarily to have gone
wrong and provisions were running low, "our men began to
grumble, and my especiall consort to speake out", but they were
appeased when Jobson spake them fair and with his fowling-piece
replenished the larder by bringing down a large duck.

Jobson's party passed the Barrakunda Falls on 15 January 1621.
He made a slow and tedious journey owing to the low state of the
water. The boat had twice to be carried over shallows, but eventually
on 26 January the party reached Tenda. There to their intense
satisfaction they found Buckor Sano, who "liked our drinke so well,
he suckt it in". After he had recovered from his potations he showed
the utmost friendliness to the English. He procured for them the
good will of the local chiefs and obtained permission for them to
trade with the inhabitants. He also gave Jobson a lot of information
regarding the wealth and commerce of the countries farther in the
interior. A market was opened on the river banks, where the goods
brought by the English were exchanged for ivory and native cloths.
Jobson was also offered a number of slaves for sale, but answered
that "We were a people, who did not deale in any such commodities, neither did wee buy or sell one another, or any that had
our owne shapes." Though John Hawkins had fifty years earlier
carried slaves from Cape Verde to the West Indies, the English
national conscience had not yet become entirely blunted. The servant of the courtiers and monopolists could still set his face against
the traffic in human flesh. It was left to the opponents of monopolies
and the supporters of the Commonwealth government to start this
trade between the River Gambia and our West Indian possessions.

Jobson stayed at Tenda until 10 February, when he decided to return owing to the falling of the river. Before leaving he conferred upon Buckor Sano the title of "Alkali of the white men", and at the same time gave the name of St John's Mart to the place where he had established his market for the exchange of goods. The Barrakunda Falls were reached in five days. On 13 March Jobson reached the *St John* and learnt that things had been going far from well with those he had left behind. Lowe himself had been using the other shallop to trade up and down the river. He had taken with him a butt of sack and a hogshead of aqua vitae. Although "in himselfe carefull enough, as his experience might well advise him, having spent many yeares and made many voyages upon that continent; yet towards his people hee carried at sometimes such an oversparing hand, that they fell to practise how they might deceive him, making use of all advantages to steale those hot drinks from him, which, being purchased as it were from his niggardly nature, they would divide as a spoyle with great greediness amongest themselves, and thereby wrought their owne confusions, that those of the people he carried with him, they eyther died before he came back to the shippe, or shortly after, some two at the most excepted, who escaped with daungerous sicknesse".

On the return journey down the river they also found that there had been further mortality. Two of the three men left at Mangegar had died. The master of the *Syon* "after our passage from Dartmouth, which was in October untill the middle of March after, about which time he died, was never twenty dayes sober". The ship's surgeon and other officers had shared in his carousals and they likewise paid the penalty in the same manner. When Jobson reached the ship on 21 March, there were not above four able bodied men left in the ship's company.

In April the *Syon* and *St John* sailed down to the river's mouth. The crew camped ashore in Kombo whilst caulking their ships and received a friendly visit from the "king" of Kombo. On 9 May they left the river, but were so short of carpenters that they had to put into Rufisque to obtain workmen.[1]

One result of Jobson's expedition was to show that the Portuguese had ceased to be a force to be reckoned with in the River Gambia. None the less Portugal still made lingering pretensions to sovereignty. In 1652 the Governor of St Jago made an indirect attempt

---

[1] Jobson, *op. cit. passim*; Purchas, *op. cit.* VI, 234 *seq.*

to oust the English from the river.[1] Ten years later a certain Manoel Vas de Franco, who lived at Bintang, claimed to hold a commission from his king as commander-in-chief in the river.[2] In 1714 the Governor of the Azores made a last attempt to assert his royal master's claims to the river,[3] but long before these dates both the government at Lisbon and the Portuguese dwelling on the river banks had realised that it was impossible to exclude the English from the river, and in fact that those few of their own nationals, who remained there, could only remain on the sufferance of and in dependence upon their supplanters.

Other results of the expedition were to prove that friendly relations could be established with the natives and that there was a possibly lucrative trade to be acquired if communication were established with the countries lying near the head waters of the river. The one tangible result of the voyage was a cargo of hides, ivory and wax, which sold for £1386. 12s. 8d. This, however, meant a nett loss to the Guinea Company of close on £600 on the voyage alone. As the return cargo of the St John on its previous voyage had only realised the paltry figure of £80 and as the voyage of the Catherine had yielded nothing at all, the Company found itself in debt to the tune of close on £6000.[4] In the circumstances it is not surprising to learn that, despite Jobson's glowing accounts of the prospects of another voyage, the adventurers hesitated before sending another expedition to the Gambia. The year 1621 was one of a financial crisis in England and great difficulty was experienced in raising any capital for any commercial enterprise.[5]

Jobson none the less laboured hard to persuade his masters to renew their interest in the Gambia. In 1623 he wrote his The Golden Trade, or A discovery of the River Gambra, and the Golden Trade of the Aethiopians and also addressed a treatise to James I, in which he demonstrated that he had discovered the route to the land of Ophir. The Golden Trade was duly published and put up for sale at the entrance to the Royal Exchange, but Jobson had to confess

---

[1] Cf. Chapter iv.

[2] Journal of Robert Holmes, 1 January 1664, Pepys Sea MS. 2698; Affidavit of Stephen Ustick, 7 June 1664, ibid. and C.S.P. Colonial (America and West Indies), 1661–1668, p. 213.

[3] William Cooke to R.A.C., 14 June 1714, P.R.O., T. 70/3 and T. 70/5.

[4] "Account of three several voyages sett forth for the River Gambra", P.R.O., S.P. 1/124, f. 115.

[5] W. R. Scott, Joint Stock Trading Companies to 1720, ii, 13.

regarding the other treatise that "some reasons lead me to conceave (it) might or did miscarry, the rather in regard I was never called to any accompt of the same". In 1624, however, he was able to prevail upon certain of the original patentees to entrust him with the command of another venture to the Gambia. But things went wrong with the expedition from the very start. Jobson afterwards complained that "the hinderaunces have bin such since my accompt of the discovery by reason of the differences between the gentlemen and the merchants, who should enjoye it, as hath spoiled the proceeding". A London merchant named John Davies, who was an original adventurer under the patent of 1618, claimed £500 from the Guinea Company and took in satisfaction thereof a complete assignment of all the Company's monopoly of the Guinea trade. In 1623 Humphrey Slaney, another London merchant, fitted out a ship for Guinea, which Davies seized in satisfaction of his debt. The matter was referred to the Privy Council and by that body to James I, who announced that he "doth utterly dislyke that his gracious favour intended for a generall good should be changed into the nature of a monopoli for the private turne to one man". Slaney's vessel was therefore ordered to be released. The dyers and clothiers also attacked the monopoly and petitioned Parliament, alleging that the patentees had raised the price of gum and red-wood. Upon the question being put on 24 May 1624 in the House of Commons, it was voted that the patent was "a grievance both in creation and execution and shall be presented to His Majesty".[1]

Whilst these disputes were still going on certain of "the gentlemen" amongst the patentees looked about for a vessel to equip for the projected expedition. They were probably not very lavish in their proposed expenditure and it may be, as Jobson alleged, that there was some "secret practise of the marchants" to hinder their projects. Whatever the reason, the only vessel which could be obtained for their purposes was a Spanish ship lying in the River Thames, of which the owners appear to have been only too anxious to get rid. The persons recruited for the expedition gave Jobson and others cause for dissatisfaction.

It was much to be doubted, he afterwards wrote, *amongst some of the zealous mynded gentlemen that were adventurers, so also even*

---

[1] "The Discuvery of the Cuntry of Kinge Solomon", Royal MS. 18 A, LVIII; *Acts of the Privy Council,* 1621–1623, pp. 477–478; 1623–1625, p. 247; *Commons' Journals,* I, 710, 794.

amoungst some of ourselves that were to goe the voyage, whether our
designe could prosper, in regard many of the gentry that made upp the
Adventurers were Romish Catholicke, by meanes whereof they had
ship't amoungst us divers of their owne faction; whereby wee were
devided even here at home before wee went.

When the ship eventually did sail, it "proved rotten and so omynous
to their proceeding, hazarding the lives of us all that were ingaged
in her ". After beating up the Channel for a short distance, it became
evident that the ship must founder and the expedition put back
ignominiously to Dover. As Jobson wrote, "many of us resolve the
stoppe of this last voyage was God's blessed hinderaunce".[1]

Jobson still did not despair of arousing interest in his land of
Ophir. In 1625 he penned *The Discuvery of the Cuntry of Kinge
Solomon his rich trade and trafique within twenty daies saile of
England* and dedicated it to Charles I. The manuscript was received
by the new king and carefully preserved, but Jobson did not, as he
had hoped, obtain the opportunity to enlarge upon his plans in the
royal presence. In the following year Charles did so far interest himself in the affairs of the Guinea Company as to take a share in the
venture of a ship to Guinea,[2] but the voyage appears to have been
projected to the Gold Coast and not to the Gambia. During the few
remaining years of the patent the grantees appear to have confined
their energies to privateering and to exacting licences from such
traders as were prepared to risk a voyage to West Africa. Though
some of these individual traders ventured to the Senegal, there is
no evidence of any of them having entered the Gambia. Interest in
the latter river was not even revived when in 1631 Charles I granted
a new patent to another set of adventurers. The Gold Coast had
proved capable of yielding more immediate and more profitable
returns than the Gambia and attention was therefore concentrated
on trade in those parts. For close on thirty years after the fiasco
of Jobson's last expedition the English showed little or no interest
in his reputed golden trade and land of Ophir.

Mention has been made on a previous page of a memorial, which
Jobson addressed to James I. Though Jobson complained that he

---

[1] "The Discuvery of the Cuntry of Kinge Solomon", Royal MS. 18 A,
LVIII, ff. 1–3.

[2] Warrant for furnishing and delivering the St Anne to the Guinea and
Binney Adventurers, 17 October 1626, *C.S.P. Domestic*, 1625–1626, pp. 439,
576.

received no intimation that the king had taken any notice of it, it had not in fact been consigned to the royal waste paper basket. It had been perused by a Scotch chaplain named Forbicher (Frobisher) and shown by him to the Lord High Admiral, the Duke of Buckingham, who in his turn had communicated its contents to a Frenchman named Gerbier Douilly. This last named used this information to publish a map of the River Gambia and to append thereto an account of the reputed wealth of the country.[1] The result was momentarily to revive French interest in the river. French traders had hitherto confined their attention mainly to the gum trade in Senegal, but were beginning to feel the effects of Dutch commercial rivalry. In 1617 the States General had established a company for trading in Africa between the Tropic of Cancer and the Cape of Good Hope. In 1621 this Company had acquired a footing on the island of Goree lying off Cape Verde and only ninety miles from the mouth of the Gambia. Rouen merchants began to fear that the Dutch might take steps to oust them from the trade of the neighbouring coast and accordingly in 1626 formed a company to exploit the regions of the Senegal and Gambia. The undertaking proved unprofitable. They endeavoured to keep out foreign competitors by forcible means and in 1629 seized an English ship, which was trading in the Senegal,[2] but the Dutch proved less easy to handle and the company was further hampered by the competition of its own compatriots. In 1633 therefore they obtained from Cardinal Richelieu the exclusive privilege of trading for thirty years between the Senegal and the Gambia, including the courses of those rivers, but the grant did not have much effect upon the fortunes of the Gambia. The Senegal trade was already firmly established and voyages to the Gambia tended to lead to possible embroilment with the Dutch at Goree. The French therefore preferred to stick to the beaten track rather than venture along one which was comparatively unknown and which might not lead to trade of any great value.[3] Between 1627 and 1636 the Groningen Chamber of the Dutch West India Company sent several ships to the Gambia, but they were mostly small vessels and the voyages were intermittent—facts which suggest that at that date trade in the river was not deemed lucrative.[4]

---

[1] "La Rivière Gambia et la Ville de Cassan en Afrique", Add. MS. 16,731 n.
[2] Petition of Nicholas Crispe, 1629, *C.S.P. Domestic*, 1629–1631, p. 145.
[3] P. Cultru, *Histoire du Sénégal*, pp. 37–41.
[4] Pereira, *Historia da Companha das Indias Occidentales*, 1623–1636, p. 645.

IV: Cavalier and Roundhead in the Gambia, 1650–1652

In 1631 Charles I had granted a new patent for the exclusive trade to Africa between Cape Blanco and the Cape of Good Hope to Sir Richard Younge, Sir Kenelm Digby, Humphrey Slaney, Nicholas Crispe and William Clobery.[1] The three last mentioned grantees had three years previously sent two ships to the River Senegal and had lost one through capture by the French.[2] Slaney has already been mentioned on earlier pages as having attempted to impeach the transfer of the monopoly of the previous adventurers to William Davies. But there is no record that any of the grantees ever concerned themselves in the trade of the Gambia. All the members of this new Guinea Company were royalists. When the civil war broke out, their privileges were attacked by the parliamentarians. In 1650 Samuel Vassall, a London merchant and member of Parliament, led a demand for the revocation of a monopoly which he alleged had been obtained "by the procurement of courtiers". Vassall had been one of those who had refused to pay tonnage and poundage, and professed to make his demand out of public spirit and a desire for more free trade. He also contended that he and his associates could import £300,000 of gold dust in the first year and double that amount after six years. But these professions of public spirit and dislike of monopolies were illusory. As the members of the Guinea Company said in reply to this attack, "we humbly conceive that they speak not against the East India company because most of them are members thereof".[3]

Whatever the justice of their case, policy made it inevitable that the holders of the royal patent should be deprived thereof. It was obvious that this trade could not be left in the hands of political opponents of the Commonwealth. It was most undesirable that such opponents should be given the pretext and the opportunity of equipping armed vessels, which might be used against the

[1] Rymer, *Foedera*, xix, 370; *C.S.P. Domestic, 1631–1636*, p. 186.
[2] Petition of Nicholas Crispe, 1629, *C.S.P. Domestic, 1629–1631*, p. 145; P. Cultru, *Histoire du Sénégal*, p. 41.
[3] Answers of the Guinea Company, 25 May 1650, *C.S.P. Colonial, 1514–1660*, p. 339.

Commonwealth. Furthermore, there were other more far seeing considerations which prompted the change. During the years of the civil war the old Company had done very little in the way of trade in Africa and it was clear that Dutch influence in those regions was in the ascendancy. Certain Baltic states were also known to have their eyes fixed on Africa. It was evident that, if the trade in those parts was left exclusively in the hands of a Company which lacked the money to make any further expansion, what small foothold England had on the West African coast would soon be entirely lost. Accordingly in 1651 a new patent was granted to Rowland Wilson, and other London merchants.[1] The patent granted them the exclusive right for fourteen years to trade in the regions of Cormantine on the Gold Coast and Sherboro in Sierra Leone on condition that they fortified those places and secured them for the Commonwealth. The trade along the rest of the coast was thrown open to all comers.[2] At the same time, as an incentive to trade in Africa, the Navigation Act of 1651 prohibited the introduction into any territory of the Commonwealth of produce of Africa, unless it was conveyed in vessels owned by Englishmen or the inhabitants of English colonies and manned by crews of which more than one-half were of English nationality.

The new patentees decided to try to open up the trade of the River Gambia. Soon after obtaining their grant they sent ships and factors thither under the charge of a Mr Langley. The expedition was instructed to follow up Jobson's discoveries above the Barrakunda Falls. On arrival in the river Langley found that he had been preceded by certain subjects of the Duke of Courland, who were engaged in building a fort upon St Andrew's Island. Remembering the scriptural allegory of the man who built his castle upon the sand, the Englishmen did not regard these Courlanders as very formidable rivals. They themselves proceeded to Bintang Creek and made their base at Bintang itself. Langley led a party as soon as possible up the river to the Barrakunda Falls to prospect for gold. He established a post at these falls and evidently either proceeded personally or else sent men up beyond the falls to Tenda. It would appear that they found some alluvial gold in the creeks. They also

---

[1] It would appear, however, that Wilson had certain royalist proclivities. In 1648 he lent the future Charles II the sum of £500. *Hist. MSS. Comm. Rep., Pepys MSS.* p. 285.

[2] Order of Council of State, 9 April 1651, *C.S.P. Colonial*, 1574–1660, p. 355.

received reports of the existence of a mountain of gold in the interior of the continent.[1]

At the end of 1651 Wilson and his associates equipped the *Friendship*, the *Supply*, and the pinnace *John* to carry further supplies to the Gambia and to trade there for hides, wax, teeth, gold, ambergris and other merchantable commodities. James Pope was placed in charge of the expedition and was instructed to settle factories on the river banks. He was also told to buy slaves and ship them to Barbadoes, where the successful introduction of the sugar cane had created a demand for labour and whither the Irish royalists captured at Drogheda had already been conveyed as slaves. Finally, Pope was instructed "to acquire from some of that country Marybucks' books of the Mahomitants' religion and send them if cheape".[2]

Of the dolorous voyage of John Blake, master of the *Friendship*, we learn something from two letters which he sent home to his masters and to his wife. His ship and the *John* left the Downs in October 1651, and reached the river a month later. The *Supply* followed in December. They proceeded to Bintang, where they found that Langley was dead as well as all his company except three. Blake himself fell ill but recovered. The heat was overbearing and the English were burned for want of air. There was no breeze except what came from the shore and that was so hot that they were almost stifled by it. In the middle of the night Goodman Bourton drank a bottle of ink in mistake for a bottle of water and so was poisoned. Mr Bowles, one of the factors, was sent up to Barrakunda. After he and his goods had been landed, he, "being taking a pipe of tobacco in one of the negroe's pipes", went to the gold chest, which had been left there by Langley and which was full of gunpowder. The gunpowder blew up and destroyed part of the house. The fire spread to adjacent houses and most of the town was burnt down. All the ivory and other goods which had been purchased were destroyed, as well as the goods which Bowles had brought up with him. The unfortunate Bowles was brought down in a wherry to Bintang. He was carried on board the *Friendship* but only survived two days, dying "a most miserable creature, being almost eaten up with

[1] John Blake to Rowland Wilson, 15 February 1652, *Hist. MSS. Comm. Rep., Portland MSS.* ii, 31.

[2] Rowland Wilson to James Pope, 17 September and 9 December 1651, *Hist. MSS. Comm. Rep., Portland MSS.* ii, 31.

maggots, they being so long coming down".[1] None the less, Blake and Pope strove to make the best of a difficult and heartbreaking task. A factor was sent up Bintang Creek to Sangrugo (Geregia), where he managed to buy a quantity of hides, ivory and wax.[2] Friendly relations were established with the chief at Portudal and the *John* was prepared for a trading venture there.[3] Notwithstanding the disaster which befell Bowles at Barrakunda, great hopes existed that the party which had been sent there would come back with a priceless cargo of gold.[4]

Though the promised Eldorado was a myth and though many of the men were sick and dying, John Blake might none the less have brought his three ships back to England with more or less profitable cargoes but for an attack which came from a wholly unexpected quarter. After the execution of Charles I, Prince Rupert collected a few ships in foreign ports and organised most successful raids on English commerce on the high seas. In February 1652 he and his brother Maurice reached the Cape Verde Islands with the *Swallow*, *Revenge*, and *Honest Seaman*. He received a welcome from the Governor of St Jago, who not only provisioned his ships but also informed him of the presence of the three English ships in the Gambia. He also offered him pilots and the cooperation of a caravel of soldiers, if he would attack these vessels. Rupert readily concurred and the four ships set sail on February 21. The Portuguese caravel disappeared the first night out at sea and, as the weather was fair, the English decided that her abandonment of the voyage was deliberate. Rupert, however, sailed on and made his landfall at Rufisque on 25 February. Two days later they made the mouth of the River Gambia. The *Crocodile*, a Courlander vessel of ten guns, was lying off Banyon Point. Peter Schulte, the commander, came on board Rupert's flagship, informed him of the whereabouts of the English vessels, and offered his services as a pilot.[5]

Rupert's squadron sailed into the river under Schulte's pilotage. Somewhere near Dog Island they met the pinnace *John* outward

---

[1] John Blake to Rowland Wilson, 15 February 1652; John Blake to his wife, 18 February 1652, *Hist. MSS. Comm. Rep., Portland MSS.* II, 31.

[2] Samuel Carington to John Blake, 24 January 1652, *Hist. MSS. Comm. Rep., Portland MSS.* II, 31.

[3] Warburton, *Memoirs of Prince Rupert and the Cavaliers*, III, 358.

[4] *Ibid.* III, 359.

[5] Warburton, *op. cit.* III, 351–358; H. Diedrichs, *Herzog Jacobs von Kurland Kolonien an der Westküste von Afrika*, pp. 25, 26.

bound for Portudal. She was very speedily made a prize and Major Robert Holmes placed in command of her. The four English ships and the Courlander then anchored near Lamin Point. Schulte proceeded to St Andrew's Island and informed the commander, Major Fock, of what had transpired. Though the Duke of Courland was connected by marriage with the Stuarts and had even secretly supplied them with money and munitions, he had from reasons of prudence recognised the Commonwealth government.[1] Fock was not unnaturally alarmed by reason of Schulte's unneutral conduct. Both he and the pastor, Eberling, upbraided him strongly, but Schulte was defiant. He told them that they were both incompetent and that, if he was not allowed to do as he wished, he would either take service with Rupert or else proceed to Europe, take service with the King of Denmark, and return with Danish ships and take possession of the Courlander settlements in the name of Denmark. He even went as far as to offer iron and hides belonging to the Duke of Courland for sale to Rupert. As there were four armed English vessels and one potential rebel Courlander vessel lying off the fort, Major Fock decided that the only way of preserving his master's fort was to fall in with Schulte's plans. He therefore went at night on board Rupert's flagship to pay his respects to the prince and to assure him that he would render any assistance he required. He was thanked for his offer and given a salute of guns when he returned to the island.[2]

At that time a Spanish ship of ten guns and an English ketch were lying in the shallow water off the north bank of the river opposite to St Andrew's Island. Major Holmes was sent in the *John* prize to try to cut them out. But as soon as the rest of the squadron was sighted rounding Lamin Point, the two ships slipped their anchors and headed past St Andrew's Island for Bintang Creek. Rupert's squadron gave chase. As it passed the fort on the island, the Courlanders fired all their guns as a salute and Rupert replied. Doubtless Fock hoped thereby to convey the impression that he was defending the fugitives and not aiding the pursuers. The Spanish ship was outsailed and captured, but the ketch got into Bintang Creek. As it was low water, Rupert's squadron was unable to

---

[1] "An impartial account of the true state of the case concerning the island of Tobago", *C.S.P. Colonial (America and West Indies)*, 1685–1688, p. 342; *Clarendon Papers*, II, 174, 842; Diedrichs, *op. cit.* p. 28.

[2] Warburton, *op. cit.* III, 358: Diedrichs, *op. cit.* pp. 25, 26.

follow. When the tide rose, the ships tried to enter the creek, but the flagship was in danger of running aground and so dropped anchor. Prince Maurice proceeded farther in and got sight of Blake's ship, the *Friendship*, but owing to the fall of darkness was compelled to anchor before he could come up with her. A party was landed to fire on the *Friendship* so as to prevent the crew from handling the sails, but the parliamentarians made use of the tide to bring their vessel up to the town of Bintang.[1]

Next day Prince Maurice stood up to Bintang and opened fire on the *Friendship*. Most of Blake's crew were debilitated by fever and the reply was feeble. After a brief exchange of shots Maurice offered good quarter and Blake his freedom. The *Friendship* then struck her flag. Pope, the supercargo, was on shore at the time and had not been included in the terms of capitulation. Some dispute arose in consequence. Maurice thereupon offered to release the ship and fight her again, but the Commonwealth sailors "rather obeyed the first conditions than hazard their lives". The ketch, which had evaded capture two days previously, was found to be hiding a little farther up the creek and was speedily made a prize by a pinnace. Another vessel was said to be hiding farther up the creek and the captured ketch was manned and sent in pursuit of her. In the hope of ingratiating themselves with the victors, the natives attacked the crew of the fugitive vessel and killed seven of their number. Rupert, "abhorring to countenance infidels in shedding Christian blood, signified his displeasure thereof through the Portuguese living amongst them".[2]

Either from papers, which he found on board his prizes, or else from information supplied to him by members of the captured crews, Rupert learnt that the river was one of great trade. He was given to understand that 300 leagues up near its source there was a gold mine, which was "reported to be a rock of firm gold of a great bigness, which might counter avail the greatest charges as may be expended in the finding of it. But, whether it be so or no, certain it is that the first discoverers were so satisfied, as they never used the sea afterwards". He therefore sent a party up as far as Elephant Island to intercept the gold prospectors as they came down the

---

[1] Warburton, *op. cit.* III, 358–359.

[2] Warburton, *op. cit.* III, 358–360; Remonstrance of Guinea Company, 21 June 1652, *C.S.P. Colonial*, 1574–1660, p. 333; Report of Dr Walker, 8 October 1653, *C.S.P. Domestic*, 1653, p. 194.

river. But the party from the Barrakunda Falls never arrived and, as Rupert understood that the season of tornados was approaching and was therefore anxious to leave the river, he was unable to make his much desired haul. Realising that he himself could not take advantage of this discovery, he wrote a letter to the Duke of Courland urging him to avail himself of the information. He likewise communicated the report to the Courlanders on St Andrew's Island, telling them that this gold mountain would yield five Dutch ducats' worth of gold in every pound of sand.[1]

Rupert's squadron had been in a very parlous state when it sailed for the Gambia. He had only three weeks' bread on board his ships and nothing to drink but water.[2] His ships were also foul, and rapidly becoming unseaworthy. The three prizes were therefore a real godsend. Prince Maurice transferred his flag from the *Revenge* to the *Friendship*, which was renamed the *Defiance*. The captured crews were distributed amongst those of the *Swallow*, *Revenge*, and *Honest Seaman*. The Spanish prize was condemned as unfit for further service and therefore broken up. Her cargo, hulk, and guns were handed over to the Courlanders on St Andrew's Island, with whom Rupert was on the best of terms. The prince also got into friendly communication with the son and brother of the "king" of Juffure, who lived on the north bank opposite to St Andrew's Island.[3]

Rupert left the river with his six ships on 13 March and made his way up to Cape Verde. Near Rufisque he had some trouble with the natives, who made prisoners of Major Robert Holmes and another officer. In the subsequent attempt to save them Rupert himself was wounded by an arrow, but eventually managed to rescue his officers. Thence he made his way to the Cape Verde Islands and subsequently to the West Indies. Whilst still in the region of the Cape Verde Islands he lost the *Revenge*. This ship got separated from the rest of the squadron. William Coxon, the former second mate of the *Supply*, had been put on board this vessel after the capture of his own ship. With the aid of other members of the captured Commonwealth ships, he took the opportunity to surprise the royalist crew and, after seizing the ship, brought her safely to England.[4]

---

[1] Warburton, *op. cit.* III, 361; Diedrichs, *op. cit.* p. 27.
[2] Narrative of William Coxon, ? June 1652, *C.S.P. Domestic*, 1651–1652; pp. 308–312.   [3] Warburton, *op. cit.* III, 362, 363.
[4] Warburton, *op. cit.* III, 363–369; Narrative of William Coxon, ? June 1652, *C.S.P. Domestic*, 1651–1652, pp. 308–312.

When news of Rupert's raid was brought to England by the *Revenge*, the Guinea Company were loud in their protests. The part played by the Governor of St Jago was quickly made known. After capturing the *Friendship* Prince Maurice had informed John Blake that he owed his capture to the information supplied by the Governor and had further added "See what friends you have of the Portugals; for, had it not been for them, we had never come hither and taken you." Furthermore, on his return to St Jago Rupert had openly made a present to the Governor of some eight to nine hundred hides, which he had obtained in the Gambia. In June 1652, the Guinea Company presented a petition and remonstrance to the Council of State asking that the Portuguese Government should be called upon to indemnify them for their losses, which they placed at £10,000. The Council of State was in a delicate position. Portugal had just recently thrown off the Spanish yoke and England and Spain were on the verge of war. Friction with this newly liberated kingdom and potential ally was therefore to be avoided, if possible. Further petitions had to be presented before the Council could be persuaded to move. Eventually, in June 1653, commissioners were appointed to take accounts of the reparations due by the Portuguese to the injured parties. The commissioners submitted a report in the following October. They found the value of the *Friendship* to be £3200 and allowed a further sum of £384 for interest exclusive of wages and loss of freight. They reported that they had got into touch with commissioners appointed by the King of Portugal and that those commissioners declined to take any further steps, as they declared that it was the Governor of St Jago, and not their King, who was affected.[1]

The Guinea Company had to rest content with this report. The Governor of St Jago was a man of straw, from whom there was no more likelihood of exacting compensation than there was from Prince Rupert himself. The assistance rendered by the Courlanders to Rupert does not appear to have come to light. Perhaps the blank ammunition, which Major Fock blazed off from St Andrew's Island, really did have the effect of hoodwinking the Guinea Company's servants. The Company certainly never presented any remonstrance

---

[1] Petitions of the Guinea Company, 21 June 1652, and 31 July 1653; Petitions of Nathaniel Goodlad, 4 and 22 March 1653, and 8 June 1653; Report of Dr Walter Walker, 8 October 1653, *C.S.P. Colonial*, 1574–1660, pp. 383, 405; *C.S.P. Domestic*, 1652–1653, pp. 41, 225, 393; 1653, p. 194.

regarding his conduct or that of Schulte. Had they done so, it might have been received with the same apathy as their remonstrance against the Portuguese. The Duke of Courland was the ruler of a prosperous Baltic state, was a relative of the exiled Stuarts, and he was further known to be anxious to enter into close commercial relations with England's trade rival, Holland. He was therefore a person to be won over to the interest of the Commonwealth. The lodging of a claim against him in respect of the vicarious acts of his officers in the remote parts of Africa would have been impolitic.

The Commonwealth Guinea Company's venture in the Gambia was therefore even more disastrous financially than that of its predecessor in the days of James I. It is not surprising to learn that they made no further attempt to open up the Gambia. None the less, though Rupert's raid on the Commonwealth's shipping in Bintang Creek has at first sight all the appearance of wanton and purposeless destruction for the gratification of political revenge, it brought about in actual fact the permanent establishment of British influence in the Gambia. Throughout all his wanderings of the next eight years Rupert never forgot the story of the gold mountain at the headwaters of the river. When his cousin Charles II came to his own again, he brought his information to the notice of that king. It is even said that he volunteered to lead a squadron personally to the Gambia in search of this wealth and that he was only prevented from doing so because his royal cousin objected to his risking his life in such a climate.[1] Be that as it may, he was one of the principal promoters of the Company which was formed in 1661 to revive English trade in West Africa and in particular in the Gambia. When plain merchant captains brought home tales of fabulous wealth in a tropical river, business men and courtiers alike hesitated to invest their money in any undertaking, until they had seen something tangible suggesting that the report was true. But when the king's own cousin brought home similar tales from the same place, the matter was different. People were far more ready to subscribe their money for an undertaking proposed by a prince of the royal blood, who had some pretensions to being a scientist, than they were for one proposed by a humble person such as Richard Jobson. Rupert's visit to the River Gambia may therefore be said to mark the real beginning of the permanent establishment of the British interest in those regions.

[1] Warburton, *op. cit.* III, 360.

V: The Courlanders in the Gambia, 1651–1661

Mention has been made in the last chapter of the fact that the English, who arrived in the Gambia in 1651, found some subjects of the Duke of Courland building a fort on St Andrew's Island. In this chapter it will be necessary to retrace our steps and give some account of this Courlander experiment in colonisation.

Courland was formerly a Baltic province of Russia. To-day the greater part of it is included in the Republic of Latvia and the rest in the Republic of Lithuania. In the seventeenth century it was an independent duchy, which acknowledged Polish suzerainty. The capital, then as now, was Mitau and its principal seaports on the Baltic coast were Libau and Windau. James, Duke of Courland, who succeeded to the duchy in 1640 at the age of thirty, was a godson of James I of England. According to a current rumour in Courland James I had given his godson the island of Tobago as a christening gift.[1]

The Duke of Courland had travelled considerably in his youth and had visited England and Holland. The country, which he was called upon to rule, was a buffer state of no great extent and with a small population. He realised that he had no chance of territorial expansion in Europe and that he lacked the means to make his duchy into a first class military power. He therefore came to his task resolved to live, if possible, in peace with his neighbours and to increase his country's prosperity by the encouragement of commerce. He had been particularly impressed by the commercial enterprise of the English and Dutch and had returned to his own country thoroughly imbued with all the ideals of the mercantilist system. His Baltic neighbours in Denmark and Brandenburg had already made attempts to obtain part of the commerce of Africa and the East. On his own accession to the Duchy the Duke of Courland decided to follow their example. In the summer of 1650 he instructed Henry Momber, his agent in Amsterdam, to organise a

---

[1] Georg Fökkersam to Heinrich von Galen, 20 September 1672, O. von Mirbach, *Briefe aus und nach Kürland während der Regierungsjahre des Herzogs Jakob.*

company for purposes of trade in Guinea and to equip two ships to proceed to Africa to select a suitable place for a fort. As Momber pointed out that the proposed company might excite the hostility of the Dutch, the Duke sent Franz Hermann von Puttkammer to the Hague to explain his plans and to offer to place all territory, which he might occupy, under the protection of the States General, as, nevertheless, his own personal property and that of his heirs. Puttkammer was instructed to ask for a categorical answer. The reply, which he received, was that "His Excellency will in the future be left unhindered in what he thinks he is able to do suo jure." In answer to this evasive statement the Duke instructed Puttkammer to say "If you will accept our proposal, all will be well and no injury done to you, but rather you will have great profit from it, if we purchase in Holland all the goods which we send to those places." If the Dutch refused to accept the proposal, Courland would have no alternative but to combine with her neighbours and put into practice the maxim *unita virtus fortior*.[1]

No reply was apparently received to this message, but the Duke of Courland, who had just previously declined to join with the Margrave of Brandenburg in a venture to the East Indies, did not put into execution his threat of setting up a Baltic combination in rivalry to the Dutch. He decided to launch his own scheme unaided. It is not exactly clear what induced the Duke to acquire land in the Gambia, but it may be conjectured that one reason was that neither the English, nor the French, nor the Dutch were at this date particularly interested in the trade of the river and that therefore he had hope of obtaining a foothold without any great fear of molestation on the part of more powerful European trade rivals. Another motive no doubt was that the Duke hoped to obtain from thence slaves for his settlement in Tobago, which had been granted by the English crown to the Earl of Warwick, who had parted with his proprietary rights to the Duke of Courland. In any event, whatever the motive, the Duke had by the end of 1651 in exchange for a small annual payment acquired St Andrew's Island from the King of Barra as well as a small plot of ground at Juffure on the north bank of the river opposite to that island. He similarly acquired Banjol (St Mary's) Island at the mouth of the river from the King of Kombo. A little later he obtained another plot of land up the river

[1] H. Diedrichs, *Herzog Jacobs von Kurland Kolonien an der Westküste von Afrika*, pp. 14–20.

at Gassan—the scene of the former massacre of the English by the Portuguese.[1]

Major Fock was sent out in charge of the original settlers. He proceeded to construct a fort on St Andrew's Island. John Blake in the English Guinea Company's service saw this fort abuilding in the early days of 1652 and likened the builder to the man who built his house on the sand, believing that when the rains came it would all be washed away.[2] But the scriptural allegory was not fulfilled and Fock showed himself no mean architect. Despite bombardments, deliberate destruction, years of neglect, and the ravages of tropical vegetation much of his handiwork still stands to-day. He built according to the recognised rules of contemporary military engineering. The main building was in the shape of a rectangle and was flanked at each corner by four bastions, which proximately faced the four cardinal points of the compass. These bastions were triangular. It might perhaps be a fair criticism of them to say that the apex of each one of them was too acute.[3] Another defect from a military point of view was the fact that the island had no water supply. It was for this reason that the plot of ground was acquired at Juffure, but the garrison none the less depended for its water upon the keeping open of communication between the island and the shore and the goodwill of the King of Barra and his subjects.

Another small fort was built on Banjol Island at Banyon Point (Half Die). There is no contemporary description of it. It appears to have been abandoned at an early date and in 1661 its ruins were scarcely visible.[4] There is no record of any fort having been constructed either at Juffure or Gassan.

The Duke's intention was not only to develop the trade between the Gambia and Courland and Tobago but also to establish a permanent settlement of his own subjects on St Andrew's Island. Married people were therefore sent out and a pastor appointed to look after their spiritual needs. The first of these was Gottschalk Eberling. He was followed in about 1655 by Joachim Dannefeld. This latter was instructed by the Duke "especially to see that the

[1] Diedrichs, *op. cit.* p. 20; Wolffrath to the delegates in the Courland business, 1664, *C.S.P. Colonial (America and West Indies), 1661–1668,* p. 94.

[2] John Blake to Rowland Wilson, 15 February 1652, *Hist. MSS. Comm. Rep., Portland MSS.* II, 31.

[3] Plan of St Andrew's Island in Diedrichs, *op. cit.* at the end.

[4] Warburton, *Memoirs of Prince Rupert and the Cavaliers,* III, 539.

heathen souls are brought to a true and a right understanding of God" and was enjoined for this purpose to learn the languages of the negroes of the country. He was further bidden to abstain in the pulpit from all religious controversy and invective, which could only arouse scandal and bitter feelings amongst the negroes and Christians belonging to other faiths. Finally, he was instructed "to employ everywhere gentleness and mildness, whereby souls might be better saved".[1] A contemporary plan of St Andrew's Island shows a small church built of cane work with a thatched roof just outside the walls of the fort near the south bastion, where doubtless both Eberling and Dannefeld ministered to their congregations. One of the duties, which these pastors had to perform with distressing frequency, was the burial of the dead. The same plan shows a cemetery hard by the church with a large number of graves.

Sickness and death were not the only things which retarded the prosperity of the settlement. Peter Schulte, whose mutinous and unneutral conduct has been mentioned in the preceding chapter, arrived at Mitau early in 1652, bringing with him Prince Rupert's letter about the gold mountain in the upper reaches of the river. This information made the Duke resolve to send a well-equipped expedition to exploit this alleged discovery. But he at once found himself confronted by a serious difficulty. He suffered from the disadvantage that few of his own subjects had the experience which qualified them for responsible posts in the new settlement. He consequently had to rely on foreigners and not a few of these proved to be pure adventurers. On 6 September 1652 he appointed a Dutch sea captain, Jacob du Moulin, as his Director in Gambia in all matters military and political with a Courlander named Frederick William Trotta von Treyden as his lieutenant. Little is known of du Moulin's antecedents except that he was a rolling stone, who had at one time sought his fortune in Denmark and had quitted that country leaving behind him a large number of debts and a none too savoury reputation. His commission from the Duke gave him wide powers. He was instructed to endeavour to form a company to exploit the source of the river, to enlist Norwegians to work in the mines and Danes as artisans. Three ships, the *Crocodile*, the *Patientia*, and the *Chur*, were placed at his disposal. The expedition reached Copenhagen in October. There du Moulin managed to recruit a number of Danes and to make up the number of colonists to 140. But

[1] Diedrichs, *op. cit.* pp. 23, 24.

difficulties at once arose. Du Moulin's past record was better known to the Danish authorities than to his employer. The Danish Government was full of mistrust and demanded that their nationals should at once be put on shore. The expedition was consequently unable to sail. The officers found their forced inactivity irksome and gave vent to their feelings by sending complaints to Courland regarding du Moulin on 15 November 1652; the Duke was constrained to write to them bidding them pay proper respect to their commander in accordance with their oaths.[1]

Subsequent events proved, however, that the complaints against du Moulin were far from groundless. He obtained the sum of $1300 from the Duke's agent in Copenhagen so as to pay the members of the expedition. Only sixty men on board the *Crocodile* received their pay. The balance of the money was used to liquidate a number of personal debts which du Moulin had contracted before he joined the Duke's service. Later he obtained two other sums of $100 and $600 and likewise embezzled them. Finally, in order to defray absolutely necessary expenses, he sold a quantity of iron which had been put on board the ships for use as barter on their arrival in Africa. On 15 December 1652 von Treyden wrote to the Duke complaining bitterly of his superior officer. "Du Moulin", he wrote, "handles your Excellency's affairs like a light-hearted knave (*als ein leichtfertiger Kerl*)". He had communicated certain of the Duke's secret instructions to foreigners. Everything was going wrong. Captain Schönberg was a good enough soldier but lacked judgment. Fiscal Muthreich knew nothing at all about his duties and was simply a fifth wheel to the waggon. Francisco Marco de Magelhan, a Portuguese in the Duke's service, wrote to confirm what von Treyden had said. Du Moulin was a satisfactory "hombre de practique" in the morning, when he was usually sober, but in the afternoon he became "as angry as an ass or a pig and quite unfit for business".[2]

In the meantime the ships lay idle in Danish waters. At the end of December 1652 du Moulin ordered Treyden to proceed on the voyage with *Patientia*, promising to follow himself in the *Crocodile* three months later. Treyden declined to obey this order. As the days passed, the murmurings of the officers and men grew louder. On 10 January 1653 the officers forwarded a formal complaint to the Duke requesting that du Moulin should be prosecuted civilly and criminally for his many misdeeds. At length in March, after

[1] Diedrichs, *op. cit.* pp. 29–32.   [2] Diedrichs, *op. cit.* pp. 32, 33, 34.

drawing another three hundred rix dollars to satisfy the demands of the crew of the *Crocodile*, the three ships left Helsingfors. But trouble began as soon as the coast of Norway was reached. Provisions had run low and du Moulin lacked the money to revictual the ships. The crew of the *Crocodile* mutinied and brought their own and the other two ships back to Windau. On 25 April 1653 they addressed a letter of complaint to the Duke, declaring that they were under the necessity of returning home, "because our supply of butter, bread, stock fish, and everything else no longer exists. Also the beer was finished on February 25. Since then we have drunk water with the result that the people are very ill and full of scurvy". They had been thirteen weeks at sea and had spent nine of these weeks in the Sound. They were ready to serve the Duke faithfully and loyally according to their oaths, "but we can in no wise go to sea with only beans, flour, and water". The Duke at once ordered the arrest of the mutineers, but further enquiry disclosed the full measure of du Moulin's misdeeds and he was arrested. After spending two years in prison he was released on signing an obligation to repay the amount of his defalcations to the Duke. Needless to say the obligation had less value than the paper upon which it was written.[1]

Despite his past experience of foreign adventurers, the Duke of Courland decided to entrust his affairs in the Gambia once more to a kindred spirit to du Moulin. His second choice was a Danish soldier of fortune, Lieutenant-Colonel Philip von Seitz, who had foregathered with du Moulin at Copenhagen and learnt a great deal from him of the Duke's plans. This individual made his way to Mitau and ingratiated himself with Louisa Charlotte, the Duke's consort. Through her mediation the Duke was persuaded in 1654 to make Seitz Governor of the Gambia and to entrust him with four ships. No sooner had they sailed than the Duke repented of his choice and wrote in haste to Danzig to say that he believed that Seitz intended to hand over St Andrew's Island to the Spaniards. Seitz, however, had not the slightest intention of going so far afield as Africa. He got as far as Hamburg, where after disembarking he pledged the Duke's credit to the tune of 15,000 rix dollars and sent the ships back to Courland. Somewhat wisely, he himself remained in Hamburg. The Duke endeavoured to have him arrested, whereupon he fled to Altona. The King of Denmark's aid was then

---

[1] Diedrichs, *op. cit.* pp. 34–37.

invoked but Seitz disappeared without ever being brought to justice.[1]

At length learning wisdom by past experience, the Duke decided to rely in future upon his own subjects. Captain Otto Stiel, who had been to the Gambia in 1653, was appointed Governor and commandant of St Andrew's Island and, as these pages will show, proved the most loyal and most faithful of all the Duke's servants. He spent five years in the Gambia and despite many setbacks did something to retrieve the squandered fortunes of his master.[2]

But an unkind fate further hampered the Duke's colonial dreams. In 1652 war broke out between England and Holland. It was the Duke's desire to preserve a strict neutrality. He had no desire to quarrel with the Dutch, who had a fort at Goree within little more than a hundred miles of St Andrew's Island. Personal inclinations did not dispose him in favour of the Cromwellian régime, but his ships had to sail through English waters and prudence required that he should keep on good terms with the new Protectorate. None the less, he was during the next two years to find that his ships were frequently detained by both belligerents. In October the Dutch seized the *Wallfisch* and the English seized the *Innocentia* and *Pietas*, which were carrying a cargo of wine, salt, ivory, and rice.[3] In March 1653 the *Louisa Charlotta* was condemned in the English Admiralty Court on a false confession by the master that he was carrying contraband.[4] In August 1653 the Dutch seized the *Temperantia, Invidia,* and *Lux* for use against the English.[5] Of these the first mentioned was captured a few months later by the English.[6] In May 1654 the English seized another richly laden Courlander ship in the belief that it was a Dutchman, but released it two months later on discovery of its true nationality.[7]

[1] Diedrichs, *op. cit.* pp. 37–39.

[2] *Ibid.* p. 39.

[3] Diedrichs, *op. cit.* pp. 22, 28; Duke of Courland to the English Parliament, 28 November 1652, Tanner MS. 53, f. 156.

[4] Petition of Duke of Courland, 3 March 1653, *C.S.P. Domestic, 1652–1653,* pp. 301, 302. This ship was again seized by the English in 1661 whilst trading between Malaga and Brazil: Petition of Philip Freher, 11 October 1661, Register of Privy Council, P.R.O., P.C. 2/55.

[5] Diedrichs, *op. cit.* pp. 28, 29.

[6] Captain Benjamin Sacheverell to General Monk, 8 February 1654, *C.S.P. Domestic,* 1654, p. 394.

[7] Captain Rich to Admiralty, 7 May 1654; Captain Roberts to Admiralty, 3 July 1654, *C.S.P. Domestic,* 1654, pp. 487, 516.

The fate of the *Leopard* shows the many hazards of a voyage between Courland and the Gambia at this date. This ship left Courland in April 1653, under the command of Klaes Friedericksen. She put into Amsterdam, where she was loaded with copper bars and other merchandise. Thence she sailed unmolested to the Gambia, where her cargo was traded for slaves. Whilst in the river the captain died and was succeeded in command by Cornelius Friedericksen. She then carried her cargo of slaves to the French island of Martinique, where they were disposed of and other merchandise bought. On her way back to Europe she put into St Kitts. There Cornelius Friedericksen died and a third captain was appointed. From St Kitts she sailed for Amsterdam, but ran into foul weather, and lost part of her sails and tackle. The master, mistaking his course, found himself in St George's Channel. He decided to put into Bristol to revictual and refit. On arrival there a certain "Mr Gill, an informer," announced that the vessel was carrying contraband from St Kitts. The *Leopard* was thereupon seized and her crew put on shore in a strange land "to the prejudice of the said Duke, the losse of the voyage homewards, and the undoinge of the company of the said shipp".[1]

As the Duke could get no satisfaction from the English government for these violations of his neutrality, he sent Rudolf von Struch as a special envoy to Cromwell. Struch arrived in October 1656, but after waiting nine months he returned to Courland having obtained no satisfaction in regard to the ships and loud in his complaints of the dilatory manner in which the English conducted their business. He was back again in June 1658, but was unable to present his credentials and found that the Commonwealth Government, "ignorant of the formalities observed by other princes", was corresponding direct with his master instead of through him. Two months elapsed before he could even obtain an audience.[2] Then events, which will be referred to later, supervened to prevent him from obtaining any satisfaction.

After du Moulin and Seitz had quitted the scene, the settlement in the Gambia had a chance to develop. Indigo, coffee, ebony, wax,

---

[1] Remonstrance of the Duke of Courland, April 1655, *Thurloe Papers*, III, 410.

[2] Francesco Giovanni to Doge of Venice, 6 October 1656, 27 July 1657, 28 June and 1 December 1658, *C.S.P. Venetian*, 1655–1656, p. 270; 1657–1659, pp. 90, 205, 213, and 286; Diedrichs, *op. cit.* p. 42.

spice, ivory, and small quantities of gold were obtained in exchange for salt, iron, and brandy. An attempt was also made to start a pearl industry. As already noted there also was a traffic in slaves to the West Indies, but the slaves appear to have come from the interior of the continent. The Courlanders lived on the best of terms with the inhabitants on the river banks. The ruling chiefs were kept on good terms by timely presents. In 1652, for instance, "the great king", presumably my lord of Barra, was given a golden robe. In 1680 the Duke sent a letter of condolence to the "king" of Kombo. As was only right and proper, when the ruler of one state corresponded with that of another, the letter was written in the recognised language for diplomatic correspondence, namely, Latin. The credit for these good relations with the natives appears to be with Otto Stiel and stood the Courlanders in good stead at a later date. Some of the Duke's factors still proved dishonest. In 1656, for instance, Nicolas Grünwald was short in his accounts to the amount of $20,000 dollars, but Otto Stiel proved a man of worth and there appeared to be every reason for hoping that the settlement could be turned into a source of revenue and profit.[1] In 1657 Richard Bradshaw was sent by Cromwell as an envoy to Courland and concluded a commercial treaty with the Duke,[2] who thereby obtained a potential ally in the event of any aggression on the part of the Dutch at Goree.

The wheel of fortune was, however, very soon to take a most disastrous turn for the Duke and for his settlements in Tobago and the Gambia. The Duke acknowledged the suzerainty of the King of Poland. The result was that he became embroiled in disputes between Poland and her neighbours and rivals. In 1656 Charles X of Sweden declared war on Poland. In September 1658 Major-General Douglas, a Scottish officer in the Swedish service, made a raid on Mitau and captured the Duke of Courland and his whole family.[3] The unfortunate Duke was carried off into exile and remained a captive for close on two years. In the meantime his settlement in the Gambia was cut off from all communication with Courland and all opportunity of obtaining the necessary money and supplies for

[1] Diedrichs, op. cit. pp. 24–25, 39–42.

[2] Francesco Giovanni to Doge of Venice, 31 May 1658, C.S.P. Venetian, 1657–1659, p. 205; Thurloe Papers, VI, 357, 656; VII, 456; Diedrichs, op. cit. p. 42.

[3] K. W. Cruse, Curland unter den Herzogen, I, 176; Thurloe Papers, VII, 456.

the purpose of carrying on. As soon as the news of the Duke's capture reached Holland, the Amsterdam Chamber of the Dutch West India Company got in touch with Henry Momber, the Duke's commercial agent in Holland, and offered to send the necessary supplies to the Gambia, provided they were allowed to take over St Andrew's Island. If anybody was the accredited political agent of the Duke in Holland, it was a certain Adrian Wicquefort. Momber had no instructions from the Duke and therefore acted entirely on his own responsibility in the transactions which followed. As it was evident that the settlement would have to be abandoned and that there was nothing to prevent the Dutch from seizing it, whether or not it was abandoned, he made what were in the circumstances probably the best terms he could have made. On 4 February 1659 he entered into an agreement with the Burgomaster and Treasurer of Amsterdam and two directors of the Amsterdam Chamber.[1] That agreement began by expressing doubts as to its own legality. It recited the fact that the Dutch West India Company, "thinking with themselves how that in the condition to which things now are reduced, the forts and strongholds might easily be taken by others and so the commerce and traffic, which His Highness doth possess and exercise upon the River Gambia be troubled", had agreed to certain proposals of Momber, "who otherwise in some affairs doth serve His Highness". It recognised the difficulty that Momber had in binding the Duke in any way by his signature, but the Company was "wanting an occasion to make a transaction of these things either with the Duke, or with his plenipotent commissaries, who by a special command he might have entrusted with a full and absolute power".[2]

By the terms of the agreement the Company undertook to send the Duke's servants a garrison with ammunition and victuals, upon the condition that every person of whatsoever office or quality should take an oath of fidelity to both the Duke and the Company. All the merchandise and goods in the forts were to be delivered up to Momber as commissary of the Duke upon payment of the freight and price of the ammunition and victuals. The Company undertook "to protect, keep and maintain the place, forts, and negotiations in the Gambia until the Duke shall be pleased to defend the forts". Until such time as the Duke re-demanded the forts, the Company was to possess and enjoy them and to pay and maintain the garrisons.

[1] P.R.O., C.O. 1/16, ff. 191, 192.   [2] *Ibid.*

The Company undertook to hand back the forts without payment as soon as the Duke should demand them again, and for the further assurance of its good faith in the transaction agreed to submit to the judgment and sentence of a court of law, if "the aforesaid articles should not be precisely executed at the appointed time". Momber subscribed his name declaring that, although "he has no power or commission to transact or conclude anything,... so far as it lies in his power and so far as he does not intermix with any of these things,...he is ready to omit nothing that may serve to protect and conserve the forts" for the Duke.[1]

Wicquefort, the Duke's accredited resident at Amsterdam, was never informed of this transaction. It did not reach his ears until the following September, when he wrote and informed the Duke and asked to be allowed formally to denounce the agreement. But this action was taken too late. After signing the agreement Momber wrote to Stiel in the Gambia, acquainting him with its terms and informing him that he had omitted his name from it, because he did not know the actual position of affairs in the Gambia. If Stiel was in a position to maintain the forts unaided, Momber advised him to ignore the agreement; otherwise, it would be advisable to abide by its terms. In the meantime the Dutch sent a ship with soldiers to take possession of St Andrew's Island. When the Dutch commander showed Stiel Momber's agreement, Stiel declared that it would be a violation of his oath to the Duke to act upon it. The Dutch, however, acquainted the soldiers of the garrison with the position of affairs in Courland, pointing out how remote was their prospect of receiving any pay from that quarter and informing them that under Momber's agreement the Dutch West India Company guaranteed them their pay. On learning of these things the garrison mutinied and put Stiel in irons. They then handed over the fort to the Dutch and took passage for the Netherlands on the ship which had brought out the new garrison. Stiel was released shortly after the departure of the ship and given a passage to Holland on the next ship sailing thither.[2]

At the beginning of 1660 news reached Holland that the West India Company had lost St Andrew's Island. A French privateer in the Swedish service had surprised the fort by night, expelled the garrison, plundered the island, and carried off all the artillery and provisions. He had subsequently met a merchant belonging to the

---

[1] P.R.O., C.O. 1/16, ff. 191, 192.   [2] Diedrichs, *op. cit.* pp. 42–47.

Groningen Chamber of the Dutch West India Company and sold the fort to him for a sum of money to be paid in Groningen. There followed an extraordinary example of lack of communication and co-operation between two chambers of the same Company. Without consulting the Amsterdam Chamber, the Groningen Chamber declined to honour the agreement with the French privateer or to take possession of the island, "because it belongs to the Duke of Courland", and informed Momber of the position of affairs.[1]

Otto Stiel had been living in Holland ever since his return to Europe. Momber promptly got in touch with him. Stiel collected a number of soldiers and in April 1660 sailed from Texel for the Gambia in a ship supplied by the Groningen Chamber. He reached St Andrew's Island in June, where "he challengeth and redemands his Prince's isles and forts and, having challenged and redemanded them, they were restored and rendered unto the power of the Duke of Courland".[2] Several weeks later three ships belonging to the Amsterdam Chamber anchored off the island and demanded its surrender. Stiel refused to comply. The Dutch then sent an armed party in boats, which effected a landing and brought a heavy fire to bear on the fort. Stiel's garrison comprised a mere handful of men. He found it impossible to maintain any prolonged resistance and was soon forced to surrender. The Dutch promptly made him a close prisoner on board one of their ships. They then proceeded to set their newly acquired possession in order, but were interrupted from what was to them evidently a wholly unexpected source. As already mentioned, the Duke of Courland held St Andrew's Island at an annual payment to the "king" of Barra. When that chief saw his tenant evicted by a strong hand and a multitude of people and the ejectors assume possession of the island without any reference to himself, he decided to take steps to show that he had some voice in the matter. A party of Dutchmen landed at Juffure to obtain water. The people of Barra captured them and word was sent to the ships that they would not be released until Stiel was once more put back on the island. It was further intimated that the Dutch would not be allowed to obtain wood or water until they had complied with this request. In the meantime the "king" of Kombo and other chiefs were asked to join forces with those of Barra. In the course of the next four weeks a large number of natives mustered with

---

[1] Diedrichs, *op. cit.* p. 47.
[2] Memorial of Adolf Wolffrath, 30 July 1662, P.R.O., C.O. 1/16, ff. 195–197.

obvious hostile intentions. The Dutch commander realised at length that the position was in the circumstances untenable and submitted with the best grace he could. He removed all the goods and provisions, spiked the cannon, partially destroyed the fort, and then handed it back to the Courlanders. Otto Stiel and his handful of men once more hoisted the Duke's flag and the Dutch sailed for Goree, promising as a parting shot that they would speedily return and hang Stiel on a gallows.[1] Stiel then set to work with his few men to put the fort in some order hoping against hope that somehow or other help would come from Courland before the Dutch returned to fulfil their threat. His master was too much engaged in setting to rights the troubled affairs of his own duchy to render Stiel any immediate assistance. None the less Stiel was destined to have a respite of eight months. During that time his small garrison was reduced by death and other causes to the number of seven Europeans including womenfolk, but these few managed to put the twice plundered fort into some sort of a condition of defence and to remount seven cannon.[2] But though he and his six hard tried companions were not wanting in the courage or the will, it was clear that without relief they lacked the power to offer any prolonged resistance to another attack on the fort.

[1] Diedrichs, *op. cit.* pp. 48, 49.
[2] Journal of Robert Holmes, 18 and 19 March 1661, Pepys Sea MS. 2698.

VI: The capture of St Andrew's Island by the British, 1661

Those who have read the diary of Samuel Pepys, the future Secretary of the Admiralty, will remember that in April 1660 he accompanied "my Lord", the future Earl of Sandwich, to the Hague in order to bring back Charles II to his kingdom. They will also remember that on 3 October 1660 Pepys was at Whitehall and "heard the Duke (of York) speak of a great design that he and my Lord of Pembroke have, and a great many others, of sending a venture to some parts of Africa to dig for gold there. They intend to admit as many as will venture their money and so make themselves into a company. £250 is the lowest share for every man. But I do not find that my Lord (of Sandwich) do much like it." Acting on "my Lord's" expression of opinion, Mr Pepys did not subscribe any of his money to the proposed venture. As subsequent events showed, "my Lord's" advice was prudent, but the result was that little or no reference was made in the diary and correspondence of Samuel Pepys to the fortunes of these new adventurers to Africa. From the point of view of the historian this is to be regretted, but none the less it is to Mr Secretary Pepys, the archivist, and to his industrious collection of materials for a history of the English navy that we owe much of our information regarding the history of the Gambia immediately after the Restoration.

The proposed new venture, to which Pepys referred in his diary, was to become incorporated under the title of "The Royal Adventurers of England trading into Africa". It had just claim to the prefix "Royal" inasmuch as the prime movers therein were closely related to Charles II. It is clear that the project owed much of its inception to Prince Rupert, who had returned to England with memories of the story of the gold mountain at the headwaters of the Gambia and with a personal knowledge of the demand in the West Indies for a labour supply, which could be recruited very cheaply in Africa. Through him James, Duke of York, also became interested in the exploitation of Africa. When the project for reviving the African trade was being mooted, he showed himself ready to assist in every way possible in his dual capacity of heir presumptive to the throne and Lord High Admiral. Weekly meetings of the adventurers were held in his lodgings at Whitehall, at which he was constantly present.[1] He not only persuaded the King and his consort, Catherine of Braganza, to become adventurers, but, what was more to the point, also promised to provide ships from the royal navy to assist in the first establishment of the trade.

The new adventurers were undoubtedly for the most part an aristocratic body. They included the King and Queen, the Duke of York, Prince Rupert, the Duke of Albemarle and Buckingham, and Lord Ashley. Despite the misgivings, which he had expressed to Pepys, the Earl of Sandwich was also persuaded to embark his capital. Amongst their number were also members or the sons of members of earlier Guinea Companies. Sir Allen Apsley, the son of one of James I's patentees, was one adventurer. Sir Nicholas Crispe, one of Charles I's patentees, was another. John Ladd, who had been one of the members of the Commonwealth Guinea Company, also took a prominent part in the affairs of the new adventurers.[2] A joint stock of £17,400 was eventually raised. The avowed objects of the Royal Adventurers were to supply negroes for the West Indian and American plantations, who were to be sold at £17 a head or for 24,000 pounds of well-cured Muscovado sugar,[3] and for the erecting of forts and the settling of garrisons to secure the whole trade of the River Gambia, "from whence a plentiful harvest was rationally to be expected, and hath been, and yet more abundantly may be reaped".[4]

At the latter end of 1661 preparations were set on foot in anticipation of the grant of a royal charter. The Duke of York promised the assistance of H.M.S. *Kinsale, Henrietta,* and *Assurance.* The command of the expedition was entrusted to Major Robert Holmes, who had been with Rupert at the time of his visit to the Gambia in 1652. Pepys, who was afterwards to know him well, once described him as "a rash, proud coxcombe"[5] and also recorded the fact that a brother-officer considered him "an idle, proud, conceited, though stout fellow".[6] Holmes' own journal is written in much the same vein as

[1] *Continuation of the Life of Edward, Earl of Clarendon,* II, 233.

[2] *A List of the Royal Adventurers of England trading into Africa,* 1662.

[3] *The Publique Declaration and Invitation of the Company of Royal Adventurers of England trading into Africa,* 12 January 1663; Duke of York to Lord Willoughby of Parham, 10 January 1663, *ibid.*

[4] *Answer of the Company of Royal Adventurers trading into Africa to the Petition...exhibited...by Sir Paul Painter* (1667).

[5] *Diary of Samuel Pepys,* 16 June 1665.   [6] *Ibid.* 24 October 1666.

that of Pepys, full of much of the same sly humour and many of the same shrewd comments, but lacking the *naïveté* of the immortal diarist. In fact this journal and correspondence show that an earlier estimate by Pepys of Holmes' character came very near to the truth —"a cunning fellow, and one, by his own confession to me, that can put on two several faces, and look his enemies in the face with as much love as his friends",[1] but, remembering the times, one must perforce repeat with Samuel, "Good God! What an age is this, and what a world is this! that a man cannot live without playing the knave and dissimulation." In fine, Robert Holmes, dissimulator though he could be, was a stout soldier and sailor, who might have been a more honest man in more honest times and at any rate loyally served his country according to the best of his lights.

A number of officers were selected to serve under Holmes. The second in command was Captain John Stoakes, a former naval officer of the Commonwealth, who was addicted to corpulence and a love of creature comforts, which hardly fitted him for the expedition on hand. A French military engineer, named La Prairie, was entrusted with the task of constructing the proposed forts. Colonel John Vermuyden, a Dutchman and protégé of Prince Rupert, was to lead an expedition in search of the gold mine. Captain Francis Kerby was to take charge of the garrisons of the proposed forts with Lieutenant Morgan Facey as his second-in-command.

On what was apparently the advice of Prince Rupert it was proposed to erect a fort one hundred miles up the river on Elephant Island, but if "there be strong reasons for another place, which reasons are to be sett downe in writing with the names of the assenters and dissenters, and the decision to be made by the major part of the voyces", some other place might be selected instead.[2] The *Kinsale* was to remain in the river for the protection of the fort until such time as it should be thought fit to send her home with news of the gold mine or any other important news. It was left to the discretion of Holmes as to how long the other ships should stay in the river.[3] The *Henrietta* was, however, to proceed to the Gold Coast as soon as she could be spared in the River Gambia. The *Amity, Sophia,* and *Griffin* were to be employed in trade. The factors

[1] *Diary of Samuel Pepys,* 1 September 1661.

[2] "Captain Francis Kerby, Commander of the Fort, his instructions" (1660), Pepys Sea MS. 2698.

[3] "Instructions to Captain Stoakes" (1660), *ibid.*

were to endeavour to obtain as soon as possible a cargo of slaves, who were to be sold in the Azores or Madeira, or if they could not be disposed of there, at Cadiz or Lisbon.[1] Prince Rupert sent a special list of instructions for the gold prospectors. They were to be supplied with barges as soon as possible and to make their way up river. La Prairie was to accompany them and to make an exact map of all places where gold was discovered. As the expedition was likely to arrive in the river only just before the rainy season began, it was realised that very little might be achieved on the first journey up river, but Vermuyden was to prepare for a second voyage as soon as the weather permitted.[2] Notice of the royal patent of the Adventurers was to be given "to all factors of our owne or any other nation there that soe they may not be supprised, or pretend to be soe, when they shall hereafter to be disturbed in their traffique there".[3] It is not clear how far the Adventurers were acquainted with the position of affairs in the Gambia *vis-à-vis* the Duke of Courland and the Dutch West India Company. But it is clear that the patent assumed the right of the English Crown to grant territorial and commercial rights in Africa regardless of the consent of the local chiefs and of the rights acquired by treaty or otherwise from such chiefs by other nations.

The expedition was delayed by a number of accidents. The *Assurance*, which was originally designed for the expedition, capsized at Woolwich on 9 December 1660, in a sudden gust of wind, and twenty of her men were drowned.[4] Two days later another ship collided with the *Kinsale* and brought down her mainmast, "which", said Pepys, "makes us think it ominous to the Guiny voyage to have two of her ships spoilt before they go out".[5] The *Assurance* was, however, replaced by the *Amity* and the last of the ships sailed from the Downs at the end of January. The whole fleet made its rendezvous off the Portuguese coast and, passing Goree, anchored at Rufisque on 2 March 1661. They found a French factory at this place and warned the factor that he was not to trade within the limits granted by the King of England to the Royal Adventurers.

---

[1] "Instructions for the factors in Gambia, 1660", Pepys Sea MS. 2698.
[2] "Private instructions to them that goe up to the myne in Gambia, 1660", *ibid.*
[3] "Instructions to Captain Stoakes" (1660), *ibid.*
[4] *Pepys' Diary*, 9 December 1660.
[5] *Ibid.* 11 December 1660.

A similar warning was also despatched to the Dutch commander at Goree.[1]

The fleet reached the mouth of the Gambia on 4 March 1661, entered the river the following day and dropped anchor off Dog Island. There they found a French ship, which Holmes prohibited from trading any more in the river and which thereupon departed for Rufisque.[2] A council of war was held that day, at which it was decided to land the soldiers and their tents on Dog Island until such time as Elephant Island could be surveyed and reported upon. It was further agreed to send La Prairie to view Elephant Island at the first opportunity and in the meantime to send him to Juffure to inform the natives of the arrival of the English fleet.[3] The *Griffin* was sent to Juffure that afternoon and on 6 March the soldiers were landed on Dog Island, which was renamed Charles Island. Though Holmes does not mention the fact in his journal, the *Griffin* was charged with the delivery to the Courlanders on St Andrew's Island of a message to hand over the fort on that island to the English within ten days. The *Griffin* returned on 6 March with some Portuguese-speaking natives and communication was opened with the "king" of Barra. On 7 March two of the smaller frigates were sent up to Juffure to look for a suitable landing-place and a place to settle a factory.[4]

Otto Stiel and his six companions had watched the movements of the English with considerable anxiety. It was obvious to them that, if the English intended to do so, they could blockade St Andrew's Island and speedily compel its garrison to surrender. Stiel was not made of the stuff which was ready to submit without striking a blow, but it was clear that resistance to any determined attack was out of the question. The only hope lay in creating the impression that the fort was manned in greater strength than it actually was and thus inducing the aggressors to abstain from their threatened attack. Accordingly, when the two English frigates arrived off Juffure, about nightfall on 7 March, Stiel fired one of his cannon at them. The frigates were well out of range but sufficiently

---

[1] Warburton, *Memoirs of Prince Rupert and the Cavaliers*, iii, 538, 539.

[2] Holmes' Journal, 4, 5 and 9 March 1661, Pepys Sea MS. 2698.

[3] "A Councell of Warr held at the arrivall in Gambia, the 5th March, 1660(−1)", *ibid.*

[4] Holmes' Journal, 5 and 6 March 1661, *ibid.*; "Relation of Otto Steele", 13 March 1662, P.R.O., C.O. 1/16, f. 193; *The Kingdoms Intelligencer*, 29 July–5 August 1661, p. 484.

near to realise that they had been fired at. Next day they returned
to Dog Island and reported the incident to Holmes.[1] In the meanwhile, remembering the stead in which the "king" of Barra had
stood him some eight months earlier, Stiel circulated to the best of
his ability reports amongst the natives that the English had come to
enslave the local inhabitants. It would appear that his propaganda
was to some extent successful and that the people of Barra did arm
themselves for their own preservation.[2]

It is not clear how far Holmes was acquainted with the position
on St Andrew's Island, but at any rate he abstained from further
action against the Courlanders for another eight days. He was busy
in the meantime landing materials and stores on Dog Island. He
was also assiduously endeavouring to cultivate the friendship of the
natives, whom he "caressed and entertained very civilly to gaine
their friendship to our people and interest".[3] A number of natives
visited him on board the *Henrietta*. On 13 March he paid a visit of
state to the "king" of Kombo, of which he gives the following very
lively account:

*This day I went ashore with Captain Stokes and divers others to see
the watering place at Combo and to visit the king of that place, with 2
boates of armed men along with us for guard, in case the blacks should
prove false for us. The king liveing 10 miles up in the country, wee
walkt up thither, where I was very civilly received by that king after
their manner. It was a very hott day—no breath of wind stirring. The
king accommodated me with the only horse that was there to be hadd, but
being young and strong, and Captain Stokes old, fatt, and burley, I let
him ride and I walked, which was one of the hardest taskes that I ever
undertook, the sun shineing so very hott, and all our way upon dry
sand. It was soe very hott that our chirurgeons mate, whom I took along
with me for fear of any accident, not able to walk and keep us company,
fell down dead upon the way, and soe did a greyhound I had with me.
Nay, one Mr Fowler, a factor, walking along with me, carrying a gun
upon his shoulder, the excessive heath of the sun fired it upon his
shoulder, which I would not have believed, if I had not taken the gun in
my hand and felt the heat of it and found the cock stand at half bent.*

---

[1] Holmes' Journal, 8 March 1661, Pepys Sea MS. 2698; Diedrichs, *Herzog
Jacobs von Kurland Kolonien an der Westküste von Afrika*, p. 49; *The Kingdoms Intelligencer*, 29 July–5 August 1661, p. 484.

[2] *The Kingdoms Intelligencer*, 29 July–5 August 1661, p. 485.

[3] Holmes' Journal, 10, 11 and 12 March 1661, Pepys Sea MS. 2698.

When I went ashore, I gave orders to all the officers of the shipps that they should fire no guns except they saw some shipps coming into the river—then to fire severall guns to give me notice, that I might make the more haste on board after my tedious hott march in the morneing. I was not sat above one quarter of an houre by his majestie, who had sent for some palm wine for me and my company to drink, but the guns began to fire on board the shipps; which when I heard, I scarce took leave of his majestie but flung out of his doores and marched towards my boates as hard as I could goe, leaving my horse with Captain Stoakes. It was in the very heate of the day that I began to march with five or six and twentie men with me. The rest came with Captain Stoakes, who could not endure the heat, but put himself in the wood under the shadow of the trees till the coole of the evening. And my cockswaine fell down 2 or 3 times, but the poor fellow, having a great kindness for me, did endeavour to gett to the boate soe soon as I did, all the rest of my company left upon the ground gasping for breath. When I got to the boates, I ordered my pinnace to row me on board and the rest of the boates to stay for those that were left behind. I got on board early that afternoon. Presently at my arrival on board I called the officers of the shipps to know the reason of the fireing of the guns. They told me they could not tell—that they were fired on board Captain Stoakes his shipp. I ordered the gunner of that ship to be sent for. When come on board, I asked him whether he had not orders from his captaine not to fire any guns, unless he saw a fleet of shipps coming into the river. (He told me) that his captain had said nothing and the occasion of his fireing was that they had struck 10 or 11 of his guns at Gravesend, which they hoysed up and mounted yesterday and scaled them this day. Now I did heartily repent me of letting Stoakes have the horse, for I was soe angry with him that I would have been well contented to have seen him hanged. I was 3 or 4 daies so dazed in my head that I thought I should never have recovered.

After spending two days in recovering from heat stroke, Holmes decided to deal with the Courlanders on St Andrew's Island. His motives for his action are thus described in his journal:

There being a small island up the river near Julyfree (Juffure), called St Andreas, inhabited by some Dutchmen pretending to be the Duke of Courland's subjects, who had a small factory there and a little factory (sic), conceivinge its vicinitie to be prejudiciall to the Royal Companies tradeing in that river and that it would prove of worse consequence if the Hollanders should gett it into their hands, it was resolved in a councell of officers and factors that I should gett possession of it for the Royal Company by faire or fowle means, especially the blacks being desirous the English should have it.

These words have all the appearance of an air of candour, which, however, is belied by what Holmes wrote some years later. In 1673 he was asked for information regarding the incident and then wrote to say that he knew nothing about having taken any fort from the Duke of Courland. He admitted to having taken "a little fort that had two men and a boy in it", but he always understood it belonged to the Dutch.[1] As Stiel had recruited his garrison in Holland, it may be that there were some Dutchmen amongst their numbers, but this fact could have done no more than afford Holmes the pretext for asserting that they were all "Dutchmen pretending to be the Duke of Courland's subjects". The Duke's flag flew over the fort. It must have been obvious that the Dutch with their two forts at Goree would have had no reason to resort to any subterfuge regarding the ownership of St Andrew's Island and, if they had been the owners, would have manned it in far greater strength. Holmes in fact gives himself away in his own journal. He clearly knew the fort belonged to the Duke of Courland. If he had believed it really belonged to the Dutch, he would no more have dreamt of attacking it than he did of attacking the two Dutch forts at Goree. He knew perfectly well that the fort was weakly manned and that it belonged to the ruler of a minor European state, who was powerless to resist or to retaliate. His only excuse was that "it would prove of worse consequence if the Hollanders should gett it into their hands".

In pursuance of the resolution of the council of war the *Griffin* went up as far as St Andrew's Island to take preliminary soundings. This operation was successfully carried out without any attempt at molestation on the part of the Courlanders. On 18 March the whole fleet weighed and made sail for the island. The *Griffin* ran aground but the other four ships proceeded to within half range of the fort. The lieutenant of the *Henrietta* was sent on shore "to let the Governor know that he had behaved himself verie uncivilly to His Majestie of Great Brittaines shipps to fire at them for coming peaceably to fetch water and without the least provocacion given

---

[1] Holmes to Sir Edward Walker, 24 May 1673, *C.S.P. Colonial* (*America and West Indies*), 1669–1674, p. 492.

him; and upon that account his continuing there would be very obnoxious to the interest of the Royall Company and their tradeing on that coast. I would have him quietly surrender it into my hands; otherwise I would have it by force, which I hope his prudence would prevent."[1]

With only seven Europeans—and at least two of them women— to man seven cannon, all resistance was obviously out of the question. Stiel realised that the only chance of preserving the fort for his master lay in inducing Holmes not to commit a gross violation of the rights of a friendly state. He therefore went on board the *Henrietta* and explained that, as the flags above the fort showed, he was the Governor of the Duke of Courland. He explained that he had no hostility towards the English and that he had fired on the frigate at Juffure because it had arrived at night time and he was unable to recognise the flag. Holmes, however, insisted upon an immediate surrender. At the same time he promised to give Stiel and his people transport to Europe and to allow them to remove whatever they had in the fort and to compensate him for such things as he was unable to move. He also offered to testify to Stiel's honour as a soldier by giving him a written certificate to the effect that he had surrendered to superior force. Stiel had no alternative but to agree to these terms. Accordingly on 19 March 1661 the Courlanders marched out of the fort and a party was landed from the English fleet to take possession thereof. The island was at once renamed James Island.[2]

Holmes subsequently sailed for Sierra Leone and the Gold Coast and eventually reached the Downs on 28 July 1661.[3] As soon as news of his exploits in the Gambia reached Europe, protests were lodged both by the States General and by the Duke of Courland. It is evident that the States General were not fully informed as to the exact situation in the Gambia at the time of Holmes' arrival, for they lodged a formal complaint on behalf of the Dutch West India Company. It is also equally clear that on his return home Holmes did not give very accurate information regarding that situation. On 14 August Charles II informed the States General

[1] Holmes' Journal, 18 March 1661, Pepys Sea MS. 2698.
[2] Holmes' Journal, 18 and 19 March 1661, Pepys Sea MS. 2698; Diedrichs, *op. cit.* p. 49; "Relation of Otto Steele", 13 March 1662, P.R.O., C.O. 1/16, f. 193; *The Kingdoms Intelligencer*, 29 July–5 August 1661, pp. 484, 485.
[3] Holmes' Journal, Pepys Sea MS. 2698.

that he absolutely disclaimed Holmes' proceedings against any Dutch subjects in Africa and promised to obtain further information in regard to them and to give the necessary orders to prevent any prejudice or wrong being done to the Dutch West India Company. As the English Government made no further report regarding the affair to the States General, the Dutch Ambassadors presented a further memorial on the subject to Charles II on 19 October.[1] The reason for this inaction is explained by a letter which the Duke of Courland had addressed to Charles II on 1 September. In that letter the Duke reminded Charles II of the friendship which had always existed between his family and the House of Stuart, informed him that he had purchased his possessions in Africa with a great sum of money, and asked for their restitution, asking that Philip Freher, his agent in London, could be granted an interview, at which the whole matter could be explained in full. The Duke received no satisfactory answer to this letter. In order to put his claim on firm ground he wrote on 6 May 1662 to the States General requesting them formally to renounce any pretensions on their part to St Andrew's Island. As the Dutch realised by this time that they had no valid claim to the island and also that they could not themselves wrest it from the hands of the English, the States General replied that, "having with ourselves deliberated about this thing, we could not but choose to return unto your Highness this friendly answer, that it is true that the aforesaid governors (sc. of the Dutch West India Company) and also this company is (*sic*) ready and willing according to equity (to do) what they have promised" by the agreement concluded with Momber in 1659.[2]

The Duke of Courland now decided to send a special envoy to England to assert his rights. With that strange lack of discernment, which seems to have dogged the Duke throughout his life, instead of selecting one of his own subjects he chose for the task a Mecklenburger from Rostock, named Adolf Wolffrath. The only commendation which Wolffrath had for the post was that he had spent two years studying in London.[3] His correspondence still survives in the archives at Mitau. It is full of vainglory and well-turned sentences, but lacking in substance. He was a master of the art of finding excuses for himself and of concealing the simplest matter in a cloud of

[1] Memorial of Dutch Ambassadors to Charles II, 19 October 1661, *C.S.P. Colonial (America and West Indies)*, 1661–1668, p. 58.

[2] P.R.O., C.O. 1/16, f. 194.   [3] Diedrichs, *op. cit.* p. 51.

empty phrases. He was given a yearly salary of 500 rix dollars and a dollar a day for expenses and was instructed not to stay in England more than three weeks and to deliver and get a reply to the following request: "Your royal majesty, having had time enough to think over this matter, will you give us an answer, if you have come to any resolution?"[1] Wolffrath stayed in London considerably longer than the prescribed three weeks, but he was not entirely to blame for this. He was captured by a Portuguese privateer on his voyage from Copenhagen and lost all his papers. On arrival in England in June 1662, he fell out with Freher, the Duke's agent, and each of the two wrote a number of mutually recriminating letters to their master.[2] Finally, when he set to work on his appointed task, he found himself up against innumerable forms of obstruction. In reporting his arrival in England to the Doge, the Venetian Ambassador observed that Wolffrath's demand would not be pleasing to the English Government and "will only encounter the dilatoriness and tedious procrastination habitual at this court".[3] On 28 June 1662 Wolffrath delivered a memorial to Charles II asking for the restitution of the Duke of Courland's African possessions, and declaring therein that the Duke had no intention of closing the River Gambia to the English or of hindering them in their commerce, but would be perfectly willing to let them build houses and construct forts there.[4] As no reply was received, Wolffrath presented a further memorial on 26 July. In it he reiterated the intention of the Duke not to hinder the English from trading in the river. He further sought to reassure the English Government by declaring that the Duke would never abandon his forts to the prejudice of Charles II's subjects. If Charles II assisted the Duke, the forts could never be taken by any other state. All that was asked was that the subjects of the King and those of the Duke might live peaceably together and build and plough within their own territories. The English with their many great ships could have as much profit as the Duke of Courland with his little ships could ever have.[5] On 14 August Wolffrath wrote to the Duke of York urging that English delegates should be appointed to discuss the matter with a

---

[1] Diedrichs, *op. cit.* pp. 51–53.   [2] *Ibid.* p. 54.
[3] Francesco Giovanni to Doge of Venice, 14 July 1662, *C.S.P. Venetian, 1661–1664*, p. 162.
[4] *C.S.P. Colonial (America and West Indies), 1661–1668*, p. 98.
[5] *Ibid.* p. 100.

delegate from the Duke of Courland.[1] With the letter he enclosed a memorial for the consideration of the proposed delegates, in which he set forth the history of the Duke of Courland's possessions in the Gambia and asked "Is it that the prince has at some time or other neglected to rise at the nod of His Majesty? Or that with his little ships he has hindered the course of the mighty English ships, for which he must pay as a penalty his islands and his forts, which he bought and exstructed at a great cost? The prince knows not how to deceive and would rather suffer an injury without imitating it."[2]

The result of all this epistolary effort was that he obtained an audience at Hampton Court, where Charles II gave him fair words but no promises. Mr Secretary Morice was requested to look into the matter but that did not bring the business much further ahead. The Privy Council was approached. Wolffrath's proposals were read and then filed without any further action being taken.[3] The Duke of York came the nearest to being frank with the Duke's agent, when he suggested, according to Wolffrath, that the Duke was not in a position to maintain the forts and had better sell them to England for the best price possible. At length on 4 September Charles II was graciously pleased to give a reply to the Duke's request and to gratify the self-esteem of the Duke's agent by presenting him with a gold chain with his own royal portrait attached. The exact terms of the reply are unknown. Freher, the Duke's agent, wrote to his master to complain that Wolffrath had refused to let him look at the letter and had only read him a couple of sentences from it. On 12 September Wolffrath wrote to the Duke claiming that he had surmounted all intrigue and obtained complete satisfaction for his master.[4]

Freher had, however, a very different report to make. According to him Wolffrath was living in the lap of luxury and doing nothing at all. He had engaged two footmen, two pages, and two interpreters—all at the Duke's expense. He was calling himself an ambassador extraordinary and styling himself "Excellency". Finally he complained that "We have sent him as an envoy and he is more of a letter-writer than an envoy—a lackey or other lowborn knave. If we had wanted to send a legate, we would have done

[1] C.S.P. Colonial (America and West Indies), 1661–1668, p. 103.
[2] Ibid.
[3] Register of Privy Council, 3, 8 and 12 August 1662, P.R.O., P.C. 2/56.
[4] Diedrichs, op. cit. pp. 53–56.

better to have brought over a qualified man from our own people instead of such a foreigner as this." [1]

Wolffrath in the meantime announced his intention of proceeding to Courland. On the strength of his assurance that Courlander ships would be allowed to proceed to the Gambia, the Duke had equipped a number of vessels which were ready to sail as soon as official confirmation of this news arrived. The Duke waited nine weeks and no envoy appeared. Eventually he received a letter from Wolffrath at Danzig asking for more money to enable him to continue his journey to Courland. By this time the Duke realised that he was dealing with a very plausible knave and through the influence of his agent in Danzig caused him to be thrown into prison. [2]

The Duke now decided to correspond direct with the English Government. He wrote to Mr Secretary Morice asking for the return of St Andrew's Island to him and for the repayment to him of the money which he had lent to Charles I and Charles II during the Civil War. Morice replied on 23 September 1663. He regretted his inability to give the Duke a favourable answer. The English African Company had informed him that, at the time it was captured, the fort was not in his possession but in that of the Dutch West India Company and that that Company had never given the Duke the undisturbed possession of the island. Furthermore the Duke was unable to guarantee that the possessions, which he claimed in Africa, would not be seized by some more powerful state. Furthermore Stiel had fired on the English flag and Holmes had in the circumstances no alternative but to take the island. If the Duke wished to have the fort restored to him, he would have to pay the African Company all their charges and expenses and also give a guarantee that no other nation would be allowed to take forcible possession of the fort. He must further conclude a treaty, by which he would undertake that the fort would protect the trade of the company and all English subjects and would also permit the English to erect their own fort on the island for the protection of their trade. [3]

The Duke came to the conclusion that the only possible course for him was no longer to insist on his full rights but to make some sacrifice and play England off against Holland. War broke out between these two countries in 1664. At the outbreak of that war the Dutch were in possession of the Island of Tobago. As mentioned in the

---

[1] Diedrichs, *op. cit.* pp. 55, 56. [2] *Ibid.* pp. 56–58.
[3] *Ibid.* pp. 58, 59.

previous chapter, the Duke of Courland had acquired certain proprietary rights in the island from the Earl of Warwick and had established a settlement there. At the time of his capture by the Swedes that settlement had shared the same fate as St Andrew's Island. Some private Dutch adventurers, who had also settled on the island, managed to seize it by employing methods similar to those employed by the West India Company in the Gambia. The Dutch had managed to hold on to Tobago and the Duke of Courland had been unable to obtain restitution.[1] He now decided to try to regain Tobago by invoking English aid on promises of renunciation of his rights in the Gambia and of assistance in the war against the Dutch.

This offer met with some success. On 17 November 1664 an agreement was concluded between Charles II and the Duke of Courland. By that agreement Charles II granted to the Duke, his heirs and successors, liberty of trade and commerce for such ships as personally belonged to the Duke, his heirs and successors, but not for the ships of his subjects, in any of the rivers or havens in Guinea. Such trade was to be limited to merchandise to the value of £12,000 yearly and the Duke was to have liberty to erect warehouses for the storage of such merchandise under the English forts. In consideration of this grant the Duke made over to Charles II the fort of St Andrew in Guinea and all other forts, fortifications, and "sconces" belonging to the Duke in Guinea. He also promised to pay Charles II a duty of 3 per cent for customs on all goods imported into or exported from Guinea. In return Charles II granted the island of Tobago to the Duke subject to certain restrictions as to the persons who should be entitled to settle there, and as to the destination of any goods exported thence. The Duke acknowledged that he held Tobago under the protection of Charles II and agreed that, when the King of England should so require it or should be engaged in a war against any foreign state except Poland, he would place one good man-of-war, furnished with forty great iron guns, and the necessary officers and men, at the King's service for the space of one year.[2]

---

[1] "An impartial account of the true state of the case concerning the island of Tobago", *C.S.P. Colonial (America and West Indies)*, 1685–1689, p. 342; Baron Blombergh to Captain Poyntz, 11 June 1695, *ibid.* 1695, p. 568; *Acts of the Privy Council*, 1685–1689, p. 342; *Thurloe Papers*, VII, 456; H. I. Woodcock, *A History of Tobago*, pp. 25–26; Cruse, *Curland unter den Herzogen*, I, 176.

[2] *Tobago, or a Geographical Description*, pp. 37–42; Diedrichs, *op. cit.* pp. 60–61; *C.S.P. Colonial (America and West Indies)*, 1661–1668, p. 255.

Charles II appears to have had every intention of honouring this agreement. On 25 November 1664 Lord Willoughby of Parham, Governor of Barbados, received orders to render all assistance to any Courlanders who settled in Tobago.[1] The English captured the island in 1664 but were speedily driven out again by the Dutch before the Duke could send a ship to take possession. Thereafter the island became a sort of no man's land—alternately possessed and lost by the English, Dutch, and French. In 1667 England and Holland concluded a treaty of peace. The Duke of Courland made an attempt to have his claims to Tobago considered during the negotiations, but the belligerents were more concerned with their own interests than his rights. The Dutch asserted that they held the place by right of conquest and the English were not prepared to jeopardise their own claims by standing up for the Duke's rights.[2]

The Duke had little better success in his trading ventures to the Gambia. The Royal Adventurers had been granted the monopoly of the trade to Guinea and they regarded Charles II's agreement with the Duke as an infringement of their rights. Soon after the conclusion of the agreement two ships were sent from Courland to the Gambia. In order to make assurance doubly sure, they were both provided with passes from Charles II. On arrival in the Gambia both were turned back by the Governor of James Island[3] and one was wrecked on the journey home. The Duke tried to secure better protection for a third ship by fitting it out at Newcastle and obtaining a pass for it from Charles II, but it shared the same fate at the hands of the English in the Gambia.[4] An attempt to establish a trading post on Dog Island proved disastrous. At low tide there is a dry passage between the island and the mainland and the natives took advantage of this fact to surprise the post and cut all the Courlanders' throats.[5] In 1669 Otto Stiel once more revisited the Gambia. In one respect he had better fortune than other Courlanders, as he appears to have been allowed to trade. But his ship was wrecked off the coast of Ireland on the way home. He lost all his property and both his legs were frost-bitten as the result of

---

[1] *C.S.P. Colonial (America and West Indies)*, 1661–1668, p. 257.
[2] "The Pretentions of the Duke of Curland to the Island of Tobago", Egerton MS. 2395, f. 591.
[3] "Mr Fanshaw's paper", June 1680, Rawlinson MS. A, 181, f. 297.
[4] Diedrichs, *op. cit.* p. 61.
[5] Barbot, *A Description of the Coasts of North and South Guinea*, p. 73.

exposure. After many hardships and sufferings he reached Danzig penniless, where the chief chaplain of the Duchess of Courland gave him four rix dollars to carry him home.[1] This is the last we know of Otto Stiel. He had proved himself a very brave and very loyal servant in times of adversity and one would like to think he lived to receive some recognition of and compensation for his many sufferings in the Duke's service.

If Stiel was allowed to trade, it was because of the temporary inability of the Governor of James Island to prevent him. Later Courlanders were less fortunate. The Duke was so far obstructed in his rights that in March 1670 the English Privy Council was ordered to investigate the validity of his claim.[2] But that body took a long time deliberating. On 12 December 1672 the Duke was constrained to write to Charles II to ask that he might receive some satisfaction. He was full of apologies for his insistence, but reminded his kinsman that it was a troublesome conjuncture. His necessities were great. He was growing old and was then in his climacterical year called Magnus. It would be a great consolation to him before his death, if his children might see him satisfied for his faithful services to the House of Stuart. If his pretensions could not be satisfied in money, he asked that some island or other equivalent might be given to him.[3] No answer appears to have been received to this letter. A second memorial was therefore addressed by the Duke to Charles II in 1673[4] and was followed on 7 April of that year by a letter from John Lucas Lyon, the Duke's agent in England.[5] As the Duke's oldest son was at this date serving as a volunteer with the Dutch in the war against England, the moment for the renewal of negotiations was hardly opportune.[6] Charles II replied that he did not think the agreement of 1664 could still be deemed alive, but none the less he promised his good offices.[7] The Privy Council was asked to look into the matter and on 17 May caused enquiries to be made of Holmes and the African Company as to the circumstances in which the English had acquired James Island. Holmes' answer was dishonest. He knew nothing about having taken a fort from the

[1] Diedrichs, op. cit. p. 49.
[2] Sir Edward Walker to Sir Richard Browne, 17 May 1673, C.S.P. Colonial (America and West Indies), 1669–1674, p. 490.
[3] Ibid. p. 443.   [4] Ibid. p. 544.
[5] Ibid. p. 480.   [6] Cruse, op. cit. I, 192.
[7] "An impartial account of the true state of the case concerning the island of Tobago", C.S.P. Colonial (America and West Indies), 1685–1689, p. 342.

Duke of Courland. He had captured "a little fort that had two men and a boy in it", but he always understood it belonged to the Dutch. The Royal Adventurers took up the attitude that they had been granted the exclusive trade in Africa prior to the agreement of 1664 and that Charles II had therefore been "surprised" in his grant to the Duke of Courland, who therefore had no right to trade in Guinea or any part thereof.[1] Whether or not the legal standpoint of the Adventurers was correct, it clearly behoved the English Government either to enforce the Duke's rights or else to compensate him for the partial failure of the consideration for the agreement of 1664. But neither of these courses was adopted.

In 1677 the Duke of Courland's ships were stopped on the flimsy pretext that, albeit they had a pass from Charles II, they had no pass from the Duke of York as head of the African Company.[2] His ships were again hindered in 1679.[3] On 6 February 1680, the Duke wrote to Abraham Marin, his agent in London, that "there could be no right or justice in England, if they allow our property to be taken from us", and instructed him to urge that he at least be allowed to occupy the land which he had purchased close on thirty years before at Gassan.[4]

As nothing was effected by approaching Charles II through the correct and proper channels, the Duke's agent decided to resort to the backstairs. On 27 February 1680, he informed his master that he had paid a large sum of money to Mistress Eleanor Gwynne to induce her to exert her influence with the king to obtain restitution for the Duke of his African possessions. "Pretty, witty Nell" did her best to earn the money. She took a suitable opportunity to ask Charles II, "Sir, how does Marin's business please you?" The king replied, "Since he came here, he has importuned me more than any other servant of the Duke in the last ten years." Nell Gwynne then asked why, if the Duke had right on his side, Marin was not given a friendly answer. To this Charles II replied, "We will see what can be done in the matter." This conversation at least bore fruit to the extent that Marin was given an audience of the King a few weeks later, but the only result of the interview was a promise that Charles II would give the matter his further consideration.[5]

[1] C.S.P. Colonial (America and West Indies), 1669–1674, pp. 490–492; Acts of the Privy Council, 1680–1720, p. 58.

[2] Diedrichs, op. cit. pp. 61, 62.   [3] Ibid. p. 63.
[4] Ibid. pp. 63, 66.   [5] Ibid. pp. 65, 66.

In the following June the Duke addressed yet another memorial to his kinsman. He requested therein that either he should be given liberty of commerce in the Gambia in accordance with the terms of the agreement of 1664 or else that his possessions there should be restored to him, in which case he would allow the English free liberty to trade in the river.[1] Following upon this memorial his agent Marin had a further audience of Charles II, who said he would give the matter his further consideration, would to the best of his ability prove that he was not ungrateful to the Duke for his past services, and would refer the matter to Mr Secretary Jenkins. Nearly two months elapsed and nothing was done. Marin then had another audience on 3 November, only to be informed that Mr Secretary had been asked for an early report.[2] On 11 January of the following year, 1681, the Duke urged Marin once more to press his claims on the English Government, because "the Moors will not leave them in possession, and we must prevent this, as they still have under consideration the question of giving it back to us". But the Duke's "climacterical year" was long past. He was now over seventy and there is all the hesitancy of an old man about his next letter to his agent. He had learnt of the dissensions between Charles II and his parliament and on 22 February wrote instructing Marin not to press his claims until there was a better understanding between the two.[3]

On 28 October 1681, James, Duke of Courland, was gathered to his fathers. By his will made four years earlier he left Tobago and his fort on the Guinea coast to his second son, Ferdinand, and the debts owing to him by Charles II to his daughters. These last-mentioned legacies proved of little value.[4] From 1669 to 1678 the English monopoly in the Gambia was underlet by the Royal Adventurers to a body known as the Gambia Adventurers. It would appear that during the period of this underlease and for a short time after its expiration the Dukes of Courland were allowed to send ships to the Gambia to trade and that they did manage to do a certain amount of commerce, principally in hides. But after the resumption of control by the Royal African Company the reversioners insisted that Charles II's grant in 1664 was an infringement of his earlier grant to the Royal Adventurers in 1661. When therefore in

---

[1] "Mr Fanshaw's paper", Rawlinson MS. A, 181, f. 297.
[2] Diedrichs, *op. cit.* pp. 67–69.   [3] *Ibid.* pp. 64, 66.
[4] Cruse, *op. cit.* I, 182, 192.

1682 their chief agent at James Island reported that Courlanders were trading in the river,[1] instructions were sent to put a stop to the practice. The result was that when the new Duke sent ships in 1684 and 1690, they were all turned back.[2] Attempts to colonise Tobago proved like failures owing to obstruction from England.[3]

On the death of Frederick Casimir in 1698 Courlander visions of overseas dominions finally ceased. In 1741 Ernest John de Biron, the last Duke of Courland, was deposed and his country overrun by Russian troops. It was not until 1918 that Courlander nationalism was once more able to reassert its independence as part of the Latvian Republic.

Sufficient has been said in this chapter to make it clear that even under more favourable conditions James, Duke of Courland's, attempt to found an overseas empire would in all probability have been destined to failure. Not only was he hemmed in in his own duchy by more powerful states, who were quick to take advantage of his weakness, but he clearly lacked both the man-power and the officers of the necessary stamp to carry through his experiment successfully. Courland in his time was in the process of emerging from feudalism to mercantilism. The government was in the hands of a baronage, who clung to the traditions of the past and whose out-look was confined more or less entirely to the limits of their feudal domains. A middle class of merchants, soldiers, sailors, and the like was coming into being but it still lacked the power and influence to make itself felt and the experience and training to fit it for leader-ship. Though a curious fatalism seems to have induced the Duke to choose the worst type of foreign adventurer for his work, the fact none the less remains, and is proved by the history of Tobago as

---

[1] John Kastell to R.A.C., 11 May 1682, P.R.O., T. 70/10.

[2] Diedrichs, *op. cit.* p. 70.

[3] Cruse, *op. cit.* I, 194; Baron Charles de Blombergh to Captain John Poyntz, 11 June 1695, *C.S.P. Colonial (America and West Indies)*, 1699, p. 568; Sir Henry Dutton to Council of Trade, 30 June 1681, and 3 January 1682, *ibid.* 1681–1685, pp. 79, 181; "An impartial account of the true state of the case concerning the island of Tobago", *ibid.* 1685–1688, p. 342; *Acts of the Privy Council*, 1680–1720, pp. 58, 62, 330; *Calendar of Treasury Books*, 1681–1685, p. 1033; Sir Leoline Jenkins to Duke of York, 9 May 1682, *C.S.P. Domestic*, 1682, p. 201; Petition of John Poyntz, 26 February 1683, *C.S.P. Colonial (America and West Indies)*, 1681–1685, pp. 399, 467, 575; Petition of Nicholas Dupin, 7 March 1700, *ibid.* 1700, p. 114; Petition of John Poyntz, 24 June 1702, *C.S.P. Domestic*, 1702–1703, p. 432; Poyntz, *The Present Prospect of the Famous and Fertile Island of Tobago*.

well as that of the Gambia, that it was hard to find many men of the necessary experience and the right stamp amongst the Courlanders themselves. Men like Fock and Stiel were undoubtedly officers of proved merit and ability, but there were few others fit to hold positions of responsibility overseas.

The attempt by a small nation to establish an isolated settlement several thousands of miles from Courland in a sphere of influence which England, France, and Holland, then the three most wealthy and most powerful trading nations in Europe, each regarded as their own, was practically courting failure. It was more or less inevitable that one or other of these three countries would take a suitable opportunity to seize the island. There can be no question that St Andrew's Island would have passed into Dutch hands, if Holmes had not stolen a march. This serves to explain, but not to excuse, the conduct of Charles II. One must not judge seventeenth-century conduct in international affairs by the modern code as laid down at Geneva, but, after making every allowance possible for political expediency, one cannot get away from the fact that our mode of acquisition and subsequent retention of James Island was far from creditable. It was a case of taking and retaining property merely because the owner was known to be unable to defend or recover it or to retaliate in any other way. The subsequent legal casuistry, which was employed to evade our treaty obligations to the Duke, does not alter the fact that both the law and public opinion give such conduct a hard name. Charles II no doubt was personally anxious to be fair in his dealings with his kinsman, but he had to contend with the influential members of a powerful trading company, and without the aid of a parliament, with which he could not agree, he lacked the means to make the necessary amends. Again, this explains, but does not excuse, his failure to do justice. If the Duke of Courland had been a stranger in blood to the House of Stuart, the conduct of the English Government would still have called for condemnation. But when the wrong was done to a kinsman, who had given two Kings of England practical sympathy and aid in the shape of men, arms, ammunition, and money in the time of their adversity and had never been repaid for that generosity, one could wish that this episode in our colonial history could remain hidden for all time.[1]

[1] Diedrichs, *op. cit.* p. 28; "An impartial account of...Tobago", *C.S.P. Colonial (America and West Indies)*, 1685–1688, p. 342; *Clarendon Papers*, II, 162, 174, 202.

VII: Dutch rivalry, 1661–1678

In the last chapter we left the settlers newly established by Holmes on Dog Island and James Island to describe the Duke of Courland's vain efforts to recover his African possessions. In the present chapter we must return to follow the fortunes of those English settlers.

Before leaving for Sierra Leone Holmes arranged one or two important matters. He naturally decided to consolidate his position on James Island and accordingly brought twenty men under Lieutenant Morgan Facey from Dog Island to garrison the fort. Stephen Ustick and a Mr Fowler were also sent there as factors with a supply of goods. Two other factors were sent with a sloop to establish another factory in the Kombo country near the mouth of the river. The *Kinsale* was sent up river with Colonel Vermuyden and Monsieur La Prairie to report on Elephant Island as a possible site for a fort and to prosecute the search for gold. La Prairie returned on 24 March 1661, to report that the proposed fort on Elephant Island was out of the question.[1]

Vermuyden appears to have returned to James Island with La Prairie. He at any rate did not prosecute his searches very far at this date.[2] On 4 December he again proceeded up the river in a boat manned by seven other Europeans and four natives, of whom one was a marabout who spoke Portuguese and was intended to be employed as an interpreter.[3] He subsequently compiled a map setting out his alleged discoveries.[4] If he is to be believed, he got farther inland than Jobson and in fact than any other European until Mungo Park's time. According to himself he passed Jobson's Tenda and the confluence of the Neriko, which he named Pembroke River. He also claimed to have passed Jallacotta, where he professed to have seen "stoan houses", and to have arrived at another tributary of the Gambia, which he called "Stoak River", and which may be the Niokolokoba, and then was finally stopped in April 1662 from further progress by two falls or barrages, "where arriving I found

---

[1] Holmes' Journal, 19, 20, 23 and 24 March 1661, Pepys Sea MS. 2698; "A description of the Elephant Island, the 21st March, 1660(–1)", *ibid.*; Warburton, *Prince Rupert and the Cavaliers*, iii, 539, 540.

[2] Warburton, *op. cit.* iii, 540.

[3] Moore, *Travels into the Inland Parts of Africa*, App. III, p. 13.

[4] Royal MS. cxvii, 96.

the long expected end of our most toilsome and long voyage: for I believe never any boat, nor any Christians, have been so high in that river, as we. Here, upon the first trial I made, the exceed of gold was so much, that I was surprized with joy and admiration". He subsequently informed Prince Rupert concerning his discoveries, which he was resolved "never to divulge either for love or force; to which end I expect according to your faithful and solemn vows of secrecy, both of the business itself and likewise of which I would not be known to the King for £1000, being content with what proportion it hath pleased God to assign me, as well as with the King's revenue. Nor shall I wholly or fully discover the vast proportion of gold I discovered there, being so much, not fit to be communicated to paper, as not knowing to whose eyes or to whose hands this may come. I shall only tell you, I was more troubled to obscure its abundance from my fellows than to bring down what I got".[1]

Vermuyden's claim to have discovered rich veins of gold is clearly a gross exaggeration, but on his own showing he admittedly was not a petrologist. Bartholomew Stibbs, who followed in his tracks in 1725, alleged that Vermuyden was inaccurate in several respects in his description of the upper reaches of the river. Stibbs found the river far too shallow to allow a boat to get even so far as Tenda.[2] This, coupled with his palpable inaccuracy regarding his discovery of gold, does in a measure cast doubt on his assertions as to the distance which he travelled. But Thomson and Jobson had been able to get their boat as far as Tenda. Moreover, Stibbs appears to have made his attempt in a year when the river was exceptionally low and furthermore is not entirely accurate himself in his allegations of discrepancies in Vermuyden's journal.[3] On the whole therefore the weight of the existing evidence suggests that Vermuyden may well have got as far up the river as he claims, though his alleged discoveries of gold must be dismissed as vainglorious exaggeration. If he did not succeed in getting as far up the river as he alleged, at any rate the information obtained by him as to the upper

[1] Moore, *op. cit.* App. III, p. 13.

[2] *Ibid.* pp. 281, 285, and 294.

[3] On 21 February 1725, Stibbs refers in his journal to "York River, which the journalist of Anno 1661 mentions to be but 17 leagues above Barracunda, although I reckoned myself near 20 leagues above it already". He repeats this statement in a letter of 26 February to Robert Plunkett. Moore, *op. cit.* pp. 285 and 294. In actual fact "York River" (Grey River) is more or less where Vermuyden placed it on his map.

reaches was remarkably accurate. The one thing that is certain is that gold did not as a result of his discovery become one of the chief articles of export from the Gambia.

Whilst Vermuyden was prospecting up the river, the settlements at Dog Island and James Island were going through critical times. Holmes left the Gambia for Sierra Leone with the *Henrietta* and *Griffin* on 2 May 1661, leaving the *Assurance, Sophia, Amity* and *Kinsale* behind. Of these all except the last-mentioned returned to England before the end of the year.[1] During the last seven months of the year the number of soldiers, sailors, and factors was considerably reduced by sickness and death. Captain Francis Kerby was one of those carried off. He was succeeded in command by his lieutenant, Morgan Facey. Dog Island was for some reason retained as the headquarters of the settlement. At the beginning of 1662 there were 119 men there, but only forty-seven of them were capable of doing duty. There were twenty-nine men on James Island, of whom five were unfit for duty.[2] These were all called upon at the end of 1661 to go through a very anxious time.

As mentioned in previous chapters, the Dutch West India Company claimed to be entitled to the possession of James Island by reason of the agreement concluded in 1659 by the Amsterdam Chamber with Henry Momber and had through the States General formally protested against the seizure of the island by Holmes. As nothing came of this remonstrance, the officers of the Company at Goree decided to take matters into their own hands. At the beginning of December 1661 the Company's ship *Black Eagle* appeared in the river and anchored off Dog Island. It had on board thirty soldiers and two factors from Goree, of whom the chief was a certain Peter Justobaque. Justobaque landed on Dog Island and had an interview with Morgan Facey. It was subsequently alleged that, in order to secure for himself freedom from molestation, he produced a forged pass, which purported to be under Charles II's sign manual and to allow him freedom of trade in the river. He appears to have enlarged upon the precarious position of the English on James Island. He alleged that the Royal Adventurers would have to give it up and that in the circumstances the best course for them to

---

[1] Holmes' Journal, 2 May 1661, Pepys Sea MS. 2698; *Pepys' Diary*, 23 and 26 December 1661.

[2] Resolution passed at Charles Island, 25 January 1662, Pepys Sea MS. 2698.

adopt was to accept payment for themselves in money and goods for the surrender of the place. According to Justobaque himself certain of the officers on Dog Island, including Morgan Facey, were disposed to accept his offer and subsequent events suggest that his statement was true.[1]

As, however, there was reason to doubt whether the commander at James Island would fall in with that proposal, the *Black Eagle* proceeded thither. The English commander was a factor, named Stephen Ustick, who was then about twenty-five years old. According to him the two Dutch factors landed "and after a long discourse they told him they were come to treate with him about a busyness, which concerned him very much and all the rest that belonged to him. At last they told him it was about delivery of James Island into their possession, for which they would give him 1000 peeces of eight in hand and whatsoever fine goods he would choose out of their cargoe to the value of 500 peeces of eight more, and that they would give him goods and provisions for 6 moneths. And they told this deponent plainly, namely, Justobaque the chiefe, that he had 30 soldiers, which he brought from Cape de Verd on purpose to settle on James Island, and that he had some assurance from one, who had a greater command than this deponent had, which startled him very much. But this deponent replied, though another had a greater command than he, yet he should never command him to betray his trust, and wished them to leave of their discourses, for he scorned both their money and their goods, and, as long as he had powder and shott, they should never effect their desire. Upon which severe answer they went away for a place called Vintan (Bintang) to trade".[2]

Soon after this incident Captain Quick of the *Kinsale* and a factor named Patrick Robertson arrived at James Island from Dog Island. They tried to induce Ustick to change his mind, "telling him it was better to let them have the said island for soe much goods than to keep it, considering in what a low condicion he and his men were and that those goods should keep them at Charles Island a long time; and they were sure, if ever any shipps arrived in the river of Gambia

---

[1] Affidavit of Stephen Ustick, 7 June 1664, *C.S.P. Colonial (America and West Indies), 1661–1668*, p. 213; Holmes' Journal, 1 January 1664, Pepys Sea MS. 2698.

[2] Affidavit of Stephen Ustick, 7 June 1664, *C.S.P. Colonial (America and West Indies), 1661–1668*, p. 213.

from the Royall Company that James Island would be sleighted. And many other persuading words they used, which this deponent utterly refused to condescend unto".[1]

Meanwhile Justobaque and his companion, after holding some converse with the Portuguese at Bintang, crossed over to the north bank of the river to a place called Barcarem. At this date the King of Barra was lying on his deathbed. As they could not see him, they interviewed a "duke" of the country called Tambo. They paved the way for their proposals by bestowing "severall presents of brandy and lynen" and informed Tambo that they had come from Goree with all sorts of goods and pointed out that the English had no goods and only a small force of men. They therefore suggested that, if the people of Barra would make war against the English by land, the Dutch would do the like by sea and that, after the English had been expelled, they could trade together as formerly without any disturbance.[2] Though before his departure Holmes had assiduously "caressed" the natives and though one of his officers claimed that the natives "were so far won by their civil deportment that they showed themselves ready to lend them their utmost assistance",[3] the natural cupidity of the inhabitants led them to welcome the proposal. With them it was not a question of morals or politics. They were perfectly ready to support any newly arrived trader as long as he was ready to stock the goods they needed and to undersell his rivals. If he in his turn was followed by another trader who was ready to undersell him, their custom went to the new trader. Stiel had been unable to live up to the commercial standards which they preferred, and the English had bribed them with new goods. Consequently the Courlanders were thrown over for the English. Now for precisely the same reasons the English were to be thrown over for the Dutch.

After making this proposal Justobaque returned to Goree. The people of Barra were so impatient to carry out his advice that they did not wait for his return so as to conduct combined operations by sea and land. Some time at the end of 1661 or the beginning of 1662 they seized a sloop, which was sailing between Dog Island and James Island. They further took advantage of the dark and of low water to

---

[1] Affidavit of Stephen Ustick, 7 June 1664, *C.S.P. Colonial (America and West Indies)*, 1661–1668, p. 213.

[2] Attestation of William Quick, 1 June 1662; Affidavit of Stephen Ustick, 7 June 1664, *C.S.P. Colonial (America and West Indies)*, 1661–1668, pp. 91, 213.

[3] *The Kingdoms Intelligencer*, 29 July–5 August 1661, p. 485.

cross the dry channel between the former island and the mainland and to attack Charles Fort. They were successfully repulsed "with shame and loss", but none the less the situation was growing critical. In the latter part of January 1662 it was clear that a large number of canoes were assembling in the river with obviously hostile intentions. It was believed that the inhabitants of Foni and Kombo on the south bank were joining forces with those of Barra. Communication between the two forts became precarious. It could not be maintained by means of boats owing to the risk of their being cut off. The *Kinsale* had to be detailed for this duty and her voyages between the two forts were very uncertain owing to wind, weather, and tide.[1]

In this posture of affairs the *Black Eagle* once more reappeared in the river. She appears to have sailed past Dog Island without anchoring and made her way straight to James Island. What happened at James Island is best told in the words of Stephen Ustick.

The foremencioned factors they came again with their shipp before James Island and, rideing at anker, both the factors came presently on shore to this deponent; and falling to their former discourse about the said island, telling him that now they hoped his mind was altered and that he would give his consent to deliver them the present possession of the foresaid island and they would immediately performe that they had promised him, telling him that it was impossible for him to keep the said island, considering the warr the English had with the negroes and that by treachery they would surely cutt them off. For, said they, the natives are soe full of treachery that, upon the least suspition they have of your wants, they will attaque you or your boats; likewise telling him, this deponent, that the Royall Company were now no more a companie but were parted, (and) that he must expect no more shipps from England. But, however, they could give him a shipp to carry him and his men away with provisions and all other necessaries. But this deponent, seeing them soe earnest about his personal deliverie of the said island, commanded them forthwith from thence to depart and sett sail immediately, or else he would proceed against them as enemies. Upon which answere they soon after set saile and went down before Charles Island, where they stayed 2 daies.[2]

[1] Resolution passed at Charles Island, 25 January 1662, Pepys Sea MS. 2698; Smith, *A New Voyage to Guinea*, p. 32. Affidavit of Stephen Ustick, 7 June 1664, *C.S.P.* (*Colonial America and West Indies*), 1661–1668, p. 213.

[2] Affidavit of Stephen Ustick, 7 June 1664, *C.S.P. Colonial* (*America and West Indies*), 1661–1668, p. 213.

Justobaque evidently tried the same methods of persuasion at Dog (Charles) Island and was so far successful as to induce the English there to hold a council of war and pass a resolution to evacuate James Island "for want of experienced persons for managing any assault" and to concentrate their forces on Dog Island.[1] That resolution was communicated to Stephen Ustick at James Island, but one is not in the least surprised to learn that he did not comply with it. Having failed by peaceable means, the Dutch decided that it was not advisable to resort to aggression and therefore left the river.

After their departure the people of Barra realised that the Dutch were not going to give them the promised assistance or trade. The old "king" of Barra had died. The new "king" was not sufficiently firmly seated on his throne to feel that he could continue to prosecute the war against the English. Accordingly before June of that year a peace was patched up.[2] On 19 June, shortly after the making of peace, Justobaque once more appeared in the river with two ships. On this occasion the people of Barra, who felt they had previously been left in the lurch, declined to render the Dutch any aid. Instead, the "king" of Barra sent warning overland to Stephen Ustick. The Dutch sailed past Dog Island and arrived off James Island at seven o'clock on the morning of 21 June.

They came, said Ustick, *before the wind with a fresh gale. As soon as they arrived within shott of the fort, this deponent fired one gun a head of them with a shott to bring them to anchor, but they would not come to anchor. Soe he fired againe at them. Then they strud their topsailes and made as if they would anchor, but drove up still and did not anchor; which this deponent seeing fired a shott into one of them, and they presently answered it with another, which went just over the Kings flagg, and withall hoysed their topsailes, and made what saile they could to pass by the said island. But this deponent fired at them again severall times and they at the English, still aimeing at the flagg. Severall shotts fell within the fort, but, the wind being strong, they passed by after this deponent had shott above 20 guns at them and they about 15 or 16 at the flagg flying.*

They then went to a place called Vintan (Bintang), where they declared to Captain Manuell Vas de Franco, commander in chief for the

---

[1] Resolution made at Charles Island, 25 January 1662, Pepys Sea MS. 2698.
[2] Attestation of William Quick, 1 June 1662, C.S.P. Colonial (*America and West Indies*), 1661–1668, p. 91.

*King of Portugall in the river of Gambia, and Manuell Alves de Britto,
two of the chief Portuguese merchants in this river, that though the
young fellow at James Island was soe quick at their coming in, they
were resolved to have the said fort as they went out and did hope to coole
his courage, for they had now about* 100 *men in both shipps, with whom
they hoped to do their busyness; whereof the said merchants did speedily
give advice to this deponent. On the* 2d *day of July they came by again
about* 12 *of the clock at night, which this deponent espyeing fired at the
biggest ship and shot away her topmast. But they drove by in the night.
Soe he could not do more execution upon them.*[1]

The wind and tide carried the Dutch ships past James Island and,
without making any attempt on Dog Island, they sailed out of the
river. As mentioned in the previous chapter, the States General had
before the date of this incident formally renounced on behalf of
themselves and the Dutch West India Company all claim to James
Island in favour of the Duke of Courland. No doubt therefore the
Company sent instructions to their servants at Goree not to take
any further steps for the recovery of the island.

During the next eighteen months the English lived unmolested in
the river. They felt their position sufficiently secure to allow the
Kinsale to depart.[2] On the other hand there is no record of any
ships having arrived in the Gambia from England with either reinforcements, provisions, or stores, and it is evident from Holmes'
Journal that the Royal Adventurers were in more or less complete
ignorance of events in the river. At the end of 1663 Holmes was
again sent out in the *Jersey* to West Africa. Some rumours had
reached England that the Dutch had been guilty of high-handed
conduct both in the Gambia and farther down the coast. Holmes
was therefore commissioned by the Duke of York as Lord High
Admiral to escort the Adventurers' ship *Katherine* to Africa and to

---

[1] Affidavit of Stephen Ustick, 7 June 1664, *C.S.P. Colonial (America and
West Indies)*, 1661–1668, p. 213. Ustick appears afterwards to have got into
trouble with his employers, as is evidenced by the following entries in the
Minute Book of the Royal Adventurers:

15 August 1664. "Resolved that Lieutenant Ustick's petition be referred
to the Committy and that by reason of some misdemeanours alledged against
him the payment of his sallary (as Lieutenant) be referred until he hath
releaved himself of the same."

26 August 1664. "That Lieutenant Ustick's account for his services be
adjusted and paid off" (P.R.O., T. 70/75, ff. 16, 19).

[2] The *Kinsale* was paid off in England on 26 August 1662, *Pepys' Diary*.

make his way as quickly as possible to the Gambia, where he was
to acquaint himself with the position of affairs. He was instructed
to abstain, if possible, from any acts of hostility against foreigners,
but "in all cases, where the King's subjects in the service of the said
Company shall be attacked, or in any way indangered, you shall
indeavour to defend them". He was particularly enjoined to keep
a look out for the *Golden Lion*, a vessel which belonged to the Dutch
West India Company, was commanded by a Scot named James
Johnson, and was alleged to have done great injury to the Company's
shipping.[1]

Holmes left Queenborough on 21 November 1663, and reached
Cape Verde on 25 December. There he became wind-bound and
hung round the Cape for two days. On 27 December he sighted a
Dutch ship called the *Crown and Brill*, which he ordered to heave to.
He then proceeded to examine her papers and alleged that he found
amongst them an express order to the Governor at Goree to establish
settlements in the Rivers Gambia and Nunes. In the circumstances
he felt justified in detaining her and carrying her as a prize to the
Gambia, where he arrived on 30 December.[2] On arrival he proceeded to unload building materials and other stores out of his prize
for the use of the two forts. He was of course fully informed as to
Justobaque's exploits two years before.[3]

Whilst he was engaged in unloading stores a Portuguese vessel
arrived in the river with the news that a thirty-six gun ship had
arrived at Goree. Holmes thereupon summoned a council of war.
It was surmised that the man-of-war at Goree must be the obnoxious
Golden Lion. It was also realised that her commander would soon
get information of the seizure of the *Crown and Brill* by Holmes and
that he would in all probability retaliate by attacking the forts in
the Gambia as soon as the *Jersey* and *Katherine* had departed. It
was therefore resolved that the *Jersey*, *Katherine*, and *Coaker*, a
small frigate belonging to the Adventurers, should proceed with all
expedition to Goree and "there either take, sink, burn, or drive her
away to the southward before us".[4]

The three ships sailed on 15 January 1664, but owing to adverse
winds did not reach Goree till 20 January. They found the place

[1] Duke of York to Holmes, 10 November 1663, Pepys Sea MS. 2698.
[2] Holmes to William Coventry, 10 February 1664, *ibid.*
[3] Holmes' Journal, 1 January 1664, *ibid.*
[4] "The Result for Cape de Verd, 11 January 1663(–4)", *ibid.*

manned by a garrison which was greatly weakened by sickness and death. The forts were bombarded on 21 January and after a faint-hearted reply surrendered the following day.[1] The Dutch were allowed to remove their private property and the goods on board ships in the road were handed over to the Dutch West India Company's agents.[2] Holmes then sent a request to the Gambia for as many men as could possibly be spared to be sent to hold the two forts. Captain John Ladd, who was in charge in the Gambia, arrived with a small force, which was placed under the command of Captain Morgan Facey.[3]

Holmes and Ladd left Goree on 10 February and reached Cape St Mary the next day. Holmes did not enter the river but Ladd returned to assume command there, whilst the *Jersey* hung round the Cape to see if her presence was further required.[4] On 13 February Ladd wrote to complain that "the little time of my absence hath brought my busyness into such a labyrinth, that I am much troubled to find the right end of it, what with the inabilitie and carelessness of our storekeeper and the many things I had ordered, which I found undon".[5] But three days later he was able to report that all was well and the *Jersey* weighed and made sail for Sierra Leone.[6] Holmes' further exploits, which led to the actual declaration of war between England and Holland, do not concern the Gambia.

As soon as news reached England of the capture of Goree, it was at once apparent that the Dutch would make an early effort to recapture it. It was therefore resolved to strengthen the garrison by sending troops from England. These reinforcements arrived on 2 October under the command of Sir George Abercrombie, who landed and took over from Morgan Facey with great pomp and ceremony. He found that Facey had done little or nothing to put the island in a state of defence. Many of the guns were unmounted and the breaches caused by Holmes during his bombardment had not been repaired. Nine days later the Dutch Admiral de Ruyter appeared in the road with thirteen sail. Both the garrison and ships

---

[1] Holmes' Journal, Pepys Sea MS. 2698.

[2] Examination of Holmes, 3 March 1665, *C.S.P. Colonial* (*America and West Indies*), 1661–1668, p. 285.

[3] "The result of the factors and agents at Gambia, 26th of January, 1663(–4)", Pepys Sea MS. 2698.

[4] Holmes' Journal, Pepys Sea MS. 2698.

[5] Ladd to Holmes, 13 February 1664, Pepys Sea MS. 2698.

[6] Holmes' Journal, *ibid.*

appear to have been taken completely by surprise and the English surrendered almost without the semblance of striking a blow.[1] De Ruyter granted the English very fair terms. He gave them provisions and transport for Gambia and Sierra Leone. In pursuance of this agreement Abercrombie and sixty men were embarked on board the English ship *Good Hope* for the Gambia. As the master of the vessel was compelled to discharge part of his cargo so as to take on board the soldiers, he was promised compensation payable in Holland by the Dutch West India Company for the cargo thus discharged.[2]

In the words of a shrewd contemporary commentator the English were "beaten to dirt at Guiney by De Ruyter with his fleete;... it being most wholly to the utter ruine of our Royall Company, and reproach and shame to the whole nation, as well as justification to them in their doing wrong to no man as to his private property, only taking whatever is found to belong to the Company, and nothing else".[3]

The garrison in the Gambia, who had sent a frigate to the Gold Coast to warn the English there of the arrival of the Dutch fleet, waited in anxious expectation of an attack by De Ruyter.[4] But the Dutch Admiral passed by the river and made his way to the Gold Coast. His instructions were merely to perform the rôle of guardian of the peace and to put back Dutch subjects into possession of property which had been wrongfully taken from them by the citizens of another country. The States General was not making war on the English nation. It was merely seeking to obtain redress for the wrong done by the servants of an English trading company to their own subjects. But though De Ruyter to the best of his ability carried out his instructions, it was inevitable that the war should finally become general between the two nations.

After the recapture of Goree there were no further hostilities in the regions of the Gambia, but the effect of this reverse was that the Royal Adventurers became apathetic regarding the Gambia itself. They alleged that De Ruyter's reprisals had involved them in a loss

---

[1] "Particulars of a voyage in Captain Reynold's ship, April 1665", *C.S.P. Colonial (America and West Indies)*, 1661–1668, p. 294; *Pepys' Diary*, 24 December 1664.

[2] G. Brandt, *La Vie du L'Amiral de Ruiter*, pp. 226–229; Dapper, *Naukerige Beschrijveringe der Africaansche Gewesten*, p. 85.

[3] *Pepys' Diary*, 22 December 1664.   [4] Brandt, *op. cit.* p. 228.

of £50,000[1] and they made several vain applications for compensation. In 1667 the Treaty of Breda left each belligerent in the position of *uti possidetis*.

The apathy of the Adventurers in regard to the Gambia is best shown by the paucity of references to these regions in the Adventurers' Minute Book and the character of such few references as do occur therein. They do not appear even to have troubled to send an annual ship to those parts. On 23 January 1666, a certain "F.B." wrote to them from Oxford recommending that "a fly boate should be hired to send to Gamboa to bring home the 400 tunns of teeth, wax, and hides 'tis said Ladd hath on his hands". Twelve days previously the committee had agreed to send out an assortment of goods not exceeding £1000 in value.[2]

In the meantime Dog Island was abandoned. In view of the fact that it was connected with the mainland at low water and was consequently extremely vulnerable, it is perhaps surprising that it was not abandoned earlier. In the middle of 1667 there was a serious rising of the slaves on James Island. The slaves managed to get possession for the time being of the island and killed thirty-one or thirty-two of the English. Fortunately the *John* of London was anchored off the island and with the aid of her crew the rising was put down. About forty of the slaves were killed and the rest fled.[3]

Evidently the cargo brought back by the *John* did not come up to expectations, for on 3 October 1667 the Adventurers decided merely to employ the proceeds of sale in purchasing fresh goods for the Gambia and also "referred to the Committy to consider of the best way of how to carry on the trade of Gambia and to report it to the next court of assistants". Four days later the Minute Book recorded the fact that a number of persons had offered to furnish a stock of £15,000 to carry on that trade. On 14 October the Adventurers agreed to subscribe one-fifth of this sum. On 18 October it was agreed to give the subscribers to this stock the exclusive right to trade in the north parts of Africa until August 1668. The subscription list was to be confined in the first instance to the Adventurers, but was to be thrown open to the public if an insufficient

---

[1] Petition of African Company, 2 January 1665, *C.S.P. Colonial* (*American and West Indies*), 1661–1668, p. 266.

[2] Minute Book of Royal Adventurers, P.R.O., T. 70/75, ff. 40, 43.

[3] John Lysle to Sir Joseph Williamson, 16 September 1667, *C.S.P. Colonial* (*America and West Indies*), 1661–1668, p. 499.

number of them subscribed. These subsidiary Adventurers were to pay the grantors 13 per cent on all goods sent out to their sphere of trade.[1]

On 14 November 1668 the Adventurers intimated that they were ready once more to sublet their trading rights in the northern parts of Africa. Four days later proposals by a body of adventurers, who afterwards came to be known as the Gambia Adventurers, received the assent of the Royal Adventurers. It was agreed to grant the exclusive trading rights in those parts for a period of seven years commencing 1 August 1669, at an annual rent of £1000. The new stock was to be between twelve and twenty thousand pounds and the new adventurers were to give security in the sum of £20,000 for the due performance of the terms of the agreement. The new adventurers appear to have been for the most part the members of the previous joint stock.[2] The principal amongst them were Captain George Cock, Henry Johnson, and Thomas Crispe, who had been husband of the Royal Adventurers in 1663. Like their predecessors, the majority, if not all, of them were also Royal Adventurers and they had their offices in Africa House, the headquarters of the parent company.[3]

The minute books and correspondence of the Gambia Adventurers have not been preserved. Consequently very little is known of the Gambia during the period of their administration. They took over all the Royal Adventurers' forts and ports between Cape Blanco and Cape Palmas. In 1664, shortly after the departure of Holmes, factories were established in the river in Kombo, at Brefet in Foni, Gassan, "Forba" and Mangegar and also at Sierra Leone and in the Rio Nunes.[4] In the following year there were also factories at Rufisque (within a very few miles of the Dutch at Goree), Portudal and Joal, and in the Rio Grande.[5] The English appear

[1] Minute Book of Royal Adventurers, P.R.O., T. 70/75, ff. 60–63, 83.

[2] "That the new grant be not delivered before paying the arrears of 13 p. cent for the last goods sent out by the Adventurers due to the Company", Minute Book of Royal Adventurers, 27 November 1668, P.R.O., T. 70/75, f. 83.

[3] "That it be referred to the Committy that made the report to agree with the Adventurers of Gambia what share of house rent they shall allow towards their convenience of meeting at Africa House", Minute Book of Royal Adventurers, 6 April 1669, P.R.O., T. 70/75, f. 88.

[4] Ledger of James Island, 1684–1685, P.R.O., T. 70/827.

[5] Petition of African Company, 1665, *C.S.P. Colonial (America and West Indies)*, 1661–1668, p. 266.

therefore to have suffered no serious molestation from the Dutch after the departure of De Ruyter from Goree. In 1665 rumours reached England that an attempt was to be made to expel the English from the Gambia and that the local Portuguese had offered their assistance,[1] but nothing at all serious appears to have happened. The local servants of the English and Dutch trading companies appear to have worked on the principle of "live and let live" and without any reference to the state of the relations between their respective home governments. Dutch ships were evidently allowed to trade in the Gambia free from molestation.[2] About 1666 a Dutchman named William Block was at Gassan and described in his journal the necromantic powers of the "king" of Great Gassan called Magro. As this chief allowed English, French, Dutch, and Portuguese alike to trade in his country, it is clear that the Gambia Adventurers made no effective attempt to claim a right to exclude other European nations from the river,[3] though they maintained a small force of soldiers, who were evidently intended for protection primarily against native aggression.[4] In 1672 the local agent of the Adventurers in Sierra Leone did seize a French vessel, but Rice Wight, their chief factor in the Gambia, repudiated his conduct, as did the Adventurers themselves on learning of it.[5] In about April 1674 an English ship called the *Elizabeth* was taken by a Spanish

[1] Prince Rupert to Earl of Arlington, 12 September 1665, *C.S.P. Colonial (America and West Indies)*, 1661–1668, p. 322.

[2] "There is at present in the river a Dutch ship of 450 tons to buy teeth, wax and hydes, belonging to the Dutch West India Company, and an Englishman, by name Captain Elton, for slaves, the ship belonging to the Duke of Ormond, as he reports. If they be suffered to trade here, you cannot expect as large returns as if some means were taken to hinder them. I never yet had any orders from the Gamboa Adventurers to seize them, nor as yet from you", Thomas Thurloe to R. A. C., 28 May 1678, P.R.O., T. 70/10.

[3] Dapper, *op. cit.* pp. 418–420; Ogilby, *Africa, being an accurate description of...the land of Negroes*, pp. 355–358. In 1850 Lieutenant-Commander Selwyn of H.M.S. *Teazer* handed over to the Royal Military Repository, Woolwich, one of the earliest examples of a breach-loading cannon. He discovered it in the Commissariat Yard at Bathurst but learnt that it had been taken from the "king" of Barra in a war of about 1820. It bore the date 1650 and the inscription CONRAET WEGEVERT ME FECIT HAGAE, P.R.O., W.O. 44/524.

[4] Petition of the Adventurers trading to the northern parts of Africa, 23 February 1670, *C.S.P. Colonial (America and West Indies)*, 1669–1674, p. 57.

[5] Gambia Adventurers to Charles II, 9 July 1672, *C.S.P. Colonial (America and West Indies)*, 1669–1674, p. 502.

ship in the Gambia and carried as a prize to Portudal, but the reason
for this act and the upshot thereof is not clear. For some reason the
Captain of H.M.S. *Phoenix*, who convoyed one of the Adventurers'
ships to the mouth of the river shortly after this incident had occurred, did not feel either disposed or impelled to take any action
in regard thereto.[1] War broke out once again between the English
and Dutch in 1672, but there is an entire absence of any record of
hostilities between the two nations in the regions of the Gambia.
In fact, it would appear that the Dutch actually granted the
English licence to trade in time of war in the vicinity of Goree.[2]
In 1677 the French captured Goree and this capture was confirmed
to them by the Treaty of Nimeguen in the following year. In consequence all fear of danger from the Dutch West India Company was
removed.

The rule of the Gambia Adventurers in this part of Africa came
to an end almost at the same time as that of the Dutch West India
Company. The reversion of their grant had come into the hands of
a new trading company, called the Royal African Company, which
had on 27 September 1672 been incorporated as a body politic to
take over the territories of the bankrupt Royal Adventurers on payment of a sum of £34,000.[3] The Gambia Adventurers themselves
suffered from the same financial embarrassment as the original
grantors. At the beginning of 1675 they were in arrear with the rent
payable for their grant to the extent of £1080. 13s. 0d.[4] This and
various other matters in difference were the subject of protracted
discussion during that year, and finally the Duke of York was called
in as a mediator. Eventually at the Duke's suggestion it was agreed
that the Company should either forgo £1000 of the arrears of rent
or else extend the agreement with the Adventurers for a further
two years.[5] The Adventurers decided to try to retrieve their fortunes

---

[1] Log of the *Phoenix*, 5 April 1674, P.R.O., Ad. 51/3933.

[2] In 1695 Alexander Cleeve informed a Committee of the House of Commons
that, when he was in the Gambia in 1686, the French seized an English vessel
off the coast "under colour that our trade there was under a patente of the
Dutche and that wee had not a right to trade there", Notes by Robert Harley,
Harleian MS. 7310, f. 217.

[3] John Roberts, "An Account of the First Establishment on that part of the
Coast of Africa called Guinea", Royal MS. 200, f. 5.

[4] Minute Book of R.A.C., 12 January 1675, P.R.O., T. 70/76.

[5] Minute Book of R.A.C., 3 September, 5 October, 9 and 30 December 1675,
ibid.

by accepting the latter alternative.[1] The Adventurers' grant expired on 1 July 1676, but it was some time before they handed back the properties to the Royal African Company. Disputes arose as to the amount payable to the Adventurers for their property in Africa. On 8 January 1678, Philip Heron was appointed by the Company to proceed to the Gambia, Sierra Leone, and Sherboro and there to appraise the goods of Adventurers.[2] On 31 October the Adventurers submitted a demand for £12,000 in respect of the appraised value of these goods. Of this sum £6814. 8s. 2d. represented the value of property on James Island.[3] The reply to the demand was given on 10 December and was to the effect that "the thinge being under examination the Company are not yett prepared to give answeere".[4] The reason for this reply was because the Company considered that Heron had not performed his duties properly.[5] In 1679, after various attempts at amicable settlement of the differences between the two companies, the Adventurers commenced proceedings in Chancery.[6] The litigation was protracted, partly owing to efforts of the Duke of York to settle the matter out of Court,[7] but in June 1680 the Adventurers obtained an interim decree for the payment of £5000[8] and directing that the further matters in dispute should be referred to arbitration.[9] The arbitrators were even longer coming to a decision than the Court of Chancery, but on 1 February 1681 an interim award gave the Adventurers a further sum of £8000.[10] Matters still lingered on till 24 June 1684, when fresh arbitrators had to be appointed to bring the dispute to a final determination.[11]

The Royal African Company's Minute Books show that the process of handing over in the Gambia was for various reasons a protracted one. The extended period of the grant expired in 1678, but the Adventurers were still engaged in trade as late as 1683.[12]

[1] Minute Book of R.A.C., 13 September 1678, P.R.O., T. 70/78.
[2] Ibid.
[3] C.S.P. Colonial (America and West Indies), 1677–1680, p. 822.
[4] Minute Book of R.A.C., P.R.O., T. 70/78.
[5] Minute Book of R.A.C., 18 December 1680, ibid.
[6] Minute Book of R.A.C., 25 March 1679, ibid.
[7] Minute Book of R.A.C., 23 September 1679, ibid.
[8] Minute Book of R.A.C., 29 June 1680, ibid.
[9] Minute Book of R.A.C., 8 July 1680, ibid.
[10] Minute Book of R.A.C., 24 June 1684, P.R.O., T. 70/80.   [11] Ibid.
[12] "That the Gamboa Adventurers have liberty to sell their sugar at the said sale", Minute Book of R.A.C., 2 January 1683, P.R.O., T. 70/80.

In 1677 the Royal African Company began to appoint factors there.[1] They also took over a number of the Adventurers' servants on the spot, including Thomas Thurloe, the chief factor.[2]

With the exception of the ship seized by the Spaniards the Gambia Adventurers do not appear to have suffered from wars, tumults, and the acts of princes. None the less they were handicapped by the poaching of interlopers upon their preserves.[3] They also complained that they were handicapped by evasion of the Navigation Acts. They complained in particular in regard to their export from Africa of redwood, which was one of their principal commodities and was imported into England for dyeing purposes. On 29 November 1672 they petitioned to the Privy Council against the importation by the Dutch East India Company of sanders wood, which was "a very fading cheeting dye". Their petition was referred to the Council for Trade and Plantations, who in due course reported that in abuse of their monopoly the Adventurers had advanced the price of redwood from £26 to £80 a ton, that English clothiers could not buy it under the rate of £5 the hundredweight, and that the dyers of London were ready from experience to demonstrate that sanders wood was as good for dyeing purposes, as regards both quality and colour, and could be imported at between £10 and £12 a ton. They therefore recommended the encouragement of the Dutch to import sanders until such time as the English East India Company could furnish a sufficient quantity of it.[4] The result was that the

---

[1] Security bond of Joseph Pott "for Gambo", R.A.C. Security Books, P.R.O., T. 70/1428, f. 8.

[2] "Though I did undertake the Gamboa Adventurers' service for the small remainder of their time for £100 p.a., yet it was with a designe only to capacitate myself to serve you as cheif, for at my coming hither I was wholly ignorant allmost of the name of Guiny, much more of the trade of it, and not understanding the language", Thurloe to R.A.C., 29 May 1678, P.R.O., T. 70/10. "The kings of Phonio (Foni) and Barra, hearing of the change of Company, have each of them presented you with a negro boy", Same to same, 14 May 1678, *ibid.*

[3] Cf. letter from Thurloe to R.A.C., dated 28 May 1678, and cited in note 2 on p. 85; Minute Book of R.A.C., 12 November 1678, P.R.O., T. 70/78; Privy Council to Governor of Barbadoes, 1 March 1676, P.R.O., C.O. 268/1, f. 29; Samuel Pepys to Captain Dickenson, 29 May 1676, Pepys MSS. 2903, 3027, 3081; Samuel Pepys to Captain Peter Heywood, 17 August 1678, Rawlinson MSS. A, 214, f. 137 b.

[4] *C.S.P. Colonial (America and West Indies)*, 1669–1674, p. 438; *C.S.P. Domestic*, 1672–1673, pp. 190, 217; 1673, p. 142.

Gambia Adventurers were prohibited from importing redwood until September 1673.[1] At the end of their time they had a quantity of this wood on their hands, which was lying rotting for want of a purchaser.[2]

Other articles exported from Africa by the Adventurers were ivory[3] and slaves, who were carried to the American continent[4] and to the West Indies, where they were exchanged for sugar, which was brought to England.[5] The principal articles of barter, which were used for the purpose of acquiring commodities in the Gambia, were beads,[6] crewel[7] and "battery ware".[8]

Except for what they were able to reap as fruits of their protracted litigation with the Royal African Company, the Gambia Adventurers made little out of their grant. As already mentioned on a previous page, they fell into arrears with their rent. Even after the Company had accepted £200 worth of beads in part satisfaction of the debt, the arrears still amounted to £1080. 13s. 0d.[9] When petitioning the Privy Council in 1672 in regard to the prohibition of importation of sanders wood, the Adventurers alleged that they had "been at vast charges and expence for that end and suffered damage and losse almost to the totall decay of their stock by warr and other accidents; yet some trade still (is) being carried on for

[1] Memorial of Gambia Adventurers, 28 July 1673, *C.S.P. Domestic*, 1673, p. 464.

[2] Minute Book of R.A.C., 29 August 1682, P.R.O., T. 70/78.

[3] Licence to the Adventurers to import 1301 elephant teeth, 3 December 1669, Privy Council Register, P.R.O., P.C. 2/62.

[4] "This Company doe not hold themselves obleiged to provide shipping to fetch home the effects of the Gamboa Company....Notwithstanding, they paying such freight as the Company are to pay and can agree for, this Company ...will speedily have another ship for them and permitt them to lade fourscore negroes on the Aribella for Virginie, they bearing the charges and mortallity in proportion with those laden on the Company's account", Minute Book of R.A.C., 13 September 1678, P.R.O., T. 70/78. The ledger books for the period do not record any purchase of slaves in large numbers. For example, only sixty-six were purchased in 1664, P.R.O., T. 70/827.

[5] On 26 October 1677, eight lots of Jamaica sugar were sold by the Royal African Company on behalf of the Gambia Adventurers, Minute Book of R.A.C., P.R.O., T. 70/77.

[6] Minute Book of R.A.C., 7 and 12 January 1675, P.R.O., T. 70/76.

[7] Licence to the Gambia Company to export 500 lbs. of "cruel" to the Gambia, Register of Privy Council, 4 February 1670, P.R.O., P.C. 2/62.

[8] Register of Privy Council, 24 September 1669, P.R.O., P.C. 2/61.

[9] Minute Book of R.A.C., 12 January 1675, P.R.O., T. 70/76.

those parts ".[1] Doubtless it suited their immediate purpose to paint a somewhat highly coloured account of their financial embarrassment, but other evidence suggests that their statement was not far from the truth.

[1] Register of Privy Council, 29 November 1672, P.R.O., P.C. 2/63.

VIII : French rivalry, 1678–1689

Between March and May 1678, Thomas Thurloe, the former chief agent of the Gambia Adventurers in the River Gambia and the newly appointed chief agent of the Royal African Company in those parts, wrote a number of letters to his new employers acquainting them with the general position of affairs. In his estimation the trade of the river would yield yearly between five and six hundred slaves, who could be purchased at thirty bars of iron each. The other commodities were ivory, which was purchasable at eighteen bars per hundredweight, and wax purchasable at sixteen bars per hundredweight. Some fourteen to fifteen tons of ivory and wax could be purchased annually. The only other commodity of any value was hides, of which 10,000 could be purchased in a year at a price of about three bars each.[1]

Although the Gambia Adventurers were said to have had seventy men on the island in 1672,[2] it is clear that on the eve of their withdrawal they had reduced their staff almost below a bare minimum. Thurloe had to recruit his staff locally. He gives the following as the factors at the time his new employers assumed control:

Mr James Peers, who is generally imployed off the island in sloops up the river.

Mr John Camp, a Dutchman, who is very well verst in the trade of Cape Verde, being a factor there for the Dutch till Goree was taken. Then I entertained him for £40 p.an.

Mr Richard Fuller, who having some skill in navigation is master of the Agent *frigatt. At his first comeing hither he was sent to be mate of the* Gamboa Adventurer, *but is a fitter man to be a factor and would do you good service in that way. He hath £30 p.an.*

Edmund Hedge, a youth about 16 years old, who in a short time will be very serviceable to you, speaking Portuguese well and the negroe language indifferently. He hath at present £30 p.an.

Mr John Jolliffe, who is at present factor on the Santa Maria *yacht and is very fitt for that imploy. If ever he come again, he hath £40 p.an.*[3]

---

[1] Thurloe to R.A.C., 15 March 1679, P.R.O., T. 70/10. The bar was at this date reckoned at four shillings, Minute Book of R.A.C., 29 January 1680, P.R.O., T. 70/78.

[2] *C.S.P. Colonial (America and West Indies)*, 1669–1674, p. 412.

[3] Thurloe to R.A.C., 28 May 1678, P.R.O., T. 70/10.

This was a very small staff indeed to control the operations of trade between Cape Verde and the Rio Grande. Thurloe wrote on 15 March 1678, to say that he needed at least forty soldiers and thirty sailors to man the Company's coasting ships.[1] On the following 29 May he declared that it was impossible to carry on at headquarters and to give proper personal supervision to the trade unless he had an accountant and two warehousekeepers.[2] A year later he complained that there was nobody left on board the *Hopewell* to navigate her and that the one person on James Island who was capable of navigating her, declined to go on board the ship.[3]

A nominal roll sent home from James Island shows the position six years later when the African Company had had more time to arrange things on a satisfactory footing. John Booker, the "second", was in charge. The garrison on James Island comprised a gunner, sergeant, corporal, and twelve soldiers. There were also seven European artisans and servants on the island and Edward Salisbury, the surgeon. The factors and writers were all at out factories or else trading on board coasting vessels. One factor was at Barrakunda with a soldier. Another was with the surgeon's mate in "Jemarrow" (Fuladu West), apparently at Buruko near MacCarthy Island. A third factor, William Quinn, who was destined to prove a source of great trouble, was at "Sangrigoe" in the Bintang Creek. There was also a writer at "Furbroh". One of the factors was on board the *Gambia* ketch, on the way to Cape Verde "to be settled" near that point. A soldier was in charge of the Company's plot of ground at Juffure and another soldier was stationed at Banyon Point (Half Die). The *Ann* and *Agent* sloops were plying up and down the river between James Island and the outlying factories. The *North* smack was at Bur Salum just to the north of the Gambia and the *Santa Maria* had gone to "Felan" to buy salt. The *Coaster* had just arrived from Barbadoes.[4]

One of the many troubles that beset the Company's servants in the Gambia was poaching by English interlopers, which the Gambia Adventurers had been more or less powerless to prevent. On 28 May 1678, Thurloe wrote to England to say that an English ship was then in the river claiming to be owned by the Duke of Ormond and that in a recent voyage to Cape Verde the *Convert* had

---

[1] P.R.O., T. 70/10.   [2] *Ibid.*
[3] Thurloe to R.A.C., 29 March 1679, P.R.O., T. 70/10.
[4] Nominal Roll of James Island, 18 March 1684, P.R.O., T. 70/1441.

been unable to do good trade by reason of the fact that another English or Irish interloper had offered better prices to the natives. "If they be suffered to trade here," he complained, "you cannot expect so large returnes as if some meanes were taken to hinder them. I never had any order from the Gamboa Adventurers to seize them, nor yet from you; therefore desire that you would be pleased to give me full instructions."[1] On 12 November of the same year the African Company, as empowered by the terms of their charter, ordered commissions to be drawn up to seize interlopers and to take them to Cape Coast for condemnation by the Vice-Admiralty Court there.[2] On 22 June 1680 Thurloe's successor, Thomas Forde, wrote to say that he had seized the *Phoenix* by virtue of this commission but, lacking the means of sending her to Cape Coast, had been compelled to release her on bond with the presumable result that she would continue to poach on the Company's preserves.[3] Previous to this, in March of the same year, another commission had been issued to Thurloe empowering him to seize interlopers and constituting a Court of Admiralty at James Island.[4] In 1681 an interloper, named How, killed one of the Company's slaves. The agent retaliated by seizing eight of his men, but apparently had to release them and to write to his employers of his "want of commission to return blowes for blowes".[5] A subsequent and less aggressive interloper complied with an order to leave the river,[6] but owing to the irregularity of communication with England the agent in 1683 felt himself obliged to purchase "a barque a longee" from another of the fraternity.[7] Condescension to such dealings hardly strengthened his hands for dealing with other interlopers. By 1685 interloping had become so persistent that the services of the *Orange Tree* frigate were obtained from the Government to cope with the offenders. This frigate turned a number of ships away from the river,[8] seized a ship and a sloop, and carried them to Cape Coast to be condemned.[9] Captain James

[1] P.R.O., T. 70/10.
[2] Minute Book of R.A.C., P.R.O., T. 70/78. On 14 November 1678 it was resolved by the Company "that there be a Court of Admiralty settled at Gamboa", *ibid*.   [3] P.R.O., T. 70/78.
[4] Minute Book of R.A.C., 18 and 23 March 1680, P.R.O., T. 70/78.
[5] John Kastell to R.A.C., 11 August 1681, P.R.O., T. 70/10.
[6] Same to same, 20 February 1683, P.R.O., T. 70/10.
[7] Same to same, 14 October 1683, P.R.O., T. 70/10.
[8] Alexander Cleeve to R.A.C., 9 March 1685, P.R.O., T. 70/10.
[9] *The Case of William Wilkinson.*

Jobson in the *Ann* sloop seized another interloper about the same time, which the agent at James Island condemned in his Admiralty Court and declared forfeit to the Company. As he lacked the necessary officers to man the prize, he had to recommission it in the Company's service under the same master.[1] The owners, however, were not prepared to acknowledge the legality of the condemnation and, when in 1688 Jobson returned to England, they caused him to be arrested at their suit for an illegal seizure and at the same time commenced proceedings against the Company.[2]

Naturally the strongest objection to the interlopers was that they sold their goods cheaper and bought the local commodities at higher prices than the Company in its own interest thought desirable. The methods employed by many of them were also a source of anxiety. The Company had a permanent stake in Africa and was therefore anxious to maintain a reputation for fair dealing with the natives. It also had the advantage of being able to exercise some measure of disciplinary control over its local agents. But the case was very different with the interlopers. "Few or none of them", wrote one of the Company's partisans, "had any consideration in view than barely the ready disposal of all such cargoes as they carried along with them (no matter to whom or which way) and the speedy procuring of negroes, or any other commodities, which they could get on the coast, whether by purchase or otherways, so as not to stay long there; for accomplishing which design they stuck at nothing, but were too frequently guilty of such sinister practices, as proved not only very injurious to the private interest of the Company, but likewise disgraceful and pernicious to the British interest in general among the natives; insomuch that the Company's agents were frequently obliged to vindicate the Company by making the natives sensible they were none of the Company's ships or servants."[3] In 1692, for instance, the Company's agent in the Gambia reported that an interloper named Plowman had kidnapped two of the "king" of Joal's subjects and urged the Company to take steps to recover them and send them back, as such "actions will endanger many men's lives".[4]

---

[1] Alexander Cleeve to R.A.C., 9 March and 30 November 1685, P.R.O., T. 70/11.

[2] Minute Book of R.A.C., 9 July 1688, P.R.O., T. 70/82.

[3] D'Avenant, *Political and Commercial Works—Reflections upon the Constitution and Management of the Trade to Africa*, v, 89.

[4] John Booker to R.A.C., 20 July 1692, P.R.O., T. 70/11.

Interlopers were not the only obnoxious visitors to the River Gambia. Pirates hung round the coast to prey on shipping from Africa and America. In November 1683, a pirate named Anderson entered the river with a small pink of seven or eight guns and anchored off James Island. It happened to be an extremely sickly season. Between 21 November of that year and 30 July of the next year no less than twenty-two of the Company's servants died, another was drowned, and two were killed by the natives. Anderson therefore found the island in a more or less defenceless state, which was not improved by the discontent prevailing amongst the garrison. Six of the Company's servants deserted to the pirate. Anderson also helped himself without any real opposition to such provisions and tackle as he wanted for the purposes of his trade. Then he learnt that there was a French ship trading in the Rio San Domingo (River Cachau). He went after her, took her and brought her back to the Gambia. As she was more seaworthy than his pink, he transferred his flag to her and sold the pink to Alexander Cleeve, the chief agent at James Island. It was further alleged on the very doubtful statement of the pirate himself that Cleeve bought a lot of property he had obtained by plundering the Cape Verde Islands, but there is no confirmation of this. Cleeve had, however, subsequently to admit that he had bought the pink and that her sheathing boards needed replacement at the time of such purchase. He further had to admit that he omitted for close on four months to inform his employers in England of the transaction.[1] Needless to say, the African Company's many enemies sought to make a great deal of capital out of an incident "to the everlasting discredit of the Union Flag, which hung on the fort, blushing to be made the mortal enemy of mankind and the patron of the vermin of the sea".

Native affairs also gave ground for anxiety. In 1686 Alexander Cleeve somewhat unwisely took the opportunity at the death of one "king" of Barra to intervene in the matter of selecting a successor. In the end Cleeve's candidate was accepted but very probably he did not owe the slightest bit of his success to the Englishman.[2]

[1] Wilkinson, *Systema Africanum*, pp. 10–11; Cleeve to R.A.C., 18 March and 10 May 1684, P.R.O., T. 70/11; Nominal Rolls of the Gambia, P.R.O., T. 70/1428.

[2] The kingship of Niumi (Barra) belonged to seven families, each of which took it in rotation to succeed. Macklin, "Queens and Kings of Niumi", in *Man*, May 1935, pp. 67, 68.

Cleeve, however, thought his influence had turned the scale and that "Gennow" Sonko, the new king, could be treated as the Company's nominee. Gennow was of a different opinion and soon intimated the fact. Upon one occasion he made a very extortionate demand for compensation for an assault, which had been committed by a captain named Hodges[1] upon one of his subjects, and seized the agent at Juffure in order to enforce his demand. Cleeve decided to go to the mainland to have an interview with the "king". One account of that interview comes from an admittedly hostile source but it clearly contains some degree of accuracy and is too diverting to omit.

The king...arose from his place to come and commune with the said agent concerning the matter, and coming to the town of Jillefree, sent the agent word he was coming to speak with him, but the agent returned answer to the alcade, that, if the king would speak with him, he should make haste, for he would depart with the next high water. At which the king said "I will go, if my master commands"; and so went to the agent's pallisadoes, and there sat down at the foot of a great tree to await his master Cleeve's approach, who was no sooner come into the king's presence, but with a great deal of impudence said, "How now, old Gennow, how is it?"

But one of the grandees, by name Sambalama, taught him better manners by reaching him a box on the ears, which beat off his hat, and a few thumps on the back, and seizing him, disarmed him together with the rest of his attendance, amongst which was Benedict Stafford, commander of the Margaret, *now in London (who made his escape and ran like a lusty fellow to his ship) and William Bramble, commander of the* Coaster, *now in London, and several others, who together with the agent were taken and put in the king of Barrow's pound and stayed there three or four days till their ransom was brought, value five hundred bars.*

It was apparently through the good offices of the ruling chief of Foni that the ransom was fixed at so low a price. Needless to say, the Company censured Cleeve for his indiscretion in incurring the

---

[1] Hodges is the "Capitaine anglais Agis" of *Le Premier Voyage du Sieur de la Courbe*, pp. 203–204, 270–272 and Labat, *Nouvelle Relation de l'Afrique Occidentale*, iv, 277–279; v, 7–11. According to these works he was once guilty of a particularly brutal and revolting murder, but, though what is elsewhere recorded of Hodges does not paint him in at all a favourable light, it must be said in justice to him that the same story is told of another Englishman farther down the coast. In either case every allowance must be made for distortion of a widespread rumour amongst the natives.

risk, which he did run. Being a strictly commercial body, they also instructed him to demand the return of the five hundred bars' worth of goods. It is equally unnecessary to say that the demand was never complied with.[1]

Cleeve was also guilty of equally indiscreet conduct a few months later. The Company had a factory at Geregia (Sangrugo), which was in charge of an Irishman named William Quinn. Unlike most of his colleagues he was a good French scholar, but this was not regarded as a recommendation by the chief agent. When in June 1686 La Courbe, the chief agent of the French Senegal Company, paid a visit to Quinn's factory, Cleeve's worst suspicions seemed to be fulfilled. He accused Quinn, rightly or wrongly, of betraying the Company's interest to the French and of embezzlement of the Company's property. Quinn was therefore requested to submit his accounts forthwith. He declined to do so and on 1 January 1688 "hee declared himself to bee no longer the Company's servant, having the promiss off the king of Sangrigoe for his protection".[2] In order to be sure of that protection he handed over all the Company's goods to his protector. He also threw away all his papers.[3] The chief agent appears to have requested the chief to hand over Quinn, but the chief either declined to do so or else made no reply to the demand. The agent then decided to make a demonstration in some force so as to procure his servant's surrender. An armed vessel was accordingly sent up the Bintang Creek to Geregia. But on arrival it was received with a heavy fire from a number of musketeers, who had taken cover in the surrounding scrub. According to a French account several of the crew were killed. At any rate so many bullets fell in or near the vessel as to make the English deem it expedient to retire.[4] An attempt was then made to induce the chief to pay the debt of the defaulting factor. As was only to be expected, he declined to do so.[5] Quinn, however, soon found himself in an intolerable position. He was entirely dependent for his life and liberty upon the good will of a capricious native chief, was unable to procure any means of

[1] Wilkinson, *op. cit.* pp. 11–12; Cultru, *Le Premier Voyage du Sieur de la Courbe*, pp. 270–272; Cleeve to R.A.C., 5 March 1687 and 25 January 1688, P.R.O., T. 70/11.

[2] Ledger of James Fort, 1687–1688, P.R.O., T. 70/832.

[3] John Booker to R.A.C., 12 February 1689, P.R.O., T. 70/11.

[4] Cultru, *Le Premier Voyage du Sieur de la Courbe*, pp. 204, 208.

[5] Booker to R.A.C., – July 1688, P.R.O., T. 70/11.

livelihood, and was unable to leave the chief's territory for fear of arrest. After six months of very uncomfortable existence at Geregia, he sent word to say that, though he declined to come to James Island, he was ready to discharge the debt due by him to the Company.[1] His ability to fulfil this latter promise depended entirely upon the good will of his protector. No opportunity was given to him of keeping his word. It was hopeless for him to expect ever to return to Europe unless he could make his peace with his former employers. Eventually therefore he was forced to surrender. He obtained a passage to England either on one of the Company's ships or else that of an interloper. On arrival he was arrested by the Company for debt and thrown into prison, but was released from the Wood Street Compter at the beginning of 1691, on giving a signed acknowledgment that he owed the Company £292. 1s. 0d.[2]

The Company's slaves were an even greater source of trouble and danger than contumacious factors. At the end of 1681 or beginning of 1682 there was a serious mutiny on James Island itself. In subsequent letters home the agent, John Kastell, had to admit that the garrison was completely taken by surprise. One Englishman was killed and eight wounded. The soldiers entirely failed to rise to the emergency, but with the assistance of a factor, named Booth, and a few loyal natives the mutiny was suppressed. Thirty-four of the mutineers were killed and forty wounded.[3]

Added to other troubles, the free inhabitants of the adjacent mainland were not infrequently hostile. In 1684 the mate of the *Anne* and another of the Company's servants were murdered and two other servants met with the same fate in the following year.[4] In 1685 a carpenter was murdered by the natives.[5] Later there was also trouble between the natives farther down the coast and the Company's coasting vessels. In September 1686 the *John and Sarah* pink was attacked at Cachau, apparently with the connivance of the Portuguese governor, and the master and a cabin boy killed. In November of the same year, whilst in the Rio Nunes, the native crew of the *Agent* sloop mutinied and murdered one of the European

---

[1] Nominal Rolls of Gambia, 30 June 1688, P.R.O., T. 70/1442.

[2] Minute Book of R.A.C., 20 January and 27 February 1691, P.R.O., T. 70/ 83. Security book of R.A.C., 27 February 1691, P.R.O., T. 70/1428.

[3] Kastell to R.A.C., 24 January and 14 October 1682, P.R.O., T. 70/10.

[4] Nominal Rolls of James Island, P.R.O., T. 70/1441.

[5] Ledger Book of James Island, P.R.O., T. 70/832.

sailors. The sloop was then seized by the natives of the country and had to be redeemed.[1]

But unsatisfactory servants, troublesome native chiefs, interlopers, pirates, and mutinous slaves were far from being the most serious obstacles to the promotion of the Company's trade and influence in the River Gambia. The Royal African Company's charter of 1673 was granted in the same year as the purchase in France by a company known as the African Company of the remainder of the term of the French West India Company's rights in Africa.

The Royal African Company's assumption of control in the Gambia more or less coincided with the transfer in 1681 of the French African Company's rights to another Company known as the Senegal Company.[2] It also more or less coincided with the capture in 1677 by Admiral d'Estrées of the Dutch forts at Goree. The consequent disappearance of the Dutch from the regions of the Gambia was followed by the appearance of a nation, which was to prove a far more formidable rival, and of a powerful trading corporation, which in the first flush of victory was ready to go to great lengths to exclude all other nations from what they claimed as their sole sphere of influence.

When d'Estrées captured Goree on 1 November 1677, one of his captains, named Ducasse, proceeded to Rufisque, Joal, and Portudal with a forty-gun ship. He easily captured these three places and then proceeded to make treaties with the local chiefs, which assured the monopoly of all trade to the French in exchange for annual presents. In 1678 Ducasse entered the River Gambia[3] and apparently established a short-lived post on Dog Island, which came to an abrupt end when the natives surprised and massacred the French.[4] In 1679 the chiefs at Portudal attacked the French factory

[1] Cleeve to R.A.C., 25 January 1687, P.R.O., T. 70/11; Ledger Book of James Island, P.R.O., T. 70/832.

[2] Tallot, *La Colonie Française du Sénégal*, p. 25.

[3] Durand, *Voyage au Sénégal*, pp. 40, 41.

[4] This appears to be the only date assignable for the massacre of the French on Dog Island, to which reference is made by Le Maire (1695) in his *Voyages... aux Iles Canaries, Cap-Verd, Sénégal et Gambie*, p. 191, and Barbot (1732) in his *Description of the Coasts of North and South Guinea*, p. 73. It is remarkable, however, that there is no mention of the occurrence in contemporary English records. The only alternative date to assign for the massacre is 1612, the year of de Briqueville's abortive settlement in the Gambia, which is referred to in *Mémoire du Voyage aux Indes Orientales du Général Beaulieu* in Thevenot's *Collection des Voyages*, p. 128. That account, however, attributes the failure

and plundered the goods. Ducasse landed 800 men and marched into the interior. He brought the chief of Baol-Salum to terms, regained possession of Rufisque, and forced the chief of Cayor to submit. He obtained treaties from these chiefs whereby France was given the overlordship of the whole country between Cape Verde and the River Gambia for a distance along the coast of thirty leagues and extending into the interior for a distance of six leagues.[1] These territorial cessions gave the French proprietary rights on the north bank of the River Gambia as far up as Juffure opposite to James Island. Though the chiefs themselves treated the documents as scraps of paper and were ever ready to make concessions to the peoples of other nations, which infringed the terms of their treaties with the French, the documents none the less had some value in Europe and could be used as evidence of title, when it came to international disputes regarding the merits of rival claims of different European nations.

By 1681 in consideration of a monthly payment of four bars of iron the French had obtained a grant from the ruling chief of Barra of a small plot of ground at Albreda, which lies on the north bank nearly opposite to James Island.[2] Thereafter French and English factors traded side by side in the adjacent village of Juffure and French ships anchored off Albreda without saluting the flag flying over James Fort.[3] The chief agent of the African Company was subsequently blamed for permitting this state of affairs, but it is clear that he was not in a position to oppose it either directly or indirectly. Though the charter of the Company granted them the exclusive right of trade in the Gambia and elsewhere, neither the existing Company nor their predecessors had ever had the wisdom to do what the French did in other places, namely, to obtain a grant of a monopoly from the local chiefs. The Company seemed to think that their grant and the grants to their predecessors in title conferred upon them some sort of prescriptive right to such a monopoly, but the local chiefs not unreasonably and perfectly justifiably

of the expedition of 1612 to sickness and not to native hostility. It is in any case remarkable that neither Le Maire nor Barbot gives any details of the massacre.

[1] Cultru, *Le Premier Voyage du Sieur de la Courbe*, p. xli; Labat, *op. cit.* IV, 118–120.

[2] John Kastell to R.A.C., 23 May 1681, P.R.O., T. 70/10; Cultru, *Le Premier Voyage du Sieur de la Courbe*, p. 200.

[3] Wilkinson, *op. cit.* p. 10.

thought otherwise. The question for the local inhabitants was whether or not it was advantageous that another trader should set up in business in their district, and the answer to such a question was obvious. Nothing short of a very material and very advantageous inducement from the trader on the spot could have altered that decision. The English on James Island lacked the power, the influence, and the money to exclude the French from Albreda. All that agent Cleeve could report to his employers was that, whilst the ruling chief of Barra was perfectly ready to entertain the French, he still gave the English good words.[1]

The French settlement at Albreda was a very temporary affair consisting apparently at first of a single native hut, which was burnt to the ground early in 1686.[2] It was then replaced by buildings on an equally unpretentious scale. Five huts were erected, of which one was a store, another a kitchen, and another a chicken house. The post was placed in charge of a single factor named La Coste, whose only European colleague was a sailor named Hugues Maret.[3] But the post none the less served as a base for trading voyages up the river, and after 1681 French boats went past James Island unmolested.[4] In 1684 a French ship lay in the river for seven months, and on its departure the commander announced his intention of returning again the following year.[5] Chief agents on James Island constantly wrote home to say that the French were ruining the English trade and pointing out their powerlessness to obstruct or hinder them.

In 1686 Jean Jajolet de la Courbe, the Director General of the Senegal Company, paid a visit to Albreda. For reasons, which will be explained later, he deemed it inadvisable to pay a state visit to James Island, but he paid an informal visit to the English factor at Juffure. He much admired the fruit and vegetable garden there. His host entertained him with punch, which he served out of a silver bowl. La Courbe very much appreciated the drink but did not allow his appreciation to let him neglect his duty of eliciting from his host

---

[1] Cleeve to R.A.C., 30 November 1685, P.R.O., T. 70/10.

[2] Cultru, *Le Premier Voyage du Sieur de la Courbe*, p. 123.

[3] Cultru, *Histoire du Sénégal*, p. 115; *Le Premier Voyage du Sieur de la Courbe*, p. 270.

[4] John Kastell to R.A.C., 23 May 1681, P.R.O., T. 70/10; Alexander Cleeve to R.A.C., 30 November 1685, P.R.O., T. 70/11.

[5] Alexander Cleeve to R.A.C., 31 May 1684, P.R.O., T. 70/11.

full information regarding trade prospects on the south bank of the river. Embarking on a shallop he left Albreda and, keeping a discreet distance from James Island, entered Bintang Creek and made his way up to Geregia, where he visited the English factor, made him a present of brandy, and pursued his enquiries regarding trade. He also paid a visit to the "king" of Geregia. Leaving Geregia he made his way overland to the Portuguese settlement at Bissao and thence back to Goree.[1] One of the immediate results of this journey was that a French factor was sent to establish another post at Geregia.[2] Another result was a change in the attitude of the Portuguese in the regions of the Rio Grande towards the English.

The two French settlements in the Gambia were not, however, destined to be as formidable rivals as was at first feared. Like the African Company, the Senegal Company were not always fortunate in their choice of servants. In 1687 rumours reached Goree that the factors at Albreda and Geregia were not giving satisfaction. The Governor therefore sent two officers to investigate. It was believed that La Coste, the factor at Albreda, had embezzled eight ounces of gold, which had been consigned to him to hand over to Sidi Sonko, one of the leading chiefs of Barra. The investigating officers found that he had destroyed some of his papers and that his books had not been properly kept. They were unable to discover the missing gold but believed he had handed it over to a mulatto woman, named Lucia, whose house they were, however, afraid to search for fear of being murdered by the natives.

Cristaye, the factor at Geregia, flatly refused to allow his papers to be examined, declaring that it would cost the life of anyone who attempted to inspect his strong-box. He destroyed his papers and threw them into the creek, swearing that he would not in any circumstances return to Goree. Both he and La Coste were, however, arrested and taken to Goree. Some days after their arrival the two made their escape along with two factors named Ronzy and La Fonte, who were likewise accused of embezzlement. They were able to seize a boat laden with merchandise and to make their way to Joal. There the natives seized the boat and robbed the four of everything they had. The fugitives then made their way overland to the Gambia, where they joined forces with an Englishman—probably the contumacious William Quinn at Geregia. Eventually the four

[1] Cultru, *Le Premier Voyage du Sieur de la Courbe*, pp. 190–233.
[2] Cultru, *Histoire du Sénégal*, p. 115; Wilkinson, *op. cit.* p. 10.

took service under a pirate. The immediate result of their misdeeds was that the factories at Albreda and Geregia had for the time being to be closed by the French.[1]

Rival French factories in the River Gambia need not in any case of themselves have been a cause for serious alarm. Good business management and tactful handling of the local inhabitants might easily have made those factories so unprofitable as to induce the French to close them down. But the line of action taken by the newcomers along the coast to the north of the river afforded good reason for serious alarm. As has been mentioned on previous pages, the English had at one time or other established factories at Rufisque, Portudal, and Joal. None of these factories was permanent. They were periodically closed down, when either the African Company lacked the necessary staff to man them, or the local inhabitants proved unfriendly, or local trade made them unprofitable. At the time of the capture of Goree by the French there were no English factories at any of these three places, but they none the less claimed the right to establish themselves at these places with the consent of the local chiefs. As already mentioned, the French had in 1679 extracted treaties from those chiefs conferring upon them the exclusive right to trade in those regions. It does not appear whether the French communicated the purport of these treaties to the English or whether the local chiefs really understood their meaning. Even if the chiefs knew what they had purported to concede, they did not attach any sanctity to their agreements and were perfectly willing for good terms to let any nation trade in their territories.

In 1680 the sloop *Mary* was sent by the chief agent at James Island with a cargo to trade at Joal and Portudal. When she arrived off the latter place, she was seized by an armed French vessel and carried to Goree, where the crew were detained for six weeks. The vessel was released subsequently on a protest being made by the agent at James Island, compensation being paid for her cargo and her detention.[2] But in the following year the incident was repeated when the African Company's ship *Margaret* was similarly seized off Portudal and carried to Goree. On protest being made this vessel was also released with her cargo intact, and Joseph Bramant, the

---

[1] Cultru, *Histoire du Sénégal*, pp. 115–116; *Le Premier Voyage du Sieur de la Courbe*, p. 270.

[2] Wilkinson, *op. cit.* p. 15; Labat, *op. cit.* IV, 330; John Kastell to R.A.C., 2 March and 23 May 1681, P.R.O., T. 70/10.

commander of the French vessel, was dismissed for his action.[1] Hostile critics of the Royal African Company were indignant that the chief agent in the Gambia did not resort to reprisals, but it is clear that he was powerless to do so and that a firm protest was at this date sufficient to meet the situation. For a variety of reasons the French were not in a position to affirm effectively their alleged rights of monopoly and for the time being made no more seizures of the English Company's ships.[2]

In 1684 the English had re-established their factories at Portudal and Joal, and their ships were trading up and down the coast between Cape Verde and the River Gambia.[3] The French at Goree sent a summons in that year to the chief agent at James Island to remove these factories, but the agent declined to comply with the demand and for the moment nothing further was heard of the matter.[4] It would appear in fact that the French and English in Africa arrived at a tentative agreement without any intervention of their respective home governments. The agreement apparently was that the English would abstain from trading in the River Senegal, that the French would similarly abstain from trading in the River Gambia, and that the whole of the trade of the coast should be thrown open to both nations.[5]

But the agreement, whatever its terms, was not destined to endure long. As mentioned on a previous page, when La Courbe visited Albreda in June 1686, he did not visit the chief agent at James Island. After he had departed for Geregia the commander of the *Catherine*, the vessel which had brought La Courbe to Albreda, anchored off the island and sent word on shore that he had orders from the Senegal Company to seize any of the African Company's ships which might be found trading along the Cape Verde coast. This message was delivered on 25 June. On 2 July in sight of James Fort the French commander fired on one of the African Company's vessels, and forced her to strike. The vessel was then boarded and searched, but was allowed to go with a message to the English

---

[1] Wilkinson, *op. cit.* p. 15; Labat, *op. cit.* IV, 330; John Kastell to R.A.C., 24 January, 11 May, 14 October 1682, P.R.O., T. 70/10.

[2] *The Case of the Royal African Company of England* (1730), p. 19.

[3] Nominal Rolls of Gambia, 18 March, 31 May and 30 September 1684, P.R.O., T. 70/1441.

[4] R.A.C. to Duke of Newcastle, 18 March 1725, P.R.O., C.O. 267/5.

[5] Evidence of Richard Harris, *Journal of Board of Trade*, 18 August 1720; Commissioners of Trade to R.A.C., 22 August 1720, Add. MS. 14,035, f. 14.

agent that the French "would doe the same to all English ships to discover such as are going or have been trading at Cape de Verd".[1] After this the *Catherine* left the river. When out at sea, her commander stopped and seized an English ship, which was taken to Martinique and there condemned "under colour that our trade there was under a patente of the Dutch and that we had not a right to trade there".[2]

Alexander Cleeve resolved, when a suitable opportunity came, to assert the English claims to trade along the coast. On 12 August 1687 he informed his employers that he proposed to contest French pretensions by sending a ship to the Senegal coast to trade for gum.[3] The officer sent in charge of the vessel was James Jobson, who had commanded the *Mary* at the time of her seizure in 1680. He was therefore anxious to wipe out an old score. When he was off Portudal in February 1688 he was stopped by a French sloop. He allowed a boat to board him and then seized four of the crew. He then returned with his prisoners to the Gambia, where they were held as hostages in the event of any interference with English trade on the coast. Eventually the captives were released.[4]

Jobson's act had little more effect than to court reprisal. In 1688 a French man-of-war commanded by Monsieur la Fonte, arrived in the Gambia with four other vessels. They made no attempt to attack James Island, but got into touch with the natives. It was afterwards learnt that "their discourse to the natives was to the disparagement of our king". They announced their intention of seizing every English vessel which they found outside the river, and that there were more ships to follow, which would seize the fort. After this they sailed for Bissao in the Rio Grande. The African Company's ship *Lady Mary* was at the time trading in that river at Gossada. On 26 May 1688 the French sent an armed party in a long boat to attack her. The English offered the best resistance they could. Samuel Lee, the commander, was shot in the shoulder and stomach and a sailor, named John Dickenson, was killed. The surgeon and one other seaman were made prisoners. William Heath, the factor,

[1] Memorial of R.A.C., 18 December 1686, Lansdowne MS. 1152 B, f. 262, Rawlinson MS. A, 139 B, f. 9.

[2] *Commons' Journals*, xi, 114; Harleian MS. 7310, ff. 219, 226.

[3] P.R.O., T. 70/11.

[4] Cleeve to R.A.C., 3 February and 20 June 1688, P.R.O., T. 70/11; "Damage which the Royall African Company have sustained by the French in the northern parts of Guinee" (1688), Sloane MS. 2902, f. 92; Labat, *op. cit.* iv, 331.

and a number of the native crew managed to escape to the shore. The natives robbed them of everything they had and seized the slaves. The free people were allowed to make their way back to the Gambia as best they could. The French carried the *Lady Mary* to Brest. This disaster meant a loss to the African Company of close on £5000. It was followed a few weeks later by the seizure by La Fonte of three other vessels belonging to the African Company in the Rio Nunes. The Company endeavoured to move the French Government through an English merchant in France to restore the *Lady Mary* and her lading. The French Government offered to restore them, if a French vessel, which had been seized off the Scilly Isles for contravention of the revenue laws, was also restored. The African Company therefore petitioned the Privy Council to procure the restoration of the French ship. Before any further action could be taken war broke out between England and France.[1]

With the exception of a brief interval after the Peace of Ryswick England and France were to be at war with one another for the next quarter of a century. Affairs in the Gambia were in no way the direct origin of that war, though indirectly the commercial rivalry of the two nations in this as in other parts of the globe largely contributed to make such a war inevitable. It is perfectly clear that the disputes between the two rival trading companies were leading up to the embroilment of the two respective governments and that, unless both those governments were ready to acquiesce in conciliatory methods and to take the necessary steps to see that their respective subjects respected international comity, there would certainly have been further bloodshed and the consequences must as certainly have been that, as in the days of Holmes and De Ruyter, the two nations would be dragged in to spill more blood in other parts of the world. Louis XIV's desire to set James II back on the throne of England may have precipitated the war, but the almost certain repetition of such incidents as the seizure of the *Lady Mary* would have made that war inevitable in any case.

---

[1] Wilkinson, *op. cit.* p. 16; Labat, *op. cit.* iv, 331; Alexander Cleeve to R.A.C., 20 June 1688, P.R.O., T. 70/11; R.A.C. to Cleeve, 4 October 1688, P.R.O., T. 70/50; Ledger Book of Gambia, 1688–1689, P.R.O., T. 70/832; Petition of R.A.C., 28 March 1689, P.R.O., P.C. 2/73; "Damage which the Royall African Company have sustained by the French in the northern parts of Guinee", Sloane MS. 2902, f. 92; Minute Book of R.A.C., 11 September and 2 October 1688, P.R.O., T. 70/32; Minute Book of R.A.C., 9 June 1691, P.R.O., T. 70/33.

IX: War with France, 1689–1697

On 28 February 1689 the Royal African Company wrote to inform John Booker, their chief agent in the Gambia, that the happy and glorious revolution had placed William of Orange and his consort Mary on the throne of England.[1] In an outburst of strong party feeling the name of their island and fort was changed to that of William and Mary and memory of the recent misdeeds of a bad king was allowed to obliterate the memory of a Lord High Admiral, who had in the past done much for the English navy and for overseas trade and settlement.[2] Despite political rancour the old name of the island still persisted and was allowed to perpetuate the memory of a prince, to whom, whatever his shortcomings, the Royal African Company owed much—and not least of all their acquisition of James Island.

John Booker, who had charge of affairs when war broke out between England and France, had only arrived at James Island the preceding year.[3] There is something refreshing and invigorating about his correspondence, which is often lacking in that of his contemporaries. He had his failings and his letters are not entirely free from complaint, but despite frequent illness he showed an energy which was unusual in promoting both politically and commercially the interests of his employers under exceptionally difficult circumstances. English prestige was low in the regions of the Gambia when he was called upon to take charge. His predecessor, Cleeve, had very recently been made a prisoner by the "king" of Barra and had met with a serious rebuff when he tried to force the hand of the "king" of Geregia. A squadron of French ships had paraded in the river in open defiance and contempt of the English at James Fort and had only just recently taken the *Lady Mary* by force. The one feeble attempt at reprisal for similarly high-handed acts had proved a miserable failure. In native eyes therefore there can be no doubt as to which was regarded as the more superior nation. There consequently could be no reliance or dependence on native assistance if matters came to a head with the French at Goree. Added to this the fort was out of repair, the garrison was seriously depleted, and the

[1] P.R.O., T. 70/50.
[2] Labat, *Nouvelle Relation de l'Afrique Occidentale*, IV, 302.
[3] Security Book of R.A.C., P.R.O., T. 70/1428.

107

remnant of the Company's European servants (soldiers included) had little or no stomach for active service. It was therefore no easy task which confronted Booker when he took charge at James Island.

On 11 June 1689 the African Company wrote to inform Booker that war had been declared against France. At the same time they forwarded to him a commission "to act in a hostile manner". He was authorised by them to send expeditions against the French. Of the plunder one-tenth would go to the Crown and the remainder to the Company, who would, however, distribute one-third of their share amongst those who participated in any such action.[1] Booker had in the meantime made some attempt to reassert the Company's authority in the river. He had done his best to prevent the French from passing James Island and had seized two sloops which had attempted to do so.[2] He hailed the declaration of war with delight. Immediately upon receipt thereof he informed the "king" of Barra, who promptly seized all the French property at Albreda.[3] He had released one of the two captured sloops before receipt of the declaration of war, but appropriated the other. The letter bringing the news arrived just at the moment when he had learnt that a French ship called the *Augustine* was in the vicinity. His commission had been brought to him by Captain Robert Perry of the *Speedwell*, whom he requested to go and seize the Frenchman. Booker communicated the Company's offer of prize money to Perry, but Perry refused to move until he had been promised something more. Booker "was forced to use many arguments and threats to Captain Perry before he would be willing to proceed with his shipp to take the French prize". Eventually the promise of two slaves for himself and one for his crew made Perry amenable. He sallied forth and captured the *Augustine*.[4]

As only one month previously Booker had confessed that he "durst not venture the ships out to trade on the coast being infested with French privateers",[5] he was not unjustly proud of having drawn the first blood. He, in fact, felt so confident that he wrote

---

[1] P.R.O., T. 70/50.

[2] Booker to R.A.C., 12 February and – July 1689, P.R.O., T. 70/11.

[3] Froger, *Relation d'un Voyage de la Mer du Sud*, p. 34; Durand, *Voyage au Sénégal*, p. 78; Booker to R.A.C., 19 August 1689, P.R.O., T. 70/11.

[4] Booker to R.A.C., 19 August 1689 and 17 June 1691, P.R.O., T. 70/11, T. 70/1433; Edward Parsons to R.A.C., 23 April 1690, P.R.O., T. 70/1433.

[5] Booker to R.A.C., – July 1689, P.R.O., T. 70/11.

urging the Company to send ships to take Goree and Senegal. He pointed out that the Dutch would in all probability make an attempt to take the former place and that, if they did so, it "would be of ill consequence". He therefore advised the Company to anticipate these allies of England. According to his information Senegal was weakly defended and he urged an attempt on the place "though at 12000£ charge", as "the riches there will repay the charge of taking it".[1]

But the Company were slow to fall in with his recommendations and to supply him with the means of carrying out his proposals. As owing to the difficulties of communication it was deemed probable that Sierra Leone was not likely to repay current expenditure, it was decided in 1690 to reduce the staff there and to send John Case with as many men as could be spared to reinforce James Island.[2] But this addition did little more than bring the garrison there up to the minimum strength necessary for the defence of the fort. Drafts and supplies from home were even less serviceable and ammunition was found to be short on delivery.[3] Three soldiers were sent out in 1689 in the *Speedwell*. When they arrived, Booker declared that "they will not deserve their victualls and, if they do not dye, he will discharge them by the first shipp".[4] The period of engagement of a number of the men on the spot had expired and Booker felt it his duty to detain them over their time. This action caused considerable discontent and several letters were sent to England complaining of the agent's action. One writer, James Lacey, complained not only of being forcibly detained but also of having been flogged.[5] The only concession that Booker felt that in the exigent circumstances could be made was to allow time-expired men to live at Brefet in Foni "as Portuguez...being ready at an allarm to assist the island".[6] As Lacey threatened his employers with legal proceedings on account of their agent's action, the Company, whilst approving of his allowing time-expired men to "live amongst the natives as the Portuguez doe and trade for themselves",

---

[1] Booker to R.A.C., 19 August 1689, 25 April 1690 and 7 June 1690, P.R.O., T. 70/11.

[2] R.A.C. to Booker, 7 January 1690, P.R.O., T. 70/50.

[3] Booker to R.A.C., 25 April 1693, P.R.O., T. 70/1443.

[4] Same to same, 19 August 1689, P.R.O., T. 70/1433.

[5] James Lacey to R.A.C., 17 June 1691; Pears Raniker to R.C.A., 16 June 1691, P.R.O., T. 70/11.

[6] Booker to R.A.C., 17 June 1691, P.R.O., T. 70/11.

felt none the less impelled to rebuke Booker for harsh treatment of his subordinates.[1]

In the meantime trouble with the local natives impeded Booker in his designs upon the French forts. The "king" of Geregia was "very abusive" and not to be trusted,[2] and the "king" of Barra was guilty of "several ill attempts", not the least of which were the poisoning of the well at Juffure[3] and the murder by some of his people of certain of the Company's slaves.[4] Peace was, however, made in 1692.[5]

As the result of forced inaction, the tide turned for the moment in favour of the French, who captured two English members of the Gambia establishment in 1690 as well as four of the Company's ships together with their cargoes to the value of over £2000.[6]

But this success was only momentary. For the next two years no French ship appeared off this part of the African coast. Finally at the end of 1691 it was reported that a ship from Havre called *L'Héreux* had sailed from Goree to Bissao "as a spye shipp". Captain Brome of the *America* was in the River Gambia at the time. On 10 December 1691 Booker embarked on board Brome's ship. Thirteen days later he wrote exultingly from Bissao to say that he had captured the Frenchman, and on 5 January he brought his prize triumphantly to James Island.[7]

Immediately after this Booker had a set back. An armed vessel appeared and seized an interloper and the Company's sloop *Assistance* with her crew of eight. It then proceeded to Sierra Leone and seized another interloper. Booker consequently had to delay the *America*'s voyage to the West Indies for fear of further attacks on English shipping. Eventually the crew of the sloop arrived back overland with the news that their captor was a pirate and not a French man-of-war.[8]

[1] R.A.C. to Booker, 25 October 1691, P.R.O., T. 70/50.
[2] Booker to R.A.C., 17 June 1691, P.R.O., T. 70/11.
[3] Same to same, 25 April 1690, P.R.O., T. 70/11.
[4] Same to same, 29 July 1692, P.R.O., T. 70/11.
[5] Same to same, 25 January 1692, P.R.O., T. 70/11.
[6] *Hist. MSS. Comm. Rep., House of Lords MSS.* ii, 79–82; Nominal Rolls of James Island, P.R.O., T. 70/1443.
[7] Booker to R.A.C., 10 and 23 December 1691 and 25 January 1692; John Case to R.A.C., 25 January 1692, P.R.O., T. 70/11; R.A.C. to William Hanbury, 27 August 1695, P.R.O., T. 70/50.
[8] Booker to R.A.C., 15 February, 17 A.C. and 20 July 1692, P.R.O., T. 70/11.

Booker none the less never despaired of putting into execution his plan for the capture of the French settlements. By dint of persuasion and by his own enthusiasm he induced his fever-ridden and half-hearted colleagues to fall in with his schemes. At the close of 1691 the arrival of the *Anne* and the *America* from England put him in a position to carry out his long-cherished design. The Company's recent offer to increase the share of prize money to be paid to ships' crews from one-third to one-half made the commanders of those ships more ready to fall in with Booker's proposals.[1] One of the officers of the French ship, which had been captured at Bissao, was a Huguenot sub-lieutenant, named Larrouy, who had been compelled as a result of the Revocation of the Edict of Nantes to abjure his faith, but who now took the opportunity of returning to it. He had previously served at Senegal and undertook to pilot the English over the bar of the river. Booker embarked 100 men on the *Anne* and *America* and arrived off the mouth of the Senegal on 30 December 1692. Two days later the French Governor surrendered on terms and was allowed to march out with the honours of war. A small English garrison was put in charge of the fort. Booker then decided to attack Goree, but was opposed in his design by the two ships' captains. He afterwards reported that "on the 26th January Captain Leech (of the *Anne*) delivered me a paper signed by himself and Captain Brome (of the *America*), in which they deny acting any longer offensively, except I should condescend to their demands, and which I was forced to mittigate by the best meanes I could to their satisfaction, that my designes might not be frustrated and your interest lost....You wilbe judges whether their demands were reasonable or noe, they being far different from your instructions to me, and I think very unreasonable." Eventually Booker was compelled to give the two his personal bond for the share of the plunder demanded by them. After he had signed this, the two captains agreed to proceed to Goree, where they arrived on 1 February 1693. The French at Goree put up a slightly longer resistance than those at Senegal. Their forts were bombarded for four days and then Booker landed with 100 men. He summoned the defenders to surrender before he had landed his cannon. The French then asked for terms and were allowed to march out with the honours of war and were promised free shipping to Europe. On 8 February the forts were handed over to Booker. He lacked the troops to man them and

---

[1] R.A.C. to Booker, 27 September 1692, P.R.O., T. 70/50.

therefore contented himself with demolishing them as far as time would allow, and then sailed with his prisoners of war for the Gambia.[1]

A number of misfortunes followed immediately upon this highly successful expedition. Captain Brome loaded a cargo of slaves to carry to Jamaica. Of these slaves "the Jaloffs rose, and the Bambarras sided with the master", but it was only with the armed assistance from Booker that the rising was suppressed.[2] Captain Leech of the *Anne* met with a greater disaster, but proved himself a better man than his conduct before Goree might have suggested. The goods, which were removed from Senegal and Goree, were placed on board his ship to convey to England. Off Land's End he fell in with some French privateers, who promptly attacked him. He kept up a determined fight for several hours, but, at length realising that he was overpowered and about to be boarded by the enemy, he blew up his ship.[3]

The consequence of this disaster was that Booker's own letters regarding his success only reached England by the circuitous route of the West Indies in November 1693.[4] Vague reports of Booker's success had, however, previously reached England, but the African Company were chary about dealing out praise. On 5 September 1693 they wrote to Booker to inform him that they understood he had captured Senegal and Goree and had subsequently abandoned the latter place. They offered no word of congratulation or thanks but desired Booker to "advise us how you found Goree, and the reason that induced you to demolish it and quit it, in regard we are informed it would have bin made a place of greater strength and security than Gamboa and as convenient for carrying on and preserving our trade in those parts".[5] Later, when Brome brought Booker's letters to England, the Company did so far unbend as to say they wished Booker to know "how great a sense wee have of

---

[1] Barbot, *A Description of the Coasts of North and South Guinea*, pp. 423–424; Froger, *op. cit.* p. 11; Cultru, *Histoire du Sénégal*, pp. 120–121; Booker to R.A.C., 14 March 1693, P.R.O., T. 70/11 and T. 70/1433; William Heath to R.A.C., 12 December 1693, P.R.O., T. 70/11; Nominal Rolls of James Island, P.R.O., T. 70/1443.

[2] Booker to R.A.C., 25 April 1693, P.R.O., T. 70/11.

[3] D'Avenant, *Political and Commercial Works—Reflections upon the Constitution and Management of the Trade to Africa*, v, 309.

[4] R.A.C. to Booker, 9 November 1693, P.R.O., T. 70/50.

[5] P.R.O., T. 70/11.

your good successe and service done", but they still harped upon the abandonment of Goree and, as good men of business, added that "as soone as wee received these letters wee examined your manifest for goods" and had found it unsatisfactory in a number of details, which they proceeded to enumerate.[1]

But by the time these letters reached the Gambia, Booker was beyond censure or praise. Many of his letters home show that he had been constantly ill for some time previous. He fell sick again on the voyage back from Goree and asked leave to return to England, but loyally offered to stick to his post until relieved, as his second-in-command, John Case, was proceeding home, and there was no-body on the spot fit to take charge if anything befell himself.[2] He had latterly been worried by the criticisms, which he had received in letters from home, of the manner in which he was performing the commercial side of his duties, and in regard to his treatment of his subordinates, and by the want of recognition of his loyalty to his masters. On 8 June 1693 he died a broken-hearted man.[3] A month before this—on 10 May—he had penned his last letter to the African Company. That letter is no longer extant, but the entry made by a clerk in London in the Company's register speaks for itself. He described it as "Agent Booker's letter on his deathbed in vindication of himself".[4]

If ever a dying man had no need of self-vindication, it was John Booker. No employers ever had a more loyal servant and few employers have been less generous in their recognition of this fact. Booker had much of the genius, which two generations later took another writer in another company's service from his stool in a counting house to lead his countrymen to victory at Plassey. Furthermore, without in any way belittling the achievements of Clive, Booker worked under greater difficulties. He had no band of trained native troops upon whose loyalty he could depend. He could not expect assistance from any powerful native ruler. All that he had was a fever-ridden and dispirited handful of Europeans, who for the most part did not profess to be fighting men at all and had little or no stomach for soldiering. A kinder fate might have allowed John Booker a resting-place in some temple of fame instead of in an

[1] R.A.C. to Booker, 9 November 1693, P.R.O., T. 70/11.
[2] Booker to R.A.C., 14 March 1693, P.R.O., T. 70/11.
[3] William Heath to R.A.C., 12 December 1693, P.R.O., T. 70/11.
[4] P.R.O., T. 70/11.

unknown grave beneath the tumbled ruins of a bastion on a lonely island in an African river.

Booker's work was all undone almost immediately after his death. He had left a factor named Throgmorton Humphreys in command at Senegal. All that he had been able to spare for the garrison was a surgeon, a carpenter, a sergeant, and fifteen soldiers.[1] Three of this number died in the course of the next few months. It was obvious that without reinforcements this garrison could not possibly hope to hold out against any superior force. The chief agent at James Island could not render any further assistance and owing to the destruction of Captain Leech's ship news of the capture of Senegal did not reach England in time for the African Company to send out any reinforcements. About June 1693, a French vessel appeared off the place and the English speedily surrendered, having offered little or no resistance.[2] It did not take long subsequently to reoccupy the abandoned forts at Goree, but Booker's demolitions had been so thorough that no effort was made to rebuild them until after the close of the war.[3]

The English in the River Gambia lacked the numbers and the enterprise to recover the two places. The African Company itself took no steps in the matter. The only hope of recovering the lost forts rested on an expedition which was being fitted out in the West Indies. Apparently on Booker's suggestion the Governor of the Bermudas gave commissions to two privateers to proceed to Africa to assist the English in the Gambia in capturing Goree. The two captains were George Dew and Thomas Tew. Little is known of the former except that he was engaged in the slave trade between the Gambia and West Indies.[4] The following is the description given by a contemporary of the latter:

Tew appeared to me not only a man of courage and activity, but the greatest sense and remembrance of any seaman that I have ever met with. He was also what is called a very pleasant man, so that sometimes after the day's labour was done, it was divertisement as well as information to one to hear him talk. I wished in my mind to make him a

[1] Nominal Rolls of James Island, P.R.O., T. 70/1443.

[2] Labat, *op. cit.* IV, 126; William Heath to R.A.C., 12 December 1693, P.R.O., T. 70/11.

[3] Barbot, *op. cit.* p. 424; Labat, *op. cit.* IV, 126; Cultru, *op. cit.* pp. 120–121; William Heath to R.A.C., 12 December 1693, P.R.O., T. 70/11.

[4] R.A.C. to Thomas Corker, 24 November 1698, P.R.O., T. 70/51.

*sober man and in particular to cure him of a vile habit of swearing.
I gave him a book for that purpose and, to gain the more upon him,
I gave him a gun of some value.*[1]

On 8 January 1693 Captain Tew and the owners of the good ship
Amity entered into a prize money agreement with the crew of that
ship. The intended voyage was therein described very cryptically.
The *Amity* was "to saile on such voyage or expedition as the commander and company shall think fitt for the best advantage of the
said owners and company".[2] Thereafter Captains Dew and Tew set
sail for Africa. By that time they were of course too late to have
rendered any assistance to Booker, who had already taken both
Goree and Senegal, but they might have arrived in time to prevent
the recapture of those places by the French. As it happened, they
ran into a storm a few days out from port. Dew sprang his mast
and, losing sight of his consort, put back to refit. The pleasant and
diverting Captain Tew then proceeded to show that he had at least
one other failing besides those of insobriety and profane swearing.
He altered his course for the Cape of Good Hope and, after rounding
that point, pursued a highly successful career as a pirate in the
Indian Ocean and Red Sea.[3]

With Tew's lapse from the path of virtue all hope of recovery of
Senegal and Goree came to an end. Furthermore, the English lost
the ascendancy at sea which they had won in Booker's time. La
Courbe was sent out from France to take charge at Goree. In 1694
William Heath, Booker's successor, sent a ship to Portudal to trade.
On a bare rumour that La Courbe was on the coast, John Hanbury,
the factor in charge, turned back and on the return voyage in some
unexplained manner managed to wound himself. Heath sent the
ship out again under another officer. On this occasion La Courbe
swooped down upon it and carried it and the crew captive to Goree.[4]

It was further apparent that the French would one day take a
suitable opportunity to try by attacking James Island to free their
settlements at Senegal and Goree from further molestation. All that

---

[1] Benjamin Fletcher to Council of Trade, 24 December 1698, *C.S.P. Colonial
(America and West Indies)*, 1697–1698, p. 587.   [2] P.R.O., C.O. 37/2.

[3] Johnson, *A General History of the Pirates*, p. 10; Edward Randolph to
Commissioner of Customs, 16 August 1696, John Graves to Council of Trade,
19 February 1697, *C.S.P. Colonial (America and West Indies)*, 1696–1697,
pp. 74, 379.

[4] William Heath to R.A.C., 7 and 9 March 1694, P.R.O., T. 70/11.

the African Company could do to prevent the capture of their fort was to send out reinforcements and to urge upon their chief agents the duties of continual vigilance and of keeping the fort in good repair. In 1690 two of the flanking bastions and two gun platforms below the bastions were reported to be out of repair and unserviceable.[1] Booker had been instructed that "what can be done without great charge to fortifie our fort, lett it not be neglected".[2] On 25 January 1692 he had reported to the Company that the fort was "almost new built", but that the houses and quarters would have to be rebuilt.[3] Realising the dependence of the garrison for their water supply upon maintenance of communication with the mainland, the Company obtained in 1685 from a certain John Short "an engine for turning salt water into fresh for James Island in Gamboa",[4] but, after the machine had been set up on the island, it was reported that the garrison got "little helpe from it".[5] Mr Short's invention was replaced by a tank, which in its turn was reported by Booker as not capable of holding water.[6]

The garrison was reported to be unreliable. As already mentioned, Booker himself had found great difficulty in dealing with the time-expired men. On 12 December 1693 his successor reported that "all the old standers will desert, if not releived, as three have done".[7] Three months later he reported that two carpenters with French names had deserted to the French.[8] In February 1695 the arrival of a contingent of twenty-six soldiers, a gunner, and ten sailors and artisans made a welcome addition to a depleted and discontented garrison.[9] Desertions, however, still continued. In July 1695 the long-expected French attack was launched. A squadron of six ships, which were bound for the South Seas under the command of Monsieur de Gennes, put into Goree on the third day of that month. On arrival they learnt from a deserter from James Island that the English garrison there were nearly all ill and

[1] Booker to R.A.C., 25 January 1692, P.R.O., T. 70/11. Wilkinson, *Systema Africanum*, pp. 12–13.
[2] R.A.C. to Booker, 4 October 1688, P.R.O., T. 70/50.
[3] P.R.O., T. 70/11.
[4] Minute Book of R.A.C., 15 October 1685, P.R.O., T. 70/81.
[5] Cleeve to R.A.C., 25 January 1687, P.R.O., T. 70/11.
[6] Booker to R.A.C., 12 February 1689, P.R.O., T. 70/11.
[7] Heath to R.A.C., P.R.O., T. 70/11.
[8] Nominal Rolls of James Island, 18 March 1695, P.R.O., T. 70/1443.
[9] *Ibid.*

were short of provisions. On 19 July the French ships sailed for the Gambia, which they entered three days later under an English flag, arriving off James Island at five o'clock the same evening. An officer was landed that night at Juffure to get in touch with the "king" of Barra and to try to persuade him to allow a force to be landed so as to prevent the English from obtaining provisions and water. "But the king announced that he did not wish to enter into our differences and, if we took the fort, it would be a ground for hatred on the part of the English, which he could only resent by flight." He, however, offered to supply the French with any necessaries they required.[1]

Next day Monsieur de la Roque was sent to summon the fort. John Hanbury, the chief agent, was away on the mainland and he was received by the second-in-command, Charles Daval, a Huguenot refugee. La Roque subsequently gave the following account of his reception:

His eyes were bandaged and he was taken to the governor's house, where in his absence he was received by the Lieutenant of the king, to whom he explained the object of our visit, and that he had come to summon him to surrender before any hostile act was done. Monsieur de la Roque was regaled magnificently and the healths of the King of France and the King of England were drunk several times to the sound of artillery. When the meal was finished, Monsieur de la Roque returned on board with three English officers, whom Monsieur de Gennes treated with reciprocal magnificence. They asked for several days for deliberation, which could not be granted to them. They were only allowed till six o'clock the following morning. The result was that they went back to the fort discontented.

Later the same day Daval sent word that "we are resolved to wait for you and to fight you until death, before we surrender, and we do not doubt that we shall meet an honourable enemy".

During the night several vessels were intercepted whilst carrying provisions to the fort. Chase was also given to a canoe which, under cover of darkness, was carrying chief agent Hanbury back to the island. Hanbury only escaped capture by jumping overboard and swimming to the mainland. Later that night he found other means of reaching the fort.

The following day two shallops were sent up the Bintang Creek to Brefet, where they captured and destroyed two armed boats,

[1] Froger, *op. cit.* pp. 5, 6, 21, 22.

which had gone to fetch wood. At eight o'clock that morning two bombs were fired at James Island but fell short. They, however, served their purpose. Mr Hanbury, who had not partaken of the potations of the previous day and had got very wet the previous night, was in a very different frame of mind to his second-in-command. He sent a flag of truce to de Gennes to ask for terms. The French commander agreed to let the English march out with the honours of war, to allow them to retain their private property and to grant them transport to Europe. These terms were readily accepted. On 27 July the French took possession of the island, but after holding a council of war, it was resolved to destroy the fort. The walls and bastions were accordingly mined and such cannon as could not be removed were spiked. All the arms, ammunition, and stores were carried on board the French ships. A French privateer from San Domingo, who arrived on 14 August to see what he could pick up, was given some of the artillery and ammunition and the "king" of Barra subsequently sent to discover what ill-considered trifles had been left behind. The English were embarked on 14 August on one of the ships for Cayenne. Part of the spoils were two hundred and twenty slaves. One hundred and fifty of them were put in the hold of the same ship which was to carry the English, "for fear they might save themselves. These unfortunate people being hardly able to breathe threw themselves one upon the other as if in despair and thirty-four of them were stifled." On 22 August the mines were successfully sprung and two days later the French left the river.[1]

After the departure of the captured English for Cayenne no attempt was made by the African Company to reoccupy James Island until after the close of the war. It furthermore appears that the French did not attempt to reoccupy Albreda or Geregia. There were a number of reasons for their failure to do so. The "king" of Barra had watched the operations of de Gennes with considerable disapproval. As already mentioned, he had for very prudent reasons refused to co-operate even indirectly in the attack on James Fort. After its capture he had done his best to prevent the African Company's slaves and other property at Juffure from being taken by the French. De Gennes had been so far incensed by this attitude as to meditate a raid on the mainland, but the "king" had made a timely submission. None the less the resentment still remained at being

[1] Froger, *op. cit.* pp. 22–48.

compelled to surrender what in his eyes had escheated to him.[1] Despite a present of brandy the "emperor" of Foni was similarly annoyed at the destruction of the two English vessels in Bintang Creek.[2] Both these chiefs clearly felt that the French had merely been destructive and had made no attempt to replace what they had destroyed. The English had proved good store-keepers. The French had failed to come up to commercial requirements and had destroyed the only satisfactory mart in the river. In the circumstances, the native feeling against them was fairly strong. As they had only a precarious footing at Goree with a mere handful of men, the French deemed it advisable not to risk establishing settlements on the banks of the Gambia. Furthermore, the finances of the Senegal Company were in grave disorder. In 1694 they had been compelled to liquidate their debts by selling the nineteen years' unexpired residue of their grant to a new company.[3] Until peace was concluded the new company was not prepared to embark on any considerable enterprise in Africa.

The surrender of James Island inevitably aroused intense indignation—more particularly in the Royal African Company. De Gennes had subsequently said that, "if the Governor had done his duty, the Fort had been almost impregnable".[4] There can be no doubt, however, that if de Gennes had been able to maintain an effective blockade for any considerable length of time, lack of a water supply would have compelled the garrison to surrender. In so far as armaments went, the French and the English were almost equally matched, but the former were placed at the disadvantage of being unable owing to wind, tide, and current to bring all their artillery constantly to bear on the fort. They were further operating in a by no means friendly country 100 miles from the nearest base at which they could reprovision or refit. If the guns of James Fort had been used, the French would certainly not have found their task an easy one and might have been induced to withdraw. The discreditable thing about the surrender was that it took place before the defenders had even come under real fire. All the evidence shows that this pusillanimity was entirely attributable to the chief agent, John Hanbury. There were clearly men of sterner stuff amongst his subordinates.

---

[1] Froger, op. cit. pp. 34–36.

[2] Labat. op. cit. IV, 294; Durand, Voyage au Sénégal, p. 80.

[3] Tallot, La Colonie Française du Sénégal, p. 25.

[4] "Some general observations...touching the contents of the Royall African Company's peticion", 3 February 1708, P.R.O., T. 70/175.

X: Between two storms, 1698–1702

During the preliminary negotiations leading up to the Treaty of Ryswick the African Company made an attempt to obtain the insertion of a clause whereby the French might be excluded from the River Gambia,[1] but, though they were able to obtain an agreement from the French to compensate them for the seizures made off the coast in 1687 and 1688,[2] they were unable to make the River Gambia their peculiar preserve. The treaty left the rights of both nations between the Senegal and Gambia as they were before the war.

The conclusion of peace therefore found the African Company faced once more with French competition, but what they regarded as perhaps even more serious was that Parliament decided that their monopoly should cease. As these pages have shown, English interlopers had persistently encroached upon their preserves for a good many years. Furthermore, public opinion in England regarded the monopoly as distasteful. After the Revolution of 1688 outcries against it became loud in the press, amongst pamphleteers, and in Parliament. The African Company had not the financial, political, or legal backing which enabled the East India Company to ward off similar attacks on their exclusive grant. They therefore with some strategic astuteness petitioned Parliament for leave to establish a new company rather than wait for the expected request for the formation of a regulated company.[3]

Legislation on the subject had, however, to wait until conclusion of the war with France. In 1698 a bill was introduced in Parliament to regulate the African Trade. The Company realised that it could not resist the opening of the trade on the Gold Coast to all comers, but, when the bill was in committee, it endeavoured to preserve its monopoly in the Gambia and Sierra Leone. It was urged that the slave trade there was inconsiderable—"but few negroes, and those the worst in esteem"—and that therefore the American and West Indian planters, who were amongst the chief opponents of the

---

[1] R.A.C. to Council of Trade, 29 June 1697, *C.S.P. Colonial (America and West Indies)*, 1697–1698, p. 643; Matthew Prior to Sir William Trumbull, 9–19 July 1696, *Hist. MSS. Comm. Rep., Marquis of Bath's MSS.* iii, 192.

[2] Journal, etc., relating to the Peace of Ryswick, *Hist. MSS. Comm. Rep., Marquis of Bath's MSS.* iii, 524.

[3] Scott, *Joint Stock Trading Companies to 1720*, pp. 19–21.

Company's monopoly, were little concerned with it. It was in fact asserted that the result of the proposed imposition of a duty on private traders would be "that the plantations would have no benefit by their bill, in having their negroes cheaper". It was further pointed out that James Fort would have to be rebuilt at a cost of from sixteen to twenty thousand pounds and would then require an annual expenditure of £6000 for its maintenance. As the annual yield of the trade from those parts was not expected to exceed £10,000, it was urged that a special case had been made out for preserving the Company's right of exclusive trade there.[1] Strong opposition was offered to the proposal by the English clothiers, who alleged that the Company's virtual monopoly of the import of redwood, which came almost exclusively from the Gambia and Sherboro, had enhanced the price of that commodity from twenty to as much as seventy or ninety pounds a ton. The Company then rejoined that the clothiers also used sanders wood, which could be bought far more cheaply than redwood, if that latter commodity rose above a certain price, but that they would be prepared to consent to throw open the trade, provided that they could charge private traders a higher duty than was proposed for the Gold Coast so as to recoup themselves for the charges of re-establishing their posts in the Gambia.[2]

The Committee was at first disposed to allow the Company to charge private traders a double duty for trading in the northern parts of Africa,[3] but in the Act, which eventually became law, no differentiation was made as regards duties between the Gambia and the Gold Coast. That Act entrusted the Royal African Company with the maintenance and upkeep of the forts in Africa, but threw the trade in those parts open to all English subjects. Persons who were not members of the Company were to pay a duty of 10 per cent on all goods and merchandise imported from Africa into England or

---

[1] Notes for Lord Ambassador Williamson, 28 March 1698, *C.S.P. Domestic,* 1698, p. 103; *Considerations on the Trade to Africa humbly offer'd to the Honourable House of Commons on behalf of the Bill now before them,* p. 3; "Proposals of the Royal African Company for the Preservation of Trade to Africa", Sloane MS. 2902, ff. 88, 89.

[2] *Reasons humbly offered by the Merchants and Traders to Guinny and West Indies against the Bill for settling the Trade to Affrica: Considerations on the Trade to Africa humbly offer'd to the Honourable House of Commons on behalf of the Bill now before them,* p. 3; *Commons' Journals,* XII, 185.

[3] Notes for Lord Ambassador Williamson, 28 March 1698, *C.S.P. Domestic,* 1698, p. 163.

America. This duty was to be appropriated towards the maintenance and upkeep of the forts. Subjects of England trading to Africa were to have the same protection as the Company and might settle factories in Africa without molestation by the Company.[1] Thereafter in the Company's correspondence private traders ceased to be referred to as "interlopers" and were given the hardly less contemptuous title of "ten per cent men". The same correspondence directed their servants in Africa to give the ten per cent men their legal rights, but not to go out of their way to assist them.

Owing to the uncertainty which prevailed whilst this bill was passing through Parliament, the African Company delayed to send any party from England until October 1698.[2] They had in the meantime instructed Thomas Corker, their agent at Sierra Leone, "to resettle Gambia and the factory there in case he could find to do it with conveniency and security and with no great expence".[3] Corker had specially asked to be appointed to the post, but he was slow to take it up. He suffered from gout and it perhaps may have been to suit his own convenience that his arrival at James Island was delayed till April 1699.[4]

In the meantime in anticipation of the legalisation of their trade by Parliament innumerable private traders had despatched vessels to the coast. Dutch interlopers also arrived to trade.[5] Lastly, the French Senegal Company made a very determined effort to re-establish their former trade and political influence. For this purpose they sent out André Brue as Director-General. He arrived at Senegal in August 1697. On 10 September of that year he sent a vessel into the River Gambia and was able to conclude a number of treaties with the "king" of Barra and other chiefs. On 13 April 1698, he sent a chief factor and fourteen other Frenchmen to re-establish the factories at Albreda and Geregia. A very determined effort was made to exclude the English private traders from the river. One vessel, which was carrying 100 slaves, was seized near Albreda. But private traders were offering good prices for slaves

[1] 9 and 10 Will. III, c. 26.

[2] Passenger lists of R.A.C., P.R.O., T. 70/1446; R.A.C. to Thomas Corker, 5 April and 2 July 1698, P.R.O., T. 70/51.

[3] R.A.C. to Francis Bowman, 27 January 1698, P.R.O., T. 70/50.

[4] Complaints to R.A.C., P.R.O., T. 70/1434.

[5] R.A.C. to Thomas Corker, 26 October and 16 November 1699, P.R.O., T. 70/51.

and the "king" of Barra resented the interference with persons who were prepared to pay more than double the former price for a slave and to purchase such slaves in almost unlimited quantities. He therefore demanded the instant release of the Englishmen. As the factory at Albreda was defenceless and could easily be plundered, the French had no alternative but to comply with this demand.[1]

Outside the river the French met with greater success in checking the activities of the English private traders. Early in 1699 an English ship obtained the leave of the chief at Portudal to trade there. An armed vessel was despatched from Goree to seize it. The chief entered a protest and eventually the English ship was released on the condition that it proceeded to the Gambia and did not attempt to trade on the coast. In March of the same year the *William and Jane* appeared off Portudal. It also was seized and carried to Goree. On this occasion Brue refused to release the ship. Her cargo of slaves was confiscated and sent to America.[2] Later a third vessel called the *St George* was also seized and condemned.[3]

The task which confronted Corker on his arrival at James Island in April 1699 was therefore by no means easy. He determined to assert his Company's rights both in and beyond the river. He not only settled a factory at Geregia close to that already settled by the French, but also settled other factories on the coast at Joal and Portudal. He was also accused by the French of endeavouring to stir up the chiefs on the coast against them, but the French chronicler of these events records with some glee the misfortunes of the two English factors who were sent to the Damel of Bur Salum. They brought a quantity of goods with them with the object of underselling the French. They were at first graciously received by the Damel, but subsequently he carried them with him from village to village until their provisions and stock in trade were exhausted. Then, as he no longer had any further use for them, the factors were cavalierly dismissed without any repayment for the value of the goods received.[4]

---

[1] Labat, *Nouvelle Relation de l'Afrique Occidentale*, IV, 293–298.
[2] Labat, *op. cit.* IV, pp. 198–204, 339–345; Petition of William Bird— William Popple to William Bird, 10 June 1700, *C.S.P. Colonial (America and West Indies)*, 1700, pp. 307, 339, 346, 352, 386; *Journal of Council of Trade*, 17, 20 and 28 June 1700; Abraham Stanyan to Matthew Prior, 30 December 1699, *Hist. MSS. Comm. Rep., Marquis of Bath's MSS.* III, 389.
[3] Labat, *op. cit.* IV, 337.　　　　[4] *Ibid.* IV, 300.

In the River Gambia itself Corker very clearly demonstrated that he did not propose to allow the French to trade above James Island. He insisted that any French boat, which wished to proceed above this point, should obtain a pass from him. Several vessels, which tried to sail past the fort, were fired on and compelled to turn back. Eventually a certain Monsieur Desnos obtained leave to send his shallop up to Kau-ur to collect debts, but on arrival there embarked in trade. He was then ordered to leave the place. On arrival at James Island he informed Corker that the French would soon destroy his fort. This so enraged Corker that he seized and detained the shallop.[1] Brue sent complaints regarding Corker's actions to France and in due course a formal complaint was lodged by the French Ambassador in London.[2] This complaint caused the African Company some alarm and they wrote out to the Gambia to their agents to say they could "not answere the seizing of any ships or effects of other nations, but your method must rather be to hinder them from tradeing by some other means. It had been excusible, if the agent first forbid them trading and, upon bringing any vessell to the castle, discharged them again immediately upon promising of departing the river, allways taking care not to offer them any violence and not to suffer their vessells or goods to be plundered or embezelled in the least, but, if need, to conduct them out of the river to the leeward and to let them goe, but not seize or to detain their effects, except our effects should be stopt or our trade mollested by them; then in such case detaining the effects of theirs to come to a fair understanding."[3]

In the meantime counter complaints had been made by the English Ambassador at Versailles regarding the seizure by Brue of the *William and Jane*.[4] Both governments realised that some *modus vivendi* must be established in Africa. The same fact was also realised by the two rival trading companies. The Senegal Company was having considerable trouble with local chiefs.[5] Both the African and the Senegal Companies were badly hit by the competition of the

[1] Senegal Company to R.A.C., 8 March 1700, P.R.O., T. 70/51; Labat, *op. cit.* iv, 301, 302, 304, 307.

[2] *C.S.P. Colonial (America and West Indies)*, 1700, p. 336; *Hist. MSS. Comm. Rep., House of Lords MSS.* iv, 452.

[3] R.A.C. to Paul Pindar, 13 February 1700, P.R.O., T. 70/51.

[4] *C.S.P. Colonial (America and West Indies)*, 1700, p. 386.

[5] Labat, *op. cit.* iv, 198–331.

English private traders. It was alleged that between January and June 1698 these traders had carried off 8600 slaves to America and that they had raised the price of slaves from between fifteen and seventeen bars to forty bars each.[1] On 8 March 1700 the Senegal Company opened up negotiations with the African Company. In their letter they recognised as "a truth worthy of anger" the fact that an English Act of Parliament permitted English interlopers to trade on the coast and that the African Company was powerless to prevent this, "but, seeing the French Company have expedients in that matter, which will produce all the effect that can be desired, but cannot trust the same to paper, it will be necessary that the English Company give order to some trusty person at Paris, with whom to conferre and take measures". They suggested that a common tariff should be fixed for the sale of European merchandise on the coast, that each Company should "oblige the negro kings and the Laptaux to trade but with the Companyes" and also take steps "to remove as far as possible all interlopers and to hinder them upon the coast of Africa".[2]

On 18 March 1701 the Company wrote to their servants in the Gambia as follows:

We have in our severall letters recommended to you the settling and improving our trade in amity with French Senegal Company. The method wee would have you use in order to the better carrying in the same is to consult with Monsieur Bruson (sc. Brue), the Generall of that Company, or such other persons as he shall direct to treat withall, upon propositions for your mutuall agreement and the promoting the joynt interest of both Companyes. For wee apprehend that, by a good understanding between your selves, you may engage the natives to a fair and just correspondence and oblige them to live in peace and amity amongst themselves and remove all obstructions in trade by not hindring the trading people of the upland rivers to come down with their effects.

And that, when any wrong or robberies are done or that the natives impose any things against reason or justice to European traders, you may by this method procure the aggressors to be severely punished by their own superiors, and, when they are brought under the obligacion of fair dealing, they will be more punctuall in performing such agreements as you shall make with them, which we have in all our letters to you ordered you to contract with them for all the returns that can be procured.

---

[1] Labat, *op. cit.* iv, 297–298.   [2] P.R.O., T. 70/51.

*The aforesaid Royal Senegal Company have advised that they re-
commend this method to their Generall, Monsieur Bruson, in their
several letters of the 8th May, 8th July, 20th September, 29th March,
12th June, 8th October, and 17th December past, and that they will
frequently renew their instructions for their agents to consult with you
in every part that may conduce to the joynt interest of both Companies.*

*Wee would have you act in this and all other concerns of this nature
very prudently and with such caution, that neither the French Company
nor the natives may make any particular advantage to our prejudice
upon any account whatsoever, but take care that wherein you agree with
them for the publick good wee may reap an equall advantage with them,
and in all cases, where you have any treaties, call to your assistance such
of our servants in any capacity that are intirely in our interest as you
can gett to be aiding and assisting to you therein. And let the minutes
and resolutions of all your proceedings be duely entred in a book for
that purpose.*[1]

Before receipt of this letter Corker had already on 10 November
1699 sent one of his factors to André Brue at Senegal with heads of
certain proposals. He offered to concede to the French the right to
trade at Albreda and Geregia, provided the English were allowed
similar rights at Portudal and Joal. Brue replied that he claimed
the right to trade above James Island and that he could not accept
Corker's pretensions to trade along the coast, alleging that the
African Company's commerce was solely confined to the River
Gambia. He urged upon Corker the necessity for fixing a tariff
common to both Companies for European merchandise and for
slaves and for putting a stop to the private traders.[2]

Brue decided, however, to follow up these pourparlers by a personal interview with Corker. For that purpose he arrived off James
Island on 9 April 1700. On arrival off the island he saluted the
English flag with nine guns, to which the fort replied gun for gun.
An officer came on board his ship to inform him that Mr Corker was
indisposed, but would receive him as soon as he was well enough.
His official reception took place on 12 April. Brue himself proceeded
to the island in two canoes with trumpets and hautboys. Not to be
outdone, seven English vessels in the river dressed ship and gave
him a salute as he passed. He was received at the landing place by

---

[1] R.A.C. to Thomas Gresham, P.R.O., T. 70/51.
[2] Labat, *op. cit.* IV, 303–308.

the officer commanding the soldiers with a guard of honour and drums and was escorted to the gate of the fort, where Mr Corker was waiting to receive him in state. The only thing, which tended to mar the ceremony, was the fact that Mr Corker's gout compelled him to appear in slippers. Brue and his officers were entertained to a magnificent repast, at which the factors acted as servitors. The healths of the Kings of France and England, the two Companies, and the two chief agents were drunk to the accompaniment of salvoes from the artillery of the fort and ships. Brue took his departure at two in the morning for Albreda, being saluted on his way by the English ships in the same manner as in the morning. Two days later Corker paid a return visit to Albreda and was treated to the same profuse hospitality.[1]

On 19 April the two officers got down to business. A conference was held on board an English vessel between Albreda and Juffure. Brue insisted that the English factories at Portudal and Joal should be closed down, but was prepared to allow the African Company to trade at those places, provided his own Company's ships were allowed to proceed above James Island. According to Brue, Corker was personally prepared to accept these proposals, but he asked for an adjournment of the conference so as to consult his brother officers and the ships' captains. After consulting his colleagues he announced that he was prepared to allow the French to trade at Albreda and to proceed as far as Geregia, but, as long as the English were hindered from trading in Senegal, he was not prepared to allow any further extension of the French trade in the Gambia. The question of Portudal and Joal was under discussion by their respective governments and he was prepared to abide by their decision.[2]

Discussions continued until 23 April when the *Ann and Sarah* arrived from England with somewhat disquieting news for Corker.[3] Complaints had reached his employers that he was embezzling their property and indulging in private trade on his own account.[4] Instructions were therefore sent to him to hand over to his second-in-command, Paul Pindar, and to return by the first available boat to England.[5] Orders were further sent that force should be used, if

---

[1] Labat, *op. cit.* IV, 309–312.
[2] *Ibid.* IV, 313–323.
[3] *Ibid.* IV, 313; R.A.C. passenger lists, T. 70/1436.
[4] Complaints to R.A.C., P.R.O., T. 70/1434.
[5] R.A.C. to Corker, 20 February 1700, P.R.O., T. 70/51.

he refused to obey these instructions.[1] These letters came at an extremely awkward moment for Corker. He had some time previously been censured for allowing Dutch interlopers to trade in the river.[2] He had then atoned for past neglect by seizing a Dutch dogger, but had freighted it for a trading venture on his own account to the Rios Nunes and Pongas. The dogger had not yet returned when the *Ann and Sarah* arrived. The captain of this latter vessel had left it to trade in another river, leaving the mate in charge. Corker went on board and, despite the mate's protest, broke open the captain's chest so as to peruse the packets from England. Having read and digested the contents of the letters, he resealed and replaced them. He refused to allow the crew of the *Ann and Sarah* to land and himself embarked on board a private trader, whither he removed all his property under an armed guard of slaves. We are further told that he "called a councell of his confederates and desired them to give him their best advices how he might defend himself against the Company, when he should get to England. Their opinions were various, but one of them, Mr Chidley by name, swore the best way was to move off of the island all things of value and sett the counting house and stores on fire, and then (he said) all his accounts would be made up at once. But Corker refused his advice and said he had four thousand pounds in ready cash by him; and Corker further said, if the Company and he could agree and they would give him a generall release, he would give the Company two thousand pounds of that money, but, if not, he would keep it and defend himself with their money." Realising that he would have one day to face his employers in England, he resolved to comply with their request and took his departure on a private trader's ship.[3] Brue, who was fully aware of the fact that Corker had amassed a considerable private fortune in the brief space of two years, sent him a letter of farewell. He felicitated Corker "on the pleasure, which he must have, in quitting a country, which was so detrimental to his health and in going to enjoy in peace in his own country the fifty thousand livres, which he was alleged to have acquired".[4] But Corker's plans went all awry. He was unable to wait for the return of his Dutch dogger, which was subsequently seized for indulging in illicit trade. Another

[1] R.A.C. to John Walter, 27 February 1700, P.R.O., T. 70/51.
[2] R.A.C. to Corker, 26 October and 16 November 1699, P.R.O., T. 70/51.
[3] Complaints to R.A.C., P.R.O., T. 70/1434.
[4] Labat, *op. cit.* IV, 313.

vessel, which he had purchased on his account, had also to be left behind. Part of its cargo was captured by a pirate and the ship itself was eventually lost in the River Gambia.[1] Corker himself did not live to enjoy his rapidly acquired fortune, but died at Falmouth soon after his arrival home.[2]

This interlude interrupted Brue's negotiations and he returned to Goree without having come to any satisfactory arrangement. As negotiations in Europe also proved abortive, the African Company induced the Admiralty to send out the *Rochester*, "a stout ship, and an excellent sailor, Captain Maine, Commander", to protect their interests.[3] Captain John Maine reached James Island on 12 March 1701. The same day he sent a written demand to Brue to restore the English ships, which he had seized, but received no reply. After spending three weeks in interviewing the leading chiefs of Barra and Foni, he decided to proceed to Goree and repeat his demand in person. On his way he sighted a French ship of thirty guns, to which he gave chase. Shots were exchanged between the two vessels but eventually the Frenchman made good his escape.[4] Maine arrived off Goree on 8 April. He sent his lieutenant ashore in a boat under a white flag. On landing, this officer demanded of Brue whether it was peace or war. When Brue replied that it was peace, the lieutenant took umbrage because the forts had not saluted His Britannic Majesty's flag. Brue replied that it was not the custom of the Most Christian King's fortresses to return the salutes of visiting men-of-war and certainly not to give them in the first instance. The lieutenant then formally demanded the restitution of the *William and Jane* and the *St George*. Brue asked for time to give a written reply which he delivered in four hours' time. Therein he pointed out that the *St George* was not even licensed to trade under the English Act of Parliament and would have been seized by the African Company's servants themselves. As regards the *William and Jane* her condemnation by an arrêt of the Conseil d'Etat in Paris disposed of the matter and for Maine's information he enclosed "the condemnation in print".[5]

The legal document nonplussed Maine. Feeling that he was out

[1] Complaints to R.A.C., T. 70/1434.
[2] R.A.C. to Thomas Gresham, 3 October 1700, P.R.O., T. 70/51.
[3] Same to same, 3 December 1700, P.R.O., C.O. 267/5.
[4] Log of H.M.S. *Rochester*, 12 March–9 April 1701, P.R.O., Ad. 51/4312/6; Berlioux, *André Brue*, p. 180.
[5] Labat, *op. cit.* IV, 335–345; Log of H.M.S. *Rochester*, 12 March–9 April 1701, P.R.O., Ad. 51/4312/6.

of his depth, he returned to James Island to report and to ask if he could be of any other service to the Company. He was asked to assist in settling trade at Portudal.

Accordingly in May he proceeded thither with a number of factors. "King Damell" proved a difficult person to deal with. He kept postponing his promised visit but eventually arrived after a week of waiting. At a "pallavera" on 15 May "he promised to protect them in a free and secure way of trade in his port, but must look to themselves as to the sea". Next day Maine went ashore "with a cradle wee gott made for him" as a present to the chief. Whilst Maine was attempting to extract a confirmation of his agreement of the previous day from him, three sail appeared in the offing. Maine promptly went on board his ship and gave chase to them. They proved to be three Dutchmen, whom he ordered to follow him into Portudal road. The next day "the king sent to know wherefore we did not let the Dutch commanders come on shore to trade, but they answered they came not to trade, nor to go on shore to no place, neither did they intend any trade, but were bound to St Jago". But "King Damell" resented this forcible interference with persons, whom he believed might be good customers, and showed his resentment by refusing to hand over the slaves, whom he had sold. Officers were therefore sent on shore "to persuade him what they could". The "pallavera" lasted well into the night. Finally on 19 May, the trouble having been adjusted, the *Rochester* sailed with the Dutchmen in company for the Cape Verde Islands.[1]

Little else of moment happened in the short breathing space before war again broke out with France. The visit of the *Rochester*, which was shortly afterwards followed by that of H.M.S. *Bonaventura*,[2] afforded a certain measure of protection to the Company's trade on the west. Moreover, Brue was having sufficient trouble with the local chiefs to prevent him from actively interfering with English shipping.[3] None the less English trade on the disputed coast did not flourish. A "ten per cent ship" carried off a slave at Joal without paying for him. In retaliation the local chief seized the English factory and goods. He was offered a slave by the chief agent but refused to return the Company's goods.[4]

[1] Log of H.M.S. *Rochester*, 1–19 May 1701, P.R.O., Ad. 51/4312/6.
[2] R.A.C. to Nathan Pile, 22 July 1701, P.R.O., T. 70/51.
[3] Labat, *op. cit.* IV, 210–215.
[4] Nathan Pile to R.A.C., 4 March 1701, P.R.O., T. 70/175.

Though the negotiations between Corker and Brue had broken down, the African and Senegal Companies at home still endeavoured to come to some working arrangement in Africa. Early in 1702 they came to a reciprocal arrangement whereby they agreed to hand over each other's deserters.[1] Even after the declaration of war on 2 May 1702 both Companies were anxious to make Africa a neutral zone. On 24 September 1702 the African Company wrote to Henry Bradshaw, their chief agent at James Island, informing him that "wee approve of your maintaining a correspondence with the French at Senegall with reference to regulating the trade with the natives, so as that you be very cautious, now the war is broke out between us, France, and Spain, that you give them no advantage to surprize or circumvent you in our trade or effects".[2]

On James Island itself affairs were far from well. Corker's successor, Paul Pindar, died a few months after his predecessor's departure.[3] Thomas Gresham, who then took charge, also died within a very short space of time.[4] There was a good deal of sickness, and after the expenditure of much work and materials a number of buildings were burnt to the ground through the carelessness of a slave.[5]

The correspondence received at this date by the African Company from their servants in the Gambia does not show a very happy feeling prevalent amongst those servants. The reason for it is not far to seek. Doubtless by reason of the lack of confidence induced by Corker's defalcations the Company decided to encourage a very unhealthy system of espionage amongst its servants in the Gambia. When on 3 March 1702 Hugh Hutchinson received his appointment as chief surgeon at James Island, he was instructed to send home from time to time reports on his colleagues and their characters "from the highest to the lowest".[6] Two days later the Company penned a somewhat similar missive to William Hacket, chaplain at James Island, telling him that they expected him "to send us by the *Supply* a full and true character of all our servants, that wee may know who are active and endeavour to promote our interest,

[1] R.A.C. to Henry Bradshaw, 24 February 1702, P.R.O., T. 70/51.
[2] P.R.O., T. 70/51.
[3] R.A.C. to Thomas Gresham, 3 October 1700, P.R.O., T. 70/51.
[4] Nathan Pile to R.A.C., 4 March 1701, P.R.O., T. 70/175.
[5] R.A.C. to Thomas Gresham, 3 October 1700, P.R.O., T. 70/51.
[6] P.R.O., T. 70/51.

and who either obstruct it by preferring their private advantage to ours, or are unactive or uncapable of performing the service they are imployed in, and who by their ambition, avarice, or debauchery are a hindrance to our affairs ".[1] When the fact is also mentioned that prior to writing this letter, the Company had heard that Hacket "has been afflicted and much out of order of his mind and thereby not able to perform the office of his place "[2] and that the letter of instructions to him opened with the expression of hope that he had recovered from his malady, one is led to wonder what value any reasonably minded person could attach to the chaplain's confidential reports.

As will be seen in the next chapter, this system of confidential reports and mutual espionage did not act as a check on the dishonesty of dishonestly minded servants, but it did engender ill-feeling and mutual recriminations, which proved highly detrimental to the Company's interests in the Gambia.

[1] P.R.O., T. 70/51.
[2] R.A.C. to Henry Bradshaw, 24 February 1702, P.R.O., T. 70/51

XI: The War of the Spanish Succession, 1702–1713

As mentioned in the previous chapter, both the African and Senegal Companies attempted to create a neutral zone in Africa on the outbreak of the War of the Spanish Succession. The negotiations did not proceed far. Even had they gone further than they did, they would not have secured entire neutrality in those regions inasmuch as the ships of war of either king and privateers holding letters of marque from the two governments were not bound by a purely commercial agreement between two trading companies and could carry on hostilities wheresoever they desired.

It was not until six months after the outbreak of the war that the first blow was struck in the Gambia, but that blow was a singularly effective one. Captain de la Roque, who had been with de Gennes at the capture of James Island in 1695, and Captain St Vaudrille arrived in the Gambia in November 1702. Very few details are given in contemporary records regarding their attack on the fort, but, as de la Roque was killed, it is evident that the English on this occasion offered some resistance. Humphrey Chishull, the new chief agent, had only arrived a few days before. He subsequently declared that he was forced to surrender "the island being week and destitute of men by reason of the mortality among us". Immediately after the surrender all the Englishmen were taken on board the French ships and kept in close confinement for seven days. Like de Gennes, St Vaudrille had a commission from the Most Christian King, but, unlike de Gennes, he believed in the exploitation of his initial success to his own advantage rather than to that of his royal master. He offered to spare the fort from demolition if the African Company's servants would ransom it. He in fact so far pressed his offer that he announced that he would convey all his prisoners to the island of Principe and maroon them there if his offer was not accepted. After seven days of captivity Chishull and his colleagues agreed to these terms. They drew three sets of bills on the African Company for the sum of £2000 each and further gave their personal bonds to secure payment of that amount in the event of the Company refusing to honour the bills. As a further collateral security for payment

133

St Vaudrille carried off as a hostage a newly arrived factor named William Pitts.[1]

In addition to taking the fort St Vaudrille also captured the *Supply*, which had only just brought out the new chief agent, and the *Gambia Galley* both belonging to the African Company.[2] Learning that the *Christopher*, another of the Company's ships, was up-river trading, he followed and captured her, but, as she appeared to be unseaworthy, he contented himself with taking her cargo and destroying her papers.[3] After taking such of the Company's goods as his own ships could carry and after having extracted the bills from Chishull, St Vaudrille set sail for Europe. Being a good man of business, he handed over his bills to a firm of Parisian bankers for collection. The African Company refused to honour them.[4] One consequence of this action was that at the end of the war a special clause was inserted in the treaty of peace to settle the question of their liability. Another more immediate consequence was that the unfortunate William Pitts was detained for three years or more a prisoner, firstly at La Rochelle and subsequently at St Malo, whence he wrote piteous letters to his employers imploring them for financial assistance, if they could not or would not procure his release.[5]

On 26 March 1703 Joseph Major wrote from James Island to the African Company to report that "since the departure of the French, there have been strange divisions in the castle, and no inventory of goods taken from time to time, each accusing the other of embezzlement. The agent has sent by Captain Johnson sixty slaves for Bermudas, of which I doubt you'l have a sorry account, the agent himselfe having once thought of going off with Johnson.[6]

---

[1] Barbot, *A Description of the Coasts of North and South Guinea*, p. 427; *Journal of Board of Trade*, 25 August 1719; Humphrey Chishull to Daniel Johnson, 2 February 1703, P.R.O., H.C.A. 1/16; R.A.C. to Earl of Nottingham, 4 June 1703, P.R.O., C.O. 267/5.

[2] Thomas Carter to R.A.C., 4 February 1703, P.R.O., T. 70/13; Account of losses of the R.A.C., 1695–1713, P.R.O., T. 70/175.

[3] Affidavit of Daniel Johnson, 4 May 1704, P.R.O., H.C.A. 1/16.

[4] R.A.C. to Earl of Nottingham, 4 June 1703, P.R.O., C.O. 267/5.

[5] William Pitts to R.A.C., 13 September 1703, 25 June and August 1704, and June 1705, P.R.O., T. 70/13 and T. 70/14; Sir Charles Hedges to Comte de Pontchartrain, 15 July 1704, *Hist. MSS. Comm. Rep., House of Lords MSS.* VII, 160, 161.

[6] This transaction is referred to in *C.S.P. Colonial (America and West Indies)*, 1703, pp. 700, 1158, and 1704–1705, p. 621. Various affidavits and statements in regard thereto are also to be found in P.R.O., T. 70/1434. There was clearly

The castle is much out of repair consisting of 14 men and 3 or 4 boys. The agent lives most at Gillefree (Juffure) and (has) no command and Mr Plunkett is the man that most applys to business. They have had a palaver with the emperour of the south shoar (sc. Foni), who promises the English protection to the utmost of his power."[1]

The documents which deal with these "strange divisions" are innumerable and indicate a good deal of hard swearing on the part of a good many people. What is clear from them is that Chishull was quite unable to keep his subordinates in hand. A none too reliable correspondent described him as "a man not to be intrusted in any imploy, being continually drunk when he can get liquour".[2] He was on very intimate terms with a certain "Madam Esperance", with whom he entered into a trading partnership on his own account, using the Company's goods for the purpose.[3] His excuse for this conduct was that he doubted whether the African Company would honour the bills, which he had given to St Vaudrille, and because he feared the French might return at any time and try to exact payment from him personally or seize him as a prisoner, if he failed to pay.[4] Others were equally, if not more, dishonest. Though the chiefs of Kombo and Geregia carefully preserved and returned a large quantity of goods, which had been left in their territories in the Company's factories, it is clear that a number of the Company's servants endeavoured to conceal their embezzlement of the Company's property under the pretence that such property had been carried off by the French.[5]

a good deal of hard swearing on both sides. Johnson was eventually arrested at the instance of the African Company on a charge of piracy. In September 1704 he had handed over certain documents to the Company proving his innocence. He was none the less brought to trial before the Admiralty Court and the documents in question were suppressed by the African Company until they were compelled by the court to disclose them. The result of the trial was that Johnson was very properly acquitted; cf. proceedings in P.R.O., H.C.A. 1/16, and in particular the affidavit of William Wigglesworth of 16 November 1704.   [1] P.R.O., T. 70/13.

[2] John Chidley to R.A.C., 2 April 1704, P.R.O., T. 70/13.

[3] Thomas Weaver to R.A.C., 5 May 1704, P.R.O., T. 70/13; "A list of debts due to the Company at the time James Fort was taken by the French", P.R.O., H.C.A. 1/16.

[4] Humphrey Chishull to Daniel Johnson, 2 February 1703, P.R.O., H.C.A. 1/16; *Journal of Council of Trade*, 25 August 1719.

[5] Complaints to R.A.C., P.R.O. T. 70/1434; "A list of debts due to the Company at the time James Fort was taken by the French", P.R.O., H.C.A. 1/16: Account of the expenditure of Daniel Johnson, 1704, *ibid.*

The news from the Gambia made three things perfectly clear to the African Company. In the first place, a new chief agent had to be sent out with all possible despatch. In the second place, they could not hope to hold James Island without assistance from the navy. Thirdly, so long as Goree could be used as a naval base by the French, their foothold in the Gambia would remain precarious.

Their new agent was Thomas Weaver, one of their sea captains, but with a strange lack of discrimination they not only chose as his third assistant a certain John Chidley, but also resolved to give him certain powers independent of the chief agent. Chidley had been one of Agent Corker's confederates,[1] and the Company's selection of him betokens the absolute failure of their system of encouragement of mutual espionage and of the rendering of confidential reports by their subordinates upon one another.

In order to ensure the relieving contingent's safe arrival at James Island it was arranged that Weaver and his party should embark upon H.M.S. *Deptford* and *Lowestoft*. The commanders of these men-of-war were further instructed to proceed to Goree and Senegal and to take the forts.[2] If they were successful in this latter purpose, the new chief agent was to evacuate James Island and make Goree his headquarters, whilst the fort at Senegal was to be demolished.[3]

For convenience, what little there is to say regarding this latter operation may be recorded first. The men-of-war sailed in company with two of the Company's ships, the *Hunter* and the *Swan*. Off the Canary Isles the *Deptford* managed to capture a French dogger, but that was almost the end of her achievements. The *Deptford* and *Lowestoft* arrived off Goree on 3 December 1703. An attempt to take the place by a night attack with boats failed because the boats were overloaded with the result that one sank. The next day Captain Wooden, the Commodore, sent a flag of truce to the island to see if the French would surrender on terms. Their reply was that "they were bound to defend themselves as long as they were able; nevertheless, if we did take them by force of arms, we should be as welcome as any nation". To quote again from the *Deptford's* log—"upon this answer our captain thought it convenient to goe after the ship that our prisoners said was gone for provisions". The ship

[1] Complaints to R.A.C., T. 70/1434. Cf. also p. 128.

[2] R.A.C. passenger lists, P.R.O., T. 70/1436.

[3] Earl of Nottingham to Privy Council, 2 July 1703, *C.S.P. Domestic*, 1703–1704, p. 432; R.A.C. to Thomas Weaver, 11 January 1704, P.R.O., T. 70/52.

in question was a thirty-two gun ship and was accompanied by a dogger. The dogger was soon outsailed and captured, but the ship escaped by running ashore and being set on fire by her crew. After this the English proceeded to James Island to land the new chief agent and his party. At the beginning of 1704 the ships returned to Goree, but beyond cruising off the island and sending a flag of truce ashore to demand the surrender of the forts they did nothing. The summons met with an answer similar to the previous one, and after a month of passive blockade the men-of-war returned to the Gambia to report that the forts were too strongly manned and the batteries too well armed to be taken by a force of their strength.[1] As the African Company wrote on learning of the utter failure of this expedition, all hope of dispossessing the French of Goree or Senegal was at an end.[2] The men-of-war had been so far of service as to act as an efficient convoy to the Company's ships. By holding French armed vessels in check at Goree they gave the new chief agent a breathing space wherein to put matters to right in Gambia. Subsequently the *Lowestoft* afforded protection to one of the Company's ships when trading at Portudal.[3] Both ships allowed some of their sailors and marines to engage in the Company's service. The crews of the two men-of-war were also detailed to put James Fort into a better state of defence, but they refused to work unless they were paid. The agent was forced to come to terms with them and pay them in gold, which he borrowed from certain of the naval officers upon bills drawn on the African Company.[4]

It is now necessary to return to Thomas Weaver on James Island. He gave the following report to the Company of the state of the island on his arrival:

The seventh of December (1703) *he came to the River Gambia and sent the pinnace with Mr Chidley to James Island and Gillifree (sc. Juffure) for a pilot. The eighth he returned with one and that night came to an anchor before James Island. The ninth a small boat came from Chishull to acquaint him that they had not one grain of powder to salute him with. Soon after he and the gentlemen landed and saluted the man*

[1] Labat, *Nouvelle Relation de l'Afrique Occidentale*, IV, 129; Log of H.M.S. *Lowestoft*, 1703–1704, P.R.O., Ad. 51/4247; Log of H.M.S. *Deptford*, 1703–1704, P.R.O., Ad. 51/4160.
[2] R.A.C. to Thomas Weaver, 22 September 1704, P.R.O., T. 70/52.
[3] Log of H.M.S. *Lowestoft*, 1703–1704, P.R.O., Ad. 51/4247.
[4] Thomas Weaver to R.A.C., 4 and 7 May 1704, P.R.O., T. 70/13.

of war with a barrell of powder borrowed from the commodore, which salute they returned.

They found in the island Mr Chishull and seven more white men belonging to the same island and only 5 men and 3 women slaves.

The walls of the bastions defensible. The servants' houses no roof. The negro house all uncovered. The great store house so open that any person might go in without going through the door.

The gunns were but fifty four in number (the rest being carried away by Captain Johnson)[1] and were either on the ground or on useless carriages—most rotten or without wracks or platforms—and some of them splitt up. The whole island left naked. The sibbies cutt down and the outer walls round the island had not one stone upon another. They found but few valuable goods in the stores, the rest being disposed of by Mr Chishull before their arrivall.[2]

. . .The eighth December Mr Chishull took thirty two cakes out of the storehouse and sent it (sic) to Mr Pymonds at Vintan (sc. Bintang), but Mr Weaver has had the wax delivered again. The same night he sent away the books and papers of the factory with the wax and (Weaver) was forced to use abundance of threatnings and perswasions before he could gett them again.

The said Chishull insisted to have the goods on the island for securing his ransom from the French and said they were none of the Companies goods, but belonged to the French.

He has discovered. . .that he (sc. Chishull) has lodged eight kintalls of teeth with one Roger Freerwood, formerly a servant of the Company, (who) now lives at Piemont's. The teeth are restored to the Company.[3]

With singular lack of foresight the Company did not include any masons or bricklayers in the contingent which accompanied Weaver, but the Commodore lent the agent some men. The Company also failed to supply any building materials to the Gambia. Weaver therefore had to make his own lime. As this work had to be done on the mainland and as there was only one boat on the island, re-building progressed slowly. Weaver was able to begin rebuilding on 21 December 1703. In the following year on 15 January he inter-cepted a sloop, which was owned by a Portuguese, but had a French-man on board and was carrying French merchandise. As the sloop

[1] Cf. p. 134, *supra.*
[2] Thomas Weaver to R.A.C., 4 May 1704, P.R.O., T. 70/52.
[3] Same to same, 8 May 1704, P.R.O., T. 70/13.

refused to come to, it was attacked and a Portuguese subject was killed. The sloop was then seized and employed in carrying materials from the mainland.[1]

All went on well until 14 February when Weaver had to report that "a dismall fire broke out at nine in the morning. The damage thereby suffered may be computed at 1000£. During which conflagration he had only time to snatch up a small trunck, which contained his commission and other papers and 5 small books of account of the factory during the whole time of Mr Chishull's being agent. The greatest loss susteined by the Company is seventy barrells of brandy."[2]

Fortunately the *Deptford* and *Lowestoft* returned from their abortive expedition to Goree on 1 March and with the assistance of their crews Weaver was able to repair the damage. He was able to report "the walls of the four flankers are very strong and were finished the twenty sixth Aprill and are about eighteen feet high as they were before. On the twenty eighth Aprill the sailors raised a large sheers of topmasts and they with the assistance of proper officers raised twenty-one guns upon the flanckers and placed them on trucks, so that the fort on all sides looks formidable."[3]

It seems clear that Weaver was a person of considerable energy and that he might have put the Company's affairs in the Gambia in tolerable order, if he had had sufficient time for the purpose. He, however, died on 4 September 1704. A letter from Gambia to the African Company informed them that he was shot, but no details are given of the incident causing his death.[4] William Smith, the second chief merchant at James Island, had on 22 May been captured by the French in the *Hunter* whilst on a voyage to Sierra Leone.[5]

Weaver was therefore succeeded by John Chidley, the third chief merchant, who was in charge of the Company's factory at Joar, near Kau-ur. As mentioned on a previous page, he had been Corker's confederate in a number of his malpractices, but the Company were apparently ignorant of this fact. He was evidently a most plausible

---

[1] Same to same, 4 May 1704, P.R.O., T. 70/14; Antonio Deagujar to R.A.C., 8 March 1705, and R.A.C. to John Chidley, 8 November 1705, P.R.O., T. 70/52.
[2] Thomas Weaver to R.A.C., 4 May 1704, P.R.O., T. 70/15.   [3] *Ibid.*
[4] Nominal Rolls of Gambia, P.R.O., T. 70/1445; R.A.C. to Robert Plunkett, 8 November 1705, P.R.O., T. 70/52.
[5] Thomas Monck to R.A.C., 5 June 1704, P.R.O., T. 70/13.

person. A number of his letters to his employers are still extant and show him to have been a thorough-paced hypocrite. In one letter he begged the Company to send out a parson, because his colleagues "live more like heathens than Christians" and he deplored their custom of making temporary wives of the local "senhoras", who were the frequent cause of embezzlement of the Company's goods.[1] The Company replied that "we agree intirely with you in opinion that the greatest reason why our servants wrong us is their taking women, who oblige them to live extravagantly and waste our estates in presents, and hope you will by your example depress such debauched practices".[2] The extent, to which Chidley fulfilled those hopes, may be gauged by the fact that he was himself the father of a child by a female slave on whom he bestowed large quantities of the Company's property including some gold, slaves, "and a great deal of brandy, wine, beer, and severall other things"[3] and that he had acquired the mother in exchange for two of the Company's slaves.

His desire for a parson may have been born of a longing for self regeneration, but his conversation on religious topics shocked honest sea captains, who visited him at Joar. After one conversation with him one captain reported that he "never in his life heard any person speak more atheistically than the said Chidley".[4] Another reported that he once heard Chidley say "he did not believe there was any Hell, and this when he was very free from being in drink".[5] Other specimens of his atheistical utterings are extant. Without being blasphemous they disclose the ill-formed conceptions of a half-educated man.

The African Company was in the habit of shipping coins of the value of about a Dutch rix dollar, called zealots, for the purpose of purchasing goods and slaves from the natives of the Gambia. Amongst Chidley's personal baggage was a coining mould. He used it to manufacture counterfeit zealots for the Company's business whilst he retained the genuine coin for his own use. In February 1704 one of the Company's ships was at Joar. As the captain

---

[1] 2 April 1704, P.R.O., T. 70/13.

[2] R.A.C. to Chidley, 28 September 1704, P.R.O., T. 70/13.

[3] Captain Charles Cook to Gawin Corbin, 24 January 1706, P.R.O., T. 70/1434.

[4] Affidavit of John Tozer, 10 June 1704, P.R.O., T. 70/1434.

[5] Affidavit of Richard Eaglesfield, 10 June 1704, P.R.O., T. 70/1434.

wished to purchase a cow for the ship's provisions he applied to Chidley for the necessary money. Chidley gave him two zealots, "whereof one was a false coined one made of copper". The captain asked for a genuine coin and was told he could not have one as "the natives did not know good from bad". Chidley also proceeded to inform the captain that he "had made false dollars, but curst and swore bitterly at those, that he said had stole away his moulds, that he could not make more, and that he had writt to England for more moulds, and (in) a little time would get a thousand pounds by itt".[1]

At the time of appointing him as their chief merchant the African Company for some extraordinary reason decided to give Chidley quasi-independent powers, to make the up-river trade more or less his own peculiar province, and to grant him the privilege of trading for himself and a commission of six slaves for every 100 purchased by him.[2] This contract had been the cause of considerable friction between himself and Weaver. Chidley had demanded of the African Company that "Mr Weaver may have positive orders not to send any other factor up the river above this place (sc. Joar) and that the governor may be directed to send from time to time such goods as he may want".[3] This demand invited a very stern rebuke from the Company for attempting to attribute to himself the sole trade above Joar "as if by your articles we had made you our farmer and not our factor".[4]

Much could have been forgiven Chidley if, despite his innumerable acts of dishonesty, he had kept James Fort in proper state of defence against any possible attack by the French. But his cupidity would not let him rise even to this. He made fictitious muster-rolls of the garrison and "placed severall persons on the account as souldiers, who never was such but were Portugueez and others, who lived ashore, but their wages and diett is charged to the Company". The rate of pay for soldiers was thirty shillings a month and Chidley so entered the amount in his accounts but there were "none paid so but corporalls and two or three old souldiers, and the rest at 20s. p. mensem".[5] In the circumstances one is not surprised to hear what

[1] Affidavit of Richard Eaglesfield, 10 June 1704, P.R.O., T. 70/1434.
[2] Thomas Weaver to R.A.C., 10 June 1704, and John Chidley to R.A.C., 2 April 1704, P.R.O., T. 70/13.
[3] Chidley to R.A.C., 2 April 1704, P.R.O., T. 70/13.
[4] R.A.C. to Chidley, 28 September 1704, P.R.O., T. 70/13.
[5] "Remarks on Mr Chidleyes indirect proceedings", P.R.O., T. 70/1434.

happened when Henri Baton, a French privateer from Martinique, appeared off the island at the end of 1704 in the brigantine *Fanfaron*. His crew of over 100 men was quite sufficient to alarm Chidley, who was also anxious to preserve his own private hoard from plunder. As a privateer, Henri Baton had to consider the financial side of his undertaking. He was therefore perfectly willing to follow the example of St Vaudrille in 1702. He plundered the fort of all that he could carry away and then demanded bills drawn on the African Company, "under the notion of ransom, for some things which they could neither take with them, nor make any advantage of in any other way".[1]

After Baton had sailed away with his bills, the soldiers on James Island refused to serve unless they received the full pay to which they were entitled. Chidley complied with their demands for one month but then reverted to his old practice of appropriating part of their pay to himself.[2] The rest of the deeds of John Chidley, first and last, and of all his ways, behold they are written in the books of the Royal African Company on many pages of paper. It was not only that he was actively dishonest. He also by his high-handed conduct excited many of the native chiefs against the English. He attempted by a show of force to obtain the return of a number of runaway slaves from the "king" of Kiang. The only result was that the king attacked and captured a number of vessels trading up river. Chidley also seized "severall of their country priests", including the "king" of Jarra's brother, with the result that local chiefs refused to supply James Fort with wood or water. Eventually native hostility made the place too hot for him. The natives "forced him to quitt the factory at Saker (sc. Sikka near Juffure) and move to the castle at eleven or twelve o'clock at night and the same he was forced to do at Barrowfatt (sc. Brefet in Foni). Otherwise they had killed him and all his men in the boat. Chidley finding the negroes averse to him, he thought it the best way to quitt the castle in time, whilst he had wherewithall, if at any time the Company should call him to an account, that he would hold them in law with their own money, that he had gott by the death of Weaver and the Portugueez ship, which he made a prize off. So, takeing his leave of the castle, he imbarkt himself on board of Captain Crookshankes his ship and a considerable parcell of negroes, also a great deal of gold, teeth, wax, and two

[1] R.A.C. to Council of Trade, 1727, P.R.O., C.O. 267/5.
[2] "Remarks on Mr Chidleyes indirect proceedings", P.R.O., T. 70/1434.

very large bales of linning, which he took out of the Portugueez ship, and a great deal of silver plate, that was fitt for any Governour's table in America or elsewhere, and went with the aforesaid goods to Pantuxet in Maryland." The night his ship fell down to Lamin Point eleven of the Company's slaves disappeared from Foni in Brefet and their irons with them. As the chronicler of all these events says, "I leave you to think what became of them."[1] The only consoling feature about the whole business was that Chidley, who openly boasted that he had given a fidelity bond for £2000 and that "he could easily pay that and not vallue the Affrican Company", did not prosper in his land of refuge. He lost a large quantity of gold, which he had embarked on the *Hazardous* man-of-war, as well as a large amount of his money in land speculation in Virginia, but he escaped the clutches of the law.[2]

The African Company was for a long time in complete ignorance of what was transpiring in the Gambia. Communication was subject to constant interruption owing to the raids of French men-of-war and privateers. In 1703 the *Success* was captured on its voyage home from the Gambia. The same fate befell the *Swan* in 1705.[3] Furthermore, it is perfectly clear that neither Chidley nor any of his subordinates took the trouble to attempt to inform them of what was happening. The news of Henri Baton's capture of James Island reached them indirectly from the Senegal Company.[4] The reason for the communication of this information by the Senegal Company was because that Company was anxious to make the north-west coast of Africa a neutral zone. It had come to their ears that Le Maitre, their Director-General in Senegal, had instigated Baton's attack and they feared possible retaliation on their own settlements. When this news reached them, they had already commenced negotiations with the African Company and, as earnest of their disapproval of Le Maitre's part in the affair, they announced that they had recalled and replaced him by Jean Jajolet de la Courbe.[5] These negotiations had

[1] Charles Cooke to Gawin Corbin, 24 January 1704, P.R.O., T. 70/1434.
[2] Gawin Corbin to R.A.C., 12 February 1708, P.R.O., T. 70/1434.
[3] Account of losses of R.A.C., 1698–1713, P.R.O., T. 70/175.
[4] R.A.C. to Chidley, 13 September 1705, P.R.O., T. 70/52.
[5] *Ibid.* Le Maitre was in fact recalled principally on grounds of mismanagement of the Senegal Company's affairs in regard to other matters. Any assistance which he may have given to Baton in his attack on James Island was a very subsidiary reason for his recall. Berlioux, *André Brue*, p. 203.

begun in 1704, when the African Company wrote to their servants in the Gambia the following letter:

This serves to acquaint you of the offers and promises of the French Senegal Company from Mr Le Porstre, residing here in London, that they will not molest the Company's trade in these parts within the limits of the French Senegal Company (which is from Cape Blanco to the River Sierra Leone) or disturb any ships, vessels, bark, boat, canoe or other effects belonging to the English Company, and they will prevent the same to be done by any ships of war, privateers, or ships in their service, and give directions accordingly to their chief agents; and also that they assist you and all this Company's servants from any disturbance from the natives; and, to remove all jealousies, they will give directions that their factory at Albadar be discontinued during the war, and not concern themselves with the trade of that river. These things we hold to be our interest, and, if it appears so they have given such directions, and their chief in all things comply thereto, you may likewise, so far as is in your power, maintain the same civilities.[1]

On 8 June 1705 articles of neutrality were drawn up and signed by the directors of both Companies. It was thereby agreed that both parties should give orders to their agents in Africa to live in peace and good accord and mutually to assist each other against the natives and any others, who might come to interrupt their trade. Each Company undertook not to attack the forts and factories of the other between Cape Blanco and Sherboro. It was mutually understood that neither Company could be held responsible for any violation of the agreement by men-of-war, privateers, or pirates belonging to the other nation, but it was agreed that each Company should approach its own Government with a request that their men-of-war and privateers should be instructed not to attack or insult the vessels or habitations of the other Company.[2]

When la Courbe was sent out to Senegal in 1705 he was instructed to see that this agreement was honoured. He even undertook to despatch letters from the English in the Gambia to the African Company, as all other means of communication had apparently failed. As further evidence of their desire to honour their agree-

[1] D'Avenant, *Political and Commercial Works—Reflections upon the Constitution and Management of the Trade to Africa*, v, 312–313.
[2] Labat, *op. cit.* iv, 347–349; Durand, *Voyage au Sénégal*, pp. 81–82.

ment, the Senegal Company undertook to restore the goods plundered from James Island by Henri Baton.[1]

La Courbe's appointment more or less coincided with that of a new chief agent in the Gambia. On 9 April 1706 the African Company wrote to inform Chidley that they were of "opinion that the greatest part of the elephant's teeth, that came home by the *Oxford* and *Hastings* men of warr lately, were purchased by you" and to instruct him to come home and render an account of his stewardship.[2] As already said, Chidley anticipated all awkward enquiries either at home or from his successor in office. He sailed with his ill-gotten gains for Virginia on 22 June in the *Olive Tree* belonging to a private trader.[3] He left a certain Joseph Dakins in charge, "who has managed it with as much frugallity as the other for his own ends".[4] Chidley's successor, Tozer, stayed only four months and then left "for want of health"[5] after complaints had been received that he "carries himself very strongly to the factors".[6] He was succeeded by John Snow.[7]

Not only had Chidley "drained, or rather robbed, the factory of what was valluable, leaving little but damaged goods",[8] but the affairs of the Company were in a bad way in every other respect. Many of the men's engagements had expired and there were murmurings about their being detained beyond their time.[9] The walls of the fort were reported "as partly blown up and no otherwise repaired than by a heap of stones and rubbish confusedly put together";[10] and the buildings were thatched with straw instead of tiles.[11] The tank was out of order. Water had to be obtained from the mainland. Owing to "the selfish knavery of the negroes" even that supply was precarious. When the "king" of Barra upon some pretext or other stopped the drawing of water at Juffure, "the pallaver cost a hundred bars".[12]

[1] R.A.C. to Chidley, 13 September 1705; R.A.C. to John Snow, 22 March 1707, P.R.O., T. 70/52.   [2] P.R.O., T. 70/52.
[3] John Tozer to R.A.C., 21 October 1706, P.R.O., T. 70/175; D'Avenant, *op. cit.* v, 178.
[4] Tozer to R.A.C., 10 December 1706, P.R.O., T. 70/5.
[5] Same to same, 15 February 1707, P.R.O., T. 70/5.
[6] Joseph Holmes to R.A.C., 23 October 1706, P.R.O., T. 70/5.
[7] John Snow to.R.A.C., 2 December 1706, P.R.O., T. 70/5.
[8] Thomas Adcock to R.A.C., 21 October 1706, P.R.O., T. 70/5.
[9] Tozer to R.A.C., 10 December 1706, P.R.O., T. 70/5.
[10] *A View of the State of Trade to Africa*, p. 6.
[11] Tozer to R.A.C., 10 December 1706, P.R.O., T. 70/5.
[12] Snow to R.A.C., 9 August 1707, P.R.O., T. 70/5.

Agent Snow endeavoured to come to some working arrangement with La Courbe. Despite the promise of the Senegal Company to restore the goods taken from James Island in 1704 their servants on the spot did nothing. On 22 March 1707 the African Company wrote to Snow instructing him to press for fulfilment of this promise "and in all respects to prevent the impositions they shall pretend to put on you by reason of any promises on the part of this Company, whilest they have no regard to their owne. But in all things consider your present circumstances, and doe not give them any jealousy of needless disputes, whereby the Companyes settlements may be again in danger of being assaulted, but rather bring them to complyance by argument and by perswading them 'tis their interest."[1] Snow had some correspondence with the French Governor at Goree and the Director-General of Senegal, but the letters are no longer extant[2] and do not appear to have resulted in any practical agreement. The difficulty under which both parties laboured in arriving at any such agreement is witnessed by an incident which occurred in March 1707 when a shallop entered the Gambia with letters from the French at Goree. Captain Frisby, who commanded the *Young Margarett*, "a ten per cent ship", seized the shallop. Despite Snow's expostulations he clung to his prize. All that Snow could do was to explain to the Governor of Goree that it was out of his power to prevent the seizure and to send him "some small presents of beer etc" and somewhat untactfully to wind up his apologies by a request that the French would honour their agreement by restoring the goods plundered from James Island in 1704.[3] La Courbe did in reply promise to return any of the goods, which might be found at Goree, but after a lapse of three years this promise was not likely to be capable of fulfilment.[4] As Snow was subsequently told by his employers that "we do not approve of your concerning yourself between the French and ten per cent men",[5] the task of recovering the property and of coming to an amicable arrangement with the French was not rendered any the more easy.

In the meantime trade languished. In 1706 two of the Company's ships were captured with their cargoes on their way to the Gambia.[6]

---

[1] P.R.O., T. 70/52.   [2] Letters received by R.A.C., P.R.O., T. 70/1511.
[3] Snow to R.A.C., 2 June 1707, P.R.O., T. 70/5.
[4] Same to same, 9 August 1707, P.R.O., T. 70/5.
[5] R.A.C. to Snow, 14 September 1708, P.R.O., T. 70/52.
[6] Losses of R.A.C., 1698–1713, P.R.O., T. 70/175.

The result was that it was found impossible owing to lack of goods to open up a number of factories either in the river or along the coast despite the pressing invitation of the native chiefs.[1] The interruption of communications prevented the men on the spot from being relieved when their agreements expired and thus gave rise to a spirit of intense discontent.

In May 1708 the garrison of James Island mutinied. The ringleaders were the warehousekeeper, the surgeon, Thomas Weaver, the sergeant of the soldiers, and Millward, the cooper, who "was a great rogue when in England". Eighteen of their number alleged subsequently that they had been harshly treated by Snow, but one of them subsequently alleged that he "was on a wrong account drawn in to rise against Mr Snow".[2] Snow himself afterwards informed the African Company that "there was no cause for the mutiny—only a design to rob you of six hundred barrs".[3] There can, however, be no doubt that however slight their grounds of complaint may have been, a number of men, cooped up on a small island and despairing of any immediate relief from home, could easily magnify their grievances and constant airing of those grievances could soon make them desperate men. The immediate cause of the outbreak was because Snow refused to comply with their demand to hand over certain of the Company's goods, which he said he wanted for purposes of trade, "on which they entered his room and made him a prisoner, taking from him his keys and extorted from him a note to pay them six hundred barrs. After which he broke them into parties and disarmed them and has brought several of them to repent being concerned therein." The six hundred bars' worth of goods were not handed over. A timely present of sixteen gallons of rum to the soldiers allayed further trouble.[4] The "king" of Barra speedily heard of what had happened on James Island and so took advantage thereof to seize the Company's goods at Juffure and to demand payment of forty bars for their redemption.[5] On 8 September 1708 a French privateer from Martinique commanded by Monsieur Parente appeared off James Island. Snow, who after

[1] Joseph Holmes to R.A.C., 29 November 1706; John Snow to R.A.C., 31 March 1707, P.R.O., T. 70/5.
[2] Letters received by R.A.C., P.R.O., T. 70/1511.
[3] Snow to R.A.C., 9 May 1708, P.R.O., T. 70/2 and T. 70/5.
[4] Same to same, 8 May 1708, P.R.O., T. 70/2 and T. 70/5.
[5] Same to same, 8 and 10 May 1708, P.R.O., T. 70/2 and T. 70/5.

the mutiny had begged for leave to return home,[1] was sick at the time as were many of his men. These facts, the hopeless disrepair of the fort, and "the having such rascalls under him" persuaded him that resistance was out of the question. Following the examples of Chishull and Chidley he decided to redeem the fort. The Frenchman carried off thirty slaves, two to three tons of ivory, eighteen ounces of gold, "and had fifty slaves more as a ransom for the fort and the redemption of the goods".[2]

Thirteen days later four more French privateers under the command of Nicholas Germaine appeared in the river and captured the Company's ship *Bridgewater* in sight of James Fort just as she was on the point of sailing for the West Indies with a cargo of 213 slaves and some ivory. The Senegal Company's ship *Amazon* was with them. According to Snow, La Courbe was on board her and had instigated the raid.[3] The privateers allowed the English passengers and crew to land on James Island and also handed back some of the goods which they found on board the *Bridgewater*.[4] Eight of the passengers and crew were dead before the end of the year.[5]

Snow's last letter to the African Company is dated 20 May 1709. Therein he reported the loss of the *Bridgewater*, that he was so far destitute of goods which he had had to borrow from La Courbe, that he had bought fifty slaves with the borrowed goods and sold them to a private trader.[6] A letter written by Francis Cole, a factor, on the following 15 June was the last the Company was to receive from James Island for over four years.[7] When H.M.S. *Scarborough*, which was detailed to the end of 1709 to cruise off the coast, arrived in the river, her commander found James Island abandoned and the factory demolished.[8] Some time before the man-of-war's arrival the few remaining Englishmen left the island and settled down on the river banks as private traders. After spiking the guns, they took with them what little was left of any value in the fort. Some of them

---

[1] Snow to R.A.C., 8 and 10 May 1708, P.R.O., T. 70/2 and T 70/5.

[2] Examination of Snow and Captain Gordon, 20 April 1726, *Journal of Council of Trade*; Barbot, *op. cit.* pp. 427, 428; Snow to R.A.C., 21 January 1709, P.R.O., T. 70/5; Francis Cole to R.A.C., 15 June 1709, P.R.O., T. 70/5.

[3] Snow to R.A.C., 20 May 1709, P.R.O., T. 70/2 and T. 70/5.

[4] Papers received by R.A.C., P.R.O., T. 70/1511.

[5] Nominal Rolls of Gambia, P.R.O., T. 70/1445.

[6] P.R.O., T. 70/5.   [7] *Ibid.*

[8] R.A.C. to Snow, 27 December 1709, P.R.O., T. 70/52; Examination of Captain Milward, 6 July 1711, *Journal of Council of Trade*.

no doubt died. Others probably eked out a very precarious existence, but some of them evidently prospered. Snow, for instance, remained in the river until 1719 and at a later date proved a thorn in the flesh of his former employers.[1]

The evacuation of James Island left English private traders in the river wholly at the mercy of the French. Fortunately for them the garrison at Goree was not in a position to be aggressive. The one recorded attempt to drive the English out of the river ended disastrously. On Christmas Eve, 1710, a French corvette tried to capture a private trader at Kau-ur. The Englishmen offered a determined resistance for an hour and a half and suffered a number of casualties. Eventually a band of 100 of the local inhabitants came to his assistance and the Frenchman withdrew.[2]

In 1709 the Senegal Company had fallen into financial straits, had been compelled to go into liquidation, and to sell their rights to some Rouen merchants.[3] The new company found it impossible to launch any ambitious scheme until after the close of the war. Despite the occasional success of a French commerce raider the English navy had more or less the command of the sea. Communication between France and her African settlements in fact became so precarious that at the end of the war the garrison at Goree was in a state of semi-starvation.[4] Consequently during the four years following the abandonment of James Island English private traders were able to visit the Gambia with comparative freedom and at the conclusion of peace in 1713 the trade of the river was for the most part still in English hands.

---

[1] Examination of John Snow, 20 April 1726, *Journal of Council of Trade*; William Cooke to R.A.C., 26 July 1714, and Francis Mackenzie to R.A.C., 16 October 1714, P.R.O., T. 70/3 and T. 70/5.

[2] Barbot, *op. cit.* p. 26.

[3] Tallot, *La Colonie Française du Sénégal*, p. 25.

[4] William Cooke to R.A.C., 2 January 1714, P.R.O., T. 70/3 and T. 70/5.

XII: Pirates, 1713–1721

At the close of the war in 1713 the Treaty of Utrecht left unaltered the position of Great Britain and France on the north-west coast of Africa. The eleventh article of the treaty provided for the appointment of commissioners to enquire into the claims of French subjects against the African Company and its servants in respect of the bills which were given at the time of the capitulations of James Island in 1702 and 1704. The African Company not unnaturally disclaimed responsibility for the unauthorised acts of their agents, which had been done under duress, and further counterclaimed against the Senegal Company for the seizure of their ships in time of peace. The enquiry was a protracted one. In 1719 the British Government announced that the African Company repudiated liability for the claims of the French and that it pressed for satisfaction to be given for seizure of the Company's shipping. The enquiry still hung fire and in 1727 the African Company informed the Board of Trade that "we are so far from having reaped any benefit from this enquiry's being hitherto deferred, that we have great reason to wish it had been made and finished long since".[1]

The African Company hesitated for some time before deciding to reoccupy James Island. The claims, which the French had lodged with the treaty commissioners at Utrecht, were no doubt one cause of their hesitation. Another and more important one was their disastrous experience in the Gambia ever since the Treaty of Ryswick. An anonymous contemporary writer summed up the history of James Island after Booker's death in 1698 pretty accurately in the following words:

Ever since that time it has been in a ruinous condition. The mortality of some sent since by the Company has brought it generally into the hands of unqualified, knavish, sottish and ignorant persons, who have never transmitted regular accounts to the Company, and yet, though the Company has been basely cheated there, it has been by such poor fools as never make themselves worth anything.

[1] Mr Popple to Richard Harris, 12 August 1719, *C.S.P. Colonial (America and West Indies)*, 1719–1720, p. 209; *Journal of Council of Trade*, 14 August 1719; Wickham-Legg, *Diplomatic Instructions, France*, 1689–1721, II, 203; R.A.C. to Council of Trade, 1727, P.R.O., C.O. 267/5.

It has several times been plundered by the French in the late warr and severall times the storehouses (which are usually covered with thatch instead of tile) have been set on fire and have served to balance their accounts, which could not otherwise have balanced.

The goods have been spoiled for want of warehouses being floored; the men have died for want of refreshments, medicins, and skilful physicians; and the want of a few things necessary hath often occasioned the loss of the whole.

The losses by the French have not a little contributed to these things. The disappointments the Company have met with have prevented their supplying them regularly and so this factory has for many years been very unfortunate; yet, were it well managed, it might be turned to good accompt.[1]

Another writer estimated that the trade would not justify more than the despatch of two ships of 120 tons each yearly and that the profit on their cargoes was only likely to be £2600.[2]

It was only at the latter end of 1713 that the African Company decided to resettle in the Gambia. They directed William Cooke, their newly appointed chief agent, to consider on arrival whether any place would be more suitable than James Island for the settlement. They supplied him with a copy of an agreement, which was apparently made by Paul Pindar some ten years earlier with the "emperor" of Foni for the purchase or lease of an island at the mouth of the Bintang Creek, which was called Pindar's Island, and requested him to consider its suitability for the purpose. Cooke was further instructed to approach the Portuguese traders in the river and "oblige them to your interest". He was further instructed that "you must enquire what English traders remain in the country and propose to entertain them in the Company's service". If they refused this offer, he was to inform them that they would be dealt with as trespassers.[3]

Cooke and a party of merchants, factors, soldiers and artisans arrived at James Island on 13 November 1713. "Next morning wee went ashore on the island, which was found in a most ruinous condition. The walls within are almost irreparable. The outer walls

---

[1] "Some Observations on the Trade to Africa", Gough MSS. Somerset, 7.

[2] "A Scheme for carrying on the Trade to Africa", Gough MSS. Somerset, 7.

[3] R.A.C. to William Cooke, 13 September and 8 October, 1713, P.R.O., T. 70/52.

blown up with powder in severall places—particularly the two western flankers from the very foundation. Wee found thirty six guns, both small and great,—yet has all their nutts and pavillions broke of and drove into their muzzells, and all their vents filled up with smiths' punchers or the like, so that of all the thirty six there is but one poor small gun, that can be put upon carriages, and it's all eat up with rust. Wee have not found one bitt of useful timber upon the island; no, not so much as the very sibbies that was about the fort, but all are burnt and broke down to the ground."[1]

Immediate reoccupation of the island was in the circumstances out of the question. Cooke inspected Pindar's Island, but could find no fresh water there. He also tried without success to persuade the "king" of Barra to allow him to build a fort to secure the well at Juffure.[2] Therefore it was decided to rebuild the fort at James Island and to keep the *Royal Anne* as the Company's headquarters until such time as the fort should be fit for habitation. For many reasons the work of rebuilding was slow and it was not until 1717 that the fort was ready for partial occupation.[3]

Cooke was one of the best correspondents whom the African Company ever had in the River Gambia, but his letters are loud in the complaints of the difficulties which confronted him. Inefficient subordinates, English interlopers, French, Dutch and Portuguese traders, troublesome chiefs, and the unreasonable demands of his employers were all matters calling for his scathing comments. He had in particular much to say about his subordinates. Richard French, the third chief merchant, died on 13 December 1713, and Richard Gibbs the steward of the *Royal Anne* was appointed to his post, "he writing a good hand and a good accountant", but later Cooke had to report that "upon tryall wee do not find him to bee the man we took him for, so must alter our resolution and make him what wee can with safety".[4] In the circumstances it was not surprising that the Company complained regarding the manner of furnishing reports and returns to them in London. On 13 April 1714 Cooke replied that "you must not expect everything to be so

[1] William Cooke to R.A.C., 2 January 1714, P.R.O., T. 70/3 and T. 70/5.

[2] *Ibid.*

[3] David Francis to R.A.C., 30 April 1717, P.R.O., T. 70/6.

[4] Cooke to R.A.C., 13 April and 10 July 1714, P.R.O., T. 70/3 and T. 70/5.

formarly and regularly done as if wee had people to doe it".[1] On the following 24 July he wrote as follows:

Below you have a list of the dead, by which you may see what condition wee are in to keep books and accounts. One of us continually troubled with the gout, and the other ailing, and the other being necessitated to goe to Portodally to buy slaves for your hired ship.[2]

But incompetent clerical assistants were far from being Cooke's greatest cause of annoyance. His soldiers and artisans were always a constant source of trouble. Desertions were frequent. On 10 February 1714 ten of them went off with a pinnace. On 8 June three more went off with a canoe, and a month later two deserted to take service with a private trader.[3] Of those who remained Cooke had but a small opinion. On 26 July he wrote to the Company as follows:

Wee have sent you in this ship James Irish, said to be a bricklayer, and Richard Shapland, said to be a carpenter, by which your honors may partly see how wee can carry on your business; and, were it not to have countenance of so many white faces, wee might have sent four parts of the five parts of those that remains, for they are rather objects of charity than anything else.[4]

Others of his fellow countrymen equally excited Cooke's indignation. John Snow, the late chief agent of the Company, was living in the Gambia. Cooke alleged that he and other private settlers "exasperate the natives against the Company's interest, insomuch that the hands he has can scarce defend him from their insults".[5] On another occasion he wrote to say that the river "was more and more infested with interlopers", but vowed he would "hinder them all they can without touching their lives",[6] but finally on 14 July 1714 he had to confess he "is brought low with grief that he cannot be revenged on the interlopers".[7]

But interlopers and private traders were by no means the menace to the Company's interest that foreign traders were. The Portuguese took advantage of the delay of the African Company to resettle

[1] P.R.O., T. 70/3.   [2] *Ibid.*
[3] Cooke to R.A.C., 24 July 1714, P.R.O., T. 70/3 and T. 70/5.
[4] P.R.O., T. 70/3.   [5] Cooke to R.A.C., 26 July 1714, P.R.O., T. 70/5.
[6] Same to same, 26 July 1714, P.R.O., T. 70/3 and T. 70/5.
[7] P.R.O., T. 70/3 and T. 70/5.

James Island and attempted to reassert their former sovereignty in the river. Shortly after Cooke's arrival an armed Portuguese vessel arrived from the Azores. This vessel spent fifteen days in the river, during which time the commander endeavoured to stir up the "king" of Barra against the English. Cooke saw that a strong line of action must at once be taken. "I was obliged", he said, "to make a prize of her, or to have gone out of this river and to have left it to the Portuguese and interlopers. He layd in readiness to fight me three days, and, when I got my small gang together and came along his side, his heart failed and he yielded his ship as a prize."[1] This prompt action so far impressed the Portuguese that a year later one of their ships consented to pay the African Company the 10 per cent dues exacted from English private traders.[2]

As was only to be expected, the French were a greater cause of anxiety to Cooke than any other nation. André Brue was sent out in March 1714 to resume charge of the French Company's affairs.[3] As stated in the previous chapter, the financial position of this Company was none too satisfactory at the close of the war. Brue himself was for some years personally concerned with the affairs in the northern parts of his Company's sphere of influence, but a number of private French traders had established themselves in the river towards the close of the war[4] and the factory at Albreda was resettled soon after the signing of the Treaty of Utrecht.[5]

Cooke demanded a commission "to fight the French in case they offer hostilities as they daily threaten".[6] It is clear that they claimed the right to exclude the English from trade on the coast, but the African Company managed to carry on a somewhat furtive trade by means of coasting vessels at Portudal and Joal.[7] Private traders were less fortunate. Two of their ships were seized off the coast in 1715 and it was alleged that the French "by combination with the king of Portodally draw ignorant people in and commit piratical depredations, the French commonly taking the ships, and the king the goods (as was the case of the Neptune during the last

[1] Cooke to R.A.C., 26 July 1714, P.R.O., T. 70/3 and T. 70/5.
[2] David Francis to R.A.C., May 1715, P.R.O., T. 70/3 and T. 70/6.
[3] Labat, *Nouvelle Relation de l'Afrique Occidentale*, v, 309.
[4] "Some Observations on the Trade to Africa", Gough MSS. Somerset, 7.
[5] Cooke to R.A.C., 26 July 1714, P.R.O., T. 70/3 and T. 70/5.
[6] Same to same, 22 April 1714, P.R.O., T. 70/3 and T. 70/5.
[7] *Ibid.*

peace)". As the French Senegal Company were alleged to be "worth little or nothing", legal redress was out of the question.[1]

None the less the position of the French in the Gambia was in fact for a time at least as precarious as that of the English. During the war both the African and the Senegal Companies had very rightly appreciated the fact that it was to their mutual advantage that hostilities should not be allowed to be carried on in front of the natives. The few hostile incidents which had occurred in the river during the war had been damaging to the prestige of either nation. The evacuation of the fort on James Island had removed the one possible deterrent to pillage by the natives of Europeans' goods in outlying trading ports. The characters of some of the French and English private traders, who had settled in the river after the evacuation of the fort, had done little to enhance European prestige. The obvious weakness and lack of combination of those traders had shown the ease with which they could be plundered without fear of reprisal. Consequently the natives—and more especially those of Barra—had by the end of the war developed a spirit of lawlessness and contempt for the foreign trader which had theretofore been unknown. The only possible means of suppression of this spirit could have been by the combination of both the companies and the private traders. But that was out of the question for the time being. Commercial jealousy not only prevented any such combination, it also led to the servants of the two companies and the private traders more or less actively fomenting trouble between the natives and their trade rivals.

The servants of the African Company were comparatively secure from attack on the *Royal Anne*, which was anchored in mid river, but the French ran considerable risks in their defenceless factory at Albreda. Matters came to a head in 1715, when the natives of Barra attacked a store belonging to an English private trader named Nathaniel Bugby. The attack was made at night. Bugby was forced to submit to seeing his goods plundered and was then strangled. When news of this outrage reached the African Company's servants on board the *Royal Anne* they made no attempt to avenge it but expressed their satisfaction because "it makes the interlopers look blank".[2] This attack was followed by one upon two private French

---

[1] *Journal of Council of Trade*, 24 November 1715.
[2] Labat, *op. cit.* v, 312, 313; David Francis to R.A.C., 28 January 1715, P.R.O., T. 70/3 and T. 70/6.

traders named Godiveau and du Buisson who lived close to Albreda. They left their goods in the hands of the natives and fled to the French Company's factory.[1]

By 1716 native hostility had become so serious that the African Company petitioned the Council of Trade that a ship of war might be sent to the Gambia for their protection.[2] In the following year the natives of Barra were so far emboldened as to make an unsuccessful attempt to surprise James Island and to assassinate the chief agent.[3] Knowledge that the French had a fort at Goree and that they had been strong enough to take James Fort on four occasions during the past twenty years restrained the natives from attacking Albreda, but it was realised that that feeling of restraint might disappear at any time. In June 1716 the Governor of Goree removed most of the goods from Albreda, leaving there only a single agent to collect debts. In August 1717 this agent was also withdrawn.[4]

At the end of 1717 André Brue found time to turn his attention to the Gambia. On 16 December of that year one of his subordinates visited Albreda. He interviewed the "king" of Barra, who denied that he had in any way counselled or connived at the insults previously offered to the French. But the agent was not entirely credulous and decided to show the displeasure of the French by refusing to re-establish a trading depot in the king's territories until he should prove more amenable. In order, however, to preserve a *locus standi* at Albreda he left a reliable native as caretaker. He then proceeded to Bintang, where the "emperor" of Foni gave him leave to establish a factory.[5]

The establishment of the factory at Bintang brought the "king" of Barra to reason. He sent to L'Eglise, the chief factor there, begging him to settle a factory at Albreda and guaranteeing the safety of the occupants. In order to make it appear that the French were not in the least anxious to resettle there the request was not complied with until it had been renewed several times. Finally in March 1718 the French agreed to re-establish their factory. Brue took the

[1] Labat, *op. cit.* v, 313, 314.

[2] *Acts of the Privy Council (Colonial)*, 1676–1783, p. 107; *Journal of Council of Trade*, 16 November 1716.

[3] Cultru, *Histoire du Sénégal*, p. 175.

[4] Labat, *op. cit.* v, 314; David Francis to R.A.C., 21 December 1716, P.R.O., T. 70/6.   [5] Labat, *op. cit.* v, 314–319.

opportunity to visit the river and to enter into negotiations with the English on James Island for an offensive and defensive alliance against the natives and in particular against the "king" of Barra. At the same time he decided to establish the factory at Bintang on such a footing that it would in his opinion be impossible for the English to dispute his right to trade there or send ships past James Island into the creek. He accordingly instructed Pelletier, whom he had decided to place in charge at Bintang, to place himself under the protection and to declare himself a naturalised subject of the "emperor" of Foni. He further on 31 July 1718 entered into a fictitious contract for the sale of the brigantine *Postillon* to the "emperor", being careful at the same time to obtain a collateral document declaring that the vessel was held by the "emperor" in trust for the Senegal Company. At the same time Brue instructed Pelletier not to do any act which might give any ground of complaint to the English at James Island, and to make a point of saluting the English flag when passing the fort. But Pelletier lacked the tact required for a delicate situation. He passed the fort without paying his respects to the chief agent and speedily found his brigantine detained. Brue had to intervene to prevent its seizure.[1]

From the letters and returns of the African Company's servants in the Gambia it is clear that Brue very much over-estimated the power of the English to hinder French competition. Those letters tell a doleful tale. Death put an end to Cooke's gout and other troubles before 1714 was out.[2] His successor, David Francis, died on 9 October 1717[3] and was succeeded by Charles Orfeur. There was a heavy mortality amongst the subordinate officers. Twenty-two had died within seven months of Cooke's arrival.[4] Many of the others deserted and escaped on board private traders.[5] No reliefs and no stores came out from England after 1715. In May of that year Francis wrote to inform the African Company that he had been compelled to fill his depleted ranks by enticing members of the crews of private traders into the service and that "their commanders threaten me what they will doe, when they come to England".[6] On the following 30 August he informed the Company

---

[1] Labat, *op. cit.* v, 316–322.
[2] David Francis to R.A.C., 2 January 1715, P.R.O., T. 70/3.
[3] Charles Orfeur to R.A.C., 21 March 1718, P.R.O., T. 70/6.
[4] Cooke to R.A.C., 24 July 1714, P.R.O., T. 70/3 and T. 70/5.
[5] Francis to R.A.C., 22 May 1715, P.R.O., T. 70/6.   [6] P.R.O., T. 70/3.

that he had been compelled to sell slaves to private traders so as "to supply his wants and sort his cargo".[1]

For lack of workmen and materials the work of repairing the fort went on very slowly. In August 1715 only ten of the guns had been mounted on the flankers and the rest were still lying on the ground.[2] Headquarters still remained on board the *Royal Anne*. It was not until 30 April 1717 that Francis was able to report that he proposed moving the Company's effects into the fort and taking up his residence there[3] and it was not until close on twelve months later that the move actually took place.[4] When on 21 March 1718 Charles Orfeur reported that he had taken command, he also reported that he had "made shift to put the fort in a little better order than it was. Has nobody to assist him but Mr Allen Rogers. Has had great mortality...and several have deserted. The sloop, boats, and all the buildings are rendered almost unserviceable. The *Royal Anne* has parted her cables and lost her anchors."[5]

This was the last letter which the African Company received from the Gambia for three years. During the period of silence a fresh disaster had befallen James Fort. The close of the War of the Spanish Succession had been followed by an outburst of piracy in the Atlantic. For a time the pirates devoted their attention to other regions than the Gambia, but in May 1719 a certain Edward England appeared in the river. Between 26 and 29 May he made a splendid haul. Five ships belonging to private traders fell into his hands as well as a sloop belonging to the Company.[6]

Shortly afterwards England was followed by one of his former apprentices to the trade named Howel Davis. In his *General History of the Pirates*[7] Charles Johnson has given a very graphic account of Davis' exploits at James Island, but in the interests of historical accuracy it has to be recorded that the story has been much em-

---

[1] P.R.O., T. 70/6.
[2] Francis to R.A.C., 30 August 1715, P.R.O., T. 70/6.
[3] Same to same, P.R.O., T. 70/6.
[4] Allen Rogers to James Mallett, 30 March 1718, P.R.O., T. 70/6.
[5] P.R.O., T. 70/6.
[6] Johnson, *A General History of the Pirates*, I, 54; Petition of Francis Sitwell, 29 January 1720, Henry Lascelles to Council of Trade, 16 February 1720, Council of Trade to Secretary Craggs, 19 February 1720, *C.S.P. Colonial (America and West Indies)*, 1719–1720, pp. 309, 356, 362; Mr Popple to Robert Walpole, 22 December 1720, *C.S.P. Colonial (America and West Indies)*, 1720–1721, p. 221.   [7] I, 106–110.

bellished. Davis did not, as Johnson would have us believe, by an elaborate stratagem overpower an armed guard and in the course of a banquet surprise and seize a Governor with a strong predilection for strong waters. The man with whom he had to deal was Charles Orfeur, who had only joined the African Company's services as a writer some thirty months before,[1] and the Europeans, whom Orfeur had with him, mustered only fourteen, of whom some were on board the *Royal Anne* and some up-river trading in a sloop.[2] Davis may, as Johnson alleges, have effected his landing on the island by posing as a law-abiding merchant in quest of legitimate trade, but André Brue is a witness that he did not gain the fort without a blow being struck. Orfeur "had been partly bred on board a man of war"[3] and had not forgotten the traditions of the service to which he once belonged. He offered some resistance and was wounded by the pirates. He certainly never, as Johnson alleges, ransomed either himself or the fort.[4] Johnson is, however, accurate when he says the pirates put their prisoners on board the *Royal Anne*, which was despoiled of her sails and cables, dismantled the fort, dismounted the guns and carried off all the goods they could. Seven of the fourteen men comprising the garrison turned pirate and sailed away with Davis.[5]

After the departure of Davis, Orfeur's subordinates decided to divide amongst themselves what little had been left behind of the Company's effects. Orfeur was powerless to prevent this.[6] He in fact appears to have abandoned the island temporarily and to have taken refuge in the upper reaches of the river from fear of the "king" of Barra, who fully realised how easily he could take possession of James Island.[7]

André Brue was eager to seize the opportunity to gain possession of James Island and arrived in the river at the end of 1719 expressly for that purpose. He found, however, that Orfeur had returned to the island. He endeavoured to attain his end by offering to lend Orfeur some French soldiers. Orfeur refused, declaring that his acceptance would amount to handing over the fort to the French.

---

[1] R.A.C. Passenger lists, P.R.O., T. 70/1437; R.A.C. Security Books, P.R.O., T. 70/1429, f. 44.

[2] Nominal Rolls of Gambia, P.R.O., T. 70/1432; Henry Glynne to R.A.C., 9 August 1722, P.R.O., T. 70/4.

[3] Smith, *A New Voyage to Guinea*, p. 10.   [4] Cultru *op. cit.* p. 178.

[5] Nominal Rolls of Gambia, P.R.O., T. 70/1432.

[6] Henry Glynne to R.A.C., 9 August 1722, P.R.O., T. 70/4.

[7] Cultru, *op. cit.* p. 175.

Brue then asked for freedom of trade in the river. Orfeur replied that that would be tantamount to ceding the whole river to the French. It was then suggested that the English and French should trade in common. Orfeur said he must await instructions regarding this. Brue then offered to supply him with a stock of goods so that he could trade for himself and the Senegal Company. Orfeur again said he must await orders. Finally Brue asked him to prevent English private traders from trading above James Fort. Orfeur replied that, if he did so, he would be more treacherous to the people of his own nation than the pirates who took the fort and that, though the African Company had lost a great deal of money, they would lose more still by consenting to Brue's proposal. Brue then left him.[1] With only six companions of very doubtful loyalty Orfeur could easily have been overpowered. But Brue evidently realised that forcible seizure of the island might lead to trouble in Europe or even to an attack on himself by the English private traders in the river. Also one would fain believe that the dogged pluck of the young Englishman aroused the admiration and chivalry of a great French colonial administrator.

Rumours of the destruction of James Fort only reached the African Company indirectly through their chief agent in Sierra Leone.[2] On receipt thereof they made no attempt either to resettle the place or to investigate the matter. Charles Orfeur was left to his own devices for over eighteen months. Three of his six companions died during that time.[3] How the survivors managed to subsist is not known. Possibly they set up in trade on their own account or else entered the service of private traders. Orfeur was the only one who even nominally remained in the Company's service at the beginning of 1721.

The apathy of the African Company was born partly of their past bitter experience in the Gambia and partly of their own financial difficulties. It seems clear that at one time they seriously considered the entire abandonment of the Gambia. What probably induced them to change their minds was the possibility of being supplanted in those regions by one of the innumerable companies, which were floated in 1719, the South Sea Bubble year. Four at least of those flotations were designed ostensibly for carrying on trade in Africa,

---

[1] Cultru, *op. cit.* pp. 177, 178.
[2] Robert Plunkett to R.A.C., 16 April 1719, P.R.O., T. 70/6.
[3] Nominal Rolls of Gambia, P.R.O., T. 70/1432.

one of them being for carrying on a trade at Arguin, which had hitherto been carried on by the African Company from the Gambia.[1] Having resolved to resume their activities in the Gambia, the Company further resolved to create an establishment which would be of sufficient strength to protect their fort from the depredations of Frenchmen and pirates and to overawe the natives. For this purpose they decided to appoint a military governor and to give him a company of three officers and eighty soldiers. Colonel David Dunbar was originally appointed as Governor, but he did not proceed.[2] Consequently Colonel Thomas Whitney was chosen in his place. This officer had over thirty years of military service, had been present at Blenheim, Ramillies, and Malplaquet, and had in 1712 been promoted to a brevet lieutenant-colonelcy for distinguished service under Marlborough.[3] His commission appointed him "to be our Governor of Gambia and captain of a company there, to take upon you the care and charge of rebuilding our forts and castles and re-establishing our settlement on that river and defending the same against all assaults or opposition whatsoever and...to do and perform all things that belong or appertain to the duty of Governor and Commander-in-Chief...and to be president of the Council to be held their (sic) for the better dispatch of the Company's affairs and to have a vote therein whenever you shall be present with them".[4] He was instructed also to endeavour to obtain a plot of land at Barra Point opposite to St Mary's Island and to erect the fort and principal factory there.[5]

Two merchants—Henry Glynne and William Ramsey—were associated with Whitney in the government. As Whitney declined "to have any concern in the trade, or the accounts thereof to be kept with the Company, but only to take upon him that part of the service, which appertains to military matters", the commercial side of the administration was entrusted solely to these two, subject however to the Governor's vote in council in all matters relating to the Company's service.[6] Of these Henry Glynne had at the beginning

[1] Scott, *Joint Stock Trading Companies to* 1720, III, 449, 450.
[2] R.A.C. to Colonel Thomas Whitney, 1 December 1720, P.R.O., T. 70/55.
[3] Dalton, *The Blenheim Roll*, pp. 2, 7, 48.
[4] Commission dated 1 December 1720, R.A.C. Agreements, P.R.O., T. 70/1433.
[5] R.A.C. to Henry Glynne, 13 September 1721, P.R.O., T. 70/55; Henry Glynne to R.A.C., 2 January 1722, P.R.O., T. 70/7.
[6] R.A.C. to Whitney, 1 December 1720, P.R.O., T. 70/55.

of the War of the Spanish Succession been the second chief factor of the Company at Sierra Leone and subsequently at Sherboro. Both these places had been captured by the French in 1704 and 1705 respectively. The Company had in consequence accused him, not entirely with justice, of cowardice. He had then become a private trader and one of the most bitter opponents of the Company.[1] Subsequently in 1719, when pirates were infesting Sierra Leone, where he was trading on his own account, he showed himself "an honest and a generous gentleman and of so much integrity, that though he had suffered by the pirates when they first landed, yet he would never accept of any goods from them, which they often pressed him to receive for his own use. This conduct, with an engaging deportment, so gained him the goodwill of the pirates, that they were ready to oblige him in whatever they were requested."[2] That influence was exerted on behalf of the African Company and earned him his reappointment to the Company's service.

The military officers under Whitney were Captain-Lieutenant John Massey, Lieutenant John Shute, and Ensign James Alexander Desoulies. Of these the last mentioned was to combine with his military duties those of steward "in providing for the publick table". Shute was to act as fort major and Massey, "as occasion shall require, to act as engineer".[3] Massey had served in Marlborough's campaigns "with great applause". Amongst the extant papers of the African Company there is a letter of attorney allotting half of his salary to his wife. One can picture both him and his commanding officer, soldiers to their finger tips, unfitted by years of campaigning for return to civilian life, with wives and families to maintain and attracted to posts in which they believed the work would be congenial to their upbringing.

In addition factors, writers, soldiers, artisans, a surgeon and surgeon's mate were appointed and a chaplain. A number of the soldiers and artisans were permitted to bring their wives and families out with them and instructions were given to provide these with free diet on condition that "the said women be employed as nurses to look after the sick as occasion shall require".[4] Some of the party were recruited in Ireland and the rest in England. The Irish party

---

[1] John Pery to William Popple, 4 February 1708, P.R.O., T. 70/175.
[2] Snelgrave, *A New Account of some parts of Guinea*, p. 224.
[3] Agreements of R.A.C., P.R.O., T. 70/1430.
[4] R.A.C. to Whitney, 1 December 1720, P.R.O., T. 70/55.

sailed on 1 December 1720 on board the *Otter*. The English party was distributed between the *Martha* and the *Gambia Castle*, which sailed on 5 February 1721 under the escort of H.M.S. *Swallow* and *Weymouth*. In all close on 170 persons, including twenty women and children, were despatched to the Gambia.[1]

Things did not go any too well with any of the three transports. The *Otter* reached the Gambia on 4 February 1721, but there had been trouble on the way. Charles Storey, the chaplain, had been so barbarously treated by the captain that he left the ship at Madeira and returned to England to lodge a complaint.[2] The *Gambia Castle* was found unseaworthy soon after leaving port and had to put back to Portsmouth.[3] Eventually her passengers had to be transhipped to the *Bumper*, which was renamed the *Gambia Castle*, and they did not reach the Gambia until 9 May 1721.[4] Captain Massey was amongst the passengers who thus transhipped. In an evil hour for himself he found that the second mate of the new vessel was a certain George Lowther. The *Martha* made the most successful voyage, reaching the river's mouth on 31 March 1721, but there was an ominous stumbling at the threshold. In order to create a suitable impression amongst the natives, Colonel Whitney embarked on H.M.S. *Weymouth* to proceed to James Island in some state. On the way the ship ran aground near Barra Point and it was four days before it got off.[5]

On arrival at James Island Whitney found Charles Orfeur there to receive him. The handing over was brief and is thus recorded by Whitney:

Pursuant to your honours' instructions we . . . demanded accounts of Mr Orfeur, who acted as commander in chief until our arrivall, but not finding anything to inventory except seventeen old guns unfit for service, nor no accounts or papers of the Companyes, except the enclosed of Mr Orfeur's, we cannot send any inventory. Mr Orfeur has undergone great hardships in your honours' service here, as he setts forth in the inclosed memorial, and we believe deserves your consideration.[6]

[1] R.A.C. passenger lists, P.R.O., T. 70/1437.
[2] R.A.C. to Whitney, 16 May 1721, P.R.O., T. 70/55.
[3] Francis Lynn to Josiah Burchett, 4 January 1721, P.R.O., Ad. 1/3810.
[4] Petition of John Massey, 22 July 1721, P.R.O., C.O. 28/17.
[5] Atkins, *A Voyage to Guinea, Brazil, and the West Indies*, p. 57; Log of H.M.S. *Weymouth*, P.R.O., Ad. 51/1057.
[6] Whitney to R.A.C., 24 June 1721, P.R.O., T. 70/4.

Whitney then turned his attention to re-establishing the settlement. It was reported that "the Company's presents...were well received by the king of Barra, and he has given the factors leave to build a fortification at Gilliflee (Juffure), a town commanded by a woman, about 15 miles up the river; made a duchess by Captain Passenger, from whence the custom has I believe been taken up of distinguishing the most deserving fellows at trading towns by the titles of knights, colonels, and captains, which they are very proud of. This Duchess of Gilliflee has become very much the factory's friend there, and gives all possible assistance in their settlement."[1]

The *pied-à-terre* at Juffure was a very urgent necessity. James Island with its ruined fort could not possibly receive the full complement of men, women, and children, who had been sent out. Quarters on the mainland were primitive to the last degree and the sufferings of the men were great, Juffure "not producing anything to drink but water that the negros daily wash in". It is not surprising to learn that sickness broke out almost at once with fatal results in many cases. Two men died in February, eight in March, and three in April. Lieutenant Shute died on 5 May and Peter Graham, the surgeon, three days later. Seven of the soldiers died in the same month. Ensign Desoulies and the surgeon's mate died on 9 June. Five more soldiers died that month.[2] The sole surviving surgeon's mate "lay at the point of death, they (*sic*) sick lyeing in a languishing condition, vizitted once in three or four days by the ship's doctor, and had no other prospect but to dye, there being no due care, provision, nor lodging suitable for any Christian".[3] Even more distressing was the fate of the women and children. Nineteen of them died in the course of five months. Only three women and one child ever lived to get away from the river. On 12 July 1721 the first coroner's jury sat in the Gambia to view the body of Helen Patteson, the wife of Robert Patteson, drummer, and to find that she "cut her own throat". Doubtless what had preyed on this unfortunate woman's mind was the fact that three weeks before she had been deserted by her husband, who left her to join in an exploit which had perhaps an even more tragic ending than her own.[4]

[1] Atkins, *op. cit.* p. 57.
[2] Nominal Rolls of Gambia, P.R.O., T. 70/1432.
[3] Petition of John Massey, 22 July 1721, P.R.O., C.O. 28/17.
[4] Nominal Rolls of Gambia, P.R.O., T. 70/1446.

Captain Johnson has told part of the story of that exploit in his *General History of the Pirates*. Part of it can also be gleaned from the returns of the Royal African Company, the pen of one of the leading actors, and the notes of the Judge of the Admiralty Court. In order to arrive at a proper understanding thereof we must go back to 9 May 1721, the day on which Captain Massey first set foot on James Island. He arrived with forty-seven soldiers and a number of artisans. " All our people ", he subsequently wrote, " were in perfect health when arrived. I was ordered to land them upon James Island, a sterrile place not afording anything that was necessary for man.... While upon James Island, in a few days after the men were landed, they were in general seased with flux, which proceeded from eating salt provisions without any sort of bread and having nothing to drink but bad water. The men under my command, besides thirty black slaves, have been twenty-four hours without water and, when supply hath come, it hath been salt water."[1]

Primarily the duty of seeing that the soldiers were properly housed and fed should have fallen upon Colonel Whitney, whom Massey's loyalty led him to describe as " a man of honour and integrity, and hath served the Affrican company as far as the merchants in Affrica did permit him. (But) the Governour being very old, and hath not had one hour's health since his landing, which caused the merchants to usurp and tyranize over him."[2] No doubt twenty years of campaigning in Flanders had not fitted a man of fifty for his first experience of service in the tropics, but it has to be confessed that, as the African Company wrote later, Whitney's inertia was not entirely excusable on the score of ill health. He did not attempt to share the hardships of the men under his command, but, as soon as the *Gambia Castle* arrived, moved on board of her together with the chief merchants, Glynne and Ramsey. It may be that he was ill and that it was difficult to insist with the chief merchants on greater liberality of treatment for the soldiers, but Whitney was not so ill that he could not look after his family's interests. His son had come out with him enrolled ostensibly as a private soldier. When Shute died, Desoulies was promoted to the vacant lieutenancy and young Whitney obtained Desoulies' post of ensign. When a month later Desoulies died, young Whitney stepped into the lieutenancy. Three weeks later he was promoted

---

[1] Petition of John Massey, 22 July 1721, P.R.O., C.O. 23/17.　　[2] *Ibid.*

captain.[1] On receipt of this information the African Company rightly observed that "he is very young and unfitt for such a post".[2]

As Whitney declined to move on behalf of the soldiers, Massey held that duty compelled him to stir in the matter. He approached Glynne and Ramsey but got no satisfaction. According to Johnson[3] Massey told them "that he did not come here to be a Guiney slave, and that he had promised his men good treatment and provisions fitting for soldiers; that, as he had the care of so many of His Majesty's subjects, if they would not provide for them in a handsome manner, he would take suitable measures for the preservation of so many of his countrymen and companions". According to Massey "some of the weekly men, that had money due to them, desired of the merchants to support them on account of their wages. They answered that there was no allowance granted from the Company. Neither would they supply them with what was necessary upon any terms, but proposed to shoot three or four men for an example to prevent the rest making their just complaints."[4] When every allowance is made for natural exaggeration on the part of a man placed in trying circumstances, there is clear evidence that high words passed between the military and civilian officers and that the latter were not only grossly unsympathetic to the unfortunate soldiers but even oppressive. The merchants in fact virtually admitted so much when later they wrote to the Company to complain that "Colonel Whitney would not punish the soldiers, who insulted them".[5]

Trouble was also brewing elsewhere than on James Island. The original instructions of the African Company had been that the *Gambia Castle* should remain in the river as a guardship and that the *Martha* should take a cargo of slaves to Maryland.[6] When the original *Gambia Castle* put back to Portsmouth and was replaced by the *Bumper* the captain contracted with the crew in England that they should make the voyage to America.[7] On arrival in the Gambia a dispute arose as to which ship was to remain as guardship

---

[1] Nominal Rolls of Gambia, P.R.O., T. 70/1446.
[2] R.A.C. to Henry Glynne, 27 June 1722, P.R.O., T. 70/55.
[3] *Op. cit.* pp. 166, 167.
[4] Petition of John Massey, 22 July 1721, P.R.O., C.O. 28/17.
[5] Henry Glynne to R.A.C., 2 January 1722, P.R.O., T. 70/7.
[6] R.A.C. to Colonel Whitney, 1 December 1720, P.R.O., T. 70/55.
[7] Petition of John Massey, 22 July 1721, P.R.O., C.O. 28/17.

and which ship was to sail for Maryland. Charles Russell, who commanded the *Gambia Castle* (late *Bumper*), worked hard to have his ship sent to Maryland in place of the *Martha*. In order to do so, he impeached the seaworthiness of the *Martha* and demanded a board of survey upon her, although none of her officers had found fault with her. That survey was held. The commander of the *Martha* was not placed upon the board. On the other hand Russell, who had a distinct motive for the change of plan, was a member thereof. Later the African Company not unjustly commented on "the partiality it was carried on with". The result of the survey was inevitable. The *Martha* was duly condemned, but the result was that she was ordered to return to England whilst the *Gambia Castle* was ordered to remain in the river as a guardship.[1]

The decision that the *Gambia Castle* was not immediately to return to England caused great dissatisfaction amongst her crew. Rumours spread of the fate of the *Royal Anne*, which had been, as already seen, detained in the Gambia from 1714 to 1718, and of the mortality amongst her crew.[2] The leader of the discontent was the second mate, George Lowther. On 11 June the crew actually mutinied. Russell ordered Lowther to be placed in irons as the ringleader, but the order was respited, according to Johnson[3] because "the men took up handspikes and threat'ned to knock that man down, that offered to lay hold of the mate".[4]

Before this Russell and Massey had held several conversations and, in Johnson's words,[5] "they aggravated one another's grievances to such a height, that they resolved upon measures to curb the power that controul'd them, and to provide for themselves in another manner". On the day following the mutiny Colonel Whitney with Glynne, Ramsey, and Russell went on shore to Juffure to meet the "king" of Barra. In Russell's absence the crew rose and seized and confined the chief mate. Lowther then sent a message ashore to Massey on James Island informing him of what he had done. According to Massey himself at a later date, "he being hastily vexed at the ill usage he and his men had met with, he told them that now was the time to save their lives and free themselves and that, if they would follow him, he would carry them back to

---

[1] R.A.C. to Colonel Whitney, 13 September 1721, P.R.O., T. 70/55.
[2] Petition of John Massey, 22 July 1721, P.R.O., C.O. 28/17.
[3] *Op. cit.* p. 108.
[4] *Ibid.*   [5] *Ibid.*

England."[1] One of the two sergeants, both the corporals, a drummer, thirty-five common soldiers, and eight artisans took Massey at his word and embarked on the *Gambia Castle*.[2] The chief mate was put on shore and wine and provisions were fetched from James Island. According to Massey he brought away all the sick men that were upon the island, but could not for obvious reasons fetch the sick on the mainland at Juffure. He then proceeded to discharge the ship's cargo, retaining only what was declared to be necessary for the voyage on hand.[3]

Meanwhile what was transpiring came to the ears of the officers at Juffure. Massey "sent to the merchants in order to have treated with them for the sustenance of life and sent sundry times to the Governor".[4] According to reports received later by the African Company, "in case Massey could prevail with the soldiers to come to treat, they were to make a signall, upon sight of which the Governor was to meet them half way in a boat".[5] But Colonel Whitney's supineness would not allow him to run "some little hazard, if there had been any", and the opportunity of averting disaster was thus lost.[6] "Instead", wrote Massey, "of any one comeing to do us justice thereof, the ships that lay in the harbour fired at us, likewise fired from the fort, which obliged us to put the ship we are now in in a posture of defence and get ready for the sea with a small quantity of water and provisions."[7]

The *Gambia Castle* stood out of range, but allowed the merchants to send for such cargo as they wanted. The deserters even returned them one pipe of wine, when they desisted sending for the rest of the cargo.[8] In the afternoon of 22 June the *Gambia Castle* started to weigh her anchors. As it was growing dark the crew only weighed one anchor and slipped the other. The result of this hasty operation was that the vessel ran aground. According to Johnson,[9] "Massey

---

[1] Mr Justice Penrice to the Lords Justices, 9 July 1723, P.R.O., S.P. Dom. 35/44; Examination of Alexander Thompson, 2 March 1723, P.R.O., H.C.A. 1/55.

[2] Nominal Rolls of Gambia, P.R.O., T. 70/1446.

[3] Petition of John Massey, 22 July 1721, P.R.O., C.O. 28/17; Mr Justice Penrice to the Lords Justices, 9 July 1723, P.R.O., S.P. Dom. 35/44; Examination of Alexander Thompson, 2 March 1723, P.R.O., H.C.A. 1/55.

[4] Petition of John Massey, 22 July 1721, P.R.O., C.O. 28/17.

[5] R.A.C. to Colonel Whitney, 13 September 1721, P.R.O., T. 70/55.

[6] *Ibid.*   [7] Petition of John Massey, 22 July 1721, P.R.O., C.O. 28/17.

[8] *Ibid.*   [9] *Op. cit.* p. 109.

showed himself a soldier upon this accident, for as soon as the misfortune happen'd, he left the ship with about sixteen hands, and rows directly to the fort, remounts the guns, and keeps garrison there all night, while the ship was ashore; and obliged some of the factory to assist in getting her clear".[1] Whilst the ship was aground, Captain Russell put off in a boat to try to bring the deserters to reason, but he had the reputation of being a hard man with his crew and was not likely to bring the malcontents to a different frame of mind. According to one of the crew of the *Gambia Castle*, "Captain Massey ordered him to keep off and ordered his men to fire, kill or not kill".[2] Next morning they got the ship afloat. Young Whitney and one or two others, who were not willing to continue in the exploit, were put on shore, and the ship sailed down the river after exchanging without any effect one or two shots with the *Martha* and *Otter*.[3]

Massey subsequently declared that he and his men sailed "with the full resolution to make the best of our way to England....Our designes was onely to fly from the apparent death of perrishing, as they rest of our country men did for want of necessary sustenance."[4] There are certain small pieces of evidence which all go to prove the truth of this assertion. In the first place, the fact that they landed part of the cargo hardly suggests that either the soldiers or the crew were at the start bent, as was afterwards alleged, upon piracy.[5] In the second place, when legal proceedings were subsequently instituted against Massey and the African Company was anxiously searching for any scrap of evidence against him of robbery on the high seas, an information was sworn that, "when they came from the River Gambia aforesaid, they brought from thence some perukes, which were then on board the said ship and which belonged to Colonell Whitney, the governor of the aforesaid castle, which were taken from the rest of his said things by the said Massey, when the rest were sent on shoar to the said Colonell".[6] Whatever the

---

[1] This statement is in part confirmed by the evidence of Alexander Thompson at Massey's subsequent trial, who deposed that "they sent for more help and got her off". Mr Justice Penrice to the Lords Justices, 9 July 1723, P.R.O., S.P. Dom. 35/44.

[2] *Ibid.*   [3] Johnson, *op. cit.* p. 109.

[4] Petition of John Massey, 22 July 1721, P.R.O., C.O. 28/17.

[5] *Ibid.* Evidence of Alexander Thompson as reported by Mr Justice Penrice to the Lords Justices, 9 July 1723, P.R.O., S.P. Dom. 35/44.

[6] Examination of Alexander Thompson, 2 March 1723, P.R.O., H.C.A. 1/55.

significance attached by a certain type of mind to such an incident, the omission of Massey to send on shore these perukes along with the rest of his commanding officer's effects does not suggest piratical intent to the ordinary mind but rather that Massey's intentions were what he asserted them to be. Finally, amongst the *Gambia Castle's* passengers were Kelran Tucker, the wife of Thomas Tucker, soldier, and her boy.[1] These two were certainly no pirates and would hardly have been allowed to board a ship on piracy bent. Small and insignificant as these items of evidence may seem, they do tend to confirm Massey's own story.

When, however, the *Gambia Castle* was out at sea, Lowther showed that he had very different intentions. He mustered the company "and told them it was the greatest folly imaginable to think of returning to England, for what they had already done could not be justified by any pretence whatsoever, but would be look'd upon, in the eye of the law, a capital offence; and that none of them were in a condition to withstand the attacks of such powerful adversaries, as they would meet with at home; for his part he was determined not to run such a hazard; and therefore, if his proposal was not agreed to, he desired to be set on shore in some place of safety; that they had a good ship under them, a parcel of brave fellows in her, that it was not their business to starve, or be made slaves; and therefore, if they were all of his mind, they should seek their fortunes upon the seas, as other adventurers had done before them".[2]

One of the crew of the *Gambia Castle* subsequently asserted that this proposal was received with acclamation by all on board, Massey included.[3] But for certain reasons this witness cannot be regarded as entirely reliable and there is evidence to suggest that under the restraining influence of Massey the soldiers hung back for some little time. It is undoubtedly true that it was only when they had put to sea that many of those on board realised the full legal consequences of their act. As Lowther said, they had rendered themselves liable to punishment on a capital charge. A statute passed in 1699[4] had enacted that any person who endeavoured to make a revolt on board a ship should be adjudged a pirate and a robber and liable to the same punishment as a pirate or a robber. Even though there

[1] Nominal Rolls of Gambia, P.R.O., T. 70/1446.
[2] Johnson, *op. cit.* pp. 109, 110.
[3] Examination of Alexander Thompson, 2 March 1723, P.R.O., H.C.A. 1/55.
[4] 11 and 12 Will. III, c. 7, s. 9.

was a real grievance to redress, it was no answer to a charge of attempting to make a revolt.[1] It was therefore painfully obvious to those on board the *Gambia Castle* that their return to England would almost inevitably result in their arrest and prosecution for an offence for which the penalty was death. They were in any case dependent for the navigation of the vessel upon Lowther and the sailors. It was clear therefore that the originally projected voyage to England was out of the question. They had perforce to fall in with Lowther's proposal that they should make their course for the West Indies. But it was not until five or six weeks later that the first act of piracy was committed off Barbados.

Before that, on 22 July 1721, Massey penned a lengthy petition to the King, which he managed by some means to send ashore to the Governor of Barbados. It is a badly spelt and not entirely coherent document, in which the writer says:

We humbly implore Your Majesty's gracious pardon for the reliefe of Your Majesty's miserable subjects, who are now tossing upon the seas depending upon Your Majesty's unparalled (sic) *goodness and clemency, not dareing to come near any Christian port.*

But soe long as our small store will support us, we shall live in the hopes that Your Majesty's royall pardon will be extended to the enlargement of Your Majesty's miserable subjects, who, if not relieved before our small stores be expended, necessity will oblige us to take some irregular method we never designed.

The unexpressible misserys of Your Majesty's dutifull subjects, who now hopes to receive Your Majesty's mercifull pardon, is intollerable, not haveing any conversation nor hopes of any but what we have a version to. But so soon as Your Majesty's great goodness shall grant the royall permission for our return, we will not only bring home the aforesaid ship and the remaining part of her cargo with her with our dutifull acknowledgement of Your Majesty's gracious favour, but will use our utmost endeavours to perswead all ships, which shall use any irregular practice, to return with us.[2]

It would almost appear as if, at the time this petition was penned, Massey was still endeavouring to exert all his influence against any resort to piracy, but that he realised that, unless a promise of pardon came soon, circumstances would be too great for the men under

---

[1] Cf. *R. v. Quelch* (1704) 14 *State Trials*, 1067.   [2] P.R.O., C.O. 28/17.

him. It was a last forlorn appeal and it did not turn the inevitable tide of events. The Governor of Barbados forwarded it to the Council of Trade on 23 August. It was not received by the Council until 16 October. It was read in Council the following day and then duly docketed and filed without any further action being taken thereon.[1] Long before that those on board the *Gambia Castle* had taken to the "irregular method", which Massey had feared. Within a week or so of the writing of the petition they seized a Boston brigantine off Barbados. Thence they made their way to the vicinity of Dominica, where they seized a French ship. From Dominica they proceeded to Hispaniola, where they chased and captured a small schooner.

Here according to Alexander Thompson, one of the crew of the *Gambia Castle*, "the said Massey and Lowther having quarrelled, he, the said Massey, with the informant and twelve soldiers left the Gamboa Castle and went on board the schooner and he, the said Massey, then declared they would take the first ship they should meet, but, there not being any sailor on board besides him, the informant, they were obliged to put into Jamaica, where they surrendered themselves to Sir Nicolas Laws, the Governor, who thereupon sent out a small man of war to seek for the said Gamboa Castle".[2]

Thompson was an accomplice and therefore not a reliable witness, but it is significant that he gives Massey the credit for parting company with Lowther on arrival at the first land touched by the *Gambia Castle* after its departure from the River Gambia. At the very least this would seem to tend to prove that Massey had never actively assented to any act of piracy and that he may even have been a reluctant spectator thereat.

The sloop which was sent in search of Lowther failed to find him. Lowther continued his career for another year and eventually died by his own hand.[3] Massey decided to return to England. When he reached London, he wrote a letter to the Royal African Company informing them that he would be found at a certain place and would stay there till his employers sent to arrest him.[4] In that letter he set out all that had transpired and "owned that he deserved to dye

[1] P.R.O., C.O. 28/17.
[2] Examination of Alexander Thompson, 2 March 1723, P.R.O., H.C.A. 1/55.
[3] Johnson, *op. cit.* pp. 114–120.
[4] Francis Lynn to Charles Delahaye, 11 July 1723, P.R.O., S.P. Dom. 35/44.

for what he had done; yet, if they had generosity enough to forgive him, as he was still capable to do them service as a soldier, so he should be very ready to do it; but if they resolved to prosecute him, he begg'd only this favour, that he might not be hang'd like a dog but to die like a soldier, as he had been bred from his childhood, that is, that he might be shot".[1] The only answer to this letter was "that he should be fairly hanged".[2]

We are told that "Massey resolved not to be out of the way, when he found what important occasion there was likely to be for him, but takes a lodging in Aldersgate-Street, (and) the next day went to the Lord Chief Justice's chambers and enquired if my lord had granted a warrant against Captain John Massey for piracy. But, being told by the clerks that they knew of no such thing, he inform'd them he was the man, that my lord would soon be apply'd to for that purpose, and the officer might come to him at such a place where he lodged. They took directions in writing and in a few days, a warrant being issued, the tipstaff went directly by his own information and apprehended him without any further trouble than walking to his lodging."

"There was then no person in town to charge him with any fact, upon which he could be committed. Nor could the latter be proved to be of his handwriting, so that they had been oblig'd to let him go again, if he had not helpt his accusers out at a pinch. The magistrate was reduc'd to putting this question to him, 'Did you write this letter?' He answer'd, 'He did', and not only that but confess'd all the contents of it; upon which he was committed to Newgate, but was afterwards admitted to a hundred pounds bail, or thereabouts."[3]

But the evidence was not deemed sufficiently satisfactory for the arraignment of Massey before a judge and jury. The African Company therefore looked about for better evidence. They found that evidence in Rotherhithe, where dwelt Alexander Thompson, the one member of the *Gambia Castle's* crew, who had deserted Lowther for Massey. On 2 March 1723 Alexander Thompson swore an information. He seems to have had a desire to be an honest man. There are a number of alterations in the original information, which indicate that he had no desire to blacken Massey's character too far, but he himself was admittedly an accomplice and was actually himself

---

[1] Johnson, *op. cit.* p. 113; Mr Justice Penrice to the Lords Justices, 11 July 1723, P.R.O., S.P. Dom. 35/44.

[2] Johnson, *op. cit.* p. 113.   [3] *Ibid.*

threatened with arrest on the same charge.[1] The temptation therefore was strong to avert the consequences of his own acts at the expense of another. He swore that Massey had actively participated
in the piracies off Barbados and Hispaniola. The prosecutors were
anxious to show that there had also been some act of larceny on
board the *Gambia Castle* whilst still in the River Gambia, which
could be construed as robbery on the high seas, but Thompson
would not go as far as the Royal African Company wished. There are
heavy erasures in his information at this point. All that he would
depose was that Massey had not sent on shore Colonel Whitney's
perukes with the colonel's other effects.[2]

On 5 July 1723 Massey was brought to trial before the Admiralty Court at the Old Bailey on this information and additional
evidence obtained from Colonel Whitney's son and Captain Russell,
both of whom had returned to England. He was arraigned on three
charges of piracy in the River Gambia, off Barbados, and off
Hispaniola. It was not until over 100 years after this date that a
prisoner charged with felony was allowed legal aid. Massey therefore had to defend himself as best he could. In justice to Sir Henry
Penrice, the presiding judge, it must at once be said that throughout
the trial he did his utmost to follow out the great judicial tradition
of protecting the interests of an undefended prisoner. Unfortunately
Massey did not assist him in this task and equally unfortunately Mr
Justice Penrice made what to-day would be recognised as a serious
omission in his direction to the jury. The evidence of Russell and
Whitney amply confirmed that of Thompson regarding the carrying
away of the *Gambia Castle*. Such an act had been declared to be
piracy by the previously mentioned statute of 1699.[3] Massey was
undoubtedly guilty on that charge regardless of the paltry question
of Colonel Whitney's perukes. But the only evidence on the other
two charges was that of Alexander Thompson, a self-confessed accomplice, who gave his evidence with a halter round his own neck.
As already said, he seems to have had some honesty in him and to
have been minded to be as truthful as circumstances and self interest
would permit. But there must be grave doubt as to whether or not
he succumbed to the temptation to exculpate himself at Massey's
expense. He, for instance, alleged that Massey threatened to shoot

---

[1] Notes of the Lords Justices, 11 July 1723, P.R.O., S.P. Dom. 35/44.
[2] P.R.O., H.C.A. 1/55.   [3] 11 and 12 Will. III, c. 7, s. 9.

Russell when he came out in a boat to make a last attempt at conciliation, whereas Russell said nothing of this in his evidence. Whilst a conviction on such unconfirmed testimony is not unlawful, it is highly dangerous and to-day a judge would strongly advise a jury to acquit in the absence of any corroboration of such a witness. Unfortunately this was not a well-established rule of practice in 1723 and Mr Justice Penrice omitted to direct the jury on this point.[1]

Massey made a statement in his own defence. The judge afterwards described it as "a very long rambling speech" and further stated that "his behaviour during the whole course of his tryal and defence was in a strange, wild, careless, rattling manner, that shewed him not to be in his senses". Unfortunately Massey's own friends did him little good. The judge had intimated during the course of the trial that insanity could be the only possible defence to the charges. A clergyman and an apothecary, who had gone bail for Massey after his committal for trial, went into the witness-box to give evidence on this point. They said "they had advised him to escape and were willing to forfeit their recognizances rather than he should suffer, but he told them he could not in honour let them suffer on his account, so would surrender. These witnesses deposed that they had known him a great while and that he was a strange, extravagant, half witted man, and by no means fit for a command or to go upon such an expedition."[2] The apothecary went so far as to say "he could not tell how it happened the Company took him into their service, but it was in 1720[3] when all the world was mad".[4]

There was only one possible verdict in the circumstances for the jury to return. The evidence of possible mental eccentricity fell far short of that degree of insanity which exempts a man from criminal responsibility for his acts. The jury returned a verdict of guilty on all three counts with a strong recommendation to mercy. That recommendation was fully endorsed by Mr Justice Penrice in his report to the Lords Justices, who held a commission of regency during George I's temporary absence in Hanover.[5] The Lord Justices took time to consider the case. They decided to make

---

[1] Sir Henry Penrice to the Lords Justices, 9 July 1723, P.R.O., S.P. Dom. 85/44.

[2] *Ibid.*   [3] *Sc.* the year of the South Sea Bubble.

[4] Sir Henry Penrice to the Lords Justices, 11 July 1723, P.R.O., S.P. Dom. 85/44.   [5] Same to same, 9 July 1723, P.R.O., S.P. Dom. 85/44.

certain enquiries of the African Company, who on 11 July 1723 sent certain information coupled with the acknowledgment that "the Court of Assistants are duely sensible of the regard their Excellenceys the Lord Justices have had to the Company in requiring this account" and the intimation that Mr Peters, their solicitor, would attend upon Their Excellencies to supply any further information which they might require.[1] Mr Peters accordingly attended. His information was given in the absence of the prisoner and of any person representing the prisoner. It may be that his instructions were not as full as they might have been, but it is certain that evidence regarding incidents occurring at James Island, which might be urged in extenuation and which was then in the possession of the African Company, was not communicated to the Lords Justices. Mr Peters then withdrew and Mr Justice Penrice was called in. He made a very powerful appeal for "an unfortunate man and an unhappy object of great compassion", but it was in vain. After his withdrawal and a short debate he was recalled and "told the excuse not admitted. The law to take its course."[2]

After this further efforts were made to save the prisoner's life. His unhappy wife, a former brother officer, and one of the jurors made strenuous appeals on his behalf.[3] But humbler folk were hardly likely to succeed where the judge of the Admiralty Court had failed. The Lords Justices did so far hesitate as to grant a reprieve for seven days[4] but would relent no further. On 26 July Massey paid the extreme penalty at Execution Dock.[5]

Such was the melancholy end of an officer who had once served "with great applause" under Marlborough. It must always remain a matter of doubt how far he was accessory to Lowther's acts of piracy after leaving the River Gambia. He was undoubtedly guilty of statutory piracy in carrying away the *Gambia Castle* from that river. If, when the law says the penalty for an offence is death, that penalty should invariably be carried out, Massey was "fairly hanged". But if the prerogative of mercy should be exercised in the case of any such offence, the judgment of history must be different.

[1] Francis Lynn to Charles Delahaye, 11 July 1723, P.R.O., S.P. Dom. 35/44.
[2] Notes of the Lords Justices, 11 July 1723, P.R.O., S.P. Dom. 35/44.
[3] William Wogan to Charles Delahaye, 17 July 1723; William Andrews to Charles Delahaye, 18 July 1723, P.R.O., S.P. Dom. 35/44.
[4] Robert Walpole to Sheriffs of London, 19 July 1723, P.R.O., H.C.A. 1/55.
[5] Warrant dated 24 July 1723, P.R.O., S.P. Dom. 35/44.

It is clear that the prosecution by the African Company, who had lost a valuable ship and had had the safety of their settlement in the Gambia jeopardised, was most vindictive. As mentioned, evidence was suppressed which might have told with the Lords Justices in Massey's favour, and the fact cannot be passed over without comment that this was not the first occasion upon which the African Company had been guilty of suppression of evidence, when prosecuting one of their servants.[1] There is no denying that Massey was a most misguided and unwise man and was guilty of the grave military offence of mutiny, but the only civil offence, of which one can be satisfied that he was guilty, was committed by him under most trying circumstances for the good of others. If ever a man went to the scaffold as much sinned against as sinning, it was Captain John Massey.

[1] In 1704 the African Company prosecuted Daniel Johnson for piratically seizing the *Christopher* in the River Gambia. Before his arrest Johnson handed to a friend certain documents proving his innocence with a request that they should be laid before the African Company. These papers were suppressed by the Company for ten months and then only disclosed after evidence had been given of their handing over. Johnson was ultimately acquitted. Information of William Wigglesworth, November 1704; Affidavit of John Pery, 21 July 1705, in *Regina* versus *Daniel Johnson*, P.R.O., H.C.A. 1/16.

XIII: A private war between two trading companies, 1720–1729

In the last chapter we digressed from the history of the Gambia to follow the history of the mutineers who sailed away in the *Gambia Castle*. In this chapter we will return to those who were left behind in the Gambia.

When the mutineers left the river deaths and desertions had reduced the settlement from one hundred and sixty-five to seventy persons. On 3 September 1721 there were only one sergeant and twenty-two private soldiers in the garrison. Colonel Whitney died on 6 October, and the government of the settlement devolved upon the chief merchant, Henry Glynne.[1]

Whatever may have been Glynne's mistakes in regard to the handling of the soldiers' grievances, it cannot be denied that he was a hard working and loyal servant of the African Company. The Minutes of the Council of James Fort and records of the African Company showed that he was a competent and energetic officer in matters of purely civilian and commercial administration. He assumed charge after a long period in which, owing to French activity, piracy, and mutinies English prestige had sunk very low in the eyes of the local natives. By judicious and diplomatic handling of the local chiefs he managed to raise it to a higher position.

The Minutes of the Council of James Fort are still extant and give a very full account of the dealings of Glynne with the local chiefs. His principal dealings were naturally with Barra. In 1722 the chief of this district was not over well pleased with the African Company because "they had afronted him in high degree by giving the fine sadle that came over to the King of Biole (Baol-Salum), which he was sure was designed for him and worth more than all that was given to him". Glynne therefore "proposed that to quiet the mind of the King of Barra and to engage him more heartily, that we do by the first opportunity write to the Company to desire them to send us a handsome sadle for the King of Barra". A cask of thirty gallons of corn brandy in the meantime partially propitiated the chief, who agreed to allow the establishment of a factory at San

---

[1] Nominal Rolls of James Island, P.R.O., T. 70/1446.

178

Domingo, near Juffure, and empowered the Company "to seize and putt in irons all such persons as they should find stealing the Company's effects and to force away all such persons as came there without trade or other business".[1] A month later he proved that he was ready to fulfil his promises, when a "fellow" was "seized for stealing the apron off the gun", and he sent word that "he should remain on the island a slave to the Company, unless redeemed by his master for another slave". Glynne observed that "this was the first piece of justice the King had shown the Company since our arrival" and in recognition of the fact sent him one gallon of French brandy and five gallons of corn brandy.[2]

The "emperor" of Foni was a little more difficult to handle. He was having trouble with his "Floops" or Jolas and their rebellion was spoiling the Company's trade at Bintang. The "king" of Barra had been approached in regard to these troubles and asked "'to make peace with the Floops or to suffer the Company to make a free trade with them from the port on the south side of the river, that belongs to him as prince of that countrey; to which he answered that he could not enter into any such agreement without the consent of the other kings, who was at warr with those people, but, if they were willing we should have a trade with them, he would not be against it". It was therefore decided to send the "emperor" of Foni twenty gallons of brandy in order to induce him to make peace with the Jolas and to allow the Company free trade in his territory.[3] Glynne therefore proceeded to Foni Brefet only to find that his imperial majesty had just been severely defeated by the Jolas and was mourning the death of nine members of his own family. Glynne was invited to the "cry" for these losses, but "as he was well acquainted with these country cryes and knew them to be a drunken, tumultuous ceremony", he sent his present of brandy to the "emperor" by a Portuguese trader. On receipt of the present, the "emperor" declared that "God Almighty must have put it into the Company's heart to send him just at that time", made a number of vague promises, and offered to meet Glynne at Brefet at a later date.[4] But the chief procrastinated and "by the trifling excuses he made to avoid coming to meet him at Barrafatt had a design only to gett a large present from the Company without doing them any

---

[1] Minutes of Council of James Fort, 16 October 1722, Rawlinson MS. c. 747.
[2] *Ibid.* 28 November 1722.   [3] *Ibid.* 16 October 1722.
[4] *Ibid.* 22 October 1722.

service for it". None the less the alcaide of Bintang proved more accessible and more helpful and a factory was established at his town.[1]

Glynne took active steps to develop the trade of the Company outside the River Gambia. It was to him that Gambia owed its participation in the gum trade at Portendic, which lasted until its final renunciation by a convention with France in 1857. The Portuguese had occupied the island of Arguin just to the south of Cape Blanco and erected a fort there in 1455. The Dutch captured the fort in 1638 and held it until 1678, when it was wrested from them by the French and ultimately ceded to France by the Treaty of Nimuegen. As, however, the French did not effectively occupy the island, it was reoccupied by the Dutch. As a means of legal evasion of the terms of the Treaty of Nimuegen they took care to occupy in the name and under the flag of the Elector of Brandenburg. For various reasons, which need not be discussed here, the French were unable to oust the intruders until 1721. The Dutch then occupied Portendic a few miles to the south of Arguin and persuaded the Trarzas, the local Moorish inhabitants, to attack Arguin, which was retaken on 11 January 1722.[2] Glynne took advantage of this turn of events to send the *Clarendon* in 1721 and the *Bonetta* in 1722 to Arguin and Portendic for gum in exchange for goods of which the Dutch stood in need.[3] On hearing of these voyages the African Company characterised them as "a very hazardous enterprize" and one likely to create trouble with the French.[4] None the less the voyages went off without any untoward incident and good cargoes of gum were obtained. But the recapture of Arguin in 1724 by the French put an end temporarily to British trade in these regions.[5]

Trade on the coast between Goree and the mouth of the Gambia proved somewhat more precarious. The chief at Portudal was found to be actively hostile. He had a long-standing grievance against the British. In 1714 the *John Galley* had been there to buy slaves. Whilst the supercargo was on shore a strange sail was sighted. Fearing it was a French vessel from Goree—though it was in actual

---

[1] Minutes of Council of James Fort, 24 November 1722, Rawlinson MS. c. 747.
[2] Labat, *Nouvelle Relation de l'Afrique Occidentale*, I, pp. 55–131.
[3] Letters received by R.A.C., 2 August 1722, P.R.O., T. 70/1512; Examination of William Ramsey, *Journal of Council of Trade*, 20 April 1726.
[4] R.A.C. to Glynne, 27 June 1722, P.R.O., T. 70/55.
[5] Labat, *op. cit.* I, 156–210.

fact a Bristol interloper—the commander set sail with fifty women and children on board, none of whom had been paid for "and the greatest part good for nothing".[1] The supercargo was allowed to make his way to Joal after making a promise to pay for the slaves carried off, but it appears that owing to the constant change of officers, lack of funds, and the troubled times which followed, this promise was forgotten. The visit in 1722 of Ramsey, the second chief merchant, provided the opportunity for retaliation. The chief accepted the presents sent by the Company and allowed the trade goods to be landed, but at once placed an embargo upon them and threatened to seize Ramsey, who hastily returned to James Island. Later, a Portuguese trader, who had dealings with the Company, was actually seized and detained for this unpaid debt.[2]

In the following year Glynne decided to try personally to establish better relations with the people of Portudal. He accordingly sailed on 17 March 1723 in the *Clarendon*. They met with a good reception from the natives but three days after their arrival an armed French vessel, the *Duc du Maine*, arrived in the road. On 28 March the French commander seized the *Clarendon* and carried her with Glynne and the other British officers on board to Goree. The commander sent word of the seizure to André Brue at St Louis, who, realising that his subordinate had gone too far, ordered the release of the ship.[3]

Glynne returned to James Island, but died ten days after his departure from Goree. On 21 April the other members of the council of the fort entered the following resolution in their minutes:

Mr Glynn being deceased, and the burthen of the Royal African Company's affairs centring in our prudent management thereof, we do in council resolve that the deceased be enterred in as good a form as we can possible, and do agree that his coffin be lined with black bayes within and without, and that, as we have no pall, that we now order one on this occasion and when please God to call any one of us; and that as soon as day that the gunner have orders to fire 10 gunns and to hoist the flag half mast, that the burial be on the north east bastion, being the

[1] William Cooke to R.A.C., 22 April 1714, P.R.O., T. 70/3.
[2] Glynne to R.A.C., 9 August 1722, P.R.O., T. 70/4.
[3] Narrative of the Proceedings of the French East India Company, P.R.O., C.O. 267/5; Minutes of Council of James Fort, 7 April 1723; Rawlinson MS. c. 747; Charles Orfeur to R.A.C., 5 May 1723, P.R.O., T. 70/7.

most proper; that the commanders be invited and that they hold up the pall, assisted by Mr Charles Orfeur, first factor, and that Mr Willey and Mr Hairstens follow the corps and the rest of the gentlemen in order as to post and seniority, and that the soldiers be drawn up in form, and that after the service for the deceased that the officer have orders for ordering three vollies of small armes and then to be followed with twenty minute guns of artillery.[1]

The control of the Company's affairs now devolved upon Joseph Willey. His letters and the minutes of the Council suggest that he was a somewhat excitable person. A day or two before his death Glynne had ordered the French factors at Albreda to prepare a ship and leave the river. That order had not been complied with in Glynne's life-time and his successor lacked the means to enforce it. On 17 May 1723 a French vessel arrived in the river and anchored off Albreda. Willey at once sent to demand the purpose of the visit. The commander of the ship sent back word that he was unable to say until he had opened his packet. Willey sent to ask if the ship was intended to remove the French factors from Albreda in compliance with Glynne's orders. No actual reply was sent, but both the French sloop and factory hoisted their national colours and proceeded to fire off guns in derision. Thereupon on 21 May a very excited Mr Willey assembled the council and told them "it's demanded in writing from you your opinion in this case and wether it is for the Company's interest that the former affront be confirmed by this. I take it to be a more gross one as under the nose of our fort and grand factory. If you have any respect for the service you are now in, give your sentiments in this case full and vou'l oblige." His colleagues cautiously recommended that an officer should be sent to Albreda to ask for an explanation of this conduct and that, unless and until such explanation had been refused, there should be no resort to strong measures. Accordingly Charles Orfeur and Patrick Massey were deputed to visit Albreda—the latter because he had "lived in France and we suppose understands the French tongue".[2]

The envoys were able to discharge their duty satisfactorily. The Frenchmen realised that they had gone rather further than good

[1] Minutes of Council of James Fort, 21 April 1723, Rawlinson MS. c. 747.
[2] Narrative of the Proceedings of the French East India Company, P.R.O., C.O. 267/5; James Willey to R.A.C., 23 June 1723, P.R.O., T. 70/7; Minutes of Council of James Fort, 21 May 1723, Rawlinson MS. c. 747.

taste permitted and apologised for not sending a proper answer to James Fort. They also declared that the French Company would give ample satisfaction for the seizure of the *Clarendon* and that the British would not be molested in future if they sent their ships to Portudal. In the circumstances they therefore suggested that their countrymen might be allowed to remain at Albreda. On receipt of this message the council of James Fort decided to await further instructions from England before insisting on the departure of the French.[1]

As for the rest of Mr Willey's worries and troubles are they not written at length in the minutes of the Council of James Fort? They show him to have been a fussy individual but none the less a hard working and loyal servant of his masters, who little deserved the strictures passed upon him by Bartholomew Stibbs in his *Journal of a Voyage up the Gambia*. On 28 October 1723 he died on duty whilst visiting the Company's factory at Joar. He was buried close to his predecessor on the north-east bastion, whilst the fort fired sixteen minute guns, to which the one ship in the offing replied with ten.[2]

Prior to Willey's death the African Company had begun to consider plans for the further and better exploitation of the resources of the River Gambia. This revival of interest was in a large measure stimulated by James Brydges, first Duke of Chandos (1673–1744), who promoted a scheme for increasing the Company's capital so as to develop the local resources of Africa and was a liberal subscriber to the new stock.[3] At his suggestion it was decided to try to develop the agricultural resources of the territories on the river banks. For this purpose John Lyle, apothecary, was appointed on 1 September 1721, "to take upon him the case of examining and making tryall of all manner of dying and other woods, druggs, vegetables, gums, oyls, salts, mineralls etc., which grow and (are) to be found in the parts about and up the said River Gambia".[4] The Company's servants were also instructed to encourage the natives to plant indigo, pepper, and cotton.[5]

[1] *Ibid.*   [2] Moore, *Travels into the Inland Parts of Africa*, p. 239.
[3] "An Article for Proposal made to a General Court of the African Company, Decr 12th, 1723, by their Court of Assistants for reducing their Capital", Gough MS. Somerset, 7.
[4] Agreements of R.A.C., P.R.O., T. 70/1423, ff. 77, 78.
[5] R.A.C. to Colonel Whitney, 16 May, 1721; R.A.C. to Glynne, 23 January 1722, P.R.O., T. 70/55.

It was also decided to make an attempt to discover Jobson and Prince Rupert's Ophir at the headwaters of the river. Despite sixty years of occupation of James Island the Company had done little to promote discovery since Vermuyden's expedition in 1662. In 1681 John Kastell had sent a sea captain named Hodges[1] to explore the river above the Barrakunda Falls. He came back to report that the river was "navigable above the falls and in 3 rivers—one for teeth, one for gold, one cambells". He said the upper reaches were in a country "whose king is a necromancer" but he also claimed to have been given a friendly reception by this king, from whom he obtained eleven slaves and the promise of an annual caravan of 100 slaves.[2] Subsequent explorers reported that his journals, which are no longer extant, were "not authentik".[3] None the less French contemporaries give him the credit of having made his way down the Faleme to a point close to its junction with the Senegal in Bambuk.[4] According to the same authority he was married to a native woman of Portuguese extraction and on his return from this expedition barbarously murdered her infant child on suspicion of infidelity on her part.[5]

Hodges returned to explore the upper river in 1688. He claimed to have got as far as Tenda, "beyond which he was not permitted to pass. They poysoned him in their milke, which was prevented by timely antidotes."[6] He tried to find a route to "Cumbo Cunda, where are gold and teeth", but eventually returned to report that the only feasible route thither was by the Senegal.[7] After that the French wars prevented any further voyages of discovery.

In 1716 the Earl of Yarmouth proposed another expedition in search of the gold mines, but in the unsettled state of affairs in the Gambia at that date all that could be promised was the sending of "a judicious inhabitant for a true account of the position of those mines and some of the sand".[8] In 1721 it was, however, decided to

---

[1] Cf. note 1, p. 96.

[2] John Kastell to R.A.C., 24 January 1682, P.R.O., T. 70/10.

[3] Richard Hall to R.A.C., 2 July 1726, P.R.O., T. 70/55.

[4] Labat, *op. cit.* v, 10.

[5] Cultru, *Le Premier Voyage du Sieur de la Courbe*, p. 204.

[6] Alexander Cleeve to R.A.C., 20 June 1688, P.R.O., T. 70/11.

[7] John Booker to R.A.C., 12 February and – July 1689, and 16 September 1690, P.R.O., T. 70/11.

[8] David Francis to R.A.C., 22 May 1716, P.R.O., T. 70/6.

send a special expedition to look for the mines. A number of Cornish miners were engaged. Nicholas Baynton was appointed to take charge of the expedition. Richard Hull was appointed as "chymist and surgeon" to analyse any minerals which might be discovered. Another surgeon and a surgeon's mate were also engaged as medical officers to the party. But the plan failed. A number of the miners deserted before the ship sailed. Though they were replaced by others, the majority of the members of the expedition never reached the Gambia. They were embarked on the *Otter*, which sailed from England on 6 January 1722, but was lost at sea. Baynton, Robert Richardson, the newly appointed chief merchant, and John Lyle, the botanist, perished with her. Fortunately, Richard Hull and a few other members of the expedition had embarked with a quantity of stores and equipment on another ship and reached the Gambia safely. But the loss of the *Otter* put an end for the time being to all projects of exploration.[1]

The African Company were not deterred by the disaster to the *Otter*, but decided to send out another expedition under the command of Captain Bartholomew Stibbs.[2] The journal of that expedition has been published in Francis Moore's *Travels into the Inland Parts of Africa*. Stibbs arrived at James Island on 7 October 1723. Willey had gone up to Joar before his arrival and died there at the end of the month as did the surgeon, who was specially assigned for the expedition, and the ensign in command of the soldiers. These deaths caused a delay in equipping the expedition, but Charles Orfeur, who succeeded Willey, gave every possible assistance. Stibbs' first mate and the captain of the miners died before the party set out and Henry Rose, who was appointed to take charge of the boats, refused to go unless he got an increase of salary. This further delayed the expedition, but on 27 December, "after having several high words with the governor about dilatory fitting of the canoas", Stibbs embarked with fifteen Europeans and thirty-eight natives on the *Dispatch* and weighed anchor. The Barrakunda Falls were not reached until 3 February 1724. Stibbs proceeded thence in five canoes, but found the river very shallow and was only able to

---

[1] Agreements of R.A.C., 29 September 1721, P.R.O., T. 70/1423, ff. 93, 94; R.A.C. passenger lists, P.R.O., T. 70/1437; R.A.C. to Henry Glynne, 2 January and 3 December 1722, P.R.O., T. 70/55.

[2] R.A.C. to Glynne, 3 December 1722, 3 March, 15 and 21 August 1723, P.R.O., T. 70/55.

make his way sixty miles above the Falls. He returned to report that he had been unable to discover any minerals and that he considered the journal and map, which Vermuyden had compiled in 1661, to be mythical. After perusal of his journal one is forced to the conclusion that a little more energy might have been productive of better results and that the difficulties of exploration were somewhat exaggerated.[1] Stibbs certainly did not do Vermuyden entire justice and it is clear that his own observations regarding the country were not entirely accurate. Howbeit, the result of his report of his voyage was to discourage the African Company from further exploration.

During the absence of Stibbs up-river Robert Plunkett arrived to take up the post of Governor.[2] His correspondence shows him to have been an excitable and not over tactful person. He had previously been in charge of the Company's factory at Bunce Island, Sierra Leone. He was there in 1720 when a pirate named Bartholomew Roberts arrived and attacked the settlement. Plunkett put up a stout resistance until his ammunition was exhausted. He was then captured as he was trying to escape. "Roberts swore heartily at him for his Irish impudence in daring to resist him. Plunkett, finding the bad company he had gotten into, fell a-cursing and swearing faster than Roberts, which raised much laughter among the pirates, who bid Roberts hold his tongue, for that he had no share at all in the palaver with Plunkett. However, it is said that by mere dint of swearing, old Plunkett saved his life."[3] In the Gambia he fell gravely foul of two private traders. A certain Captain Smyth arrived off James Island and offered to buy slaves from the Company. Plunkett refused and further forbade him notwithstanding the Act of Parliament to proceed up the river. Smyth ignored the Governor's order and went up stream and a shallop was sent from James Island to bring him back.[4] The *Hope* (Captain Perry) sailed past the fort to Joar without bringing to. On his

---

[1] Moore, *op. cit.* pp. 235–297; Richard Hull to R.A.C., 2 July 1724, P.R.O., T. 70/7.

[2] R.A.C. to Joseph Willey, 31 October 1723; R.A.C. to Robert Plunkett, 31 October 1723, P.R.O., T. 70/55; Agreements of R.A.C., 18 November 1723, P.R.O., T. 70/1423, ff. 134–139.

[3] Smith, *A New Voyage to Guinea*, p. 86.

[4] Evidence of Captain Smyth, *Journal of Council of Trade*, 12 January 1750.

return Plunkett fired at him and brought him to anchor. He then seized Perry's yawl as it was carrying goods to some Portuguese at Juffure. Perry came to the fort and, to Plunkett's intense indignation, disputed the African Company's authority to prevent him from trading and refused to show his clearances.[1]

French activities very easily roused Plunkett. On 2 December 1723, shortly before his arrival, the French factor in charge at Albreda had asked permission for himself and his canoe to proceed to Tankular. Permission was refused, whereupon the Frenchman announced to the Governor and council "that he would go up the river, as high as he pleased, and when he pleased, without asking leave". Three days later he set off. A sloop was sent after him from James Island. It overtook the canoe at the entrance to Bintang Creek, but the French factor made his escape overland to the town of Bintang. The canoe was declared to be forfeited and handed over to Stibbs for his expedition.[2]

On the following 26 February Plunkett sent a sloop in charge of Charles Orfeur and Henry Rose to resettle the factory at Portudal. He at the same time wrote to the French Director-General at Senegal announcing what he was doing and demanding to know what reparation he would make "for the late affronts and disturbances they had given our trade there". No answer was sent to the letter. In view of its tone and the recent seizure of a French canoe in the River Gambia this was perhaps only to be expected. On 25 March a French sloop with soldiers on board came into Portudal road and seized the British sloop. Orfeur was on shore at the time and an armed party was sent to seize him, but the local chief protected him. A few days later the Governor of Goree arrived in person and "by force assisted by bribes to the king got Mr Orfeur into his power". The British sloop was then taken to Goree. On 2 April Plunkett wrote to the French Director-General requiring him to remove the French factories at Albreda and Bintang by June or "otherwise (he) would seize them till the matter should be decided at home". No immediate answer was sent to this letter. But after the passing of further correspondence the British sloop was released

---

[1] Robert Plunkett to R.A.C., 4 February 1724, P.R.O., T. 70/7; Letters received by R.A.C., August 1724, P.R.O., T. 70/1512; Moore, *op. cit.* p. 296.

[2] Moore, *op. cit.* pp. 242, 243; Narrative of the Proceedings of French East India Company, P.R.O., C.O. 267/5.

on 26 April. Though its hatches had been sealed, it was discovered that a quantity of goods had been pilfered.[1]

On 5 June, as the French Company had declined to remove its servants and effects from the River Gambia, a party was sent from James Island to Albreda. The French factors were forewarned and had made their escape overland to Goree. The factory was left in charge of some natives, "who made some resistance but soon submitted". All the effects of the French were taken to James Fort and inventoried. On 25 June similar action was taken at Bintang. The goods of the French were inventoried "and with their servants transported to the fort. The French gentlemen at their own request had liberty to proceed to Goree or Senegal whenever they pleased."[2]

This action led to difficulties with the "king" of Barra. Plunkett "acquainted him with the proceedings of the French and desired him to stand neuter, as it is a palaver between the 2 companies and no relation to him, which he promised to do". At the same time he considered that the price of his neutrality ought to be some share in the goods which had been seized at Albreda. When he was informed that he could not have it, he took grave offence and began to make other demands. As these demands were not complied with, he seized some of the Company's servants at Juffure and demanded a ransom of a thousand bars worth of goods for them. He further was reported to have planned to seize Plunkett himself, when he landed at Juffure to confer with him. It so happened that at this juncture H.M.S. *Leopard* was at the mouth of the river cruising in search of pirates. Plunkett sent a letter to the captain, in which he expressed regret that he was "so tied up as not to be able to perform the commands you are designed upon in these parts. We know not if this is through ignorance of those, who represented the river, or not.... We ask for a hundred of your hands, to which we will join thirty or forty more, to seize the king in his own town and his officers, who actually occasioned these disturbances. We will procure guides and send such sloops, long boats or canoes as you require." In a hasty postscript he added

By this tide we have dispatched our sloop and long boat, which with your long boat will be sufficient, being resolved to seize the king of Barra

[1] Plunkett to R.A.C., 3 August and 20 September 1724, P.R.O., T. 70/7; Charles Orfeur to R.A.C., 3 August 1724, P.R.O., T. 70/7; Letters received by R.A.C., August 1724, P.R.O., T. 70/1512; Narrative of the Proceedings of the French East India Company, P.R.O., C.O. 267/5.   [2] *Ibid.*

at Jillifree, if your aid comes before he departs from thence. We beg your men may be dispatched without delay. If the king leaves Jillifree before their arrival, we ask that your officers may be told to follow our instructions and to proceed where we think proper to send them.

Captain Medley of the *Leopard* sent his barge back to James Island to find out the precise position of affairs and, on learning that Mr Plunkett was a very excitable person, decided that his ship and crew ought not to be embroiled in a purely domestic quarrel between the Company's servants and a local chief. Accordingly, to Plunkett's intense indignation, he weighed anchor and sailed for Sierra Leone. Eventually through the good offices of the "emperor" of Foni some sort of a peace was patched up with Barra.[1]

Peace with Barra was only just made in time. On 25 August a French forty-four gun ship and two sloops arrived at Albreda. Two days later a message was sent to James Fort demanding the goods, which had been seized at Albreda and Bintang, and announcing that "the said factorys should be re-established without the least consideration in lieu thereof, and that we should make them satisfaction also for the damages they have sustained for their lost time and for obstructing their trade". Plunkett replied "that their insults upon the Royal African Company had occasioned those settlements being seized and broke up, and that he had transmitted home to England an account of the goods, which had been so taken, and therefore could not restore them without orders from England, nor suffer them to resettle their factorys in the River Gambia before the dispute about Portodally and Joally was settled by the two Companys at home; and therefore they were determined to be on their guard in defence of the Companys interest".[2]

At two o'clock in the morning of the following day the French tried to cut out the Company's brigantine *Advice*, which was lying off James Island, but, "being timely discovered, were prevented". For the next three days the French took no action, but at three o'clock in the afternoon of 1 September they opened fire on James

[1] Plunkett to R.A.C., 3 August 1724, P.R.O., T. 70/7; Plunkett to Captain Medley, 26 July 1724, *Hist. MSS. Comm. Rep., Du Cane MSS.* p. 24; Log of H.M.S. *Leopard*, P.R.O., Ad. 51/533.

[2] Plunkett to R.A.C., 20 September 1724, P.R.O., T. 70/7; Narrative of the Proceedings of the French East India Company, P.R.O., C.O. 267/5.

Fort and kept up the bombardment for two hours. That night they made another unsuccessful attempt to seize the *Advice*. On the ten following days they kept up an intermittent fire on the fort. On 11 September the bombardment lasted from early morning till sunset and over 300 shot were fired. The night happened to be a very dark one and a boat was able to cut the cables of the *Advice* and carry her off. Subsequently the French plundered the Company's factories at Bintang and Brefet in Foni, making a prisoner of Matthew Wilson, the factor at the former place. A similar attempt on the factory at Geregia would have been successful, "if the king of the country had not protected them". The French continued at Albreda for a whole month. On 27 September they seized a British vessel as it was entering the river. The following day they fell down the river and finally sailed away on 1 October.[1]

Plunkett wrote home to say that it was common report amongst the natives that the French "were resolved to take the fort, and the reason they gave for not proceeding then was that they waited the arrival of another ship, when they would put their design in execution, but, if they should fail therein, their orders were from the General of Senegal to blockade the fort fourteen months to oblige them to surrender".[2]

Though Plunkett wrote to England in apprehension of a further visit from the French,[3] the Director-General in Senegal realised that matters had been allowed to go to too great a length and that the last incident might lead to complications in Europe. As was only to be expected, a great deal of correspondence poured home from the servants of both Companies. But neither the British nor the French Government appears to have taken much note of the matter. Neither party was ordered to return the property of the other nor to make compensation for any seizure. The *Advice*, which had been carried off from under James Fort, was retained by the French[4] and there is no record of the handing over by the British of the goods seized at Albreda and Bintang. Apparently the two respective governments regarded the incidents as the ebullitions of one or two excitable people in the tropics, which had done no particular or permanent

---

[1] Plunkett to R.A.C., 20 September 1724, P.R.O., T. 70/7; Narrative of the Proceedings of the French East India Company, P.R.O., C.O. 267/5.

[2] *Ibid.*

[3] Plunkett to R.A.C., 27 October 1724, P.R.O., T. 70/7.

[4] Daniel Pepper to R.A.C , 21 December 1728, P.R.O., T. 70/7.

harm, and that the net result of mutual reprisals was that the honours were even.

Plunkett continued for another year in mixed moods of despondency and excitability. He tried to retaliate upon the "king" of Barra by sending the *Gambia* sloop up-river to seize the canoes and people of Barra, but had to confess in the end that he could not "make up the palaver with the king of Barra, who is too powerfull for them".[1] He also bemoaned the lack of letters from home, and complained "they are neglected by the Company, which discourages them from continuing there longer". He therefore earnestly begged to be recalled.[2]

His troubles were, however, soon to end. On the night of 1–2 November 1725 the powder magazine blew up and destroyed a large portion of James Fort. The cause of the disaster is not known, but it was believed to be lightning. There were fortunately only nineteen Europeans upon the island at the time, but eleven of them perished. Amongst the killed were Plunkett, Edward Drummond, the second merchant, the officer in charge of the soldiers, and two of the four remaining soldiers. The mortality amongst the native servants and slaves is not recorded, but "Superansa, formerly slave of Mr Plunkett, who lost her leg by the fort being blown up in 1725", was for ten years afterwards a pensioner of the Company. Fortunately the tradesmen and artificers slept in barracks outside the fort and so escaped injury. Richard Hull, the chief factor, had a miraculous escape. He was sleeping inside the fort and the surrounding apartments caught fire, but he managed to make his escape with a number of valuable accounts and papers.[3]

Fortunately for himself and the Company Anthony Rogers, the third merchant, had proceeded only two days previously up-river on a trading voyage. He at once returned and with the help of Richard Hull set to work energetically to rebuild the fort. Captain Rodwell of the Company's ship *Diligence* was anchored off the island

---

[1] Plunkett to R.A.C., 27 October 1724 and 14 September 1725, P.R.O., T. 70/7.

[2] Plunkett to R.A.C., 27 June 1725, P.R.O., T. 70/7.

[3] Smith, *op. cit.* p. 33; Anthony Rogers to R.A.C., 24 November and 19 December 1725, P.R.O., T. 70/7; Richard Hull to R.A.C., 14 March 1726, P.R.O., T. 70/7; Nominal Rolls of James Island, P.R.O., T. 70/1446; Accounts of James Fort, 1733, P.R.O., T. 70/1451, f. 249; Accounts of James Fort, 1735, P.R.O., T. 70/1452, f. 209; "A Gambia Diary book commencing November 1, 1725", *Journal of Council of Trade*, 20 April 1726.

at the time and he also rendered invaluable assistance. There was, however, trouble with the surviving soldiers and tradesmen, who took advantage of the disaster to strike for higher pay, and owing to the urgency of the work their demands had to be granted. In contrast to this conduct all the neighbouring chiefs, including the "king" of Barra, whose objection to Plunkett appears to have been purely a personal one, showed their sympathy in a practical manner by allowing the Company free access to and use of building materials in their territories. Within a year of the disaster the Company's surveyor was able to report that James Fort "was again rebuilt with many alterations for the better".[1]

When news of the disaster reached England it was predicted to the Council of Trade that "the French would do what they pleased there",[2] but the servants of the French East India Company did not take any immediate advantage of their rival's misfortune. Late in the following year they sent to enquire of Rogers if he intended to abandon James Island. When he assured them that he had no such intention, they decided to spy out the land. On 18 February 1727 to the very great alarm of Rogers, two large ships and a sloop sailed up the river and anchored within gun shot of the fort. They sent a boat ashore with a letter announcing that the Deputy Director-General was on board. Next day this officer landed and dined with Rogers. He announced that his visit was quite peaceable and expressed his concern and regret for the attack on James Fort in 1724, "which action was condemned in Paris and the then Governor of Senegal ordered to be hanged". He further expressed his desire that the two Companies should come to some amicable arrangement. With this object he proposed that the African Company should allow the French to return to Albreda and Bintang in exchange for recognition of their right to trade unmolested at Portudal and Joal. He also issued a cordial invitation to Rogers and Hull to pay a visit to St Louis to discuss further terms. Rogers was sufficiently impressed by his visitor's protestations of good will as to agree provisionally to allow the French to resettle at Albreda, provided the African Company were allowed to send one ship yearly to Portendic to trade for gum. At a later date, however, he reported that there were difficulties about the proposed agreement and asked the

[1] Smith, op. cit. p. 33; Anthony Rogers to R.A.C., 24 November 1725, 24 January and 24 February 1726, P.R.O., T. 70/7.
[2] Journal of Council of Trade, 26 April 1726.

African Company not to confirm it.[1] On receipt of news of the arrangement the Company wrote to say

We can by no means approve the permission you have given the French to resettle again at Albreda, nor the narrow demand you made of one ship yearly to trade on the gum coast: yet we are willing to excuse what you have done therein for the present as being occasioned by the apprehensions you might be under of being compelled to do it by force. And as you have permitted them to settle at Albreda, so we think proper to acquaint you that, if the French Company at Paris should make any overtures to us for ratifying the articles lately concluded between you and their agents, we shall be very far from agreeing to them without considerable alterations and having due regard to the Company's interest, and also some compensation made to our servants there in the losses and damages they sustained in the late attack the French made upon our fort.[2]

The French Company did not approach the English Company.[3] At a later date the latter Company recommended Rogers "to revise the said orders and instructions, and to act as you shall judge most for our interest, either by removing the French out of the river, if they offer to give our ships any interruption in their trade on any part of the coast, except where their own settlements lye, or permit them to remain some time longer at Albida, but not to proceed further up the river till you receive our further orders in relation to that affair".[4] In the meantime by a more or less tacit understanding on the spot the British were allowed to trade at Portudal and Joal.[5]

In the midst of the troubles with the French there occurred the last attempt at piracy in the River Gambia. From 1720 onwards the British navy had made strong efforts to stamp out piracy in the Atlantic Ocean, but it needed constant and frequent patrolling to deal with this offence. The opportunities for lawless plundering were very great and the opportunities of suppression were but few. In

---

[1] Anthony Rogers to R.A.C., 15 and 29 March and 19 May 1727, P.R.O., T. 70/7; Council of Trade to R.A.C., 26 January 1727, Add. MSS. 14,035, f. 35.
[2] R.A.C. to Rogers, 14 September 1727, P.R.O., T. 70/55.
[3] R.A.C. to Council of Trade, 11 July 1764, P.R.O., C.O. 267/7.
[4] R.A.C. to Rogers, 11 September 1729, P.R.O., T. 70/55.
[5] Smith, *op. cit.* p. 32; Letters received by R.A.C., 16 November 1728, P.R.O., T. 70/1512.

1721 the crew of a small brigantine from Bristol had turned pirate after leaving the River Gambia.[1] In September 1726 the *Ark* from Rhode Island arrived in the river to slave. Edmondson, the commander, avowed his intention of turning pirate, but a number of the crew refused to follow him and informed Rogers on James Island of their commander's intentions. When he found that his plans were known, Edmondson hastily weighed anchor so as to get out of the river. The Company's sloop *Gambia* was sent under the command of Charles Orfeur to bring him back. Edmondson, who had only a crew of three white boys and six recently purchased slaves, refused to surrender, when called upon, and fired at Orfeur. The fire was returned and Edmondson was badly wounded. Orfeur then boarded the *Ark*. Edmondson threw himself overboard and was never seen again. The captured vessel was then taken to James Island.[2] It was fitting that the last outbreak of piracy in the River Gambia should be suppressed by that one of the Company's servants who had suffered most at the hands of the pirates in defence of the Company's property.

It is clear that under the energetic guidance of Rogers and Hull, despite the disaster of the explosion, trouble with the French, sickness, mortality, and other hindrances, the affairs of the Company in the River Gambia made a remarkably rapid recovery. Not only was trade opened up with Portudal and Joal, but also in the River Casamance and at Cachau in Portuguese Guinea. Factories which had been closed down just before Willey's death were reopened on the banks of the River Gambia. Relations with the native chiefs were good and the Company's prospects in these regions looked particularly bright.[3]

Unfortunately, there was a rift in the lute. The Company were not entirely appreciative of the work done by their servants in the Gambia and of the difficulties under which it was done. Those in control in London were extremely critical in regard to petty details and omissions to render accounts and returns in the precise forms which they desired, and their commendations for good work done were very few and far between. They furthermore were not very

---

[1] Johnson, *A General History of the Pirates*, ii, 179.

[2] Smith, *op. cit.* pp. 10–12; Anthony Rogers to R.A.C., 2 October 1726, P.R.O., T. 70/7; R.A.C. to Anthony Rogers, 6 July 1727, P.R.O., T. 70/55.

[3] Anthony Rogers to R.A.C., 30 October 1726 and 15 March 1727, P.R.O., T. 70/7.

energetic in sending out ships to replace casualties and to supply James Island with trade goods or the necessities or minor amenities of life. Little care was exercised to see that the quality of such supplies was satisfactory. In 1728, for instance, a supply of bread, which was sent out in the *Clarendon* and was intended to last the settlement on James Island for several months, was found to be absolutely unfit and had to be thrown away on arrival.[1] In the circumstances it was hardly surprising that the men on the spot felt discouraged and that Rogers wrote home in strong terms resenting the tone of the Company's letters and their allegations of "unaccountable management".[2]

It is also not surprising that in a tropical climate and in their confined and cramped conditions the men on James Island fell out amongst themselves. Rogers and Hull had worked well together immediately after the disastrous explosion of 1725, but they subsequently quarrelled. The precise cause of their dispute is not known. The upshot was that Hull was dismissed or dismissed himself from the Company's service, but was eventually reinstated on making a very abject submission.[3] When the Company got to hear of these quarrels they sent out stern letters of rebuke. Rogers was informed that

You should have more business on your hands and a greater concern for the good and interest of the Company, by whom you are employed, than to quarrell amongst yourselves and by your private piques to put their affairs under such difficulties, as they needs must be, by Mr Hull's being dismissed the service, a step taken by you, which they do not think you had sufficient authority to do. And therefore I am to recommend it to you to settle matters so between you, since it is not supposed that Mr Hull is yet come away, so that he may return to his duty in the Company's service at least untill such time as he has the Company's leave or they can meet with a proper person to relieve him.

I am ordered likewise to tell you the Court take notice of the extraordinary manner of your writing to them, which they think ought to be grave and respectfull, whereas your late letters are filled with jests and ludicrous turns instead of serious observations and remarks, which might tend to the advantage of the service.[4]

[1] R.A.C. to Richard Hull, 18 June 1728, P.R.O., T. 70/55.
[2] Rogers to R.A.C., 24 April and 25 May 1727, P.R.O., T. 70/7.
[3] Rogers to R.A.C., 10 July 1727, P.R.O., T. 70/7.
[4] R.A.C. to Rogers, 23 November 1727, P.R.O., T. 70/55.

The following letter was addressed to Hull:

The Court are extremely surprized to find such dissentions and dis-putes amongst you as to give you cause to relinquish their service before they knew of it, or have found out a proper person to relieve you. They were in hopes you had more regard to the interests of your employers than to carry your piques and resentments so high as to let their affairs suffer thereby, and therefore recommend it to you (as they have to Mr Rogers) to adjust your differences and to return again to your duty in the Company's service. . . . I am ordered further to observe to you that the Court very much resent the uncommon stile, in which you have of late wrote to them. Your letters are filled with jests and ludicrous turns.[1]

But matters did not mend after these exhortations. On 19 February 1728 the Company had to write to complain of two letters received from the Gambia, "both of which, being for the most part written in so confused and unintelligible a manner and with so little regard to decency and good manners, we shall deferr answering them till we receive your further explanations upon them". The Company took the strongest possible exception "to your late insolent manner of writing" to complain about the alteration in the scale of allowances for diet, which were the same as were in force "before any of you knew the River Gambia". In view of the tone of the letters, which they had recently received, they had regretfully to record that

We did intend to have sent you by this ship a commission under our common seal, empowering and enabling you to have taken the most proper and effectuall measures for mantaning and securing unto us the benefit of all our rights and priviledges in the River Gambia and other places under your command against the invasions and incroachments of all other persons whatsoever, but we are sorry you give us cause to tell you that we must wait for better proofs of your abilitys, address, steadiness and inclinations to serve us in the common way of business, before we can resolve to intrust you with powers of such importance to our interest.[2]

On 25 March 1728 Rogers wrote to announce that the position was intolerable and that he intended returning home, leaving Hull in charge.[3] On 7 September 1728 Hull wrote home to apologise for the tone of his previous letters but still protested against the alteration

[1] R.A.C. to Hull, 23 November 1727, P.R.O., T. 70/55.
[2] P.R.O., T. 70/55.   [3] P.R.O., T. 70/7.

in the scale of allowances for diet.[1] Before this letter reached England the Company had decided to take action with Hull. On 18 June 1728 a letter was sent to James Island expressing the strongest possible disapproval at his attempts to incite the Company's servants to disobedience and mutiny in regard to the new diet regulations and announcing that

Since you (Mr Richard Hull) have not thought fit to give us such satisfaction as to these and like particulars as we had just reason to expect from you, and since you are so plain as to tell us you either cannot or will not send us such accounts for our affairs and trade as may enable us to judge for ourselves, and that you have taken upon you not only to neglect, but to disobey, orders, the regard, which becomes us to have for the honour as well as the interest of the Company, obliges us to take this opportunity to tell you that from the day of receipt of these our orders, you are discharged and we do accordingly hereby discharge you from the Company's service.[2]

Hull arrived in England to report that "the Company's affairs were in great disorder".[3] Charles Cornewall, who succeeded him, reported that the new scales of pay and diet "had like to have raised a mutiny".[4] Reports reached England that very drastic measures indeed had been taken in dealing with several refractory subordinate officers and on 14 August 1729 the Company felt constrained to write to James Island to say

We must observe to you that your method of punishment by putting persons in irons is what we can by no means approve of and has in it so much barbarity, that we are surprized it should be put in practice amongst gentlemen in a country, where the best accommodations of life are attended with inconveniencys and uneasiness. In case any of our servants are refractory or negligent of their duty, the way of punishment we have always directed is the discharging them from the service and sending them home.[5]

In the meantime death had carried off Charles Cornewall and many of the senior officers on James Island and the command had devolved upon Daniel Pepper, whose acts and deeds will form largely the subject of the next chapter.

[1] *Ibid.* [2] P.R.O., T. 70/55.
[3] R.A.C. to Rogers, 27 November 1729, P.R.O., T. 70/55.
[4] Charles Cornewall to R.A.C., 14 November 1728, P.R.O., T. 70/7.
[5] P.R.O., T. 70/55.

XIV: A conspiracy and an interlude of peace, 1729–1745

Daniel Pepper, who, as mentioned at the end of the last chapter assumed charge of the Royal African Company's affairs in the Gambia in the middle of 1729, was not a very frequent correspondent with his employers in London. The tone of the few letters which he did write gave these employers grave cause for offence. In one such letter he "banters the Company about the encouragement they give their servants abroad" and was further guilty of a "second banter about Mr Rogers being sent out as governor".[1]

Being clad with little brief authority and having the certain knowledge that he was soon to be superseded by a new Governor from England, Pepper determined to make hay whilst the sun shone. He kept no proper accounts, falsified such accounts as he did keep, and embezzled the Company's property. But that was not the sum total of his sins of omission and commission. He made not the slightest attempt to exercise any control over his European or native subordinates. He neglected to supply the slaves with food with the result that during four months over eighty ran away. One batch of fugitives carried off the Company's long boat and, though they remained in sight of the fort for two days, Pepper refused to make any effort to recover them. On another occasion twenty to thirty slaves went off *en masse*. When Pepper was urged to invoke the assistance of the native chiefs to recapture them, he was heard "swearing great oaths that he cared not if all the slaves of the Company ran away, that he would give himself no trouble to send after them. Let them, said he, that are coming out (meaning the Governour and Captain Stibbs) send, for he would not." Most of the other slaves, being in want of food, went off unhindered to the mainland and stayed there until the new Governor arrived.[2]

His neglect of duty was due as much as anything else to the fact that he appears to have been continually drunk and devoted his few sober interludes to fresh schemes for defrauding his employers. In his more intoxicated moments he was really dangerous. In one such

[1] Pepper to R.A.C., 20 September 1729, P.R.O., T. 70/7.
[2] Minutes of Council of James Fort, 29 November 1729, Rawlinson MS. c. 747.

drunken fit he killed a brother of the "king" of Barra without the slightest provocation. Fortunately for the safety of the other Europeans at James Island the "king" expressed his willingness to be consoled for his bereavement by pecuniary compensation. That compensation was duly paid out of the Company's goods. Pepper also quarrelled with the "emperor" of Foni, who had always been consistently loyal to the English, and with the leading Portuguese and native traders. One of his favourite recreations was "suffering no canoas to pass or repass but what he would fire at, when he was upon the fort, which was not often; for it appears that for one day he was upon the fort he was three days ashore, where his behaviour was so odd that it rendered himself so ridiculous, that he became a jest to the countrey".[1]

On 4 October 1729 H.M.S. *Adventure*, under the command of Lord Muskerry,[2] anchored off Barra Point. In accordance with instructions from the Admiralty his lordship did not take his ship further into the river but sent his lieutenant up in the barge to James Island to enquire whether there were any pirates in the vicinity or whether the Company's servants were at war with the local chiefs. The lieutenant arrived off James Island, flying the King's colours, but to his surprise was greeted with a shot from the fort. Nothing deterred, he proceeded to land—only to find the gates of the fort closed against him. After a little parleying he induced Pepper to open the gates and to accord him an interview. When he asked for an explanation for the insult offered to the British flag, Pepper said "he apprehended him to be Governour Rogers and Captain Stibbs, for whom he had a brace of pistolls ready charged, whenever they came". On receipt of this information the lieutenant returned to the *Adventure* and reported to his commanding officer that he did not consider any useful purpose would be served by remaining in the river.[3]

---

[1] *Ibid.*

[2] Robert MacCarthy, Viscount Muskerry and titular Earl of Clancarty, was son of a Jacobite Irish peer, but entered the British navy and was Governor of Newfoundland, 1733-1735. After having made an unsuccessful attempt to recover the family estates, which his father had forfeited in 1690, he left the navy, went over to France, and devoted himself to the Stuart cause. He died in 1769. Sir Charles MacCarthy (1770-1824), who was responsible for the re-occupation of the Gambia in 1816, came of the same family.

[3] Minutes of Council of James Fort, 6 October 1729, Rawlinson MS. c. 747; Log of H.M.S. *Adventure*, P.R.O., Ad. 51/12.

Lord Muskerry was about to weigh anchor when the African Company's ship *Bonetta* hove in sight. She had on board Anthony Rogers, whom the Company had re-appointed as Governor, and Bartholomew Stibbs, the third chief merchant. Lord Muskerry spoke the *Bonetta* and informed the new Governor of the extraordinary reception which had been accorded to his lieutenant. As he anticipated further trouble when the *Bonetta* reached James Island, he embarked with a number of his officers and men on that vessel so as to be ready to render assistance in case of need. Pepper did not, however, give Rogers the reception which he had promised. He had wasted all his powder in firing at passing canoes and had been compelled to borrow from the French at Albreda. Apparently almost the last charge of this borrowed powder had been expended upon the reception given to the *Adventure's* barge. When Rogers landed he found there was no powder at all in the fort and gladly accepted the offer of Lord Muskerry to supply him with fifteen barrels.[1]

Lord Muskerry stayed at the fort for four days. Rogers was very much perturbed that he was unable to entertain the son of a peer of the realm fittingly, "considering the confusion and ill state we found the fort in", but gratefully acknowledged the assistance he had rendered in enabling him to effect a peaceable entry into the fort. When therefore Lord Muskerry announced his intention of returning to his ship, he ordered the Company's sloop *Dispatch* to be made ready to convey him to the river's mouth. Rogers, Captain Livingstone of the *Bonetta*, and the chief French factor at Albreda accompanied his lordship to the *Adventure*. After having received some hospitality on board the man-of-war, Rogers ordered the *Dispatch* to make ready to return to James Island. Captain Henry Smith, the commander of the *Dispatch*, had also partaken of the navy's hospitality and was decidedly the worse for liquor. When Rogers ordered him to weigh anchor, he refused point blank to do so. Rogers then gave him a written order to weigh. Smith "did not only refuse the same order in writing to proceed to the fort, but did in the most mutinous manner make several attempts to gett at the arms, cursing and swearing that he would shoot that man, that would offer to weigh the anchor or obey any orders but his; but,

---

[1] Minutes of Council of James Fort, 10 October 1729, Rawlinson MS. c. 747; Log of H.M.S. *Adventure*, P.R.O., Ad. 51/12; Rogers to R.A.C., 10 October 1729, P.R.O., T. 70/7.

being prevented in the attempt, he then fell upon the governour, collared him and in the most scandalous manner grossely abused him without the least regard to the French governour's being there; and, not being content with this usage to the governour, behaved in the same manner to Captain Livingstone, who then had the governour's orders to take upon him the charge of the sloop; whereupon he not only denied any power of authority the governour or Company had over him or his sloop, but publickly avowed revenge and threatned to run away with the sloop, for he then had, as he said, more than three hundred pounds sterling on board, and that he would not lye within reach of the fort's gunns".[1]

Fortunately Livingstone was able to control the crew and the party got back to James Island. Smith was duly hailed before the Council the next day and asked to explain his conduct. He replied that "he did not fear anything that we could do, alledgeing he could justify everything he did except the personal abuse of the governour, for which he said he was sorry for, and that he was in liquor, but insisting then, when sober, that the governour or Company had not the power to act by him as he, the governour, did". The inevitable result of this speech was that Smith was deprived of the command of the sloop.[2]

Smith's conduct made it clear that some of the Europeans on James Island were in a very ugly mood and that further trouble was likely to arise. Following upon the incident on board the *Dispatch* reports were received from a French private trader named Lemaigre that Smith had been embezzling the Company's property and that Pepper was privy to such embezzlement.[3] It was also clear that Pepper had a number of allies amongst the old hands, who were determined to do everything they could to flout and undermine the authority of the new Governor, but matters came to a head in an unexpected manner and with unexpected rapidity.

On 14 October Roger Gillingham and William Roberts, two of Pepper's particular cronies, were having a bowl of punch in company with David Willson. Gillingham and Roberts began to grumble saying they had had nothing to eat for supper. Gillingham suddenly said "Come, let us take the fort" and Roberts rejoined "With all my heart". As Willson believed that these words were uttered "out

---

[1] Minutes of Council of James Fort, 16 October 1729, Rawlinson MS. c. 747; Anthony Rogers to R.A.C., 6 April 1730, P.R.O., T. 70/4.
    [2] *Ibid.*   [3] *Ibid.*

of such a merry, jocose temper", he said nothing more than "Pray, gentlemen, don't talk so foolish, for you will have somebody hear you". The conversation then turned to other topics and Willson attached no significance to the remarks he had heard.[1]

Two days later in the afternoon Gillingham entered the apartment, which Willson shared with a newly appointed writer, named Andrew Rutherford, and said to Willson, "What sort of a cock is the gentleman that lies in the room with you?" Willson replied, "Why, what do you want with him?" Gillingham did not reply but went in search of Rutherford. When he found him, he took him outside the gate and asked him whether he liked the country or wanted to go home. Rutherford replied "that I did not know, that I believed that governour Rogers would not hinder me, if I was no use to him, and that I could go in any ship". Gillingham informed Rutherford that, "if I had a mind, he knew of a gentleman that would supply me with one that was worth three or four hundred pounds and that he and three or four more were designed to leave the factory, but he desired me to say nothing of it".[2]

The factors and writers assembled together for supper that evening. "They were all at table and was very uneasy for want of something to eat at supper." After an unsatisfying meal a number of them adjourned to Crossley Middlemore's apartment to console themselves with a bowl of punch. Amongst them was William Lloyd, the factor at Juffure, with whom Pepper had shared in a number of drinking bouts on the mainland. The talk in Middlemore's room returned to the topic of food. Lloyd started up and exclaimed, "Damn it, let's take the fort for some victuals. We live more like beasts than gentlemen." A few moments later Gillingham burst into the room, said the Governor had ordered him to hand over his keys to Thomas Saxby, and shouted out "Damn me, if I will be used ill by anybody. It is not justice for one to be chose third merchant, who has never given security, nor the Company never saw." Lloyd and Roberts at once swore in good round oaths that the keys would not be handed over to Saxby. One or two of the milder spirits proposed that a deputation should be organised to wait on the Governor to protest against this and other similar treatment, but Roberts, Lloyd, and Gillingham would have none of it. The more peaceable members of the party realised that the meeting was getting noisy

---

[1] Minutes of Council of James Fort, 17 October 1729, Rawlinson MS. c. 747.
[2] Ibid.

and that the conversation was growing dangerous. They therefore withdrew one by one from the room.[1]

Andrew Rutherford was one of the first to leave. Outside the room he met David Willson and said, "I am glad you are from amongst them gentlemen, for they make such a noise they will be taken notice of". Willson replied, "I wish they may have no ill design, for I heard Mr Roberts saying they would take a factory over the water and I believe they will surprise the fort". Rutherford said, "I do not think they have such a design, nor do I think it practicable, should they attempt it". But, following as it did upon his conversation with Gillingham, Willson's information caused Rutherford some uneasiness. He therefore went in search of Gillingham and found him with Pepper, Lloyd, and Roberts on one of the bastions. He called Gillingham aside and told him, "I am afraid you will injure yourself by talking at the rate you do", and, after telling him what Willson had told him, asked him what he designed to do. Gillingham said, "We will not endure the usage we have". Rutherford again asked him what his designs were. Gillingham then said, "We will blow up the long room. We have long since laid a scheme to do it. Mr Pepper, Mr Lloyd, and Mr Roberts are the persons. The cooper, serjeant, and gunner with all the old standers will stand by us." Rutherford then said their proposal was a dangerous one and asked what reason they had. Gillingham said, "Mr Rogers did use to whip his people and put them in irons and throw them amongst the slaves", and then, growing suspicious of his questioner, "suddenly gave it this turn, that they would put the design in execution, if Mr Rogers use them ill". Rutherford at once went to look for the Governor.[2]

William Blackstone had also become alarmed at the turn the conversation had taken and had communicated his fears to James Davis. The latter went to the bastion, where Pepper and his companions were, and overheard Pepper saying he had pistols to execute the design. He at once went to look for Captain Stibbs. James Conner, a newly appointed writer, who believed that Pepper and his companions had merely spoken idle words in liquor, went and told them what Davis was doing. Pepper announced, "If we meet Mr Davis ashore, we will make a spread eagle of him". Davis had in the meantime informed the Governor and Captain Stibbs, who went to

[1] *Ibid.*   [2] *Ibid.*

search the suspects' apartments, whilst Davis kept watch on them on the north bastion. Davis saw Pepper slap his hand upon his breast and heard him say, "The Governor is affrighted out of his wits and afraid of his life, but I have pistols and we can still execute our design". Roberts then exclaimed, "Have you, by God? Then we will do it." Lloyd, who was apparently very drunk indeed, said, "We had better die like lions than live like beasts".[1]

Apparently nothing incriminating was found in the apartments of any of the suspects, but Rogers decided as a measure of precaution to place all four of them under close arrest. Next day statements were obtained from a number of the officers and each of the four suspects was brought in front of the Council singly. The statements were read to them and they were each asked separately if they could clear themselves of the charge of conspiracy. Lloyd appears to have been very scared indeed. He owned that "he was very much in liquor and appeared very much concerned for what had past (sic) and with greatest submission begged pardon". As he had only come to the fort from Juffure a few hours before the conversation took place, he was acquitted of having participated in the conspiracy, received a severe reprimand, was ordered to return at once to Juffure, and informed "that his future conduct should determine our resolutions".[2] His death two months later solved all problems as to his future retention in the Company's service.[3]

The other three suspects "all pretended ignorance as to any designed conspiracy, that if any such words or actions passed as the informations specifyed, they said it was the effects of liquor, but all of them (Mr Lloyd excepted) appearing not in the least concerned nor any ways desirous of being forgiven". All except Pepper admitted that they had been talking together, but alleged "it was of things indifferent". Pepper categorically denied everything and "declared further it was a designed contrivance to ruin his character, promising himself to be revenged of the authors, whenever opportunity offered".[4]

The Council found the charge of conspiracy proved against Pepper, Roberts, and Gillingham. They ordered that the two latter "be lodged without the gates separate, one in the tradesmen's, and one in the soldiers' barracks, with strickt orders they have no conversation

[1] Minutes of Council of James Fort, 17 October 1729, Rawlinson MS. c. 747.
[2] *Ibid.*   [3] Nominal Rolls of James Island, P.R.O., T. 70/1447, f. 24.
[4] Minutes of Council of James Fort, 17 October 1729, Rawlinson MS. c. 747.

with each other, their (*sic*) to continue till the first opportunity offer to send them home to England, unless we find great probability of amendment".[1] Gillingham was sent a month later to Cape Coast Castle.[2] Roberts was allowed to remain in the Gambia until 1732, when further misconduct on his part made the Governor inform him that "we look upon you as a lost man, and one (whilst you continue that insatiable thirst after liquor) incapable of rendring the Company any service", and ordered him to return to England.[3]

Different treatment had to be meted out to Pepper. He had not yet handed over the Company's effects to Rogers or submitted any accounts. It was therefore decided that he "be allowed liberty in the day time to join with governour and Captain Stibbs to finish the survey of goods, stores, etc.", but "that in the night time he be under arrest to prevent further mischief either to himself or other people". He was allowed until 21 October to deliver up his books of accounts and, pending such delivery, his future disposal was to remain in abeyance.[4] 21 October came and the books of accounts were not forthcoming. Pepper was allowed further time and still did not comply with orders. Eventually it transpired that he had destroyed a number of documents, tried to persuade a private trader to give him a false voucher for some ivory, which he had embezzled, and had made a number of entries, which were proved by reliable witnesses to be false. Not only that, but whilst under arrest, he was guilty of "ill treatment to the country traders, when they came to the fort, wounding one with a sword, Senor Alexander Jelloiff, and his ridiculing in a publick manner the governour and councill, and threatning to be revenged upon them in a very desperate manner, which caused a general dissatisfaction even among the natives and traders, insomuch that they publickly declared, if he was not removed from the fort, that they should think themselves not safe, when they came and while he continued on".[5] It was therefore decided that in the public interest any attempt at making him go through the formality of handing over should be dispensed with and that he should be sent back to England by the first available ship.[6]

---

[1] *Ibid.*
[2] Nominal Rolls of James Island, P.R.O., T. 70/1447, f. 24.
[3] Moore, *Travels into the Inland Parts of Africa*, pp. 104, 105.
[4] Minutes of Council of James Fort, 17 October 1729, Rawlinson MS. c. 747.
[5] Minutes of Council of James Fort, 22 November 1729, Rawlinson MS. c. 747.   [6] *Ibid.*

On his arrival home he disappeared and later took service with a private trader on the Gold Coast.[1] The African Company never recovered his ill-gotten gains or managed to call him to account for his innumerable misdeeds.

There can be no doubt that Pepper was a desperate and a dangerous man, who was determined to raise up trouble and to go to almost any length to effect his ends. But how far he had managed to induce his brother officers to enter into a conspiracy with him must remain a matter of some doubt. The judges in the proceedings before the Council at James Fort were also the accusers. The evidence of some of the subordinate officers may for certain reasons have been in a measure coloured. Putting it at its strongest, there is room for doubt whether the utterances of Roberts were not idle drunken words. Gillingham would appear to have been more deeply incriminated, but to what extent must be doubtful. None the less, it is clear that there was a spirit of grave discontent brewing, and in the confined conditions existing on James Island the constant airing of real or fancied grievances by a number of drunken malcontents might have led to a very serious situation indeed. Memories of the mutiny of the soldiers in 1721 and of the explosion in 1725 were all too recent. What had at first been mere idle words might by constant repetition have come to be uttered in all seriousness. The mutiny of 1729 may have only been in a state of embryo but there can be no doubt that it would inevitably at some time have broken out but for Rogers' prompt action.

As the correspondence of the African Company and Francis Moore's *Travels into the Inland Parts of Africa* show, the African Company had by no means rid themselves of dishonest, insubordinate, and incompetent servants in the Gambia, but, as the same records show, the years immediately following the dismissal of Pepper were the most prosperous of all the years of the Company's rule in those regions. Rogers undoubtedly had his faults. As Moore's book and the Company's records show, he was a hard task-master and not an easy man with whom to work. It was subsequently alleged that he had been guilty of falsification of his books and that he had indulged in private trade with a certain Senhora Angela, but the information comes from his successor, Richard Hull, with whom, as mentioned on a previous page,[2] he had formerly had a violent quarrel and must

---

[1] R.A.C. to Rogers, 30 July 1730, P.R.O., T. 70/55.   [2] P. 195.

therefore be taken with some measure of caution.[1] It is quite possible that his standard of commercial morality was no higher than that of his times, but it is very evident that he did a great deal to promote his employers' interests and that under his administration the affairs of the Company prospered. During his governorship a very large number of out-factories were established on the river banks even as high as Fattatenda. Efforts were also made to encourage the planting of economic crops by the local inhabitants.[2] The Company's trade was also developed along the coast. Sloops were sent to Portuguese Guinea and the Casamance as well as to Portudal. Relations with the French were on the whole satisfactory. As the French were anxious to retain their foothold at Albreda for the purposes of the slave trade, they did not interfere with the Company's ships in their trade between Cape Verde and the River Gambia.[3]

Rogers was recalled by a letter dated 7 February 1733 because of the number of irregularities appearing in his accounts.[4] It does not appear that he was proved guilty of actual embezzlement, but it would appear that he had been secretly indulging in private trade to the prejudice of his employers.[5] He was succeeded by Richard Hull.[6] Though Hull had a good deal to write about Rogers' mismanagement, it is clear that he found the Company's affairs in the Gambia in a more prosperous condition than they had been for over fifty years. This prosperity continued under Hull's own management. Hull died on 16 January 1737[7] and was succeeded by Charles Orfeur.

Orfeur had been twenty-one years in the Company's service at the time of his appointment to the chief post in the Gambia. He was to

---

[1] Richard Hull to R.A.C., 11 July 1733 and 5 December 1734, P.R.O., T. 70/4; R.A.C. to Hull, 4 July and 2 November 1734, P.R.O., T. 70/55.

[2] Rogers to R.A.C., 10 June 1731 and 2 February 1732, P.R.O., T. 70/7. Agreement dated 7 July 1730, with Joseph Bick, citizen and chandler of London, to serve three years in the River Gambia and "to use his best endeavours to refine all such beeswax as he shall receive" and to send samples to England, Agreements of R.A.C., P.R.O., T. 70/1423, ff. 265, 266.

[3] Rogers to R.A.C., 2 April 1731, 25 April and 20 June 1732, P.R.O., T. 70/7; Letters received by R.A.C., September 1731 and 13 May 1732, P.R.O., T. 70/1447.

[4] P.R.O., T. 70/55.

[5] R.A.C. to Richard Hull, 7 November 1734, P.R.O., T. 70/55.

[6] Agreements of R.A.C., 25 January 1733, P.R.O., T. 70/1423.

[7] R.A.C. to Charles Orfeur, 29 September 1737, P.R.O., T. 70/55.

remain in that service another eight years.[1] During the whole of that period he had only one short spell of absence in England. He had from time to time been unfavourably reported upon by his superiors, but, as other incidents mentioned on previous pages and his general record show, he was a very loyal servant. Though under his administration the fortunes of the Company in the Gambia began to decline, the reason for this cannot be attributed to him.

During the fifteen years following the suppression of Pepper's abortive conspiracy in 1729 there was little of great moment which happened in the River Gambia. As Moore's *Travels* and the Company's correspondence show, there were occasions when factors, writers, and others grossly misconducted themselves and even went so far as to threaten violence to their superiors. But these were isolated acts and the majority of the Company's servants appear to have conducted themselves reasonably well. There was occasional trouble with the natives but nothing which developed to any serious proportions. Great Britain and France were at peace and the relations between their respective subjects in West Africa were quite friendly. When, for instance, on the night of 17 November 1780 the factory at Albreda caught fire, the Governor and twelve soldiers from James Island went over promptly to render what assistance they could.[2]

After being expelled from Bintang by Plunkett in 1724, the French confined themselves to Albreda. They also confined themselves there almost entirely to the slave trade and found great difficulty in competing therein with the African Company and the English private trader. On 14 May 1740 Orfeur entered into an agreement with Peter Felix David, Director and Commandant-General in Senegal for the French East Indies Company, whereby the English Company agreed to deliver yearly 100 prime slaves at Albreda in exchange for an annual supply of 360,000 pounds of gum. The agreement, which was to last for ten years, attempted to provide for neutrality in the event of war between the two countries. The English Company were to endeavour to obtain a safe conduct for the French Company's ships whilst in the River Gambia "so that the said ships be not sett upon by any English ships, while they are staying there to unload,

---

[1] Orfeur was not in charge during the whole of this period, but the intervening periods, during which other governors sent out from England were in charge, were so brief that he may be said to have been virtually in charge from 1737 to 1745.   [2] Moore, *op. cit.* p. 51.

and be it not allowed them even to follow them till twenty-four hours after they have passed the broken islands going out of the said river ". If the English Company were unable to obtain this safe conduct, the French were not to be required to deliver the gum at James Fort, "but the Company of England must be furnished with the gum by other means that shall be agreed by the Companies ".[1] This agreement was approved in advance by the African Company.[2] It worked on the whole satisfactorily. Deliveries from the French did not quite come up to the annually stipulated quantities[3] and it was also alleged that the French entered into the slave trade in the River Gambia in violation of their agreement,[4] but it would appear that the English Company failed in their turn to supply the stipulated number of slaves. The result of the contract was that the English were enabled to establish a factory at Portendic.[5] The agreement was observed by both parties even after their respective countries had in 1743 taken opposite sides in the War of the Austrian Succession.[6]

The African Company's anxiety to secure the gum trade led to a renewal of their attempts to explore the interior of the continent with the hope of discovering the gum forests and diverting the traffic to the Gambia.[7] John Hall was sent up the Bintang Creek above Geregia in 1733 and reported that the country could produce a quantity of cotton, hides, and indigo as well as gum.[8] In 1735 an exceptional opportunity presented itself for endeavouring to explore the country lying at the head-waters of the Senegal and to discover the gum forests.

In 1731 a Fula of Bondu, who is commonly referred to in contemporary records as Job ben Solomon, but whose real name was Job Jallo, was kidnapped by some Mandingos on the banks of the Gambia near Joar and sold as a slave to a private trader, who carried him to Maryland. He was a Mohammedan, and during his captivity his devout observance of the rites of his religion attracted the attention

[1] Agreements of R.A.C., P.R.O., T. 70/1424, ff. 174–176.
[2] R.A.C. to Orfeur, 18 March 1740, P.R.O., T. 70/56.
[3] Letters received by R.A.C., P.R.O., T. 70/1514.
[4] Roberts, "An Account of the First Establishments on that part of the Coast of Africa called Guinea", P.R.O., C.O. 267/5.
[5] Moore, *op. cit.* p. 211.
[6] Charles Orfeur to R.A.C., 25 June 1743, P.R.O., T. 70/4.
[7] Moore, *op. cit.* pp. 209–212, 217, App. IV, pp. 18–20.
[8] *Ibid.* App. IV, p. 18.

of a number of benevolent Marylanders. Eventually through the good offices of General Oglethorpe he procured his release and was sent over to England.[1] On 27 December 1733 the African Company granted him formal letters of manumission and liberty to proceed to Africa in one of their ships.[2] On 4 July 1734 the same Company wrote to Richard Hull regarding Job in the following terms:

We do earnestly recommend it to you to use him kindly while he stays and to take particular care that none of his things be lost or imbezzled; and when the season comes for sending him up the river, we desire he may be sent up with all his things to such of our factorys in the river as lye nearest and most convenient for him to get to his own country under the care of such a person as you can confide in....If the person you should send up river with him should be willing to accompany him into his own country, possibly he might by that means be able to do the Company good service by opening and settling a trade and correspondence between the natives of those parts and our highest factorys.[3]

Originally Richard Hull proposed to make the journey to Bondu in company with Job, but was prevented from doing so owing to the dry season, the scarcity of water, and the fact that the other more urgent affairs of the Company had to receive his attention.[4] Job eventually set out in 1736 in company with the Governor's kinsman, Thomas Hull.[5] This latter kept a diary of his journey, which is, however, apparently no longer extant. The following letter from the African Company to Richard Hull indicates what became of it and the probable nature of its contents:

We received Mr Thomas Hull's diary of his progress with Job to Boonda, his stay there, and his return from thence; and, as His Grace the Duke of Montague[6] *was informed of such a diary having been brought over, his curiosity induced him to desire to see it, with which we readily complied, but were obliged to order the best excuse we could to be*

[1] Bluet, *Some Memoirs of the Life of Job*, pp. 1–31.
[2] Agreements of R.A.C., P.R.O., T. 70/1424, f. 18.
[3] P.R.O., T. 70/55.
[4] Moore, *op. cit.* pp. 223–225, 230, 231, App. IV, p. 19.
[5] R.A.C. to Richard Hull, 13 January 1737, P.R.O., T. 70/53.
[6] John, second Duke of Montagu (1688–1749), had interested himself in Job whilst he was in England. A letter, which was sent by Job to the Duke by Francis Moore and is dated 5 April 1735, is to be found in the Buccleuch manuscripts, *Hist. MSS. Comm. Rep., Buccleuch MSS.* p. 385.

made for the brevity and other defects of that diary. We were concerned
to see it barren of the usefull observations and remarks that might un-
doubtedly have been made by Mr Thomas Hull during the long time of
his residing there, but we must impute that defect to his youth and in-
experience. We observe you have sent him on another progress to
Bambou(k) and Nettico; and, as we doubt not but you have given him
proper and full instructions for his conduct therein, we hope his diary
of that progress will give us more satisfaction; and, according as he
behaves, we shall be glad to give him suitable encouragement.[1]

Job sent two letters to England to the African Company to thank
them for the assistance, which their servants had rendered to him.
These letters were in Arabic script and were handed over for trans-
lation to a certain Melchior de Jaspas, "an Armenian, native of
Diarbekir, the capital city of Mesopotamia". It was ascertained
that this interpreter was well acquainted with the Arabic of Job's
country and "is capable of learning any language in a short time".
It was therefore thought that he might be a useful person to the
Company in promoting trade between the Gambia and the interior.
He was therefore engaged as an "assistant to be employed by our
chief merchant or agents for the time being at James Fort, Gambia,
for carrying on and improving our inland trade up the River Gambia,
to reside at Boonda or such other place inland as our chief merchant
or agents shall judge most proper". He was accompanied by a
Persian boy slave, named Joseph, and James Anderson, who, "besides other languages, understands and writes French very well and
is very desirous of accompanying Mr de Jaspas into the inland countries and be assisting in making discoveries". De Jaspas was also
given presents to take to Job and the "king" of Bondu as well as
a letter to the former asking for his assistance in the promotion of
trade.[2]

Nothing much came of the appointment of de Jaspas. He did not
get on with the Company's servants on the spot and reports reached
England that he "has mett with most inhumane treatment from
several persons at James Fort". Eventually he, at his own request,
was discharged from the Company's service, which led the Company

---

[1] R.A.C. to Richard Hull, 19 May 1737, P.R.O., T. 70/55.
[2] *Ibid.*; R.A.C. to "Mr Job at Boonda in Africa", 19 May 1737, P.R.O.,
T. 70/56; Warrant to de Jaspas dated 12 May 1737, P.R.O., T. 70/1424, f. 55;
Nominal Rolls of Gambia, P.R.O., T. 70/1447, f. 85.

to inform their chief merchant that, "had he but received at James Fort the treatment in general that is required and ought to be expected from persons supposed to be civilised, though residing in a barbarous country, allowances might have been made for any defects on his part". They further declared that, if de Jaspas had returned to James Fort, "we hope you that were there have had the discretion to receive him back again into the Company's service and to treat him kindly".[1]

A Mandingo-speaking Fula named Lahamin Jay had been kidnapped and carried to Maryland along with Job.[2] After his release from captivity Job wrote to the Duke of Montagu asking him to procure the release of his companion.[3] Through the Duke's good offices Lahamin was redeemed and was sent by the African Company in 1738 to the Gambia.[4] When he arrived, de Jaspas had just returned to the Company's service and it was decided to send him with Lahamin to Bondu. De Jaspas came back thence in 1740 with Job, who received a very warm welcome at James Fort and was given a number of presents before he returned together with de Jaspas to his own country. No material advantage was derived by the Company from these visits to Bondu. With a blissful ignorance of geography and the physical difficulties of such an undertaking, the authorities in England then suggested that de Jaspas should be despatched with a European officer to find a way to Cape Coast. That recommendation was never carried out. In 1744 de Jaspas undertook a journey overland to Cachau in Portuguese Guinea. After that date the Company's records are silent concerning him.[5] The only outward and visible sign of any promotion of the Company's trade by reason of these journeys was an agreement of doubtful value, which de Jaspas concluded with Haji il Mouctari, marabout of "Portobar", "in the noble college of religion" and "the sinful servant of God", on behalf of "Habibila of the family of Portobar, an university in the kingdom of Gannara". By this agreement Habibila purported to guarantee to the Royal African Com-

[1] R.A.C. to Asher Levy, 16 March 1738 and R.A.C. to Charles Orfeur, 22 March 1739, P.R.O., T. 70/56.

[2] Bluet, op. cit. pp. 29–31.

[3] Job ben Solomon to Duke of Montagu, 5 April 1735, Duke of Montagu to Job, 16 April 1736, Hist. MSS. Comm. Rep., Buccleuch MSS. p. 383.

[4] R.A.C. to Charles Orfeur, 2 February 1738, P.R.O., T. 70/56.

[5] Charles Orfeur to R.A.C., 19 June 1740; P.R.O., T. 70/4; R.A.C. to Charles Orfeur, 18 March 1740, 26 March 1742 and 11 October 1744, P.R.O., T. 70/56.

pany the exclusive right to all gum exported from his country and
to deliver at Colar at the head of Jawarra Creek.[1]

In 1743 war broke out between Great Britain and France. The
rival companies of the two respective nations were anxious to create
a neutral zone in Africa. The English Company approached the Duke
of Newcastle on the subject,[2] but nothing came of the proposal. In
1745 H.M.S. *Sutherland* and *Gosport* arrived at the mouth of the
river convoying a number of merchant vessels. They captured a
French sloop bound from Albreda to Goree off the mouth of the
river on 20 May. After seeing their convoy into the river they proceeded to the mouth of the Senegal but did not attack St Louis. On
7 June they returned to the Gambia and nine days later sent their
prize, a long boat and a barge with 100 men to destroy the French
factory at Albreda. The French factors had been forewarned and
escaped, but the factory was destroyed and the goods handed
over to the Governor at James Fort. The French made no attempt
to reoccupy the place until 1748 after the Treaty of Aix-la-
Chapelle.[3]

Before this last-mentioned date Charles Orfeur's career had ended.
No details of the incident are forthcoming, but he was murdered in
1745 on the mainland by certain subjects of the "king" of Barra.[4]
On 8 December 1737 the Company had felt constrained to inform
him that his letters were "so triffling, short, and unlike persons bred
to any business, that we cannot but be dissatisfyed with such a
highly loose and careless way of correspondence",[5] but seven years
later they showed what was for them unusual appreciation of long
and loyal service by granting him an addition to his salary of £100
per annum.[6] The records of the Company show that he undoubtedly
had his failings and his faults, but he had stuck loyally to his post
in 1718 and had proved his fidelity on numerous other occasions
during his thirty years of service. With him disappeared almost the

---

[1] Agreement dated 11 January 1742, P.R.O., T. 70/1424, f. 196.

[2] R. Spence to Thomas Corbett, 10 December 1744, P.R.O., Ad. 1/3810.

[3] Log of H.M.S. *Sutherland*, P.R.O., Ad. 51/951; Log of H.M.S. *Gosport*,
P.R.O., Ad. 51/400; Roberts, "An Account of the First Establishments on that
part of the Coast of Africa called Guinea", P.R.O., C.O. 267/5; Cultru,
Histoire du Sénégal, p. 199.

[4] R.A.C. to James Conner, 11 December 1746, P.R.O., T. 70/56; Joseph
Debat to Secretary of State, 26 February 1766, P.R.O., C.O. 267/13.

[5] P.R.O., T. 70/56.

[6] R.A.C. to Orfeur, 11 October 1744, P.R.O., T. 70/56.

last of a school of colonial servants, who with all their shortcomings had proved themselves men and who for little reward had served their masters often under the most trying conditions with a fidelity which was not always appreciated at its true worth. Though the Gambia was to remain under the control of the African Company for another five years, Orfeur's death virtually marks the close of one epoch of British administration in West Africa.

XV: The African Committee's Administration, 1750–1765

Except for the destruction of the French factory at Albreda there were no warlike operations in the regions of the Gambia during the War of the Austrian Succession. None the less that war had a disastrous effect upon the affairs of the African Company. Communication between Africa and England became precarious. Ships had to be despatched under naval convoy at rare intervals.[1] Even before the outbreak of war returns had begun to fall off. War conditions accentuated the Company's financial difficulties and recourse was had to very questionable means in an endeavour to retrieve the situation. From 1730 the Company had been assisted by an annual parliamentary grant for the maintenance and upkeep of their forts.[2] The enemies of the Company asserted that this money was not used for the purpose for which it was allocated, but was employed in the purchase of goods for the purposes of trade and that in the case of James Fort the accounts which were submitted were largely fictitious.[3] The accounts of James Island as submitted to Parliament during that period are still extant[4] and were passed annually by the House of Commons.[5] They show that items were debited against the vote, which in strictness ought not to have been so debited, were passed without surcharge, but they do not suggest that there was any actual falsification. Parliament, or more probably the Treasury examiners, who reported on the accounts to Parliament, evidently regarded the vote in the light of a subsidy to enable a public corporation to keep going and had no particular desire to scrutinise its expenditure too closely. But public opinion looked on this mode of audit with disfavour and under its influence the House of Commons refused to renew the grant in 1747.

Other practices of the African Company were certainly far more open to reprobation. Some of the methods adopted to evade seizure

[1] R. Spence to Thomas Corbett, 4 April, 20 September, 16 and 25 October, and 10 December 1744, P.R.O., Ad. 1/3810.

[2] Astley, *A New General Collection of Voyages and Travels*, II, 160.

[3] *A Detection of the Royal African Company* (1749), p. 11.

[4] P.R.O., T. 70/1451 and 1452.

[5] *Calendar of Treasury Books*, 1731–1734, p. 568; 1735–1738, p. 441; 1742–1745, pp. 5 and 451.

of the Company's property by its creditors can only be described as absolutely dishonest. The Company stands convicted in one instance at least on the clearest possible documentary evidence furnished by itself. In 1746 a quantity of gum, ivory, and beeswax was shipped in the Gambia on board two hired vessels, the *Loyal Judith* and the *Expedition*. Instead of consigning this cargo to England it was shipped to Cape Coast Castle, where on instructions from the Company in London it was transhipped on board of a man-of-war under a bill of lading in favour of the Company's nominee, James Goddard, merchant of London.[1]

When the Company was thus reduced to such straits in order to evade its creditors, it is not surprising to find that it had the greatest possible difficulty in stocking its forts and factories with trade goods. The inevitable result was that its commerce declined. The Gambia was perhaps more hard hit than the forts and factories farther down the coast. Up to 1744 the trade in the river had been relatively prosperous. In that year there were still six outfactories on the river banks.[2] But in 1749 Captain Pye of H.M.S. *Humber* had a very different tale to tell. He subsequently reported that he found James Island "in a most miserable condition, the people in a melancholy situation for want of goods to carry on a trade for the support of their garrison, not having had any supplies for upwards of five years past and not being allowed to trade for themselves—the consequence of which was they were obliged to call in their outfactors on the continent, which were many, and, if properly supplied, one of the best branches of trade on the coast for wax, slaves, teeth, and gold, but by being so long neglected the chief trade is gone down the River Senegal to the French factory".[3]

A merchant, who visited James Island in 1750, reported that at that date in the garrison "so great a mortality had taken place that they were reduced to five or eight, by which means a common soldier had succeeded to the command of the troops. The garrison had consisted of a company of from twenty-five to thirty men. I had also the opportunity of remarking the very sickly appearance of all the Europeans, both French and English, who were most of them labouring under fluxes or fevers, but chiefly the former, insomuch

---

[1] *A Detection of the Royal African Company* (1749), p. 17; Agreement, dated 26 December 1745, between R.A.C. and James Goddard, P.R.O., T. 70/1424.
[2] *Calendar of Treasury Books*, 1742–1745, p. 451.
[3] *Commons' Journals*, XXVIII, 274.

that I did not see above two persons apparently in health appearing in the character of gentlemen or officers. The accounts given of the unhealthiness of the climate to the captain of the ship, in which I was, induced him to give orders that no person should sleep ashore in the fort".[1]

Eventually the Company's affairs were reduced to so parlous a state that they found themselves in Chancery and their secretary in prison. It became evident that, unless Parliament stepped in, the British trader in West Africa might find himself driven out by foreign competitors and a valuable source of commerce might be lost not only to Great Britain but also to the American and West Indian colonies. The Council of Trade was therefore instructed to evolve a scheme for the reorganisation of the African trade. In 1750 an Act of Parliament[2] was passed creating a regulated "Company of Merchants trading to Africa". By means of this new body "it was hoped to avoid both the monopolistic tendencies of rule by a joint-stock company, and the expense of government by officers commissioned and paid by the Crown".[3] The details of the new organisation need not be discussed here at any length. The principal characteristics, in which the new company differed from any of its predecessors, was that the Company was prohibited from all trading in its corporate capacity. The affairs of the Company were to be controlled by an executive committee comprising nine members chosen from the merchants of London, Liverpool, and Bristol, who were likewise prohibited from trading during their period of office. The income of the Company was to be derived from the fee of forty shillings payable by each member thereof and an annual grant from Parliament for the upkeep of the forts. The committee were empowered to make regulations for the better carrying on of the African trade, provided they should not "tend to lay any restraint whatsoever" upon persons trading to the coast. Provision was also made in the Act for the removal by the Commissioners of Trade of any member of the committee, who was guilty of misbehaviour, for the annual submission of the Company's accounts to the Exchequer, and for the submission to Parliament of all orders and

[1] Evidence of Mr Call, Minutes of a Committee...respecting a Plan for transporting Felons (1787), P.R.O., H.O. 7/1, ff. 43, 44; *Commons' Journals*, XL, 958.

[2] 23 Geo. II, c. 31.

[3] Martin, *The British West African Settlements*, 1750–1821, p. ix.

regulations made by the committee under the powers conferred by the Act.[1]

As the claims of the Royal African Company's creditors had still to be examined and satisfied, it was not found possible at once to divest the old company of its property in Africa and to transfer it to the new company. The investigation of those claims took a long time and it was not until 1752 that an Act[2] could be passed formally divesting the old company of its charter. In the meantime the two companies existed side by side. The members of the old organisation were not predisposed to be helpful and administrative action by the members of the new organisation was hampered by a section in the Act of 1750,[3] which enacted that they should act in all matters concerning the forts and garrisons in Africa "so far as the said African Company shall assent". A grant of £10,000 from Parliament had enabled the new company to purchase necessary stores and goods for the forts and garrisons in Africa. Two ships were chartered to carry these stores to the Gambia and Cape Coast Castle, but the old company refused to confirm the appointments of the officers, who had been selected by the new company for their disposal. The ships were unable to sail. An appeal was made to the Council of Trade, who declined to intervene as the new company's control could only become operative after the dissolution of the old company. Petitions were addressed to Parliament on 25 March 1751, and 10 April 1752, but it was not until the passing of the divesting Act in 1752 that the new company was able to work with a free hand.[4]

The result of this dual control was particularly disastrous in the Gambia. As mentioned on a previous page, the old company's affairs in those regions were in a very parlous state. Their officers were being gradually diminished in numbers by sickness and death and they almost entirely lacked the means wherewith to carry on trade. The Treaty of Aix-la-Chapelle had not attempted to deal with Anglo-French disputes in West Africa. The French seized the opportunity to re-establish themselves at Albreda and to make a very determined effort to capture the entire trade of the river. Messieurs de la Brue, Director-General of the French East India Company, de Saint Jean, Governor of Goree, and Michel Adanson arrived in the river on 20 February 1750 and stayed there till 12 March.[5]

[1] Martin, op. cit. pp. 9–13.   [2] 25 Geo. II, c. 40.
[3] 23 Geo. II, c. 31, s. 5.   [4] Commons' Journals, xxvi, 146.
[5] Adanson, A Voyage to Senegal, pp. 156, 174.

During that time they were able to arrange with the "king" of Barra to resettle Albreda.[1]

After the departure of de Brue and his colleagues the French agent at Albreda crossed over to James Island ostensibly to pay a complimentary visit to John Gootheridge, the Governor, but in reality to spy out the nakedness of the land. As Gootheridge's successors subsequently reported, "we...must say that Mr Gootheridge was very much to blame for allowing them so much liberty; they came often to make him a visit, and make their observations on the strength and situation of the fort, and [he] even told them of their weak condition, in regard to the want of both a supply of men and goods, which was acting very imprudent".[2]

The information, which they gleaned during these visits, made the French resolve to make very determined efforts to oust the British from the river and, despite the fact that the two nations were at peace, to take strong measures for this purpose. In June 1750 Gootheridge was superseded by James Alison, who reported that on his arrival he found "Mr Gootheridge, being so impaired in his health (believe he cannot live long), Mr Smith was fully resolved to take his passage with the first ship home; the rest that would have remained would inevitably have plundered the fort, and so would have left it to the first that had a mind to take possession: all this the French governor had information of. As we have given you a small hint of their characters that would have remained, we believe it will appear pretty plain to you that that would have been the case, had anything happened to Mr Gootheridge".[3]

On Alison's arrival the French "came to pay their respects to us, as formerly they had done but met with a cold reception. After some talk we told them that they must immediately shut up their factory and depart this river; if not, we would be obliged to make them by force of arms: likewise told them, that we would give them a limitted time to carry off their effects, we not wanting to make any reprizalls: they begged to have time for an answer from the Governor of Senegal, which we granted. The answer of their letter is not yet come. Likewise, told them, that we expected men of war soon in this river, and that they might expect to be served in the

[1] *Journal of Council of Trade*, 13 September 1750.
[2] James Alison to R.A.C., 13 June 1750, P.R.O., C.O. 267/5.
[3] *Ibid.*

same manner they were formerly by Captain Pocock,[1] which was to seize their effects, and drive them out of the river".[2]

The promised reply from the Director-General at St Louis was never communicated to the Governor at James Island. During the next four months the French worked sedulously to undermine British prestige with the natives of Barra. As the French were well supplied with trade goods and the British for a long time were not supplied at all, the task was not very difficult. In October the effect of anti-British propaganda was clearly demonstrated. After his supersession Gootheridge was placed in charge of the Company's factory at Juffure. He died there in October. The "king" of Barra claimed all the goods in the factory as escheating to him by native custom and seized them. He also seized four of the slaves, who were in charge of the Company's well at the adjacent village of San Domingo. The result was that the inhabitants of James Island had to send all the way to Kafuta in Kombo for water. This was followed up by a letter from the French Governor at Goree, "wherein he calls us interlopers and says we have no right in this river" and "several threatening and impertinent letters from those upstarts at Albreda".[3]

At the same time by offering high prices the French at Albreda virtually monopolised the whole of the trade. After three months' residence at James Island Alison reported that "they have purchased and sent off above fifty slaves since we have been here; beside beeswax, gold, teeth etc., as we have been credibly informed: and poor we have not purchased one slave, for all we are properly assorted with goods; they giving so high a price that it is not possible for us to purchase anything, excepting what they refuse". They further evaded the attempts of the Governor at James Island to prevent them from trading above that island by entrusting their goods to native and Portuguese traders.[4]

On 11 December 1750 the *Penelope*, a private trader, arrived in the river and anchored within two miles of Albreda. Within an hour of anchoring she was fired at from the French factory. The Commander, Anthony Gother, then sent a boat to James Island, which was also fired at from Albreda. The Governor of James Island came

---

[1] *Sc.* in 1745, cf. p. 213.
[2] James Alison to R.A.C., 13 June 1750, P.R.O., C.O. 267/5.
[3] *Ibid.* 8 January 1751, P.R.O., C.O. 267/5.
[4] *Ibid.*

off to the *Penelope* and, after consulting Gother, decided to send to the French to demand an explanation. Monsieur Aubert, the French agent, came off to the ship. "We insisted", wrote Gother, "on their departing, which they promised; but when they got on shore again, they sent word off they would not depart, but had sent to Goree for four ships to come and destroy our ship and take the fort into their possession, and got the natives so strenuously in their favour, that we could not send on shore for water or provisions for fear of being seized or destroyed. Upon this their daily threatening we were obliged to fire at the French factory and they with a large number of natives did the same at us. On the 17th a French brig arrived. The governor of the English fort came down and desired my assistance, which I readily complied with and sent two boats and twenty-one men. They brought the brig up and we put men on board of her to prevent her landing any goods,...and sent several messages to the French on shore to send off their goods and effects and embark and go away. They still refusing and threatning to destroy us and the castle, when we had got the brig ready to sail, His Majesty's ship, *Prince Henry*, Captain Jasper, arrived.[1] We petitioned him for assistance, who immediately sent up his pinnace with a number of men. We weighed our anchor and ran down abreast of the French factory, and the *Betty Snow*, Samuel Sacheverall, master, the Company's sloop, and the man of war's long boat, and landed a number of men and spoke with the headman of the town and desired them to send the Frenchmen off, which they promised, if we would embark, which was done. And they then got together a very large number of men to withstand us. We fired on each other for four days running but could not bring them to any terms, our fourth mate receiving a shot in his right arm."[2]

On 31 December the *Prince Henry's* long boat and barge took the captured French brig down to their ship at the mouth of the river, but Captain Jasper, realising that the seizure might lead to international complications, sent the brig back again and decided to take his own ship up to investigate affairs. Owing to wind and tide this movement could only be carried out by the tedious operation of warping and it took two and a half days to proceed from Banyon Point (Half Die) to Albreda—a distance of only fifteen miles. The

[1] *Sc.* on 24 December, Log of H.M.S. *Prince Henry*, P.R.O., Ad. 51/4299.
[2] Anthony Gother to Messrs Brasnett and Pole, 9 January 1751, P.R.O., Ad. 1/3810.

man-of-war warped into Albreda Bay on 7 January 1751, and spent
part of that day and the next in firing spasmodically on the French
factory and native town of Albreda. The bombardment appears to
have had little effect. The French had by this time entrenched themselves and the people of Barra had assembled in such large numbers,
and were so obviously hostile, that it was deemed inadvisable to
land a party to destroy the factory. On 9 January the *Prince Henry*
departed.[1]

In reporting to his employers on the incident Gother had scathing
criticisms to make of the Company's servants at James Island.

I have, he wrote, *inspected the situation of the castle and find it but
of very poor order, and also weakly manned, and that, if attacked, would
make but a poor defence. . . . The fort would not make any trade, nor
have I bought one slave or a pound of goods of any kind, the French
having ingrossed all themselves and incensed the natives against us to
that degree, that we cannot send any boats on shore not so much as for
water. I am much afraid that what the natives complain of is true; the
agents of the castle not having used them well, nor so much as ever given
the great men a bottle of brandy, but treated them roughly. I am certain
if you do not send out abler heads and also strength immediately, as also
a vessel to cruize off the river's mouth, the French will in a short time
have the river and the castle in their possession. I have according to my
promise assisted the castle and done all I could to rout the French out,
but find the agents willing and ready to drive them out with words, but
not willing to be at any expence, for which reason I shall not be concerned with them any more.[2]*

At the time of the bombardment of Albreda there was an interregnum in Barra following upon the death of the late "king". The
new "king", Gelawley Casa, was chosen shortly after that incident.
He had been duly impressed by the might of the British navy and
was anxious to keep on good terms with what he believed to be the
strongest party, but his subjects at Albreda and in the vicinity were
definitely pro-French. On 20 May 1751 he paid a visit to James
Island and explained the situation. He said he would turn the
French out as soon as he could persuade his people to that line of
action and "told us at the same time that, [if] we chose to turn them

---

[1] Log of H.M.S. *Prince Henry*, P.R.O., Ad. 51/4299; John Hopkins to R.A.C.,
8 January 1751, P.R.O., C.O. 267/5.

[2] Gother to Messrs Brasnett and Pole, 9 January 1751, P.R.O., Ad. 1/3810.

out directly, none of his people should give them any assistance".[1]
The ultimate result was that the French found native opinion turned
against them and temporarily abandoned Albreda.[2] Needless to say,
protests were sent to Europe and forwarded to the British Government against the action taken by the Commander of the *Prince
Henry* and orders were given for a French squadron to proceed to
the Gambia "to regulate the incident".[3]

James Skinner, the first governor of the new company, was ordered
to occupy the vacated factory at Albreda, but, having received reports of the threatened visit of the French squadron, abstained from
doing so.[4] The visit did not, however, take place. It was apparently
realised by the two governments and those in control in Europe of
the affairs of the two rival companies that their servants and others
on the spot had carried matters too far and that what had happened
in the Gambia was hardly worth the description of an international
incident. The French were in fact instructed from Paris to adopt a
more conciliatory attitude and to endeavour to recover their foothold in the Gambia by less chauvinist means. In 1754 Arsenac, the
new Governor of Goree, thought a favourable opportunity had come.
The British had fallen out once more with the people of Barra who
were boycotting British ships by refusing to allow them wood or
water. Accordingly a sloop was despatched from Goree to Albreda
in February of that year. Skinner reported that

*We endeavoured by bullying and other safe expedients to deter them
from their purpose and had almost prevailed in turning them away, but
the natives persisted so strong in their having possession, that they
hauled the sloop on shore; and two days ago we received a message from
the king desiring us in a mild manner to send for our goods and give
the French possession, which we was obliged to do.*[5]

A week or two later the slaves on board a Liverpool ship rose and
overpowered the crew. In the fight the vessel ran aground on the
Foni shore. The "emperor" of Foni tried to claim the ship as a sort
of deodand, but a Carolina slaver came to the rescue and got the

---

[1] James Skinner to Committee of Merchants, P.R.O., C.O. 267/5 and Ad.
1/3816; *Journal of Board of Trade*, 1750–1753, p. 232.

[2] Joseph Debat to Captain Richard Graves, 1765, P.R.O., C.O. 267/5.

[3] Cultru, *Histoire du Sénégal*, p. 199.

[4] Skinner to Committee of Merchants, 12 February 1753, P.R.O., C.O.
267/5.   [5] Skinner to Committee of Merchants, P.R.O., Ad. 1/3810.

ship off. After that the "emperor" of Foni and the "king" of Barra appeared off James Island with a large number of canoes. "As", wrote Skinner, "this gave us great reason to suspect they had no good design and was agreeable to the advice we had received of their coming to do mischief, we were provided for them, and ordered them away immediately, as well the Barrah as the Phoney canoes; and as we thought them tardy in obeying our orders, we pointed three six pounders and fired them just over their heads. They then hurried off and in the scuffle we seized the ringleader of the whole affair, as well as the cause of our late loss at Albreda, Tom Banja, the king's brother, the identical fellow that brought the French back again. ...We clapped him in double irons, and he continued so with a centry over him four hours. In that time the king was leaving us with a promise of his being with us again in a day or two. He kept his word and yesterday we saw him and had a very serious palaver, the substance of which was our detaining his brother as a hostage in the fort, which he agreed to; and we now have him in custody and hope, as he is the chief machine the French have at work, we shall yet rout them. Hitherto they have landed but little goods, and are making no preparations for the rains, which encourages us to think they have but an ill opinion of their situation."[1]

As in 1748 the Treaty of Aix-la-Chapelle had said nothing about the respective rights of the two countries in West Africa, Monsieur Arsenac, the Governor of Goree, resolved to be firm in asserting the right of the French to Albreda but none the less was anxious to avoid any actual clash with the British in the river. He therefore endeavoured to adopt a conciliatory attitude. In the early part of 1754 a number of British private traders had been trading on the coast of Bur Salum. Two Carolina traders and a settler at the Banana Islands had behaved there in a most outrageous manner, virtually levying war on the inhabitants and kidnapping the free inhabitants of the country. The inevitable result was that the Damel seized three of the crew of one of the ships. One died before he could be ransomed, but Arsenac advanced goods to ransom the other two and obtained the restoration of some of the goods, which were pillaged from the ship. He took the opportunity to address a letter to the Governor of James Island, in which he assured him of his readiness to assist the British in any manner possible but at the same time to

[1] Skinner to Committee of Merchants, 22 March 1754, P.R.O., Ad. 1/3810.

insist on the incontestable right of the French to trade in the River Gambia and to request that the factory at Albreda should not be molested. He therefore recommended to the Governor at James Island that he should "not continue to work on the same principles which you have put in use hitherto. You will find us no more in the same dispositions and expect from us no other marks of moderation than those you will use yourselves to us. These, Sir, are at this day our intentions, which it is good you should not be ignorant of; for if you make as little of the captain of the sloop, who carries this letter, and use the same difficulties to him, as you did to Monsieur Faucheur in the last voyage, which he made to the Gambia, expect, Sir, to find in this one as much resistance to your wills, as you have met with in the other. You will find him in like manner equally disposed to oblige you".[1]

Skinner on James Island was not prepared to be conciliatory. He wrote home demanding that a man-of-war should be sent to "rout the French out" and the Committee of Merchants in London asked the Admiralty to assist in taking "such measures to dispossess the French as may be thought most prudent and necessary".[2] Skinner in the meantime tried to induce the "king" of Barra to expel the French, but found that he was "entirely governed by a man, who was compelled to leave the country during the last king's time, and was factor at Albreda. He is a greedy fellow and will do anything for a large present, which we intend to offer him soon, provided he will get the king to burn the French factory". Fearing both British and native aggression, the French decided to postpone trading in the river and merely to content themselves with an assertion of their right to Albreda. They therefore landed no goods but left "two black butlers there to hoist their colours every Sunday".[3]

Matters remained in this position until February 1755, when a British sloop went to Kahone in the River Salum to trade. On its way back it was attacked by a French sloop, seized, and carried to Goree. The French did not profess to make this seizure in assertion of their old claim to the exclusive trade in those regions, but alleged that the supercargo of the British vessel had endeavoured to in-

[1] Arsenac to Skinner, 24 April 1754, P.R.O., C.O. 267/5 and Ad. 1/3810; Skinner to Committee of Merchants, 5 June 1754 and 28 March 1755, P.R.O., Ad. 1/3810.
[2] Samuel Poirier to John Cleveland, 22 October, 1754, P.R.O., Ad. 1/3810.
[3] Skinner to Committee of Merchants, 5 June 1754, P.R.O., Ad. 1/3810.

stigate the local natives to murder the French. This allegation was denied by the supercargo. The opportune arrival of H.M.S. *Gosport* enabled Robert Lawrie, the Governor of James Island, to proceed to Goree to demand restitution of the sloop. Monsieur St Jean, Governor of Goree, received him in a friendly manner. He described his subordinate's action in seizing the sloop "as a very rash inconsiderate act", but remonstrated against the conduct of Phillips, the British supercargo. He also informed Lawrie that the Director-General at St Louis had instructed him to "forgive" Phillips and that he had not only sent him and his sloop back, but, as further evidence of his desire to live on friendly terms with the British, had also sent with them the crew of a Liverpool ship, which had been wrecked off the coast of Barbary.[1]

St Jean took advantage of the returning British sloop to send two factors to Albreda.[2] These factors proceeded to claim the right to trade above James Island and sent a boat over to Brefet in Foni. Lawrie instructed them to desist: "otherwise I shall be under a necessity of taking measures, which I assure you my indispensable duty oblige me to". The chief factor at Albreda forwarded Lawrie's letter to Goree. Correspondence passed subsequently between Goree and James Island. It was heated on Lawrie's part, but the tone of St Jean's letters was conciliatory. The apparent upshot of it was that the French at Albreda were advised from Goree to abstain from any action, which might give possible cause of offence.[3]

In 1756 the Seven Years' War broke out. Considerable anxiety was felt in England about the probable fate of James Island.[4] In 1755 a military engineer had examined the fort and reported that it was very much out of repair and not in a proper state of defence.[5] Strenuous efforts had been made by Tobias Lisle, the Governor, and Robert Caulton, the surveyor, to put the fort in a better condition,[6] but it was known that the garrison was weak. On 30 September

[1] Robert Lawrie to Committee of Merchants, 5 February and 28 March 1755, P.R.O., Ad. 1/3810.

[2] Lawrie to Committee of Merchants, 28 March 1755, P.R.O., Ad. 1/3810.

[3] Robert Lawrie to Porquet Duprez, 7 August 1755; Duprez to Lawrie, 7 August 1755; Estoupan St Jean to Lawrie, 19 August 1755; Lawrie to St Jean, 30 September 1755; Lawrie to Committee of Merchants, 30 September 1755, P.R.O., Ad. 1/3810.

[4] *Journal of Council of Trade*, 17 and 18 September 1755.

[5] *Commons' Journals*, xxviii, 275; Plans of the English West African Forts, P.R.O., C.O. 267/11.   [6] *Commons' Journals*, xxviii, 280, 288, 523.

1754 Lawrie had described the situation as "little better than deplorable. For some time past we have been reduced to the necessity of making centinels of the castle slaves, who, as they are naturally lethargick, we think are not too much to be depended on, especially if a war should break out".[1] An inspection of the fort on 13 July 1756 by a naval officer disclosed the fact that there were only thirty soldiers in the garrison and that nearly half the cannon were still unmounted.[2]

Nearly a year of the war elapsed before hostile operations took place in the Gambia. Until then the French were allowed to remain at Albreda—probably from fear that any attempt to oust them would be visited by retaliation on James Island. On 4 October 1757 two French privateers entered the river under British colours. By this ruse they managed to surprise and take a Liverpool privateer, which was lying four miles below James Fort. The one shot, which the Liverpool ship was able to fire before her capture, warned the fort. But the garrison was in a very unfit state to offer any resistance to an attack. The gunner had been ill for the past six weeks and was unable to stir from his room. There "was not a man on the island that knew the right way to put a handspike to a carriage". But Captain Ingledon of the sloop *Speedwell* was lying off the fort and "he being a skillful man gave all the assistance he could". The Governor mustered every occupant of the fort, including the castle slaves, and divided them into watches and the guns of the fort were prepared for action.[3]

The French made no attempt to surprise the fort that night owing to darkness coming on. Next day they bore down on James Island flying English colours, but realised that their nationality had been discovered and stood in to Albreda. They were fired at from the fort but were out of range. During that and the two following days the garrison on James Island stood to arms and made a show of preparation by firing a morning and an evening gun. On 7 October the French decided that James Fort could not be taken and stood down the river taking their prize with them.[4] Shortly after leaving the river the two privateers were captured by a British man-of-war.[5]

[1] Lawrie to Committee of Merchants, 30 September 1754, P.R.O., Ad. 1/3810.   [2] *Commons' Journals*, xxviii, 279.

[3] Tobias Lisle to Committee of Merchants, 23 October 1757; Robert Caulton to Committee of Merchants, 23 October 1757; Journal of Proceedings of Council of James Fort, 1757, P.R.O., Ad. 1/3810.   [4] *Ibid.*

[5] An account in French of the capture of Goree, 1758, P.R.O., C.O. 267/1.

Early in 1758 H.M.S. *Isis* arrived in the river. The commander landed a party at Albreda, but "the Frenchmen went according to their usual custom among the negroes, till the man of war was gone, who the very next day came and settled their factory".[1] But the tide had by this time definitely turned against the French. On 2 May 1758 Commodore Keppel took Senegal, and followed up this success by taking Goree three weeks later.[2] H.M.S. *Rye* and *Harwich* proceeded from Goree to James Island. On 6 June Albreda was bombarded, but a landing party of sixty men was compelled to return to the ships because of the hostility of the natives. The place was again bombarded three days later. On this occasion the landing party was more successful. The factory, which had already been abandoned by the French, was set on fire as well as the native town, but not until after a very determined resistance by the natives, who killed three of the *Rye's* crew.[3] One of the terms of the capitulation of Goree was that all merchandise and effects at Portudal, Joal, and Albreda should be handed over to the British.[4] Subsequently a French commerce raider captured a British merchantman in the Atlantic on its way from Liverpool to the Gambia,[5] but the settlements in the Gambia remained unmolested until the conclusion of peace in 1763.

At the Treaty of Paris the French settlement at Senegal was surrendered to the British, but Goree was handed back to the French.[6] The reasons for this settlement need not be discussed, but the cession of Goree obviously created a source of future trouble. Before the war had ended, strong representations were made to the British Government that one of the terms of the treaty of peace should exclude the French from the River Gambia,[7] but nothing came of them. The position of the two nations in the Gambia was not touched upon by the terms of the Treaty of Paris.

---

[1] John Roberts, "An Account of the First Establishments on that part of the Coast of Africa called Guinea", P.R.O., C.O. 267/21.

[2] *Annual Register*, 1758, p. 75.

[3] Log of H.M.S. *Rye*, P.R.O., Ad. 51/825.

[4] *Annual Register*, 1759, p. 63; Committee of Merchants to Council of Trade, 11 July 1764; An account in French of the capture of Goree, 1758, P.R.O., C.O. 267/6.   [5] Williams, *The Liverpool Privateers*, pp. 489–490, 665–667.

[6] *Annual Register*, 1762, pp. 61, 238.

[7] Joseph Debat to Committee of Merchants, 15 June 1760, P.R.O., C.O. 267/6; Committee of Merchants to Council of Trade, 19 May 1761 and 24 December 1762, P.R.O., C.O. 267/6 and Add. MS. 14,035, ff. 114, 149.

Immediately after the close of the war the French determined to make the most of what was left to them of their West African possessions. Goree was reoccupied and at once made a base for operations in the Gambia. In September 1763 they reoccupied Albreda, proceeded to surround their factory with a palisade, erected two bastions on the river bank, and mounted some cannon. In July 1764 the Governor of Goree arrived in a thirty-gun frigate with a hundred soldiers. He landed with full military honours and mounted a military guard at Albreda. As a result of the war the "king" of Barra had become an ardent supporter of the British interest. When he learned of the impending visit of the French Governor, he tried "to fling himself into the arms of the fort", but was prevented. He none the less refused to see his unwelcome visitor. The French Governor stayed at Albreda for two months. He announced his intention of passing above James Island, "if not by fair methods to use foul", but was prevented from carrying out his design owing to an outbreak of sickness amongst his crew. None the less he managed to send agents overland to endeavour to divert caravans from up-river towns to Albreda.[1] After his return to Goree the French Governor seized the Committee's store ship, imprisoned one of the officers on what was alleged to be "a frivolous pretence", and refused to return the ship until Joseph Debat, the Governor at James Island, had delivered up four slaves, who, according to him, "had been bought by a trader in a fair and just manner".[2]

All these difficulties were in due course reported to England and representations were made to the Government that active measures should be taken to exclude the French from the River Gambia. As the journal of the Council of Trade shows, a great deal of the year 1764 was taken up with discussions between that Council and the Committee of Merchants as to the legal position, but it was not until the end of the year that a decision was taken to invoke the aid of the Admiralty.[3] Captain Thomas Graves was instructed to proceed to the spot in H.M.S. *Edgar* and to lend what assistance he could to

[1] Joseph Debat to Committee of Merchants, 26 May and 20 July 1764; Joseph Debat to Captain Thomas Graves, 1765; Memorial of Joseph Kitching and others, 4 July 1764; Memorial of James Songster and others, — April 1764, P.R.O., C.O. 267/13.
[2] Joseph Debat to Captain Thomas Graves, 1765, P.R.O., C.O. 267/13.
[3] Lords of Admiralty to Earl of Halifax, 15 December 1764, *C.S.P. Home Office Papers*, 1760–1765, p. 473.

the Committee's servants in restraining French activities. But his instructions were vague and he was not informed as to the precise legal position or as to the lengths to which he could be empowered to go.[1]

Fortunately Graves was not only a person of some resource and initiative but was also a person of some discretion. He proceeded to the Gambia with the *Edgar, Shannon*, and *Hound*. First of all he sent a frigate to Goree to inform the French Governor that he would not be allowed in any way to fortify Albreda and that steps must at once be taken to remove any military stores, which were there. He then proceeded to James Island in the *Hound* sloop. On 15 April 1765 he landed with a party of marines at Albreda. Information had already reached the French of his intended visit and they had stirred up the natives of Barra to oppose any attempt at the removal of the stores. Shortly after Graves landed, he and his small party were surrounded by a large party of armed natives. There was a scuffle and the marines were only able to make their way back to the boat by firing into the crowd. The surgeon of the *Hound* had been sent to attend Girard, the French factor, who was ill. He was cut off and captured by the natives. A message was sent on shore to the French informing them that they would be held responsible for his personal safety. The surgeon was consequently released. On 19 March a French sloop arrived from Goree and in compliance with Graves' orders removed the six small cannon, which had been mounted at Albreda and conveyed them to Goree. The British ships then left the river, but the *Hound* returned at intervals during the next three years to see that the French made no attempt to re-fortify Albreda.[2]

Senegal had been occupied by a military garrison until the end of the Seven Years' War. After the conclusion of peace it was handed over to the Committee of Merchants.[3] But two years of the Committee's administration showed that they were not sufficiently strong to develop British influence in those regions and at the same time to cope with French activities. Early in 1764 the Council of Trade became very much perturbed at the reports of French

[1] Lords of Admiralty to Earl of Halifax, 15 December 1764 and 11 May 1765, *C.S.P. Home Office Papers*, 1760–1765, pp. 473, 549.
[2] Lords of Admiralty to Secretary Conway, 29 July 1765, *C.S.P. Home Office Papers*, 1760–1765, p. 581; Log of H.M.S. *Edgar*, P.R.O., Ad. 51/301; Log of H.M.S. *Hound*, P.R.O., Ad. 51/462.   [3] 4 Geo. III, c. 20.

aggression received from the Gambia and proceeded to investigate the political situation there. After careful deliberation the Board recommended that the British possessions in Senegal and the Gambia should be revested in the Crown and administered as a colony. This recommendation was adopted by Parliament and on 25 May 1765 the royal assent was given to an Act divesting the Committee of its authority in the Senegal and the Gambia and re-vesting it in the Crown.[1] Though the Committee nominally resumed charge of the Gambia eighteen years later, this Act marked the real close of Company rule in those regions.

Apart from the troubles with the French there is very little to record concerning the Committee's period of administration in the Gambia. One marked feature of the change of administration was the tendency of the Committee's servants to avoid initiative and for the Committee to be called upon to decide a number of questions, which, in view of the uncertainty of communications and the time which necessarily elapsed in the passing of correspondence between England and Africa, obviously ought to have been decided by the man on the spot. The Committee in its turn was loath to take the responsibility of giving advice and referred matters to the Council of Trade. The result was that the decisions, which were reached, were often peculiarly ineffective. When, for instance, in 1757 the "king" of Casinka proved troublesome, the whole matter was re-ferred home to the Committee, who in their turn referred it to the Council of Trade. This latter body could only consult somebody who knew the country and who advised "that it would be most advisable to endeavour the putting an end to these disputes by gentle methods and a few presents to the principal people". After a week's deliberation the Council of Trade recommended that the Committee's servants should be instructed "to endeavour to ac-commodate the differences, which had arisen, in an amicable way and to pursue such methods as should in their opinion prove most effectual".[2] One feels that under the former regime the trouble and its adjustment would have been reported as *faits accomplis* and not referred to England for advice, which in the circumstances was in-evitably platitudinous.

Four years later one of the Government slaves was suspected of poisoning several castle slaves and others. One would have thought

[1] Martin, *op. cit.* pp. 57–64.
[2] *Journal of Council of Trade*, 19 and 26 January 1758.

this a case for immediate action on the spot, but it was referred to the Committee in England on 30 March 1761. Nearly eight months later, on 13 November, the Committee, after due deliberation, decided that they were not competent to advise, referred the matter to the Council of Trade, and "desired their lordships' sentiments and directions upon it". The Council of Trade deliberated the matter at three meetings and finally, after consulting a person who claimed to be acquainted with West African affairs, announced that, "as he was not able to inform their lordships, and as it did not appear from any other circumstances what the practice and usage had been upon the coast in cases of a like nature, their lordships declined to give any opinion of what directions it might be proper for the Committee to give on this occasion".[1]

The prohibition, which was placed by law upon trading on the part of the new Company in its corporate capacity and of the members of the Committee of management, considerably reduced the friction, which had existed under the old regime, between the company and private traders. None the less the conduct of some of the captains and crews of ships, which visited the regions of the Gambia, gave cause for grave anxiety to the Committee's servants. The Committee's servants had no executive control over these traders and could therefore do little except threaten or remonstrate. Instances of misconduct by some of these traders have already been given in this chapter. The refusal of Liverpool and Bristol ships to pay the customary dues claimed by the "king" of Barra was largely responsible for the friction between that chief and the Committee's servants on James Island. This refusal was so persistent that representations had to be made to the Council of Trade, who wrote to the Master of the Merchants' Hall at Bristol and the Mayor of Liverpool asking them in future to give directions to masters of ships so as to avoid any just cause of complaint on this score.[2] Others were guilty of far worse practices. The activities of three masters of ships in Bur Salum in 1754 led Skinner to inform the Committee that, "if there is not a stop put to those proceedings, 'twill be dangerous for vessels to come in this river, especially strangers, who generally send their boats along the coast to find out the river's mouth".[3] Of another captain, whose misconduct is set out at

---

[1] *Journal of Council of Trade*, 11, 13 and 20 November 1761.
[2] *Journal of Council of Trade*, 26 March 1760.
[3] Skinner to Committee of Merchants, 5 June, 1754, P.R.O., Ad. 1/3810.

length, Skinner wrote that "he is not a proper person to purchase slaves in this river; besides his uncommon behaviour to his linguister, which Mr Lisle was witness to, he treated the natives in so opprobrious a manner, that was it not out of the respect that's held for the Company, it's a matter of doubt if he had not been cut off".[1]

Perhaps Skinner would have been nearer the mark if he had said that it was not so much respect for the Company that upheld British prestige in the River Gambia as the moral force behind the Company. The Act constituting the new Company provided for the regular inspection of the Company's forts by men-of-war, which were sent to cruise along the coast.[2] The result was that James Island was far more frequently visited by the navy under the new than under the old regime and very convincing proof was given to the local inhabitants of the power which lay behind the Committee.

[1] Same to same, 28 February 1754, P.R.O., Ad. 1/3810.
[2] 23 Geo. II, c. 31, s. 30.

XVI: The Province of Senegambia, 1765–1776

The constitution of the Province of Senegambia was deliberately modelled on the type of that of an American Colony subject to certain differences to meet local conditions. There was a Governor and Council entrusted with legislative and administrative responsibilities and a Chief Justice in charge of a far too elaborate and complicated judicial system. Headquarters were to be at St Louis on the banks of the River Senegal. The River Gambia was placed under the charge of a superintendent of trade, who was to reside at James Island.[1] This superintendent was to be paid a salary of £200 per annum.[2] In 1766 his title was changed to that of Lieutenant-Governor.[3] He was to be subordinate to the Governor at St Louis and to obey all orders received from him. He was to do nothing prejudicial to a free trade in the river and was prohibited from indulging in private trade. One of his duties was to act as mediator between British subjects and the natives in all cases of dispute and "palarver". He was in particular instructed that, "in case any trader shall attempt to carry off any native or free negroe subject of the King of Barrah or any other sovereign or chief in alliance with or living under the protection of His Majesty's fort, he do use his best endeavours to bring the authors of such unwarrantable and inhuman practices to due punishment". Friendship and a good understanding was to be cultivated with the "king" of Barra and other chiefs, "who either have acknowledged or shall acknowledge His Majesty's authority in these parts, and either have or shall put themselves under His Majesty's protection".[4]

The superintendent was further instructed to keep a close watch on the French at Albreda and to do his best to counteract any attempts by them to alienate the natives from the British interest. With this object in view he was to encourage the establishment of factories in the river by British subjects.[5]

[1] Martin, *The British West African Settlements*, 1750–1821, pp. 66, 67.
[2] *Commons' Journals*, xxx, 636.
[3] Joseph Debat to Earl Shelburne, P.R.O., C.O. 267/13.
[4] Instructions to the Superintendent of Trade in Senegambia, 6 December 1765, P.R.O., C.O. 268/2, ff. 25 *seq.*   [5] *Ibid.*

Amongst others of his duties were those of assisting any British vessels on the coast in distress and of reporting periodically to the Commissioners for Trade and Plantations on the possibility of opening up fresh avenues of trade.[1]

Three independent companies of foot, known as O'Hara's Corps, were raised for the defence of the newly created Province and instructions were issued to the Governor that one of these companies should proceed to the River Gambia with such number of soldiers and others as the Governor should direct.[2]

The first Governor of Senegambia was Colonel Charles O'Hara of the Coldstream Guards. He has been described as "not a man who claimed a large place among the biographies of national worthies, and a personal characteristic which brought him into trouble with the Colonial Secretary, adds to the difficulty of sketching a full-length portrait of him. He had apparently an overmastering aversion to correspondence, and his dispatches are so spasmodic that they give a very incomplete picture both of his doings as Governor and of the fortunes of the Province under his rule".[3]

An additional criticism of a historian of the Gambia must also be that during his eleven years of governorship he appears to have concentrated his energies almost entirely upon the Senegal and to have taken very little interest in the Gambia, except as a penal settlement to which to transport convicted felons from St Louis.[4] Though the British Government's intention was that the Lieutenant-Governor should be a civilian officer, whose principal task was to be the development of British trade, O'Hara's military training gave him a

---

[1] *Ibid.*

[2] J. C. Roberts to Charles O'Hara, 1 January 1766, *C.S.P. Home Office Papers*, 1765–1769, p. 1. After O'Hara's departure from Senegal this corps became known as the African Corps. It was disbanded in 1784 (P.R.O., W.O. 4/125, ff. 1, 2, 9), but was reformed in 1800 under the command of Colonel (afterwards General Sir) John Fraser for the purpose of garrisoning Goree (P.R.O., W.O. 4/180, ff. 222, 402, W.O. 26/30, f. 227). The corps was finally absorbed in 1840 with three supernumerary companies of the First West India Regiment into a corps designated as the Third West India Regiment, which was disbanded in 1870 (Ellis, *The History of the First West India Regiment*, pp. 209, 302).

[3] Martin, *op. cit.* p. 76.

[4] "The convicts not to return from James Fort to Senegal until the time they are sent there has expired without an order from the Governor or Commandant at Fort Lewis to send any particular convicts to Senegal." Instructions of O'Hara to William Myres, 28 June 1774, P.R.O., C.O. 267/16.

bias in favour of appointing a military person to that post. He therefore ruled that on a vacancy in the post the commandant of the
troops, whether an officer or a non-commissioned officer, should act
as Lieutenant-Governor and recommended that any civilian officer,
who did not desire to be superseded in that post by a non-commissioned officer should enrol in O'Hara's Corps as a supernumerary
sergeant. "Any civil officer not consenting to the proposed plan
renders it impossible for him to become an occasional commandant
of James Fort."[1] Eventually, O'Hara received an official rebuke
for his marked antipathy to the preferment of civilian officers. On
16 December 1774 Lord Dartmouth had to inform him that the
assumption of power by the senior officer of the troops would be un-
warranted, whilst there was a Lieutenant-Governor in the Province.[2]
It would further appear that O'Hara only twice visited the Gambia.
The first occasion was after the lapse of nearly three years from his
appointment as Governor.[3]

A purely personal matter appears further to have led to the neglect of the Gambia by colonial headquarters. Neither O'Hara, nor
his successors, were on good terms with their Lieutenant-Governors.
When William Myres called at St Louis on his way to assume charge
at James Island in 1774, he reported that:

*I was politely received by the Governor etc. and I presented His
Majesty's appointments, which he requested I would leave with him.
Some days after he told me he had carefully perused them, also his
instructions and acts of parliament respecting the establishments of the
Governor of the Province of Senegambia.*

*That he looked upon such appointments as totaly illegal and un-
constitutional, that no such officer as Lieutenant-Governor was in the
establishment, nor was there any emolument or allowance whatever for
such; such officer could not have any power or duty during his (the
Governor's) residence in the province; and that, in case of his death or
absence, he was well satisfied the oldest officer of the troops (then resident
in the province) would take command in pursuance of his instructions
and the acts of parliament for the establishment; but that, in consideration of my being sent out here and having been put to so much incon-*

---

[1] Instructions of O'Hara to William Myres, 28 June 1774, P.R.O., C.O.
267/16.

[2] P.R.O., C.O. 267/16.

[3] O'Hara to Lords of Treasury, 15 September 1768, P.R.O., C.O. 267/13.

venience etc., he had determined to send me down to the Gambia as Lieutenant-Governor or Comandant with such instructions as appeared to him proper and that the illegality and impropriety of such appointments might be examined into by those, who wished to engage in such matters.[1]

On his arrival at James Island his reception by the military officer in charge was equally chilly. On 12 February 1774 he wrote to Lord Dartmouth that:

On the morning after my arrival I presented my appointment to Mr Sugden, a Lieutenant of the troops, and who has been commandant here for about two years and three months. At my request he inserted in the orderly book a parole for the day and also that His Majesty had been pleased to appoint me as Lieutenant Governor of this Province. At the same time he informed me that he could not give me up such book, any command of the fort, or any account of His Majesty's property here; that he was sent here by Governor O'Hara and looked upon himself as accountable to him only; that this was a province and the Governor upon it; that he had various accounts to settle with him, not having seen him during his residence here, but hoped he should hear from him, and have his particular direction on the occasion in a short time.

In this manner three weeks have now gone, but I should be doing an injustice to Mr Sugden, did I not acknowledge that his behaviour to me as a private gentleman has been polite and friendly.[2]

The procedure, which the home Government sanctioned, of allowing the Lieutenant-Governor to correspond without reference to the Governor direct with the Secretary of State tended further to accentuate these personal differences and to diminish the Governor's interest in an outlying and detached portion of his province.

The dependence of the Gambia for supplies upon headquarters at St Louis was very unsatisfactory. Communication was precarious and the cost of transport was expensive. As Myres once wrote, as much as ten or twelve months sometimes elapsed before the garrison on James Island could be relieved.[3]

The control of the Gambia passed from the Committee of the Merchants to the Crown in April 1766, when a detachment of O'Hara's Corps took possession of James Island. Joseph Debat, the

---

[1] William Myres to Earl of Dartmouth, 14 July 1774, P.R.O., C.O. 267/16.
[2] P.R.O., C.O. 268/4.   [3] *Ibid.*

Committee's last governor, was continued as Superintendent of Trade and ultimately as Lieutenant-Governor. Lieutenant Philip du Perron, the officer commanding the troops which took over the fort, reported that "the only persons they found there were the Committee's Governor with a few clerks and slaves. This fort had likewise been very much neglected by the Committee and was in want of a general repair".[1] As already mentioned, O'Hara himself deferred visiting the river until 1768. On 27 January 1767 he informed the Board of Trade that he was unable to give a particular account of James Fort, as the two officers whom he had sent there had died before making any report, but that he had received information that the Committee had left the place almost bare of stores and that he had therefore been compelled to deplete the very inadequate supply of ordnance stores at St Louis to make good deficiencies.[2] On 15 September 1768 he explained his inability to make a personal inspection of the fort by the fact that at that date he had only one other officer with him at St Louis and he was sick.[3]

O'Hara's instructions warned him to keep a sharp look out upon the activities of the French at Goree and in the River Gambia, "keeping a watchful eye upon all their proceedings and preventing by all possible means any communication or correspondence between them and those inhabitants of our island of Saint Louis, who were formerly subjects of France or connected in interest with them".[4] Unfortunately those instructions made no attempt to define the international position in the Gambia or to intimate to him the extent to which he was empowered to act so as to frustrate French activities in those regions. Equally unfortunately O'Hara did not issue any precise instructions on the subject to his subordinates in the Gambia. The consequence was that several critical situations arose between the British on James Island and the French at Albreda.

The French Government claimed that the treaty of peace empowered their nationals to trade in the river by merchant vessels, but not by means of armed barks.[5] They none the less proceeded to

---

[1] Minute for the Province of Senegambia, Royal MS. 200, f. 35.
[2] P.R.O., C.O. 267/14.
[3] O'Hara to Lords of Treasury, 15 September 1768, P.R.O., C.O. 267/14.
[4] Instructions to O'Hara, 6 February 1766, P.R.O., C.O. 268/2, ff. 66, 67.
[5] Lords of Admiralty to Earl of Halifax, 11 May 1765, *C.S.P. Home Office Papers*, 1760–1765, p. 549.

refortify Albreda, where they mounted five pieces of cannon. They also re-established their factories at Portudal and Joal.[1] Trouble began when a Liverpool merchant contracted with a French merchant in London for the delivery by the latter of 300 slaves. A French ship was despatched from Honfleur to Albreda to ship the slaves. Lieutenant du Perron, who was in charge of the troops on James Island, seized the ship as it lay at anchor off Albreda. He subsequently released it on an undertaking that it would return at once to Honfleur.[2] When the incident was reported to O'Hara, he wrote to du Perron that:

I am supprised you should interfere in so delicate a department as that of trade, uninstructed and uninformed, especially as His Majesty has appointed a Superintendent of Trade for the River Gambia.

... You must therefore take such measures as you think most prudent to vindicate the step you have taken and for the future confine yourself to the instructions, which you receive from me and I shall then be answerable for your conduct, which I cannot be if you exceed your authority.[3]

O'Hara did refer the matter to the Board of Trade and enquired whether the practice of English merchants shipping goods from the Gambia in foreign ships was not a breach of the Navigation Acts.[4] But the Board was too cautious to commit itself and O'Hara and his subordinates were left to interpret the Navigation Acts and peace treaty as best they could.

The incident caused considerable indignation amongst the French. O'Hara accused them of causing the next trouble which arose in the river. In 1765 a native of Barra had shipped as "linguister" on board a British merchant vessel bound for the West Indies. He returned thence in another British ship two years later. On the voyage he attempted to shoot the master. He was promptly clapped in irons and handed over to Lieutenant-Governor Debat on the ship's arrival

[1] O'Hara to Council of Trade, 28 May 1766, P.R.O., C.O. 267/1, C.O. 267/13, and Royal MS. 200, f. 25.

[2] Lieut. Du Perron to O'Hara, 30 August 1766, P.R.O., C.O. 267/13; Same to same, 15 September 1766, Royal MS. 200, f. 32; Petition of Miles Barber, 23 February 1767; Affidavit of John Allen, 3 October 1766, P.R.O., C.O. 267/13; Earl of Shelburne to Commissioners for Trade, 26 February 1767, P.R.O., C.O. 267/1; Commissioners for Trade to Earl of Shelburne, 5 March 1767, P.R.O., C.O. 268/2, f. 108; *C.S.P. Home Office Papers*, 1765–1769, p. 161.

[3] P.R.O., C.O. 267/13.   [4] 12 January 1767, Royal MS. 200, f. 32.

at James Island. Debat was at the time having some trouble with the "king" of Barra and he decided to keep the prisoner in custody "till he could find a favourable opportunity of making a merit with the king of Barrah by releasing him". The chief, however, was not thereby reduced to amenableness. He intimated his displeasure by refusing to visit O'Hara on the occasion of one of the latter's rare visits to James Island in February 1768. Three months later the "king" made a further request for the man's release. Debat decided that the moment was opportune for giving his consent and fixed a day for handing the prisoner over. What happened next arouses a considerable measure of suspicion. Debat's subsequent version of the affair was that "the King of Barrah arrived at the Fort, and Lieutenant Governor Debat sent immediately on board the Snow for the negroe, but was informed by the Snow's people at the return of the boat that the day before the negroe had broke from his confinement, jumped into the sea and that they had seen him eaten by a shark".[1] This story may or may not be true, but, whether true or false, it infuriated the people of Barra. They seized four Europeans and twelve slaves, who happened to be on the mainland, and refused to allow the inhabitants of James Island to fetch wood or water. Debat consequently had to send to Bintang for these commodities, but reported that "I pay for water as I do for wine".[2]

In April a small reinforcement of troops arrived at James Island, and Debat, who on one occasion had been unable to obtain water for the garrison for five days, decided to attack Albreda. The officer commanding the troops subsequently reported that

Before daylight in the morning of the 23d of April, being St George's day, every man having a St George's cross in his hat, we surrounded the town, but was rather too soon, being discovered by the outguards and the barking of dogs; but to complete my design and my orders, immediately began the attack, when a smart engagement and a warm fire ensued. In less than an hour I was master of the place, burnt the town to ashes, destroyed everything that I could in that time come at, made many prisoners and embarked the troops with little or no loss. The prisoners are all here, among whom is the Queen of Baragh, who had been upon a visit in this place, it being like Bath in England, where the better sort

[1] O'Hara to Lords of Treasury, 15 September 1768, P.R.O., C.O. 267/14.
[2] Debat to O'Hara, 27 May 1768, P.R.O., C.O. 267/14.

*of people come for the benefit of their health. Her Majesty was so un-
fortunate as to have three of her fingers tore off by one of our hand
grenades. I have taken all care in my power of her, also the governor;
and she is now attended by our surgeons.*[1]

Debat held the royal lady and thirty-eight other prisoners as
hostages for the safety of the captives taken by the Barra people.[2]
This, however, did not bring his opponents to terms and Debat, who
was evidently badly overwrought at the time, decided to go to St
Louis to appeal personally to O'Hara for reinforcements. He left in
charge a certain Ensign Fury, "lately arrived on the coast, totally
unexperienced in the manners and genius of the people, and subject
to those violent excesses to which he soon died a martyr".[3]

Soon after his arrival at St Louis Debat fell dangerously ill.
O'Hara realised that he had been through a trying time and subsequently made an attempt to extenuate his conduct to the home
Government, but at the same time he could not disguise the fact
that Debat's attempt to exact reprisals with a totally inadequate
force and his subsequent departure from James Island at a very
critical moment were highly imprudent. As soon as Debat was sufficiently well to travel, he was ordered back to James Island with an
officer and twenty-three soldiers. O'Hara warned him that he fully
believed that he would "find James Fort in the hands of the blacks".
If he should find that this disaster had occurred, he was to take every
step possible to regain the fort. He was further enjoined that, "if
you should dispossess the blacks of James Fort, I would recommend
to you the utmost severity, even bordering upon cruelty, upon those
you may find upon the fort. The insolence is so new and the example
so fatal to the well being of the white people upon this coast, that
the severity of your punishment must be in proportion to the injury
we have received".[4]

O'Hara's worst fears were very nearly, but fortunately not quite,
fulfilled. At four o'clock in the morning on 14 July 1768, 500 men in
twenty canoes attacked James Fort. The garrison comprised forty
soldiers, but a number of them were sick. Ensign Fury had allowed

---

[1] *Annual Register*, 1768, pp. 149, 150.
[2] Debat to O'Hara, 27 May 1768, P.R.O., C.O. 267/14.
[3] Viscount Weymouth to O'Hara, 15 December 1768, P.R.O., C.O. 267/14.
[4] O'Hara to Debat, 11 August 1768; O'Hara to Commissioners for Trade,
15 September 1768, P.R.O., C.O. 267/14.

discipline to become very lax and no proper watch was being kept. Fortunately Williams, the clerk of the cheque of the ordnance, rose to the occasion. "So bad a look out was kept that they were nigh ashore before the least alarm. The troops got into the gates just in time with the castle slaves. Fury was ill and Williams managed the whole affair. They attempted at one place only to scale the walls and were beat off. Two soldiers and two blacks were killed on our side, which is all our real loss. A tolerable number of the blacks were cut off. The whole might have been destroyed with ease had the guns been properly pointed to destroy their canoes."[1] "The retreat of the assailants from the island was so precipitate and confused that they left their scaling ladders behind. Now the natives were never known to have a thing of that kind in their possession before, nor even the most intelligent one among them either genius to invent or tools to make one." Strong suspicion was therefore aroused that this attack was due to French instigation.[2]

After the attack was driven off, there were further alarms. Ensign Fury got into a state of panic. The soldiers were housed in barracks outside the fort and he brought them all inside. The accommodation was hopelessly inadequate. In a few days an alarming sickness—apparently yellow fever—broke out and seventeen of the forty died. When Debat arrived back at James Island, only four of their number were capable of doing duty.[3] Had it not been for the assistance offered by the crews of certain trading vessels, it would have been impossible to have manned the fort. The hostility of the natives became so widespread that a number of British trading vessels, which were further up the river, were attacked and some of them captured.[4]

Fortunately at the time when Debat was ready to return from St Louis to James Island, H.M.S. Phoenix and Hound arrived off the mouth of the Senegal. These ships not only conveyed Debat and the reinforcements to James Island but also by their presence had a very salutary effect on the people of Barra. Captain Tonyn, commanding the Phoenix, decided to remain on the coast for several months and

---

[1] Debat to O'Hara, 3 September 1763, P.R.O., C.O. 267/14.
[2] Captain Tonyn to Lords of Admiralty, 28 August 1769; O'Hara to Lords of Treasury, 15 September 1768, P.R.O., C.O. 267/14.
[3] Debat to O'Hara, 3 September 1768, P.R.O., C.O. 267/14.
[4] Memorial of Richard Evans and others, 31 August 1768, P.R.O., C.O. 267/14.

both vessels made further visits to the River Gambia. Though the navy indulged in no warlike operations, its presence created a proper impression. They further assisted the garrison at one critical moment "by a timely supply of every article of which they stood much in want". Governor O'Hara himself paid two visits to James Island and saw that the fort was put into a proper state of defence. By May 1769 the people of Barra had decided to abandon hostilities and resume friendly relations.[1]

After 1769 comes one of those regrettable gaps in O'Hara's correspondence with the home Government. The little information, which can be gleaned about affairs in the River Gambia, has to be gleaned from other sources. Considerable anxiety was felt regarding French activities, but it seems clear that the fears were exaggerated. The French East India Company had become bankrupt. Goree was proving of little commercial and very doubtful military value. At this date Albreda was proving to be of a far greater commercial importance than Goree, but the refusal of the British to allow the French to proceed above James Island prevented any great development of trade there. Le Brasseur, the Governor of Goree, therefore advocated the abandonment of both places and the establishment of a settlement at the mouth of the River Salum.[2] By 1771 even Albreda was in a very low state. An English officer, who visited the place about that time, reported that he found there "only one French woman, all the men except her husband being dead, and he was gone up river trading, and while I was there, she heard he was dead and all the white men with him, which was a very common case, for she had five husbands in three years".[3]

France's West Indian possessions were in urgent need of slaves and after the dissolution of the East Indies Company a number of projects were launched for the development of those regions in West

[1] Lords of Admiralty to Richard Sutton, 8 August 1768, P.R.O., C.O. 267/14; Viscount Weymouth to Lords of Admiralty, 1 December 1768, *C.S.P. Home Office Papers*, 1765–1769, p. 388; Lords of Admiralty to Viscount Weymouth, 5 December 1768; Debat to John Hollwell, 18 January 1769; O'Hara to Captain Tonyn, 16 March 1769; O'Hara to Captain Male, 4 July 1769; Captain Male to Lords of Admiralty, 25 July 1769; Captain Tonyn to Lords of Admiralty, 3 August 1769; Captain Tonyn to Philip Stephens, 28 August 1769, P.R.O., C.O. 267/14; Log of H.M.S. *Hound*, P.R.O., Ad. 51/462.

[2] Cultru, *Histoire du Sénégal*, p. 219; Douin, *Plan d'un Etablissement à former dans l'Intérieur de L'Affrique Occidentale*, p. 2. Add. MS. 19,884.

[3] Evidence of Sir George Young before Parliamentary Committee, 2 May 1785, P.R.O., H.O. 7/1, ff. 9, 10.

Africa, which still remained to her. The British Government viewed these schemes with considerable alarm and demanded an assurance from the French Government that there was no intention on their part of erecting fortifications in the River Gambia or the parts adjacent thereto.[1] In 1773 four ships left Havre with the avowed object of establishing a considerable settlement on the coast.[2] The expedition was in charge of a certain Abbé du Manet, who had once been chaplain to the garrison at Goree but had a "visionary, profligate character" and had been sent home "for repeated indiscretions and ill conduct". He sent a vessel to Albreda to purchase slaves and subsequently sent two more to Portendic. But his plans came to nothing.[3]

After five years of more or less complete silence O'Hara returned to epistolary virtue in 1774. His principal reason for so doing was the trouble, which he was experiencing with his Lieutenant-Governor at James Island. Ensign Matthias MacNamara was described by his contemporary, Edward Morse, Chief Justice of Senegambia, as "a man without education, extremely brutal, vulgar, and avaricious, but possessed of an uncommon share of natural parts".[4] His correspondence betrays the fact that he must have been a singularly unlovable and unpleasant person—conceited and a venomous backbiter. How he came to obtain the appointment is not at all clear. He passed over the heads of a number of senior officers. His selection for the post was extremely unpopular and he did nothing to allay that unpopularity. The predominant notes of his correspondence with the home Government are the complete self-satisfaction of the writer and the underhand attacks which he makes on his brother officers.

He first attempted to assert his authority by taking very high-handed measures with the French. A canoe belonging to an English trader was either stolen or went adrift. It was salved near the mouth of the river by a native and by him sold to the resident at Albreda. When MacNamara heard of it, he demanded immediate restitution.

---

[1] Earl of Rochford to Earl of Hillsborough, 6 April 1772, *C.S.P. Home Office Papers*, 1770–1772, p. 475; Earl of Hillsborough to Earl of Rochford, 12 April 1772, *ibid.* p. 482.

[2] Earl of Dartmouth to O'Hara, 18 August 1773, P.R.O., C.O. 268/3.

[3] O'Hara to Earl of Dartmouth, 24 January 1774, P.R.O., C.O. 268/4; Douin, *op. cit.* pp. 2, 10, 11. Add. MS. 19,334.

[4] Morse to Lord Townshend, 12 August 1782, P.R.O., C.O. 267/20.

The resident refused to hand it over unless he was reimbursed the price which he had paid for its purchase. MacNamara thereupon wrote as follows:

If said boat is not immediately returned, I shall cause it to be seized as also all the persons concerned. Shall look upon them as thieves and they shall be punished accordingly....Prudence is recommended, as I am determined to have her back or the person, who sold her without six-pence expence. Therefore he must take what follows....I cannot omitt saying that the gentleman might easily find a genteeler method of furnishing himself with a boat.[1]

The French resident still stood out for compensation. MacNamara then informed him:

Now, Sir, you having declared to the messenger your having no further to do in this affair, and their (sic) is no other recourse left but applying to where we think it will be found, which I think will not be very pleasing to the persons, in whose possession she is found, as I am determined they or he shall pay very dear for the boat.[2]

The canoe had in fact been handed over to a French sloop at Albreda. MacNamara sent a shallop with some soldiers to seize it. When the shallop reached the sloop, a Portuguese mulatto on board the French ship fired at the British. This may have been, as was subsequently alleged, or may not have been due to a misunderstanding of the French captain's orders. It at any rate afforded a pretext for retaliation. The British opened fire and killed two or more of the crew and wounded several others. Some of the French crew jumped overboard. The British boarded the sloop, made an easy prize of her, and carried her and the crew off to James Island. Two of the captives managed to seize a boat and make their escape to Albreda. The remaining four were placed in irons and MacNamara wrote to St Louis to announce his intention of shipping them on board a British vessel bound for the West Indies.[3]

It was small wonder that O'Hara was greatly perturbed when news of these events reached him. Captain John Clarke was hastily despatched to the Gambia to try to put matters to rights. He at

---

[1] MacNamara to Chevalier Moubeg, 15 January 1775, P.R.O., C.O. 267/16.
[2] Same to same, 16 January 1775, P.R.O., C.O. 267/16.
[3] The whole of this incident forms the subject of a very voluminous correspondence in P.R.O., C.O. 267/16.

once ordered the French sloop to be handed back and released all the prisoners save the master. When the incident was reported to England, Lord Dartmouth severely censured MacNamara for having acted with more zeal than discretion and expressed the opinion that he "has a great deal to answer for". He ordered the immediate release of the master and directed that a somewhat qualified apology from the French Governor at Goree for the conduct of his fellow countrymen should be accepted as closing the incident.[1]

Shortly after its release the French sloop was again seized by the armed colonial vessel *Lord Dartmouth* for trading elsewhere than at Albreda. The French resident at that place made preparations to retake her by force of arms. On this occasion MacNamara had sufficient wisdom to release the sloop before there was any bloodshed, but his attitude of mind is fully revealed in his report of the incident to the Secretary of State.

The French, he wrote, *thinking her in our possession sent two long boats from their shipping manned and armed to retake her. I, who was (with my glass) on the bastions laughing at their disappointment, thought it an instance of their audacity. Had it been otherwise, I must have sent force to oppose them as I could not suffer an affair of such a nature to be carried on in my sight, which might have been the cause of bloodshed.*[2]

In the same letter he announced that the natives had become "desperate insolent", that the people of Sikka had fired on one of his boats and killed a castle slave, that he was paying the people of Barra "almost as much liquour as he received water", that he could only get water on the mainland under the protection of an armed guard, and that the garrison had been at one time reduced to a pint of water a day. All this information was announced with the utmost complacency and the confident assurance that, if only he were given sufficient men and ships, the position of affairs would soon be altered.

In the circumstances it is not surprising that O'Hara wrote to inform him that

I am afraid you may be considered as the author of all the disturbances in the Gambia so ruinous and destructive to the trade of that

[1] Dartmouth to O'Hara, 20 April 1775, P.R.O., C.O. 268/3; O'Hara to Dartmouth, 13 May 1775, P.R.O., C.O. 268/4; Dartmouth to O'Hara, 27 July 1775, P.R.O., C.O. 268/3.

[2] MacNamara to Dartmouth, 8 June 1775, P.R.O., C.O. 267/16 and 268/4.

river. As you have thrown the whole River Gambia into confusion, you shall have the merit of restoring it to tranquillity again, if possible. You have constantly acted for yourself as if you was entirely independent of me in your command.

The only response to this criticism was a long letter, which was written behind O'Hara's back to Lord Dartmouth setting forth at length MacNamara's many merits and virtues and O'Hara's innumerable demerits and failings.[1]

A month later O'Hara set sail for England. The government then devolved upon the Lieutenant-Governor. According to MacNamara, O'Hara never informed him of his impending departure and left the senior military officer, Captain Joseph Wall, in charge with instructions not to hand over to him. Whatever the truth of this allegation, MacNamara overrode all obstacles by proceeding at once to St Louis and taking control of affairs, though it "caused disagreeable measures to bring them to a sense of duty".[2] He followed up this success by collecting materials for charges against his predecessor on the grounds of immorality, dishonesty, oppression, and general neglect of duty. His lengthy indictment was investigated by the Board of Trade, who found none of the charges proved, but none the less recommended O'Hara's dismissal on the ground that finding obstructions in the way of carrying out his instructions he had failed to report the matter to the home Government. For this reason they recommended his dismissal after ten years of service. The verdict of history must undoubtedly be in the words of the historian of Senegambia. "Whatever the justice of the Board of Trade's conclusions on O'Hara's shortcomings as Governor, and those shortcomings were unmistakably evident, Senegambia suffered a severe loss in his removal from office at a most critical time in the history of the province."[3]

[1] MacNamara to Dartmouth, 26 October 1775, P.R.O., C.O. 267/16 and 268/4.

[2] MacNamara to Dartmouth, 26 January 1776, P.R.O., C.O. 267/1 and 268/4.

[3] Martin, *op. cit.* pp. 88–90. O'Hara subsequently served with distinction in the American War of Independence and in the war with France, 1793–1802. He attained the rank of general and was Governor of Gibraltar from 1795 until his death in 1802.

XVII: Wall versus MacNamara, 1776–1778

Having brought the officers at St Louis to a sense of duty by "disagreeable measures", Acting Governor MacNamara proceeded to take steps to ensure that he met with little opposition in the future. Captain Joseph Wall of O'Hara's Corps had been his principal opponent. His removal was easily effected by appointing him Lieutenant-Governor of the Gambia. This move was an astute one. It had all the appearance of magnanimity towards a rival, but it was in fact intended as a punishment. Shortly after assuming the post of Governor, MacNamara informed Lord Dartmouth that after his fifteen months' residence at James Island he regarded the Gambia as a very suitable place whereto to send convicts.[1] In effect Wall was sent to James Island as a deportee.

Joseph Wall was an Irishman with a varied career. He had at one time been a student of Trinity College, Dublin, where it is said "he made himself thorough master of the Greek, and wrote the Latin language with a degree of purity and elegance to which few scholars are capable of attaining". But he exchanged the pen for the sword, taking a commission in the Royal Marines. He served with distinction at the taking of Havana in 1762. Subsequently he entered the East India Company's service, but left it on account of a none too creditable duel. In 1773 he obtained a commission in O'Hara's Corps. His letters suggest that he was a man of a very much superior education to most of the officials serving in Senegambia and it is clear that O'Hara placed considerable confidence in him. He was evidently a person of some military and administrative ability, but he lacked proper balance and suffered from a very short temper. MacNamara was equally short tempered and it was inevitable that there should be a clash between the two.

After his arrival at James Island Wall decided to regard himself as holding an independent command and to treat the orders of the Governor with contempt. MacNamara had created a precedent for such conduct by his treatment of O'Hara, but he was not prepared to tolerate the like conduct in others.

---

[1] MacNamara to Dartmouth, 5 August 1776, P.R.O., C.O. 268/4.

There were no marked signs of hostility between the two in the early days of Wall's lieutenant-governorship. Both shared the same antipathy for the French and both were equally prepared to resort to strong measures to prevent them from trading in the Gambia. In March 1776 a French vessel was found trading on the southern shore in the Foni country. Wall instructed the commander to confine his trade to Albreda. The reply was that the French and English had equal rights to trade below James Island and "no English governor or commandant should prevent him from it". It was discovered that the Frenchman had agents at Pirang and Brefet and attempts to oust them were opposed by the natives. In the circumstances Wall decided that the only course was to seize the vessel.[1] His action was endorsed by MacNamara, who, however, subsequently offered to release the vessel—an offer, which the owner declined to accept.[2] Three months later the French attempted reprisals by seizing a long boat, which got adrift at James Island. They carried it to Albreda but made no attempt to resist its recovery by the armed colonial vessel *Lord Dartmouth*.[3]

But smooth relations between MacNamara and Wall very soon ceased. Rumours reached St Louis that Wall was resorting to extraordinarily high-handed measures with his subordinates. MacNamara gave a very ready credence to these rumours. It is difficult to say now how far these reports were true. The whole matter was investigated twice—firstly, by the Governor and Council of Senegambia and then by a judge and jury in the English Court of Common Pleas. The evidence was conflicting and there were allegations, which cannot be entirely disregarded, that MacNamara was guilty of subornation of perjury. Furthermore, it is clear that the witnesses on either side were strongly biassed. However, even if one discounts entirely the contradicted evidence given on behalf of MacNamara, there remain sufficient admissions on the part of Wall's witnesses to show that MacNamara's suspicions were not entirely groundless.

The trouble began when Wall proceeded to ignore letters addressed to him by MacNamara. The latter had treated O'Hara in the same cavalier manner, but he could not tolerate the like conduct

[1] Wall to MacNamara, 14 July 1777, P.R.O., C.O. 267/6.
[2] MacNamara to Lord George Germaine, 18 July 1777, P.R.O., C.O. 276/6.
[3] Wall to MacNamara, 14 July 1777, P.R.O., C.O. 267/6.

in another. Finally on 22 July 1776 MacNamara wrote to Wall in the following terms:

Finding you disobey and neglect any orders and instructions, I now command you to give an answer to every sentence contained in my different publick letters on His Majesty's service from the time you took command of Fort James, setting forth both your reasons for not answering such letters before with your reasons at large for disobedience of my orders and instructions.

After enumerating several instances of Wall's misconduct, MacNamara enjoined him "not to obstruct, but give every assistance to inforce my commands". The letter concluded in the following language:

It is extraordinary to me you should not procure a surgeon for your garrison—still more so, since Schotte has been relieved, you have not demanded one from me. I now send one, a stranger, who I engaged for that purpose, no person here of that profession but would prefer to be shot than serve under your command from your unprecedented severity.

I strictly forbid you the confining of any person above the degree of noncommissioned officer in any other place than that allotted for his abode before offence or crime is committed. This you are to insert in the Book of General Instructions and to make it known immediately to the other magistrates.

> *I am, Sir, your obedient humble servant,*
>
> *Matthias MacNamara.*[1]

The reply to that letter was unexpected. On the night of 8 August Governor MacNamara was sitting in his quarters at St Louis, when the door opened and in walked his Lieutenant-Governor. Wall was a powerful man standing well over six feet. MacNamara, though professedly a soldier, was not a particularly brave man. He confessed as much when he reported the incident to Lord George Germaine. "Your Lordship will be able to judge what I must feel on being alarmed at the sight of a man entering my room between eight and nine o'clock at night, whom I thought was at his command. However, I immediately recovered myself and asked him why he had quitted his command, to which he answered with as

[1] P.R.O., C.O. 267/16.

insolent an air and manner as the following words could be spoke—
'Your ill treatment to me made me quit my post'."[1]

MacNamara then sufficiently recovered his presence of mind to
call a sentry and order Wall into close arrest. Wall, who as a matter
of fact was a sick man, offered no resistance. He was a few days
later placed on board a vessel and sent back to James Island with
instructions to the officer commanding there to keep him in close
confinement until His Majesty's further pleasure should be known.[2]
Wall remained in durance for nearly ten months. His gaolers evidently had the humanity to disregard the instructions of Mac-
Namara so far as to accord him a little liberty of movement on the
island, but the fact none the less remains that he was kept a very
close prisoner. He was not allowed to communicate with anybody.
His place of confinement stands to this day. It was the guardroom
on the ground floor of the tower of James Fort. Subsequently a
witness, who was distinctly hostile to Wall, informed the Governor
and Council of Senegambia that it was a room six feet by eight feet,
that it had two windows and a long hole without a frame, that he
was uncertain if the windows had shutters, and that "he has seen
things stuffed in the hole".[3]

Three months later MacNamara proceeded to James Island to
collect evidence against Wall. Certain of that evidence was easily
forthcoming. Whatever he may have done, Wall had made himself
none too popular with his subordinates in the Gambia. Furthermore, if a Governor for personal reasons descends to take the rôle
of investigating police officer, it is not very difficult to elicit the
statements, which he wants to obtain, from his subordinates—
especially from common soldiers and others occupying minor posts.
Finally, when he left James Island to take charge at St Louis,
MacNamara had left a very useful spy behind him.

This spy was a certain Thomas Sharpless. This individual had
once upon a time enlisted in the 10th Foot, but had subsequently
deserted. He was later apprehended and confined as a prisoner in
the Savoy, but had been pardoned upon condition that he enlisted
for service in Africa in O'Hara's Corps.[4] There he had managed to
work his way up to the rank of sergeant. He was posted to James

---

[1] MacNamara to Germaine, 15 August 1776, P.R.O., C.O. 267/3 and 268/4.
[2] *Ibid.*
[3] Evidence of Thomas Sharpless, 7 June 1777, P.R.O., C.O. 267/3.
[4] Memorial of Edward Morse, 26 March 1778, P.R.O., C.O. 267/4.

Island during MacNamara's Lieutenant-Governorship and, owing to deaths and other casualties amongst all the officers of commissioned rank, obtained the command of the troops. As was subsequently proved at an enquiry held by the Council of Trade, during his sojourn in the Gambia MacNamara had indulged in private trade—more particularly with the French at Albreda. Sharpless was hand in glove with him in this trade. He had been left in charge at James Island, when MacNamara proceeded to St Louis to take over the governorship of the province. When Wall was sent to James Island, he received instructions from MacNamara to discharge Sharpless, who thereupon set up as a private trader at Bintang. He was financed for this purpose by MacNamara. For some reason Wall appears to have had no suspicions regarding Sharpless and, if Sharpless is to be believed, said a great many things to him and entered into a number of transactions with him of a very questionable nature. All the information, which Sharpless could give to damn Wall, was very readily supplied to MacNamara, when he visited James Island in search of evidence.

History is silent as to whether or not MacNamara and Wall met each other during the latter's visit. What is clear is that MacNamara insisted that his orders regarding the confinement of his victim should be rigorously enforced. The Governor's soldier-servant, John Fowlis, was seen speaking to Wall. He alleged that he was guilty of "no other crime than having paid his duty to his captain". He paid for his disobedience of orders by being placed successively in the pillory and the stocks.[1]

After collecting this evidence MacNamara returned to St Louis. He subsequently obtained from the revenue the sum of £237 18s. 4d. for his contingent expenses for this visit to James Island.[2] He made no attempt to bring Wall to trial. His subsequent excuse for his failure to do so was that he could not muster sufficient officers to constitute a court martial,[3] but that excuse did not subsequently hold water with Lord Mansfield and a jury in the Common Pleas and cannot hold water in the judgment of history. Certain of Wall's alleged misdeeds were offences in the eyes of the civil as well as the military law. There was a Chief Justice at St Louis and Wall could have been arraigned before him. Furthermore, there was the

[1] Memorial of Edward Morse, 28 February 1778, P.R.O., C.O. 267/4.
[2] Accounts of Lt.-Gov. MacNamara, P.R.O., C.O. 268/2.
[3] Wall v. MacNamara, *English Reports*, xcii, 1239.

council of the Province of Senegambia, which could have held a disciplinary enquiry. The real truth appears to have been that MacNamara lacked the confidence in his own cause, which might have induced him to submit it to the arbitrament of the Chief Justice or Council. Edward Morse, the Chief Justice, appears to have been a sane and level-headed man, though perhaps too much of a formalist and a stickler for procedure. But there can be no doubt that to the best of his ability he would have dealt justice impartially without fear or favour. Most of the members of the Council, which included Morse, were honest men and apparently ready to do justice according to the best of their lights. But it is clear that the affair had become so personal that MacNamara did not want justice. As neither the Chief Justice nor the Council were ready to be domineered, Wall remained an untried prisoner on James Island.

In one respect Wall's continued confinement operated to his advantage. His health was badly impaired and there is no doubt that, as after events showed, his mind was in some measure affected. But his prolonged punishment without trial led to a reaction in his favour. He had for very good reason not been popular with his subordinates, but the unjust treatment, which was meted out to him, aroused their sympathy. Wall's gaoler, Ensign George Fall, had risen from the ranks and was described by Chief Justice Morse as "a very illiterate, ignorant man",[1] but he had a kindly heart beneath a rough exterior. He relaxed, as far as he dared, the restrictions which had been imposed on Wall's liberty. When he had first arrived at James Island as Wall's subordinate, he had been none too fairly treated by Wall, who had sent him, when he was very ill indeed, in an open boat on a mission to the Portuguese at Bissao, but he readily forgot this and did much to assist Wall in the preparation of his defence. Within a few days of MacNamara's departure Sergeant Richard Hill swore an affidavit retracting every allegation he had made in a previous affidavit sworn before MacNamara. He declared that his previous affidavit had been dictated to him by the Governor's aide-de-camp and that he had felt compelled to put his name to it.[2] Later he announced that he swore the previous affidavit "through dread and fear" of MacNamara. "The men

---

[1] Morse to Thomas Townshend, 12 August 1782, P.R.O., C.O. 267/20.

[2] Affidavit of Richard Hill, 15 November 1776, P.R.O., W.O. 1/111, f. 143.

were always in dread and fear of him....He was forced to swear the deposition for fear of being punished....He had no reasons for swearing to the deposition than that of being struck on (sic) duty and that reason was enough."[1]

MacNamara had amongst other things accused Wall of paying the soldiers at James Island in beads and iron instead of money and of valuing these commodities at an exorbitant rate and pocketing the difference between the price thus charged and the cost price. Twenty of the soldiers subsequently came before Lieutenant William Lacy, who had succeeded Fall at James Island, and deposed to the fact that Wall was doing no more than following a practice instituted by MacNamara himself, when he was at James Island, and that they felt no cause of complaint.[2]

Wall's confinement might have been indefinitely prolonged, if MacNamara had been allowed to remain in charge of the province. Wall's arrest had been reported by MacNamara to the Secretary of State but nobody at home appears to have had the slightest idea as to the manner in which he was being confined. But MacNamara's other activities had given the home Government great cause for concern. Rumours had reached England that he had been guilty of most oppressive conduct to other people—if not actual barbarity. How far the statement had any foundation in fact cannot be said, but it was reported from a French source that he had erected a "maiden" or guillotine and had actually decapitated a negro for not raising his hat to him.[3] But the greatest cause of anxiety arose from his continued high-handed treatment of French vessels trading along the coast. He caused one such ship to be seized at Portudal and announced that he intended to distribute the captured crew amongst British vessels bound for the West Indies.[4] Diplomatic protests were at once made. As the American colonies had by this time revolted and it was known that the French Government was disposed to render them assistance, the British Government was very anxious to avoid any international incident, which might afford a pretext for the declaration of war. It was therefore decided

[1] Evidence of Richard Hill, 16 July 1778, P.R.O., C.O. 267/3.
[2] Declaration of James Waddams and others, 15 May 1777; Affidavit of Robert Mitchell, 2 June 1777, P.R.O., W.O. 1/111, ff. 140–142.
[3] Le Brasseur, Governor of Goree, to ——, 31 August 1776, P.R.O., C.O. 267/6.
[4] MacNamara to Dartmouth, 5 August 1776, P.R.O., C.O. 268/4.

that MacNamara must be replaced as soon as possible. Captain John Clarke was therefore sent out from England as Governor and instructions were sent to MacNamara to return home at once to answer the charges preferred against him by the French ambassador.[1]

Clarke arrived at St Louis on 8 April 1777, "to all appearances in good time to put a stop to the very extraordinary proceedings carrying on in this province".[2] At a later date he reported that "on my arrival I found matters so circumstanced that they could not have continued in the same situation much longer without some fatal consequence". MacNamara declined to return home. Shortly before Clarke's arrival, he had sent to James Island ordering Lieutenant William Lacy to come to St Louis to answer certain complaints. Lacy "absolutely refused in obeying his orders to come up, giving for reason in writing to Captain Lang, then commandant at Gambia, the horror of a long imprisonment: Captain Lang, taking upon himself to vindicate Lieutenant Lacy's non-compliance with the Lieutenant-Governor's orders, kept him at Fort James".[3]

Clarke found a great many things to put to rights amongst the undisciplined troops, the chaotic disorder of every Government department, and the "very complicated scene of public fraud, embezzlement, and perjury",[4] but he got to work on Wall's case as soon as he could. He decided to hold an enquiry before the Council. The personnel of this tribunal was open to criticism. Nothing could be alleged against the impartiality of Clarke himself or Morse, the Chief Justice, nor probably against William Bishopp or John Peter Demain. On the other hand, it is clear from what has just been mentioned that Lieutenant Lacy must have been distinctly prejudiced against MacNamara. But as a sort of counter-balance the remaining member, John Peter Schotte, had personal reasons for disliking Wall and actually gave evidence against him during the course of the enquiry. Clarke had, however, to make use of the personnel, which he had available.

The enquiry opened on 2 June 1777, when MacNamara handed in a list of charges against Wall. They were twenty-three in number. The first alleged disobedience of orders by coming from James Island to St Louis without leave. Nine others alleged overt attempts to undermine MacNamara's authority as Acting Governor including

[1] Germaine to MacNamara, 5 February 1777, P.R.O., C.O. 268/3.
[2] Clarke to Germaine, 4 July 1777, P.R.O., C.O. 268/4.
[3] Same to same, 26 July 1777, P.R.O., C.O. 268/4.   [4] *Ibid.*

(*inter alia*) allegations that he "has studied to take away my life" and openly avowed his intention of coming to St Louis in order to do so, that he "has declared that he had put the whole province of Senegal in confusion", and that MacNamara was in his power and he would "smash" him. Others alleged oppression to his subordinates, the wrongful confinement of some in the black hole at James Fort, and the wrongful dismissal of others. The remaining charges asserted embezzlement, indulgence in private trade, and general disregard of MacNamara's instructions. A copy of these charges was furnished to Wall, who was given three days in which to reply.[1]

Wall conducted his own defence. He has generally been given the reputation of being a blusterer, but at this date he was clearly badly broken down in health and in no mood for bluster. He appears to have behaved with some degree of dignity and the record of the proceedings shows that he cross-examined his opponent's witnesses with some ability. MacNamara did not appear in person to prosecute his charges. He alleged that he "was in a most desperate state of health" and sent his brother, Francis MacNamara, to examine the witnesses. Subsequently he alleged that his brother was treated by the Council with great abuse and threatened with confinement in the black hole, but, as there is only MacNamara's word for this allegation, it should be discounted.[2]

There can be no doubt that subconsciously the tribunal was predisposed in Wall's favour. He was not a lovable and had never been a popular man. If he had been brought to trial soon after his arrest, it might well have been that MacNamara would have carried the day. There was no getting over the fact that Wall's conduct had more than once been high-handed and that some of his pecuniary transactions were highly suspicious. At the time of his arrest there was undoubtedly a strong, though possibly not entirely reasonable, prejudice against Wall. As the months rolled on, Wall's sufferings aroused an equally strong and more reasonable reaction in his favour. He came before the tribunal broken down in health and an object of compassion. His opponent's absence aroused the strong, though not altogether reasonable, impression that there was no case for Wall to answer.

---

[1] Minutes of Council of Senegambia, P.R.O., C.O. 267/1 and 267/3.
[2] MacNamara to Germaine, 7 July 1777, P.R.O., C.O. 268/4.

The first witness called on behalf of MacNamara did a great deal to damage his case. This was Wall's former gaoler, Ensign Fall. One of MacNamara's allegations was the inhumanity of Wall in sending this officer in an open boat to Bissao, when he was seriously ill. Fall demolished this allegation by saying that he was ill at the time "but not so ill as to prevent his going on command". The record suggests that he was an honest witness. He did depose that the soldiers on James Island had complained of being paid in kind instead of in money, but stated their murmurings were appeased when the goods received were supplemented by Wall with linen goods.[1]

The next witness was Thomas Sharpless. His examination extended over ten days. If he was to be believed, Wall had never disguised his dislike of MacNamara. In July 1776 Wall had shown a native of Barra a hanger and had announced that "that was what he intended paying the Lieutenant-Governor a visit with and that he would sharpen it for the purpose. He had then a pair of pistols on a bench alongside of him and said he had been practising with one of them at an ace of cards, but could not tell the ace. There were two balls not far from the card on the door; and Captain Wall asked the deponent if they would not be near a man, if he stood there". Sharpless also said he had heard Wall let drop such expressions as "he would dry shave without ball or razor", that "he would sever the Lieutenant-Governor's head from his body, if he did not take care", and that "he had put Senegal in confusion". This evidence was, however, largely discounted by the admission of the witness that he did not take the first opportunity to inform MacNamara of this intemperate language. His excuse that he "did not choose to interfere between gentlemen" was not very convincing. Sharpless also deposed to certain acts of embezzlement by Wall. If he was to be believed, he was Wall's accomplice in most of these transactions and he broke down rather badly on cross-examination.[2] Sharpless also gave evidence to the effect that Lieutenant Mallard, commanding the colonial sloop *Lord Dartmouth*, Thomas Parkin, the agent victualler, and John Peter Schotte, the surgeon, had been confined in the black hole of Fort James. In cross-examination he admitted that the so-called black hole was the guard-room under the gate.

[1] Minutes of Council of Senegambia, 5 and 6 June 1777, P.R.O., 267/3 and 270/1.

[2] Examination of Thomas Sharpless, 7, 10–14, 16–18, June 1777, and Minutes of the Council of Senegambia, P.R.O., C.O. 267/3 and 270/1.

All three of the alleged victims were in St Louis to give evidence, but only Schotte, who was a member of the tribunal, was called as a witness. He was a native of Hesse-Cassel, who apparently spoke only broken English. He said he had been confined for ten days in the black hole for writing "errors excepted" on a victualling return, which he had made out at Wall's dictation. He thought the black hole "a very nasty place", full of mice, centipedes, and cockroaches, where new bought slaves were usually confined. Schotte protested that "it was not a place of confinement for gentlemen", but had not been moved to another place. In cross-examination he admitted that "the affair was seemingly made up between deponent and Captain Wall before deponent left Fort James.... He does not know that it was in consequence of the affair being made up that Captain Wall did not report deponent's crimes to the Lieutenant-Governor. ...[But] the Lieutenant-Governor on deponent's arrival at Senegal desired him to lodge a complaint against Captain Wall.... He told the Lieutenant-Governor the affair was made up, but that was not deponent's reason for not complaining.... On deponent's refusing to lodge a complaint the Lieutenant-Governor called him no names". Reading his deposition, one is left with the impression that he was a truthful witness, but a timid creature, easily bullied, and supremely anxious to live on good terms with his superiors whatever wrongs they might do him.[1]

MacNamara did not call either of the other alleged victims, Mallard and Parkin, for a very good reason. Parkin had filed a number of suits against him for assault and on other grounds.[2] Mallard also had a strong dislike of MacNamara and on 19 July 1777 signed a document to the effect that in the performance of his duty he had been "constrained by threats, personal abuses and severe contradictions" on the part of MacNamara.[3] Both he and Parkin therefore were likely to say as little as they possibly could to substantiate the charges against Wall. The fact none the less remains that Wall never attempted in his cross-examination of either Sharpless or Schotte to refute the allegations regarding Parkin and Mallard. According to Schotte, Parkin complained that rats had run away with his clothes during the night he was in the black hole,

[1] Examinations of Thomas Sharpless and John Peter Schotte, 7, 10–14, 16–18, 25–26, 30 June, and 1 July 1777, P.R.O., C.O. 267/3 and 270/1.
[2] Memorial of Edward Morse, 28 February 1778, P.R.O., C.O. 267/4.
[3] P.R.O., C.O. 267/3.

but neither he nor Mallard had been confined for longer than one night, probably because they were more vocal than Schotte.

In the course of the evidence of Sharpless the fact was elicited that MacNamara had on his visit to James Island in October–November 1776 taken certain evidence on oath professedly before his Council. He had, however, retained the depositions in his own personal custody and had not handed them over to his successor. On 18 June 1777 he was ordered to produce these documents but it was not until 3 July that he produced them.[1] This apparent suppression of evidence clearly militated very strongly against him.

The enquiry went on until 16 July. A number of soldiers were examined regarding Wall's alleged acts of embezzlement and indulgence in private trade, but not very much was elicited from them. MacNamara then applied for an adjournment so that further evidence could be obtained from the Gambia. On 17 July the Council passed the following resolution:

Lieutenant Governor MacNamara having occasioned a very heavy expence to government in sending a vessel twice to Gambia for witnesses to support his charge against Captain Joseph Wall, and the Council having reason to suspect that the said Lieutenant Governor is trifling with this Honourable Board; ordered, that Matthias MacNamara, Esquire, do on Saturday next deliver to this Board a list of names of such persons as he intends to call in support of the several charges and allegations brought by him against Joseph Wall, Esquire, and that no persons whatsoever be examined as witnesses on behalf of the said Matthias MacNamara, whose names shall not be in such required list.[2]

On 19 July MacNamara appeared before the Council and announced "that he had not had time to make it out, and that he would not give in any list, that he had a great many witnesses to examine and could not tell but one might offer himself on his going out of the Court, or that others might rise up at the last moment of his examination". He was then informed that the Council thought he was only trifling with them, but that they would allow him till 21 July to submit his list. MacNamara refused to do this. "He then produced a paper, which he called a representation of some matters. The Council having suffered him to read a part of it and finding that

[1] Minutes of the Council of Senegambia, P.R.O., C.O. 270/1.
[2] P.R.O., C.O. 270/1.

it contained a very indelicate attack on His Excellency the Governor, whose conduct in all the proceedings, and particularly those wherein the Lieutenant Governor was concerned, cannot but be highly approved, the Council therefore put a stop to his reading any more of it and dismissed it." The members further resolved that MacNamara had "treated the said Board with great contempt and that the conduct of the said Lieutenant-Governor since the commencement of the said matters be taken into consideration".[1]

After examining the captain of a passing merchant vessel in regard to one of Wall's alleged transactions, on 30 July the Council by a majority came to the following resolution:

Resolved, that it is the opinion of this Board that the several charges exhibited by Lieutenant-Governor MacNamara against Captain Joseph Wall are frivolous, groundless, and vexatious, contradicted by his own witness, that the long confinement the said Captain Wall suffered at Fort James, Gambia, in a very small room destitute of every convenience was malicious, that the said Matthias MacNamara has trifled with this Board, and treated it with the most injurious and insolent contempt.

Resolved, that the said charges be dismissed, and that it be recommended to His Excellency the Governor to release the said Captain Wall from his arrest, if His Excellency shall think proper, and that the Clerk of the Council do furnish the said Captain Joseph Wall with an attested copy of the said charges and depositions.[2]

The one dissentient was Schotte. Whether it was due to the sense of his own personal grievance or his ignorance of the English language, for once he deviated from an ingrained habit by venturing to disagree with his superior officers.

Immediately after his acquittal Wall proceeded to turn the tables on MacNamara. When he paid his unexpected visit to St Louis in August 1776, he had brought with him some goods chiefly comprising wine and wax. After Wall's arrest MacNamara had seized the goods and had them sold. Wall now brought an action for trover claiming £4000 damages. The case was tried before the Chief Justice and a jury. MacNamara made no attempt to defend the action. During the hearing evidence was given that the official, who made the seizure, had been approached by MacNamara to write a document purporting to be a request to MacNamara to keep the goods

---

[1] P.R.O., C.O. 270/1. [2] *Ibid.*

in safe custody, whereas the official in question had been ordered by MacNamara to hand the goods over to him. The jury eventually awarded damages amounting to £1527 14s. 6d.[1] One comment on the case is that the nature of the claim itself suggests that there was very substantial foundation for MacNamara's allegations that Wall was indulging in private trade.

When Wall commenced his next action for false imprisonment, Morse decided that local prejudice was so strong that a fair and impartial enquiry on the spot was out of the question. As both the parties were proceeding to England, he recommended that the action should be tried there. He dealt similarly with an action commenced by Parkin against MacNamara for assault and conversion and one commenced by John Fowlis for false imprisonment.[2] Criminal proceedings were also started against several of Mac-Namara's adherents. Sharpless was arrested for embezzlement and Thomas Wallace for subornation of perjury.[3] Morse wrote to England to explain that "the incompleat state of the civil establishment of this province, added to Mr Sharpless's own request has determined Governor Clarke to send him home for tryal.... We have had a very fatiguing time, but thank God its now over".[4] This decision did not prevent Sharpless from alleging that he was being sent home against his will.[5]

Meanwhile, evidence was being collected as to MacNamara's innumerable misdeeds whilst Lieutenant-Governor of the Gambia. In August 1775 Alexander MacDowell, master and part owner of the *Friend*, had arrived in the river. He had had trouble with his crew, who had mutinied and wounded him in the arm. He therefore appealed to MacNamara for assistance. This was refused unless he agreed to sell the Lieutenant-Governor his sloop. MacDowell protested that "it was his little all that fortune had left him". Mac-Namara then "joined and sided with the malicious complaints of a disappointed piratical crew of sailors, who would have sworn anything to escape the punishment they themselves meritted". He assaulted and beat MacDowell and threw him into the black hole. The unfortunate master then agreed to sell his sloop for £200 payable

---

[1] Memorial of Edward Morse, 28 February 1778, P.R.O., C.O. 267/4.
[2] *Ibid.*
[3] Warrants dated 23 June and 14 August 1777, P.R.O., C.O. 267/4.
[4] Morse to Robert Browne, 14 August 1777, P.R.O., C.O. 267/4.
[5] Petition of Sharpless, s.d., P.R.O., C.O. 267/4.

by bills of exchange upon London. MacNamara then released the master, put his crew in irons, and confined them in the black hole. MacDowell asked for something in writing regarding the sale of the sloop and the Lieutenant-Governor "damned him for a rascal and a scoundrel, and that he would never pay him" and ordered him to leave James Island at once. MacDowell was penniless and asked for a trifle wherewith to buy food. He was told that he would be put in close confinement and fed on bread and water, if he did not at once remove himself. He was a sick man at the time and, thanks to MacNamara's conduct, the natives on the mainland were very hostile at the time to white men. MacDowell, however, could not choose but go. He "fortunately met with a generous benefactress" in a mulatto woman, who fed him for four months. He then had the offer of a passage on a vessel bound for the West Indies, but being unable to pay the small fare asked of him approached Sharpless, who refused to give him anything unless he gave a receipt in full satisfaction of all claims against MacNamara in respect of the sloop.[1]

This was by no means the sum total of the charges, which were brought against MacNamara. He was alleged to have suborned perjury by inducing William Stevenson, a soldier at James Fort, to swear falsely that certain accounts were true and correct. Just before MacNamara's departure from James Island for St Louis to assume the post of Acting Governor, Stevenson had a quarrel with Thomas Sharpless. For this he was placed in irons by MacNamara. Three months later he was brought to St Louis and released on his promising to swear to the accuracy of the accounts. According to affidavits sworn later, Stevenson expressed great uneasiness because he knew the accounts were not true, but as he had "already experienced very severe treatment from the said Lieutenant-Governor, he, this deponent, was absolutely afraid to refuse complying with the order".[2] As a result an indictment for subornation of perjury was presented against MacNamara and on 1 June 1777 a jury at St Louis found a true bill.[3]

Finally, allegations were made that MacNamara had been guilty of a number of irregularities, including the carrying on of private

[1] Affidavits of Robert Dam and Alexander MacDowell, 27 January 1777, P.R.O., C.O. 267/4.
[2] Affidavit of William Stevenson, 22 May 1777, and Affidavit of Thomas Parkin, 31 May 1777, P.R.O., C.O. 267/3 and 4 June 1777, P.R.O., C.O. 267/4.
[3] P.R.O., C.O. 267/4; Clarke to Germaine, 4 July 1777, P.R.O., C.O. 268/4.

trade with the French at Albreda.[1] Both MacNamara and Sharpless demanded an immediate trial. Morse, the Chief Justice, knew that he could not empanel a proper jury, as he lacked the means for setting the proper legal machinery in motion. He shrewdly suspected that the two made their demand for this very reason. "I consulted", he subsequently wrote, "with Governor Clarke what steps were best to be taken in such a critical situation. He begged that I would not let the weak state of the civil power be known, that I would endeavour to form a grand jury, draw a bill of indictment and submit it to them, adding, that if they found the bills true bills, he would send the prisoners home. The bills were accordingly found and the prisoners sent to England....Soon after my arrival Messieurs Mac-Namara, Wallace, and Sharpless...entered into a conspiracy against me and presented complaints to the Lords of Trade against me for maladministration. On hearing it, it appeared that I had acted consistently with justice and equity and with as much legal form as the circumstances of the province would permit. I was consequently honourably acquitted of the charges."[2]

Governor Clarke was subjected to a like attack, the Board of Trade being inundated with petitions, which they forwarded to him for "such proofs and depositions in answer thereto as you shall think necessary for your vindication and defence".[3]

The battle was now to be fought out in England. MacNamara was brought before the Council of Trade to answer the various charges relating to his administration. His defence to the charge of trading with the French at Albreda was that he had been compelled to sell slaves to them so as to buy necessaries for James Fort, which the English traders were unable to supply.[4] After hearing the evidence, the Council held that this and certain other charges were proved and recommended that it would not be for the royal service or the public welfare that MacNamara should be continued in the post of Lieutenant-Governor.[5] MacNamara appealed from this decision to the

---

[1] Examination of Thomas Parkin, 16 January 1778, P.R.O., C.O. 267/4.
[2] Morse to Thomas Townshend, 12 August 1782, P.R.O., C.O. 267/20.
[3] MacNamara to Board of Trade, 12 December 1777, P.R.O., C.O. 267/4; Petition of Matthias MacNamara, 21 January 1778; Petition of Thomas Wallace, 27 January 1778; Petition of Francis MacNamara, 5 February 1778; Petition of Thomas Sharpless, 24 February 1778; Petition of Benjamin Duley, s.d.; Board of Trade to Clarke, 7 April 1778, P.R.O., C.O. 268/4.
[4] Examination of Thomas Wallace, P.R.O., C.O. 267/4.
[5] Board of Trade to the King, 3 March 1778, P.R.O., C.O. 268/2, ff. 296–303.

Privy Council, but the Committee of that Council for Plantation Affairs saw no reason to differ from the finding and the appeal was dismissed.[1] On 28 August 1778 he received formal notification of his dismissal[2] and on the same date Governor Clarke was informed that the post vacated by his dismissal had been filled by the appointment of Captain Joseph Wall.[3]

In the meantime Wall was prosecuting a suit in the Common Pleas against MacNamara for malicious imprisonment. MacNamara could not plead that information, which he had obtained subsequent to Wall's arrest, was legal justification for that imprisonment. He could only justify that arrest on the grounds that at the time of making it he had reasonable and probable cause for believing it to be justified. The presiding judge, Lord Mansfield, held that the imprisonment might have been at first legal inasmuch as Wall, as a soldier, had been guilty of an offence under the Mutiny Act by leaving his post without the leave of his commanding officer. But he proceeded to direct the jury as follows:

It is admitted that the plaintiff was to blame in leaving his post. But there was no enemy—no mutiny—no danger. His health was declining and he trusted to the benevolence of the defendant to consider the circumstances in which he acted. But supposing it to have been the defendant's duty to have called him to a military account for his misconduct, what apology is there for denying him the use of common air in a sultry climate, and shutting him up in a gloomy prison, where there was no possibility of bringing him to trial for several months, there not being a sufficient number of officers to form a court martial? These circumstances, independent of the direct evidence of malice, as sworn by one of the witnesses, are sufficient for you to presume a bad malignant motive in the defendant, which would destroy his justification, had it been within the powers delegated to the defendant by his commission.[4]

The result was that the jury awarded Wall £1000 damages.

Apart from any legal aspect of the case there can be no doubt that Lord Mansfield's criticism of MacNamara's conduct is the judgment of history in regard to this long drawn out fight. It is true that Wall

[1] Order in Council, 19 August 1778, P.R.O., C.O. 267/6.
[2] Germaine to MacNamara, 28 August 1778, P.R.O., C.O. 268/3.
[3] Germaine to Clarke, 28 August 1778, P.R.O., C.O. 268/3.
[4] Wall v. MacNamara, *English Reports*, xcix, 1239.

had been guilty of insubordination. There can further be no doubt that Wall had acted in an oppressive manner towards his subordinates and that there was a very strong suspicion that he had indulged in private trade. But the charges had been grossly embellished and exaggerated at MacNamara's instigation. In any event it was a case of the pot calling the kettle black. MacNamara had been guilty of at least as many, if not more, delinquencies. His venting of his personal spite by his thoroughly vindictive and oppressive treatment of his opponent is one of the blackest of the regrettably many dark pages in the history of the Gambia.

MacNamara passed out of the history of the Gambia after his dismissal. Wall will be mentioned in future pages. His end was a tragic one. In 1782, whilst Governor of Goree, he caused three soldiers to be flogged to death. He subsequently fled to the continent and was not brought to justice till twenty years later. He was then tried in the King's Bench for murdering a sergeant named Armstrong, found guilty, sentenced to death, and duly executed. Despite the defence which he raised there can be no doubt that he was rightly convicted of a very brutal and callous murder. Certain political considerations prevented the executive from exercising the prerogative of mercy and perhaps it was not a case for clemency. It must, however, be said in Wall's favour that at the time of the offence he was in a bad state of health and that he was dealing with a thoroughly mutinous set of soldiers, who had been recruited from most of the gaols in England. It must further be remembered that his ten months of oppressive and unjust confinement on James Island had undoubtedly had a lasting effect upon his mind. Joseph Wall was justly and properly convicted of the murder of Sergeant Armstrong, but a great deal of the moral responsibility for that crime rested with Matthias MacNamara.

XVIII: The last days of the Province of Senegambia, 1776–1783

After having got the affairs of MacNamara and Wall disposed and the two adversaries embarked for England, Governor Clarke wrote to the Secretary of State saying: "I cannot but think the situation of the Province retrievable notwithstanding the severe shocks it has received within these two years past by the misconduct of the Lieutenant-Governor."[1] In more favourable circumstances there seems to be little doubt that Clarke might have fulfilled his promise, but fate was against him.

Whilst MacNamara and Wall had been bickering, the American colonies on the other side of the Atlantic had revolted. For a time the war had few repercussions in West Africa. Instructions were sent from England to seize all American ships, which arrived off the coast, and it was one of MacNamara's allegations against Wall that he had disregarded these instructions and had later allowed the masters of the seized vessels to redeem their ships with bills of exchange payable to Wall himself.[2] In 1778 France took sides with the revolted colonies and the war was carried into Africa. The French at Goree were not in a position to be aggressive, but no more were the English garrisons at St Louis and James Island. At the end of 1778 both these places were reported to be badly in need of provisions and much reduced below their establishments.[3] Furthermore the activities of French men-of-war and privateers resulted in the frequent interruption of communication with England.

Great Britain's commitments on the other side of the Atlantic distracted attention from the very defenceless state of their West African colonies, but at least one person in France had taken full note thereof. This was the Duc du Lauzun, whose attention was drawn to the position of affairs by an article, which he had read in an English magazine. He propounded a plan of campaign to the French Government, which was subsequently adopted. A combined

---

[1] Clarke to Germaine, 12 September 1777, P.R.O., C.O. 267/3.

[2] MacNamara to Germaine, 18 August 1776, P.R.O., C.O. 267/3 and 268/4; Charges against Captain Wall, P.R.O., C.O. 267/3.

[3] William Knox to Agent for Senegambia, 28 November 1778, P.R.O., C.O. 268/3.

military and naval force was equipped and despatched at the end of 1778 in seven ships to attack St Louis and James Island. The Duc du Lauzun was placed in command of the land forces and the Marquis de Vaudreuil of the sea forces. Instructions were given to attack and capture St Louis and then to remove thither the garrison at Goree after having destroyed the forts at this latter place. Instructions were also issued to take James Fort, where "it is presumed that the defence will be very feeble and that the commandant will soon ask to capitulate". The fortifications were then to be razed, the buildings and store houses burnt, and the banks and piles, which served to enlarge the island, were to be destroyed. All ships and vessels in the river were to be seized.[1]

This expedition started at a very inopportune time for the British in Senegambia. Governor Clarke died on 18 August 1778.[2] Wall had not yet arrived as Lieutenant-Governor and the administration therefore devolved upon Lieutenant Lacy, who was in command at James Island. Ensign Fall took over command at St Louis and sent a letter by the *Gambia* packet to notify Lacy of Clarke's death. The packet was, however, captured soon after leaving Senegal and it was not until November that Lacy heard of the death of Clarke. On 24 November 1778 Lacy wrote to the Secretary of State to inform him of the position of affairs. He reported heavy losses by death at St Louis, but added that the French at Goree had lost all their officers except one. None the less the French had been so far active as to intercept three packets, which he had tried to send overland to St Louis. The garrison on James Island had been short of provisions for seven months and he was in hourly expectation of being attacked.[3]

The French fleet reached the mouth of the Senegal on 28 January 1778. It found a very easy task before it. Lacy had instructed Ensign Fall to hand over to Lieutenant Stanton of the artillery. Fall had refused to do so and had later come into conflict with some of the troops, who had shut him out of the fort. The result was a small war and on 30 January the French fleet settled the dispute between the two opponents by taking possession of the fort.[4]

---

[1] J. Montheilet, "Le duc du Lauzun, gouverneur du Sénégal", *Bulletin de Comité d'Études Historiques et Scientifiques de l'Afrique Occidentale Française* (1920), pp. 215–235.

[2] List of deaths in Fort Louis, Senegal, P.R.O., C.O. 267/18.

[3] P.R.O., C.O. 268/4.

[4] J. P. Schotte to Germaine, 29 March 1779, P.R.O., C.O. 267/19.

The Chevalier de Pontdevez was then despatched with a corvette to Goree to pick up reinforcements and to proceed thence to the Gambia. Information of the arrival of the fleet had reached the French at Albreda who had been allowed to remain there unmolested by the British. They at once circulated the information amongst the people of Barra. The seed, which they sowed, yielded good fruit. A number of British vessels and factories up the river were attacked and destroyed and the merchandise carried off. As he was powerless to carry out reprisals or to afford protection, Lacy ordered every trader up the river down to James Island to devise a scheme of defence.[1]

The garrison at Goree numbered only forty-eight men, but Boucher, the French Governor, lent Pontdevez an officer and twenty men as well as a corvette. In addition twenty-two free mulattoes volunteered for service and two private vessels were placed at Pontdevez's disposal. The expedition left Goree on 6 February 1779, but was delayed by fog. Albreda was reached on 9 February. Lacy had at his disposal one other officer and twenty soldiers, fifteen merchant captains and traders, and seventy-eight castle and other slaves "bred on board their craft, as good as whites", but he was short of provisions. On 11 February he surrendered at discretion without a blow having been struck. As was inevitable, he was afterwards severely censured. He had a heavier armament than the ships opposing him and might have been able to beat off an attack, but, if de Vaudreuil had subsequently reinforced Pontdevez, the fate of James Island would have been inevitable.[2]

Lacy and the other prisoners of war were taken off to St Louis. One of the French corvettes was sent up the river to take possession of any British vessels and factories, which they might find there. Pontdevez set to work to raze James Fort. The task was not a difficult one. "The angles of the bastions were so acute they admitted of no defence and were easily destroyed by a few barrels of powder. It is now an entire heap of ruins. The faces of the bastions and the centre of the curtains were undermined, and on the explosion the whole elevation of the work was brought to the ground.... The French destroyed the piles, which protected it from the encroach-

---

[1] Roberts, "An Account of the Situation of Senegal and Gambia", P.R.O., C.O. 267/19 and Egerton MS. 1162 A, f. 242.

[2] Montheilet, *op. cit.* pp. 526–539; Thomas Parkin to Thomas de Grey, 11 February 1779, P.R.O., C.O. 267/20.

ments of the river." [1] Except for a brief reoccupation by a sergeant's guard after the close of the Napoleonic wars James Island from this date ceases to figure in the history of the Gambia.

In accordance with the instructions received from the French Government Goree was abandoned, and the forts demolished, and the garrison transferred to St Louis. [2] As soon as news of the loss of St Louis and James Island reached England, it was decided to make an effort to recapture these places. Captain Joseph Wall and a contingent of the African Corps were therefore embarked upon the ships of a squadron, which was bound for the East Indies under the command of Sir Edward Hughes. The squadron made no attempt against St Louis but proceeded direct to Goree, which they found abandoned. A small force was landed to occupy the dismantled forts and on 24 May 1779 four men-of-war proceeded to the Gambia with part of the African Corps under Wall's command. Information as to the position of affairs in the river was meagre. It was believed that James Island might be in French occupation and Wall was instructed that "in case he shall find that settlement in the possession of a superior French force, he is then to make the best of his way to the Leeward Islands". [3] James Island was reached on 31 May. The fort was found to be in so ruinous a condition that a military engineer reported that it could only be restored by removing the existing debris and rebuilding it from its very foundations. Wall therefore decided to make no attempt to reoccupy it and proceeded with the squadron to Barbadoes. [4]

The history of the remnants of the Province of Senegambia during the closing months of the American War of Independence does not particularly concern us. Goree remained in British hands until the end of the war and the French abandoned Albreda, but retained St Louis. No attempt was made to reoccupy any place in the Gambia, but British merchant ships took advantage of the protection afforded by Admiral Hughes' squadron to renew their activities in the Gambia. [5] Shortly after Wall's departure from Goree, it was

[1] Captain Daniel Houghton to Rt Hon. Thomas Townshend, 24 February 1783, P.R.O., C.O. 267/20.   [2] Montheilet, op. cit. p. 209.

[3] Lord Macleod to Germaine, 10 May 1779; Lt.-Col. Rooke to Germaine, 25 May 1779, P.R.O., C.O. 268/4; Annual Register, 1780, p. 11.

[4] Wall to Germaine, 5 July 1779, Lt. Robert Beatson to Wall, 9 July 1779; Rooke to Germaine, 19 June 1779, P.R.O., C.O. 268/4.

[5] Log of H.M.S. Actaeon, 23 May 1779; P.R.O., Ad. 51/3: Log of H.M.S. Vesuvius, 31 May 1779, P.R.O., Ad. 51/1034.

reported that "the river of Gambia still continues open, there being no garrison upon it at present".[1] In course of time, relying upon the protection which could be afforded by the garrison at Goree, British merchants began to trade once more in the river.[2] During the next three years settlements were established at various places on the river banks. One such was established as far up the river as Nyanimaru. Bintang was reoccupied as well as Juffure and Brefet in Foni district.[3]

The people of Barra remained aggressive and complaints were received that they committed depredations on various traders, but the people of Foni and Kiang showed a very friendly disposition.[4]

No attempt was made from Goree to re-establish a military post in the River Gambia, but Government vessels occasionally visited the river to obtain wood, oyster shells for lime, and other building materials. In October 1780 Captain Daniel Houghton was sent with eighty men and four vessels to Bintang to cut timber. Whilst the party was engaged on this task, the French frigate Sénégal[5] under the command of Monsieur Allery entered the river. Houghton was compelled to abandon his ships and take refuge amongst the Jolas of Foni. They proved good friends in the hour of need. The "emperor of Foni ordered Houghton's party to be housed and supplied with provisions. Four hundred Jolas were mobilised to prevent the French from landing and destroying the factory of a British trader at Bintang. They stood to arms for three successive nights. The French frigate approached within one hundred yards of Bintang and opened fire. Availing themselves of every scrap of cover afforded by the bush, the Jolas returned this fire with such effect that the French did not attempt to land. Five of the frigate's crew were killed and four of the Jolas. Eventually the French withdrew taking the four British transports with them.[6]

News of the activities of the Sénégal reached Goree just at the moment when H.M.S. Zephyr (Lieutenant John Inglis) called there.

[1] Lieut. Winter to Germaine, 30 May 1779, P.R.O., C.O. 268/4.
[2] Same to same, 21 April 1780, P.R.O., C.O. 268/4.
[3] Daniel Houghton to Thomas Townshend, 24 February 1783, P.R.O., C.O. 267/20; Evidence of Thomas Nesbitt, 3 May 1785, P.R.O., H.O. 7/1, ff. 11, 12.
[4] Wall to Germaine, 22 August 1780, P.R.O., C.O. 268/4.
[5] The original name of this ship was the Racehorse. It had been captured by the French from the British. Nelson had served in the Racehorse in Captain Hon. C. J. Phipps' Arctic expedition in 1773.
[6] Houghton to Thomas Townshend, 24 February 1783, P.R.O., C.O. 267/20; Annual Register, 1781, p. 246.

The *Zephyr* and the privateer *Polly* at once proceeded to the Gambia. They arrived off Barra Point on 2 November where they found the *Sénégal* and her four prizes. As soon as the British ships were sighted, the French set fire to two of their prizes and the *Sénégal* proceeded to get under weigh. The *Zephyr* carried only fourteen guns to the French ship's twenty-two, but she at once bore down on her opponent. When both vessels were within pistol shot, they exchanged broadsides and for the next hour there was a very hot engagement. Both ships eventually ran aground off Barra Point. The *Zephyr* was in such a position that she could only get one gun to bear on her opponent, but by lightening the ship forward and with the help of the tide Lieutenant Inglis managed after seventy minutes to swing round on his keel and bring four guns into action. For the next three hours he kept up an incessant fire on the *Sénégal*, which struck at six o'clock, having lost twelve men killed and twenty-eight wounded. The British losses were two killed and four wounded, but during the action the *Zephyr's* main yard and maintopmast were shot away, and the lower mast, maintopsail yard, and rigging badly damaged.

After the action Captain Houghton's party was rescued and taken with the prize to Goree. The prize blew up for some unknown cause a few days after its arrival at Goree and twenty-three of the prize crew perished with her.[1] Inglis' action had a very decisive effect upon the history of the Gambia. The *Sénégal* had been a real source of danger to British shipping and, had it not been for Inglis' very plucky fight, there can be no doubt that British influence in the Gambia would have been entirely supplanted by that of the French. Inglis was not, however, destined to receive much credit for his conduct at the time. He did receive some very belated and much begrudged praise from Wall, who had by this time assumed command at Goree.[2] Unfortunately for Inglis, Wall had found occasion to fall out with him, as he had with practically every other officer with whom he was brought in contact. The withholding of that praise was the more ungracious because Inglis had assisted in the suppression of an incipient mutiny against Wall of the troops at Goree.[3]

---

[1] W. L. Clowes, *The Royal Navy*, IV, 58; *Annual Register*, 1781, pp. 246 *seq.*; Log of H.M.S. *Zephyr*, P.R.O., Ad. 51/1100.

[2] Wall to Germaine, 3 July 1781, P.R.O., C.O. 267/20 and 268/4.

[3] Log of H.M.S. *Zephyr*, 4 and 5 August 1780, P.R.O., Ad. 51/1100.

The *Zephyr* remained on the coast and visited the River Gambia on two other occasions. The first visit was for the purpose of embarking some of the castle slaves from James Island, who were at Juffure, and of salving a twenty-four pounder from the ruins of the fort. Both these tasks were accomplished. Just before leaving the river a native sloop put in to Albreda. Inglis tried to intercept it, but, being unable to do so, fired several broadsides into Albreda. His reason for so doing is not clear. It was afterwards alleged that he had received instructions to do so from Wall,[1] but Wall himself informed the Secretary of State that this had been done "for reasons and motives unknown to me".[2] As Wall had previously reported that the Barra people were giving trouble and that, "when I am permitted to take command of the garrison of Goree, I am flattered that the face of affairs in this country will give satisfaction to the king and your Lordship",[3] one is disposed to doubt his repudiation of Inglis' conduct. One doubts it the more, when one learns that on the *Zephyr's* next voyage to the Gambia, an artillery officer was sent to entice and detain on board the ship several natives of Barra.[4] Such evidence as there is seems to point to the conclusion that Wall, whose mind had clearly been affected by his past ill-treatment, believed that a policy of occasional "frightfulness" was the best means of upholding British prestige in the Gambia. There seems little doubt that, as Captain Houghton wrote, Wall's "unfriendly treatment of the natives and others shut up all intercourse with the continent and defeated our most sanguine expectations".[5]

Some interest was shown in West Africa during the negotiations preceding the Treaty of Versailles. No attempt was made to secure the restitution intact of the Province of Senegambia, nor was it suggested that Goree should be exchanged for St Louis. The French were very anxious to retain this latter place so as to purchase slaves for their West Indian possessions and the British were anxious to retain the gum trade at Portendic. The right of the British to the Gambia was duly recognised.[6] An attempt was made to induce the

---

[1] Charges exhibited by Houghton against Wall, 1783, P.R.O., C.O. 267/20.
[2] Wall to Germaine, 3 July 1781, P.R.O., C.O. 267/20 and 268/4.
[3] Wall to Germaine, 22 August 1781, P.R.O., C.O. 268/4.
[4] Charges exhibited by Houghton against Wall, 1783, P.R.O., C.O. 267/20.
[5] Houghton to Thomas Townshend, 24 February 1783, P.R.O., C.O. 267/20.
[6] Wickham Legg, *Diplomatic Instructions*, 1745–1789, VII, *France*, pp. 188, 199.

French to renounce their claims to Albreda, but the French representative offered so determined an opposition to the proposal that the British representative did not press it, hoping that "a disposition on our part to oblige France in this article may give us a claim to a like facility on her part as to the establishment of any factories which may find it expedient to erect on the Gum Coast".[1] The definitive treaty of peace was signed at Versailles on 3 September 1783. By it Great Britain ceded St Louis, Podor, Galam, Arguin, Portendic, and Goree to France and France guaranteed the possession of James Island and the River Gambia to Great Britain. It was further agreed that the English should have liberty to carry on the gum trade in the vicinity of Portendic but that they should not form any permanent settlement in those regions. In all other respects English and French subjects were to be allowed to "continue to resort thereto, according to the usage which has hitherto prevailed".[2]

In December 1783 H.M.S. *Bulldog* arrived in the Gambia to show the flag. The arrival was opportune as in the course of a month no less than four French ships entered the river. They were all stopped and sent back to Goree.[3] The *Bulldog's* action was of questionable legality, but it did have the effect of giving British merchants, who arrived just after the close of the war, a market free from foreign competition. Furthermore, the first French arrivals in the river did not create at all a favourable impression with the natives. The crew of the corvette *La Blonde* were guilty of high-handed conduct at Albreda, which led to retaliation. In December 1784 a French merchant captain died at Albreda and the "king" of Barra seized his goods as having escheated to himself. It was not until 1785, when the French Governor of Senegal paid a special visit to the river, that these differences were settled. By a treaty concluded on 14 April of that year the boundaries of the French concession at Albreda were delimited and the French were given the right of free trade in Barra, to place a resident there, to ditch and palisade their factory, and to erect batteries.[4]

[1] Martin, *The British West African Settlements*, 1750–1821, p. 100.
[2] Hertslet, *The Map of Africa by Treaty*, II, 713.
[3] Log of H.M.S. *Bulldog*, P.R.O., Ad. 51/144; Richard Parker, the ringleader of the mutiny at the Nore, was at the time a midshipman on the *Bulldog*, *Navy Records Society*, *Spencer Papers*, II, 161.
[4] Golberry, *Voyage en Afrique*, II, 169–181.

Shorn of what had been regarded as the most important and most profitable portion thereof, the remnants of the Province of Senegambia were clearly no longer suited for the elaborate machinery of Crown Colony government. It was therefore decided that the Province should cease. The Crown decided that it would be put to no further expense in regard to the Gambia and accordingly an act of parliament was passed[1] revesting those regions in the Committee of the Company of Merchants trading to Africa. The military members of the former establishment were for the most part absorbed into other units, but the civilian officers, such as Chief Justice Morse, were left to their own devices and to find a new livelihood as best they could. The African (formerly O'Hara's) Corps was disbanded.[2]

"The revesting of what remained of the Province of Senegambia in the much-criticised Company of Merchants is in itself something of a commentary on the experiment of the first Crown colony in West Africa. The scheme prepared in 1765 had not in practice proved a device suited to the particular circumstances of the country for which it was framed. 'As in the American colonies' had not been a satisfactory constitutional guide in administration making for tropical Africa. The whole machinery had been too cumbersome and elaborate for a province where the white population was scanty and fluctuating. A governor was almost forced to choose either, as O'Hara did, to disregard his instructions as impracticable, or, as Clarke did, to attempt to carry them out fully and run the risk of being charged with deviation from strict legality by so doing. The judicial system was too elaborate for a population entirely unaccustomed to the English methods of trial by jury, and there were not enough Europeans in the colony to carry it on without the natives. The same difficulty affected the most important part of the civil administration, the Council. As the garrison were the only permanent English residents in the colony apart from such officials as the chief justice, the Council could be little more than a board of military officers, since there was no thought of admitting natives."[3]

The effect of Crown Colony government in the Gambia is best summed up in the words of Chief Justice Morse:

[1] 25 Geo. III, c. 65.
[2] P.R.O., W.O. 4/125.
[3] Martin, op. cit. pp. 101, 102.

The River Gambia, although part of the Province of Senegambia, felt not the least benefit from its civil establishment on account of its great distance from Senegal, the seat of government. A subaltern officer was usually there with about thirty men and the necessary people for the fort. Sometimes a captain was sent there, and latterly a lieutenant-governor, but no civil officers. The consequence was the trade for want of proper regulations dwindled almost to nothing.[1]

---

[1] Morse to Lord Sidney, 6 March 1783, P.R.O., C.O. 267/7.

XIX: Laissez faire, 1783–1807

Except for the despatch of H.M.S. *Bulldog* to show the flag in the River Gambia and the formal transfer of that river from the Crown to the Committee of Merchants no steps were taken by the British Government to assert the right of possession, which had been guaranteed to it by the Treaty of Versailles. The Committee of Merchants were equally supine but for a very intelligible reason. The River Gambia had been taken away from them eighteen years before because they were not deemed capable of its administration and it was now handed back to them as a *damnosa hereditas* with a ruined fort and no tangible assets of any description.

An attempt was made to get financial aid from the Government to set up an establishment for the administration of the Gambia. On 12 June 1783, when it was known that the Gambia was to be handed back to the Committee, certain members of the Committee waited upon Lord North to ask for such aid. They were, however, unable to furnish a proper estimate of the cost of rebuilding the fort until a proper survey should have been made, but they estimated the annual charges of the proposed establishment, which was to comprise thirty-two Europeans, at £5500.[1] An engineer was sent out to make a report, but that report was never communicated to the Committee. On 28 May 1784 they pressed for information regarding the report, but there is no evidence that any reply was sent to their letter.[2] Petitions were presented to the House of Commons on 27 April 1787 and 9 May 1788, asking for financial aid so as to rebuild James Fort, but they do not appear to have met with any reply.[3] Thereafter the Committee's interest in the Gambia ceased entirely. No attempt at all was made to control or administer those regions. In 1791 a number of merchants trading in the Gambia, who included MacNamara's friend, Thomas Sharpless, presented a memorial to the Board of Trade complaining that illicit trade was being carried on with the French settlements in the river to the prejudice of legitimate British commerce. The memorial was referred on 20 September to the Committee. On 21 October the Secretary

---

[1] Committee to Lord North, 17 June 1783, P.R.O., C.O. 267/20.
[2] Committee to Lord Sidney, 4 October 1786, P.R.O., C.O., 287/21; Committee to Edmund Nepean, 28 May 1784, P.R.O., C.O. 267/8.
[3] *Commons' Journals*, XLII, 694; XLIII, 466.

of the Committee replied "stating the said Committee have no information whatsoever on the subject in question, but they are of opinion that practices such as are stated in the memorial are highly injurious to British commerce and navigation".[1]

One reason for the unwillingness of the Government to assist the Committee was an equally strong reason for the Committee's reluctance to spend any money in the Gambia. It was more or less of an open secret that the Government might at any moment want to take back the river as a convict settlement. The problem of relieving the pressure on the dangerously overcrowded jails in England had for more than a century been a very serious one. A partial solution had been found by transporting convicted felons to the American colonies, but the secession of those colonies had put an end to that means of relief. The British Government therefore looked about to find other countries in which to dump its surplus prison population. A few convicts had from time to time been transported to West Africa—chiefly to serve as soldiers—but the time had come for transportation on a wholesale scale.

In 1776 very soon after the outbreak of the American War of Independence MacNamara had recommended the establishment of a convict station at Bintang.[2] Three years later John Roberts, a former Governor of Cape Coast Castle, submitted a scheme for a convict settlement farther up the river at Nyanimaru.[3] In 1783 Chief Justice Morse advocated the sending of convicts to the Gambia but condemned Roberts' scheme of a convict settlement, recommending in its place the interspersing of the convicts—"and those not the most abandoned"—amongst free settlers.[4] In 1784 the Government decided that the possibility of using the banks of the River Gambia as a penal settlement was one worth serious consideration and accordingly sent Commodore Edward Thompson to survey the river.[5] As a result of his survey it was decided that Lemaine (now MacCarthy) Island would be a suitable place for

[1] Minutes of Council of Trade, 20 September and 21 October 1791, Add. MS. 38,393, ff. 128, 138.

[2] MacNamara to Germaine, 5 August 1776, P.R.O., C.O. 268/4.

[3] Egerton MS. 1162 A, ff. 282, 284.

[4] Morse to Lord Sidney, 6 March and 23 June 1783, P.R.O., C.O. 267/8; Morse, "A Sketch of a Plan for erecting a Colony in the Territory belonging to the River Gambia in Africa", P.R.O., C.O. 267/8.

[5] Thompson to Secretary of State, 2 December 1784 and 5 January 1785, P.R.O., C.O. 267/8 and 267/9.

establishing a convict settlement. On 5 January 1785 the Government informed the Committee that they proposed to purchase the island and stated that they were, "from the absolute necessity of clearing the gaols determined to execute the said plan before the proper season of the year shall expire by sending one hundred and fifty persons".[1] Before this letter had been written, a certain Richard Bradley had already been sent to purchase it from the local chief. He landed at Juffure in February of that year and then proceeded by sloop to Junkakunda, where a British trader, named Michael Dove, was settled. Bradley found that the ways of African diplomacy were circumlocutory and that presents for the expediting of negotiations were necessarily very frequent. He first of all had to send a messenger ahead overland from Juffure to announce the purpose of his intended visit. On a.rival at Junkakunda he had to fee the "tobab mansa"—or official intermediary between the Europeans and the local chiefs—to procure an interview with "the king or master of the island Lemain". On arrival that potentate expected a gratuity for condescending to make the visit. He announced that he was perfectly willing to cede the island for an annual tribute of thirty bars, but it then transpired that he could not make the cession without the consent of five of his principal men. These five individuals therefore had to be paid a fee for according an interview. Then both they and the "king" had each to receive further presents for giving their consent to the cession. Then a further present had to be "paid privately to the king at the conclusion of the purchase, and which was agreed should be concealed from the above five chiefs, or they would have agreed on the like sum to each". All these presents and the incidental expenses of the voyage to Junkakunda had to be paid in goods to the value of £374 15s. 0d. Bradley then applied to Michael Dove for goods to that value, but Mr Dove was not doing well in business and insisted on the purchase of his whole stock in trade for £579 8s. 0d. After which His Britannic Majesty obtained full livery of seisin of Lemaine Island.[2]

In the meantime a Committee of the House of Commons, which had been appointed to consider the question of the disposal of convicted prisoners, began to take evidence as to the suitability of

---

[1] King's Servants to Committee, 5 January 1785, P.R.O., C.O. 267/21.

[2] Richard Bradley to Secretary of State, 29 November 1785, P.R.O., C.O. 267/8.

Lemaine Island as a penal settlement. John Howard's *State of Prisons* had been published eight years before and John Wesley had long denounced the treatment of convicted offenders as worse than anything " on this side hell", but the evidence of certain of the witnesses before the Committee reveals how little the humanitarian movement, which was so long overdue, had at this date influenced the minds of educated men in England. When one realises their attitude to the more unfortunate of their own kith and kin, one can fully understand the difficulty which Granville Sharpe and Wilberforce encountered in combating the African slave trade.

The most astonishing evidence was that of Mr Evan Nepean of the Home Office. He explained that 200 convicts—"the worst of both sexes "—were to be transported almost immediately by a contractor to the Gambia. When questioned as to whether Lemaine Island was ready for their reception, he had to admit that " we have not yet any territorial right, but it is probable we may have such a right soon: it belongs to some native chief". Questioned as to the disposal of the convicts on arrival, he explained that it was proposed to land them about sixty miles below the island. They were then to be supplied with framework for huts and agricultural tools and marched to Lemaine, where they were to fend for themselves. The Government was ready to provide a medicine chest for their use on the island, because " he had heard that among the convicts were some medical persons". A guardship was to be stationed between Lemaine Island and Nyanimaru to prevent the convicts from escaping and to protect trade. The Committee viewed with some doubt the question of expense, but Mr Nepean was able to reassure them on this point. " They would not cost the government more in the first year than they did on the hulks at home: and in the second and third years the expence would be much reduced, *though all the settlers should live!*"

It must, however, be recorded that other witnesses did exhibit a more humane attitude towards the subjects of the proposed experiment. Several merchant captains and naval officers, who had visited the Gambia, denounced the scheme as cruel. Sir George Young, for instance, hinted very strongly that the proposal fell little short of one of murder.[1]

---

[1] *Commons' Journals*, XL, 955–958; Minutes of the Committee of the House of Commons regarding the transportation of convicts to West Africa, 1785, P.R.O., H.O. 7/1.

Eventually on 28 July 1785 the Committee of the House of Commons condemned the scheme, not on humanitarian grounds, but because "the outcasts of an old society cannot form the foundation of a new one; therefore it is impossible to form a colony solely of convicts".[1] The 200 convicts destined for Lemaine Island were ordered to be sent to Das Voltas, lying between Angola and the Cape of Good Hope.[2] The Gambia was preserved from at least one experiment in colonisation, which would inevitably have ended disastrously. Apart from any question of humanitarianism, a convict establishment would inevitably have led to embroilment with the local inhabitants, have destroyed legitimate forms of trade, and generally had a disastrous effect upon the economic prosperity of the country. The first year's rent of Lemaine Island had been paid by Bradley at the time of purchase. Presumably the default in payment of any subsequent rents rendered the island forfeit to its original owner.

Having found other lands for the establishment of penal settlements, the British Government ceased to interest itself in the Gambia. But interest in these regions was kept alive by others besides the few traders who frequented the river. The Society for promoting the Discovery of the Interior Regions of Africa, which was founded in 1783 by the Duke of Northumberland, the Earl of Galloway, Richard Watson, Bishop of Llandaff, was very anxious to learn whether communication could be opened up with Timbuktu and the upper reaches of the Niger by way of the Gambia. With this object they sent out Major Daniel Francis Houghton, who has figured in the previous chapter with the rank of captain. Houghton arrived in the Gambia in November 1790, and made his way overland to Medina near the Barrakunda Falls. From Medina he went in the company of a native trader into Bambuk; after which nothing further was heard of him. He was certainly robbed of all he possessed and either died of disease and starvation or else was murdered.[3]

It was realised that Houghton had been sent out with very inadequate equipment and in 1794 the Association decided to invoke

---

[1] *Commons' Journals*, XL, 1161.

[2] *Ibid.* Instructions for Commodore Edward Thompson, s.d., P.R.O., C.O. 267/10.

[3] *Proceedings of the Association for promoting the Discovery of the Interior Parts of Africa*, 1792 and 1797; *Elucidations of the African Geography*, 1793; Park, *Travels in the Interior Districts of Africa*, pp. 103–104.

Government assistance for the promotion of further schemes of exploration. It was represented to the Government that "the jealousy of the slave traders in the Gambia (whose intrigues endangered the safety of Major Houghton in his passage up the river and whose attempts were repeated with more effectual success on his approach to Timbuctoo) can only be prevented by persons, who carry with them the sanction of a public character and the respect that is paid to a representative of the British government. If assurances of protection on the River Gambia (unquestionably a part of the British dominions) could be given to British merchants, there is reason to believe that intercourse from the Gambia to the Niger would be opened by mercantile houses of good character in London". They therefore recommended the appointment of a British consul for Senegambia, who should be instructed to proceed to Bambuk to open up trade.[1]

The Government agreed to appoint a Consul and promised a sum of £3000 per annum for two years towards the expenses of the proposed undertaking. James Willis was on 10 April 1794 appointed Consul-General "in that part of Africa, which is distinguished by the name of Senegambia, with the object of promoting trade with Bambouk".[2] Provision was to be made for the raising of a corps to be known as the Senegambian Corps, which was to assist him in the carrying out of his duties. This corps was to comprise three officers and sixty other ranks and was to be stationed at or near Fattatenda, near the Barrakunda Falls.[3] Willis' instructions were to proceed to the Gambia as soon as shipping and a convoy could be provided and to make his way to Fattatenda and there or in that vicinity to erect a mud fort for the protection of the persons accompanying him. He was then to take such steps as he should judge proper for obtaining the friendship of those African chiefs, with whom he should find it necessary to communicate, for the furtherance of British interests. He was also to endeavour by every means in his power to open up communication between the Gambia and the Niger.[4]

The original scheme was largely the product of a member of parliament, named Henry Beaufoy, who was also a member of the

[1] Proposals submitted to the Rt Hon. Henry Dundas by the Committee of the Association, P.R.O., W.O. 1/768, ff. 86–88.   [2] *Ibid.* f. 189.

[3] Lieut. Benjamin Barbauld to Secretary of State, 12 May 1794; Willis to William Huskisson, 18 April 1795; Willis to John King, 22 December 1795 P.R.O., C.O. 267/10.   [4] Instructions to Willis, P.R.O., C.O. 267/10.

African Association. Some mystery attaches to the selection of Willis as prospective Consul-General. He was apparently not known to any member of the Association and there is no record as to what were his particular qualifications for the post. He was to receive a yearly salary of £600 with the stipulation that such salary was not to commence until his arrival at his destination. At the same time he was given a fairly free hand in regard to the purchase of stores and materials for his expedition and he took full advantage of this.[1] The war with France delayed the sailing of the expedition. On 5 June 1795 Willis reported that all the ordnance, stores and ammunition had been embarked, but that he was waiting for a convoy. He at the same time expressed the opinion that he ought not to sail before September, because the rainy season in the Gambia would prevent him from making any progress.[2]

September came and passed and still Willis had not sailed. In the meantime the Government began to feel uneasy about the small return shown for the money, which Willis had been allowed to expend. As a letter of Willis shows, there was some difficulty in running him to earth and obtaining accounts from him,[3] but eventually he submitted an account in the early days of 1796. This showed that he had been allowed to draw £7437 17s. 1d. and had expended £5816 18s. 0d.[4] The Government was very much perturbed at the heavy expenditure, which till then had yielded no practical results at all and submitted the accounts to the African Association with an intimation that Willis must look to the Association if he wished to draw any further money for the expedition. The Association replied that, being a society supported entirely by voluntary contributions from a limited number of members, it could not possibly undertake any large financial commitments in respect of the expedition. They also reported that the Senegambian corps was in a most unsatisfactory state. The lieutenant had died and the ensign had absented himself without leave. Furthermore, Willis had been granted sums of money exceeding by more than one-half what had originally been

[1] Proposals submitted to Rt Hon. Henry Dundas, 11 July 1794, P.R.O., W.O. 1/763, f. 38; Sir Joseph Banks to Secretary of State, 24 December 1795, P.R.O., C.O. 267/10; Dundas to Duke of Richmond, 17 October 1794, P.R.O., W.O. 6/142 and C.O. 267/10; Evan Nepean to Secretary of Board of Ordnance, 18 January 1795, P.R.O., W.O. 6/142.

[2] Willis to Dundas, 5 June 1795, P.R.O., C.O. 267/10.

[3] Willis to Duke of Portland, 31 December 1795, P.R.O., C.O. 267/10.

[4] John King to Charles Long, 8 January 1796, P.R.O., C.O. 267/10.

deemed necessary to execute the entire plan. They further pointed out that according to reports received from the Gambia the river was more than usually infested by privateers. They therefore concluded by saying:

> They submit therefore to His Majesty's Ministers whether it will not be better for the present to pause for a little rather than forward the undertaking at a time when the hopes of its success are certainly less flattering than they were some time ago and than they are likely to be some time hence.[1]

On receipt of this reply the Government came to a quick decision. Willis was informed on 15 February 1796 that the expedition was postponed indefinitely.[2]

The African Association's reluctance to bear any part of the expense of the proposed Senegambian establishment was due in part to the fact that they had already committed themselves to financing an unofficial journey of exploration to discover a route between the Gambia and the Niger. Anticipating that the Government would appoint a consul with the necessary establishment, they had selected a young surgeon to send on a private expedition of discovery hoping that that expedition would be afforded some sort of additional protection by the near presence of a representative and an armed force belonging to the Crown. The person selected was Mungo Park, who had attracted the attention of Sir Joseph Banks by reason of his botanical researches when serving as an assistant surgeon during the voyage of an East Indiaman to Sumatra. The African Association delayed sending Park to Africa in the expectation that he would be able to sail under the aegis of Willis.[3] But when Willis' departure was delayed, they took a passage for him in a small trading vessel, which left Portsmouth on 22 May 1795. Park's instructions were "to pass on to the river Niger, either by way of Bambouk, or by such other route as should be found most convenient. That I should ascertain the course and, if possible, the rise and termination of that river. That I should use my utmost exertions to visit the principal

---

[1] Report of the Committee of the African Association, 13 February 1796, P.R.O., C.O. 267/10.

[2] Willis to Secretary of State, 22 February 1796, P.R.O., C.O. 267/10.

[3] Park, *Travels in the Interior Districts of Africa*, p. 3; *Proceedings of the Association for promoting the Discovery of the Interior Parts of Africa*, 1797, pp. 16, 20 and 21.

towns and cities in the neighbourhood, particularly Timbuctoo and Houssa". He reached Juffure on 21 June and proceeded thence to Pisania (Karantaba) above MacCarthy Island. There he was be-friended by Dr John Laidley, under whose roof he lived for six months studying Mandingo and collecting information regarding the countries into which he was to penetrate. He left Pisania on 2 December with only a negro boy, a horse, and two asses. After severe hardships he reached Segu and the Niger and eventually re-turned to Pisania on 10 June 1797. Most of the episodes of his re-markable journey do not concern the history of the Gambia, but those who wish to read a true story of indomitable courage, which is very modestly told, should read Park's *Travels in the Interior of Africa*.

After Park's return to England the African Association once more attempted to revive the proposal for the appointment of a consul for Senegambia. At a meeting held on 25 May 1799 it was resolved to send a memorial on the subject to the Government pointing out that Mungo Park had proved that the regions between the Gambia and the Niger had great commercial possibilities,[1] but the war with France prevented anything from coming of these re-presentations.

Unfortunately, contemporary records give very little information of the repercussions in the Gambia of the wars with France, which lasted from 1793 to 1815. It is evident that hostilities were carried on in the river, but there are very few details of any particular incidents. The French with a base at Goree began the war with a distinct advantage over the British private traders, who no longer had such protection as James Fort had afforded in previous wars or the hope of any permanent protection by the British navy. In 1794 a French vessel of the line and a frigate entered the river and cap-tured every English merchant ship, which was trading there.[2] No particulars are given in any contemporary record of this exploit, but in speaking of the Jolas of Foni at the time of his visit in 1795, Mungo Park states that "during the present war they have more than once taken up arms to defend our vessels from French priva-teers; and English property of considerable value has frequently been left at Vintain for a long time entirely under the care of the Feloops (sc. Jolas)".[3] But he gives no details of any particular

[1] Memorial of African Association, 25 May 1799, P.R.O., C.O. 267/80.
[2] Pelletan, *Mémoire sur la Colonie Française du Sénégal*, p. 85.
[3] Park, *Travels in the Interior Districts of Africa*, p. 16.

fighting. One of the grounds, which induced the African Association to recommend the indefinite postponement of the proposed expedition of Willis to Fattatenda, was that in 1796 the river was reported to be more than usually infested with hostile privateers.[1]

These raids and the pillaging in 1794 of the newly established colony at Sierra Leone induced the British Government to take some steps to check French activities in West Africa. In 1800 a squadron under Sir Charles Hamilton captured Goree.[2] This success appears to have put an end not only to raids in the Gambia by French privateers but also for the time being to the French factory at Albreda. But on the conclusion of the Treaty of Amiens in 1802 the French Governor at St Louis sent an agent named Bonnard to resettle the factory. This agent was subsequently reported to have weakened British influence considerably by means of intrigues with the "king" of Barra. On the renewal of the war with France H.M.S. *Imogene* entered the river and captured a French sloop lying off Albreda, but part of the crew managed to escape on shore. The *Imogene* made no attempt to destroy the factory and left the river with its prize. Soon after its departure an English cutter arrived at Sikka with a valuable cargo. Monsieur Bonnard furnished "a pirate Portuguese named Anthonio" with letters of marque from the French Government, and with a number of armed men who captured the vessel. The "king" of Barra was bribed into connivance with this act, and despite a protest from the British officer commanding at Goree, refused to assist in obtaining restoration of the vessel.[3]

In 1803 the officer commanding at Goree had to report that a French privateer from Senegal had seized several vessels, which had been sent to the Gambia to obtain rice for the garrison at Goree, and that the schooner, which he had sent to deal with this raider, had itself been captured by two French privateers off the Cape Verde Islands.[4] In fact the British at Goree lacked both the men and shipping to retaliate or to offer any protection to their countrymen in the River Gambia.

In January 1804 Goree had to surrender to a French squadron commanded by Chevalier Mahé. Two months later four British

---

[1] Report of the Committee of the African Association, 13 February 1796, P.R.O., C.O. 267/10.   [2] *Annual Register*, 1800, p. 213.

[3] George Otley to Major Richard Lloyd, 18 August 1804, P.R.O., C.O. 267/10.

[4] Colonel Frazer to Lord Hobart, 11 December 1803, P.R.O., W.O. 1/351.

men-of-war under the command of Captain E. S. Dickson recaptured the place.[1] But during those two months Bonnard managed to be extremely active at Albreda. Another British schooner was seized in the vicinity of that place and a French privateer proceeded up river as far as Nyanimaru and destroyed a valuable British ship.[2]

The recapture of Goree did not put an end to French raids into the Gambia, as the French privateers continued to use Senegal as a base for their operations. The garrison at Goree was able to do little to check the activities of these raiders. In 1805 a Liverpool merchantman and two small vessels from Goree were captured and another vessel from the same port was with difficulty rescued by a detachment of troops sent specially from Goree.[3] As late as December 1808, another French vessel from Senegal made a sudden swoop and captured a British vessel belonging to Goree. Another vessel only managed to save itself by reason of a timely warning from the alcaide of Juffure.[4]

There is very little to record as to reprisals against the French. Some little satisfaction was, however, obtained in 1805 when Spain threw in her lot with France. A number of Spanish slave traders had been in the habit of resorting to the Gambia. In January 1805 Lieutenant James Martyn of the Royal African Corps, who was a few months later to accompany Mungo Park on his last expedition, was able to report that a party of volunteers under his command had managed to capture a Spanish schooner lying off Juffure.[5] But captures such as these were but a poor set off for the more numerous prizes made by the French. In 1809 English traders in the Gambia still complained that owing to the lack of a naval force at Goree they were "open to the insults of any armed vessel from Senegal".[6] In 1810 a French ship was able to ship a cargo of slaves at Sikka, near Albreda, but was captured five days out at sea by Sir Thomas Cochrane.[7] It was only when Senegal was captured in 1809, and

---

[1] *Annual Register*, 1804, pp. 526–530.

[2] Otley to Lloyd, 18 August 1804, P.R.O., C.O. 267/10.

[3] Major Lloyd to Viscount Castlereagh, 23 November 1805, P.R.O., C.O. 268/7; Major Lloyd to Earl Camden, 16 August 1805, P.R.O., C.O. 268/7.

[4] Major Maxwell to Viscount Castlereagh, 15 January 1809, P.R.O., C.O. 267/32.

[5] Lieut. Martyn to Major Lloyd, 14 January 1805, P.R.O., C.O. 267/22.

[6] Maxwell to Castlereagh, 2 April 1809, P.R.O., C.O. 267/32.

[7] Washington, "Some account of Mohammedu Sisei", *Journal of Royal Geographical Society*, VIII, 448.

French privateers consequently deprived of their base, that this spasmodic harassing of British shipping in the Gambia came to an end.

British traders may possibly have exaggerated the extent of French influence with the inhabitants of the river banks, but there can be no doubt that the impunity with which French privateers swooped down and carried off prizes did not enhance British prestige and led to difficulties with a number of the chiefs. In 1806 the officer commanding at Goree reported that the "king" of Barra tried to prevent small armed vessels from proceeding up the river, but had changed his attitude on being informed that recourse would be had to strong measures if he persisted in his course of obstruction.[1] But this attitude does not appear to have been shared by all the "king's" subjects. The alcaide of Juffure, for instance, appears to have been well disposed to the British. In 1792 he made an agreement with Lieutenant Wickham of the Royal Navy fixing the scale of customary dues to be paid by ships entering the river and was then reported as being "a good man and one who is a particular friend to the English". Mungo Park reported equally well of him in 1805.[2]

Park's discoveries and the capture of Goree did revive some interest in the River Gambia. In 1802 Sir Joseph Banks and Zachary Macaulay called attention to the danger of the spread of French influence in those regions, unless the British Government took some active measures to check French activities.[3] In 1804 Colonel Charles Stevenson, who was in command at Goree, made a proposal to intercept trade between the interior and the French at Senegal by the erection of a blockhouse at Fattatenda[4] and to garrison it with a regiment of West Indian negroes.[5] A very elaborate military expedition was eventually projected. A second battalion of the Royal African Corps was to be raised. Half of its personnel was to be European and the remainder African. The former element was to be recruited in part from volunteers from the existing battalion and in part from convicts from the hulks in England. The Africans were to be recruited from the Maroon and Nova Scotian settlers at Sierra Leone. A corps of artificers and a corps of artillery were also to be

[1] Lloyd to Castlereagh, 6 April 1806, P.R.O., C.O. 267/22.

[2] Mungo Park to Lord Camden, 26 April 1805, Egerton MS. 3009, f. 40.

[3] Sir Joseph Banks to John Sullivan, 1 August 1802; Zachary Macaulay to John Sullivan, 4 September 1802, P.R.O., C.O. 2/1.

[4] Colonel Stevenson to John Sullivan, 13 and 14 January 1804, P.R.O., C.O. 2/1.   [5] Same to same, 10 March 1804, P.R.O., C.O. 2/1.

raised with Europeans and Africans in the same proportions. The interior of the continent was to be approached from several directions. A contingent of the African Corps was to proceed from Sierra Leone along the route recently explored by Thomas Winterbottom to Timbo and Labe at the head waters of the Gambia. Colonel Stevenson was to advance to the Faleme, gain possession of the French Fort St Joseph on the Senegal, and to establish military posts in Bambuk. Captain Philip Beaver of the Royal Navy, who a few years previously had had the conduct of a disastrous experiment in colonisation of the island of Bulama, was to sail up the Rio Grande. Lastly, Mungo Park was to be given a military commission and to have charge of an expedition, which was to proceed up the River Gambia.[1]

Park's expedition was to consist of 250 men of the African Corps, of whom 100 were to be recruited from the garrison at Goree, twenty men of the corps of artificers, and two or three naval officers. After picking up his reinforcements at Goree he was "to immediately proceed to the Gambia for the purpose of dislodging the French from their factory at Albreda". Having accomplished this, he was to proceed to Pisania and Barrakunda. "He should announce to the king of Wooli his arrival for the purpose of re-establishing English factories in the River Gambia, and of extending the relations of commerce with that and the neighbouring countries. Mr Park should be furnished with the means of conciliating this chief by giving him presents; and he should be directed, after having fixed a tariff of duties, to take the measures, which appear to him most proper for obtaining his concurrence and assistance towards the establishment of a post at Kooger or at some other convenient place near the north east frontier of Wooli.... It may be politick, if there should be any slaves for sale, to purchase some of them and thereby to guard against the counteraction of the slatees or slave dealers, who might otherwise throw such obstacles in our way as might materially retard our progress. The slaves might be employed to open the road and to assist in the conveyance of stores." Park was to advance from Kooger into Bondu, to enter into friendly relations with the ruler of that country, and thus to outflank the French at Fort St Joseph on one side, whilst Stevenson operated from the other side.

[1] Memorandum by John Sullivan; Memorandum of instructions for Park, 1804, P.R.O., C.O. 2/1.

After all the French dependencies on the banks of the Senegal and Faleme had been captured, Stevenson was to co-operate with Park in pressing on towards the Niger. In the meantime a party under the leadership of some selected naval officers was to proceed above the Barrakunda Falls as far as the Neriko and to endeavour to open up communication with Labe and the River Faleme.[1]

The plan was, however, far too elaborate and too ambitious to be carried out in full. The question of expense at once made the Government eager to curtail the scheme of operations. Eventually the plan was reduced to very modest and economical proportions. Park was given military rank and instructed to proceed to Goree, whence he was to fit out an expedition, which he was to lead up the River Gambia and thence along his former route to the banks of the Niger. He was to be supplied with an escort of an officer and thirty-five soldiers from the garrison at Goree. In addition he was to be given a number of convict artificers from the hulks in England,[2] but eventually recruited these from volunteers from the *Squirrel* frigate. Park reached Juffure in April 1805. The story of his expedition does not greatly concern the Gambia. The party proceeded as far as the island of Kai-ai by water and thence marched overland. The expedition had started too late in the year and met with misfortunes and disasters almost from the very start. Only Park, Lieutenant Martyn, and two other Europeans reached the banks of the Niger, where they were waylaid and massacred. The expedition had been organised on an entirely wrong scale. The percentage of Europeans was too great. The party was too numerous to escape attention and too weak to defy hostility. Except inasmuch as it stimulated others to follow in his footsteps, Park's second expedition was a lamentable failure.[3]

Whilst the Committee of Merchants declined to bestir themselves at all in regard to the affairs of the Gambia and the British Government vacillated over projects for the establishment of convict settlements, consulates, and military posts, individual British traders with little or no official encouragement managed to maintain and even to a certain degree to extend British influence in the river. When the French captured James Island in 1779, all the British settlers had congregated on the island and were transported with the

---

[1] Memorandum of Instructions for Park, 1804, P.R.O., C.O. 2/1.
[2] Park to Edward Cooke, 23 January 1805, P.R.O., C.O. 2/2.
[3] Park, *Journal of a Mission to the Interior of Africa in the year* 1805.

military garrison to Senegal,[1] but one trader returned to the River Gambia early in the following year.[2] In October 1780 a British trader was settled at Bintang trading in wax. In 1783, when H.M.S. *Bulldog* entered the river to show the flag, three British vessels were trading in the river.[3] Though the number of British vessels, which visited the river in any year, appears rarely to have exceeded three or four,[4] the voyages appear to have been, generally speaking, very profitable.

By 1783 individual British traders had established factories at Juffure, Bintang, and Brefet in the Foni country.[5] In the following year three were settled at Nyanimaru, but a visiting merchant captain reported that "they had a very poor appearance, being quite pale and emaciated, and hardly able to crawl. They told me they regularly fell sick in August".[6] In 1785, as mentioned on a previous page, there was a European trader at Junkakunda opposite to Lemaine (MacCarthy) Island.[7] In 1786 there was another factory sixteen miles above Junkakunda at Pisania (Karantaba).[8]

This last mentioned factory deserves more than mere passing notice. It appears to have been originally established by some brothers of the name of Aynsley. A Robert Aynsley was amongst the settlers, who were made prisoners at the taking of James Island in 1779,[9] and it would appear that he was already established at or in the vicinity of Karantaba at that date. He appears to have returned to the Gambia soon after the taking of Goree. In 1791 he and his brother had been joined at Karantaba by a surgeon, named John Laidley, who acted as banker to Houghton and Park and in many

[1] John Dudfield to Lieut. Lacy, P.R.O., C.O. 267/19.
[2] Lieut. James Winter to Lord George Germaine, 21 April 1780, P.R.O., C.O. 268/4.
[3] Log of H.M.S. *Bulldog*, P.R.O., Ad. 51/44.
[4] Evidence of John Barnes, 27 April 1785, Minutes of the Committee of the House of Commons regarding the transportation of convicts to West Africa, P.R.O., H.O. 7/1; Park, *Travels in the Interior Districts of Africa*, p. 25.
[5] Houghton to Townshend, 24 February 1783, P.R.O., C.O. 267/20.
[6] Evidence of John Nevan, 3 May 1785; Minutes of the Committee of the House of Commons regarding the transportation of convicts to West Africa, 1785, P.R.O., H.O. 7/1.
[7] Richard Bradley to Secretary of State, 29 November 1785, P.R.O., C.O. 267/8.
[8] Durand, *Voyage au Sénégal*, p. 83.
[9] John Dudfield, Robert Aynsley and others to Lieut. Lacy, 12 May 1779, P.R.O., C.O. 267/19.

other ways rendered these two explorers very valuable assistance.[1] Laidley died in 1797 in Barbadoes whilst on his way home to England,[2] but the Aynsley brothers carried on the tradition of assisting African explorers. Park paid a warm tribute to them on his second expedition in 1805.[3] Sometime before 1818 the factory had to be abandoned because of the hostility of raiding parties from Bondu and Wuli.[4] A monument has been erected on the banks of the river at Karantaba to commemorate Mungo Park's connection with the Gambia. It also may be said to commemorate the pioneers of one of those colonial outposts which kept the British flag flying under great difficulties and rendered invaluable aid in forwarding African exploration.

Captain Robert Heatley's career in the Gambia may in some respects be taken as typical of that of the better class of eighteenth-century "coaster". He first arrived in the river in 1763 during the last days of the regime of the Committee of Merchants. He appears to have left finally in 1788. During that time he traded principally at Nyanimaru. He made a number of voyages to North America and the West Indies, but stayed on one occasion for a period of five years in the river, on another for three years, and on another for close on one year. Heatley spoke Mandingo fluently. He dealt in ivory and wax, but his principal trade was in slaves whom he carried to Jamaica, Dominica, and South Carolina. Though his crews sometimes suffered great mortality, he himself enjoyed the best of health during his twenty-five years' residence up the river.[5]

The settlers used to complain bitterly that they were hampered by the depredations of the French, foreign competition, and want of support or encouragement from the home Government, but evidence suggests that on the whole they prospered. Captain William Lyttleton, who in 1791 had complained of the illicit trade carried on with Albreda to the prejudice of British navigation and commerce,[6] was none the less, if rumour was correct, able to retire on a

[1] *Proceedings of the African Association*, Vol. II, Part I, pp. 10–25; Park, *Travels in the Interior Districts of Africa*, pp. 3–33, 357–361.

[2] Park, *Travels in the Interior Districts of Africa*, p. 13.

[3] Park, *Journal of a Mission to the Interior of Africa in the year* 1805, pp. 1–10.

[4] Gray, *Travels in Western Africa*, p. 70.

[5] *Report on the Slave Trade*, pp. 5, 114, 132, 133.

[6] Minutes of Committee of Trade, 20 December 1791, Add. MS. 38,393, f. 128.

fortune after four years of trading at Fattatenda.[1] Mungo Park's description of the life of Dr Laidley and the Aynsley brothers at Karantaba also suggests prosperity.

The sporadic raids of French privateers have already been mentioned. They did undoubtedly upon occasion cause serious temporary set-backs to British trade, but it is clear that the French factory at Albreda was not as serious a rival to the British merchants as the latter endeavoured to make out. According to Captain Robert Heatley the French had by 1788 managed to monopolise most of the commerce in the lower reaches of the river, with the result that British ships for the most part proceeded to Nyanimaru, where they were able to intercept slave caravans and produce going down to the coast. The result of this transfer of British activities to the upper reaches of the river was that the British still retained the greater part of the trade.[2] Golberry[3] and Durand[4] estimated that in 1786 the value of French exports from the Gambia was only about one-fifth of the value of British exports. French commerce, moreover, does not appear to have increased to any large extent during subsequent years. In 1800 Pelletan estimated the French share in the trade of the river at the same percentage as in 1786 and that the majority of the French exports were purchased at second-hand from British traders. He described the factory at Albreda as "a wretched mud barrack, without fortifications, without means of defence, over which the national flag floats at the end of a mast....A resident with a salary of twelve hundred francs, sometimes a white man, sometimes a mulatto, and sometimes a negro, and three or four negro sailors inhabit this pretended factory". Furthermore, more than one of these agents had been murdered by the natives in recent years.[5] After the capture of Goree in 1804 Albreda was abandoned and French trade dwindled to nothing.

The Danes, Prussians, and Americans were also competitors with the British in the Gambia. In 1781 the *Zephyr* found two Danish ships with very sickly crews at anchor off Juffure and ordered them out of the river,[6] but in 1795 Park reported that the Danes still had

[1] Major Houghton to Mrs Houghton, 10 March 1791, *Proceedings of the African Association*, Vol. II, Part I, p. 28.
[2] *Report on the Slave Trade*, pp. 42, 43.
[3] *Voyage en Afrique*, II, 209, 210.   [4] *Voyage au Sénégal*, p. 85.
[5] *Mémoire de la Colonie Française du Sénégal*, pp. 33–35.
[6] Evidence of Captain Thomas Hills, *Report on the Slave Trade*, p. 51; Log of H.M.S. *Zephyr*, P.R.O., Ad. 51/1100.

a small share of the trade.[1] Ten years later Park also found a Prussian ship at Juffure.[2] American ships had resorted to the Gambia in fair numbers before the War of Independence. They continued to resort there soon after the outbreak of that war and one of MacNamara's complaints against Wall was that he connived at their trade.[3] After the Peace of Versailles a few American ships revisited the river in quest chiefly of slaves,[4] but in 1795 Park described these ventures as being only "by way of experiment".[5] Ten years later, however, he found the Americans very definitely established in the slave trade of the river[6] and it was largely owing to their activities in this trade that the interest of the British Government in the Gambia was so far revived as to induce it to decide to resume effective occupation of this hitherto neglected possession. The steps leading up to that occupation will be considered in the next chapter.

[1] *Travels in the Interior Districts of Africa*, p. 25.
[2] Park to Lord Camden, 26 April 1805, Egerton MS. 3009.
[3] MacNamara to Lord George Germaine, 15 August 1776, P.R.O., C.O. 267/3 and 268/4.
[4] Durand, *op. cit.* p. 84.
[5] *Travels in the Interior Districts of Africa*, p. 25.
[6] Park to Lord Camden, 26 April 1805, Egerton MS. 3009.

XX: The abolition of the slave trade, 1807–1816

In preceding chapters a number of references have been made to the slave trade, which formed a very important part of the commerce of the River Gambia for over three centuries. Though the material on the subject is abundant, it is not proposed to go into details in regard to the traffic, which in most respects resembled the traffic in other parts of West Africa. Nor is it proposed to make any more than passing reference to the campaign, which led to the abolition of the slave trade. This chapter is purely concerned with the effect which the abolition of the trade had upon the fortunes of the Gambia.

On 25 March 1807 the royal assent was given to a bill, which prescribed that from 1 January 1808, "all manner of dealing and trading" in slaves in Africa or in their transport from Africa to any other place was to be "utterly abolished, prohibited, and declared to be unlawful" and enacted penalties for dealing in slaves contrary to its provisions. The Act was promptly enforced by the British Navy as soon as it came into operation. The majority of British "slavers" found it impossible to escape the vigilance of British cruisers and, though a few bold spirits endeavoured for a few years to risk the possibility of capture, the increased penalties prescribed by an amending Act of 1811 more or less effectively put an end to British speculation in the slave trade.

The River Gambia had been recognised by the Peace of Versailles in 1783 as a British possession and the Abolition Act of 1807 therefore made slave traffic in the river unlawful. In so far as the majority of the British merchants and settlers in the river were concerned it may be said that they accepted the decision of Parliament and at once relinquished the traffic. But difficulties arose with foreign slavers visiting the river. So long as Great Britain and France were at war, the French traffic in the river was precarious owing to the risk of capture on the high seas, but as late as 1810 a French vessel managed to ship a cargo of slaves at Sikka, near Albreda.[1] The more extensive speculators in the traffic were, however, the Americans,

---

[1] Washington, "Some account of Mohammedu Sisei", *J.R.G.S.* VIII, 448.

the Portuguese, and the Spanish. Though the United States Government had passed an Act in 1807, which prohibited the further importation of slaves from abroad, a number of American citizens still continued to carry on the trade under Spanish colours. Whilst such traders always ran the risk of capture by British cruisers near the river's mouth, the necessarily limited number of ships patrolling the coast was insufficient to establish an effective blockade and foreign slavers were often to elude the vigilance of the British Navy and to carry their cargoes safely across the Atlantic.

In 1810 four American-owned vessels sailing under Spanish colours were able to carry off over 700 slaves from the River Gambia.[1] As the trade was becoming more and more risky, the type of individual who engaged in it became more and more desperate and was often ready to stoop to atrocities, which were rarely committed in the days when the trade was legitimate. The American mate of another vessel trading in the river under Spanish colours was guilty of brutality resulting in the death of two of his captives and of the rape of another. Though he was eventually captured and sent to England for trial, he escaped justice by reason of the fact that there was no court of jurisdiction competent to try him.[2]

Though the commissioners, who were appointed in 1810 to enquire into the state and condition of the West African settlements, did not visit the Gambia, the activities of the slave traders in the river were brought to their notice. They recommended that a schooner should be sent periodically from Goree to patrol the river and to suppress the trade.[3] In pursuance of this recommendation the officer commanding at Goree sent Lieutenant Moore of the Royal African Corps with the colonial vessel *George* and a small detachment of soldiers. Moore's instructions were to seize only American-owned ships and to keep his hands off Spanish and Portuguese vessels. All vessels, which were seized, were to be taken to Sierra Leone for adjudication in the Admiralty court there.[4] Moore made a most successful haul capturing five vessels. As they had only just begun to

[1] *Fifth Report of the Directors of the African Institution*, p. 107.

[2] Affidavits of Stephen Clark and others; Captain E. H. Columbine to Lord Liverpool, 24 July and 10 October 1810; Captain Robert Hall to Sir Roger Curtis, 2 March 1811; Henry Goulburn to Sir Robert Peel, 16 March 1811; T. Burkitt to Sir Robert Peel, 11 April 1811; John Barrow to Sir Robert Peel, 18 April 1811, P.R.O., C.O. 267/28.

[3] *Report on...Papers relating to African Forts*, p. 124.

[4] Governor Maxwell to Lieut. Moore, 16 June 1810, P.R.O., C.O. 267/28.

slave, the number of victims, who were liberated, amounted to only twenty-five men and twelve women and children. Unfortunately Moore had not sufficient men to man his prizes effectively. The crew of one of them managed under the cover of darkness to overpower the soldiers placed on board her and to carry them and the vessel to Cuba.[1] Moore's further activities were somewhat curtailed by a dispute, in which he became involved with Captain Columbine the Governor of Sierra Leone. He took his schooner to the Rio Pongas, which, according to Columbine, was within his jurisdiction. On Moore's arrival at Freetown, Columbine refused to let him sail, unless he gave an undertaking to proceed straight back to the Gambia or Goree.[2] To make assurance doubly sure that the George should not operate within the jurisdiction of Sierra Leone, he took all the seamen out of the vessel on the pretext that they belonged to the Navy.[3]

None the less the visit of the George considerably curbed the activities of slave traders in the Gambia for the time being. When H.M.S. Amelia arrived off the mouth of the river in November 1811, the commander of the George reported that there was only one slaver in the river and that she was dismantled, with her rudder unshipped "too far up for even our boats to get near her, especially as she was protected by the natives".[4] As was perhaps to be expected, the people of the Gambia, who had hitherto done a highly profitable middleman business in the trade, viewed the changed attitude of the British Government to that trade with strong disapproval and on more than one occasion displayed active hostility, when British men-of-war attempted to make seizures. An example of this occurred in 1812, when a person named Melbury, who had formerly commanded the Government schooner at Goree, took the American schooner Hope up the Bintang Creek to slave. The colonial schooner Princess Charlotte went up the creek in pursuit. The natives came to the Hope's assistance and the Princess Charlotte was repulsed with the loss of two men badly wounded. At this juncture H.M.S. Kangaroo arrived off the river's mouth and, on being informed of

---

[1] Spanish Ambassador to Marquis of Wellesley, 23 May 1811, P.R.O., C.O. 267/28.

[2] Columbine to Moore, 10 August 1810; Columbine to J. W. Croker, 11 August 1810, P.R.O., C.O. 267/28.

[3] Colonel H. Torrens to Sir Robert Peel, 29 August 1810, P.R.O., C.O. 267/33.

[4] Captain F. P. Irby to J. W. Croker, 30 November 1811, Report on...Papers relating to African Forts, p. 205.

the position of affairs, accompanied the *Princess Charlotte* as far as the town of Bintang. They found that the slaver had made its way fifteen miles farther up the creek. Captain Lloyd of the *Kangaroo* thereupon threatened to burn Bintang, unless the *Hope* was surrendered. After some parleying the vessel was surrendered together with her crew and sixty-seven slaves, but the commander managed to make his escape. Though the final capture was a bloodless one, a large number of the *Kangaroo's* crew were stricken down with fever as a result of this expedition.[1]

In 1814 there was a recrudescence of slave trading in the river. Early in that year a schooner under Spanish colours carried off 379 slaves and also ten of the local natives, "who had received presents and not procured the number of slaves they expected". The commander had threatened violence to the British vessels, which had endeavoured to prevent him from trading, and Sir Charles MacCarthy, who was in command at Senegal, had to report that without an adequate naval force he was unable to cope with the situation.[2]

In April of that year another slaver arrived in the river. It was a Rhode Island vessel, which had left America under Portuguese colours and had subsequently changed them at Teneriffe for Spanish colours. A party of two officers and sixty men of the Royal African Corps was sent from Goree in the sloop *Young Frederic* to capture the vessel. The slaver put up a determined resistance but the crew eventually abandoned the ship and with the exception of eight wounded men managed to make their escape. The soldiers lost eight of their number killed and nine wounded.[3]

This operation served only as a temporary deterrent to the slave traders. In February and March 1815, 600 slaves were exported from the Gambia by Americans sailing under Spanish colours.[4] MacCarthy therefore wrote to Earl Bathurst, the Secretary of State, urging the establishment of a small garrison and a battery of two or three guns on James Island to protect British vessels in the river and

---

[1] Captain John Lloyd to Commodore F. P. Irby, 8 November 1812; Lieut. W. R. Pascoe to Captain E. Scobell, 7 November 1812; Commodore Irby to J. W. Croker, 12 November 1812, *Report on...Papers relating to African Forts*, pp. 216–218.

[2] Sir Charles MacCarthy to Earl Bathurst, 19 March 1814, P.R.O., C.O. 267/38.

[3] MacCarthy to Bathurst, 2 April and 8 May 1814; Major J. Chisholm to MacCarthy, 22 April 1814, P.R.O., C.O. 267/38.

[4] MacCarthy to Bathurst, 29 June 1815, P.R.O., C.O. 267/38.

to suppress the slave trade.[1] When at the close of the Napoleonic Wars reports were received that the French intended to re-establish their factory at Albreda, he urged his proposal even more strongly.[2] Towards the middle of 1815 four American vessels arrived in the river. As they were prepared to deal in slaves and British traders were not, and as they were able to flood the market with cheap goods, they virtually captured for the time being the whole of the trade of the river—legitimate and illegitimate. On 12 July Mac-Carthy wrote to inform Earl Bathurst that he was "thoroughly convinced that, unless directions are sent out to occupy the fort of St James in the River Gambia, and foreign vessels prevented from trading there, the whole of the important trade of that river will soon be in the hands of the Americans".[3]

MacCarthy's representations bore fruit. On 20 July 1815 Earl Bathurst instructed him that, in view of the fact that Senegal and Goree would probably be restored to the French by the treaty of peace, it was deemed advisable to take some measures to suppress the slave trade in the River Gambia and ensure that British traders should continue to participate in the gum trade at Portendic. With that object in view he was authorised to reoccupy James Island, "but should you be led to believe that any other situation in that neighbourhood offers superior advantages either in point of defence or as a commercial establishment (and that there is under the Treaty of Paris no obstacle to its occupation by Great Britain), you will proceed to occupy it, reporting however in detail the circumstances which have governed your decision, and the mode in which occupation has been effected".[4]

It was known that James Fort had been reduced to a state which rendered its restoration virtually impossible or else only possible at an expenditure to which the British Government was not prepared to go. Furthermore, the opinion had been expressed more than once in the past that James Island was of very doubtful strategic value and that the military post should be established at the mouth of the river. At the time of the capture of the island by the French in 1779 a number of British traders had advocated the erection of a fort at Banyon Point (Half Die) on the island of Banjol on the south bank

---

[1] MacCarthy to Bathurst, 10 June 1814 and 16 March 1815, P.R.O., C.O. 267/38.   [2] Same to same, 3 May 1815, P.R.O., C.O. 267/38.
[3] Same to same, 29 June and 12 July 1815, P.R.O., C.O. 267/38.
[4] P.R.O., C.O. 268/14.

of the river.[1] During the latter part of the seventeenth century the Royal African Company had made one or two efforts to establish a factory on this island at Banyon Point[2] but they had come to nothing. The island was in fact a sandbank lying a considerable distance from the populated districts on the south bank of the river. According to Major Houghton, who also advocated its occupation as a military post, it was in 1783 occupied by "a few stragling natives", who were "indolent, being mostly the subjects of the King of Barra on the north side of the river, who have fled there for shelter".[3] About the same time Chief Justice Morse recommended that the island should be made the seat of a civil government and a convict settlement.[4] The African Company had also debated the question of occupying Banjol,[5] but the refusal of the Government to grant financial aid had put an end to this as well as the Company's other projects in the Gambia.

Earl Bathurst's instructions to MacCarthy did not reach the latter until 29 November 1815. As he was not able to proceed to the spot personally, MacCarthy gave orders for Captain Alexander Grant to proceed from Goree with a detachment of the African Corps. Grant sailed from Goree on 19 March 1816, with Ensign Adamson, an assistant surgeon, fifty men of the African Corps, and twenty-four artisans. On entering the river Grant landed at Banyon Point. The "few stragling natives" who had been there in 1783 had betaken themselves to some other place. Grant was impressed by the fact that Banjol offered greater scope for expansion than James Island. He therefore approached the "king" of Kombo to enquire if he would be prepared to cede Banjol. On 4 February—only six weeks before Grant's visit—a Spanish ship called the *Panchita* had kidnapped ten men, two women, and eight children, who were near relations of the chief. Grant therefore found him only too ready to make a cession of the island in exchange for British protection from such marauders.[6]

[1] John Dudfield and others to Lieut. William Lacy, 12 May 1779; Thomas Parkin to Thomas De Grey, s.d., P.R.O., C.O. 267/19.

[2] There was a factory there in 1684 (R.A.C. Nominal Rolls), P.R.O., T. 70/1441.

[3] Houghton to Thomas Townshend, 24 February 1783, P.R.O., C.O. 267/20.

[4] Morse to Lord Sidney, 6 March 1783 and 23 June 1784, P.R.O., C.O. 267/8.

[5] Rutherford to Nepean, 16 September 1783, P.R.O., C.O. 267/20.

[6] Grant to MacCarthy, 16 April 1816; Affidavit of Joseph Totosano, 2 May 1816, P.R.O., C.O. 267/42.

In pursuance of his instructions Grant then proceeded to James Island. He had a friendly reception from the "king" of Barra, to whom he explained "that the intention of the British government in again occupying St James was not with a view of depriving him or his people of any of their rights and privileges, while he and they conducted themselves with propriety and lived on amicable terms with the British; but, on the contrary, it was the wish of our government to better their situation; and, though he and his people might in the meantime conceive themselves to be losers by the non-entrance of slave vessels and the suppression of that traffic, which was one object sought in the renewal of the treaty and re-establishment of the fort, yet in a short time after the British came to be established in the river, they would find themselves amply compensated by a free and honourable commerce". The chief expressed himself quite satisfied and in entire agreement with the proposals and consented to the reoccupation of the island on an annual payment of three hundred bars (about £75). He promised every possible assistance in rebuilding the fort and his promise was confirmed by his assembled chiefs and retainers, who touched their foreheads with their hands and said "Amen".[1]

The value of the "king's" promises was soon realised. "A few days only elapsed, when an opportunity came of proving to the king that we would adhere to these resolutions and, though few in number, were determined to act with consistency and firmness. At daylight one morning a strange sail was discovered at anchor in the river about three miles below the fort. I immediately ordered Lieutenant Adamson with a small armed party to embark in one of our craft in order to ascertain what she was and to bring her to anchor under the fort. She proved to be the *Dissamparados*, a Spanish vessel for slaves, and agreeable to my instructions she was detained. The king of Barra had immediate information of this and sent his alcaide and several of his principal people to me to demand the custom for the vessel. I expressed to the alcaide my astonishment at the demand, after having so lately explained at length and apparently to the king's satisfaction the description of vessels, of which this was one, which we were determined to prevent coming into the river, or the seizure, if they did come. I then dismissed the alcaide and his people, desiring him to tell the king that, if he valued the

[1] MacCarthy to Bathurst, 16 April 1816, P.R.O., C.O. 267/42; Grant to R. W. Hay, 25 November 1825, P.R.O., C.O. 324/76.

friendship of the English, he would never again send me any such demand."[1]

As the "king" of Barra was clearly determined to honour his agreement only to the extent to which it suited him and as it was clearly impossible to restore James Fort to a condition fit to house the detachment, Grant recommended that Banjol should be occupied in preference to James Island. Pending further instructions he merely set about repairing the few remaining buildings within the ramparts for use as an outpost.[2]

On 19 April Colonel Brereton proceeded from Goree to the Gambia with a further detachment of thirty men. On arrival at James Island he found that slow progress had been made in clearing away the rubbish and putting the old walls into a habitable state of defence. After conferring with Grant he proceeded with him to Banjol. On 23 April these two officers met the "king" of Kombo, and Grant, with the approval of Brereton, entered into a treaty with that chief, whereby the chief agreed to allow the British Government to occupy Banjol with liberty to erect such buildings and fortifications as might be thought expedient and further to surrender all his right and title to the island in exchange for an annual payment of 103 bars to himself, his wife, and his principal retainers. Formal possession of the island was taken on the same day in accordance with the terms of this treaty.[3] The island was renamed St Mary's Island.

Work was at once commenced by Grant on barracks to house eighty men[4] and a battery of six twenty-four pounders and two field pieces was erected.[5] These works were expedited so that the garrison could be comfortably housed before the rainy season set in. The "king" of Barra was so far accommodating as to allow stone for building purposes to be taken from Dog Island. In order to encourage civilian settlers, Brereton on his return to Goree offered the merchants there free lots upon condition that they would enter into an engagement to erect good airy and substantial stone or brick houses within a stipulated time.[6]

[1] Grant to Hay, 25 November 1825, P.R.O., C.O. 324/76.
[2] Grant to MacCarthy, 24 June 1816; MacCarthy to Bathurst, 16 April 1816, P.R.O., C.O. 267/42.
[3] Brereton to Bathurst, 18 May 1816; Grant to MacCarthy, 24 June 1816; MacCarthy to Bathurst, 20 July 1816, P.R.O., C.O. 267/42.
[4] Now the Secretariat.
[5] Now the Six Gun Battery adjoining Government House.
[6] Brereton to Bathurst, 12 June 1816, P.R.O., C.O. 267/42.

On 20 July 1816 Earl Bathurst wrote to inform Sir Charles MacCarthy that he was prepared to approve the occupation of either St Mary's or James Island, "but you are not to consider yourself authorized to incur any expence, which may have for its object a permanent establishment, or to erect any buildings beyond what may be absolutely necessary for the protection of the small detachments of troops employed in that river under Colonel Brereton. The mere fact of its occupation by a British force will be sufficient to deter the dealers in slaves from a continuance in this illegal traffic, and, if the merchants consider that there is a prospect of carrying on from thence the same trade with the natives, which has heretofore been carried on at Senegal, they will take the same measures for making the island, which you finally determine to occupy, an adequate depot for their goods".[1] Notwithstanding this parsimonious benediction, which was thus bestowed upon the new settlement at St Mary's Island, it was decided to call the nucleus of the town, which was beginning to rise there, after the noble lord.

MacCarthy decided to withdraw all the troops from James Island except a sergeant's guard, which was left to prevent foreign vessels from proceeding farther up the river, and to concentrate the force at Bathurst. He also decided to reinforce the garrison at the latter place with one or more native companies of the African Corps, as the European troops suffered from the climate.[2] During the first rainy season the settlement consisted of a half-finished barrack, the commandant's house, and a few huts. The whole was surrounded by an intrenchment to resist a possible attack from the natives, who had shown signs of resentment at the determined efforts of the British to suppress the slave trade. None the less the settlement justified its existence. In the first three months after its inception no less than four slave vessels were seized and another shared the same fate in October.[3] These were carried to Sierra Leone and condemned, Chief Justice Hogan taking the opportunity of promulgating in the most solemn manner that the River Gambia was thenceforth to be considered wholly British and closed to the slave trade for ever.[4]

The slave trade did not entirely end in the Gambia immediately upon the establishment of the settlement at Bathurst. The French

---

[1] P.R.O., C.O. 268/18.
[2] MacCarthy to Bathurst, 5 October 1816, P.R.O., C.O. 267/42.
[3] MacCarthy to Bathurst, 5 October 1816, P.R.O., C.O. 267/42.
[4] Hogan to Bathurst, 17 June 1816, P.R.O., C.O. 267/42.

reoccupied Albreda in 1817 and it was not until fourteen years later that the French Government took any really effective steps to put down trading in slaves by its own subjects. Even after that date the disposition to co-operate with Great Britain in the campaign against the trade was for some time very spasmodic. For some years to come Albreda was a slave depôt, but the French resident was prohibited from trading above James Island, his establishment was a small one, and death and sickness led to a constant change of residents.[1] Consequently the traffic was never very considerable. In 1818 the British commandant at Bathurst seized a French cutter for trading in slaves. Though it was subsequently forcibly retaken by a French vessel,[2] in deference to the marked opposition of the British to the trade no open attempt was thereafter made to send slaving ships into the river. None the less slaves were still despatched overland from Albreda to Goree, but the volume of the traffic was greatly diminished.

Caravans were also diverted from the higher reaches of the river to the Rivers Casamance, Grande, Nunes and Pongas, where the slaves were embarked and often escaped the vigilance of the British cruisers in the Atlantic. Until foreign states could be induced to co-operate whole-heartedly with Great Britain in its fight against the traffic, that traffic could never be entirely suppressed. None the less the establishment of a military post on St Mary's Island at once fully justified its immediate purpose by striking a shrewd blow at the trade. The River Gambia provided exceptional facilities for slavers, who could often do their bartering in the upper reaches of the river free from any fear of molestation and could then bide their opportunity to slip out of the river, when no patrolling cruiser was in the offing. A military post at the river's mouth, which was constantly on the look out for and ready to search suspicious craft, made it impossible for a slave ship to hope to escape detection. In 1786 it was estimated that an average of 3700 slaves were thus exported in one year from the Gambia.[3] There is reason to believe that these figures increased in later years, but after 1816 not a single ship ever succeeded in carrying a cargo of slaves out of the River Gambia. The credit for this achievement was due to a number of people. Due

[1] P. Marty, "Le Comptoir Français d'Albréda en Gambie, 1817–1826", *Revue de l'Histoire des Colonies Françaises* (1924), pp. 240–242.

[2] *Exposé des faits relatifs à la traite des nègres au voisinage du Sénégal*, pp. 20–28.   [3] Golberry, *Voyage en Afrique*, ii, 209, 210.

praise must be given in the first place to Commodore Frederick Irby, the officers and men of the Royal Navy, who kept up an unceasing and unwearying patrol along the coast often at considerable risk and always in the most trying conditions. Credit must also be given to Sir Charles MacCarthy, whose foresight and genuine anxiety to suppress the trade saw the necessity for the reoccupation of the Gambia. Last and by no means least, due credit must be given to Captain Alexander Grant, the actual founder of the modern colony of the Gambia, and the men of the Royal African Corps. As despatches show, Grant used his utmost exertions to make the settlement a successful one. It was begun very shortly before the rainy season and but for his personal energy might have been the same failure that so many other previously attempted settlements along the coast had been. It was Grant's constant vigilance and promptness of action, which effectively put a stop to the visits of slave ships within a very short time after the occupation of St Mary's Island.

With Grant must be associated the men under his command. Military historians have very little to say that is good of the Royal African Corps. Its personnel was largely recruited from the convict hulks in England and military offenders from other regiments. The early days of Bathurst were trying ones for the rank and file, who were very far from being properly housed. Eight of their number died during the first rainy season and many more fell sick.[1] None the less the men of the Royal African Corps emulated their comrades in the senior service in their determination to suppress the slave trade. They had to serve by sea and by land. Their task was sometimes dangerous and, as these pages have shown, casualties were not infrequent. What these men were and what they did can best be summed up in the words of the historian of the British Army. "The Royal African Corps did not include, as a body, the choicest of his kind, nor were the men—outcasts on account of crime from other regiments—ideal representatives of the British private soldier....They may have been criminals; they may have been doubly-dyed incorrigible scoundrels, with backs scarred by the lash and consciences seared with a red hot iron. But when the time of trial came, they did their duty, and more than their duty, as British soldiers."[2] The Corps has long disappeared from the Army List. It

[1] Fox, *A Brief History of the Wesleyan Missions on the Western Coast of Africa*, p. 261.

[2] Fortescue, *History of the British Army*, XI, 388.

never had any regimental colours, nor any battle honours. But it was one of the few units in the British Army, which shared with the Royal Navy at a cost in life, which was little appreciated at the time, the distinction of having played an honourable part in that "unweary, unostentatious, and inglorious crusade of England against slavery", which Lecky once said "may probably be regarded as among the three or four virtuous pages comprised in the history of nations". One has only to read contemporary despatches to realise that many of the men, who were thus brought face to face with the appalling realities of the slave trade, truly believed that they were fighting a holy war.

XXI: The early days of Bathurst

The primary object of the occupation of St Mary's Island had been for the purpose of establishing a military post for the suppression of the slave trade but, as already mentioned in the last chapter, Earl Bathurst also hoped that the protection afforded by that post would induce British merchants to settle on the island. This expectation was fulfilled. A number of British merchants had settled at Goree during the Napoleonic wars. Some of them had been carrying on trade in the River Gambia. Others had participated in the gum trade at Portendic, which had been preserved for British traders by the treaty of peace. Although the Treaty of Paris stipulated that merchants, who had settled at Goree during the time of the British occupation, might remain and carry on trade there on the same footing as French subjects, it was considered very probable that direct or indirect pressure would be brought upon them to remove. Consequently most of the British merchants at Goree transferred themselves to St Mary's Island as soon as they could wind up their businesses.

In its first few years the new settlement grew very rapidly in every respect. By 1818 the population amounted to 600, including the garrison.[1] In the following year the civil population, exclusive of the garrison, was over 700.[2] In 1826 (again excluding the troops) it had increased to over 1800, of whom thirty were Europeans.[3]

During the early years of the settlement the only source of revenue was a duty levied on imports. In 1817 nearly forty vessels called at the island and discharged merchandise to the value of £1800, which yielded a revenue of £500. In 1818 the imports had increased to £40,000 and the revenue therefrom to just short of £1800. By 1823 the revenue had increased to £3500.[4]

Sir Charles MacCarthy took a very practical interest in the new settlement, which he visited in 1818 and again in 1819 and 1822. Major Gray had visited the island in 1818 and reported that it was then "nothing more than a number of thatched huts".[5] In 1820 MacCarthy was able to say

[1] Sir C. MacCarthy to Earl Bathurst, 29 March 1818.
[2] Same to same, 24 February 1819.
[3] *Report on...the State of Sierra Leone* (1827), p. 7.   [4] *Ibid.* p. 13.
[5] Gray, *Travels in Western Africa*, p. 365.

I found the settlement in an improving state, the whole of the inhabitants happy and satisfied. Many elegant and substantial houses have been built since my visit in March, 1818, and I feel it part of my pleasant duty to record that the zealous and able conduct of the present commandant, Captain Grant, of the Second West India Regiment, whom I entrusted with the formation of this place, deserves my warmest approbation. All were loud in praising his kind treatment of them and in encouraging trade.[1]

Two years later, after an extended tour of all the British Settlements in West Africa, he declared that "I can venture to say that there is more progressive improvement in commerce here than in any of the stations occupied by His Majesty's forces on the coast".[2] In 1821 Major Gray reported that the public buildings, which had then been completed, included a government house, barracks, officers' quarters and mess, a jail, a hospital and the Three-Gun Battery. According to him "the resident merchants vie with each other in the neatness and commodiousness of their private dwellings and store rooms. Upwards of twenty are finished, many more in a great state of forwardness".[3]

There can be no doubt that the tribute, which Sir Charles Mac-Carthy paid to Captain (afterwards Lieutenant-Colonel) Alexander Grant was thoroughly well earned. He had largely to make bricks without straw. Both he and his subordinates had to work under very trying conditions in a very unhealthy climate on what was no more than a barren sandbank, which was largely under water during the rainy season. Some of his subordinates and of the early immigrants to the settlement were far from desirable characters. But he proved a very capable organiser and administrator of the infant colony and heartened and inspired the early settlers. He also had the confidence of the natives. "No man", wrote a contemporary, "ever stood so high with the natives and was so capable, from his knowledge of their language and conciliating manners, of influencing their measures."[4] When in 1818 there was considerable friction with the natives of Barra, the same person informed his brother in

---

[1] Sir Charles MacCarthy to Earl Bathurst, 3 January 1820.
[2] Same to same, 18 June 1822.
[3] Gray, *op. cit.* p. 365.
[4] William Forster to R. W. Hay, 1 January 1817.

London that "the Mandingoes...want to write to England to have Captain Grant out again".[1]

The military population of the new settlement consisted almost entirely of officers and men of the Royal African Corps. Many of the former were Peninsular veterans, but, as mentioned in the previous chapter, the rank and file were for the most part recruited from military offenders from other units, who were undergoing punishment. Little good has ever been recorded of the latter. They were a real legion of the lost ones, who "considered themselves to be exiled for life from their native land, and, as they entertained no hope whatever, under such forlorn circumstances, of redeeming their character, they abandoned themselves to debauchery, and gave free vent to the most debasing tendencies of their nature".[2] After the establishment of the settlement upon St Mary's Island these men had no amenities and nothing to occupy them outside the routine of peace time soldiering. Even if many of them had been more exemplary in their lives, they lived under such appalling conditions that posting to Bathurst came very near being the equivalent of a sentence of death. In 1825 a contingent of 199 European soldiers arrived at Bathurst. As there was accommodation for only half that number, 91 were kept during the next four months at sea in the *Surrey* transport. The remaining 108 were landed. They had arrived in May just at the beginning of the rainy season. They very soon began to fall sick. The military hospital had accommodation for some 60 or 70 patients. During the next few months it was at times to accommodate from 120 to 140. It was subsequently reported that "at one time they were so numerous that it became necessary to place them in the galleries".[3] By 21 September 1825, 87 out of the 108 had died. As there was now plenty of accommodation on shore, the remaining 91, who had hitherto not suffered in health at all, were brought to the barracks. By 21 December 1825, 73 more had died. This left 39 alive out of the original 199. On 10 March 1826

[1] William Forster to M. Forster, 29 January 1818. Alexander Grant was appointed a Captain in the Royal African Corps, 31 August 1809; promoted to be Major in the Second West India Regiment, 13 December 1821; and Lt.-Col. in the Royal African Corps, 8 January 1824. He was Commandant of the Gambia Settlement, 1816–1817, 1819–1820 and 1822–1823, and acting Governor of Sierra Leone in 1820 and 1821. He resigned his commission on account of ill-health, 1 August 1826, and died at Elgin, North Britain, in October 1827.

[2] Holman, *Sierra Leone and the Gold Coast.*

[3] *Report on...the State of Sierra Leone* (1827), p. 6.

the acting Governor of Sierra Leone wrote from Freetown to inform Earl Bathurst that, "being really anxious to decrease the number of white troops serving in this garrison, who generally speaking are men of the most desperate character, I shall order one hundred to be embarked in the *Edward* transport and landed in the Gambia". Ultimately a draft of 200 was sent. Like its predecessor it arrived just at the beginning of the rainy season. The same story was repeated. Major-General Sir Niel Campbell visited Bathurst in the following August. In the hospital he found 93 out of a total strength of 116 white soldiers under the sole care of an acting assistant hospital mate, whose "inexperience makes him ignorant of the police duties and comforts, which are practised in the army in tropical climates and enforced by officers in command".[1] Between 21 June and 21 September in that year 98 men died. Eighteen more died during the following three months and of the survivors 33 were permanently unfit for any further service. In July 1827 after 276 out of 399 European soldiers had perished, it was decided that white troops could not be stationed in the Gambia and the survivors were withdrawn and replaced by African troops.[2]

Some of the original merchant settlers had been engaged in trade upon the coast for a good many years. William Waterman, for instance, had settled at Goree soon after its occupation by the British in 1800. Edward Lloyd, who was thereafter to command the Royal Gambia Militia, and Charles Johnston had set up in business there in 1806. John Wynne, who had at one time held a post under the Government, arrived at Goree in 1811. Charles Grant, a cousin of the settlement's first Commandant, had also originally been in Government service at Goree. He was destined to be a strong supporter of the Wesleyan Mission up to the time of his death in 1848. William Forster, who was in charge of the firm of Forster and Smith, which was for many years the leading business house in Bathurst, had also started to trade in Goree.[3] Thomas Chown, who was to be succeeded in his business by both his son and his grandson, arrived a little later.[4] Last, but by no means least, there came from Goree

---

[1] Sir N. Campbell to Earl Bathurst, 17 August 1826.

[2] Martin, *British Colonies*, IV, 174; Gore, *Medical History of our West African Campaigns*, pp. 3, 209; Ellis, *The Land of Fetish*, pp. 8, 9; Crooks, "The Royal African Corps", *United Services Magazine* (1917), pp. 213–219.

[3] Messrs Forster and Smith to Earl Bathurst, July 1826.

[4] *Correspondence relating to the proposed cession of the Gambia to France* (1870), p. 77.

a certain Thomas Joiner, a man with a very remarkable history. He was by origin a Mandingo from the upper Gambia and had begun life as a pagan and a griot, or professional musician. He had been kidnapped in early manhood and carried off as a slave to America. There his superior intelligence had attracted the attention of his master, who had placed him in a position of confidence. Eventually he saved sufficient money to purchase his freedom. He had then come to Goree, where he had set up in trade on a small scale before 1810. He had traded in the Upper Gambia for a number of years before the foundation of Bathurst. In course of time he amassed considerable wealth and lived in one of the largest houses in Bathurst hard by the humbler residence of Robert Aynsley, the mulatto son of Mungo Park's friend and the very man who had sold him to the captain of the American slave ship.[1]

As in the early days of the settlement no provision was made for any civil establishment, many of these merchants were called upon to do unpaid public service as sheriffs, magistrates, and in similar posts. As early official correspondence shows, they also rendered useful aid to the authorities in opening relations with the inhabitants up the river and in making agreements with a number of chiefs.

Although none of them arrived until five years after the foundation of the settlement, mention should be made of the earliest missionaries to work in the Gambia. Both of the first two societies, which sent missionaries to the country, did so at the earnest request of Sir Charles MacCarthy and Alexander Grant.[2] By 1820 the population had increased to upwards of one thousand, but no provision had been made for their spiritual needs. Grant himself formed a

---

[1] *J.R.G.S.* III, 72; *Report on...the State of Sierra Leone* (1827), pp. 3, 4; Moister, *Memorials of Missionary Labours in Western Africa*, pp. 176–178. Joiner was one of the witnesses to the MacCarthy Island treaty of 1823 and was wounded in the expedition against Kemintang in 1835. Writing of the relations between Aynsley and Joiner, Moister says: "The children of both parties attended the mission school; and I am happy to say that they lived on terms of perfect friendship and goodwill, and would occasionally allude to the circumstances here narrated with considerable good humour in social parties, where I have often met them." But as other pages in Moister's book show, the general attitude of the former captive to his quondam captor was usually, and not unnaturally, very different, if they ever chanced to meet again.

[2] *Report of the Committee managing a Fund raised by some Friends*, p. 42; Biller, *Memoirs of Hannah Kilham*, p. 172.

congregation and read prayers each Sunday morning,[1] but both he and MacCarthy realised that the time had come for the appointment of a minister of religion and that there was also a field for missionary work beyond Bathurst. In that year Sir Charles MacCarthy proceeded to England on a short furlough. During his leave he called at the Wesleyan Mission House in London and strongly urged upon the general secretaries the establishment of a mission in the Gambia.[2]

In actual point of time the first missionary to arrive in the Gambia belonged to the Society of Friends. Though this particular mission did not labour long in the country, its work deserves something more than mere passing mention. William Singleton landed at Bathurst on 21 January 1821. He was sent out under the auspices of a number of Friends, who had interested themselves in two natives of Goree and the Gambia respectively, who had arrived in London on a sailing ship. Singleton and a few other Friends had these two persons educated in England with the express object of utilising them as assistants to a party of European missionaries, whom it was proposed to send to the Gambia. Singleton went out to explore the field before the actual working party was sent out. After a visit to Tendeba he obtained from the alkali of Bakau and the "king" of the Kombo permission for the future missionaries to open a station at Cape St Mary. He subsequently paid a short visit to Sierra Leone and then sailed for England on 29 May 1821.[3]

Major Grant had shown a lively interest in the mission and had done everything to encourage it. On 8 December 1823 the working party arrived at Bathurst. The leader was Hannah Kilham, the widow of John Wesley's protagonist and founder of the Methodist New Connection, who had joined the Society of Friends shortly after her husband's death. At the time of her arrival in Bathurst she was close on fifty years of age, but she showed indefatigable energy and held views on missionary matters which were well in advance of those of her time. During his visit to the Gambia Singleton had prepared a short Jollof vocabulary. With the aid of this vocabulary and the co-operation of her two African protégés Mrs Kilham had prepared a simple Jollof phrase book and had also translated a

[1] Fox, *A Brief History of the Wesleyan Missions on the West Coast of Africa*, p. 262.

[2] Moister, *Missionary Pioneers*, p. 377.

[3] *Report of a Committee managing a Fund raised by some Friends for the purpose of promoting African Instruction.*

number of passages of the Scripture into that language before sailing
for Africa. The mission, of which she took charge, was almost, if not
quite, the earliest industrial mission in Africa. In addition to
evangelical work the missionaries set out to train their followers in
agricultural and mechanical work. Mrs Kilham was accompanied by
Richard Smith, a brother and sister named John and Anne Thompson, and her two African protégés, Mamadi and Sandani.

The alkali of Bakau gave the missionaries a plot of ground at
Cape St Mary, where the two male members of the party began to
instruct the natives in ploughing and other farming work. The
ladies took up their residence in Bathurst, where they opened a
school for girls and subsequently another school for boys. Mrs
Kilham later paid a visit to Sierra Leone to explore the mission field
there. On her return she found that a Wesleyan missionary and his
wife had arrived and were endeavouring to start work amongst
women. In a remarkable spirit of tolerance and good sense Mrs
Kilham decided that at that stage there was not scope for more than
one mission in the same place. Accordingly she handed over her
girls' school and her pupils to Mrs Hawkins, the wife of the Wesleyan
missionary. She and Anne Thompson removed themselves to Bakau,
where they opened another girls' school.

Unfortunately all the members of the mission suffered from fever.
All of them except Smith had to return to England. John Thompson
died on the voyage home. Less than one month after the departure
of the others, Richard Smith, who had gone to the Gambia at his
own expense, also succumbed to the climate. These calamities
brought the mission to an end. Mrs Kilham subsequently went to
Sierra Leone and eventually died in 1832 on her return voyage to
England. Though the Society of Friends ceased to be directly interested in missionary work in the Gambia, their interest in the country
did not wane. When in 1833 a committee was formed to start a
mission to the Fulas of the upper river, Elizabeth Fry was one of its
strongest supporters. Furthermore, in the little time during which
Hannah Kilham and her companions laboured in the Gambia they
left a permanent mark behind them. In 1837, nearly fourteen years
after their departure, in a country where memories are proverbially
short, the alkali of Bakau made particular inquiries of the Lieutenant-
Governor after his old friends, the Quakers, and expressed great
regret that they had not remained amongst his people, whilst the
Lieutenant-Governor himself saw in the progressive modes of

cultivation employed by the people of Bakau clear signs of the influence of the former missionaries.[1]

The Wesleyan Mission was second only to that of the Society of Friends by a matter of a few days. John Morgan arrived at Bathurst on 8 February 1821, and was followed shortly afterwards by John Baker, who had previously been stationed in Sierra Leone. They had been recommended to open a station up the river at Tendeba, but after visiting that place Morgan decided that the disturbed state of the country and a number of other circumstances made this out of the question. After the alkali of Bakau had refused them a plot of ground near to his village, they obtained land from the "king" of Kombo at Mandinari. Here at the beginning of the rainy season the two missionaries found temporary shelter in a native hut. Having procured some tools from Bathurst they set to work with the assistance of a few natives to fell trees and to erect a house, which they managed to complete mainly owing to their own personal exertions after six weeks of hard labour under a tropical sun. During those strenuous weeks the two missionaries regularly went into Bathurst every Saturday afternoon, returning to Mandinari every Monday morning. "We meet our little class", wrote Baker, "on Sunday morning, attend the chaplain's[2] preaching at 10 a.m.; preach at two p.m. to about one hundred people, and in the evening at six frequently more than double that number. Our intermediate time on the Sabbath is devoted to visiting the poor people; and on Monday we have an opportunity to procure anything we want for ourselves or the settlement." It is not surprising to learn that both these devoted men soon broke down in health and that Baker had to be invalided to England.

Such labour and devotion deserved to reap better fruit than actually was reaped, but Mandinari had soon to be abandoned. The spot was most unhealthy, the water was bad, and the neighbouring

---

[1] *Proceedings of a Committee for raising a Fund etc.*; Biller, *op. cit.*; Moister, *Memorials of Missionary Labours in Western Africa*; Fox, *op. cit.*; Bowdich, *Excursions in the Interior of Maderia and Porto Santo*, p. 216 and *Stories of Strange Lands*, pp. 134, 135; Kilham, *African Lessons: The Friend of the African*, p. 58; William Allen to Mr Canny, 26 October 1823. William Allen, the Quaker scientist, abolitionist and prison reformer, showed a warm interest in the Gambia. He not only was a supporter of Mrs Kilham's mission, but also did much, as official correspondence shows, to endeavour to promote and develop the agricultural resources of the river.

[2] *Sc.* the Church of England chaplain.

inhabitants showed not the least disposition to be taught Christianity. More fruitful soil was found in Bathurst itself. The opportunity came in 1823 to open a new station at a more advantageous spot up the river. With the limited staff, which was available for out-station work, it was decided to abandon Mandinari after an occupation of little over a year.

Better results were obtained in Bathurst, where much good work was done amongst the Jollofs and liberated Africans. A boys' school was opened in Jollof Town in 1822. The arrival in 1824 of Mrs Hawkins with her husband enabled the mission to take over the girls' school, which had been started by the Society of Friends. A mission house and school house were built in 1825 and on 3 December 1834 the foundation stone was laid of the still existing Wesleyan Church. By the last-mentioned date the church membership, which amounted only to half a dozen at the end of 1821, had increased to over two hundred and fifty.

But the harvest had been reaped at a very grievous price. During those thirteen years ten missionaries and six wives of missionaries had arrived in the country. Of that number three missionaries and two wives had already laid down their lives and the death roll was to mount up still further in the years to come. Every missionary society, which has sent out workers to Africa, has a long and mournful roll of those fallen in the field, but perhaps few can tell a more melancholy tale of self sacrifice and devotion than that which was unfolded in very broken English by Sally Douglas, an Ibu ex-slave girl, when on a cold grey morning in October 1830 she carried in her arms to the Wesleyan Mission House in London the emaciated, fatherless and motherless child of Richard Marshall. But if her tale was a piteous one, it also gave inspiration. A group of young men, who were preparing for the mission field, were present when she told it. One of them, William Moister, at once volunteered to fill the gap. He was followed shortly afterwards by another of them, William Fox. To these two not only the Wesleyan Mission but all races, creeds and classes in the Gambia were to owe a very great debt for their quiet and unobtrusive, but none the less unremitting, devotion to duty and to the welfare of all races and classes of the community.[1]

[1] Biller, *op. cit.*; Fox, *op. cit.*; Moister, *Memorials of Missionary Labours in Western Africa, Heralds of Salvation, Missionary Pioneers, Conversations on . . . the present state of Wesleyan Missions*; Morgan, *Reminiscences of the founding*

Although the members of other churches did not at this date share in the labours of the mission field, some reference must also be made to them. At the request of Sir Charles MacCarthy the Church Missionary Society undertook in 1820 to provide a chaplain for the garrison.[1] Robert Hughes, the first chaplain, arrived in March 1821. The Wesleyan missionaries expressed a deep appreciation of the assistance, which he gave to them. Unfortunately before the year was out both he and his wife fell victims to the country.[2] The sickness and deaths of many of his immediate successors prevented any real continuity in church work.[3] Though funds were collected by local subscription for the purpose at a very early date,[4] many years were to elapse before a church was built. Until then the services were conducted in a room in the barracks.

Last of all, but by no means least, mention must be made of the French Sisters of Charity, who in 1823 came at the request of Sir Charles MacCarthy from Goree. In view of the state of the surrounding country their work had necessarily to be confined to St Mary's Island. Despite many difficulties they did much real philanthropic work amongst the poorer members of the community. Both Mrs Bowdich and Mrs Kilham gave high praise to the Sisters for their ministrations to the sick. Unfortunately the same calamities befel them as befel the rest of the missions. Sister Adèle died and ill-health eventually compelled her companion to leave the colony.[5]

The African population came from many different tribes and arrived in Bathurst under very differing circumstances. When experience had at length proved the utter impossibility of garrisoning the island with white troops, black troops were drafted in from Sierra Leone. These for the most part comprised men who had been rescued by British cruisers from slave ships. Part of the civilian population was drawn from the same class. A number of liberated Africans, who had been apprenticed in Sierra Leone, were brought to the Gambia to assist in the building operations. In 1827 Major

of a Christian Mission in the Gambia, Wesleyan-Methodist Magazine, Wesleyan Juvenile Offering; Findlay and Holdsworth, History of the Wesleyan Methodist Missionary Society.

[1] J. Pratt to H. Goulburn, 18 March 1820.

[2] Fox, op. cit. pp. 262, 270.

[3] During vacancies in the chaplaincy a Wesleyan missionary used to conduct the garrison service.

[4] Memorial of Bathurst merchants, 28 June 1834.

[5] Bowdich, Madeira and Porto Santo, p. 203; Biller, op. cit. p. 188.

Rowan reported that the Sierra Leone Government took advantage of a request for a supply of this class of labour to rid itself of a number of undesirables by sending "a few persons said to have been convicted of offences at that settlement, and removed to the Gambia; a measure, which, considering the circumstances of the Island of St Mary, appears to have been anything but judicious. They have given much trouble, and in fact the only persons tried at the sessions held in June, 1826, were of this class".[1] In 1825, when work on public buildings had more or less come to an end, General Turner sent a number of them back to Sierra Leone, but many of them returned and took up a permanent abode in the Gambia.[2] Those of them, who were thrifty or belonged to the artisan class, managed to earn a livelihood, but the unskilled labourer, who generally lacked both the opportunity and the inclination to till the soil, was often in very great want.[3]

The liberated African formed, however, at this date only a very small element of the population. The more considerable element hailed from Goree and St Louis. A number of these were, in the words of a later Governor, "the descendants of those British colonists, who, sooner than live under the French flag at Senegal when it was ceded to France in 1814, made an exodus to St Mary's Island in the Gambia, having made country marriages with the senioras, or daughters of the very early European settlers on the coast".[4] Several of these families, and in particular those of Lloyd and Hughes, became the principal landowners in Bathurst[5] and also did much useful public service, especially as officers of the militia in some of the early native wars.[6] They resided for the most part in the quarter of Bathurst which came to be known as Portuguese Town, that being the local generic name which was bestowed at this date on persons of mixed blood.

The greater number of the immigrants from Goree were, however, either the domestic servants of the traders from that place or else artisans, who either accompanied or else were sent by their masters from that place to assist the merchants in their building operations. Many of them were slaves in their country of origin and provided the

---

[1] *Report on...the State of Sierra Leone* (1827), p. 8.   [2] *Ibid.*
[3] Kenneth Macaulay to Earl Bathurst, 28 August 1826.
[4] Governor D'Arcy to Duke of Newcastle, 20 April 1861.
[5] Horton, *West African Countries and Peoples*, p. 74.
[6] D'Arcy to Newcastle, 20 April 1861.

early administrators with somewhat difficult problems. Sir Charles MacCarthy was out to encourage civilian settlers and to give them every facility to build houses for themselves. Skilled labour was not easy to come by in those early days. If the artisan immigrants from Goree were to be emancipated forthwith, the result might well have been that both they and their masters would at once leave St Mary's Island. MacCarthy therefore effected a temporary compromise. It was arranged that an indenture of service should be granted for a short period, at the expiration of which both the servant and his children were to become free.[1]

At a very early date, however, MacCarthy announced that any slave in the Island of St Mary, who applied for it, would be issued with a document declaring him to be free.[2] This action led to a protest from the French authorities in Senegal, who in 1817 demanded the surrender of a number of slaves, who had either run away from or else refused to return to their masters. MacCarthy replied that he could not in consistency with English law surrender any person, who sought an asylum from slavery under the British flag.[3]

As the French authorities in Senegal tolerated domestic slavery, the refusal of the British authorities to surrender these fugitives often led to considerable friction. The French refused to recognise any change in the legal status of a slave by reason of his entry upon British soil and furthermore asserted that his status attached to his children. They from time to time pushed this claim to very considerable lengths. In 1836 two daughters of a discharged soldier of the Royal African Corps were detained as slaves at Goree because their mother had originally been a slave there. They were, however, released by the Governor of Goree on a formal demand for their surrender by the commander of a British man-of-war.[4] In 1839 an educated African woman, who had never left the Gambia, appealed

[1] MacCarthy to Earl Bathurst, 20 January 1820.
[2] Same to same, 20 September 1820.
[3] MacCarthy to H. Goulburn, 29 September 1817.
[4] T. L. Ingram to Lord John Russell, 6 January 1840. In his *Sketches of a Missionary's Travels*, pp. 214–215, R. M. MacBrair gives a version of this incident, which contemporary official correspondence shows to be at complete variance with the facts. MacBrair was undoubtedly badly treated by the government in respect of a certain incident at MacCarthy Island. Unfortunately his personal grievance led him to distort the facts in regard to other matters, thus making it necessary to accept his accounts of contemporary events with a considerable measure of caution.

to the British authorities for letters of protection. Her father had also served in the African Corps and had married her mother in the very early days of the colony, but, as in the previous case, the mother was a slave from Goree and had never been formally emancipated. The mother's former mistress claimed ownership of the daughter solely for the purpose of extracting money as a ransom. Needless to say, the British authorities refused to entertain the claim.[1] In 1843 Mr Fox of the Wesleyan Mission took with him to England an African boy, aged twelve years. On the voyage home the ship called at Goree, where a mulatto woman, who was more or less permanently resident in Bathurst, claimed the boy as her slave. The boy had never previously been to Goree in his life, but his mother had originally been a slave there. She had gone to Bathurst and had there married a British subject and subsequently purchased her freedom. The boy was born before her manumission and on that ground a French court at Goree formally adjudicated him a slave. Fox had to pay the claimant $150 in order to procure the boy's release.[2]

Many such cases were no doubt purely cases of blackmail, but the French authorities certainly had more legitimate grounds of complaint when this right of asylum was abused by deserters from French craft in the River Gambia and escaped convicts from Senegal.[3] The diametrically opposite attitudes of the two nations towards the question of slavery led to considerable friction in these early days. Matters reached a climax in 1841, when two French men-of-war, after sailing past Bathurst without saluting the British flag, stopped a vessel off Albreda and forcibly removed two Africans, who had long been resident in Bathurst on the pretext that they were absconding slaves. The authorities at Goree refused to surrender them, when a formal demand was made by the commander of a British man-of-war, and the men were only released after representations had been made through diplomatic channels in Europe.[4]

---

[1] Sophia Handy to Acting Lt.-Gov. Ingram, 12 December 1839; Ingram to Lord John Russell, 6 January 1840; Russell to Lt.-Gov. Huntley, 30 March 1840; Huntley, *Seven Years' Service on the Slave Coast of Western Africa*, ii, 368.

[2] Fox, *op. cit.* pp. 564, 565.

[3] Ingram to Lord John Russell, 12 June 1841; Ingram to John Mantell, 12 May 1842.

[4] Ingram to Captain Denman, 13 July 1841; *State Papers*, 1841–1842, pp. 1040–1042.

Emancipation papers therefore were often of no great value to their recipients. Not a few ex-slaves, who were undoubtedly well aware of the fact that they could obtain them more or less for the asking, never took the trouble to apply for them. Many of them had left relatives behind in Goree. If they desired to visit those relations, the documents did not secure them immunity from detention by their former owners. Furthermore domestic slavery in their country of origin was frequently very paternal and imposed upon the owner the liability to maintain his slave in sickness and old age. In the circumstances a number of the early immigrants from Goree did not trouble to go through the formality of establishing the status, which was conferred upon them by the British authorities at Bathurst.[1] For example, John Cupidon, who was born a slave at Goree and had been sent by his master to work as a carpenter at Bathurst in its very early days, preferred to ensure his freedom in both French and English territory by purchasing it from the master, whom he had left behind in Goree. On the other hand, Pierre Salla, who had been sent by his master to work as a stonemason, obeyed his master's order of recall to Goree, when building work in Bathurst came to an end. He only procured his freedom by means of a subscription, which was raised by the Wesleyan Mission. Both these men were not only respectable members of the artisan class, but also persons of some education, who eventually became assistant missionaries in the Wesleyan Mission.[2]

Others of the early settlers came from the adjacent mainland. A Jola community sprang up and took up its residence in a small village, which was some distance away from the rest of the habitations on St Mary's Island and came to be known as Jola Town. Other immigrants were Mandingos from the Kombo. Many of them had been slaves in their own country and, though it never actually led to open rupture, the refusal of the British authorities to surrender such persons on demand often caused a considerable amount of ill feeling amongst the neighbouring chiefs. Not a few of those, who thus sought an asylum under the British flag, had been enslaved in their own country for their past misdeeds. As one officer in charge of the administration said, the feeling of the chiefs was that "we are abetting their criminals and that we are receiving

[1] *Report of Select Committee on West Coast of Africa* (1844), p. 196.
[2] Moister, *Memorials of Missionary Labours in Western Africa*, pp. 136–139.

offenders flying from punishment brought upon them by their own conduct".[1] In 1829 Captain Jackson, who was temporarily in charge of the administration, entered into a treaty with the "king" of Kombo for the surrender of fugitive slaves in certain circumstances, but that treaty was honoured in the breach almost from the date of signature. It was never forwarded at the time to the home Government and, when it was unearthed over a dozen years later, it was repudiated by the Secretary of State.[2]

As was inevitable in an infant colony, which comprised so many different elements collected together in such a haphazard manner, a certain number of undesirable characters congregated in Bathurst. In 1824 a purge by the commandant removed some of the least estimable members of the community. After holding quarter sessions that year Acting Chief Justice George Rendall reported that the inhabitants "may generally speaking be called industrious, particularly since Captain Findlay removed from the settlement those pests, the griots, beggars and maraboos, all of whom were living on the public....Petty offences are not numerous, if it is considered how many bad characters have been sent here, to which class they are chiefly confined".[3] Periodically an influx of ne'er-do-wells brought about a recrudescence of serious crime. In 1826 some fresh arrivals from Sierra Leone provided a heavy calendar for quarter sessions,[4] as in 1833 and 1836 did a number of escaped convicts from Senegal.[5] But the very few presentments to the grand juries over a number of years indicate that these people of very mixed antecedents were on the whole a very law-abiding community.

To-day the inhabited portion of the Island of St Mary virtually consists of the single compact town of Bathurst, but, as originally laid out it consisted of a number of separate villages, which housed the different sections of the community.[6] Portuguese Town was the trading centre and residential quarter of the more wealthy settlers. Melville Town was mainly allotted to the artisans and servants and dependents of the early merchants. It subsequently acquired the

[1] Lt.-Gov. Huntley to Lord John Russell, 23 July 1840.

[2] T. L. Ingram to Lord Stanley, 10 January and 5 May 1842; Lord Stanley to Ingram, 14 February 1842.

[3] Rendall to D. M. Hamilton, 1 December 1824.

[4] *Report on...the State of Sierra Leone* (1827), p. 8.

[5] T. L. Ingram to Lord John Russell, 12 June 1841.

[6] Moister, *Memorials of Missionary Labours in Western Africa*, p. 114.

name of Jollof Town from the race of its principal residents.[1] The name Soldier Town sufficiently indicates the class of persons inhabiting it. The open space, which separates it from Portuguese Town and is now known as MacCarthy Square, was the original market place of the settlement. Mocam Town, which later acquired the name of Half Die, was the home of the poorer African. All these villages were separated by strips of open land. The original intention was that these open spaces should be given over to cultivation and pasturage. As late as 1844 there were still forty acres on St Mary's Island, which were under cultivation,[2] but it is clear that even in its very earliest days the soil of Bathurst never sufficed to support its African population. In fact the only evidence of agriculture on the island was once not inaptly described as "here and there...a patch of ground on which labour has been lavished, where some sickly vegetation seems to be doing violence to the poverty of the soil".[3] As the population increased, these vacant spaces were built over and the villages joined up to form a single town.

Alexander Grant was responsible for the layout of the settlement and the ground plan of Bathurst to-day is practically the same as his original design. The streets were named after Waterloo generals and sufficiently date his work, but, whatever may be said of later building operations and encroachments upon public streets, a modern regional planning expert would find little to criticise in the original layout. Grant and Captain Kelly of the Second West India Regiment were also responsible for the erection of the earliest public buildings in Bathurst. They were confronted with innumerable difficulties in this task. Their expenditure was limited to what could be collected in import duties. There were no building materials of any description on the island. Consequently stone had to be fetched from Dog Island off the Barra shore[4] and timber from the mainland. Some of those buildings have lasted until this day. Government House still serves its original purpose. The barracks are now occupied by the Secretariat and the military hospital has been converted into residential quarters for Government officials.

[1] At a later date another Melville Town arose. It began as a village for liberated Africans from Sierra Leone. It is now included in New Town.

[2] *Accounts and Papers (Colonial)*, 1844, p. 415.

[3] Dr Madden in *Report of Select Committee on West Coast of Africa* (1844), p. 179.

[4] *Report on...the State of Sierra Leone* (1827), p. 6.

These building operations at one time landed the infant colony in what might have been a serious financial crisis. Work was started on Government House in 1820. After the walls and other masons' work had been finished, reference had to be made to the Government in Sierra Leone in regard to the roofing. During the delay thus caused a severe tornado did considerable damage to the building and washed part of it down. The necessary repairs cost £2000.[1] As there were no funds to meet this expenditure, the commandant was empowered to issue colonial notes of the denomination of £1 to the extent of £2000. It was the original intention gradually to cancel these notes as revenue came in, but in 1821 further notes amounting to £1000 were issued. For several years no steps were taken for cancellation of either issue. The notes were accepted by the Government in payment of revenue at their face value, but in ordinary commercial transactions they passed for four Spanish dollars or 17s. 4d.[2] Eventually they had to be redeemed in 1826 at their market price and for this purpose £1000 had to be borrowed from the Sierra Leone Government. The immediate result was that the settlement was reported to be deeply involved in debt. "No public works of any kind have been carried on for the past eighteen months, and none can be attempted for the next eighteen months."[3]

For the first five years of its existence the settlement on St Mary's Island was in strict legality in territory, which was subject to the control of the Committee of Merchants trading to Africa by virtue of an Act of Parliament passed in 1783, but, as mentioned in Chapter xix, that body had long ceased to display any interest or to attempt to exercise the slightest authority in the Gambia. As in its origin the new settlement was purely a military post, it was for the first couple of years under the sole control of a military commandant, who was subject to the orders of the Governor of Sierra Leone. When in 1818 the civil population had begun to outnumber the military, Sir Charles MacCarthy made provision for a civil

[1] H. Wynne to General Turner, 21 December 1826.
[2] Spanish dollars were legal tender in the Gambia until 1880. In order to prevent them from being carried away into the interior and thus put out of circulation they were cut into quarters: Chalmers, *History of Currency in the British Colonies*, pp. 210–219.
[3] Kenneth Macaulay to Earl Bathurst, 28 June 1826; *Report on...the State Sierra Leone* (1827), p. 14.

government. He created a Court of Police and Equity for the trial of minor offences and cases of petty debt. At the same time he created a Settlement Court, which exercised both judicial and legislative functions. It dealt with civil appeals from the Court of Police and Equity and was also empowered to hold quarter sessions for criminal cases. It was composed of the merchants of Bathurst and the chairman was given the title of mayor. The members were never to be less than five, of whom three were to form a quorum. The Commandant and the Settlement Court were empowered to enact regulations for the peace, welfare and good government of the settlement, such regulations being subject to a power of disallowance by the Governor of Sierra Leone.[1]

In 1821 an Act of Parliament[2] divested the Committee of Merchants of all their territorial rights and jurisdiction in West Africa, which were revested in the Crown. Letters patent of the same year placed all British forts and settlements in West Africa under the authority of a central government in Sierra Leone. The effect of these two measures was to abolish the two courts which MacCarthy had created in 1818, and thus to leave the Gambia without any local machinery either for legislation or for the administration of justice. Provision was made in 1822 and 1824 for the establishment of a Court of Common Pleas and a bench of local justices of the peace,[3] but no provision was made for a local legislature. The Gambia had to depend for its laws upon the Governor and Council in Sierra Leone, who had no knowledge of local conditions in the Gambia. In 1826 the then Governor of Sierra Leone, Sir Neil Campbell, attempted to remedy this state of affairs by creating two Boards of Commerce at Bathurst. Both boards were composed of local merchants nominated by himself. Their function was to act as an advisory board to the Commandant, who was to forward their resolutions together with his observations to Sierra Leone.[4] For some reason, which is not disclosed by the correspondence, Earl Bathurst did not approve of this apparently innocuous measure for the

[1] Commissions dated 14 and 16 April 1818.

[2] 1 and 2 Geo. IV, c. 28.

[3] These courts were replaced in 1825 by a Court of Requests and a Police Court, each of which had a more limited jurisdiction than its predecessor. The result of the change was that the more important cases had to await the arrival in the Gambia of the Chief Justice of Sierra Leone: *Report on...the State of Sierra Leone* (1827), p. 15.

[4] Campbell to Earl Bathurst, 3 September 1826.

benefit of a settlement, which happened to bear his own name. Sir Neil was therefore instructed to abolish the boards.[1]

In 1827 Major Rowan, who had been appointed by Parliament to report on the state of the settlements in West Africa, pointed out the inconvenience which was caused by the delay entailed in sending all legislative proposals to a body in Sierra Leone, which had no interest in the Gambia. He therefore advocated the appointment of a Lieutenant-Governor and separate council for the Gambia.[2] The Secretary of State was not, however, prepared to go the full length of his recommendations. As a sort of half-way measure the Commandant at Bathurst was instructed to correspond direct with the home Government and to be guided by the instructions, which he might receive from that Government.[3] Acting under this authority, Major Alexander Findlay, who was then Commandant, revived the two Boards of Commerce only to receive the same rebuff as had Sir Neil Campbell.[4] In 1829 Findlay—by then a Lieutenant-Colonel—was appointed the first Lieutenant-Governor of the Gambia. By virtue of this appointment he was made directly responsible to the home Government and ceased to be responsible in any way to Sierra Leone. But he was still required to forward all legislative proposals to Sierra Leone for enactment by the council of that Colony.[5] His apparent independence was therefore very far from real. A number of administrative matters required to be regulated by law. Reference of such matters to Freetown only entailed delay. The Sierra Leone Government not infrequently took it upon itself, without consulting anybody from the Gambia, to amend the legislation submitted to it in such a manner as to alter very materially its whole purport and intention. Again, without any consultation of any responsible person on the spot, the same Government also made use of its power of legislating for both settlements to pass laws which purported to be applicable to the Gambia and which clearly betrayed great ignorance of local conditions in that settlement.

[1] Earl Bathurst to Campbell, 24 November 1826.
[2] *Report on...the State of Sierra Leone* (1827), p. 15.
[3] W. Huskisson to Governor Denham, 8 December 1827.
[4] R. W. Hay to Findlay, 25 July 1828.
[5] Sir G. Murray to Findlay, 12 December 1829.

XXII: Extension of the British sphere of influence, 1821–1837

The last chapter was confined to events on the Island of St Mary. Whilst that settlement was slowly developing, the British were at the same time extending their sphere of influence up the River Gambia. Before, however, giving an account of that expansion, it will be as well to give some account of the territories and the peoples in those regions. For present purposes it will be necessary to refer only to the four principal tribes—the Mandingos, the Jollofs, the Fulas and the Jolas.

Of these tribes the Mandingos are the most numerous. According to their traditions their original home was a place called Manding, lying in an elevated region some 700 miles in an easterly direction from the coast. They were firmly established on both banks of the river at the time of the arrival of the Portuguese. Physically they are a spare athletic race of a medium height with finer features than the average typical negro.

The Jollofs were also invaders from the east and were established in the country before the arrival of the first Europeans. Their line of invasion was, however, into the regions lying between the Senegal and the Gambia and it was only a few overflows from the main stream of invaders who arrived on the banks of the latter river. They are also a well-built people of medium height with a very dark complexion and very woolly hair, but without the flat noses which are a common feature of many other negroes of West Africa. They are intelligent and peacefully inclined, having a strong proclivity for trading, but, as past history has shown, if driven to it, they can be warlike and brave.[1]

The Fulas are, compared with the Mandingos and Jollofs, late-comers into the Gambia, but they had already begun to arrive when Jobson visited the river in 1621. They are evidently connected with

[1] The Jollofs of the Protectorate must be distinguished from those of Bathurst. As shown in the previous chapter, the Jollofs of Bathurst came for the most part from Goree in the early days of the settlement. Many of them subsequently intermarried with other races. Racially and linguistically they are virtually the same as the Jollofs of the Protectorate, but historically they are a different community.

the Fulani of Northern Nigeria. Many of them have the same European features and light skins, which are to be found amongst the pure Fulani. They are of a Libyo-negroid origin and migrated from the east towards the headwaters of the Senegal and Gambia in the sixteenth and seventeenth centuries. Thence various offshoots made their way into the Gambia. The earliest comers were for the most part semi-nomads, who lived in villages and cultivated crops during the rainy season but moved about with their flocks and herds to different pasture lands after the harvesting of their crops. Until the opening of the nineteenth century those Fulas, who were resident in the Gambia, were of a peaceful disposition and were content to submit to a good deal of oppression by their Mandingo neighbours. But early in the nineteenth century Fulas of a very different metal began to arrive in the country. Those of Bondu, Futa Toro and Futa Jallon were a warlike people and indulged more or less annually in raids upon the less warlike people living on the banks of the Gambia. One section of the tribe—the Tukolors—are for the most part Mohammedans, but Islam has not made as great strides amongst the other sections.

The Jolas, who were known to the earlier Europeans as the Feloops, are the longest resident in the Gambia. At the present time they are to be found for the most part in Foni. They live as a rule in small communal groups. They are more primitive than their neighbours and have a reputation for truculence, but they are not unintelligent and are hard working and thrifty. The Mandingos appear to have overrun Foni at an early date and to some extent to have subjugated the Jolas, but the allegiance of the conquered to the conquerors was for the most part very nominal. Such reference as is made to them in the correspondence of the servants of the Royal African Company and the later Government officials of Senegambia shows that in the late seventeenth and early eighteenth centuries they were giving their overlords a good deal of trouble. At times they were ready to be led to war by their conquerors, but at other times they were in a state of rebellion. The "emperors" of Foni were often hard pushed to hold their own against their own subjects and against neighbouring Mandingos, who invaded the country. The Sieur d'Anville summed up the political situation in this "empire" very concisely and very accurately, when in his map of 1751 he described it as "autrefois très puissant".

As the history of the Mandingos shows, invaders have moved down both banks of the river. The Gambia has never been a tribal boundary. Nor is there any geographical feature in close vicinity to the river, which makes a natural boundary. The result has been a considerable intermingling of races. There was in the past a certain amount of intermarriage, but until recent years the four tribes already mentioned have on the whole preserved their distinct tribal characteristics. To this day small, but distinct, colonies of one tribe are to be found interspersed in territories in which the people of another tribe predominate. As a consequence chieftainships have been for the most part small and have tended to be territorial rather than tribal.

D'Anville's map shows the kingdoms on the river banks in 1751. In many respects it might serve as a political map of the Gambia of to-day and certainly would have answered that purpose with a considerable degree of accuracy sixty or seventy years ago. The kingdoms of Tomani, Jemarrow (Jimara), and Eropina have been absorbed into what is now known as Fuladu, and Geregia has been absorbed into Foni. Otherwise the districts are the same to-day as in d'Anville's map and even the boundaries of those districts have altered very little since 1751. The kingdoms on the north bank, proceeding down the river from the Barrakunda Falls to the sea, are Wuli, Upper and Lower Nyani, Salum, Baddibu and Barra (Niumi). Those on the south bank are Kantora, Tomani, Jemarrow, Eropina, Niamina, Jarra, Kiang, Foni and Kombo.[1] The majority of these districts were ruled by Mandingos. The one notable exception was Salum. D'Anville's map provides the explanation. The Jollof kingdom of Bur Salum (Sine Salum) extended inland from the Atlantic for over one hundred miles. Barra and Baddibu cut it off from the Gambia for most of this distance, but between the last-mentioned kingdom and that of Nyani the Jollofs managed to drive a wedge which brought them to the banks of the river. Even to-day the connection between the people of Salum and those of French Senegal is much closer than in other parts of the Gambia.

Though these districts were for a long time dignified in official correspondence with the title of "kingdom", and in the case of Foni with that of "empire", they were always petty districts in comparison with the emirates farther down the coast. Many of them also lacked the unity and stability which really qualifies a territory for the title of kingdom. In the upper river in particular there was

[1] Certain of these districts are at the present time sub-divided for administrative purposes.

hardly such a thing as a recognised succession of paramount chiefs based upon a more or less hereditary principle. Rule in those regions was generally speaking that of war lords, who rose and fell very often with astonishing rapidity. Their warfare was intermittent and not very bloodthirsty. One warrior would from time to time carve for himself an independent district out of that of some earlier war lord and would in course of time wrest the hegemony from that chief, only in his turn to succumb in a few years' time to another aspirant for that hegemony.

Nearer the coast these kingdoms had more solidarity. This may possibly be attributed to the mode of selecting the ruler, which perhaps had its origin in the fact that the original conquerors were not a party of marauders led by a single war lord but comprised a confederation of several warlike tribal groups. In Barra (Niumi) and Kombo the kingship was in one sense hereditary. It went by a recognised rota from one of several families to another and thus guaranteed a confederacy of several royal families, each of which would be prepared to support the king regnant, if his rulership were contested by any invader or any claimant who was not of the blood royal.[1]

At the present day the predominant religion amongst these peoples is Islam, although there still exist strong pagan elements amongst the Jolas and Fulas. Islam is, however, a very recent importation to the country. It was brought from the interior by Moorish traders or the converts of Moorish traders. It is clear that at the time of Cadamosto's visit Islam had made very little headway. In Jobson's day the "marybucks" were evidently beginning to gain ground, but one gathers from Francis Moore that Mohammedans were still well in the minority in his day. D'Anville's map of 1751 shows fifteen villages in the Gambia, which were called "Morokunda" (holy city) and which were evidently the homes of Moslem communities. Their distribution is interesting—six in Nyani, three in Barra (Niumi), and one each in Tomani, Eropina, Jarra, Kombo, Salum and Baddibu. Later in the same century there were a number of indications that the religion had gained considerable ground amongst the Mandingo population. For example, a number of Mandingo captives, who had been enslaved in local wars and

[1] Macklin, "Kings and Queens of Niumi", *Man*, xxxv, 72, 73; Sir Neil Campbell to Earl Bathurst, 3 August 1827 (as to Kombo). It would further appear that the same system of election obtained in Jarra and Kiang.

shipped to the West Indies, were discovered to be Mohammedans.[1]
Place-names with an Arabic etymology began to appear on the map[2]
and the larger villages had their Koranic schools.[3]

As might be expected some of the converts were not very whole-
hearted in their new belief. Islam made its first appeal to the trading
community, who had come in contact with the Mohammedans from
the interior. It was passed on by them to the peasant class and the
humbler grades of Mandingo society, but a long time elapsed before it made much impression with the chiefs and their immediate
entourages. Islam taught a code of self-discipline, which was not
congenial to absolutists. As some pagan beliefs conferred divine
attributes on many of these chiefs and made them heads of both
church and state, and as many of the rights claimed by these chiefs
were diametrically opposed to the teaching of the Koran, it is not
surprising to learn that this section of the community was slow to
embrace the new faith and eventually accepted it with considerable
reservations.

The result was that early in the nineteenth century Mohammedans
in the Gambia had become divided into two sects with acute religious differences, which eventually became political differences.
One of these sects came to be known as the Marabouts. They were
the puritans of Islam. They told their beads, were careful in their
public devotions and abstained from intoxicating liquor. The
majority of them had received some sort of an education at a village
school. Many of them were traders. Taken as a whole, their smattering of education and their business pursuits gave them a wider
outlook than that of their neighbours.

The other sect were known as the Soninkis owing to the fact that
they did not abstain from intoxicating liquors. The warrior class and
the chiefs' retainers were mainly recruited from their ranks. Their
principal characteristics were their laxity in religious observances
and their extreme conservatism in all mundane affairs. Contemporary onlookers frequently distinguished between the two factions

---

[1] Early in the nineteenth century there was a Mandingo society in Trinidad.
Its members were ex-slaves who subscribed to redeem their co-religionists from
captivity: Washington, "Some account of Mohammedu Sisei", *J.R.G.S.* VIII,
448–456.

[2] E.g. the Medina of Mungo Park in Wuli. Lemaine Island on d'Anville's
map is a misspelling of Lamin, which in its turn is a corruption of Abd-ul-Amin.

[3] There was one such school at Nyanimaru *c.* 1805: Washington, *op. cit.*
p. 448.

by attributing all the virtues to the one and all the vices to the other, but such a generalisation was as fallacious as would be a like generalisation over cavaliers and roundheads. The members of the two factions belonged for the most part all to one race and each of them had the virtues and the failings of that race, which were leavened to a slight extent by their respective upbringings.

The Marabouts did not come into prominence until about the middle of the nineteenth century.[1] They were evidently in a minority in the earlier years of that century and lacked the power of combination. They consequently had often to undergo considerable persecution at the hands of the members of the ancient regime, but that persecution first gave them their sense of unity. They began more and more to form separate communities in villages apart from their Soninki neighbours. Though these Marabout villages were often isolated one from another, communication between them was frequent and by co-operation they began to make themselves felt as a political force in the land. Up to a point their progress was slow. The African is conservative at heart and has a great veneration for the hereditary chief. Unless they are men of very considerable force of character, would-be reformers are not as a rule very popular and do not attract large followings to themselves. It is doubtful if the Marabouts would have been able to come to power by their unaided efforts, but external events, which tended to weaken the authority of the existing chiefs, gave them their opportunity. It is clear that in the early days of their clash with the Soninkis the Marabouts were distinctly pro-British and hoped to obtain the support of the Government at Bathurst. But a combination of circumstances eventually brought them into opposition to the British authorities. Except, however, in moments of extreme fanaticism they were never really anti-British. They were anti-chief. The policy of the British Government was one of neutrality, but the chain of events led it to intervene more frequently on the side of the chiefs than on that of the Marabouts. Hence, when in the last days of the struggle the leadership was in the hands of the extremists, the Marabouts came into serious conflict with the British. When in the end milder counsels were allowed to prevail, the anti-British feeling speedily evaporated.

[1] The earliest use of the term Soninki, as opposed to that of Marabout, which I have been able to discover is in Moister, *Memorials of Missionary Labours in Western Africa*, p. 176. Moister resided in the Gambia from 1831 to 1833.

The factories on the river banks had brought the inhabitants into contact with the Europeans for several centuries. In the last days of the slave trade Nyanimaru had been the principal place where slave ships had obtained their cargoes for the West Indies, but except in Lower Nyani the people of the upper river had had less direct dealings with the white man than had the people of Barra (Niumi), Kombo and Foni. Furthermore, the opening years of the nineteenth century found the upper river in a very disturbed condition. Rival chiefs were struggling for the mastery on the river bank and the Fulas and Bambarras from the interior were taking advantage of this state of affairs to raid the countryside with comparative impunity. The result was that the European factories in the upper river began to close down and their owners removed to the lower reaches of the Gambia or, after 1816, to the greater security offered by the military post of St Mary's Island. For example, some time before 1818 the mulatto son of Mungo Park's friend, Robert Aynsley, removed to Tendeba from the factory, which his father had established some forty years previously at Pisania (Karantaba).[1]

The last of the Aynsleys is an example of the change which had been taking place in the character of the up-river traders. Though many of the European traders lived for a considerable number of years at a time up the river, none of them became really permanent residents there. The ambition of most of them was to make a sufficient competence to enable them to retire to live in greater comfort in England. They had no idea of colonisation or of founding a business, which could be handed on from father to son. As white women did not come to the country, the white traders formed temporary unions with the daughters of Heth. Many of these "senhoras" showed a remarkable aptitude for commerce. When in the later eighteenth and earlier nineteenth centuries the European trader died or took his final departure for his native country, the "senhora" not infrequently succeeded to the business and often carried it on with considerable success, eventually handing it on to her children.[2]

Besides these persons of mixed blood, another class of settler was beginning to establish himself in the river. The foundation of the colony of Sierra Leone and the abolition of the slave trade had

---

[1] Gray, *Travels in Western Africa*, p. 70.
[2] Gray, *op. cit.* p. 51; Park, *Travels in the Interior Districts of Africa*, pp. 7, 357 and *Journal of a Mission to the Interior of Africa in the year* 1805, p. 8; *Report of the Committee managing a Fund raised by some Friends*, pp. 31, 32.

brought into being an African community, who claimed either to be British subjects or else under British protection. A number of its members took very readily to trade and were prepared to venture into many parts of the coast beyond the limits of Sierra Leone. A few were beginning to find their way to the Gambia. In 1794, for instance, the Directors of the Sierra Leone Company reported that a native of the Gambia, named Cuddy, who lived on "the sloop side" of the river, had persuaded a carpenter and another African, who was acquainted with ploughing, to leave Freetown and settle at his village in the Gambia.[1] Thomas Joiner's history has been given in the previous chapter. He at one time had a factory at Fattatenda and another at Barrakunda, but lost the latter by fire. In about 1810 he was trading in Bintang Creek and sent a canoe to discover if the headwaters of the creek connected with those of the Casamance.[2] At about the time of the occupation of St Mary's Island another African, named Dean, acquired Baboon Island from a native chief and settled there with his family. How that family managed to thrive in the midst of all the alarums and excursions of war on a more or less barren sandbank, which was over one hundred miles from Bathurst and was more or less waterlogged in the rainy season, is something of a mystery, but the fact remains that his widow or his daughter was still carrying on trade there in 1840.[3] These traders had, however, a more precarious existence than had the European traders. They had as a rule very little capital and no reserve upon which to fall back, if their property was pillaged or destroyed. Furthermore, they were not in so strong a position to hold their own in the case of any aggression on the part of the local inhabitants. Consequently in the early days of the new colony there was a tendency on their part to withdraw from the upper river. Some of them appear to have fallen back as far as Bathurst itself, but a number congregated at Tendeba, which for the time being became the most important trading centre for European, African and mulatto trader alike.[4]

---

[1] Report of...the Sierra Leone Company (1794), pp. 132, 133, 143, 144.

[2] Report on...the State of Sierra Leone (1827), pp. 3, 4; J.R.G.S. III, 72.

[3] Lt.-Gov. Mackie to Marquis of Normanby, 14 June 1839; Lt.-Commander H. W. Hill to Lt.-Gov. Huntley, 10 April 1840. When Moister visited the island in 1832, he called it Dean's Island, op. cit. p. 175.

[4] Report of Edward Lloyd, president of the Bathurst Board of Commerce, 20 December 1826; Report of the Committee managing a Fund raised by some Friends, p. 30.

Though the Treaty of Paris gave Great Britain the River Gambia, at the outset the British Government had no intention of acquiring any territory except at the river's mouth. The rest of the Gambia was to be treated as it had been in the days of the Province of Senegambia and of the Royal African Company before it. The river was to be regarded as a British sphere of influence with trading posts of the old type. Individual merchants were to be encouraged to settle or to establish factories in the river, but each merchant was expected to make his own bargain with the local chief and generally to fend for himself. If a chief gave him land for his factory, he held that land by native customary tenure. The fact that he was a British merchant did not make the factory site British territory. If he was deprived of that land or was otherwise despoiled of his property, the British Government was under no legal obligation to render him any assistance and was only under a moral obligation to do so in the case of a very serious outrage. British territory proper was to be limited to the Island of St Mary and the derelict fort on James Island. Great Britain was at this date not anxious to have any further territorial commitments in West Africa.[1]

The only motive, which might induce the home Government to deviate from its policy of non-expansion, arose from the desire to suppress the slave trade, but even with this object in view Earl Bathurst was averse to the acquisition of further land, if the end could be obtained by other means. Writing on 22 April 1826 to Sir Charles Turner Earl Bathurst said:

Although it has been found necessary to withhold His Majesty's sanction from the treaties, which you have recently concluded with several of the tribes in the vicinity of your government, yet I wish you to understand that I am fully sensible of the necessity of maintaining a good understanding with them, and of keeping that influence, which is so material with a view to the suppression of the slave trade, that this country should possess over these people, who it is to be feared would, if left to themselves, be too much disposed to return to that odious traffic. I should therefore be prepared to authorize some expenditure for the purpose of enabling you to make a small annual payment to those chiefs, who possess the most influence on the coast and in the river.

[1] In 1827 W. Huskisson, Colonial Secretary, wrote to J. C. Herries, Chancellor of the Exchequer: "I quite agree that the whole of the coast of Guinea ought to be abandoned; and I am prepared to say the same of Sierra Leone": Hall, *The Colonial Office*, p. 176.

None the less a number of circumstances combined to make it inevitable that the local administration, with the somewhat hesitant consent of the home Government, should from time to time diverge from this settled line of policy.

The first piece of territory to be obtained on the mainland was acquired in 1821. The preceding four years had proved the unhealthiness of St Mary's Island and Captain Grant decided that it was necessary to have a convalescent station, where invalid officers could recuperate. At the river's mouth close to Cape St Mary the land rises sixty feet above sea level and receives all the breezes of the Atlantic. Grant decided that this would be a suitable spot for a convalescent station and also for erecting a navigation light to mark the entrance to the river. A plot of ground was therefore purchased from two natives of the neighbouring village of Bakau. The transaction was very informal. No written document appears to have been drawn up at the time. The position was not regularised by treaty until 1827 and a formal conveyance in writing of the land from the original owners to the Colonial Government was not obtained until 1840. A house, which is now known as Cape House, was erected on the plot by a number of liberated Africans. As it was not immediately required as a convalescent house, it was handed over to the Society of Friends for their use during the brief period of their labours in the Gambia. At later dates it was put to a number of different uses—a convalescent house, a fort, a residence for the Manager of the Kombo, and the Governor's country residence. The "lighthouse" consisted of a lantern hung on a neighbouring palm tree and does not appear to have lasted very long.[1]

Though it initiated a new policy, this transaction hardly deserves to be called a territorial acquisition. It was a very ordinary transfer of land by some private individuals to the representative of what was in effect a foreign government. There was no transfer of any sovereign rights along with the land. For that reason, no doubt, and also because the acreage thus acquired was infinitesimal, no objection was raised to the transaction by the home Government.

The next transaction had a very important influence on the history of the Gambia. In 1822 Bryan O'Beirne, the assistant surgeon of the colony, and Thomas Chown, a Bathurst merchant, made a

[1] *Report of the Committee managing a Fund raised by some Friends*, p. 43; Bowdich, *Madeira and Porto Santo*, pp. 213–216; *Ordinances of the Gambia*, 1875, p. 525; Hertslet, *Map of Africa*, pp. 11, 16; Hertslet, *Treaties*, xii, 11.

voyage up the river to Kantalikunda about thirty miles below the Barrakunda Falls. They met with a friendly reception all the way.[1] As a result of this voyage the merchants in the following year re-established trading posts on the river banks as far up the river as Kantalikunda. But the country was still in a very disturbed state and in the course of one of the periodical skirmishes a factory belonging to Thomas Chown was destroyed. Major Grant was consequently solicited to establish a military post up the river so as to afford the outlying traders some measure of protection. In March 1823 he accordingly proceeded to Kantalikunda, accompanied by Thomas Joiner and John Morgan of the Wesleyan Mission and a sergeant and twelve men of the Second West India Regiment. He decided that Kantalikunda was unsuitable for the purpose and returned down stream to the Island of Lemaine or Janjanbure.

It is evident from contemporary correspondence that Bradley's acquisition of Lemaine Island in 1785[2] was unknown both to the officers on the spot and to the authorities at home. In any case non-occupation by the British Government and resumption of occupation by the local natives tended to defeat any title, which might have been acquired under Bradley's treaty. The island was for the most part a sandbank with a few patches of land capable of cultivation. As the name Janjanbure denoted, it was used periodically as a place of refuge by fugitives from the mainland.[3] In 1823 a man, who is called "Woody" in contemporary documents, had formed a small village on the island, which was known as Morokunda (holy city). This man was a Marabout and it would appear that he and his followers had settled there to avoid persecution by their Soninki neighbours. The sovereignty of the island was claimed by a Soninki chief called Kolli, who styled himself "king" of Kataba. He was in actual fact one of several aspirants to the overlordship of Nyani, who had each of them carved out a small domain for themselves and was then waging kite and crow warfare against his rivals. In 1823 Kolli was doing none too well. He and a younger chief named Kemintang were indulging in a family vendetta and Kemintang was getting rather the best of it. In addition to this the Fulas and Bambarras were frequently raiding Kataba and carrying off the people and their cattle. As he believed that by ceding an island, which had very little value

---

[1] Memorial of Bathurst merchants c. 1830.   [2] Cf. p. 278.
[3] It had apparently been used as a place of refuge by the "king" of Kataba in 1810 during a raid by the people of Wuli: Washington, op. cit. p. 448.

to himself, he would be able to purchase the alliance of the British Government, Kolli very readily agreed to Major Grant's proposal to cede Lemaine Island to the British Government in exchange for an annual payment. The treaty of cession was signed on 14 April 1823. Grant took formal possession of the island the same day. He at once set to work to erect a small mud fort, which was completed in a little over a fortnight. On 30 April two small cannon were mounted on the bastions, the British flag was hoisted and a royal salute was fired. The fort was named Fort George and the island was renamed MacCarthy Island. Grant then returned to Bathurst, leaving the sergeant and twelve men as a garrison.[1]

MacCarthy Island was for a number of years a solitary outpost, but the importance of Grant's treaty lies in the fact that it gave Great Britain a permanent foothold in the upper waters of the river. When some years later there was talk of abandonment of the Gambia and when at a subsequent date the rival claims of Great Britain and France came to be considered, the existence of this small outpost turned the scales and British Gambia was allowed to continue. To Grant therefore belongs the credit of founding not only the Colony but also the Protectorate of the Gambia.

An African noncommissioned officer, Sergeant Buchanan of the Second West India Regiment, remained in charge of MacCarthy Island until 1827. During those four years he was inspected twice only by visiting governors from Sierra Leone. When he was relieved in 1827 by an officer and detachment of the Royal African Corps, both he and his men were long overdue for discharge.[1] The original mud fort stood until 1827 when Sir Neil Campbell replaced it by another fort at Fatota at the west end of the island. In the following year, however, it was decided to rebuild Fort George in the centre of the north bank of the island, but the other fort, which was called Fort Campbell, was retained as an outpost until 1850.[2] No permanent fortifications were erected, Viscount Goderich having stated in 1831 that the home Government would not sanction the erection of any kind of stone buildings.[3]

[1] Kenneth Macaulay to Earl Bathurst, 29 June 1826; Sir Neil Campbell to Earl Bathurst, 16 May 1827.

[2] Sir Neil Campbell to Earl Bathurst, 16 May 1827; R. W. Hay to Major Findlay, 30 August 1828; Lt.-Gov. Rendall to John Grant, 1 January 1833; Report of the Select Committee on West Africa (1844), p. 239; Poole, Life...in the Gambia, ii, 223.

[3] R. W. Hay to Lt.-Gov. Rendall, 31 January 1831.

MacCarthy Island lay in the centre of a very disturbed piece of country. More than once there were rumours of intended attacks upon the island, but the small detachment was sufficient to prevent any warlike bands from crossing over from the mainland. A fairly considerable population began to gather round the fort. MacCarthy Island shared with St Mary's Island the disadvantage of possessing no stone for building purposes, but in 1827 the king of Kataba agreed to allow the British to quarry stone on the mainland.[1] Bathurst merchants began to erect stores near the fort soon after the annexation of the island. The Wesleyan Mission was offered land on the island and in 1824 John Morgan opened a station. Ill health, however, compelled him to return to Bathurst and the mission was not fully inaugurated until 1832.[2] A number of discharged soldiers were induced to settle on the island and were given grants of farms. In 1826 the acting Governor of Sierra Leone reported that "I found the discharged men settled there in a very comfortable state, both in their houses and their persons, complaining of nothing but want of wives, the people round being Mahommedans, who will not inter-marry with them".[3]

"Woody" was not expropriated from his village at Morokunda, which apparently increased in population owing to the number of Marabouts and others, who sought refuge from persecution and raids on the mainland.[4] This village was allowed to remain under the government of its own alkali. In 1832 the commandant was instructed to leave the settlement of disputes between the inhabitants of the village to their own chief and to give immediate redress to any complaint by any such inhabitant against any person under his own command. At the same time, as the number of refugees was constantly increasing and as the grant to them of an asylum might lead to embroilment with the local chiefs, orders were given not to allow such people to enter the island in time of war.[5] This latter order was repeated by Lieutenant-Governor Huntley in 1840.[6]

The next acquisition of territory was due to the alarm caused by the vast increase in the civil and military establishments of the

---

[1] *Ordinances of the Gambia*, 1875, p. 507.
[2] Fox, *A Brief History of the Wesleyan Missions on the West Coast of Africa*, pp. 284, 285, 337.
[3] Macaulay to Earl Bathurst, 29 June 1826.   [4] *Ibid.*
[5] Lt.-Gov. Rendall to Rufus Coffin, 20 October 1832.
[6] *Report of the Select Committee on West Africa* (1842), pp. 236, 240.

French in Senegal and the defenceless state of St Mary's Island. The French had reoccupied Albreda in 1817. Their activities there and the unfriendly attitude adopted by the people of Barra led to the fear that the French might obtain possession of further territory on the north bank of the river. Experiments, which Major Grant had carried out in 1823, showed that the largest guns in Bathurst had not sufficient range to reach the Barra shore.[1] It was therefore apparent that in the event of a war with France, which at this date was regarded as a very real possibility, the British position in the Gambia would be very probably untenable. The "king" of Barra was approached in 1823 with a request to allow the British to erect a battery on the shore opposite to Bathurst, but he declined to do so.[2] In 1826 matters came to a head. For some time previously the "king" had been proving troublesome by reason of his exorbitant demands upon Bathurst merchants trading in his country. The Governor of Senegal paid him a visit in that year and it was clear that the "king" was coquetting with the idea of granting the French some further territory.

It so happened that at this particular juncture Kenneth Macaulay, the acting Governor of Sierra Leone, had just returned to Bathurst from a voyage up to Pisania (Karantaba), whither he had accompanied Lieutenant Owen, who was engaged on a survey of the river.[3] On his return he found Commodore Charles Bullen in port with H.M.S. *Maidstone*. Macaulay's own vessel, the *African*, was the first steam vessel to navigate the Gambia and must in itself have been an awe-inspiring sight to the local native. The acting Governor took the opportunity of this combined display of force to bring Burungai Sonko of Barra to reason. That individual appears to have lived in a more or less habitual state of intoxication, but the sight of the steamer and man-of-war appears to have reduced him to a condition of momentary sobriety.

I accordingly sent for him, Macaulay subsequently wrote, *to visit me at Bathurst, which he immediately did attended by his principal headmen. After taxing him severely with all he had said and done towards our settlement and its inhabitants, which prevented the govern-*

[1] Grant to MacCarthy, 7 July 1823.
[2] Marty, "Le Comptoir Français d'Albreda en Gambie, 1817–1826", *R.H.C.* (1924), p. 246.
[3] Owen, *Narrative of Voyages...to Africa*, II, 373, 374.

ment from considering him in any other light than as hostilely inclined, and pointing out to him the serious consequences, which must inevitably occur for him and his people, if a repetition of the same ever occurred, I was induced to conclude with him and his chiefs the convention, which I now have the honour to enclose.[1]

By that convention Burungai Sonko and his chiefs, in exchange for an annual payment, ceded to the British Government "the full, entire, free and unlimited right, title and sovereignty and possession of the River Gambia", all right to demand "customs" or other payments from British or other vessels entering the river, and (with the exception of the French factory at Albreda) the whole of the right bank of the river for one geographical mile inland, commencing at Bunyadu (Jinnak) Creek on the west and extending to Jokadu Creek on the east.[2] Immediate steps were taken to show that this was not intended to be merely a paper transaction. Commodore Bullen conveyed a couple of cannon over to Barra Point and formal possession was taken of the ceded territory in the name and on behalf of George IV to the salute of the guns of the *Maidstone, African* and the shore batteries at Bathurst. A military guard was placed over the two cannon and the site was named Fort Bullen.[3]

In 1827 the necessity of finding additional land outside of Sierra Leone for the location of Africans, who had been rescued by the Navy from slave ships, induced Earl Bathurst to sanction the opening of a new station at Fattatenda or Kantalikunda.[4] Major-General Sir Neil Campbell undertook the task personally in the colonial steamer *African*. On arrival at Fattatenda he found that the new "king" of Wuli had only recently succeeded to the turban and that he was anxious to open up his country to European trade. On 15 May 1827 he entered into a treaty of friendship whereby he agreed to put down the slave trade in his territory and to give all traders undisturbed access thereto. He did not, however, make any cession of land.[5]

On the way down stream General Campbell called at Brikama, a

[1] Macaulay to Earl Bathurst, 28 June 1826.
[2] Hertslet, *Map of Africa*, p. 8.
[3] Macaulay to Earl Bathurst, 28 June 1826; Bullen to J. W. Croker, 22 June 1826.
[4] Earl Bathurst to Sir Neil Campbell, 23 March 1827.
[5] *Ordinances of the Gambia*, 1875, p. 508; Campbell to Earl Bathurst, 16 May 1827.

port lying on the south bank of the river near to MacCarthy Island in what was then the kingdom of Jimara. He found that there had recently been a civil war in the district and that one of the under-chiefs was trying to set himself up as an independent chief, but was being hard pressed by his overlord. The underchief was only too anxious to ally himself with the British and on 29 May 1827 entered into a treaty, whereby he engaged (*inter alia*) to suppress the slave trade and, in exchange for an annual payment, to cede to Great Britain "a secure spot to be chosen by the British commandant, for a military post opposite to the island of Kayaye and close to the river, with as much territory adjoining it as the artillery can reach from this port (*sc.* of Brikama) or any other place".[1]

Sir Neil Campbell, however, received an official rebuke when he reported these transactions to England. The Wuli treaty was rati-fied, but Sir Neil was given to understand that the British Govern-ment had now done all that was required of it for opening up the river to trade and that it now remained to the Bathurst merchants to do the rest. The Brikama treaty was not repudiated but met with strong disapproval.

No very urgent necessity existed for entering into so many treaties or arrangements with the authorities of the adjacent countries. To such of the arrangements as are limited to mutual assurances of good will and friendship and to the grant of a few annual presents of inconsiderable value, I have no objection to make; and, if I do not think it necessary to signify to you my disapproval of the Brikama Convention, it is be-cause the territorial acquisition of which it is the subject matter, is of no importance. You will have the goodness to bear in mind that His Majesty's government are unwilling to sanction arrangements involving the cession of territory to this country; for, not to mention the political objections which attach to measures of this description, it is impossible to overlook the inconvenience, which must manifestly ensue from con-tracting obligations of alliance with small bodies of people, whose ex-treme weakness would be perpetually urging them to claim our inter-ference on their behalf, so that we should eventually find our influence with them much less than if we had merely kept up a friendly intercourse with them without promising them anything.[2]

[1] Campbell to Earl Bathurst, 12 May 1827; *Ordinances of the Gambia*, 1875, p. 510; Hertslet, *Map of Africa*, p. 10 and *Treaties*, xii, 7.
[2] Viscount Goderich to Campbell, 25 August 1827.

This rebuke was followed up on 4 November 1827 by positive instructions to abstain from any kind of interference in disputes between natives and to confine attention solely to the protection of such settlements as were actually in British possession.[1] No attempt was consequently made to occupy the land ceded by the Brikama Convention. That document survives as an interesting record. It was probably soon forgotten by the chiefs who signed it. Ten years later the Wesleyan Mission thought of opening a station in the Brikama country but had to abandon the project because they found the chiefs unfriendly.[2]

In 1829 William Hutton, who was temporarily in charge of the administration, made a voyage up the river to Fattatenda and Kantalikunda. Eleven Bathurst merchants had guaranteed to send up goods to the value of £7000, if he could enter into satisfactory treaties with the chiefs of those places. On 11 April 1829 Hutton entered into an agreement with the chief of the latter place, whereby in consideration of an annual payment of $50 the chief consented to allow merchants from Bathurst to erect houses and factories at Kantalikunda free of all "customs" and other expenses. Two days later he entered into another treaty with Mansa Kwiri, "king" of Wuli. In consideration of an annual payment of $200 the "king" granted to the British Government full power and sovereignty over the town of Fattatenda and one hundred acres of land adjoining thereto and further promised to use his influence with the "king" of Bondu to bring trade from that country to Fattatenda.[3] No prior sanction had been given to the making of either of these treaties and, in view of the recent instructions from home in regard to treaty making, it is not surprising to find that Hutton's conduct did not meet with the approval of the home Government. A number of reports reached England in regard to Hutton's conduct during the course of the expedition. Sir George Murray therefore instructed Lieutenant-Governor Findlay on his return to make one or two inquiries and to demand a few explanations regarding an expedition, which was "apparently for the laudable purpose of extending mercantile operations in that quarter—but, in truth, as is alleged, with

[1] W. Huskisson to Campbell.
[2] Lt.-Gov. Rendall to Lord Glenelg, 24 April 1837.
[3] Hertslet, *Map of Africa*, p. 11; *Correspondence relating to the Limits of British Jurisdiction in the Gambia* (1877), pp. 14–16; Hutton to R. W. Hay, 17 May 1829.

a view to the accomplishment of other objects ".[1] In particular, explanations were needed as to expenses alleged to have been incurred in presents to chiefs and in connection with the voyage, including a wine bill, which Hutton had debited to the Colonial Government. Hutton's explanations were not deemed satisfactory. As his conduct in regard to other matters had also given cause for dissatisfaction, he was dismissed the service.[2]

After this episode neither Lieutenant-Governors, nor their deputies, attempted to make any further treaties without prior sanction from England. In 1830 Lieutenant-Governor Findlay was approached by another chief in the upper river with an offer to allow, in exchange for a subsidy, a free passage to Bathurst for gold merchants from the interior. Findlay declined to make any present until the reciprocal promise had been fulfilled. When the incident was reported to the Secretary of State, Sir George Murray, whilst commending Findlay's caution, none the less disapproved of the promise of any reward at all. Writing to Findlay's successor in office, he said:

The engagement contracted by your predecessor must be held sacred, but, as experience has shown the fallacy of expecting any national benefit from arrangements, which rest upon a system of tributary presents, you will avoid going the length of purchasing an intercourse between our settlements in the Gambia and the natives. Some sacrifices must of course be made occasionally to obtain the good will of the influential tribes, but no expence should be incurred for that purpose exceeding what the rules of courtesy prescribe as sufficient.[3]

For a number of years thereafter there were no further attempts to extend the British sphere of influence in the Gambia. When in 1836 Lieutenant-Governor Rendall suggested the acquisition of further territory near to MacCarthy Island, Lord Glenelg said:

Such a project, founded, as you state it to be, on the assumption that this new possession will be placed under the protection of MacCarthy's Island, is so opposite to the view taken by His Majesty's government of the impolicy of extending our footing in the Upper Gambia without first

---

[1] 1 December 1829.
[2] *Correspondence relating to the Limits of British Jurisdiction in the Gambia* (1877), p. 21; R. W. Hay to Hutton, 30 April 1830.
[3] To Lt.-Gov. Rendall, 26 June 1830.

having the foundation of a strong settlement, which shall be capable of protecting itself against assault, isolated or combined of native tribes, that I cannot but very earnestly deprecate the prosecution of such a scheme.[1]

As Viscount Goderich had previously announced that he "cannot understand what necessity there is for very frequent communication from Bathurst with that island",[2] and Sir George Murray had also doubted the necessity for the Lieutenant-Governor visiting MacCarthy Island and at the same time added that "it is requisite to apprise you that His Majesty's Government will not under any circumstances sanction any expence whatever for the purpose of erecting fortifications on this spot",[3] any further project of expansion was for the time being clearly out of the question.

[1] *Correspondence relating to the Limits of British Jurisdiction in the Gambia* (1877), p. 22.
[2] R. W. Hay to Lt.-Gov. Rendall, 26 January 1831.
[3] Same to same, 7 September 1830.

XXIII: Punitive Expeditions— Liberated Africans, 1830–1837

On 23 February 1830 George Rendall, acting Chief Justice of Sierra Leone, was appointed Lieutenant-Governor of the Gambia. Except for a few fleeting visits to Madeira in order to recuperate his health, he remained at his post until his death from yellow fever on 22 September 1837. The principal landmarks in those seven years are two campaigns against native chiefs and the arrival in the country of the liberated Africans.

The first of these minor wars was with the people of Barra (Niumi). Though a somewhat trivial incident led to the actual outbreak, it is clear that trouble had been brewing for a good many years. It is evident in the first place that the "king" and people of Barra were not only disappointed, but had also taken serious umbrage, at the virtual abandonment of James Island for St Mary's Island. In the past the dependence of James Fort upon the "king" of Barra had given him and his people a certain amount of prestige and influence, which had not been enjoyed by the natives on the south bank of the river. The transfer of British activities meant that much of that prestige and influence and also a very considerable volume of trade passed from them to the "king" and people of the Kombo.

The very decided attitude, which Captain Grant had taken up in regard to the slave trade immediately after the reoccupation of James Island in 1816, had also given further offence. Until the passing of the Abolition Act in 1807 the natives of Albreda and Juffure had carried on a very profitable business with European slave traders. They had not been merely middlemen, who acted as brokers between the leaders of slave caravans and the captains of slave ships. They had taken—and in fact for very many years after 1816 continued to take—very active measures to procure slaves from the opposite bank of the river so as to sell them to the French in Senegal. In 1820, for example, two women of Brefet in Foni were kidnapped whilst working in the rice fields and carried over with nineteen other captives to Albreda, whence they were marched overland to the

344

mouth of the Salum River for purposes of sale.[1] When a year later the Quaker missionary, William Singleton, visited Tendeba, he met there the alkali of Albreda, who did not disguise the fact that he had come to pick up a consignment of slaves.[2] But, whilst a furtive trade could be carried on by marching the captives overland to Joal or Goree and evading the vigilance of the British at Bathurst, the profits were not the same as they had been in the days when ship-loads of slaves were embarked upon ocean-going ships at Albreda and Juffure. As the British had closed the river to this more lucrative mode of conducting business, their action was strongly resented.

In 1817 the attempts of the British to interfere with the slave trade brought them into open collision with the people of Albreda. The sergeant's guard on James Island saw a suspicious looking canoe coming down the river. They stopped it off Albreda so as to examine its contents. The people of Albreda at once set on the soldiers, beat them and wrested their arms from them. When an officer was sent from Bathurst to demand restitution and an apology, he was sub-jected to contumely and abuse. An armed party was then sent to Albreda, which burnt that town as well as part of the "king's" town. This brought the people of Barra to a different frame of mind. An apology was tendered and the weapons were restored.[3] As a punishment for this misconduct the recognised "custom", which had been paid to the "king" of Barra for James Island, was reduced by one-half. This act would probably not have been very greatly resented, but unfortunately the remaining half was not very regu-larly paid.[4]

The "king" and people of Barra continued to show marked hos-tility to the British. More than once rumours spread that they and the people of Kombo were combining to attack Bathurst. In 1820 the Commandant took advantage of the presence of H.M.S. *Morgiana* to proceed in her to James Island and to hold a "palaver" with the Barra chiefs, who strenuously denied any hostile intentions. They were given a few presents and, after the man-of-war had fired a few

[1] One of the women who had been sold to a mulatto woman in Goree was subsequently brought by her mistress to Bathurst, where she was given her freedom by Captain Grant: Grant to MacCarthy, 22 August 1822.

[2] *Report of the Committee managing a Fund raised by some Friends*, p. 31.

[3] W. Forster to M. Forster, 8 September 1817.

[4] Grant to R. W. Hay, 25 November 1825.

guns, they were dismissed with the information that visits of the like nature would be frequently repeated in the near future.[1] This showing of the flag apparently had the desired effect. For the next few years the people of Barra displayed a much more peaceable frame of mind.

There were, however, other grievances besides the attempted prohibition of the slave trade. In the days when Goree was still in British hands, those merchants, who visited the Gambia, had been in the habit of paying a "custom" for the privilege of trading in Barra. In those days a considerable portion of this "custom" had gone into the pockets of the headmen of such places as Albreda and Juffure. When Janies Island was reoccupied in 1816, Grant had stipulated for a reduced "custom", which was paid direct to the "king" and does not appear to have gone further than him.

When building operations started in Bathurst, Kollimanka Mane, the then "king" of Barra, consented to allow the British to quarry stone at Dog Island and elsewhere in his territory. He made no stipulation for any payment or anything else in exchange, but he made a present fully expecting that in accordance with African custom that present would be reciprocated. Unfortunately for him and his people British officials and merchants treated his act as one of extraordinary generosity. Large quantities of stone were removed from his territory, but he and his people did not get the royalty, which they regarded as their prescriptive right.[2]

In 1823 Kollimanka Mane died. According to Niumi custom his kingship passed to another family, which lived within a mile of Barra Point at Essau. Burungai Sonko, the new "king", soon proved a very unpleasant neighbour. He was described in official correspondence as "an insane drunkard". On one occasion, when he graciously condescended to give a public audience to a missionary, he did so reclining upon a very dirty couch in a state of hopeless intoxication and drinking rum out of the spout of a teakettle.[3] One of his first acts was to pick a quarrel with the French Resident at Albreda, because that officer's Government did not give him a satisfactory present on his accession. The result was

---

[1] Grant to Earl Bathurst, 26 November 1820.
[2] Kenneth Macaulay to Earl Bathurst, 28 June 1826.
[3] Moister, *Memorials of Missionary Labours in Western Africa*, p. 210.

that the Resident took refuge in Bathurst and the factory at Albreda was closed down for several months.[1]

This quarrel seems to have been picked of a set purpose. Despite the fact that the succession went according to a well-established rule a new "king" of Barra generally found that there were rival candidates for his post. Once in his chieftainship, he had to make a bid for popularity amongst those who had opposed his succession. In 1823 the general feeling of the people of Barra clearly was that Kollimanka Mane had been far too weak in his dealings with the Europeans and that he had let his people down. Burungai Sonko therefore had to win favour by a display of distinctly anti-European bias. His quarrel with the French Resident was followed by a number of exactions from Bathurst traders, who entered his country, and by encouraging his people to despoil those traders with impunity.

In 1826 the combined effects of the arrival of a British man-of-war and of the cupidity aroused by the promise of an annual payment to himself induced Burungai Sonko to sign the Ceded Mile Treaty. When immediately after that treaty was signed he and his people saw cannon brought over to Barra Point and soldiers posted there, their worst suspicions were at once aroused. As already mentioned in the previous chapter, the battery was intended as a protection against the French and the guns pointed seawards. But those guns could soon be slewed round and made to point towards Burungai Sonko's own village. To the native mind this was obviously the real purpose of the battery and the feeling arose that Burungai had opened the door to the invader. Furthermore, the Ceded Mile Treaty put an end to the right, which the people of Barra had exercised for several centuries, of demanding tolls from all ships entering the river. A large proportion of these tolls had found their way into the pockets of the underchiefs. The commuted annual payment, which was substituted by the treaty, went straight to the king. His people therefore began to murmur against the sale of their birthright for a mess of pottage, in which they had no share. Burungai Sonko began to realise that he would have to do something to regain his waning popularity. After recovering from the alarm occasioned by the visit of Commodore Bullen, he took every possible opportunity of demonstrating his hostility towards the British and of encouraging his people in the like attitude.

[1] MacCarthy to Earl Bathurst, 11 August 1823; Marty, "Le Comptoir Français d'Albreda en Gambie", *R.H.C.* (1924), pp. 246, 252–258.

British inactivity lent countenance to the belief that this policy was proving highly successful. For a number of years the only outward and visible sign of the transfer of the sovereignty of the Ceded Mile was a very temporary military post at Barra Point. The guns were still mounted in temporary emplacements and the handful of troops, who guarded them, were housed in mud huts. An attempt to induce the pensioners of the West India Regiments to settle there failed owing to the greater attractions of Bathurst.[1] The military post at James Island had never proved capable of checking illicit trade or depredations upon the mainland. As the men were housed in temporary hovels made out of the ruins of the fort and as their presence there served no useful purpose, this garrison was withdrawn in 1829.[2] This evacuation further increased the impression that the Ceded Mile Treaty could be treated as a dead letter. Except at Barra Point and at a small village near by, which was peopled by a few settlers from Bathurst, and at Juffure, where a few European traders had houses, Burungai Sonko ruled the Ceded Mile exactly as he had done before he signed the treaty.

In 1830 the treatment of Bathurst traders in Niumi became so outrageous that the Lieutenant-Governor decided, with the approval of the home Government, to suspend payment of Burungai Sonko's annual subsidy.[3] This act appears to have sobered the "king" for a brief period and he appears at least to have made a promise of reparation. But in 1831 a very small spark fired the train. On the night of 21 August in that year two men came from Essau to the small settlement that had grown up near Fort Bullen. They were armed with cutlasses and muskets and, if they had not been drinking very freely, at any rate were in a very truculent mood. After having picked a quarrel with some of the settlers they went on to Fort Bullen. Discipline at that place seems to have been extraordinarily lax, for the men were able at eight o'clock at night to enter the fort canteen and to demand to be served with rum. When the canteen keeper refused to serve them, one of them discharged his gun at him but missed him. After this both men made off in the direction of Essau. When the incident was reported to the commanding officer, he caused the alarm gun to be fired.

[1] Captain Frazer to Sir Neil Campbell, 26 December 1826 and 6 January 1827.
[2] Fox, *A Brief History of the Wesleyan Missions on the Western Coast of Africa*, p. 261; Poole, *Life...in the Gambia*, II, 96.
[3] R. W. Hay to Rendall, 1 September 1830.

The shot was heard in Bathurst and as soon as possible on the following morning a party of thirty soldiers was sent over to Barra Point. They were accompanied by a number of the local inhabitants and the captains and the crews of some merchant vessels, which were in the harbour. All might still have gone well, if those in command had taken a little time to deliberate, but, as soon as the details of the incident of the previous night were made known, it was decided that this medley of soldiers, merchant seamen and civilians should proceed forthwith to Essau and demand the surrender of the culprits. The party arrived to find that the village of Essau was surrounded by a strong double stockade. Again, there was no pause for deliberation. Orders were given for the party to fire into the village. It was at once realised that their arrival was fully expected. A large armed party, which greatly outnumbered the British, issued out of the stockade and, taking cover in the growing corn and long grass, poured a heavy fire on their opponents. The ill-organised party had perforce to beat a very hasty retreat on Fort Bullen. They were closely pursued and lost several of their number on the way. When they turned to make a stand at the fort, they found that they were hopelessly outnumbered and therefore decided to take to their boats. The embarkation took place in the greatest possible confusion. Many were cut off and killed before they could reach the boats. The enemy waded out into the sea and inflicted more casualties before the boats could get away. Altogether twenty-three soldiers and a number of civilians were killed in this lamentable affair. One of the latter was a merchant captain. Believing that he was the Governor, the Mandingos decapitated him and placed his head in triumph on a pole.[1]

When the retreating party reached Bathurst, the place was thrown into the greatest possible confusion. It was believed that the people of Barra would follow up their success by crossing the river and attacking Bathurst and that the people of the Kombo would join forces with them. The French at Albreda were warned that they were in danger and they and their movable property were brought to Bathurst. The militia was embodied. A merchant vessel was detained for any possible emergency. Urgent appeals for help were sent to the British authorities in Sierra Leone and to the French authorities at Goree and St Louis.

[1] Moister, *op. cit.* pp. 162, 163; Fox, *op. cit.* p. 337. Lt.-Gov. Rendall's voluminous despatches are completely silent as to the opening incidents of the war. Moister states facts and offers no comments.

The first to answer the call were the French. The Commandant at Goree promptly sent Commandant Louvel and the man-of-war *Bordelaise* to Bathurst. To-day Louvel's name is very rightly commemorated by one of the streets in Bathurst. He arrived on 8 September and at once took charge of the situation and set to work to put Bathurst into a state of defence. He built a blockhouse on the far side of the island and also constructed a barricade, which was composed partly of sandbags and partly of masonry, from that blockhouse to the opposite shore. His energy and that of his men encouraged the inhabitants, who threw themselves wholeheartedly into the task of putting the town in a state of defence. William Moister of the Wesleyan Mission thus describes Bathurst at this critical moment in its early history:

All, who could carry arms, were drilled and enrolled in a militia. A strong stockade was erected across the island near to Bathurst; and a new fort was built in a commanding position just behind the mission house. Sentinels were also appointed to keep a strict look out and to walk the streets during the night, that they might give an alarm in case the enemy should attempt to land on the island. Mrs Moister and her schoolgirls were busily employed in making sandbags for the erection of movable batteries; and indeed the services of every person, who could render any assistance, were required in the common defence of the settlement. Even the native women and children carried stones for the erection of the new fort, singing and clapping their hands, as they walked along with their loads upon their heads, in a manner, which showed their loyal and enthusiastic attachment to the British government.[1]

On 15 September the *Bordelaise*, accompanied by some schooners with men of the West India Regiment and the local militia on board, crossed over to the north bank to endeavour to recover Barra Point. They found the enemy strongly entrenched and were unable to dislodge them by artillery fire. An explosion of gunpowder on board of one of the attacking vessels caused a number of casualties amongst the French seamen and marines. As the forces at his disposal were limited, Louvel decided against an attempt to land and returned to Bathurst. A further appeal for reinforcements was despatched to

---

[1] Moister, *op. cit.* p. 164. Moister omits to mention the fact that at a later date he attended to the wounded under fire.

Senegal. It was answered in person by the French Governor, Renault St Germain, who arrived on 10 October with more sailors and marines.

In the meantime there had been little further in the way of hostilities. From the fact that they had strongly entrenched themselves it seems evident that the enemy had never really contemplated an attack upon Bathurst. At the most all that they wanted to do was to keep the British out of the Ceded Mile. Louvel's bombardment at any rate must have convinced them of the unwisdom of carrying the war across the river. A force of "River Fencibles", which was organised by the Bathurst merchant, Thomas Chown, patrolled the Niumi shore in schooners and diverted a number of the enemy from Barra Point.

During this lull in the hostilities there were unfortunate differences of opinion between the Lieutenant-Governor and the officers in charge of the British troops. It is unnecessary to go into details, but the upshot was that one commanding officer was, with the subsequent approval of his superior officer in Sierra Leone, suspended from duty, whilst his successor had a nervous breakdown and had to be superseded. Colonel St Germain very wisely and very properly did not attempt to attack the enemy, deeming that his duty confined him solely to the defence of the settlement until such time as British reinforcements might arrive. When those reinforcements did come, he withdrew most of his men but at the request of the British authorities left some sailors and marines to participate in the final operations.

The British reinforcements arrived from Sierra Leone on 5 November. Two days later they were embarked on H.M.S. *Plumper*, the *Panchita* transport and an armed schooner. The troops landed at Barra Point under cover of a bombardment by the ships. A heavy fire was poured upon them from the enemy trenches, but after half an hour's hand to hand fighting the position was taken at the point of the bayonet. On 17 November the troops proceeded to attack Essau. The place was bombarded with some small field pieces, but the enemy returned a vigorous fire. The artillery did little damage and after five hours' fighting ammunition began to run short. Two parties of the enemy were then seen to emerge from the town and to deploy as though to encircle the attackers. The order was thereupon given to fall back on Barra Point.

On 7 December further reinforcements arrived from Sierra Leone, but the attack on Essau was not renewed. The enemy had, however, by this time had enough of it. They had suffered heavily in resisting the three attacks on Barra Point and the people of Baddibu had invaded the Jokadu district. This attack in the rear had drawn away a large number of men and it was felt that they could not hope to repel another attack upon Essau. Overtures were therefore made for peace. On 5 January 1832 a convention was signed at Juffure. Burungai Sonko, his chiefs and people "publicly declared their sorrow for the outrages they have committed" in "an unjust and cruel war", promised never to offend in the like manner again and gave hostages from the royal family for their good faith. They furthermore confirmed the cession of the Ceded Mile in 1826 and agreed that the limits of that territory should be extended to the Atlantic Ocean.[1]

There were one or two aftermaths of the war. There was a good deal of recriminatory correspondence between Rendall and some of the military officers. The French Government asked to be reimbursed the sum of about forty thousand francs for the cost of their expeditions, but were informed by the British Government that, as these expeditions had been for the protection of French interests at Albreda as well as British interests, the claim could not be entertained. Having made this announcement, the British Government presented a claim to the French Government for the cost of transporting the French and their effects from Albreda to Bathurst. It hardly needs saying that the French Government did not accept liability. For some reason Colonel St Germain was bitterly attacked in the French press for the part which he had played. A proposal that he and Commandant Louvel should receive some special form of recognition from the British Government was met by a reply from Earl Granville that St Germain "would find in the expression of thanks of the British government a more perfect recognition of the services, which he had rendered, and the competence, which he had shown, than in a more real honour". But to the people of Bathurst the danger had been too real to make them ungrateful or oblivious. They subscribed one hundred guineas to present Louvel with a sword and rallied to the defence of St Germain in the press campaign, to which he had been subjected.

Thus ended what has come to be known as the Barra War. It had lasted for four months, during which time all trade had been brought

[1] Hertslet, *Map of Africa*, p. 12; *Ordinances of the Gambia*, 1875, p. 523.

almost completely to a standstill. The enemy's casualties are not known, but the war had cost the British and French some fifty lives as well as thrice that number wounded. Burungai Sonko was a troublesome drunkard. No doubt both he and his people were working up for trouble of some sort, but a little more judicious handling both before and at the commencement of the affair might have saved a good many lives. It was not a particularly glorious war, but it had one or two redeeming features. The chivalrous conduct of the French should not be allowed to be forgotten. The navy and marines—English and French alike—fully maintained their high reputation for courage and efficiency. The West India Regiment reached the same high standard and the Gambia and Sierra Leone militias showed that they were of the same metal. Lastly, and by no means least, the civil population of Bathurst, men, women and children, irrespective of race or creed, rose nobly to the emergency. If little else that was good emerged from the war, it had at least been shown that this fifteen-year-old community of so many mixed races and origins was wholeheartedly British.[1]

Lieutenant-Governor Rendall's next campaign took place four years later. As mentioned in the previous chapter, Kolli, "king" of Kataba, was in a state of constant war with his neighbour Kemintang. According to reports current amongst the British this latter had come to his chieftainship by means of murder. This information, which came from a hostile source, may or may not have been true, but, if true, Kemintang was not alone in having risen to power by this means. It was unfortunate for him that his reputation with the British authorities depended upon the character supplied for him by his rivals. He no doubt had all the faults of his contemporaries, but he was certainly no worse than the majority of them.

Trouble between him and the Colonial Government began in the middle of 1834. According to Kemintang a Bathurst trader, who was named Salim Jobati and had a factory at Tendeba, had seized and carried off some of his people. Two years before he had had trouble with the same man, which had ended with the seizure of

---

[1] An account of the military operations is given in Ellis, *History of the First West India Regiment*, pp. 179–182. A French account of the war is to be found in Faure, "Une expédition française en Gambie au secours des Anglais (1831)", *R.H.C.* (1925), pp. 639–640. Moister, *op. cit.* describes the events from the point of view of the civilian resident in Bathurst. Lt.-Gov. Rendall's despatches are voluminous. Though they omit certain details, they supply others which are not to be found in any printed record.

Salim Jobati's schooner. On that occasion the Manager at Mac-
Carthy Island had managed to settle the dispute and the schooner
had been released.[1] Kemintang decided to try to obtain redress on
this second occasion by the like means, but, as Salim Jobati's
schooner had departed, he seized another schooner belonging to
William Goddard, a Bathurst merchant. He detained the vessel and
two of the crew, but sent the master and the rest of the crew in a
boat down to Bathurst with a message to the effect that Salim
Jobati must be handed over to him before he released the schooner.
As shortly after this incident the Colonial Secretary issued a public
notice warning Bathurst traders as to their conduct in territories
belonging to native chiefs, it would appear very probable that
Kemintang had a genuine ground of complaint, whatever may be
the criticism of his mode of seeking redress.[2]

As was to be expected, the Bathurst merchants were very indignant at this seizure. The Lieutenant-Governor appealed to two
naval officers in succession for assistance, but they declined to intervene. An officer was then sent up river to interview Kemintang and
to demand restitution and compensation. He was also instructed to
endeavour to persuade the neighbouring chiefs "to take measures
for the punishment of the outrage that has been committed against
them as well as us". As Kemintang declined to make restitution
except upon his own terms, the officer returned to MacCarthy Island.
After consultation with the principal traders there it was decided
that the only measure, which could be adopted, was the withdrawal
of all traders and their property from the upper river. On 5 August
1834 the Lieutenant-Governor issued a proclamation placing an
embargo upon trade above MacCarthy Island.[3]

Given time, the embargo might have had the desired effect. Other
chiefs besides Kemintang suffered from the resulting loss of trade
and were consequently by no means friendly disposed towards the
author of their troubles. The "king" of Wuli in fact announced his
intention of making war upon Kemintang. In face of his increasing
unpopularity Kemintang decided to come to terms. In March 1835
he sent messengers to Bathurst to offer compensation, but the sub-

[1] Memorandum for Mr Gibbs, 1832.

[2] Lt.-Gov. Rendall to Lieut. Bryan, 13 June 1834; Lt.-Gov. Rendall to
R. W. Hay, 14 June 1834; Notice by Colonial Secretary, 18 November 1834.

[3] Lt.-Gov. Rendall to Lieut. Nicholls, 26 June 1834; Lt.-Gov. Rendall to
R. W. Hay, 21 August 1834.

sequent negotiations were dilatory and after three months no compensation was forthcoming. In June H.M.S. *Brisk* arrived at Bathurst bringing a draft of the Royal African Corps. At the same time information was received that a number of chiefs were mustering forces in the upper river in order to attack Kemintang. In the circumstances Lieutenant-Governor Rendall decided that a favourable moment had arrived to teach Kemintang a salutary lesson.[1]

The expedition consisted of 120 men drawn from the crew of the *Brisk*, the African Corps and the MacCarthy Island militia. They were met at the entrance to Sami Creek by 150 horse and foot from Wuli. Kemintang was known to be entrenched at the head of the creek in the stockaded town of Dungasseen. The expedition was conveyed in boats up the creek to the limit of navigation, whence it was a fifteen-mile march to Dungasseen. All the artillery had to be man-handled over the whole of that distance through alternate sand and mud. The ammunition boxes were given to the native irregulars to carry. Some of them deserted, either throwing away their loads or else carrying them off with them. It took eight hours to cover the first nine miles. The force then halted for the night. On the following day it took another four and a half hours to cover the remaining six miles. Any element of surprise had by then obviously disappeared. The members of the expedition were exhausted for want of water. None the less they did their best. The guns were brought into action, but after four hours of bombardment very little impression had been made on the defenders' position. It was then discovered that most of the native allies had disappeared. As the rest of the party were thoroughly exhausted and as they were fifteen miles from their boats, it was decided to retire before night set in. Fortunately the enemy did not follow in pursuit; for with the exception of the seamen and marines from the *Brisk* and a handful of others the withdrawal was carried out in the greatest possible disorder. The remainder of the native allies abandoned three of the guns on the way. The naval men managed to spike one of them, but the remaining two had to be left.[2]

[1] Lt.-Gov. Rendall to Acting Governor of Sierra Leone, 21 October 1834; Lt.-Gov. Rendall to Earl of Aberdeen, 17 March and 17 June 1835.

[2] Huntley, *Seven Years' Service on the Slave Coast of Western Africa*, pp. 271–280, gives an account of this expedition. The official correspondence fully confirms its accuracy.

On receipt of the news of the failure of the expedition Lord Glenelg expressed to the Lieutenant-Governor his regret "that your arrangements were not made with that degree of providence, which should have ensured a fortunate result to the exertions and gallantry of the officers, troops, seamen and volunteers, who were engaged in the attack....After you had determined to attack that chief, it was incumbent upon you to make the best arrangements for ensuring its success".[1] Kemintang dragged the abandoned British guns in triumph to Dungasseen and mounted them on his stockaded fort. This was a severe blow to British prestige, as both the Colonial Government and Kemintang were well aware. The news travelled very quickly up and down the river and well into the interior. When Mr Fox, the Wesleyan Missionary, visited Bondu three years later, he found that it was still the talk of the countryside.[2] Lieutenant-Governor Rendall had been warned earlier in the year against making expeditions of this nature without the prior sanction of the home Government.[3] He now tried to console himself and the home Government with reports that Kemintang had been killed in the bombardment of Dungasseen, but Kemintang was very much alive for several years to come.

The captured guns may not have been of much military value to Kemintang, but he was fully aware of the fact that the possession of them enhanced his prestige amongst his neighbours and also that they were an asset for bargaining when it came to negotiation with the British authorities. When in 1839 the attacks of some of those neighbours at length induced him to try to make his peace with the British Government, he was informed that no terms would be discussed unless and until he restored the guns. He gave a reply to the effect that "the guns may be recovered on amicable terms, but not by making it appear that he was frightened out of them".[4] Overtures consequently broke down and Kemintang went his own way until his death in 1843. He continued in the bad books of the Government—principally because he persisted in making war on the friendly "king" of Kataba. But when in 1842 Mr Fox of the Wesleyan Mission ventured to visit him in his stronghold, he did not reveal himself as the formidable tyrant that he had been painted. His looks may have been, as Mr Fox said, "depraved, determined

---

[1] 19 September 1835.   [2] Fox, *op. cit.* p. 454.
[3] Lord Stanley to Lt.-Gov. Rendall, 1 January 1834.
[4] Captain Jackson to Lt.-Gov. Mackie, 3 May 1839.

and malignant", but he agreed to send one of his sons to the mission school on MacCarthy Island for the sons of chiefs. The real truth appears to have been that he was a typical Soninki freiherr, his hand being against every man and every man's hand against him, at the same time having no real desire to quarrel with the European but rather a wish to keep on the right side of him.[1]

The other outstanding, and more important, event which occurred during Lieutenant-Governor Rendall's administration was the arrival in the Gambia of a large number of liberated Africans from Sierra Leone. British cruisers, which captured foreign slave ships in the Atlantic, were in the habit of bringing their prizes to Freetown. As time went on, the number of people thus rescued increased very considerably and the question of their disposal became a very real problem for the Sierra Leone Government. In most cases it was quite impossible to repatriate them to their own country, because, even if that country were known, repatriation would only have been followed by re-enslavement. They therefore had to be kept in British territory. Many of them were quite unable to fend for themselves and the question of finding them suitable employment became one of real difficulty. Small parties had previously been sent from time to time from Sierra Leone to the Gambia, where they had generally been placed out as apprentices. In 1831 Lieutenant-Governor Rendall decided to obtain sanction for the location of a large body of liberated Africans in the Gambia. He did so for a fourfold reason. In the first place, there was a shortage of artisans in the Gambia and he hoped to increase their number by apprenticing some of the liberated Africans to various trades. Secondly, owing to the poverty of the soil St Mary's Island was not self-sufficing. It was therefore hoped that arrangements could be made for the settlement of other liberated Africans in farm colonies near to Bathurst, where they could raise food crops for the settlement. Thirdly, it was proposed to give the able-bodied male liberated Africans some form of military training as a militia and thus build up a reserve to the regular garrison. Yet another consideration, which undoubtedly influenced a Colonial Governor with a very small revenue at his disposal, was the fact that the home Government was prepared to pay for the maintenance of the ex-slaves until they were in a position to look after themselves.[2]

During the next decade there was a great deal of official corre-

[1] Fox, *op. cit.* p. 547.   [2] *Liberated Africans* (1840), p. 5.

spondence in regard to the liberated Africans. It is not proposed to follow that correspondence in any detail or to discuss the wisdom of the plan in the light of subsequent events. It is sufficient to say here that the plan failed to fulfil original expectations. Lieutenant-Governor Huntley summed up the cause of his failure very accurately, when he said "it may be found in having carelessly applied for liberated Africans to be sent from Sierra Leone before the question of locating them upon ground adapted for the purpose of agriculture and providing them with properly qualified overseers had been sufficiently canvassed".[1] There had been a triangular correspondence between the Lieutenant-Governor of the Gambia, the Secretary of State, and various officials in Sierra Leone upon the subject of sending liberated Africans to the Gambia, but in none of that correspondence was any detailed scheme put up as to their disposal on arrival.

In 1830 the Secretary of State approved a proposal to acquire other islands in addition to MacCarthy Island for the location of liberated Africans,[2] but when the first contingent arrived, no such island had been acquired. In 1834 Lieutenant-Governor Rendall obtained Deer Island from the chiefs of Nyanibintang and Gassan upon payment of an annual rent of $70.[3] Its value to the British Government may best be given in Lieutenant-Governor Huntley's words. "The Deer Island, my Lord, as a location can never deserve the consideration of an hour from the single circumstance of the chief part being under water half the year. Purchasing such places is literally to throw money into the water."[4]

As Lieutenant-Governor Rendall himself admitted, the scheme was eventually launched at the worst season of the year. After a good deal of correspondence the first contingent, comprising 170 men and 30 women, arrived in the middle of the rainy season of 1832. As there was no other island available, they were destined for MacCarthy Island, where it was necessary for them to break up the soil for farming purposes. Though the Sierra Leone Government had been directed to supply agricultural implements to the emigrants before embarkation,[5] they had omitted to do so.[6] A number of

[1] Lt.-Gov. Huntley to Lord John Russell, 29 August 1840.
[2] R. W. Hay to Lt.-Gov. Rendall, 5 September 1830.
[3] Rendall to Hay, 9 April 1834.
[4] Lt.-Gov. Huntley to Lord John Russell, 28 July 1840.
[5] *Liberated Africans* (1842), p. 5.
[6] Colonial Secretary to Mr Campbell, 13 July 1832.

miscellaneous tools were hastily purchased on their arrival in Bathurst, but the season was too far advanced for them to make proper farms that year. A devastating fire, which was believed to be the work of an incendiary and which destroyed most of the buildings on MacCarthy Island,[1] greatly impeded agricultural work in the following year. It was followed by a shortage of rain, which ruined the crops.[2] Another fire in 1834, which was also believed to be the work of an incendiary, threw back the work another year.[3]

As the idea was that the immigrants should settle in outlying places and develop the land, it is clear that they ought to have been carefully selected, but no attempt at proper selection ever appears to have taken place in Freetown. At times the attitude of certain officials in that colony appears to have resembled that of the acting Governor, who had dumped white soldiers upon the Gambia, because they were proving too much of a nuisance in Freetown. On arrival of one of the earliest contingents in the Gambia it was found to include three Akus, who were not ex-slaves at all but had been recently concerned in some political troubles in Sierra Leone.[4]

Many of the rescued slaves, who were brought by British cruisers to Freetown, were landed there in a badly debilitated state owing to long confinement in slave barracoons, the congested and insanitary accommodation on board slave ships, the change of habits and food, and also the change of climate. Many landed only to die and many never sufficiently recovered from their past experiences ever to be able to look after themselves. These latter became a charge upon the revenue of the colony. In a number of instances that liability was transferred by the Sierra Leone to the Gambia Government. In 1835, for instance, 300 liberated Africans were embarked on board the *Governor Campbell*. At Freetown the master of the vessel detected signs of recent smallpox on some of them, but the Government surgeon passed them as fit and he was forced to accept them. He did, however, positively refuse to accept one man, who was so weak that he had to be carried on board the ship. He received a supply of blankets and clothing, but his instructions were to hand them over intact to the authorities at Bathurst. The voyage between the two ports lasted sixteen days. It happened to be the

---

[1] Colonial Secretary to John Grant, 21 May 1833.
[2] Lt.-Gov. Rendall to R. W. Hay, 16 October 1834.
[3] Same to same, 9 April 1834.
[4] Lt.-Gov. Rendall to Governor Findlay, 1 June 1833.

coldest season of the year and most of the party fell sick when four days out at sea. One man died before Bathurst was reached. Of the remainder sixty-six were so weak that on arrival at Bathurst they had to be carried from the ship to the hospital. Seventy-three more followed them there in the course of a week and of the total number forty-one died.[1]

The first party was sent from Sierra Leone without cooking utensils or the prescribed issue of clothing.[2] In 1831 a vessel was chartered to carry 180 men, women and children from Freetown to Bathurst. Many of them were sickly and three died during the course of the voyage. Apparently owing to stress of weather the master saw fit to land them forty miles down the coast from Bathurst. The overseer tried to organise them so as to march them to their destination. Four of the party were drowned whilst crossing a creek. On the way the remainder came into conflict with the local inhabitants and the overseer was killed. Fortunately news of their plight reached the British authorities. A party was sent to their rescue and eventually all with the exception of four, who were too ill to be moved, were brought to Bathurst.[3]

As many as possible of the immigrants were sent to MacCarthy Island, but the number, which could be received there, was limited. An attempt was therefore made to form the nucleus of another settlement in the Ceded Mile by apprenticing a number of liberated Africans to some discharged soldiers, who had been given grants of land at Berwick Town[4] close to Barra Point.[5] It was hoped to be able to make this place into a farming colony, which might be a granary for Bathurst, and to give the settlers some sort of a military training so as to employ them, if occasion arose, for the defence of the Ceded Mile. In 1837 the population of this settlement was sufficiently large to induce the Wesleyan Mission to open a station there,[6] but ultimately the disturbed state of the adjacent country and the greater attractions of Bathurst caused the settlers to leave.

Those, who remained at Bathurst and who were physically fit,

[1] *Report of the Select Committee on West Africa* (1842), p. 201; Medical report of Alexander Bryan, 29 December 1835.

[2] Colonial Secretary to Mr Campbell, 13 July 1832.

[3] Colonial Secretary to Thomas Cole, 25 November 1831.

[4] So called after Lieut. Thomas Berwick of the Royal African Corps, who was wounded during the landing at Barra Point in 1831.

[5] Lt.-Gov. Rendall to Lord Glenelg, 14 July 1836.

[6] Same to same, 24 April 1837.

were either indentured as apprentices, or were given plots of ground to cultivate, or were put to learn brickmaking. The system of apprenticeship did not last long as it was soon found to be open to abuse. Settlements were made for the agriculturists at Melville Town[1] and Goderich Town. The former place lay within about half a mile of the main town. Its inhabitants soon drifted into Bathurst or, if they remained in Melville Town, abandoned agriculture for casual employment in the main town. Goderich Town lay three miles from Bathurst on the bank of Oyster Creek. Lieutenant-Governor Rendall thought it a thriving place in 1833,[2] but six years later his successor reported that "this village has ceased to exist or rather has been deserted on account of its unprofitableness".[3] The brickworks were started in 1833 at Lamin in Kombo. There was never any formal grant of the land, which was merely held on a verbal gift to Lieutenant-Governor Rendall. The earth was bad. Consequently the bricks were inferior and did not find much of a market even in a place so destitute of building materials as Bathurst. It soon became clear that brickmaking was an industry at which few, if any, of the immigrants could earn a livelihood and the works were therefore abandoned in 1839.[4]

A little more success was achieved at MacCarthy Island. The work here also included instruction in brickmaking and agriculture. In addition the curriculum, which was drawn up by Lieutenant-Governor Rendall in 1832, provided for military training so as to build up a reserve to the regular garrison. A number of hours each day were to be devoted to drill and on Sundays the liberated Africans were to parade with the regular soldiers. The organisation of the other work was on a military basis, the men being divided into messes and squads, each under the leadership of one of their own number, and "periods of time and summonses to turn out are to be made known by bugle".[5] This military organisation lasted for several years. Fifty volunteers from the MacCarthy Island militia received their baptism of fire three years later in the expedition against

---

[1] To be distinguished from Old Melville or Jollof Town, which adjoined Portuguese Town.

[2] Lt.-Gov. Rendall to John Grant, 29 November 1833.

[3] Lt.-Gov. Mackie to Lord Glenelg, 1 April 1839.

[4] T. L. Ingram to Marquis of Normanby, 30 October 1838.

[5] Colonial Secretary to Mr Gibbs, 10 July 1832; Lt.-Gov. Rendall to Rufus Coffin, 20 October 1832.

Kemintang,[1] but their Sunday parades were stopped in 1837 on a protest being raised by Mr MacBrair of the Wesleyan Mission.[2]

The credit for such success as was achieved at MacCarthy Island was largely due to the members of the Wesleyan Mission. In 1838 this society took over 600 acres of land upon the island, which had three years previously been granted to a nonsectarian mission started by Dr Robert Lindoe of Southampton for work amongst the Fulas.[3] As there was no good pasturage on the island, the Fulas were not attracted to the place and the original object of the mission failed. It was then reorganised as an industrial mission[4] for the training of the sons of chiefs and the Wesleyan Mission undertook to supply the necessary training staff. In preparation for this work the mission started to develop the 600 acres and for that purpose enlisted a number of the liberated Africans. Special agricultural instructors

[1] Lt.-Gov. Rendall to Earl of Aberdeen, 17 June 1835.

[2] MacBrair, *Sketches of a Missionary's Travels*, p. 262.

[3] The mission to the Fulas owed its inception to the Rev. John Morgan of the Wesleyan Mission, who visited MacCarthy Island with Major Grant in 1823 as well as on subsequent occasions. He interested Dr Lindoe in the proposal and the scheme was launched in 1833. Though the Wesleyan Missionary Society undertook to provide the necessary staff, the supporters of the mission came from many different religious societies. Dr Lindoe himself was a member of the Church of England. The Rev. John Horton, a former Church of England chaplain at Bathurst, was one of his earliest supporters, amongst whom were also to be found Elizabeth Fry, the Quaker philanthropist, and Thomas Clarkson. Dr Lindoe subscribed very liberally indeed to the original mission as well as to the subsequent mission, which was organised in its place: MacBrair, *op. cit. passim*; Fox, *op. cit. passim*.

[4] The history of both missions is very candidly summed up in the annual report of the Wesleyan District Meeting for 1846. "The civilization department has been a failure. The objects of this department were, 1st, the benefit of the Foulahs by inducing them to abandon their wandering habits and settle upon the island. For this purpose a grant of 500 acres of land was obtained from the British government in 1836, but up to the present time (1846) not one of them has been induced to do so. It is true a few of these people come in the island in the dry season, but they invariably leave before the rains. They have been even compelled by the authorities to leave when they have sought refuge from the scourge of war.

"...II. The institution has failed. We have not now a single student, nor are we likely to obtain one on our present system. Our funds will not allow of our visiting native chiefs and giving them expensive presents, as was formerly the case.

"...III. The mission has not accomplished its primary object. It is called the Foulah mission and was designed to exert a saving influence upon that and other aboriginal tribes. To effect this the missionaries ought to reside amongst

were sent out from England. The first of these died soon after his arrival. His successor did not arrive until three years later and had to be invalided home after a residence of less than six months. The Rev. William Fox then undertook the superintendence of the work in addition to his pastoral duties and, despite lack of funds, succeeded in achieving a great deal for the benefit of the liberated African. The reports of contemporary officials show that he was indefatigable in his labours. A model village, called Lindoe, was erected in 1841. It comprised twelve brick houses of four rooms each, which were given out to such members of the Wesleyan church as showed themselves most industrious and deserving. When the acting Governor visited the island in 1843, he spoke highly in praise of the work of the mission, and in particular of Lindoe village. In reporting on the general state of the liberated Africans on Mac-Carthy Island, he said "some of them had prospered and, to judge by the comfortable and cleanly appearance of their houses, many were evidently in easy circumstances; their wives and their children were decently dressed in English costume and seemed contented and happy. A large number, however, did not present so pleasing an appearance, their huts and their persons manifesting the presence of penury".[1]

The acting Governor's concluding sentence was equally applicable to the liberated Africans in Bathurst. It was inevitable that a certain proportion of parties of immigrants, whose selection was made in a very haphazard manner, should be either undesirable or else unemployable. Some were physically unfit to do any work at all. As late as 1862 there were still a number, who had to be maintained at the public expense.[2] The women and children, moreover, presented special problems. Apprenticeship was tried in the first instance but proved most unsatisfactory. After its abolition the only

them.... But the missionaries have been unable to do this, for from the commencement there has been a society of liberated Africans, to whom they have had to discharge their pastoral duties... and attention to the native tribes has been rendered almost impossible."

In justice to the mission it should also be added that sickness and deaths amongst the staff and the constantly disturbed state of the mainland made missionary labours near MacCarthy Island far from easy.

[1] *Report of the Select Committee on West Africa* (1842), p. 186; East, *Western Africa*, pp. 287, 355, 356; Ingram, "Abridged Account of an Expedition of about two hundred miles up the River Gambia", *J.R.G.S.* xvii, 152–153; MacBrair, *op. cit.* pp. 328–332; Huntley, *op. cit.* ii, 64–68.

[2] Duke of Newcastle to Colonel D'Arcy, 4 January 1862.

solution for the women appeared to be compulsory matrimony. The Manager of MacCarthy Island was instructed in 1832 "to find good husbands for the women, taking care to marry them always to their own country people",[1] and was directed a year later to send back to Bathurst all who had been unable to find eligible husbands.[2] After considerable hesitation Mr Fox of the Wesleyan Mission was induced to acquiesce in this solution of a difficult problem. On one occasion in 1835 he celebrated thirty weddings in a single day, reflecting that "there may be an evil in this wholesale system of marrying; but when there are two evils, prudence dictates that we choose the least; and, believing this to be the least of the two, I perfectly concurred with the governor in thus uniting them in matrimony,...though it was with some difficulty I maintained my customary gravity".[3]

When Lieutenant-Governor Mackie assumed office in 1838, he utterly condemned this system of indiscriminate immigration and refused to receive any more liberated Africans from Sierra Leone.[4] Except for a party of 200, who arrived from Sierra Leone in 1861 and were settled at Kotu in Kombo,[5] there was no further wholesale immigration of alien races into the Gambia. Until his premature death in 1839 Lieutenant-Governor Mackie did much to ameliorate the condition of those who had already arrived. His work was carried on by the acting Governor, T. L. Ingram, and by Lieutenant-Governor Huntley. With limited funds and an over-full labour market the task was by no means easy, but the situation was considerably relieved in 1840 when the acquisition by the Government of part of the Kombo enabled Lieutenant-Governor Huntley to settle a number of liberated Africans on the mainland.[6]

Whilst a great deal was done by Government officials to improve the lot of the liberated African, all due credit must also be given to the missionary societies. Without their assistance the Government would have been unable to have achieved much. In Bathurst both the members of the Wesleyan Mission and of the Roman Catholic

[1] Colonial Secretary to Thomas Gibbs, 10 July 1832.
[2] Lt.-Gov. Rendall to John Grant, 1 January 1833.
[3] Fox, *op. cit.* pp. 373, 374.
[4] T. L. Ingram to Lord Stanley, 2 February 1843.
[5] Colonel D'Arcy to Duke of Newcastle, 24 March 1861; Duke of Newcastle to Colonel D'Arcy, 19 August 1861.
[6] Lt.-Gov. Huntley to Lord John Russell, 29 August 1840.

Mission, which arrived in 1849, co-operated loyally and unostentatiously with the Government in assisting the liberated Africans not only by educational work, but also in innumerable forms of social service.

Finally, a proper measure of praise must be given to the liberated Africans themselves. Neither Government officials, nor missionaries, nor any other benevolently minded person could have helped them, if they had not had a real desire to better themselves. They started under innumerable handicaps. They came from very different races with very different standards of civilisation, intelligence and morals. They had no common tongue, no common tribal organisation, and no common customs or traditions. The only tie, which could possibly unite them, was that of fellowship in past suffering. But from the very outset numbers of them showed a determination to rise to better things. Many of them made considerable personal and pecuniary sacrifices in order to secure the best available education for themselves and their relatives. Whether that education was always best suited to their needs may be open to doubt, but the fact remains that they very definitely set themselves out for self-improvement according to the best of their lights. The result was that, before the first generation had run its course, they had become a community and were holding responsible posts under the Government, in the missions, in commerce and in the professions.

XXIV : Further extension of the sphere of influence—separation from Sierra Leone, 1837–1843

William Mackie succeeded George Rendall as Lieutenant-Governor in 1838. There had been an interregnum of about a year between the death of his predecessor and his own assumption of duty. It is clear that in that period matters had been allowed very much to drift and that he found a great deal to set to rights. During his all too brief period of office he managed with very limited means to achieve a very great deal. His untimely death after only six months' residence was a great loss to the Gambia. It was followed by another inter-regnum of about six months before the arrival of Captain Henry Vere Huntley. The new Lieutenant-Governor had already had ex-perience on the West Coast of Africa, having served with distinction in the squadron for the suppression of the slave trade. He took over what was still a *damnosa hereditas*. The public revenue had been mismanaged and the settlement was in debt, the problem of em-ployment for the liberated African had not yet been solved, and British prestige in the upper river had suffered a severe blow owing to the mismanagement of the expedition against Kemintang. During the course of the next few years he managed to put all these matters to rights.

One of the earliest decisions, at which he arrived, was that the British Government must extend its territories and its sphere of in-fluence. Both Bathurst and MacCarthy Island were overcrowded and could not properly maintain the population which was already there. The Ceded Mile was not suitable for the settlement of the liberated African. Though there had been no real trouble with the people of Niumi since 1831, there were frequent disturbances in that district as the result of quarrels between the natives. It was out of the question therefore to transfer any liberated Africans to any portions of the Ceded Mile except the village of Berwick, which was covered by the guns of Fort Bullen, and that of Juffure, where the presence of a few European traders afforded some sense of security. Even at these places life was not free from anxiety. In 1834, on a false alarm that the "king" of Barra was meditating war, the pensioners at Berwick Town were ordered to sleep in Fort Bullen and their families were sent over to Bathurst.[1]

Any fresh place of settlement for the liberated African had clearly got to be in close proximity to some military post. In the upper river all the islands near to MacCarthy Island were waterlogged half the year and were therefore unhabitable. The mainland was out of the question owing to the perpetual state of warfare. Therefore the only possible spot was the south bank of the river near to Bathurst.

Soon after his arrival Lieutenant-Governor Huntley began to treat with Suling Jatta, "king" of the Kombo, for a cession of part of his territory. This chief proved a little difficult. Some of his personal slaves had fled to St Mary's Island and he announced that he would not consider any transfer of territory, unless they were surrendered. His request was refused and he declined to continue the negotiations. The Lieutenant-Governor thereupon announced that he would close the Kombo to trade because the "king" had failed to observe the article in his treaty with the British Government for the suppression of the slave trade. The "king" then became more amenable and in 1840 entered into a treaty whereby, in exchange for a payment of $100, he ceded to Great Britain the district which thereafter came to be known as British Kombo or Kombo St Mary. The area thus ceded, which was slightly enlarged by another treaty in 1853, comprised about twenty-five square miles of the mainland adjoining St Mary's Island and included the plot of ground at Cape St Mary which had been acquired in 1821.[2] On 3 August 1840, formal possession was taken of this territory. The British flag was hoisted to the firing of a royal salute at Cape House, which was converted into a barrack for a small detachment of the Royal African Corps. For a few years the "king" of Kombo continued without interruption to collect "customs" and rents in the ceded territory, but in 1850 he renounced these rights in consideration of an annual payment.[3]

---

[1] Lt.-Gov. Rendall to Lieut. MacDonnell, 10 February 1834.

[2] Huntley, *Seven Years' Service on the Slave Coast of Western Africa*, II, 117–123, 138–141, 155, 198–199; *Ordinances of the Gambia*, 1875, pp. 513, 527; Hertslet, *Map of Africa*, pp. 12, 17, 18; Hertslet, *Treaties*, XII, 28–60; *Proceedings of the Select Committee on Africa (West Coast)* (1865), p. 406.

[3] *Ordinances of the Gambia*, 1875, p. 525; Hertslet, *Map of Africa*, p. 16 and *Treaties*, XII, 47.

This transfer of sovereignty gave rise to no friction with the inhabitants of the ceded territory. By the terms of the treaty native landowners were not to be disturbed. The only village of any consequence was Bakau near Cape St Mary. As Suling Jatta's exactions from the inhabitants of this place had recently been heavy and as those inhabitants had already been brought in close contact with the British, the change was not unwelcome.[1] The alkali of Bakau was left to administer his own people as theretofore. The natives were neither expropriated nor otherwise deprived of the enjoyment of their lands, but villages were erected on the unoccupied land. A number of liberated Africans and discharged soldiers were settled there and lived on very good terms with the original inhabitants.

The upper river provided Lieutenant-Governor Huntley with some of his earliest difficulties. He was greeted on his arrival with the information that the natives had committed a number of outrages on traders and that there had been a collision between them and the troops on MacCarthy Island. Affairs at Bathurst prevented him from proceeding at once to the spot, but he took advantage of the presence of H.M.S. *Saracen* to send the commander to investigate and to restore order. Lieutenant-Commander Hill returned from MacCarthy Island to report that previous information had been unduly alarmist but that a very regrettable incident had occurred. The chief of Nyanibintang had collected a large body of men and had proceeded with them to the mainland opposite to MacCarthy Island. The motive for this muster is not apparent, but it caused some alarm upon the island itself. Hitherto the chief and his people had been well disposed towards the British and his subsequent conduct hardly suggests any intention of attacking the island. After he had been encamped for a few days the chief and a small party of armed followers crossed over to interview the civil commandant. This party was allowed to land fully armed. When they were returning from the interview the party fell out with some of the troops on duty. The civil commandant and one of the merchants proceeded to take charge of the situation. The Riot Act was read— a formality which can have had no meaning whatever to a band of non-English-speaking Mandingos and did not necessarily provide in strict law a justification for what followed. After the reading one

---

[1] Lt.-Gov. Huntley to Lord John Russell, 29 August 1843.

of the soldiers fired without orders. Fighting then became general and in the end the chief and two of his followers were killed. Captain Shaw, the senior military officer, had not been informed of what was happening and arrived on the scene too late to prevent bloodshed. He managed by his own personal exertions to separate the combatants and to get the remnant of the chief's party conveyed across the river.

As the Lieutenant-Governor informed the civil commandant, it was a most regrettable incident, which had been mishandled from the very start and might have had very serious consequences indeed. After the death of their chief the rest of the armed party dispersed to their farms. The dead man does not appear to have been very popular with a section of his people and his successor took an early opportunity of disclaiming any hostility towards the British. Little resentment was shown for what had happened. In 1844 the new chief offered land to the Wesleyan Mission. An African assistant missionary was stationed in his district for about a year, but shortage of staff and the unresponsive attitude of the inhabitants eventually led to his withdrawal.[1]

Lieutenant-Commander Hill's report also showed the real danger of increased friction between native chiefs and the British Government by reason of the irresponsible conduct of certain African agents of Bathurst traders. To give only one example, he had been instructed to enquire into an outrage which was alleged to have been committed upon one of these agents at Dumasansan in Jarra. It turned out that the agent was frequently drunk and had badly wounded a Mandingo with a sword whilst in a state of intoxication. Hill declined to intervene, saying "I cannot but feel in taking the trader's part I should be condoning the proceedings at the Mac-Carthy's Island. If the merchants employ improper people to trade in the native towns, it must be at their own risks, and they cannot expect men of war to act contrary to their own customs and laws in such cases".[2] The origin of the dispute with Kemintang shows that this was very far from being an isolated act. The criminal calendars and official correspondence of this date show that a number of African agents of Bathurst firms were indulging in a clandestine

[1] The official correspondence on the case is very extensive and the inquest proceedings are still extant. The District Meeting Book of the Wesleyan Mission gives the information in regard to the mission station at Nyanibintang.

[2] Hill to Lt.-Gov. Huntley, 10 April 1840.

traffic in slaves.[1] A large number of these agents gave no trouble at all, but the misconduct of the rest did not make the task of maintaining good relations between the Colonial Government and the chiefs at all easy.

In accordance with instructions from home Lieutenant-Governor Huntley kept aloof from the perennial disputes between the chiefs in the upper river. In order that there might not be the slightest colour for the belief that the British Government was prepared to take sides in these quarrels, he issued orders that in time of war fugitives were not to be allowed to cross over to MacCarthy Island and that no attempt was to be made to mediate in any such quarrel, unless one of the parties requested it.[2]

At the end of 1840 it became apparent that this policy of strict neutrality might prove disastrous to the people of Kataba. The "king" of that district invoked the protection of the British Government against Kemintang. An officer was sent from MacCarthy Island to interview both the belligerents and to try to arrange a peace. Kemintang professed to be anxious for peace, but procrastinated about the terms. In the middle of March 1841 the motive for his dilatoriness became apparent. A large body of Fulas and Bambarras descended the river. It at once became clear that Kemintang was only waiting for their assistance to renew his attack upon Kataba. Whatever may have been the merits of their quarrel with Kemintang, the people of Kataba deserved well of the British Government and Lieutenant-Governor Huntley decided to intervene. The "king" of Wuli had promised to refuse the Fulas and Bambarras a passage through his country, but it was clear that he was powerless to prevent them, if they persisted. The Lieutenant-Governor therefore reinforced the garrison at MacCarthy Island and moved a detachment of troops thence into the Kataba district. When news of this reached the "king's" opponents, they at once dispersed. The "king" was profuse in his thanks. He agreed to allow the British to erect a small fort in his country and to man it with a party from the Third West India Regiment. On 23 April 1841 he concluded a treaty of friendship and commerce with Great Britain. In exchange for British protection he further agreed to cede one square mile of land to the British Government and also undertook not to enter into any alliance, negotiation or communication with

[1] *Report of the Select Committee on West Africa* (1842), pp. 228, 229.
[2] *Ibid.* pp. 236, 240.

any political power in the world without the consent of the British Government.[1]

The occasion had been deemed urgent and Lieutenant-Governor Huntley had acted without prior reference to the Colonial Office. When his report arrived in England, it was not received with entire approval. On 8 November 1841 Lord Stanley wrote:

I deem it proper to instruct you that you are to consider yourself absolutely prohibited from concluding any treaty or agreement, which should have the effect of binding Her Majesty to give military aid to any African chief, or to assume any right of sovereignty or protection over any portion of the soil or waters of Africa.

Cases may occur (I hardly think it possible they should), in which it may be deemed advisable ultimately that Her Majesty should enter into such an agreement, but I repeat that in no case are you to take a step, which may fetter the discretion of the Queen's government. If at any time application should be made to you to place an African chief or his territory under the sovereignty or protection of the Queen, the utmost to be done, and this most sparingly, and in cases of extreme urgency, should be to forward such application to Her Majesty's government.[2]

The terms of this letter were somewhat modified at a later date. Instructions were given that the "king" of Kataba should be informed that, whilst those articles of the treaty, which referred to British protection and the cession of territory, could not be ratified, "so long as he shall faithfully adhere to the terms of the treaty, and take no hostile measures against his neighbours, he may appeal to Her Majesty for protection from any unprovoked aggression on their part". Sir Henry Huntley had in the meantime been transferred to Prince Edward Island. The acting Governor had been negotiating similar treaties with other chiefs,[3] but on receipt of these instructions went no further with them. He also withdrew the military detachment, which had mounted guard in Kataba and had fired a morning and evening gun every day for close on a twelvemonth.[4]

[1] Lt.-Gov. Huntley's despatches give a full account of this transaction, which is also referred to in his *Seven Years' Service on the Slave Coast of Western Africa*, ii, 361 seq. Cf. also *Ordinances of the Gambia*, 1875, p. 514; Hertslet, *Map of Africa*, p. 13; *Report of the Select Committee on West Africa* (1842), pp. 227, 242.

[2] *Index to Report from Select Committee on Western Coast of Africa* (1865), p. 426.   [3] *Ibid.* p. 427.

[4] Lt.-Gov. Huntley to Captain Findlay, 21 and 30 May 1841.

The Wesleyan Mission, who had been promised a piece of land by the "king", had to abandon the project of opening a station there.[1] But the twelve months' occupation had a good effect. Kemintang's exuberance was curbed. British prestige recovered from the shock, which it had received six years before. The marauding bands from Bondu and Futa Jallon decided that it was not advisable to carry their operations very far down the river.

Thomas Lewis Ingram, the acting Governor, took advantage of the favourable impression, which had been caused by the occupation of Kataba, to make a voyage up the river in 1843 with the object of establishing better relations with the chiefs of the upper river and of endeavouring to open up trade with the countries beyond the Barrakunda Falls. At this date very little was known about the upper reaches of the river. As mentioned in Chapter XXII, Bryan O'Beirne and Thomas Chown had gone up as far as Kantalikunda in 1822. In 1831 the Bathurst merchants had formed a company with a capital of £6000, which was known as the Tandah Company and had for its object the opening up of communication with the countries above the Barrakunda Falls.[2] The enterprise received the official benediction of Lord Goderich and an officer was detailed to assist the company by proceeding on a mission to Bondu,[3] but the Barra war interrupted the mission. Somewhere about 1831 John Grant, a Bathurst merchant, proceeded by water about a hundred miles above the Barrakunda Falls and thence made his way overland to the Neriko and Jobson's Tenda, but on his return did not report at all favourably on commercial prospects in those regions.[4] In 1838 William Fox of the Wesleyan Mission had travelled from Wuli to Bondu.[5] None the less information regarding the trade from the interior, whether from explorers or from native reports, was very scanty. In 1843 Ingram wrote that "the river is quite unknown to our traders beyond Kantalikunda and even to the natives

[1] Fox, *A Brief History of the Wesleyan Missions on the Western Coast of Africa*, p. 550.

[2] Belcher, "Observations on the West Coast of Africa", *J.R.G.S.* II, 296; "Reports received by Colonial Office", *J.R.G.S.* II, 305.

[3] Lt.-Gov. Rendall to Ensign Fearon, 27 March 1831.

[4] The date of Grant's voyage is not certain. He kept a journal, which was seen in 1849 by Governor MacDonnell. In his instructions of 27 March 1831 Lt.-Gov. Rendall refers to a merchant as having "already started for the upper river to seek a favourable spot" for the Tenda Company to open up trade. This would appear to be Grant.   [5] Fox, *op. cit.* pp. 454 *seq.*

of that place ".[1] In December 1842 Ingram himself proceeded up the river, but did not get farther than Kantalikunda owing to a war in Wuli between the Marabouts and Soninkis. He met with a good reception and concluded a number of treaties, whereby the chiefs undertook to keep the roads open to the river, to allow foreigners to enter their territories for the purposes of trade, and to suppress the slave traffic.[2]

In 1843 Major Cobbe started from Bathurst on a mission to Bondu. He managed to take the colonial steamer *Wilberforce* as far as the Barrakunda Falls, but a war between Wuli and Bondu prevented him from reaching the latter place.[3] In the following year R. G. MacDonnell, the newly appointed Chief Justice, met with greater success. He travelled by water as far as Fattatenda, where he met Monsieur Raffenel of the French navy and two companions, who had set out from St Louis in 1843 and had just visited Bondu. From Fattatenda MacDonnell proceeded on foot and—to use his own words—"after surmounting various perils from banditti and the climate", arrived at Bulibani, the capital of Bondu, where he was given a friendly reception. He learnt that Raffenel had just induced the paramount chief of Bondu to sign a treaty, which gave the French the exclusive right to the export trade of the country. He persuaded the chief to disavow that treaty and to make another, whereby he agreed to keep open the road between Bondu and the River Gambia.[4]

A change had taken place in the status of the Gambia whilst these exploring and treaty-making expeditions were being carried out. The movement to secure entire independence from Sierra Leone had begun at a very early date. It had been brought to the notice of Major Rowan in 1827, when he was sent out from England to investigate and report upon West African affairs. Between 1834 and 1842 local public opinion on the question was voiced in a number of petitions, memorials and presentments by the grand jury at quarter sessions. All these representations urged complete separation from

[1] T. L. Ingram to Major Cobbe, 14 October 1843.

[2] Ingram, "Abridged account of an expedition of about two hundred miles to the Gambia", *J.R.G.S.* xvii, 150–155; *Ordinances of the Gambia*, 1875, p. 520.

[3] Ingram to Lord Stanley, 25 January 1844.

[4] *Annual Report for* 1849; Raffenel, *Voyage dans l'Afrique Occidentale*, pp. 480 *seq.*; Ancelle, *Explorations au Sénégal*, p. 101. Bondu became a French protectorate in 1858: Hertslet, *Map of Africa*, p. 635.

Sierra Leone and were forwarded by successive Lieutenant-Governors with the strongest possible backing, but as late as 1840 Lord John Russell had expressed the opinion that separation was not practicable.[1]

The inconveniences of the Gambia's dependence upon Sierra Leone were innumerable. One, which does not appear to have been fully appreciated at the time, was the difficulty and irregularity of communication between the two places. In the days of sailing ships a vessel might be able to make the voyage from Bathurst to Freetown in three or four days, but the return voyage usually occupied anything from a fortnight to one month.[2] Sir Charles Turner, who was one of Sierra Leone's most energetic Governors and certainly tried to do his duty by the Gambia, put the matter very forcibly, but very accurately, when he informed Earl Bathurst in 1825 that "it would be easier for the general officer at Cork to take charge of the Barbadoes than for me to take charge of the three colonies" of the Gambia, Sierra Leone, and the Gold Coast.[3]

In one respect the appointment in 1829 of a Lieutenant-Governor of the Gambia had not been a change for the better. In the early days of the settlement Governors of Sierra Leone, such as Sir Charles MacCarthy, Sir Neil Campbell, Sir Charles Turner and acting Governor Macaulay, had felt it their duty to interest themselves in the Gambia and had, amid their other multifarious duties, found time to visit the river and thus to gain a first-hand knowledge of local needs and requirements. When a Lieutenant-Governor was appointed, who was made responsible direct to the home Government, those visits came to an end. As long as the officer in charge of the administration of the Gambia was entirely subordinate to the Government of Sierra Leone, that Government felt some responsibility for, and consequently some interest in, the Gambia, but, when that officer became quasi-independent, that interest ceased. But despite his apparent independence on paper the Lieutenant-Governor was still very dependent upon Sierra Leone. All legislation had to be forwarded to the government of that colony for enactment and all important civil and criminal cases had to be tried by a judge from Freetown.

The consequent feeling in the Gambia was that their affairs were

[1] Lord John Russell to Lt.-Gov. Huntley, 4 September 1840.
[2] Lt.-Gov. Rendall to Rt Hon. E. G. Stanley, 2 July 1834.
[3] Butt-Thompson, *Sierra Leone in History and Tradition*, p. 239.

being neglected by the Government of Sierra Leone and that their needs were far too often sacrificed to the interests of that colony. Allowance must be made for a parochial point of view, but the opinion, which was expressed by the commander of a visiting man-of-war in 1832, deserves to be quoted. "Had a portion of the liberality of government to Sierra Leone been extended to Bathurst and its dependencies, I feel satisfied that long 'ere this it would have acquired that character, which eventually with infinite labour it will establish for itself from its own resources."[1]

The two principal respects, in which the Gambia suffered from this dependence upon Sierra Leone, were in regard to the administration of justice and the passing of legislation. No provision was made for the appointment of any legal or judicial officer in the Gambia after the union with Sierra Leone in 1821. As mentioned in Chapter xx, petty civil and criminal cases were left for adjudication by a lay magistracy, but all the more important cases had to be tried by the Chief Justice of Sierra Leone. Parties and witnesses had either to go to Freetown for the hearing or else had to await the arrival of the Chief Justice in Bathurst. The first alternative was so prohibitive that in actual practice no litigation ever was taken to Sierra Leone.[2] Prisoners awaiting trial had perforce to submit to the second alternative. The Chief Justice had his duties in Sierra Leone to occupy him and, even when he had time to spare, the opportunities of obtaining a passage between Freetown and Bathurst were very irregular. When, however, in 1834 Lieutenant-Governor Rendall forwarded and supported a memorial from the merchants of Bathurst praying for a separate judiciary, the Chief Justice had declared the proposal to be "inexpedient" and Mr Spring Rice had concurred in that view.[3] On 16 December 1835 the same Lieutenant-Governor called the attention of the Chief Justice to the fact that there was a full calendar of prisoners, many of whom had been awaiting trial for some months, and urged him to pay an early visit to Bathurst. The Chief Justice did not arrive until the following May. Some of the prisoners had then been in custody for ten months. The grand jury was very outspoken in its comments and at the end of the session the Chief Justice had to admit that "the delay, which has occurred,

---

[1] Belcher, "Observations on the West Coast of Africa", *J.R.G.S.* ii, 296.

[2] Memorial of merchants and traders of Bathurst, 28 June 1834.

[3] Lt.-Gov. Rendall to R. W. Hay, 17 March 1835; Lord Glenelg to Rendall, 15 June 1835.

has caused, I fear, the failure of justice in some cases by the absence of witnesses, the unusually long confinement of the prisoners for trial, and the hardship of individuals being bound over for a long period in recognizances to give evidence".[1]

In 1839 and 1840 a prisoner was kept in custody nearly eleven months awaiting his trial on a charge of murder.[2] On more than one occasion witnesses had to travel from MacCarthy Island to Bathurst on receipt of information that the Chief Justice of Sierra Leone was about to visit the latter place. After travelling over 150 miles they often had to wait several months away from their homes and work only to be informed in the end that the sessions had been postponed indefinitely and that they would have to return to MacCarthy Island with the certain knowledge that they would be put to the same inconvenience again at some later date or else forfeit their recognisances. Matters reached their culminating point in 1842. In January of the previous year there had been an explosion of gunpowder in Bathurst, which had resulted in the loss of six lives. There was evidence to suggest that the ignition was the deliberate act of the employee of a certain merchant. In such case the offence was murder. In any event the powder had been illicitly stored and there was at the least a *prima facie* case of manslaughter of an aggravated kind. The suspect was arrested and committed for trial, but had to wait in custody for two years before a Chief Justice arrived to take his case. The one essential witness for the Crown was his employer, who, despite his precarious health, waited for five months for the trial to take place. At the end of that time his medical adviser insisted on his return to England. The result was that on the tardy arrival of the Chief Justice, the grand jury had to ignore the bill for want of sufficient evidence.[3]

The absence of a separate legislature had an even more hampering effect upon the progress of the Gambia. When in 1827 Major Rowan made his report on the British possessions in West Africa, he remarked that "the knowledge possessed at Sierra Leone of the local circumstances and interests of the Gambia is, as has already been stated, very limited, and with reference to trade these places may be considered as rival settlements. It is, therefore, not unlikely that

---

[1] Chief Justice Rankin to Lt.-Gov. Rendall, 19 May 1836.
[2] Calendar of prisoners tried, 7 and 9 May 1840.
[3] *Report of the Select Committee on West Africa* (1842), p. viii; Huntley, *op. cit.* pp. 309–314; T. L. Ingram to Lord Stanley, 27 November 1841.

the regulations adopted may not be equally beneficial to both; and the power of making regulations at one place will always be looked on with distrust at the other".[1] He therefore advocated the creation of a separate establishment for the Gambia subject to the control of a Governor-in-Chief at Sierra Leone, but, as already seen, the home Government was not at that time prepared to go this length.

In 1834 the merchants and traders of Bathurst protested in a memorial against "the anomaly of receiving legislative enactments from persons residing five hundred miles off, totally unacquainted with local interests, and in some cases opposed thereto". Soon after his arrival Lieutenant-Governor Huntley pointed out the impossible position in the following words:

It has often happened, and of course will happen again, that the necessity of passing a law has occurred to meet some peculiar and local case. A law has been consequently so framed and forwarded to Sierra Leone for confirmation by the Governor and Council of that Colony. At the expiration of (I understand) never less than six months the act is returned, during which period this place has been suffering from the want of it, but it has so happened that, when returned, it is found to have undergone such alterations at Sierra Leone as to render it of comparatively no effect here.

...My predecessor (Acting Governor Ingram), having written for a copy of the acts of the Governor and Council of Sierra Leone, received the reply that they were "out of print" and could not be supplied. This ...places the Colony in ignorance of the legality of its proceedings.

At this moment, my Lord, we are in want of a law to authorize the extension of the Spirit Licence Act and others to regulate the beach, streets and police generally. For these simple laws we must wait six months and then get something, which will not answer, when the whole matter may be settled here in as many hours with the additional advantage of getting what would answer.[2]

Many examples could be given in proof of the truth of the above statement. One such example may suffice. In 1840 a bill for the regulation of Bathurst harbour was sent to Sierra Leone for enactment. One of its clauses made provision at the public expense for a boat to enable the harbourmaster to attend to his duties. That clause was amended at Freetown so as to make the harbourmaster

---

[1] *Report on...the State of Sierra Leone* (1827), p. 15.
[2] To Lord John Russell, 5 June 1840.

provide the boat and the wages of the crew out of his own pocket. As Lieutenant-Governor Huntley pointed out, these expenses would entirely exhaust the harbourmaster's salary of £100 a year.[1]

In 1841 Dr R. R. Madden was sent out from England to report upon the British settlements in West Africa. On his arrival at Bathurst he was made acquainted with all the facts already mentioned as well as a good many more. His report was submitted to a Select Committee of the House of Commons, which on the strength of it recommended the complete severance of the connection with Sierra Leone and the establishment of a separate legislature and judiciary. In addition to stressing the disadvantages, under which the Gambia laboured under existing conditions, the members of the Committee expressed the opinion that "for the purposes of trade and useful communication of every kind with the interior of Africa, the Settlement of the Gambia seems to possess advantages far beyond those of any British settlement on the coast of Africa". They pointed out its advantages as a base of operations for the suppression of the slave trade, that its magnificent waterway provided a means of transport, which obviated the necessity of carrying goods by headloads and the consequent encouragement of the slave trade, and that with a very little expenditure trade with the interior could be very much developed.[2]

Parliament very speedily adopted the Committee's recommendations. The necessary act to enable the separation of the Gambia from Sierra Leone was passed in 1843.[3] On 24 June in the same year by letters patent under the great seal the Gambia was erected into a separate colony under the control of a Governor and a Legislative and an Executive Council. The Legislative Council was to consist of the Chief Justice, the Colonial Secretary, the officer commanding the troops and a justice of the peace. Three of this number were to form a quorum and the power of disallowance of any legislation was reserved to the Crown. The Executive Council consisted originally of the Colonial Secretary and the Collector of Customs. The Queen's Advocate was added to their number in 1845.[4]

---

[1] Lt.-Gov. Huntley to Lord John Russell, 27 August 1840.
[2] *Report of the Select Committee on the West Coast of Africa* (1842), pp. vii, viii.   [3] 6 Vict. *c*. 13.
[4] *Papers on the Civil and Judicial Constitution of the Settlements on the West Coast of Africa* (1854).

XXV: The groundnut trade— further punitive expeditions, 1843–1852

No very striking events occurred during the first few years after the separation of the Gambia from Sierra Leone. The immediate result of the change was the passing of a number of laws, none of which were in themselves of very far-reaching consequences, but each of which was very essential for the efficient working of the machinery of local government and the general progress of the country.

The absence of any remarkable occurrence in these early days of the new Crown Colony was in itself evidence of progress. The real history of this period is to be gleaned from the dryasdust statistics, which are to be found in blue books and trade returns. These figures reveal a steady progress, which had admittedly begun before the separation from Sierra Leone but which continued after that event had taken place. The most remarkable thing about these statistics is the record which they give not only of increased exports but also of the complete change in the character of those exports.

In the early days of the settlement the principal article of export had been beeswax. In 1817 it represented nine-tenths of the total value of all the exports. In that year the only other article which was exported in any considerable quantities was hides. These two commodities with a little gold, gum and ivory, all of which had come from regions beyond the Barrakunda Falls, were the only articles exported.[1] The export of hides increased considerably during the next few years. So to a less extent did that of wax. Gum, gold and ivory fluctuated but none of them ever formed any very large proportion of the exports. Timber—and in particular mahogany—began to be exported in 1822. About the same time one or two other local products began to appear in small quantities in the trade returns. In 1830 a new and very insignificant item first made its appearance amongst the list of exports. This was a hundred baskets of groundnuts, which were valued at half a dollar a basket or

---

[1] Sir C. MacCarthy to Earl Bathurst, 3 January 1819.

379

£10 16s. 8d. in all.[1] This item disappeared from the list in the following year and did not reappear until 1834, when 213 baskets valued at £21 16s. 0d. were exported. In the next year 47 tons were exported. In 1836 the figure rose to 129 tons and in 1837 to 671 tons. The total tonnage first passed treble figures in 1841. By 1848 it had risen to 8636 tons, which were valued at £103,778 and represented two-thirds of the total value of all exports.

This change was due to what one writer has described as "the reflex action of the Industrial Revolution" in Europe.[2] A variety of causes led to an increased demand for soap, which had hitherto been manufactured from animal fats. The available supplies of animal fats were inadequate to meet the increased demand and soap manufacturers resorted to vegetable oils. About the same time the French Government imposed high duties on most kinds of oil nuts. Consequently oil nut crushers in France began to look round for some variety of nut, which was not taxed or only lightly taxed, and found that the groundnut answered their purpose.[3]

The history of the Gambia groundnut crop is in some respects unique amongst the histories of economic crops in British tropical Africa. In some instances what is now a staple agricultural product of a tropical dependency was already being grown and exported, when the British assumed control of the country. In many other instances it was hardly grown, if at all, at the time of the advent of British rule and its growth has been promoted by the Government by means of official assistance and encouragement of the grower and by fostering and protecting the industry in its early days. Neither of these two things happened in regard to the Gambia groundnut crop. It was not grown for export in 1816 and, though from 1841 onwards large quantities have been exported from Bathurst and have contributed very largely to the colonial revenue in the shape of an export duty, yet for about half a century the crop was almost entirely grown on soil, which was not British, by natives of Africa, who were not under British rule or protection. It is one of the few instances in which the native of Africa has learnt more or less subconsciously that he has at his door a saleable product, which could fetch a good market price in Europe, and started to grow it with very little material instruction or encouragement from official sources.

---

[1] Belcher, "Observations on the West Coast of Africa", *J.R.G.S.* ii, 298.
[2] McPhee, *The Economic Revolution in British West Africa*, p. 36.
[3] *Ibid.* pp. 36, 37.

The history of the export trade in its infancy is rather obscure. The first few basket loads, which left the country in 1830 and 1834, have the appearance of samples despatched for experimental purposes. Of the forty-seven tons, which left the country in 1835, forty-one went to Great Britain. In 1839 the acting Governor reported that "the late demand for groundnuts in England and America has been the means of opening a new branch of commerce in this river".[1] In 1837 a little over half the nuts went to the United Kingdom, but thereafter, except in 1841, by far the greater majority were despatched to foreign destinations. America soon dropped out and by 1848 France had taken its place. Figures fluctuated from year to year, but those for 1847 and 1848 may be quoted. In the first of those years only 321 tons out of a total crop of 8236 tons went to the United Kingdom. In the latter year 3036 tons out of a total crop of 8636 tons went to that destination. In both years practically the whole of the remainder of the crop was consigned to France.[2] In 1859 no less than 13,000 out of the 15,000 tons exported from the Gambia went to France or French possessions, the United States receiving 600 tons and the United Kingdom most of the remainder.[3]

Perusal of the official correspondence of this period at first sight rather suggests that the groundnuts were growing under the eyes of the British administration without much encouragement on its part, but a chance sentence here and there in an official despatch shows that this was not entirely the case. In 1838 or possibly earlier an area of land was planted with groundnuts near to the brickworks, which were started at Lamin in the Kombo for the instruction of the liberated Africans.[4] The brickworks were closed down soon afterwards and in 1840 the liberated Africans were removed to settlements in the newly acquired British Kombo. There are clear indications

[1] T. L. Ingram to Marquis of Normanby, 31 October 1839. "In 1835 a mill for crushing groundnuts was erected in London, but its after-history is obscure. This is the only known attempt to establish the groundnut industry in England", McPhee, *op. cit.* p. 37.

[2] Governor MacDonnell to Earl Grey, 6 June 1849.

[3] Colonel D'Arcy to Duke of Newcastle, 12 February 1861.

[4] "My reason for appointing Mr Sleight overseer at Lamin was to avoid the loss of the crop of groundnuts, binny etc., which has been raised during the last rainy season by the liberated Africans, and which is now fit for gathering. The proceeds of the crop *this year* I have reason to hope will be considerable, although the number of liberated Africans employed at Lamin has been smaller than heretofore." T. L. Ingram to Marquis of Normanby, 30 October 1839.

that some of them had benefited by the instruction, which they had previously received at Lamin, for despatches of a few years later make frequent reference to their groundnut farms in their new homes. From them the cultivation evidently spread not only to the Mandingos of British Kombo, but also to the natives of adjacent districts.

But the credit for inaugurating and expanding the industry clearly does not rest solely with those in charge of the farm at Lamin. The spread of groundnut cultivation in the upper river appears to have been due in no small measure to the instruction, which was given by the Wesleyan Mission on their model farm at Mac-Carthy Island.[1] Due credit must also be given to a number of individual traders and merchants, who stimulated the industry but who by reason of absence of all reference to their work in official correspondence must remain anonymous. It is clear that many of these persons were not British subjects. The French do not appear to have entered into the Gambia trade in groundnuts until about 1841, when a small merchant at Rufisque named Rousseau sent forty tons to Marseilles as an experiment. The consignment met with approval and French merchants at Goree very quickly embarked upon the purchase of groundnuts. The French factory at Albreda soon became a centre for the trade, but it is also clear from export returns that a large quantity of groundnuts, which were purchased by Bathurst merchants, were consigned to purchasers in France. As aliens were debarred from possessing land, it is not certain when the first French trader set up in business at Bathurst, but an Anglo-French Convention of 1857 put French subjects in the Gambia on an equal footing as regards trade as British subjects. In 1859 the Bordeaux firm of Messieurs Maurel et Prom, which still exists in Bathurst to-day and is the parent of many other French firms now there, already had agents as far up the river as Dumasansan near Elephant Island.[2]

---

[1] "The exertions of that part of the population residing there [*sc.* Mac-Carthy Island] have with the exception of perhaps thirty to forty acres perfectly cleared the ground and [have] fair crops every year of corn, ground-nuts, rice etc....; I beg leave to acknowledge the great benefit derived from the Wesleyan Missionary establishment fixed upon the island, as it may be found in the instruction which it disseminates either as it applies to religion, morals or agriculture. The two first are daily taught in the schools and the last upon the tract of land, which this establishment has upon the island." Lt.-Gov. Huntley to Lord John Russell, 22 April 1840.

[2] D. Robertson to Sir E. B. Lytton, 20 June 1859.

This, as well as many other French firms, did much to promote the cultivation of the groundnut in the upper river. Hilaire Maurel, one of the founders of Maurel et Prom, was the inventor of an agricultural tool, which is now commonly known in the Gambia by his Christian name and which is in general use on all groundnut farms in the country.

The exploitation of the groundnut led to other economic changes. One was the advent in the Gambia of the person, who is now commonly known as the "strange farmer"—an appellation which has received official recognition in at least one local ordinance. In 1852 Governor MacDonnell reported that the groundnuts were chiefly raised by natives of the countries well in the interior, who came down for two or three years to the lower parts of the river, where they hired land from the various chiefs and planted the nuts, and, after having acquired the means of purchasing European goods, returned with those goods to their own countries.[1] A certain number of these farmers have from time to time taken up their permanent abode in the Gambia, but to this day the practice has been for the majority to sell their crops and to return home and come back again at the beginning of the next planting season. There are a number of motives prompting this custom, but the principal one appears to be the same to-day as it was when Colonel D'Arcy mentioned it to the Secretary of State in 1863.[2] The native of Africa is often smitten with wanderlust, but has the same homing instincts as any other race. As often as not his object in making long journeys in quest of work is so as to earn the means of providing himself or a relative with a dowry for a wife. If he can earn the money, or a substantial part of it, after a few months' labour in a strange land, he will naturally go to that land to earn it rather than tarry in a less fertile land working for some exacting Laban. Before the spread of the cultivation of the groundnut in the Gambia most of these temporary sojourners had sought to acquire their wealth either as bandits or as mercenaries, who were ready to hire themselves out to one of the many chiefs, who might at the time be indulging in a war with his neighbour. But the wages of the bandit or the mercenary are as uncertain as their lives and, though the process of change took many years to complete, in the gradual course of time the freebooter became a tiller of the soil and the land had peace.

[1] Grey, *Colonial Policy of Lord John Russell's Administration*, ii, 289.
[2] Colonel D'Arcy to Duke of Newcastle, 26 April 1863.

One effect of the arrival of the strange farmer was to alter the medium of exchange in the river. Hitherto trade in those regions had been done mainly by barter. The majority of the strange farmers came from territories, which were in the French sphere of influence, and had a need for actual money. The French trader appears to have realised this fact sooner than the British and was thus enabled to capture a great deal of the groundnut trade. The coin, which was put into circulation, was not British current coin but the French five franc piece, which came to be known locally as the dollar and which was recognised in the Gambia as legal tender by a proclamation of 1843.[1]

Writing on 24 May 1860 to the Secretary of State, Colonel D'Arcy said: "The fact is isolated in colonial history, but, while I write, I count thirty tricolours, six stars and stripes and but one union jack flying in the port of Bathurst." Even the British merchant sent his groundnuts to Marseilles and Bordeaux and because of the prohibitive duty, which was charged upon British ships entering a French port, he shipped his cargo under the tricolour. Naturally patriotic governors expressed some concern for this state of affairs, but it by no means meant that the trade of the Gambia was entirely in foreign hands. Though the native was no longer prepared to condescend to barter, his new purchasing power created an increased desire for articles, which had hitherto been regarded as luxuries for the more wealthy. Whilst he was anxious to buy cheaply, he was none the less a discriminating purchaser, who was not to be put off with a shoddy article. He was therefore attracted by the superior quality of most British made goods. Consequently the change in destination of the majority of the exports did not ruin British trade in the Gambia. Those exports paid a duty, which increased the colonial revenue, and there was a corresponding increase in imports, of which the majority came from Great Britain.

One other event, which took place during these years of peace, must also be mentioned. In 1849 a Roman Catholic Mission was opened in Bathurst. The first party included three Fathers from Paris and three Sisters from the Convent of St Joseph of Cluny.

---

[1] *Annual Report for* 1868; Chalmers, *History of Currency in the British Colonies*, pp. 210, 219, 220. Another piece of evidence, which showed the extent of the participation of the French in the groundnut trade, was the ordinance, which was passed in 1848 and recognised the bourdeau as a customary measure having the capacity of eight bushels.

This mission started in a very humble way with very limited funds, but was soon able to show a record of much good work, particularly amongst the poorer section of the Bathurst community. Soon after their arrival governors' reports were full of praise for their educational and other work and for their loyal co-operation with the administration in promoting social welfare. A few words in particular must be said of the work of the Sisters in their ministrations to the sick, irrespective of race or creed. When a civil hospital was opened in 1854, they undertook the nursing. When periodic scourges of yellow fever and other epidemics swept over Bathurst, their hands and their hearts never wearied or faltered. They set an example of gentle courage and unassuming devotion to their calling, which should never be forgotten in the history of the Gambia.

Turning to administrative matters, the period of office of Henry Frowde Seagram, the first Governor of the independent Colony, was cut short by his premature death six months after his arrival. He was followed in 1844 by Commander G. Fitzgerald, who was in his turn succeeded in 1848 by Richard Graves MacDonnell. The last named had in 1843 been appointed the first Chief Justice of the Colony. He has already been mentioned in the preceding chapter as having in 1844 undertaken a mission to Bondu. Soon after his promotion he showed that the exploring instinct had not departed from him. In 1849 he proceeded by boat 105 miles above the Barrakunda Falls. He returned in the following year and managed to get as far as Jallakotta on the River Neriko, where the people expressed to him a desire to have British traders. But the results of these two expeditions disappointed him. There were a number of impediments to navigation above the Barrakunda Falls, the country was found to be very sparsely populated, and there were no signs at all of any cultivation along the river banks.[1] The net result of the two expeditions was to put an end once for all to any further encouragement of projects to bring Jobson's Tenda within the British sphere of influence.

On his way back from the first of these expeditions Governor MacDonnell stopped at Tendeba to enquire into a robbery which was alleged to have been instigated by the people of Kunnong. Accompanied by two European officials and a small party of natives from Kwinella he proceeded on foot to Kunnong to interview the chief. During the course of the "palaver" the Governor's party was set

---

[1] *Annual Reports for* 1849 *and* 1851.

upon and roughly handled. The Governor's life was only saved through the timely intervention of Makali, the headman of Kwinella, and an elder of Kunnong named Burri. The people of Kwinella managed to extricate the Governor and his party and to convey them back to their steamer at Tendeba. The incident was followed up by the pillaging by the people of Kunnong of another trading post at Jamali near Battelling. Subsequently a punitive expedition was sent to deal with the people of Kunnong and those of Bambako, who had been aiding and abetting the previous outrages. The first place was completely and the latter partially destroyed. Thereafter the "king" of Kunnong sent in his submission. It appears that he was in no way responsible for the attack on the Governor, which was the work of a few hotheads amongst the younger men in the town. When a year later a medical officer visited his district on a vaccination campaign, he met with a most friendly reception from the chief.[1]

Another punitive expedition, which also took place in 1849, was undertaken for the benefit of international shipping generally. The inhabitants of the Bissagos Islands, which lie off the mouth of the Rio Grande, had for a number of years shown great hostility to European crews, whose vessels were forced there by shipwreck or by stress of weather. Nominally these people were subject to the authority of the Portuguese Governor of Bissao, but in actual fact that officer exercised no control whatever. In 1841 a London vessel was wrecked off these islands and the crew were detained as prisoners. At the request of the acting Governor of the Gambia, Lieutenant Charles Lapidge of H.M.S. *Pantaloon* went to their rescue. His landing was opposed and it was only after he had captured twenty-three of the natives and carried them off to Bathurst that the inhabitants were brought to reason. On 1 April 1842 the "king" of the Papels entered into an agreement with the British Government for the protection of shipwrecked mariners. In consideration of being allowed a fourth share of the value of any cargo, which might be salved, he undertook to use his influence to secure the humane treatment of all shipwrecked crews and to forward them and their property to the Portuguese post at Bissao or the nearest European settlement. As pledges for the performance of this engagement both he himself and each of his leading chiefs gave two of

---

[1] The correspondence, which passed between Governor MacDonnell and Earl Grey between February 1849, and March 1850, deals very fully with this incident and the subsequent punitive expedition.

their children as hostages, it being understood that these children were to be educated at the expense of the Gambia Government.[1] The "king", however, appears to have been able to exercise very little control over his people. A few months later a French vessel was wrecked off the same islands and the crew were made captive. As the French Government had previously rescued two shipwrecked British crews to the north of the Senegal, the Gambia Government now reciprocated by ransoming the crew of this vessel.[2] In 1849 a British schooner was captured by the inhabitants and the master and some of the crew were murdered. As both British and French shipping had been the victims of a number of these outrages, and as the Portuguese Government was unable or unwilling to intervene, it was resolved to send a joint expedition to teach the inhabitants a lesson. The British contingent consisted of H.M.S. *Centaur* and *Teazer* and fifty soldiers from the Bathurst garrison. The French Government sent the armed steam vessel *Rubis*. The operations were short but decisive. A party was landed at Cajecool. It met with a determined resistance, in the course of which an officer of marines was killed and one naval officer and seven naval ratings were wounded. The enemy were eventually driven back, their town was destroyed and the captured schooner was recovered.[3]

In 1852 Governor MacDonnell was transferred to St Lucia. He was succeeded in the Gambia by Lieutenant-Colonel Luke Smythe O'Connor of the First West India Regiment, who at the same time was appointed officer commanding the British troops in West Africa.

[1] T. L. Ingram to Lord Stanley, 17 February 1842; *Ordinances of the Gambia*, 1875, p. 516.

[2] T. L. Ingram to Lord Stanley, 4 June 1842.

[3] Governor MacDonnell to Earl Grey, 24 December 1849; Earl Grey to Governor MacDonnell, 11 February 1850.

XXVI: Beginning of the Soninki-Marabout War, 1850–1859

At the time of Colonel O'Connor's appointment the differences between the Soninkis and Marabouts in the territories adjacent to the British settlements were coming to a head. This was more especially the case in the Kombo. The "king" of that district and the leading families, from which the "king" was elected, were all Soninkis, but the Marabout element was rapidly gaining strength. The Soninki party mainly occupied the central portion of the district. The Marabouts were in their greatest strength at Gunjur and in the surrounding villages in the southern part of the district, where their principal leader was a young man named Fodi Kabba, who was destined to have a long and very troublesome career.[1] They were also in considerable numbers at Sabaji (Sukuta) and Brefet in the northern portion of the district, which adjoined British Kombo. They also had a number of supporters in Bathurst itself. The rights and the wrongs of the dispute between the two factions are hard to discover, but it is clear that the Marabouts wanted a share in the government, which had hitherto been denied to them by the hereditary rulers of the district. By about 1850 all the Marabout villages of the Kombo had formed a loose confederacy to contest the authority of the ruling families. There is evidence to show that the demonstrations, which began about this date, were repercussions of the pan-Islamic movement, which had caused the French much trouble in Algeria in 1847 and 1848, and that emissaries from the Mediterranean coast had arrived in the Senegal and the Gambia to preach a Jehad, or holy war, against all non-Islamic communities.

By the end of 1851 the disturbances had begun to assume serious proportions. The fighting between the two factions was of a very desultory nature and much of it was undertaken by persons who were Serahulis, Sereres and Jolas and had no interest at all in the religious differences of the two factions and were just mercenaries ready to sell their trade guns to the higher bidder. First the hirelings of one faction would raid a village belonging to the other and then

[1] Fodi Kabba's name is first recorded in a despatch from Colonel O'Connor to Sir George Grey, dated 14 June 1855.

this would be followed by a retaliatory raid. None the less it gradually became clear that Suling Jatta, the "king" of the Kombo, was losing ground. With one section of his opponents firmly established in and about Gunjur and the other section equally firmly established in and about Sabaji, he and his supporters were between two fires. The principal tie, which united the Soninki faction, was that of kinship, but it failed to create the organisation which the bond of religion had created amongst the Marabouts. The inhabitants of Sabaji and Brefet proved a particular thorn in the side of the Soninkis. They had a number of supporters in Bathurst, who often surreptitiously smuggled arms and ammunition into their villages. Though the cession of British Kombo had not been followed by any attempt to disturb the inhabitants in their lands, their customs or beliefs, it had not been entirely popular in other parts of the Kombo. The religious fanaticism of many of the Marabouts had been excited by the activities of the Wesleyan missionaries amongst the liberated African settlers in that district. Those missionaries had in actual fact confined their labours almost entirely to the new settlers, many of whom were already Christians when they arrived there. They had certainly done nothing at all to arouse religious animosity, but the mere fact that they were at work there was sufficient to feed those flames. There was a small party of level-headed men amongst the Marabout elders at Sabaji, who were certainly not out for war for war's sake, but they were outnumbered or outvoiced by the other party. Though the war party fought nominally under the cloak of religion, it is clear that Sabaji had at this date become the home of a band of lawless Adullamites, whose ideals were anarchical rather than religious.

The attitude of the Colonial Government towards the fighting was in the first place one of strict neutrality. Early in 1852 Governor MacDonnell found it necessary to issue a proclamation warning persons in British territory against supplying arms or ammunition to either of the belligerents.[1] At the same time he informed the home Government that it was evident that sooner or later the British would have to intervene in the quarrel. Though the British were under no treaty obligation to give any aid to Suling Jatta, he and his followers, whatever their other failings, had always loyally observed the terms of their treaty. Furthermore, he did represent law

[1] Sir John Palkington to MacDonnell, 5 March 1852.

and order and it was quite out of the question to recognise as the rulers of an independent district bordering upon British territory a band of malcontents, who were little better than banditti and were likely to raid British and other territory alike. The only means of restoring order therefore appeared to be to rid Suling Jatta of one set of rebellious subjects by placing them under the British flag. "All that is now required", wrote Governor MacDonnell, "is the permission of Her Majesty's Government for the Colony to avail itself of the circumstances, which the opportunity affords it—a fair chance of acquiring in its immediate neighbourhood sufficient room for the expanding needs of its population."[1]

The home Government was not prepared at that moment to give the necessary permission and Governor MacDonnell was informed that it was not disposed to interfere on behalf of either belligerent by sending an armed force into the Kombo.[2] But, as the months went on, the situation did not improve and there was an ever increasing anxiety that the trouble might spread to British Kombo. Colonel O'Connor was therefore instructed that it was desirable to put an end to the very unsatisfactory state of affairs and that, for that purpose, he should use his discretion as to approaching Suling Jatta with a proposal that he should cede part of his unmanageable territory to the British Crown on condition that the British Government allayed disturbances in other parts of his country.[3] Colonel O'Connor accordingly entered into negotiations with Suling Jatta as well as with the Marabouts. As was to be expected the proposal of cession was not received with any great liking. At length some of the members of both factions realised that the annexation might have its advantages. Suling Jatta and his followers saw that they had no chance of regaining the Sabaji district and certain of the Marabout leaders realised that under the British flag they would be free from the exactions and the oppression of the Soninkis. On 24 May 1853 Suling Jatta and a small section of the Sabaji elders signed a treaty whereby a strip of land, which included Sabaji, was added to British Kombo upon Colonel O'Connor undertaking to put an end to the disturbances in the district.[4]

[1] *Annual Report for* 1851.
[2] Sir John Palkington to Governor MacDonnell, 12 May 1852.
[3] Sir John Palkington to Governor O'Connor, 4 November 1852.
[4] *Ordinances of the Gambia*, 1875, p. 527; Hertslet, *Map of Africa*, p. 17, and *Treaties*, xii, 60.

At the time of signing this treaty it was, however, very apparent that the great majority of the inhabitants of Sabaji were opposed to it. Within twelve hours of obtaining the signatures Colonel O'Connor moved a body of troops to Jeshwang.[1] The people of Sabaji declined to be overawed and it was decided to resort to sterner measures. An armed party comprising detachments from H.M.S. *Teazer*, the three West India Regiments, the Gambia Militia, and some pensioners advanced against the town. The place was taken by storm on 1 June 1853, and the alkali and leading Marabouts were taken prisoners and lodged in Bathurst jail.[2]

Colonel O'Connor attempted without success to mediate between the Soninkis and the Marabout leader, Fodi Kabba of Gunjur, but the leaders of neither party were amenable to reason. Consequently the war drifted on. During the next two years the Marabouts gradually gathered more strength. A Moor named Haji Ismail was travelling through West Africa preaching a Jehad, or holy war. He does not appear to have visited the Gambia, but he had his agents there, amongst whom were some native traders in Bathurst itself. Another of these agents was a Moor named Omar, who had been concerned in Abd-el-Kader's rising against the French in Algeria in 1847. This man took up his abode at Sabaji. He had had some military training and showed some powers of organisation. Though his activities did not come to the knowledge of the British authorities until later, during the early part of 1855 he was busily engaged in organising a concerted attack by all the Marabouts of the Kombo on the British settlements. With some astuteness he deliberately delayed launching the campaign until the wet weather had set in, when the British would not only have greater difficulty in moving their artillery but also their shells and their rockets would not be likely to ignite the thatched roofs in Mandingo villages. He also spread abroad the very common canard of the unscrupulous African sedition monger that he had the power to turn the white man's bullets into water.[3]

On 24 June 1855 the Marabouts of Gunjur attacked Busumballa, the town of the "king" of Kombo. The attack was driven off, but Suling Jatta was shot through the heart. This does not appear to

---

[1] Minutes of the Executive Council, 25 May 1855; Colonel O'Connor to H. Labouchere, 4 June 1856.

[2] Ellis, *History of the First West India Regiment*, pp. 228–232.

[3] Colonel O'Connor to Sir William Molesworth, 15 and 26 October 1855.

have formed part of Omar's plan of campaign, but it is evidence that many of his followers were spoiling for the fight. Possibly the spark, which actually fired the train, was not due to Omar but it was treated by the Marabouts as the signal for which they had been eagerly waiting.

Early in July 1855 Fodi Osmanu, a native of Sabaji, proceeded to Jeshwang in British Kombo and forcibly carried off a woman, whose husband he already held in captivity at Sabaji. A warrant was issued at Bathurst for his arrest. As it was realised that there might be trouble in executing the warrant, the Queen's Advocate accompanied the constables together with two officers and a sergeant's party from the Second and Third West India Regiments. This party proceeded to Sabaji on 16 July, entered the town and arrested the offender. They were almost immediately attacked by a large party armed with guns. During the course of the struggle the prisoner was rescued and the Queen's Advocate and both the officers were wounded. The detachment then retreated to Jeshwang followed by the people of Sabaji. They took refuge at Jeshwang in the house of James Finden, the Colonial Engineer, who was also the officer commanding the Gambia Militia. Oyster Creek lay between Jeshwang and the Island of St Mary. It was clear that with three wounded officers on their hands the detachment would be cut off before they could reach the creek. Finden therefore advised them to make for Cape House near Bakau, whilst he and his wife made a dash for the creek to raise the alarm. Two of the soldiers remained in Finden's house to cover the retreat of both parties and were eventually captured by the enemy. Mr and Mrs Finden got safely across the creek and carried the news to Bathurst. The detachment made its way to Cape St Mary. They had a running fight for a mile and a half, but managed to get their wounded officers as far as Bakau Konko. There a former sergeant of the regiment named Sankey and a handful of pensioners hastily left their farms, ran for their guns and kept the pursuers in check. Their prompt action covered the detachment's retreat to Cape St Mary, where they arrived with their three wounded officers. Sergeant Sankey's stand was sufficient to put a stop to any further advance of the Sabaji people, who turned aside to Kotu to plunder and burn the property of Mrs Edward Hughes, the widow of one of the first merchant settlers in Bathurst. Fortunately she was not on the spot at the time.

On receipt of the news Colonel O'Connor mustered every available man and set out for the Kombo. On arrival at Oyster Creek Finden's house and the village of Jeshwang were seen to be in flames. Colonel O'Connor therefore marched straight for the Cape, where he was very much relieved to find the three wounded officers. The same evening Sergeant Sankey and twenty-five other pensioners marched in fully armed with their wives and families from Bakau Konko. They had left their village behind them in flames. Before another twenty-four hours were out, eight of this little band—all of them men over fifty and true veterans in the proper sense of that word—were to fall in the field.

Colonel O'Connor now had a force of 260 men at his disposal. It comprised men from the West India Regiments and the Bathurst Militia as well as a few pensioners. The next day he set out from Cape St Mary to attack Sabaji. A thick belt of forest lay between the two places. All the recognised military precautions were taken for traversing this ground, but a heavy fire was opened as soon as the advance guard reached the wood. It soon became very apparent that the people of Sabaji were ready for them and had been reinforced by people from other villages. It was equally clear that they were being led by somebody with a military training. Some of the enemy were seen to emerge from the wood and to make a movement as if to outflank the British troops. It was clear that the small force was outnumbered and in danger of being surrounded. Colonel O'Connor therefore gave the order to retire on Cape St Mary. Some of the militia broke, but the rest of the troops fought a stubborn rearguard action. Most of the fighting was hand to hand. Colonel O'Connor himself was twice wounded and was at one time completely surrounded by the enemy. He was saved by his interpreter, Daniel Sleight, who managed to force a way out for both of them. Eventually the column reached Cape St Mary. They had lost twenty-three killed and fifty-three wounded, or more than one-quarter of their number.

When news of this setback reached Bathurst, it caused the utmost consternation. Colonel O'Connor's force was virtually beleaguered at the Cape. The enemy held the ground between it and Bathurst. The only means of communication between the two places was by boat. Bathurst itself was practically denuded of soldiers. If the enemy had chosen to cross Oyster Creek, the town was more or less at their mercy. Dr Daniel Robertson, the Colonial Secretary, hastily armed a number of Government servants, merchants and other reliable inhabitants and at the same time sent urgent messages for help to Sierra Leone and Goree.

Fortunately the enemy failed to follow up their advantage and during the next few days very gratifying proof was given of the loyalty of the surrounding natives. Demba Sonko, the "king" of Barra, sent a message to say that he would send as many men as the British Government wanted. The new "king" of the Kombo and the chiefs of Busumballa and Brikama all sent like offers of assistance. A Serere chief, named Cherno, made his way to the Cape with eighty of his followers and placed them entirely at Colonel O'Connor's disposal.

When Colonel O'Connor had sufficiently recovered from his wounds, he made his way by boat to Bathurst to arrange for co-operation between the improvised civilian defence force and his own troops. On 26 July the defence force and Cherno's band of Sereres set out to clear the enemy out of the bush country between Oyster Creek and Cape St Mary. On this and the two following days there were several sharp skirmishes, in which the Sereres lost a number of men, but the enemy were ultimately driven back. On 27 July, whilst the issue of this fighting was still in the balance, Colonel O'Connor returned to Cape St Mary. He was accompanied by Sister Sophia and Sister Agnes of the Roman Catholic Mission, who had volunteered to minister to Captain Joseph Degrigny, an African officer of the Bathurst Militia, who was lying mortally wounded at Cape House. They stayed with the wounded man and rendered him every aid in their power until he passed away early the following morning, when they returned to Bathurst.

On 30 July the much needed reinforcements arrived at Bathurst. As in 1831, the French Commandant at Goree responded readily to the appeal for aid. He at once collected every man, whom he could spare, and despatched them to the Gambia on board the man-of-war *Entreprenant*. A day or two after their departure from Goree the steam sloop *Lavoisier* arrived from France with reinforcements for the garrison. Without landing the men, the Commandant sent the boat straight on to Bathurst. These two contingents amounted in all to 130 men and included in their number some soldiers, who had only recently returned from the Crimean War. This welcome addition to the forces marched as soon as possible for Cape St Mary.

On 4 August the combined Anglo-French force marched on Sabaji. The forest belt proved once more to be full of the enemy, but a passage was forced after some hand to hand fighting. When the

column debouched from the forest in front of Sabaji, they found that
the town, which had had no defence at all on 15 July, was strongly
stockaded and that the enemy had received further reinforcements.
Again there was clear proof that the defence had been organised by
someone with a knowledge of military strategy. An attempt was
made to outflank the attackers as they emerged from the forest, but
it was repulsed by the French and the men of the West India Regiments at the point of the bayonet. The few light field pieces which
were available then opened a bombardment upon the town. After
ninety minutes of this bombardment very little damage had been
done. Colonel O'Connor therefore gave the order for the town to be
stormed. The troops had no scaling ladders and the stockade was
still more or less intact. The men of the West India Regiments in
the centre and the French on either flank rushed to the stockade and
after a few minutes of desperate struggle under a very heavy fire
managed to pull it down with their hands. French and British
troops alike then poured through the gaps and carried the town at
the point of the bayonet.[1]

After the destruction of their town the people of Sabaji were forbidden to rebuild on the former site.[2] This prohibition was kept in
force for some years and a ring fence was put round the place to
prevent desecration of the ancestral tombs of the Marabouts.[3] The
majority of the inhabitants of Sabaji thereafter removed to Gunjur,
where they reinforced Fodi Kabba. Omar, the organiser of the rising,
managed to make his escape at the time of the assault and to flee
from the Gambia. Haji Ismail, who had been responsible for the
preaching of the Jehad throughout West Africa, was caught by the
French in the Casamance and was deported to Cayenne. A rising,
which he had instigated in the Senegal, was suppressed by the
French shortly after that of Sabaji.[4] As a result the Marabouts of

[1] *Annual Register for* 1855, pp. 119, 120; Ellis, *op. cit.* pp. 248–256, describes
the part played in the operations by the West India Regiments and the French
troops. Colonel O'Connor's despatches for the period 1855–1858 give details of
the part played by the irregular troops and civilians. They also correct one or
two minor errors in Ellis' account. One other particular should also be added.
The garrison chaplain, Rev. J. H. Monsarrat, and Father Blanchet of the Roman
Catholic Mission assisted the medical officers in attending to the wounded under
a heavy fire.   [2] D. Robertson to H. Labouchere, 9 June 1856.
[3] Colonel D'Arcy to Duke of Newcastle, 21 May 1860.
[4] Colonel O'Connor to Sir William Molesworth, 15 and 26 October 1855;
Colonel D'Arcy to Duke of Newcastle, 25 December 1863.

Gunjur could no longer depend upon outside aid in their war with the Soninkis. But the war, if it may be so called, lingered on for the best part of another year. Colonel O'Connor had at one time contemplated an attack upon Gunjur on the ground that they had assisted the Sabaji rebels, but had decided that he lacked the necessary forces for the purpose.[1] The two factions were therefore left to fight the matter out between themselves. All that the Colonial Government did was to endeavour to enforce the embargo upon the supply of arms and ammunition to either belligerent. Dissensions amongst themselves considerably weakened the Soninkis. Suling Jatta's successor died very suddenly. Rumour had it that he had been poisoned. Disputes then arose between the ruling families of Busumballa and Yundum in regard to his successor. The matter eventually went in favour of Yundum, but the interregnum gave the Marabouts a fresh lease of life.[2]

The so-called war looked as if it was going to be interminable, but at length the Marabouts realised that despite a few transient successes they had very nearly shot their last bolt. The embargo upon arms and ammunition had told more heavily upon them than upon the Soninkis. The constant interruption to agriculture and the complete interruption to trade had reduced them to poverty. They therefore sent emissaries to Demba Sonko of Barra to request his mediation with the British Government. Colonel O'Connor invited the leading Marabout chiefs to Bathurst to discuss the terms upon which he was prepared on their behalf to arrange a peace with the Soninkis. On 17 April 1856 the chiefs signed a convention whereby they mutually promised to use their best endeavours to maintain peace and to the best of their ability to compel all Marabout villages to observe the terms of the convention. The Soninki chiefs were then invited to Bathurst and nine days later signed a convention in the like terms.[3]

Although circumstances made it necessary for him to make an armed intervention in the quarrel between the Soninkis and the

---

[1] Colonel O'Connor to Lord John Russell, 21 May 1855. Demba Sonko of Barra offered to attack Gunjur, but the offer was declined; Colonel O'Connor to H. Labouchere, 22 December 1855.

[2] Colonel O'Connor to H. Labouchere, 5 February 1856.

[3] *Ordinances of the Gambia*, 1875, pp. 528, 529; Hertslet, *Treaties*, XII, 66, 67; Colonel O'Connor to H. Labouchere, 15 and 17 April 1856; D. Robertson to H. Labouchere, 9 June 1856.

Marabouts, Colonel O'Connor's governorship was marked by substantial progress in other respects. Despite the heavy military expenditure, which was incurred in the Sabaji campaigns, he was able to make a number of improvements in Bathurst itself. A number of useful and much needed public buildings were erected. Many of them are still in use to this day. They included a barrack for the troops (now used as residential quarters), a civil hospital and a public market.

Colonel O'Connor also made regular tours of the upper river, which helped materially to develop British influence. He was able to arrive at satisfactory understandings with the chiefs of Jarra, Nyani, Kataba, and Wuli for the protection of the lives and property of British subjects and for an increased reciprocity of commercial interests.[1] On more than one occasion warring chiefs accepted him as arbitrator in what would otherwise have been interminable disputes, which could only result in frequent bloodshed and constant interruption of trade. In 1853 and 1857, for instance, he successfully arranged treaties of peace between Demba Sonko, "king" of Barra, and two of his rebellious underchiefs.[2]

Colonel O'Connor was also able during the course of these voyages to settle a number of disputes between the agents of Bathurst merchants and local chiefs. Amongst other things, he was able to check a number of abuses, which had hitherto been perpetrated by African traders and which had caused the British administration to acquire a bad name.[3] He managed to place some check upon the slave trade, which was still being carried on in the higher parts of the river, and on several occasions was able to procure the liberation of a number of British subjects, who had been enslaved by the local inhabitants, and also of a number of local inhabitants, who had been acquired as slaves by African traders from Bathurst.[4]

Taken altogether Colonel O'Connor's voyages marked a very great step forward in the promotion of good relations with the chiefs and in the extension of British influence in the upper river. Evidence of this was forthcoming in the critical stage of the Sabaji rising of 1855, when chiefs living outside British territory volunteered their as-

---

[1] *Annual Report for* 1854.

[2] *Annual Report for* 1857; Hertslet, *Treaties*, xii, 62; *State Papers*, l, 628, 827.

[3] Colonel O'Connor to Sir George Murray, 21 November 1855; Colonel O'Connor to H. Labouchere, 4 March 1856.   [4] *Ibid.*

sistance. Those offers were a genuine proof of attachment to a government, which had come to be recognised as a fair and impartial arbiter in all their quarrels and an apostle of peace and order. If any further demonstration of this fact were needed, it was given in 1859 when Colonel O'Connor took his final departure from the Colony. A deputation of chiefs from the Kombo waited upon him to bid him farewell. That deputation included Soninki and Marabout chiefs alike, who despite their past wars and their still latent animosities had come to recognise the fact that the representative of the British Crown stood for impartial justice in all matters affecting their interests.[1]

[1] Sir E. B. Lytton to Colonel O'Connor, 11 May 1859.

XXVII: The French in the River Gambia, 1817–1857

Various references have been made in preceding chapters to the relations which existed between the French Government in the Senegal and the British Government in the Gambia, but so far little has been said of French activities in the River Gambia during the period in which they had an actual foothold on its banks. The French settlement of Albreda existed side by side with its neighbour of Bathurst for forty years. Though from time to time its affairs impinged upon the history of the British settlement, it had for the most part an entirely independent existence, which requires a chapter to itself.

In 1814 the Treaty of Paris gave the French the right to resettle at Albreda and the British the right to trade for gum at Portendic. As previous chapters have shown, both these rights had come into being somewhat fortuitously and the enjoyment of each had been somewhat intermittent and precarious. The result of the terms of the treaty consequently was that each nation became very tenacious of a right, which conferred little advantage on the possessor as compared with the friction engendered by insistence on the exercise thereof.

In May 1817 the Governor of Senegal despatched the brig *Argus* to the Gambia. The lieutenant in command called at Bathurst to notify the Commandant as to his instructions and then proceeded to Albreda. On arrival he renewed the ancient treaties between France and the "king" of Barra and installed Monsieur du Bonnay as Resident. This proceeding was contemptuously referred to by two Bathurst merchants as "sending a man with a pole and a white flag to hoist it on a small negro village". The British Commandant at once sent to inform the Resident that, following the precedents created by Governor O'Hara in 1775 and 1776, he would not be allowed to trade above James Island. For several years the "residency" at Albreda was a grass hut[1] and the Resident was the only European inhabitant of the enclave. By 1821 he had been joined by

---

[1] Captain Grant to Sir C. MacCarthy, 21 August 1822.

another French merchant and by 1826 the number had increased to three or four.[1]

Very soon after the reoccupation of Albreda it became apparent that the Resident was indulging in a furtive traffic in slaves and that, despite his treaty with Captain Grant, the "king" of Barra was conniving in it.[2] The mode of acquisition was by kidnapping and the operations very frequently took place on the opposite bank of the river in the Foni country. The captives were secretly conveyed across the river to Albreda. In order to evade the vigilance of the British at the river's mouth, they were then marched overland to some point on the Atlantic coast, whence they were either shipped for the West Indies or else conveyed to Goree.[3]

In 1818 this traffic very nearly brought about a serious rupture between the two governments. The Commandant at Bathurst seized a French cutter, which had been found in the river equipped for the purpose of carrying slaves. He placed an officer and crew on board with instructions to take the vessel to Sierra Leone for legal condemnation. A French ship intercepted the cutter near the mouth of the river and carried the crew and vessel to St Louis. The officer was allowed to return to Bathurst, but the cutter was retained.[4] Apparently the British authorities felt some doubt as to the legality of the original seizure and no further action was taken in regard to the recapture. In 1824 another French slaver from Guadeloupe actually came across the bar of the river to try to pick up a cargo.[5]

Another method of slave trading took the form of purchasing able-bodied men as recruits for the French colonial army. In 1822 the Resident at Albreda was instructed to ransom slaves for this purpose and to give to each of them a proper paper of enfranchisement conditional upon his serving fourteen years in the French army. He

[1] "La reprise des établissements de la Sénégambie en 1816–1821", R.H.C. (1913), pp. 546–550; Marty, "Le Comptoir Français d'Albreda en Gambie (1817–1826)", R.H.C. (1924), pp. 237–242; Sir C. MacCarthy to Earl Bathurst, 3 January 1818; R. W. Hay to Lord Howard de Walden, 21 September 1826; Messrs Hook and Dodds to Earl Bathurst, 8 August 1817; Kenneth Macaulay to Earl Bathurst, 16 June 1826.

[2] Annual Register for 1821, p. 559; Sir C. MacCarthy to Earl Bathurst, 24 September 1822; Memorial of Bathurst merchants, 10 August 1822; W. Forster to Earl Bathurst, 7 December 1817.

[3] Major Grant to Sir C. MacCarthy, 21 August 1822.

[4] Exposé des faits relatifs à la traite des nègres dans le voisinage du Sénégal, pp. 20–28.

[5] Lt.-Gov. Rendall to D. M. Hamilton, 1 December 1824.

was to avoid offending British susceptibilities and therefore "to act with the utmost discretion". The men were not all to be redeemed at one time, "so as to avoid the difficulties, which are caused to us without any reason by the English, as well as to our own station, and so that there may be no fear that the men, being taken from the same country and the same society, so to speak, will desert en masse".[1] This mode of recruiting for the French army was carried on for a good many years. In 1840 a French vessel, which had been chartered to deliver one hundred slaves as recruits for the French colonial army, was seized by the British authorities in the Gambia, taken to Sierra Leone and there condemned for slave trading.[2]

The French settlement at Albreda caused further trouble to the British authorities by reason of its use as a smuggling depot. The Resident managed to evade the restriction, which limited his right of passage to the river below James Island, by sending contraband goods up the river in native canoes.[3] The sergeant's guard at James Island proved unable to check this practice. In fact in 1824, when the soldiers took their boat from the island to Albreda to obtain water, the French Resident threatened to arrest them for espionage.[4] The smuggling was carried on on such an extensive scale that in that same year import duties at Bathurst fell from £4000 to £2000. The British Commandant at Bathurst thereupon wrote to the French Commandant at Goree to inform him that he would not allow French vessels to proceed up the river to Albreda, unless they paid import duties at Bathurst. As, however, it appeared that the possession of Albreda impliedly gave the French the right of free entry into the river, it was held that such a step would be a violation of their treaty rights and the British Commandant's letter was repudiated by Earl Bathurst.[5]

Smuggling still went on and a very considerable amount of revenue was lost every year by the British Government. The French Government showed no disposition to help, when it was approached on the subject. They contended that French vessels had a right of

---

[1] Faure, "La garnison européenne du Sénégal et le recrutement des premières troupes noires (1779–1858)," *R.H.C.* (1920), p. 34.

[2] *State Papers*, 1840–1841, pp. 242–245, 524–538 and 1841–1842, pp. 1017, 1039; Huntley, *Seven Years' Service on the Slave Coast of Western Africa*, II, 206.

[3] Marty, *op. cit.* pp. 269–271; *State Papers*, 1825–1826, p. 32; Sir C. Turner to Captain Findlay, 2 June 1825.

[4] Captain Findlay to Captain Hugan, 2 June 1824.

[5] Earl Bathurst to Maj.-Gen. Turner, 18 January 1825.

free undisturbed passage up to Albreda and declared that any attempt to interfere with that right would be regarded as an act of
hostility.[1] The Governor of Sierra Leone therefore instructed the
Commandant at Bathurst to insist that the master of any vessel,
which entered the river flying French colours, should show his papers
to the customs officers at Bathurst and to refuse entry to any ship,
which was not proved to be a *bona fide* French ship properly cleared
for Albreda.[2] This procedure was subsequently carried out—not,
however, without innumerable protests from the French, which from
time to time during the next thirty years formed the subject of a
fairly voluminous diplomatic correspondence between the two
governments in Europe.

The want of a disposition to assist in the suppression of smuggling
was not confined solely to the French authorities. A number of
Bathurst merchants took full advantage of the loophole, which was
held out at Albreda for the evasion of payment of import duties.
After the signing of the Ceded Mile Treaty in 1826 a number of
British merchants took up plots of ground within a mile of Albreda
at Juffure. About 1845 they began to obtain other plots immediately
abutting upon the French enclosure at Albreda.[3] The opportunities,
which were thus obtained for smuggling by the less scrupulous
British subjects, were obviously unlimited. In 1848 Governor
MacDonnell made an attempt to check them by stationing a colonial
vessel off Albreda. A few seizures were made of canoes, which were
hired by or else were the property of French subjects, but, as the
Governor had to confess, "in a short time, however, in consequence
of various disguises easily assumed the real ownership of the canoes
became a matter more difficult to decide, and the right to stop a native
canoe laden with native produce merely because it was bound to
French Albreda was a most questionable point and I never raised
it".[4] All that he was able to do was to put a stop to encroachments
by French subjects on territory lying outside the limits of the en-

[1] Maj.-Gen. Turner to Earl Bathurst, 3 July 1825.
[2] Maj.-Gen. Turner to Captain Findlay, 3 June 1825.
[3] Governor MacDonnell to Earl Grey, 14 January 1850. On 1 October 1845
Demba Sonko, "king" of Barra, granted to Thomas Brown, merchant of Bathurst, a plot of ground at Albreda, which adjoined the French comptoir. The
description of the boundaries of the land shows that Richard Lloyd, another
Bathurst merchant, had already acquired another plot in this locality. I am
indebted to M. Abel Rives, Belgian Consul at Bathurst, for the opportunity
to peruse this grant.   [4] Governor MacDonnell to Earl Grey, 11 May 1850.

clave.[1] In 1854 Governor O'Connor made a further attempt to suppress smuggling by stationing a small revenue vessel off Albreda. The net result was, in his own words, that the cutter "made a few paltry seizures, fomented the hostile feelings between the English and French traders, sharpened the wits of the smugglers, nearly embroiled us with the 'king' of Barra and other chiefs, increased considerably the colonial expenditure, and eventually captain, crew and cruiser became so utterly useless that all were about to be withdrawn".[2]

Albreda was responsible for yet another cause of friction between the two governments. This was occasioned by the periodical visits of French men-of-war to Albreda. The right of such vessels to visit Albreda was never denied, but for some reason French commanders displayed a strong antipathy to saluting the British flag as they passed Bathurst. The correspondence regarding this omission of an international courtesy was exceedingly acrimonious at times. When in 1821 two French men-of-war passed Bathurst without saluting the British flag, the British Commandant informed the senior French naval officer that he intended to exercise his right to stop and examine all foreign vessels, which entered the river, and that "any person hereafter violating this right must do so at his peril".[3] When this correspondence reached Sierra Leone, the Commandant received a rebuke for deviating so far from his instructions as to threaten coercive measures,[4] but the matter was brought to the notice of the Governor of Senegal with the suggestion that the omission had possibly been due to want of information and the request that French naval officers might be instructed to comply with the rule of international courtesy in the future.[5]

For reasons best known to themselves a number of French naval commanders felt it to be their duty to show that the French had equal rights with the British over the navigable waters of the Gambia. In 1826 one of them went so far in the assertion of this alleged right as to stop and search a number of small craft from

[1] *Ordinances of the Gambia*, 1875, p. 522; Hertslet, *Map of Africa*, p. 13 and *Treaties*, XII, 44; Earl Grey to T. L. Ingram, 31 July 1847; Earl Grey to Governor MacDonnell, 8 September 1848, 11 November 1850 and 12 August 1851; Governor MacDonnell to Earl Grey, 21 March and 3 May 1850.

[2] *Annual Report for* 1857.

[3] Captain J. R. Stepney to Captain Villeneau, 21 and 22 January 1821.

[4] Captain Grant to Captain Stepney, 2 March 1821.

[5] Captain Grant to Governor Le Coupe, 3 March 1821.

Bathurst off Albreda.[1] In 1841 two French men-of-war not only sailed past Bathurst without saluting the British flag, but also stopped a vessel off Albreda and forcibly removed two Africans, who had long been resident in Bathurst, on the pretext that they were absconding slaves from Goree. It was only after diplomatic representations had been made in Europe that the two men were released.[2] Quite a considerable portion of the early correspondence of British administrators at Bathurst was taken up with reports of breaches of international etiquette upon the part of French naval officers and some of that correspondence found its way into white papers.[3] One of the last culprits was no less a person than the Prince de Joinville, the third son of Louis Philippe, who passed Bathurst in 1842 without saluting the British flag. Subsequently an official rebuke was administered by the French Government to the Prince, who made some slight amends by accepting an invitation to dinner at Government House, Bathurst, of which he subsequently gave a very amusing account.[4]

In the early days after the Napoleonic wars the very determined efforts of the French to rebuild their colonial empire were viewed with considerable suspicion and anxiety by the British Government. There was a great fear that they might try to extend their foothold in the Gambia beyond the limits of Albreda and so strangle the British settlement. For this reason their activities in the river twice engaged the very serious attention of several Secretaries of State. In 1821 the foreign minister, Lord Londonderry, caused a draft letter to be drawn up instructing the British Ambassador at Paris to make a formal demand that the French should evacuate Albreda. Earl Bathurst, however, counselled greater moderation and suggested that a draft should be substituted "giving them the option, either to state on what they ground their right to Albreda in contravention of the stipulations of the treaty of 1782,[5] or to be prepared for our considering their silence as an admission of our right". Lord Londonderry's letter was therefore not sent. Neither was any other

---

[1] Marty, op. cit. p. 206; Captain Findlay to Kenneth Macaulay, 29 March 1826.

[2] T. L. Ingram to Captain Denman, 13 July 1841; State Papers, 1841–1842, pp. 1040–1042.   [3] State Papers, 1843–1844, p. 370.

[4] De Joinville, Vieux souvenirs, p. 241; Ingram, "Abridged account of an expedition...up the River Gambia", J.R.G.S. xvii, 150; Lord Stanley to Governor Seagram, 14 February and 10 April 1843.

[5] The correct date was 1783.

letter sent along the lines suggested by Earl Bathurst. The question cropped up again in 1825, when Canning, then foreign minister, declared that "it is clearly a question not of one department or the other, but for the cabinet to weigh and decide". Earl Bathurst again counselled moderation, saying "I must take the blame, if blame there be, of having been instrumental in preventing the sending of the note" of 1821. He pointed out that the wording of the two treaties of 1783 and 1814, coupled with the indisputable fact that the French had occupied Albreda between those two dates, weakened any right of the British Government to insist on the evacuation of Albreda. The matter therefore never came before the Cabinet and at the time no further steps were taken to induce the French to renounce their claims to Albreda.[1]

As events turned out, the fears of Londonderry and Canning proved groundless. In 1826 the Governor of Senegal visited the River Gambia. He came armed with a treaty already drawn up for the signature of the "king" of Barra. That treaty would have extended the boundaries of the enclave at Albreda, but Burungai Sonko refused to sign it. Shortly afterwards Kenneth Macaulay induced the "king" to sign the Ceded Mile Treaty. The result was that Albreda became hemmed in on every side by British territory and there could be no possibility of further French expansion on the north bank of the river.[2]

After the signing of the Ceded Mile Treaty the retention of Albreda gave the French no real advantage, commercial or political. The area of the enclave was under eighty acres. There was therefore no possibility of building up a large commercial settlement and the expense of maintaining a Resident and a residency exceeded any revenue which came into the settlement. More than one of the Residents fell out with the local inhabitants. In 1823 a quarrel with Burungai Sonko of Barra compelled the Resident to take refuge in Bathurst and Albreda had to be closed down until somebody, who was more of a *persona grata*, could be found to take his place.[3] In 1831 the station had to be evacuated because of the Barra war. In 1841 another Resident killed a Mandingo in the course of a quarrel. According to native customary law the homicide, whether justi-

---

[1] *Hist. MSS. Comm. Rep., Bathurst MSS.* pp. 593–595.
[2] Kenneth Macaulay to Earl Bathurst, 28 June 1826; Governor MacDonnell to Earl Grey, 3 May 1850.
[3] Marty, *op. cit.* p. 255; Sir C. MacCarthy to Earl Bathurst, 11 August 1823.

fiable or not, rendered both himself and his property liable to seizure by the "king" of Barra. It was only the intervention of the acting Governor at Bathurst and the fortunate coincidence that the "king" was at the time distracted by a war with Baddibu that prevented the seizure of Albreda by the natives.[1] In 1856 the settlement was exposed to considerable danger on account of a war between the "king" of Barra and a Serahuli underchief, named Ansumana Jagga, and an appeal was sent to Goree for protection. Acting Governor Robertson thereupon explained that he could not allow French troops to be landed at Albreda, but sent a warning to the belligerents that any attack upon Albreda would be regarded by the British Government as a hostile act. Fortunately the warning had the desired effect.[2]

French and English visitors alike painted a most disparaging picture of Albreda. When Governor Seagram visited the place in 1843, he declared that "a more paltry or miserable settlement does not bear the flag of any European power".[3] The Prince de Joinville, who had visited the place the previous year, was of much the same opinion. He described it as a "not very important factory", which was fever ridden and occupied by four white men with a crowd of attendant senhoras and slaves.[4] Acting Governor Ingram, who visited Albreda at the same time as the Prince, described the official residence "as a wretched looking dilapidated building, and so entirely surrounded by trees, jungle, rank weeds and high grass, that it could not but be unhealthy did not its low and swampy position make it so".[5]

If France had an insignificant outpost in the Gambia, from which she derived no material benefit and which merely served to cause friction with another power, Great Britain was in a like position farther up the coast. Her first participation in the gum trade, which was reserved to her by the Treaty of Paris, had been in 1722. That participation had always been very intermittent and rarely very profitable, but it was believed to be a market with very great potentialities. Both in 1783 and 1814 the British Government had

[1] T. L. Ingram to Major Perry, 9 November 1841; Ingram to M. Chenu, 29 November 1841; Ingram to Lord Stanley, 30 November 1841.

[2] D. Robertson to H. Labouchere, 21 December 1856 and 12 January 1857; Labouchere to Robertson, 8 February 1857.

[3] Governor Seagram to Lord Stanley, 17 May 1843.

[4] De Joinville, *op. cit.* p. 241.   [5] Ingram, *op. cit.* p. 150.

been prepared to relinquish Goree to the French in the firm hope that those potentialities would be realised and one of the reasons, which induced Earl Bathurst to consent to the reoccupation of the Gambia, was that he believed the new settlement would be a base for operations in a highly profitable trade at Portendic. But neither treaty conferred upon Great Britain any territorial right at Portendic. All that was preserved thereby was the right to trade. French legalists seized upon the wording of the two treaties to maintain that the right to trade did not impliedly carry with it the right to erect even temporary buildings on shore for the purpose of carrying on that trade. They asserted that it merely conferred the right to remain in an open roadstead for the purposes of receiving cargoes of gum. They further claimed that the right of the British to trade did not debar the French from competing in the same market or from making treaties with the local natives, which gave the French the monopoly of that trade. Treaties were in actual fact made with the Trarza Moors in 1785 and 1837, which gave the French this monopoly.[1] Realising, however, that from their point of view competition was preferable to a monopoly, the Trarzas honoured their treaty obligations more in the breach than in the observance.

The trade was a seasonal one, all business being done between the months of January and August. The Trarzas had always proved somewhat close in their dealings and had expected a large present before they condescended to do any business at all. During the British occupation of Senegal this initial present had been supplied by the British Government. After the reoccupation of the Gambia Bathurst merchants had talked of sending ships to Portendic, but the voyages never took place owing to the question of these presents.[2] In 1819 a representative of the chiefs of the Trarzas visited Bathurst and Sir Charles MacCarthy agreed that the Gambia Government should renew the annual payments.[3] A speculative voyage was made from Bathurst in 1820. It proved so far successful, that Bathurst merchants sent ships every year to Portendic up to

---

[1] Treaty between the Comte de Repentigny and the chiefs of Amanlow, 2 May 1785; Treaty between the Comte and Moktar, king of Braknass, 10 May 1785; Treaty between the Comte and Kouri, king of the Trarzas, 16 May 1785; Lt.-Gov. Rendall to Commander Norcott, 25 April 1837.

[2] William Forster to Earl Bathurst, 7 December 1817.

[3] Lt.-Gov. Rendall to T. Spring Rice, 27 October 1834.

the end of 1830.[1] The French had made a treaty with the Trarzas in 1821[2] and thereafter attempted in a number of devious ways to obstruct the British traders. The result was that in 1823 and subsequent years it was deemed advisable to send a man-of-war to Portendic to protect British interests.[3] In 1824 it was estimated that £12,000 worth of gum was obtained from Portendic.[4] In view of this fact the British Government not unreasonably decided that it could be left to the merchants to make the annual present.[5]

In 1830 the gum trade came to an end for the time being, apparently owing to a dispute with the Trarzas in regard to the annual present and to indirect obstruction on the part of the French. At the end of 1834 the Trarzas fell out with the French. The occasion was thought to be opportune for recapturing the gum trade. On 25 January 1835 the French declared a blockade of this portion of the coast. On 4 February a ship from Bathurst arrived off Portendic. Ten days later two French men-of-war appeared. They sent an armed party on board the British ship, took her out to sea and there left her with orders not to return to Portendic. Later another Bathurst ship, the *Governor Temple*, arrived off Portendic. She was seized and taken to Senegal for trading with the enemy. Some time previously a schooner from England had visited Portendic and had supplied the Trarzas with arms and ammunition. The Bathurst merchants denied any like intention, but, remembering the assistance, which the French had rendered at Bathurst three years previously, French resentment at the attitude of the British towards their own troubles with the natives was very intelligible.[6] The upshot of this proceeding was that Thomas Joiner, the owner of the *Governor Temple*, put in a claim for compensation amounting to no less than £88,900. 9s. 10d. The matter was taken up in Europe and dragged on for ten years. The case was first of all referred to joint British and French commissioners, who after two years' deliberation were unable to arrive at an agreement. In 1842 the King of Prussia

[1] Gray, *Travels in Western Africa*, p. 365; Lt.-Gov. Rendall to Governor of Senegal, 17 July 1834.

[2] Hertslet, *Map of Africa*, p. 634.

[3] W. Forster to M. Forster, 2 February 1823; Earl Bathurst to Sir Charles MacCarthy, 18 January 1823.

[4] *Annual Register for* 1826, p. 32.

[5] Earl Bathurst to Maj.-Gen. Turner, 19 October 1825.

[6] Alexander, *Narrative of a Voyage of observation amongst the Colonies of Western Africa*, p. 71.

was appointed as arbitrator and in 1844 an award was filed assessing the damages at £1657. 11s. 6d.[1]

The French had in the meantime agreed to withdraw their declaration of a blockade on condition that they were allowed to exercise their belligerent right of searching neutral vessels.[2] In 1836 Lieutenant-Governor Rendall proceeded personally to Portendic and concluded a treaty with the chief of the Trarzas, whereby the Gambia Government undertook to pay the annual presents and the chief of the Trarzas agreed to allow the British a site between the St John's River and the River Senegal for erecting stores for the purposes of the trade.[3] But when a British vessel arrived in the same year off Portendic, it was followed by a French man-of-war, which opened fire on the Trarzas and put an end to trade for that season.[4] In 1837 the French obtained a treaty from the Trarzas, which purported to give them the monopoly of the gum trade.[5] Thereafter no attempt was made to revive the trade until 1842.[6] It was then carried on very fitfully until 1847, when Earl Grey instructed Governor Fitzgerald to stop the annual presents to the Trarzas.[7] After that there was little or no communication between Bathurst and Portendic.[8]

At a very early date it became obvious to more than one person —French and English alike—that the enjoyment by each nation of their respective rights at Albreda and Portendic did not compensate for the annoyance caused by the disputes, which arose over the exercise of those rights. A proposal for mutual renunciation was mooted as early as 1821,[9] but it was a very long time before the general consensus of public opinion in both countries veered round to this very obvious solution of the whole trouble. Bathurst merchants and others clung tenaciously to golden dreams of a thriving gum trade and French sentiment disliked the idea of surrendering

---

[1] *State Papers*, 1834–1835, pp. 543–588; 1838–1839, pp. 122 *seq.*; 1841–1842, pp. 581–649; 1845–1846, pp. 1064, 1102.

[2] Treaty of 4 July 1836.

[3] Lt.-Gov. Rendall to Lord Glenelg, 9 July 1836.

[4] Lt.-Gov. Rendall to Lord Stanley, 9 July 1836.

[5] Lt.-Gov. Rendall to Commander Norcott, 25 April 1837.

[6] T. L. Ingram to Lt.-Com. Lapidge, 28 February 1842.

[7] 20 February 1847.

[8] Colonel O'Connor to Sir George Grey, 1 June 1855.

[9] "Tentatives commerciales anglaises à Portendick et en Mauritanie (1800–1826)", *R.H.C.* (1922), I, 34.

an inch of French ground. At length even the diehards had to submit to what was obvious. On 7 March 1857 a convention, which was subsequently ratified by an Act of Parliament,[1] was signed by the representatives of the two governments. By that convention Great Britain renounced all right to participate in the gum trade at Portendic and France ceded Albreda to Great Britain. French subjects, who were already settled at Albreda, were to be allowed to retain their property and all rights attached thereto. The French Government was at liberty to appoint a consular agent at Bathurst and French subjects were to be allowed access to the river on the same footing as British subjects.[2] On 19 May 1857 Commodore Prôtet of the Imperial French Navy conveyed Colonel O'Connor in the steamer *Dialmath* to Albreda. On arrival he explained to the inhabitants the terms of the convention and Colonel O'Connor read the proclamation of annexation, which was countersigned by the Commodore, and the French flag was hauled down.[3]

"Thus", in Colonel O'Connor's words, "a long pending vexatious question, fertile in material for correspondence, a bone of jealousy to the commercial communities of both nations in the Gambia, a pretext and covert opening for contraband traffic, and a thorn in the side of the British settlers, is removed."[4] The hauling down of the French flag, after it had flown over Albreda for more than a century and a half, further meant that from thenceforth the River Gambia was exclusively a British sphere of influence.

France naturally demanded a *quid pro quo* for the surrender of Albreda, but in actual point of fact she could well have afforded to have abandoned the place without any consideration at all. It is not possible to set out even in a very short compass the history of her successful efforts to rebuild her colonial empire in West Africa, but a few words are necessary in order to show how those efforts affected the fortunes of the Gambia.

After Waterloo Great Britain and France may be said to have started on a more or less equal footing in West Africa. France had St Louis and Goree and Great Britain had Bathurst. At that date all three settlements were no more than military posts upon the shores of the Atlantic. Neither nation possessed an inch of the

---

[1] 21 and 22 Vict. c. 35.
[2] Colonel O'Connor to H. Labouchere, 21 May 1857.
[3] *Annual Report for* 1857.
[4] Hertslet, *Map of Africa*, p. 716.

hinterland and neither nation possessed a military post in the countries lying between the Gambia and Sierra Leone. The only power, which had any permanent foothold in the country to the south of the Gambia was Portugal, which had some forts on the banks of the Rios Casamance and Grande. Portugal also claimed to exercise sovereignty over a vast extent of territory surrounding those forts, but in actual fact that sovereignty could hardly be called even nominal. The only extent, to which it could really be said that there was any assertion of that sovereignty, was in insistence on the recognition of those territories as Portuguese in anti-slavery treaties. In the course of negotiating those treaties Great Britain more than once hinted a doubt as to the validity of those claims. France on the other hand went a great deal further than hinting a doubt.

Until the close of the Napoleonic wars Great Britain, France and Portugal alike had each regarded their respective West African possessions in much the same light, namely, as coastal or riverine military posts, which afforded some measure of security to their own nationals trading farther inland in more or less savage countries. But whilst they were upon occasion prepared to intervene for the protection of those traders, they made no attempt to assert sovereign rights over the territories where that trade was carried on.

After the Napoleonic wars Great Britain and Portugal continued to treat their West African possessions in the same way as before those wars. France, however, launched upon a different policy at a very early date. She set out very definitely to obtain a full and effective control of the hinterland by entering into treaty relations with the chiefs and by establishing military posts in the interior. The process was naturally slow. The change over from the old to the new policy was gradual and was barely noticed by the outside world until the object had been actually achieved. It is quite impossible within the limits of this book to describe French progress at all adequately, but it should be mentioned that a great measure of it was due to General Faidherbe, who became Governor of Senegal in 1852.

Governors in the Gambia were fully conscious of the change, which was taking place, and were fully alive to the effect which it would probably have upon the commercial prosperity of the Gambia and also on British trading interests generally in those regions. It was more or less recognised that the close proximity of Goree prevented any great expansion of British commercial interests to the north of the Gambia, but it was felt that something could be done to secure a permanent British foothold in the regions to the south of that river. There was an extensive and profitable trade between the Gambia and places as far down the coast as the Rio Grande.[1] A great deal of it was carried on by native mechanics and liberated Africans resident in Bathurst, who had managed to save sufficient money to purchase small vessels of about fifteen tons burden, which they used for trade during the rainy season between the Rio Grande and the Salum River for rice, corn and other commodities, which were at that period of the year exceedingly scarce in Bathurst.[1] The larger mercantile firms at Bathurst also traded on a regular and more extensive scale in the same region. In 1855 Colonel O'Connor found quite a large colony of British subjects at Kanabek in the Bissagos Islands, where the shipping to and from England was on quite a large scale and where the chief was a firm friend of the English.[2] In 1861 Colonel D'Arcy visited a British settlement near the mouth of the Casamance, which was called Lincoln. Though a certain proportion of the inhabitants were absconding debtors from Bathurst, the major part were British subjects carrying on a legitimate and thriving trade. Two Bathurst houses had European agents there, who were doing a large business in groundnuts and rice in exchange for British goods.[3]

More than one Governor applied to the home Government for leave to plant the British flag along the coast. It was not until the sixties of last century that the French made any active attempt to administer the regions of Sine Salum. Until then British traders from Bathurst were frequently exposed to robberies and exactions on the part of the local inhabitants. Their only hope of redress lay in the hands of the Gambia administration. More than once Lieutenant-Governor Rendall had to send special missions to the ruling chief in order to obtain satisfaction for outrages committed upon British subjects.[4] He therefore urged that Great Britain should take over control there, but in 1835 he was informed that the home Government was not prepared to make any territorial claims beyond

---

[1] T. L. Ingram to Lord Stanley, 3 March 1842.
[2] Colonel D'Arcy to Duke of Newcastle, 20 April 1860.
[3] Colonel O'Connor to Lord John Russell, 21 May 1855.
[4] Lt.-Gov. Rendall to R. W. Hay, 14 June and 4 December 1834; Hay to Rendall, 29 January 1831.

the limits acquired by the Ceded Mile Treaty of 1826.[1] Trouble between Bathurst traders and the people of Sine Salum continued long after this date. In 1856 a number of outrages induced Colonel O'Connor to proceed to Joal and conclude a special treaty with the ruling chief for the protection of the property of British subjects.[2] At that date French settlement in the regions of Joal was limited to "three French missionaries, who had a dreary precarious life, tolerated but not encouraged".[3] In 1859 the "king" came into conflict with the French and requested Colonel O'Connor to intervene on his behalf. O'Connor, however, with the approval of the home Government, declined to do so.[4] Shortly afterwards the French erected a fort at Kaolak.[5] In 1860 as the result of further outrages committed upon British subjects in Sine Salum Colonel D'Arcy paid a visit to that river. The "king" then undertook to pay compensation, but at the end of fourteen months had failed to fulfil his promise.[6] In March 1861 he placed himself under French protection[7] and apparently decided that this act relieved him of his previous obligations. Four months later Colonel D'Arcy paid him another visit and also asked the French commandant at Kaolak for his assistance. Subsequently he was informed that his action was not approved by the home Government.[8]

Though there were very intelligible reasons for abstention from attempts at territorial expansion to the north of the Gambia, the position to the south of that river was somewhat different. Except for the shadowy claims of the Portuguese there was nothing to prevent British expansion in those regions. In 1830 the Portuguese had a fort at Ziguinchor on the banks of the Casamance. By virtue of this fact they claimed the river as a Portuguese river. In 1828, however, the French established a trading post near the mouth of the river. In 1834 Lieutenant-Governor Rendall recommended that the British should also occupy an island near the same spot,[9] but out of deference to Portuguese susceptibilities the proposal had been dis-

---

[1] Lord Glenelg to Lt.-Gov. Rendall, 14 August 1835.
[2] Hertslet, *Treaties*, xii, 64.
[3] Colonel O'Connor to H. Labouchere, 4 January 1856.
[4] Sir E. B. Lytton to Colonel O'Connor, 11 August 1859.
[5] Colonel D'Arcy to Duke of Newcastle, 14 February 1860.
[6] Same to same, 10 April 1860, and 24 July 1861.
[7] Hertslet, *Map of Africa*, p. 634.
[8] Duke of Newcastle to Colonel D'Arcy, 23 September 1861.
[9] Lt.-Gov. Rendall to T. Spring Rice, 8 November 1834.

approved. In 1836 the Governor of Senegal arrived in the river on board the man-of-war *Bordelaise*. Despite a protest from the Portuguese Governor he sailed past Ziguinchor and selected a site for the erection of a French fort higher up the river at Seju. This action called forth a number of urgent entreaties to the Lieutenant-Governor in the Gambia for his intervention. Lieutenant-Governor Rendall, however, declined to intervene.[1] In 1839, however, it was brought home to the British authorities that the French were making very determined efforts to obtain exclusive possession of the Casamance. The *Highlander*, a Bathurst vessel, called, as it had done in the previous year, at Seju to pick up a cargo of hides, rice and wax. A boatload of French soldiers boarded her, took forcible possession and announced that British vessels from the Gambia would not be allowed to trade in the Casamance "until our respective governments have decided the question".[2] The crew abandoned the vessel and returned to Bathurst. A British man-of-war was sent to investigate. An officer of the West India Regiment, who went with it, subsequently reported a very curious situation. He found a greatly perturbed Portuguese governor inside his fort at Ziguinchor. Proceeding a few miles up the river to Pinding he found another Portuguese settlement "consisting of a few huts, where a soldier is stationed to hoist the flag to keep the French from taking the place". Continuing his voyage he arrived at Seju, where he learnt that a few days previously the Governor of Senegal had acquired extensive tracts of land for the French Government by treaties with the local chiefs.[3] He found a flourishing French factory at Seju side by side with a large native town, where the Portuguese were still endeavouring to carry on trade.[4] Eventually the Governor of Senegal admitted that the seizure of the *Highlander* was illegal and agreed that the British had an equal right with the French to trade in the river.[5]

There was occasional friction in the Casamance after this incident. Another vessel was seized by the French in 1857[6] and a number of other impediments were offered to British commerce. There were also a number of trifling disputes between British and French

[1] *Report of the Select Committee on West Africa* (1842), p. 189.
[2] Martin, *Colonial Magazine* (1840), pp. 261, 264.
[3] Hertslet, *Map of Africa*, p. 634.
[4] Journal of Ensign W. H. W. Graham, 24 December 1839 to 2 January 1840.
[5] T. L. Ingram to Lord John Russell, 16 March 1840.
[6] H. Labouchere to Colonel O'Connor, 20 October 1857.

traders, all of which were amicably settled after some corre-
spondence. None the less it became apparent in course of time that
French influence in the Casamance was definitely in the ascendant
whilst that of the British and the Portuguese was on the decline.
The erection of French forts at the mouth of the river induced the
Portuguese to relinquish their shadowy control by abandoning
Ziguinchor and active competition drove the British trader away.
In 1861 the British subjects at Lincoln requested Colonel D'Arcy to
hoist the British flag, but the day was then long past when this could
be done without the risk of international complications.[1] By a convention with France in 1886 the Portuguese recognised that their
pretensions to the Casamance had to be abandoned.[2] Long before
that date it had become apparent to British subjects that Great
Britain could not contest French supremacy in that river.

[1] Colonel D'Arcy to Duke of Newcastle, 24 July 1861.
[2] Hertslet, *Map of Africa*, p. 764.

XXVIII: Continuation of Soninki-Marabout War, 1859–1866

The last chapter centred round a single event, which materially affected the after history of the Gambia, and certain other incidents which preceded and followed that event and also had an important influence on the history of the Gambia. It was an interlude, which interrupted the thread of the main narrative but which helps to throw light on later developments in that narrative. In the present chapter we must return to affairs in the Gambia itself.

Colonel O'Connor was succeeded in 1859 by another officer of the West India Regiment, Colonel George Abbas Koolie D'Arcy. The new Governor landed to find himself in the midst of an outbreak of yellow fever, the first after an interval of twenty-two years. It lasted from August to October, by which time only ten Europeans were left in the Colony.[1] After its subsidence Colonel D'Arcy set to work to improve the sanitation of Bathurst. Despite the jaundiced criticisms of Burton in his *Wanderings in West Africa* a great deal was done at this date to improve public health and sanitation. The work was, moreover, being carried out with very limited funds, upon which from time to time quite unforeseen inroads had to be made for other purposes. Modern science may be able to criticise some of the steps, which were taken at this date, but it is clear that they had the full approval of contemporary medical opinion.

When the passing of the epidemic and its aftermaths gave Colonel D'Arcy greater time to devote to affairs beyond Bathurst, he found that the upper river was in a general state of lawlessness, which was brought about by quarrels between rival chiefs and the perpetual feud between the Soninkis and Marabouts. During the course of these disturbances the goods of a number of Bathurst traders were pillaged. Colonel D'Arcy therefore sent a number of officers up the river to obtain redress. Satisfaction was given except in one instance in Baddibu.[2] The Soninki "king" of that district had been

[1] D. Robertson to Duke of Newcastle, 20 August 1859; Colonel D'Arcy to Duke of Newcastle, 24 September, 4 and 8 October 1859.

[2] Colonel D'Arcy to Duke of Newcastle, 24 December 1859, 23 March and 28 August 1860.

approached and had agreed to pay an indemnity in cattle, but deliberately delayed payment. When he was threatened with coercive measures, he tried to postpone the evil day by sending meagre instalments of the compensation. It was eventually decided to show him that no further delay would be tolerated. His country was therefore placed under a blockade. The "king" and his people continued obdurate and announced that they had not the slightest intention of paying anything further.[1]

As the people of Baddibu were defiant and the natives of neighbouring districts were exhibiting further signs of lawlessness, Colonel D'Arcy decided to resort to sterner measures. Reinforcements were obtained from Sierra Leone and an expeditionary force was formed comprising contingents from H.M.S. *Torch*, the three West India Regiments, and the Gambia Militia. Colonel D'Arcy made a final effort to arrive at a peaceful solution of the matter. The *Torch* was sent with a flag of truce to N'Jawarra Creek, but the commander returned to report that the recalcitrants were strongly entrenched and refused to hold any communication with the ship.

The expedition then embarked on the *Torch*, the colonial steamer *Dover* and a number of schooners and sailed for Suwarrakunda, which was reached on 16 February 1861. Still anxious to avoid bloodshed, Colonel D'Arcy warned the enemy through an interpreter that, if they did not abandon the earthworks within half an hour, the ships would open fire on them. The half hour elapsed without result and the bombardment began. At first the enemy returned a spirited reply, but at the end of three hours many of them were seen to be in retreat. The troops were then landed, but found that there was still a strong body of the enemy ready to offer a very determined resistance. It was only after some very fierce hand to hand fighting that the enemy finally broke and fled. After this the British force, which had been reinforced by contingents from H.M.S. *Arrogant* and *Falcon*, marched through western Baddibu and on 21 February took the stockaded town of Saba by storm. Immediately after that the "king" of Jokadu sent messengers with offers of mediation. After a short armistice a treaty of peace was signed on 26 February. By that treaty the "king" of Baddibu agreed that in future he would refer all disputes between his own people and British subjects to the Governor at Bathurst. He further agreed to pay an indemnity and gave hostages as a guarantee for the faithful performance of the

[1] Same to same, 24 November 1860.

terms of the treaty. Later in the same year he entered into a second treaty. By this latter treaty the "king" of Baddibu agreed that in exchange for an annual payment to himself he would allow British and French traders, who held a pass signed by the Colonial Secretary at Bathurst, to trade in his own country without payment of any "customs". In consideration of this agreement all except one-quarter of the indemnity was remitted and the hostages were surrendered.[1]

Only part of that remaining quarter of the indemnity was ever paid, but the default as regards the balance was due to causes over which the "king" of Baddibu had no control. Though he was a Soninki, his Marabout subjects had made common cause with him in his resistance to the British demands, which had led up to the punitive expedition. Amongst these Marabout supporters was a certain Hamma Ba, commonly known as Maba. This man had a farm close to Suwarrakunda. He had taken part in the defence of that place, but on the night of the attack came on board the *Torch* to make his submission and to beg Colonel D'Arcy to spare his own village. The Governor had agreed to do so on condition that he marched with the troops during the subsequent operations. Later he proved of great service in arranging the terms of the peace. No doubt self interest entered into his conduct, but he was in many respects a remarkable man. He had begun life as a Soninki but had later joined the other faction and had embraced all its tenets with all the ultrafervour, which is so often displayed by the convert. He had become an advanced radical in his politics and certainly started his career with one or two ideals. He had a real desire for the friend-ship of the British Government and, though he was subsequently often to violate the spirit, he never broke the letter of his promises to that government. Whatever his motives for first approaching Colonel D'Arcy, they were interpreted by the "king" as being an act of treachery. Foreseeing danger, Maba fled to Bathurst. Colonel D'Arcy offered him land in British Kombo, but he eventually patched up some sort of reconciliation with his overlord and re-turned to his own country. As most onlookers expected, that reconciliation was a very hollow one. Soon after Maba's return the "king" sent one of his sons to assassinate him. The son arrived at

[1] Ellis, *History of the First West India Regiment*, pp. 265–275; Laird Clowes, *The Royal Navy*, VII, 188; *Ordinances of the Gambia*, 1875, pp. 530, 531; Hertslet, *Treaties*, XII, 79, 82.

Maba's village, where he dined not wisely but too well. He disclosed his project in his cups to his host, who promptly informed Maba. The tables were speedily turned. The "king's" son was murdered whilst he was still sleeping off his carouse and Maba raised the standard of revolt.[1]

In an incredibly short time the Marabout faction had overrun the whole of Baddibu, the "king" had been wounded, captured and put to death, every Soninki village was in flames and practically the whole of the Soninki population had fled the country. Maba preached a real Jehad and the fighting was conducted with all the fanaticism of such a war. Throughout the war Maba adopted an unusual attitude. Subsequent events proved that he was by no means a physical coward, but, unlike most African leaders of revolt, he personally abstained from any participation in the actual fighting. He adopted the role of a Mahdi, but combined with it many of the relics of his former paganism. Colonel D'Arcy thus described his conduct in the field:

On approaching a town he intends to destroy, he dismounts from his horse, orders his praying carpet to be spread and calls for writing materials. A staff of blind Marabouts now surround him, repeating in a low chaunt that God is great and that there is only one God and Mahomet is his prophet. Mahaba then most earnestly writes grees, or charms, which he hastily distributes to his warriors, who, as they now imagine themselves doubly armed, rush to victory or heaven. It is said that Mahaba has never yet been seen under fire or even been known to carry a weapon. He is superstitious to a degree and fancies that his power will be secure for ever, if he can obtain a particular mare, which is now the property of my aide de camp, Lieutenant Stubbs of the Militia Artillery.[2]

The fighting, which followed upon this initiatory ritual, was ruthless. Any man, who was taken prisoner, was given the alternative of shaving his head, repeating the declaration of the Mahommedan faith and renouncing drink, or of being put to instant death. But, if the Marabouts were strong in their faith, many of the Soninkis were equally strong in theirs. On one occasion a European eye-witness beheld a string of Soninki prisoners, who in front of Maba resolutely declined to renounce their old beliefs and were instantly massacred.[3]

[1] Colonel D'Arcy to Duke of Newcastle, 8 August 1862.
[2] Same to same, 8 August 1862.   [3] Same to same, 5 August 1862.

At the beginning of the war the Soninkis were evidently taken completely by surprise. Many of them fled panic stricken to the banks of the Gambia. About 600 men and a few women and children were rescued by Bathurst traders and conveyed to Tendeba on the opposite bank. Colonel D'Arcy hurriedly proceeded to the spot in H.M.S. *Dart* and was able to rescue a few more women and children, who were hiding in the mangrove swamps. He also managed to get into communication with Maba, who sent a message to say the war was over, that he was disbanding his army and that he had declined the kingship because "the office was maintained by plundering the property of others and that henceforth in Baddibu the title should be dispensed with ".[1]

This declaration was a very remarkable one to come at this date from the mouth of an African leader, who had hitherto had little contact with the outside world. It was no doubt uttered at the time in all sincerity, but later events proved too much for Maba. It so chanced that at this very inopportune moment Demba Sonko, "king" of Barra, was gathered to his fathers. There was the usual interregnum and the usual wrangling before his successor, Buntung Jammi, was elected. One of Maba's captains, a Jollof named Amer Faal, took advantage of this state of affairs to cross the N'Jawarra Creek and invade Niumi. He speedily overran Jokadu, where he compelled the underking to shave his head and renounce his faith. Thence he made his way through Niumi carrying everything before him. On learning of these successes Maba collected a force and followed him. The Soninki population fled in haste to Berrending and Essau, the two chief villages of the heptarchy. The new "king" of Barra took refuge in Bathurst, but the Sumars, or headmen, of Berrending and Essau prepared to make a stand. They sent to the Governor to implore his aid or at the least an asylum for their women and children. Apart from his instructions from home Colonel D'Arcy had very recently had to deplete his garrison in order to furnish troops for an expedition to Lagos. He was therefore unable to comply with the first request, but he very readily complied with the second. Several hundred fugitives took refuge under the guns of Fort Bullen. Colonel D'Arcy undertook to protect them and at the same time sent a messenger to Maba to try to persuade him to withdraw his forces from Niumi. He also moved all his available troops over to Barra Point and sent H.M.S. *Lee* to Albreda

---

[1] Same to same, 22 May and 24 August 1862.

to evacuate the British and French subjects. Two hundred women and children, who had fled to Dog Island, were rescued in canoes by the liberated Africans of Berwick Town and brought to Fort Bullen.

A message came back from Maba that the only condition, upon which he would consent to call his men off, would be if the Soninkis would consent to have their heads shaved and become Marabouts. That was out of the question. The Soninkis abandoned Berrending after a feeble defence and concentrated all their forces in the stockaded town of Essau, where 500 of them dressed in death colours, yellow, prepared to make a last stand. On 26 May 1862 Maba invested Essau, but did not attempt to take the place by assault. That last week of May was an anxious one for Colonel D'Arcy. On the Bathurst shore crowds, which included not a few Marabout sympathisers, stood daily watching events. On the opposite shore about 1000 women and children were cowering under the few obsolete cannon mounted on Fort Bullen. A mile away Maba's forces were yelling threats of destruction upon the defenders of Essau. Between them and the women and children was a thin line of men of the First and Second West India Regiments and the Gambia Militia. They were most of them tried campaigners, but their line extended over nearly a mile and they were only 230 strong. As he rode along that line, Colonel D'Arcy may well have wondered if it would hold, if the need came, and, if it did not hold, what would be the fate of the people behind it. It only needed a single shot from some irresponsible person to set everything ablaze. Fortunately fine military discipline told and there was no incident. The British troops stood to arms for seven days. In the meantime Maba held his hand against Essau. Then on 1 June the town of Berrending was seen to be in flames and a message came from Maba to say that in deference to the Governor's wishes he had decided to withdraw his men. Later further news came through. The "king" of Sine Salum had invaded Baddibu, and Maba was hurrying back with all his forces to his own country.[1]

After Maba's withdrawal Colonel D'Arcy assembled the chiefs of both factions at Albreda and managed to arrange some sort of a peace. Soninkis and Marabouts alike implored him to take Niumi under British protection. Without instructions from home he was naturally unable to agree to the proposal, but he wrote to England

[1] Same to same, 24 May and 16 June 1862.

to urge its acceptance. He was, however, informed in reply that the proposal could not be entertained.[1]

The peace was short lived. It was broken by the Sumar of Essau, who recaptured some cattle which had been taken during Maba's advance through Niumi. Colonel D'Arcy's attempts at mediation failed and desultory fighting began once more. Maba himself had driven back the invaders of Baddibu and had then carried the war into the enemy's country, only to be utterly defeated and himself severely wounded at Kaolak, when French troops came to the aid of the "king" of Sine Salum.[2] For the time being therefore the Marabouts of Niumi had to carry on the war without outside aid, but the Soninkis had been so decimated in the previous war that it was all that they could do to hold the small belt of the river bank, which contained the villages of the seven ruling families. For some six months the operations consisted mainly in the burning of a good deal of powder with no very decisive advantage to either side. Finally at the end of 1862 Fodi Kabba and the Marabouts of Gunjur, whose movements had long been watched with considerable anxiety by the British authorities, decided to come by sea to Jinnak Creek so as to lend a hand. At the same time Maba found himself free to come once more to the aid of the Marabouts of Niumi. Colonel D'Arcy then made another effort to secure peace. Maba had never forgotten the fact that the Governor had once spared his own village and undoubtedly had the greatest possible respect for him. He agreed that the Marabouts should burn their stockades provided the Soninkis did likewise and also handed over some prisoners, whom they had taken in a raid upon Juffure. He also agreed to refrain from any further interference in the affairs of Niumi and to abide by the provisions of the second Baddibu Treaty of 1861. The Soninkis were persuaded to accept these terms. The stockades of both factions were set on fire and a formal treaty of peace was drawn up and signed on 24 February 1863.[3]

[1] Same to same, 16 June 1862; Duke of Newcastle to Colonel D'Arcy, 4 December 1862 and 21 May 1863.

[2] Colonel D'Arcy was asked by the French to co-operate in this campaign against Maba, but he declined to do so. His action subsequently received the approbation of the British government: *Proceedings of the Select Committee on Africa (West Coast)* (1866), p. 432.

[3] *Proceedings of the Select Committee on Africa (West Coast)* (1866), p. 415; *Ordinances of the Gambia*, 1875, p. 533; Hertslet, *Treaties*, xii, 101; Colonel D'Arcy's despatches to the Duke of Newcastle, 23 July 1862 to 21 March 1863.

Maba had sworn on the Koran to abide by his word to Colonel
D'Arcy and he did not break his oath. None the less he marched
straight from making the peace into Sine Salum. A month later the
single police constable at Barra Point was suddenly confronted by
a band of 2000 unarmed men, women and children. They were
Jollofs and Sereres, whose country had been devastated by Maba
and who had come to seek British protection. The sudden problem
of providing for their immediate wants was a serious one, but
eventually they were given the site of the neighbouring Soninki
town of Kanume, which had been destroyed some time previously
by the Marabouts and never rebuilt. Five months later another
band of 700 refugees arrived at Barra Point. They too had fled from
Maba's devastation in Sine Salum. They were all in a state of absolute starvation. Many had died on the way. Fourteen more died
at Barra Point before food and medical aid could be rushed over
from Bathurst. Many of the rest were far too weak to lift the food
to their mouths when it did come. The whole of the party was
eventually conveyed over to Bathurst, where temporary relief works
were organised in the form of construction of a road from the far
side of Oyster Creek to Cape St Mary. As many as possible were
given land in British and Lower Kombo and a small settlement,
which was known as Outram Town, was formed on the mainland on
the shore of Oyster Creek.[1]

In the meantime Maba was confining himself to raids on more or
less defenceless villages in Sine Salum. His defeat at Kaolak had
given fresh hope to the Soninkis of Baddibu. A son of the former
"king" made a bid to recover his father's cap. A large body of
refugees, who at the beginning of Maba's revolt had fled to Tendeba,
recrossed the river and stockaded themselves at Tunku. Maba
quickly retaliated by crossing over to the Kiang country. The
Soninkis mustered in force at Kwinella, where Maba proceeded to
attack them with a force which was said to be 5000 strong. There
followed one of the few pitched battles in this interminable war. The
end of it was that Maba fled from the field with a few horsemen,
leaving behind him over 500 dead Marabouts. He took refuge at
Sumbundu amongst some Tukolors, or Mahommedan Fulas.[2] His
power was broken, but he was still able to cause a good deal of
trouble for a few more years. In 1864 he managed to collect a band

[1] Colonel D'Arcy to Duke of Newcastle, 24 March and 11 September 1863.
[2] Same to same, 4 May, 20 June and 24 August 1863.

of men and returned to Baddibu. The fighting was no longer on the scale of his earlier days. It degenerated into the old kite and crow warfare, but on the whole Maba managed to gain ground. He was so far successful that he induced the French to recognise him as the ruler of Baddibu with the title of Almami. But his restless spirit would not allow him to settle down. In 1866 he came into collision with the French and fled to Niumi.[1] In the following year he was killed in a raid into Sine Salum.[2]

Though Maba's defeat at Kwinella marked the final collapse of his personal power, he had lit a candle which was destined not to go out. His earlier successes in Baddibu and Niumi were the signal for the Marabouts up and down the river to rise against their Soninki overlords. A letter from the Commandant at MacCarthy Island explains how the Marabouts brought the war to Nyani.

Ha Fodi with a few followers went to the town of Lamin...and secreted themselves outside the wall. When everything was quiet in Lamin and the inhabitants had retired to rest for the night, these men constructed a temporary ladder for the occasion, scaled the wall and made for the house of the chief Walli. They then murdered him in a most brutal manner. One of his wives, happening to be present, threw herself on the body so as to prevent their cutting him to pieces. The child that was on her back was beheaded. His two brothers and another follower shared the same fate. His wives carried off. The town pillaged and burned.[3]

This was followed by the sacking of the town of Junkakunda opposite to MacCarthy Island. Many hundreds of aged men, women and children took refuge on the island itself.[4] In 1863 Ha Fodi Jola was killed in attack upon the "king" of Kataba,[5] but owing to dissensions amongst the Soninkis the Marabouts steadily gained ground. By the middle of 1864 MacCarthy Island was surrounded by a number of stockaded camps of Marabouts, who manifested every intention of crossing over to the island itself. It was therefore decided to send reinforcements to the island. Their arrival brought the Marabouts to a different frame of mind. The camps were broken

---

[1] *The Times*, 17 September 1866.
[2] *Annual Report for* 1886; Guy, "Le Sine Saloum", *La Géographie*, xviii, 311.   [3] Ensign A. H. Duthie to Colonel D'Arcy, 25 September 1862.
[4] Colonel D'Arcy to Duke of Newcastle, 24 October and 24 December 1862.
[5] Same to same, 24 August 1862.

up and the fighters returned to their homes. On 14 June 1864 the Soninki "king" of Kataba and Fodi Alhaji, the leading Marabout chief of the same district, concluded a treaty whereby they agreed to refer all future disputes to the arbitration of the Commandant of MacCarthy Island.[1]

There was less trouble farther down the river, but in many places the so-called peace was maintained on the footing, which was described in 1863 as existing at Nyanimaru. "The Soninki king is bound by treaty with the Colonial government to keep open the roads and to protect the trade. At present he is quite unable to do so, for the town adjacent to the wharf is Marabout and bids defiance to the king by the erection of a stockade commanding the wharf."[2]

In the Kombo Fodi Kabba was only waiting for a favourable opportunity to fall upon his Soninki overlord. That opportunity seemed to have come in 1864, when an incident occurred, which was very far from being uncommon in this so-called religious war. The village of Manduari was situated close to the frontier between Soninki and Marabout Kombo. Fearing a possible raid by the Marabouts, the inhabitants purchased a stock of gunpowder, which they placed in the charge of their Sumar or headman. This worthy proceeded to sell the powder. On discovery of his dishonesty he fled to Gunjur, where he underwent a very rapid conversion to Maraboutism. As proof of the sincerity of his conversion he led a force against Manduari, which he took and subsequently stockaded. He then proclaimed a Jehad against all other Soninkis. The "king" of the Kombo sent to Colonel D'Arcy to ask for assistance. An officer was sent to Gunjur to persuade the Marabouts to hold their hands, whilst the Governor went to see the "king" at Yundum. The mission to Yundum was successful, but the "king" urged Colonel D'Arcy to attack Gunjur. The Governor naturally refused to do so. Thereupon the "king" said, "Then I will send and offer Gunjur to the French, who will, no doubt, take it". The next day there was a collision between the parties, in which there were over thirty casualties. A general war seemed inevitable, but some of the elders of the destroyed town of Sabaji offered to mediate between the two parties. Whilst they were endeavouring to arrange a peace

---

[1] *Report of the Select Committee on Africa (West Coast)* (1865), p. 432; *Ordinances of the Gambia*, 1875, p. 535.

[2] Colonel D'Arcy to Duke of Newcastle, 26 April 1863.

H.M.S. *Rattlesnake* arrived at Bathurst. Commodore Eardley Wilmot was requested by the Governor to proceed to Gunjur to try to negotiate a settlement. On 8 February 1864 he returned with a treaty, which had been signed by both the "king" of the Kombo and Fodi Kabba. The parties thereby consented to refer all future disputes to the arbitration of the Governor and agreed that any future act of hostility on the part of either party should be treated as an act of hostility against the British Government.[1]

Fodi Kabba, however, had not the same regard for his written word as had Maba. In October of the same year a band of Marabouts from Gunjur attacked the Soninki town of Busumballa shouting "Fodi Kabba". They were driven off leaving four dead behind them. One of the killed proved to be a Jollof Marabout from Albert Town, which lay just within British Kombo and had a headman who was known to be a strong Marabout. Four days later a band of Soninkis surrounded Albert Town alleging that the headman had instigated the raid on Busumballa. Colonel D'Arcy hurried to the spot and hastily threw fifteen men of the Kombo Militia into the town, over which he hoisted the British flag. He then proceeded to Yundum and, on promising to remove the obnoxious headman, persuaded the "king" to call off the raiders.[2]

Maba's departure had by no means ended the troubles in Niumi. The Marabouts of that district showed very little disposition to honour their treaty. In 1863 a Marabout of Juffure was arrested in the British settlement at Albreda for attempted robbery. He was brought to trial before the resident magistrate and convicted. His conviction was followed by a very ugly demonstration on the part of the headman of Juffure and a band of his followers. A few days later two slave girls fled from the Marabout town of Sikka to Albreda and claimed British protection. They were forcibly rescued from the police constable by the headman of Sikka and twenty men. The tables were, however, turned a few weeks later, when the headman, perfectly unabashed, arrived in Bathurst to demand audience of the Governor. He very quickly found himself in jail with the intimation that his release depended upon that of his captives. The slave girls were handed over within less than twenty-four hours.[3]

[1] *Report of the Select Committee on Africa (West Coast)* (1865), p. 432; *Ordinances of the Gambia*, 1875, p. 53.
[2] *Ibid.* p. 433.
[3] Colonel D'Arcy to Duke of Newcastle, 20 June and 20 July 1863.

This truculent attitude was known to be directly encouraged by Maba's former lieutenant, Amer Faal, who was living in the neighbouring village of Tubab Kolon. Amer Faal had not been a party to the treaty of peace in 1862 and was just a very ordinary type of lawless bandit. In order to counteract his influence and to relieve congestion near Barra Point, part of the 2000 refugees from Sine Salum were removed from Kanume to Banta Killing, which was renamed Fitzgerald Town, and their chief, Masamba Koki, was appointed headman of this portion of the Ceded Mile. Being a Jollof and a Soninki, Masamba Koki found it very difficult to exercise any authority in his district. Fighting very nearly began in 1864, but the arrival at Albreda of H.M.S. *Mullet* with some troops brought the Marabouts to reason. Two years later further trouble was caused when some of Amer Faal's people raided the cattle of the people of Fitzgerald Town. Colonel D'Arcy went to Albreda to try to settle the matter amicably, but the Marabouts were defiant. No alternative was left but to teach Amer Faal a lesson and a punitive expedition was sent to deal with him.[1]

The subsequent operations lasted only four days. It is perhaps for that reason that they receive no mention in the Annual Report for 1866 or in any other official publication except the *London Gazette*. They were none the less decisive and served fully to maintain the reputation of the West India Regiments. On 26 July 1866 H.M.S. *Mullet* and the colonial steamer *Dover* conveyed 270 officers and men to Albreda, where the Marabouts were taken by surprise and disarmed without any blood being shed. The column then advanced upon Amer Faal's stockaded village at Tubab Kolon. By previous arrangement they were joined there by the Soninki Sumar of Essau with 500 men. The stockade was bombarded, but the artillery was too light to make any real impression and the defenders put up a spirited reply. Colonel D'Arcy then called for volunteers to make a breach in the stockade. He was answered by Lieutenant Jenkins, Ensign Kelly, and fifteen pioneers of the Fourth West India Regiment, who advanced with Colonel D'Arcy himself under a very heavy fire. Jenkins and Kelly were killed and thirteen of the men severely wounded. The two survivors—Samuel Hodges and a man named Boswell—managed to reach the stockade and started to hack it to pieces with their axes whilst the enemy poured

[1] *Report of the Select Committee on Africa (West Coast)* (1865), pp. 431, 432; Horton, *West African Countries and Peoples*, pp. 82, 83.

a heavy fire upon them from loopholes in the stockade. Boswell was killed just as the breach had been made. Colonel D'Arcy himself was the first through the gap, followed by Hodges, who was armed only with an axe. They immediately found themselves confronted by two inner barricades, which Hodges proceeded to hew down. The remainder of the troops followed and the place was carried at the point of the bayonet after an obstinate resistance, in which the enemy had about 300 casualties. For his gallantry Hodges was subsequently awarded the Victoria Cross, being the second of the three Africans who have won that much coveted honour. There can be no doubt that, if posthumous awards had been conferred at this date, Boswell would have received the same recognition of his bravery.[1]

Though Maba's meteoric career was comparatively short and his end was violent, that short period of power had a very lasting effect upon the political history of the Gambia inasmuch as it resulted in the destruction of the old system of hereditary chieftainships. In the upper part of the river, where the Fulas and the Bambarras were making constant raids from the interior and many of the chiefs were no more than petty war-lords, this would no doubt have happened without the rise of the Marabouts to power. Though peace and good order were not likely to be evolved out of chaos, in districts where one war-lord overthrew his neighbour only to be in his turn overthrown by another of his kind a few years later, in the lower parts of the river the country was ruled by hereditary dynasties which had been established for several centuries. The petty war-lord's authority depended upon his own personality and popularity, but the hereditary ruler had the traditional loyalty of many generations behind him and that in Africa meant a very great deal. The Soninki chiefs possibly deserved to lose their power because of their many obvious failings and faults, but under careful and tactful guidance their regime might have been so reformed as to establish peace, order and good government. As it was, when their rule broke down, nothing of any permanent value was erected in its place. When revolutions break out in primitive society, a great deal more depends upon the man than upon the cause. Maba was evidently imbued with some ideals and had some power of organisation, but he lacked the balance and the personality to guide the revolution, which he had begun.

[1] Ellis, *op. cit.* pp. 19, 20; *The Times*, 9 August 1866; *London Gazette*, 4 January 1867.

His lieutenants were no more than very commonplace freebooters and he had no successor of the same ability as himself. The result of his revolt was to put back the clock for close on half a century and to reduce the more settled regions in the lower parts of the river to the same state of anarchy as had hitherto been found only in the upper parts.

The pity of the whole matter was that, apart from a few fanatics and a few lawless spirits, the rank and file in the land were yearning for the opportunity to cultivate their foodcrops and to raise and sell their groundnuts in peace. During his period of office Colonel D'Arcy was constantly receiving missives in Arabic and bad English from Marabouts and Soninkis alike imploring him to take over their land or to place them under British protection, but his instructions from home were clear and he was unable to accede to any of these petitions. It is a great tribute to him that he managed to achieve what he did towards the establishment of peace in the regions beyond British territory and that he saved the Colony from unnecessary embroilment and even possible destruction in a civil war, in which religious fanaticism and personal rancour played so great a part. He was labouring under innumerable difficulties. The constant warfare had ruined agriculture and trade. The colonial revenue was badly diminished. Furthermore, once in 1861 and twice in 1862 he was called upon during the most critical stages of the civil war to deplete his very small garrison of regular troops in order to send reinforcements to Lagos and the Gold Coast.[1] He was loyally and ably assisted by a number of officers—civil and military—but it was largely as a result of his own personal exertions and of the high esteem in which he was held by the natives of the Gambia that very serious trouble was averted at a very tense moment at Fort Bullen in 1862 and that some sort of peace was established in Niumi.

Colonel D'Arcy's experience led him to advocate the establishment of a protectorate along both banks of the river. His despatches show that he had carefully weighed the pros and cons of the proposal and that he recognised some of the difficulties, of which not the least was the problem of domestic slavery, but at the same time he urged that the arguments in favour of a protectorate strongly outweighed those against. He was not alone in his opinion. It was

[1] Colonel D'Arcy to Duke of Newcastle, 24 December 1861, 11 August and 24 November 1862.

shared by Colonel H. St George Ord, who was sent out by Parliament in 1864 to report on the British settlements in West Africa. On his return Colonel Ord expressed the following opinion:

Conscious of their weakness the chiefs and people have expressed to the government a desire to live under British rule, the simplest mode of which would be the cession of their territory, but this is impracticable from the fact that they are slave holders. There are also strong objections to the country being made a protectorate in the sense in which the word is understood in England. It would, however, be the subject of much regret if this small, harmless and useful community should be thus abandoned to destruction through fear of our being involved in unnecessary responsibilities; and it is to be hoped that the government may, without risk to itself, find some means of extending to them the protection they seek. Such a step would further our obtaining that influence on the northern side of the river of which, as has been stated, we are reaping the benefits on the south.[1]

The attitude of the home Government to the proposal must be left to the next chapter.

[1] *Report on the Condition of the British Settlements on the West Coast of Africa* (1865), p. 9.

XXIX : The proposed cession to France, 1866–1876

During the sixties of last century the attention of Parliament was drawn to West Africa by reason of the number of punitive expeditions, which it was found necessary from time to time to despatch from each of the four British settlements against natives in the neighbourhood. The garrisons of these settlements, which were provided by the West India Regiments, were a charge upon the imperial vote. The Navy was also very frequently being called upon for assistance and each of the settlements was in receipt of a grant in aid. Murmurings began to be heard amongst certain members of the House of Commons in regard to this expenditure. In 1864 the Government decided to send Colonel Ord out to West Africa as a commissioner to enquire into the state of the Settlements and to report as to what economies might be effected. Colonel (afterwards Major-General Sir) H. St G. Ord presented a report on his return and in 1865 a Select Committee was appointed to consider it and to make recommendations as to the future administration of the British West African Settlements.[1]

The Committee comprised members of both political parties. It examined a number of witnesses, but the only person summoned before them, who was at all conversant with the affairs of the Gambia, was Dr Daniel Robertson, the Colonial Secretary. It is clear from the minutes of his evidence that he had come to England quite unprepared for a summons of this nature and that he suffered from the disadvantage of being unable to consult the necessary documents, which would have given his evidence the authority to which it was entitled. It is also equally clear from the questions, which were put to a number of witnesses, that certain members of the Committee had made up their minds before they had heard any evidence at all.

Colonel Ord's conclusions may be summed up in two sentences, which are taken from his report.

The present condition...may be attributed to the want of a regular and well defined system of administration. For this, as well as for

[1] Hansard, *Parliamentary Debates*, CLXXVII, 559.

431

another evil, viz., the entire absence among the four colonies of a uniform policy of dealing with natives, the remedy that suggests itself is the placing of the whole under the control of one central authority. The principle, upon which this arrangement should be carried out, is that which prevails in our smaller West Indian colonies, each of which is permitted to raise and appropriate its revenue, to pass its laws, and generally to administer its affairs, subject only to the approval of the governor-in-chief.[1]

For this purpose Colonel Ord recommended Sierra Leone as the headquarters of the central government. He pointed out that the introduction of steam had done away with one of the disadvantages of central control, which had led to the change in 1843, but at the same time he urged that the visits of the governor-in-chief to the outlying settlements should be fairly frequent. He was strongly opposed to the entire abandonment of any of the British West African Settlements, as he was convinced that this would lead at once in every instance—and more particularly in the Gambia—to the reopening of the slave trade. His only other recommendation of any importance, which affected the Gambia, was in regard to MacCarthy Island, where he recommended the withdrawal of the military establishment and more frequent communication by the government steamer. "It is open to question whether her more frequent employment on the river would not more than compensate for any danger or inconvenience, which may be expected to result from the reduction of the military force at MacCarthy's Island."[2]

We are not concerned here with the evidence given by witnesses in regard to other parts of West Africa, but it is not irrelevant to mention that those witnesses included naval and military officers, civil servants, missionaries and merchants and that they were one and all opposed to any form of retrocession. Having heard their evidence, the Select Committee made its report on 26 June 1865. That report contained the following recommendations:

1. *That it is not possible to withdraw the British Government, wholly or immediately, from any of the settlements on the West African Coast.*

---

[1] *Report on the Condition of the British Settlements on the West Coast of Africa* (1865), p. 32.   [2] *Ibid.* p. 10.

2. *That the settlement in the Gambia may be reduced by M'Carthy's Island, which is one hundred and fifty miles up the river, being no longer occupied; and that the settlement should be confined as much as possible to the mouth of the river.*

3. *That all further extension of territory, or assumption of government, or new treaties offering any protection to native tribes, would be inexpedient; and that the object of our policy should be to encourage in the natives the exercise of those qualities, which may render it possible for us to transfer to them more and more the administration of all the governments, with a view to our ultimate withdrawal from all, except, perhaps, Sierra Leone.*

4. *That this policy of non-extension admits of no exception as regards new settlements, but cannot amount to an absolute prohibition of measures, which, in peculiar cases, may be necessary for the more efficient and economical administration of the settlements we already possess.*

5. *That the reasons for the separation of the West African Governments in 1842 having ceased to exist, it is desirable that a central government over all four settlements should be re-established at Sierra Leone with steam communication with each Lieutenant Government.*

6. *That the evidence leads to the hope that such a central control may be established with considerable retrenchment of expenditure and at the same time great increase of efficiency.*[1]

The result of these recommendations was that by a Royal Commission, dated 19 February 1866, the Gambia, Sierra Leone, the Gold Coast and Lagos were merged into one government, which had its headquarters at Freetown and was known as the British West African Settlements. The Governor was to be resident chiefly in Sierra Leone, but was to visit each of the other settlements at least once in each year. The Gambia retained its separate legislature, but the title of the officer in charge of the administration was changed to that of Administrator.[2]

On 8 February 1866 Mr Cardwell, Secretary of State for the Colonies, announced in Parliament that orders had been given for the final abandonment of MacCarthy Island not later than June of that year.[3] But Bakari Sardu, the ruler of Bondu, made that course

[1] *Report of the Select Committee on Africa (West Coast)* (1865), p. iii.
[2] Hertslet, *Map of Africa*, p. 18; *State Papers*, LIX, 1194.
[3] Hansard, *op. cit.* CLXXXI, 194.

impossible. Early in that year he invaded Wuli and then proceeded down the river towards the island, burning and destroying as he went. MacCarthy Island was occupied not only by traders from Bathurst, but also by a colony of liberated Africans, who had been settled there by the British Government, a number of natives, who in the past had fled there to claim British protection, and a Wesleyan Mission, which had been specially invited to work there by the British Government. It was obvious that the safety and liberty of all these were in danger and that they were entitled to some protection. A few troops were hastily sent up the river under the command of Captain Bridges of the Royal Engineers and the Bondu raiders retired.[1]

Bakari Sardu's raid had the result of proving that the entire abandonment of MacCarthy Island was out of the question, but on 23 May Mr Cardwell announced that "Her Majesty's Government cannot regard the upper waters of the Gambia as being under British protection and, when traders establish factories on the shores of countries beyond the limits of British jurisdiction, they must be prepared for the risks which they incur in doing so".[2]

At the same time orders were given for the withdrawal of the officer and thirty men, who formed the garrison of MacCarthy Island. These troops left the island on 18 May 1866. The only official, who was then left upon the island, was Dr J. A. B. Horton, a native of Sierra Leone, who was Staff Assistant Surgeon to the troops and had served in the Ashanti campaign two years before. The island was left without any form of civil administration. Rumours of the impending departure of the troops had reached the ears of the natives and bands of armed men had been seen assembling on either river bank. Dr Horton therefore decided upon his own responsibility to organise a provisional administration until such time as the properly appointed civil officer should arrive to take over. The members of the mercantile community, who were all of them Africans, subscribed to maintain a volunteer defence force of twelve men. Nine other persons were sworn in as special constables. All drumming, firing of arms, and any other noise was forbidden after eight o'clock at night without special permission. Owners of canoes were instructed to bring them over to the island by six o'clock in the evening and to place them under lock and key. "After the proposed

[1] *Correspondence relating to the limits of British jurisdiction in the Gambia* (1877), pp. 12, 17–21, 42.	[2] *Ibid.* p. 9.

hour, should any of them be seen on the other side, the sergeant of the (volunteer) police should give notice to the owners, and should it not be immediately brought over, he should be deprived of its use for three days or pay a fine of 2*s.* 6*d.*" The headmen of Fatota and Borabakunda were instructed not to allow more than six men to cross over from the mainland to the island after six o'clock in the evening. This provisional government lasted for a fortnight. We are told that "the whole of the inhabitants went cheerfully and heartily to work in carrying out these resolutions; there was not the least trouble experienced in enlisting the volunteers, and every one threw in his mite towards their support".[1] In June a Manager arrived with some police constables and Dr Horton handed over to him. Provision for the future defence of the island was then made by the raising of a volunteer militia from amongst the inhabitants.[2]

In March 1866, whilst the fate of MacCarthy Island was still hanging in the balance, proposals were received from the French Ambassador in London that the Gambia should be handed over to his Government in exchange for the French posts on the Ivory Coast. The proposal was considered worthy of consideration, not because of the expense of the upkeep of the Gambia but because at this date the British Government was anxious to consolidate its territories in West Africa by getting one compact block of settlements under one set of laws.[3] Further conversations took place, during which it was suggested that the French settlements on the Gaboon coast should be substituted for those on the Ivory Coast. On 22 May 1868 this last proposal was declined by the British Government, but at the same time the Ambassador in Paris was instructed to offer the Gambia in exchange for all rights on the French Coast between the Rivers Dembia and Sheba.[4]

In 1869 Sir Arthur Kennedy visited Bathurst. He had in 1859 been appointed Governor of the Gambia, but had never taken up the post. His first visit to the Gambia was seventeen years later

[1] Horton, *West African Countries and Peoples*, pp. 83–86. The cost of the provisional defence force was subsequently defrayed by the Government (cf. Appropriation Ordinance, 1866).

[2] Ordinance dated 4 June 1866.

[3] The history of the policy of successive British Governments in regard to relations with France in West Africa is very fully set out in Hall, *The Colonial Office*, pp. 177–179, and in Lord Salisbury's despatch to Lord Dufferin of 30 March 1892, which is to be found in Hertslet, *Map of Africa*, pp. 750 *seq.*

[4] *State Papers*, 1870–1871, p. 1106.

when he was Governor of the British West African Settlements. "What", subsequently asked Messrs Brown and Quin of Bathurst, "can the opinion of Sir Arthur Kennedy be worth? He never spent ten days in the Gambia, never went up the river beyond Bathurst, knows nothing of the trade and resources of the river, or of the different tribes inhabiting the banks of it." Sir Arthur Kennedy's reply was that "it requires no long residence or grasp of intellect to master the extent of the trade, resources and future prospects of the Gambia".[1] We will leave it to others to judge between Sir Arthur Kennedy and Mr Thomas Brown, whom the Earl of Carnarvon once described in a Colonial Office Minute Paper as the Gambia's watchdog,[2] and follow the sequence of events. At the end of his brief visit the Governor arrived at the conclusion that the Gambia might with very great advantage be ceded to France and so informed the Colonial Office. He urged his proposal on a number of grounds. The garrison was costing the imperial government £20,000 a year, the revenue was in its nature precarious and entirely dependent upon groundnuts, the trade was largely in French hands, and the place had no value as a military post or any mercantile value to Great Britain. To sum up, he disapproved of "the responsibility of maintaining the settlement without any result or prospective advantage", especially in view of "the hopelessness of extending civilisation among the peculiar people, which surrounds and composes the bulk of the settlement".[3]

Upon receipt of Sir Arthur Kennedy's expression of opinion the negotiations, which had rather hung fire since 1868, were revived by the British Government. The correspondence in relation thereto fills one hundred pages of a parliamentary white paper. It is not proposed to attempt even a short summary here, but it should be mentioned that, though the Liberal Government of the day came in for a good deal of criticism over the proposal, the matter was in no sense a party question and that the leaders of the Conservative party were in full agreement with the policy of the ministry.

News of the proposal was of course not slow in reaching the Gambia. The troops were withdrawn from Bathurst in 1870. In May of that year French officials from the Senegal visited the place in a

---

[1] *Correspondence relating to the proposed cession of the Gambia to France* (1870), pp. 71, 77.	[2] Hall, *op. cit.* p. 113.

[3] *Correspondence relating to the proposed cession of the Gambia to France* (1870), p. 3.

gunboat and made a careful inspection of the public buildings. In the following month the Governor of Senegal arrived in another gunboat and proceeded up the river as far as Baddibu.[1] Expenditure on public works was reduced to a minimum and many other preparations were made with a view to an early relinquishment of British control. All these things were in fact carried so far that on 5 July 1870 the British Ambassador at Paris informed the Foreign Secretary that he had been asked by the Quai D'Orsay "what was it that the British authorities meant? Should the French at once enter into the territory and take possession of it?"[2]

If these preparations somewhat mystified the French Government, they caused the greatest possible consternation amongst the inhabitants of Bathurst. Henry Finden, Samuel John Forster, J. D. Richards and a number of other leading Africans in Bathurst took counsel, as Sir Arthur Kennedy subsequently complained, of Mr Thomas Brown. On his advice they drew up a petition to which over 500 signatures were subsequently obtained. The signatories were entirely Africans and included Protestants, Roman Catholics and Mohammedans. The petitioners declared that they were British subjects, that they were ready by the enrolment of a militia force and a constabulary to undertake the protection of the settlement and that, upon retrenchment of the civil establishment, they were ready to pay the necessary taxes to make the colony self suffing and thus to avoid the compulsory transfer of their allegiance— a course to which from their knowledge of French institutions in the Senegal they were exceedingly averse.[3]

Protests against the proposal were not confined to Bathurst. When Tomani Bojang, "king" of the Kombo, learnt of the current rumours, he hastened to Bathurst to interview the Administrator and to express his own alarm and that of his people. When he learnt that the rumours had some foundation in fact, he returned to Yundum and assembled his chiefs. At their request he sent the following petition for forwarding to the Queen:

I, Tomani Bojang, thank the Queen of England for all past favours; and as Your Majesty is aware that it was war that compelled me to give up part of my territory to your people, I now beg, that should you desire

---

[1] *Ibid.* p. 65.   [2] *State Papers,* 1870–1871, p. 1117.
[3] *Correspondence relating to the proposed cession of the Gambia to France* (1870), p. 34.

to transfer your settlements to another person, I would rather you return
my territory back to me as an act of friendship. I, King of Tomani of
Kombo, wish the Queen to remember that our friendship commenced
long before war broke out in my territory; as when your subjects re-
quired a piece of land for farming or building purposes, I have never
yet refused, but always grant them a piece; and my reason for so doing is
because I love the British people and like their friendship; and they
have possession of such lands up to the present time. Even Bathurst,
which Your Majesty is about to give away to strangers, was given to
you by my grandfather, and that is sufficient proof that I and my
ancestors were kind and that we love you, as you have exhibited the same
disposition to us.[1]

When at a later date he was informed that the British Government could not accede to his request for the return of his territory,
Tomani Bojang's reply was:

I shall respect any ruling power that administers the government of
the Gambia, and would watch its policy. If it be friendly and just, I will
maintain it; but if on the contrary, I will separate from it and regret our
losing the English, who are our powerful allies and the pride of the
government of my kingdom.[2]

Other people besides the local inhabitants were also at work en-
deavouring to stop the negotiations. The three leading Bathurst
firms—Messrs Forster and Smith, Messrs Brown and Quin, and
Thomas Chown—each lodged their protest. So did the Manchester
Chamber of Commerce and the Wesleyan Missionary Society.
Members of both Houses of Parliament took the matter up. Eventually the matter was raised in the House of Lords by the Duke of
Manchester and in the House of Commons by Mr (afterwards Sir)
Robert Fowler. On 10 June 1873 the latter was informed in answer
to a question that the negotiations were still proceeding. This
answer produced a supplementary question from Sir John Hay as
to whether the transfer could take place without parliamentary consent. Hitherto all questions on the subject had been answered by
the Under Secretary of State, but this further question brought Mr
Gladstone to his feet. He said the question took him by surprise,
but he believed that the intended arrangement could not be carried

[1] *Correspondence relating to the proposed cession of the Gambia to France*
(1870), p. 48.   [2] *Ibid.* p. 106.

through without parliamentary consent and that the Government had not the slightest intention of putting it into effect without such consent. Sir John Hay raised the matter again in debate on 16 July. He expressed the opinion that "the Colonial Office had determined without consulting Parliament to carry out the arrangement". Mr Monsell, Under Secretary of State, repeated the assurance that the consent of Parliament would have to be obtained before any transfer took place and added that the French Government had been given so to understand. He further stated that the proposed terms of cession had by no means reached finality. Though no vote was taken, the speeches showed that there was a very strong opposition to the proposal.[1]

After the debate the Government decided that matters could not be hastened. The Governor of Sierra Leone was instructed "to proceed to the Gambia to inquire as to the feeling of the natives, and to endeavour, by prudent steps, to remove any opposition to the transfer of sovereignty when occasion for it shall require; and that in the meantime temporary arrangements will be made for carrying on the administration of the affairs of the settlement".[2] Finally, the outbreak of the Franco-Prussian War provided the British Government with an excuse for putting an end to further negotiations. On 13 August the British Ambassador was instructed to inform the French Government that "whilst France is at war, it will be impossible to proceed with negotiations for a cession of territory, and that Her Majesty's Government must reserve to themselves the liberty, before the renewal of negotiations, to consider the objections to the proposed transfer which have been made in the settlement and in this country".[3]

News of this decision was received in the Gambia with considerable relief, but it was felt that it was merely a respite and not a reprieve. "Temporary arrangements...for carrying on the administration of the settlement" sounded ominous and meant in fact that a number of public services were badly starved. The colonial steamer *Dover* had had to be scrapped as no longer serviceable in 1866 and was not replaced until 1875 with the result that in 1869, when there was a bad outbreak of cholera on MacCarthy Island and medical stores were urgently needed there, those stores had to be sent 150 miles upstream by a slow sailing cutter. Certain drainage

---

[1] Hansard, *op. cit.* cci, 1842–1843; cciii, 340, 353–367.
[2] *State Papers*, 1870–1871, p. 1123.   [3] *Ibid.* p. 1124.

and reclamation schemes near Bathurst, which had been declared by the medical authorities to be absolutely necessary, were suspended until the question of cession should be finally disposed of.[1]

The state of local feeling was summed up in the following words by the ministers of the Wesleyan Mission in the Gambia.

So far as trading is regarded, it is painfully evident in the circumstances of the people that even the transfer, all but universally deprecated, would be a commercial advantage compared with the embarrassing uncertainty at present existing; and the ministers testify of what is within their knowledge when they affirm that a most injurious paralizing influence rests upon British enterprise from a conviction that matters must become worse, whilst this uncertainty admits of a variety of prejudicial action on the part of those non-residents so deeply committed to the advocacy of transfer.[2]

France's own misfortunes in Europe prevented her from reverting to the matter for several years, but early in 1874 the French Government submitted a proposal for the exchange of the Gambia for Mellacori, Grand Bassam and Assini. Lord Carnarvon asked the Administrator to sound public feeling in the Gambia in regard to such a proposal, stating that "there are reasons which would induce me to look favourably upon such a proposal". The answer came in the form of two petitions. One was signed by Joseph D. Richards and 151 other inhabitants of Bathurst. It declared that the signatories "naturally feel a great aversion to being summarily transferred into the hands of a foreign power, whose language, habits, and institutions are diametrically opposed to their own, and whose policy, as evidenced at Senegal and Goree, your petitioners feel will materially interfere with their social and their religious rights". They went on to say that they were opposed to the transfer

because they are averse to French rule, because, as loyal subjects of the Queen, they are attached to British institutions, because they love political and religious liberty, and because by their industry they have acquired property in these settlements, which the projected transfer will materially affect.... The settlements are self supporting and practically independent of the mother country, have no public debt to liquidate,

---

[1] *Correspondence respecting the financial conditions of Sierra Leone, Gambia, and St Helena* (1877), p. 2.
[2] Gambia District Meeting Book, 23 January 1871.

have a revenue sufficiently adequate to their requirements, and which with a little economy and retrenchment would be more than adequate to meet their present expenditure. Should it be necessary, your petitioners are ready and willing to submit to extra taxation rather than be given to a foreign power.[1]

The other petition was even more numerously signed. The signatories included not only inhabitants of Bathurst but also the headmen of Mandingo, Jollof and Serahuli towns in the Kombo. The petitioners declared that "we do not desire to say anything against our French neighbour, but we may be permitted to remark that from our experience of the neighbouring colonies we infinitely prefer to remain as we are".[2]

In the meantime the negotiations between the two countries proceeded very slowly. The original French proposal was varied by the substitution of the territories between the Rios Pongas and Gaboon for the territory originally offered, but the discussions were protracted. They fill up 180 pages of a parliamentary white paper and were also the subject of a number of contemporary pamphlets and newspaper articles. When in July 1875 the Soninki-Marabout war looked as if it was about to be carried into British Kombo, Lord Carnarvon informed the Foreign Office that this "grave complication...affords an additional reason for pushing forward without unnecessary delay the negotiations with France".[3] By this time, however, opposition to the proposal was beginning to make itself heard. The Manchester Chamber of Commerce once more entered the lists. The Duke of Manchester also moved in the matter. The Royal Colonial Institute (now the Royal Empire Society) appointed a committee to consider the question. A report was drawn up by Sir Frederick Young, which went into considerable detail to prove "how utterly unfounded" were the French claims "for which a sacrifice of British territory was being contemplated". Subsequently the Institute sent a memorial to Lord Carnarvon protesting against the cession "on commercial, political and imperial grounds, as well as from a sense of the obligations imposed upon the British Empire

---

[1] *Correspondence respecting...the proposed exchange with France* (1876), pp. 5, 7, 178.

[2] *Copy of a petition from the inhabitants of the Gambia* (1876).

[3] *Correspondence respecting...the proposed exchange with France* (1876), p. 43.

not to abandon or hand over without their consent to a foreign power any of its subjects, who desire to retain the privileges and benefits of its rule".[1] In addition a Gambia Committee was formed, with Mr C. Wingfield as chairman and Messrs F. W. Chesson and C. Fitzgerald as honorary secretaries. This committee sent a deputation to wait upon Lord Carnarvon and also published literature protesting that "the proposal to make peaceful and industrious populations the subject of barter is no less dangerous to the tranquillity of the West Coast of Africa than it would be fraught with injustice to the people concerned".[2]

Lord Carnarvon repeated the assurance of his predecessor that no cession would take place until Parliament had had the opportunity of expressing an opinion.[3] There was a short debate on 17 February 1876 in the House of Lords, when Lord Carnarvon explained the reasons for advocating the proposed exchange. The subsequent discussion showed that there was a strong feeling in the House against the proposal.[4] The matter was therefore referred two days later to a Cabinet meeting, where, in Lord Carnarvon's words, the members were, "as usual, adverse to a bold course". It was eventually decided that Mr Disraeli should announce the appointment of a committee in the House of Commons. But the lower house was never called upon to discuss the question. The French Government suddenly withdrew their offer to cede the whole control of the coast to the east of the Gold Coast in exchange for the Gambia. Lord Carnarvon had only been prepared to consider the projected cession of the Gambia upon the terms of complete cession of this other territory. He was therefore not prepared to go any further with the negotiations.[5] On 20 March 1876 in answer to a question in the House of Commons Mr James Lowther, the Under Secretary of State, announced that, as the French Government was not prepared to cede the full control of the regions, which the British Government desired in exchange for the Gambia, all further negotiations had

---

[1] Folsom, *Royal Empire Society*, pp. 215, 224, 228; Young, "Report on the Gambia question", *J.R.C.I.* VII.

[2] Fitzgerald, *Gambia and its proposed cession to France* and *The proposed cession of the Gambia.*

[3] *Correspondence respecting...the proposed exchange with France* (1876), pp. 46, 176; Hansard, *op. cit.* CCXXVI, 444, and CCXXVII, 133.

[4] Hansard, *op. cit.* CCXXVII, 374 *seq.*

[5] Hardinge, *The Life of Henry Howard Molyneux Herbert, fourth Earl of Carnarvon*, II, 142–144.

been brought to an end.[1] On 2 May 1876 there was a short discussion in the House, which went a long way towards allaying further anxiety in the Gambia. Mr (afterwards Sir) William McArthur rose to call attention to the position of the settlement with a view to placing it on a permanently satisfactory footing and also in the interests of commerce to opening up communications in the river. He expressed a hope that no government would again attempt to hand over 14,000 British subjects to a foreign power without their consent. He further declared that it was only due to British subjects, who were engaged in trade there, that they should no longer be kept in suspense and that the Government should give some assurance as to its future policy. In reply Mr Lowther announced that it was now the Government's intention to retain the colony.[2]

Though the matter never got so far as negotiations between the two countries, there was some further talk in 1888 of exchanging the Gambia for other territory.[3] The subject has also been raised since then. In his *Dual Mandate* Lord Lugard summed up the matter in the following words:

The exchange of the Gambia...has been from time to time revived up to the present day. It would surely be an immoral and indefensible transaction, unless with the consent of the people. A French writer in the Observer *(11th November, 1917) endorses this view.*[4]

[1] Hansard, *op. cit.* ccxxviii, 272.
[3] Hall, *op. cit.* p. 178.
[2] *Ibid.* pp. 1998, 2007.
[4] P. 54, n.

XXX: The Soninki-Marabout War, 1866–1887

As mentioned in the previous chapter, the long drawn out negotiations between Great Britain and France caused great uneasiness in the Gambia, which was reflected in the decline of trade and a general inactivity in administrative affairs. Yet another severe blow to the revival of prosperity was inflicted by an outbreak of cholera, which in 1869 swept through the whole of the country on both banks of the river. The disease had its origin in Senegal, where it was rampant during the early months of that year. On 1 April it broke out in MacCarthy Island. Mr Benjamin Tanner, the Manager, was attacked but fortunately recovered. There was only one other European on the island and no medical officer. No doctor could be spared from Bathurst. All that the Administrator could do was to send up a few stores and medicines. These had to be carried by a slow sailing cutter, as the colonial steamer *Dover* had been scrapped in 1866 and had not been replaced. In the midst of all this trouble a fire broke out on the island and destroyed twenty houses. Apparently that fire had a like effect to that in London two centuries before. The plague abated, but in the course of three weeks ninety-three people had died out of a population of 400 and many of the rest had fled to the mainland.

Thereafter the disease gradually travelled down the river. Bathurst was forewarned, but limited resources made quarantine restrictions impracticable. The only measures, which could be taken, were to convert the coal depot into a temporary hospital and to evacuate the troops to Cape St Mary and Fort Bullen. On 5 May the disease claimed its first victim in Bathurst and thereafter worked its will for over two months. The Sierra Leone Government was unable to send any assistance and the French in Senegal, who had readily lent doctors in the yellow fever outbreaks of 1859 and 1866, had more than enough to do in combating the disease in their own country. The brunt of the work fell upon Staff Assistant-Surgeon Robert Waters and a single African dispenser named Chapman. Cholera was a hitherto unknown disease to the natives and many of them were panic stricken. It was left to a small band of Europeans to render the attenuated medical staff what assistance they could. Foremost amongst these were the Administrator (Rear-Admiral Patey), the Colonial Secretary (Mr Henry Fowler), Mr Thomas Brown, a leading Bathurst merchant, and the Fathers and Sisters of the Roman Catholic Mission.

A white paper was subsequently published giving an account of the outbreak. Many of its pages read like passages from Defoe. One brief letter, which Mr Brown hastily penned to the Administrator, tells much.

The cart has just left a dead body in the street and others are awaiting burial. John Bye says the horse will not draw. He is looking for men to carry the body. I fear he will not get people quickly.

Admiral Patey had to send his own horse to draw that cart. He and other European volunteers had each morning and evening personally to superintend the collection and burial of the dead.

Mr Fowler, wrote the Administrator, *the first thing every morning went round to collect the dead in the streets, lifting the bodies with his own hands into the carts, as sufficient men could not be obtained for love or money. . . .So many natives have been struck down whilst engaged in this work, it is only by the free use of brandy that one or two can be prevailed upon to take the risk of supplying their places. . . . The natives are given up to despair and drink, and it is a work to distinguish the dead from the intoxicated; the touch alone reveals the fact. The dead and dying are also left in the huts to take care of themselves, and in my regular rounds I have to go into the houses myself, with Mr Fowler, and others that are with me, before I can induce the relatives to attend to their wants, or I have to wait to see the burial party carry off the corpse, as personal example is the only means of making an impression on the panic stricken natives. . . . The bodies are placed in trenches, as time and labour do not admit of separate graves.*

During May there were for some time over seventy deaths a day and, by the time that the disease had spent itself, 1162 persons had died out of a population of 4000. It is impossible to estimate the number of deaths, which occurred between MacCarthy Island and Bathurst as the disease travelled down the river. Some villages may have escaped altogether, but when once the plague found its way into one of the many over-crowded stockaded villages, which the wars had brought into existence, it must have worked terrible havoc. It is known, for instance, that at the trading post at Dumasansan in Jarra the cholera carried off eighty persons out of a population of 300. Therefore it may well be that in the course of about three months one-quarter of the people living on the river banks fell victims to cholera. One thing is certain: for the time being trade and every other kind of business came to a standstill.[1]

A previous writer on the Gambia summed up its history during the years following the cholera as "the inactivity in the colony from 1870 to 1887". Those few words may fairly accurately summarise the history of the Colony, but they cannot be held to describe events in the upper river. Those seventeen years were no doubt years of inactivity on the part of the British administration in the upper river, but in other respects they were years of distressing activity in the shape of wars and raids amongst the natives.

The fact that the local administration did not intervene in these struggles was due to instructions from England. In 1866 Mr Cardwell had announced that the upper river was not under British protection and that traders, who settled beyond the limits of British jurisdiction, did so entirely at their own risk. Lord Carnarvon had announced in 1874 that, so long as MacCarthy Island was held by the British Government, merchants trading in the river up to that point were no doubt entitled to expect protection from the Colonial Government against unprovoked attacks by the natives, but that "they should be warned that in going beyond that place for the purpose of trading or for any purpose, they will do so at their own risk and must not look for protection or redress in part of the country where British authority does not exist". In that year and again in 1876 the acting Administrator attempted to obtain redress for two outrages committed upon traders by the natives of Karantaba (Pisania) and Barragalli. In the first case he imposed a fine on the inhabitants, which was paid. When in the second case he went to Barragalli to collect the fine, he was met with a defiant refusal by a body of armed men. When the incident was reported to Lord Carnarvon, he repeated his former declaration and expressed the opinion that in the particular case it had been imprudent to inflict a punishment, which there was no means to enforce. "After fully weighing

[1] *Papers relating to the recent outbreak of cholera in the Settlement of the Gambia* (1869); Gore, *Medical History of our West African Campaigns*, p. 216; *The Times*, 8 May and 26 June 1869.

the question of the possible risk of prestige,... I cannot consider the present to be a case in which I would advise employment of Her Majesty's military or naval forces for the punishment of the offenders." A year later Surgeon-Major Gouldsbury, who had been in the meantime appointed Administrator, proceeded to Barragalli in a gunboat to find a new chief, who was very quick to repudiate his predecessor's conduct and promised to live on good terms with the British. Prestige was thereby regained, but the policy of non-intervention in disputes above MacCarthy Island remained in force for another decade.[1]

The natives above MacCarthy Island were therefore left to settle their own quarrels and troubles by themselves. Not only had they the Soninki-Marabout quarrel always with them, but they had also to submit to constant raids from the interior. In the earlier part of the century these raids appear to have been carried out by a few adventurous spirits under some chosen leader. By the middle of the century the movement had become so universal that it had become organised on what might be called a national scale. A powerful Fula confederation had come into being, which despatched almost annually a force of several thousand men to raid the Gambia. The leaders of this confederation were Bakari Sardu, the ruler of Bondu, Sori or Alfa Ibrahima, the ruler of Futa Jallon, and a warlike chief named Alfa Molloh. Of these Bakari Sardu had received a French education and had been awarded the Legion of Honour.[2] He appears to have been a person of considerable ability, who possessed a wider outlook than most of his neighbours. He was very careful to keep on the right side of the French, but seems to have considered it necessary to give his people some outlet for their bellicosity and therefore encouraged raids into territory which was not French. Alfa Ibrahima was a typical ruler of a warlike African race, bent not so much upon conquest or the acquisition of fresh territory as upon providing his people with a means of livelihood by robbery and pillage of weaker tribes.

Alfa Molloh belonged to a colony of Fulas, who in the early days of the nineteenth century had come from Kasonko in the Sudan and had settled in the Mandingo country, which lay between the Gambia and the Casamance. His original name had been Mozzo Egué and his original occupation that of elephant hunter. According to

[1] *Correspondence relating to the limits of British jurisdiction in the Gambia* (1877).   [2] *Ibid.* p. 34.

rumour he had once been the slave of a Mandingo chief. At an early age he acquired a reputation for personal bravery and in about 1867 he raised the Fulas in revolt against the ruling Mandingos. In that year he defeated Lekuta Sona, the leading Mandingo chief, in a fight near the present French station at Kolda. After this victory he changed his name to Alfa Molloh and invoked the aid of the ruler of Futa Jallon. Alfa Ibrahima sent his son, Momodu Salif, to assist him. With this help and also that of Bakari Sardu of Bondu he gradually made himself during the course of the next few years supreme in the districts of Jimara (Jemarrow), Tomani, Eropina, Pata, Kamako, Yega and Fambantan.[1] In return for the help which he received from his two compatriots he assisted them in their wars in the valley of the Gambia.

It was easy to find a pretext for raiding the valley of the Gambia. The rulers of Bondu and Futa Jallon were by instinct anti-Marabout and in its early days many of the leaders of the new movement had fled from those countries to the banks of the Gambia. They were not as a rule welcomed by the local chiefs and generally found it necessary to set up for themselves in separate villages, which were strongly stockaded. The Soninkis and Marabouts had in fact come to blows in the upper river as early as 1843, when acting Governor Ingram was prevented from reaching the Barrakunda Falls because the two factions were fighting near Kantalikunda.[2] As many of the Marabout leaders in the Gambia were fugitives from their own countries, the rulers of Bondu and Futa Jallon had excellent pretexts for joining in these wars in the Gambia.

One such example may be given. In about 1870 a well-known Fodi, or teacher, named Simotto Moro, came from Bondu and settled on the banks of the Gambia near to Yabutenda. He was driven thence by Alfa Molloh and then settled at Tubakuta in Wuli. The fame of his teaching spread and he gathered a large following around him. As his village had become the rallying point for Marabout refugees, Bakari Sardu attacked it in 1875 but was driven off. Four years later the combined forces of Bakari Sardu, Alfa Ibrahima and

---

[1] Legrand, "Le Fouladou", *La Géographie*, xxvi, 250 *seq.*

[2] Ingram, "Abridged account of an expedition of about two hundred miles up the Gambia", *J.R.G.S.* xvii, 155, would appear to be the earliest use of the term Soninki (there written "Sononkay") in official correspondence, but the Rev. William Moister, who left the Gambia in 1833, uses the term in his *Memorials of Missionary Labours of Western Africa*, p. 176.

Musa Molloh again attacked Tubakuta and were again driven off. Simotto Moro died in 1885 and his mantle fell upon his son, Dimbo. In the following year a certain Momodu Lamin, who had been causing the French a lot of trouble in the Senegal, took refuge with Dimbo. This gave Alfa Molloh's son, Musa Molloh, the opportunity for revenge. He combined with a French force under Captain Fortin to attack and destroy Tubakuta. Momodu Lamin escaped from the sack of the place, but was subsequently captured by Musa Molloh and beheaded.[1]

Though the Soninki-Marabout disputes as often as not provided an excuse for invading the Gambia, the raiders very frequently showed strict impartiality as to the persons whom they raided. Both parties were apt to suffer alike and in the long run the Soninkis derived very little advantage from their *soi-disant* allies, who certainly did not help to make their cause popular. The result was that the Marabouts gradually obtained a paramount influence in many districts in the upper river. Kemintang had died in about 1843. He does not appear ever to have had an extensive jurisdiction, but merely to have acquired some measure of notoriety from his quarrels with the Colonial Government. Nobody of even his calibre had risen in his place. The Soninki chiefs of Nyani had been caught between two Marabout fires, which had been kindled by Maba on the one side and the refugees from the interior on the other side. Their own mutual jealousies, which not infrequently led to wars between themselves, prevented effective co-operation. In the end many of them decided to agree with their adversaries quickly by giving the Marabouts posts in their petty kingdoms. When Colonel O'Connor visited the upper river in 1858, he recorded an interview, which he had with the "king" of Kataba and his leading Marabout chief. "The former appeared not to have recovered from the state of intoxication I found him in in January 1854. The latter has but surely sapped the influence of the king and is *de facto* the ruler." There was the same story to tell in Wuli. Jatta Fodi had set up a fortified town on a bend in the river. The "king" was "a mere feeble cypher" and the power was in the hands of this Marabout freebooter, "a crafty, boisterous bully", who, however, after a few words with the Governor "soon saw his place...and promised to behave well in future".[2]

[1] Rançon, *Dans la Haute Gambie*, pp. 42-48, 116; Legrand, *op. cit.* p. 250.
[2] Colonel O'Connor to H. Labouchere, 4 March 1858.

Many of these Soninki chiefs managed to retain their positions solely by reason of the fact that they were by virtue of various treaties in receipt of subsidies from the Colonial Government. The fear that a subsidy might be withheld, if the chief were deposed, induced more than one Marabout "mayor of the palace" to leave a drivelling Childeric or Chilperic as nominal ruler of the land, but generally in the end the two would fall out, a war would follow and, as often as not, the Soninki "king" was worsted and killed or otherwise got rid of. Kataba is a case in point. In 1863 an emissary of Maba invaded the land, but the "king" managed with some difficulty to hold his own.[1] Through the mediation of Major Harley of the West India Regiment he and his leading Marabout chief came to an agreement, whereby all future differences were to be referred to the arbitration of the Commandant of MacCarthy Island.[2] But his power was rapidly waning. In 1870 both he and the chief of Nyanibintang begged the Colonial Government to place them under its protection, but in accordance with instructions this request had to be refused.[3] In 1872 Bakari Sardu decided to intervene on behalf of the Soninkis and raided the country as far as Karantaba.[4] As a freebooting expedition it was highly successful, but it did little more than stem the Marabout tide for a brief moment. It was followed by a counter-raid by Momodu N'Dare Ba, the Marabout chief of Baddibu, and the "king" of Kataba became a fugitive.[5] As he could no longer fulfil his undertaking under the MacCarthy Island Treaty of 1823 to protect British subjects, the "king" of Kataba's subsidy was taken from him and given to his conqueror.[6] But the Marabout triumph did not bring peace to Nyani. In 1876 the ruling chief of Sine Salum ravaged that district and also carried the war into Wuli, where he destroyed the "king's" town at Medina.[7]

Wuli, however, was the one kingdom on the north bank which managed to preserve its integrity. The district was used by Bakari Sardu and his allies as a corridor for their raids down the river. The ruling chiefs of Wuli realised their inability to prevent this and turned it to their own advantage by invoking the aid of the raiders

[1] Colonel D'Arcy to Duke of Newcastle, 24 August 1863.

[2] *Ordinances of the Gambia*, 1875, p. 535.

[3] *Correspondence respecting the proposed cession of the Gambia to France* (1870), p. 17.   [4] Rançon, *op. cit.* p. 129.

[5] *Correspondence respecting...the proposed exchange with France* (1876), p. 17.   [6] *Ordinances of the Gambia*, 1875, p. 541.

[7] Rançon, *op. cit.* pp. 44, 45.

against any of their rebellious Marabout subjects. Their position was, moreover, considerably strengthened in 1869 when the Manager of MacCarthy Island, on behalf of the British Government, concluded a treaty with a representative of Bakari Sardu, whereby the latter undertook to keep open the trade route between Bondu and the River Gambia.[1]

In 1875 Musa Molloh, the son of Alfa Molloh, swept down the south bank of the river as far as Kai-ai Island and then turned south into Portuguese Guinea. It was one of the few decisive invasions which have ever taken place in the history of the Gambia. He carried everything before him and the relics of the kingdoms of Tomani, Jimara (Jemarrow) and Eropina tottered to the ground. Most of the Mandingo population fled before him and his Fula followers occupied the land, which thenceforth became known as Fuladu.[2]

In 1881 Alfa Molloh died. On his death-bed he bequeathed his wives and his cattle to his brother, Bakari Dembel, but at the same time made it known that his son, Musa, was to succeed him in his chieftainship and the rest of his property. Disputes arose between the uncle and nephew regarding the inheritance, but eventually Musa Molloh, who appears to have realised the dangers of disunion in a recently conquered territory, agreed to recognise Bakari Dembel as his overlord. But a year or so later there was further trouble between the two. As Musa Molloh was the actual conqueror of Fuladu, he enjoyed very great popularity. This was strongly resented by his uncle, who instigated the people of two villages to attack Musa. The nephew was warned of the plot and retaliated by destroying the two villages. After that, being anxious to avoid a civil war, he removed himself into the southern portion of Fuladu near to the banks of the Casamance. In 1883 he entered into a treaty whereby he placed the districts, which were then subject to his authority, under French protection.[3]

Musa Molloh had not been able to subjugate the district of Kantora, but his conquests on the south bank of the river extended from Kantora to the district of Niamina, where he was brought to a halt

---

[1] *Ordinances of the Gambia*, 1875, p. 536.

[2] *Correspondence relating to the limits of British jurisdiction in the Gambia* (1877), pp. 32–34; Rançon, *op. cit.* p. 68.

[3] Legrand, *op. cit.* p. 250; *Further Correspondence relating to...the Gambia* (1892), pp. 74–76; Minutes of the Annual Meeting of the Gambia District (Wesleyan Mission), 19 January 1880, 13 December 1881 and 13 February 1883.

by the Marabouts. Neither Niamina nor the neighbouring districts of Kiang and Foni had been spared from the ravages of the Soninki-Marabout war. Though Maba's invasion of Kiang had ended disastrously before Kwinella in 1863, the setback had been only temporary. After Maba's return to Baddibu his lieutenants carried on the war. The principal of these was Fodi Kabba, who in 1875 crossed over from Baddibu to fight Musa Molloh at the time when the latter was subjugating Fuladu.[1] Fodi Kabba had the longest career of all the Marabout leaders. One of the few Europeans, who ever saw him face to face, described him as being a man of remarkably fine appearance and, even in his old age, of powerful physique, standing six feet high and broad in proportion.[2] He had begun his career as a Marabout leader whilst still in his twenties during the early fighting in the Kombo. In 1862 he had taken a party of Marabouts from Gunjur to assist their co-religionists in Niumi.[3] After the conclusion of the peace between the two factions in that district he threw in his lot with Maba and followed his fortunes. He was not devoid of intelligence and had in the course of his career picked up a smattering of French. But his general outlook on life is disclosed in the message which he once sent to the Administrator.

I beg to say I have nothing to do with groundnuts, as, where I am, I am only a stranger. Ever since I knew myself to be a man, my occupation has been a warrior; and I make it my duty to fight the Soninkis, who profess no religion whatever. If the Soninkis on the north bank of the river had accepted the Mahommedan religion, we could have lived in unity. . . . I will be very glad if the traders and groundnut planters can come to an agreement, because I will be benefited by it, as our guns, shot and powder are bought from the traders.[4]

An incident, which occurred in the early days of his fighting against Musa Molloh, brings out his character in strong contrast to that of Maba, who never forgot that Colonel D'Arcy had once spared his village. During that fighting Musa Molloh's men carried off Fodi Kabba's wives and children. When the Administrator heard of it, he

---

[1] *Correspondence relating to . . . the proposed exchange with France* (1876), pp. 37, 38.
[2] Lt.-Com. I. H. Fraser in *Further correspondence relating to . . . the Gambia* (1892), pp. 26, 27.
[3] Colonel D'Arcy to Duke of Newcastle, 24 December 1862.
[4] *Correspondence respecting the affairs of the Gambia* (1887), pp. 19, 20.

persuaded Musa Molloh to restore them to Fodi Kabba.[1] There was never the slightest expression of gratitude on Fodi Kabba's part to the Administrator or to anybody else, nor was there ever afterwards anything done by him to show that he appreciated this act of kindness.

None the less Fodi Kabba had a gift of leadership and considerable powers of organisation. Whilst he did not succeed in defeating Musa Molloh, he managed to hold up his hitherto irresistible advance. Thereafter he consolidated his own position by forming a large confederacy of Marabouts, which exercised a paramount influence in Niamina, Jarra, Kiang and Foni as well as in the regions to the south of those districts as far as the banks of the Casamance. He really ruled three districts, which were isolated the one from the other, namely, a district to the south of the Bintang Creek, another comprising part of eastern Kiang and western Jarra, and another comprising part of eastern Jarra.[2] In between those districts the Soninkis managed to maintain their independence. Furthermore his authority did not go entirely uncontested within them. The Jolas in particular showed very little disposition to show him implicit obedience.[3] But the result of his failure to obtain full control over the whole of these areas was that the evils of the Soninki-Marabout war were perpetuated and aggravated. Fodi Kabba could only hold his own by constant raids upon his opponents and could only carry out those raids by attracting to himself some of the worst elements in the country. It was very justly said of him in the annual report for 1888 that his "existence is a curse to the neighbourhood. He lives by slave hunting and robbery. None of his neighbours, unfortunately, are strong enough to drive him out, and he naturally attracts to himself all the idle and worthless ruffians, who prefer living on the industry of others to doing any honest work for themselves."

Whilst Fodi Kabba was endeavouring to carve out a kingdom for himself in the middle reaches of the river, his former associates at Gunjur were steadily gaining ground in the Kombo. The peace, which had been patched up between the two factions in 1864, was not of long duration. Even if the respective leaders had been anxious

---

[1] *Correspondence respecting...the proposed exchange with France* (1876), pp. 34, 54.

[2] *Further correspondence relating to...the Gambia* (1892), p. 102.

[3] *Annual Report for 1888.*

to abide by the terms thereof, they were quite unable to control their more bellicose subordinates. The war soon broke out again in its customary form—raids and counter-raids. But, as in the previous fighting, the Soninkis slowly lost ground. By 1873 all the Soninki towns in the Kombo except Busumballa and Brikama were in Marabout hands and many of the inhabitants had taken refuge in British Kombo. As all the regular troops had been removed from the Colony three years before, the only permanent force left to resist aggression was a local constabulary of 100 men. Ordinances were therefore passed to increase the strength of the Kombo Militia and to raise a volunteer defence force. The timely arrival of H.M.S. *Merlin* made the Marabouts hesitate before carrying the pursuit into British territory and on 24 March 1873 they concluded a treaty with the acting Administrator, whereby they undertook to maintain peace and not to allow marauding parties to molest British territory.[1] The chief of Brikama offered to cede his territory to the Colonial Government, if only he could be given protection against the Marabouts, but he had to be informed that all that the Administrator could do was to mediate on his behalf. By the middle of 1874 Brikama had fallen and Busumballa alone held out. Many of the Soninkis retreated to Sukuta, which was just on the border of British Kombo. They erected a stockade there, but the acting Administrator destroyed it, "as he considered it endangered the security of our people residing near the boundary". In June 1874 the Marabouts destroyed Sukuta and the inhabitants fled to British Kombo.[2]

The situation had now become very serious. In the same month the Administrator concluded a treaty at Sukuta with Fodi Silla, who had come to be recognised as the leader of the Kombo Marabouts. By that treaty the Administrator undertook to make every effort to prevent persons residing in British territory from leaving it to engage in war on behalf of either faction. It was further agreed to create a neutral zone by banning the erection of any town or stockade between the town of Yundum and the boundary of British Kombo. Permission was given for the land in this zone to be cultivated. It was further agreed that British subjects might plant groundnuts there, but the customary rents were to be paid to the

[1] *Ordinances of the Gambia,* 1875, p. 539.
[2] *Correspondence respecting…the proposed exchange with France* (1876), pp. 11–19.

chiefs in possession of the land.[1] Four months later, however, Fodi
Silla announced that, as Soninkis were leaving British territory to
attack the Marabouts, "they would in future show no quarter to the
conquered, but would pursue them to Cape St Mary and destroy
them".[2] As many of the constabulary as could be spared were at
once drafted to the frontier of British Kombo. Fodi Silla did not,
however, attempt to carry out his threat. It was the rainy season
and even the Marabouts were for the time being more intent upon
food cultivation than on war. The threat appears to have been
merely a piece of bluster. The allegation therein contained would
also appear to have had little or no foundation in fact. The Soninkis
were just as intent on raising food in their new homes as were the
Marabouts.

The fighting began afresh in 1875. In June of that year Busumballa, the last Soninki town, fell. Many of the inhabitants fled to
British Kombo, where they were disarmed by the police. A small
remnant under their "king", Tomani Bojang, erected a stockade at
Lamin within 400 yards of the British boundary. Hoping thereby
to put an end to an exceedingly awkward situation, the Administrator offered the "king" land in the Ceded Mile, but the offer
was refused. It now seemed almost inevitable that the war would be
carried into British territory and the Admiralty was requested to
send a ship to Bathurst.[3] Fortunately the rains broke just at this
critical moment and there was a lull in the hostilities. During this
respite the acting Administrator worked hard to prevent the war
from breaking out again. Tomani Bojang was given to understand
that, as he refused the offer of land elsewhere, he could not expect
British aid. At length on 29 September 1875 the last of a dynasty,
which had ruled the Kombo for two centuries or more, assented to a
peace on the most humiliating terms. He agreed to shave his head,
become a Marabout, adopt a Mohammedan name, lay down his
arms, and destroy his stockade. In return for which Fodi Silla
agreed to give him and his people lands, which they might cultivate
in peace.[4]

[1] *Ordinances of the Gambia*, 1875, p. 543.
[2] *Correspondence respecting...the proposed exchange with France* (1876),
p. 19.   [3] *Ibid.* pp. 41–46.
[4] *Ordinances of the Gambia*, 1875, p. 544.

XXXI: Separation from Sierra Leone, 1888

Several persons, who visited Bathurst between 1870 and 1885, have recorded their impressions of the place. Those impressions are for the most part not at all complimentary. One such writer describes how on his arrival by steamer a few leaky canoes came out to convey him and his fellow-passengers to the shore. After landing he proceeded past "four establishments for the promotion of civilisation", otherwise grogshops, and "the ghost of the engineering works" to Government House, to which he did give the credit of being "pretty and well kept". He also had a word or two of praise for missionary endeavour, but otherwise found little evidence of anything else except lethargy.

The state of the town, he wrote, *is a reflex of the apathy and listlessness of its people. Those, who have continuously lived there, scarcely recognise the place in its present condition, compared with what it was some years ago. No friendly associations exist for the advancement of the colony, and meetings for the general good are seldom held. The Europeans possess no bond of union, and avoid each other, but have not failed, with few exceptions, to gain the respect of the natives.*

...During the rains the chief part of the town is overflowed, and the people catch fish in the middle of the streets. Occasionally a crocodile from the creek makes its appearance, affording the natives considerable amusement, usually ending in its being killed near to the wineshops on the way to the cemetery. Other natives enjoy the Venetian pastime of rowing up and down the streets in boats, when the water forces its way into the barrack square to the depth of a foot. Luckily these floods soon subside, the muddy soil covered with a great coat of sand, under which the water stagnates, and becomes prejudicial to health from the air being overloaded with evil odours.

...Sanitary science is a sealed book in Bathurst and other West Coast towns, and the name of sanitary inspector is there scarcely known, although the exercise of the functions of such an officer could with great benefit be performed in Bathurst. The most appalling indifference to the existence of festering sewage in the midst of a town population pervades

the inhabitants. Thousands of gallons of putrefying animal and vege-
table refuse in uncovered, or barely covered, holes in the ground form
filthy cesspools close to the dwellings and have not been emptied for
years. The nauseating mixture of gases that arise not only from these
cesspools, but from the slaughterhouse, is intolerable, and through the
neglect and lazy indifference of the inhabitants the air is laden with the
poison they have themselves created.[1]

Another visitor was equally uncomplimentary and declared that

at present we are playing the part of the fabled dog in the manger; we
will not make use of the Gambia as a means of opening up the interior,
nor expend any money in the colony; and, although it is of no value to
us as it is, we will not give it up to another nation, to which it would be
exceedingly useful, and which is ready to make the necessary outlay for
unclosing this long closed country.[2]

Cursory impressions picked up by a casual visitor from a calling
steamer are not necessarily entirely accurate. The truth of a great
many of the foregoing assertions cannot be denied, but behind this
air of apparent stagnation successive Administrators were doing
their best with the very limited means at their disposal. The colony
was not in receipt of a grant in aid, but despite the disturbances in
the upper river and despite serious setbacks such as the yellow fever
of 1866 and the cholera of 1869, it was managing by dint of rigorous
economies not only to pay its own way but also to put by a small
balance. In 1880 that balance stood at £19,000 or the equivalent of
about one year's revenue. If part of that balance could have been
devoted to remedying the insanitary state of affairs, which has
already been described as existing at this date in Bathurst, some of
the strictures, which were passed by visitors, might have been
avoided. In 1877 sanction had been refused by the Treasury Department to a scheme of sanitary reform on the ground that the finances
of the Gambia did not admit of the undertaking.[3] The balance in
hand in 1880 would amply have covered the cost of that scheme, but
unfortunately for the Gambia it was not at this date viewed as a
separate entity. In 1869 a former Under Secretary of State for the
Colonies, Sir Charles Adderley (afterwards Lord Norton), had

---

[1] Mitchinson, *The Expiring Continent*, pp. 308–407.
[2] Ellis, *The Land of Fetish*, p. 11.
[3] *Correspondence respecting the financial condition of Sierra Leone, Gambia,
and St Helena* (1877).

written that "at this moment the Gambia's surplus makes up the Gold Coast's deficiency".[1] This view that the surpluses of West African settlements should be regarded as forming part of a common pool was not peculiar to Sir Charles Adderley and the result was that sanitary reforms in the Gambia had to wait.

Two decisions were reached on the strength of the accumulation by the Gambia of a balance of £19,000. In the first place the British Government decided that the subsidy, which had been paid out of the Imperial funds to the British and African Steamship Company for a monthly mail to the Gambia, should in the future be a charge upon the Colonial Government.[2] This in the light of existing events was not unreasonable, but, as will be seen, it ultimately proved a very serious drain on the revenue of the colony. In the second place, Sir Samuel Rowe, Governor of Sierra Leone, recommended that part of the balance should be used "in defraying the cost of a journey (in the neighbourhood of the upper river), which I propose should be made with a view to obtaining accurate information of the stream as a commercial highway and the promotion of friendly relations with the chiefs of the neighbourhood". He therefore proposed that Surgeon-Major Valesius Skipton Gouldsbury, the Administrator of the Gambia, should proceed up the river to its source in the Futa Jallon plateau and thence make his way back by Timbo to Sierra Leone. Lord Kimberley approved the plan and instructed the Administrator to inform the chiefs, through whose territory he was to pass, that "the expedition had been organised with no view to territorial acquisition or interference with their rights or customs, but solely with a wish to cultivate friendly relations with them".[3]

When forwarding his proposal Sir Samuel Rowe submitted the suggested itinerary for the expedition. As that itinerary shows, no new ground was to be explored. Mungo Park, Major Gray and Governor MacDonnell had each of them travelled as far as the Tenda regions and the last mentioned had officially reported that above the Barrakunda Falls there were a number of impediments to navigation and that the commercial prospects in those regions were disappointing.[4] The French explorer, Gaspard Mollien, had in 1818

---

[1] Adderley, *Review of the Colonial Policy of Lord John Russell's Administration*, p. 216.

[2] *Correspondence respecting the affairs of the Gambia* (1887).

[3] *Correspondence respecting the recent expedition to the upper Gambia* (1881).

[4] *Annual Report for 1849.*

travelled thence to Futa Jallon. Thomas Winterbottom had reached this last mentioned country from Sierra Leone in 1794 by way of Timbo and the last section of the route had also been covered as recently as 1873 by Dr Edward Blyden. To sum up therefore, it was already known that the Gambia had no value as a commercial highway above the Barrakunda Falls and that the prospects of promoting any considerable trade between the Gambia, which was to defray the cost of the expedition, and the countries in the upper reaches of the river were very remote. In addition there was already considerable information to hand regarding the country between Futa Jallon and Sierra Leone.

Dr Gouldsbury's expedition was not therefore destined to make any important discoveries and the details thereof do not come within the scope of this book. Treaties of friendship and commerce were concluded with the ruling chiefs of Futa Jallon and other countries,[1] but the results of the expedition were for the most part purely negative. Not a single canoe or other vessel was seen upon the river after passing the Barrakunda Falls "and from the date of Governor MacDonnell's expedition in 1849 until we appeared—a lapse of thirty-two years—its surface bore no other burden than the floating leaf, the broken branch, and the fallen tree". At the end of his journey the Administrator could only repeat what Governor MacDonnell had already said before him. He could see no near prospect of any great development of commerce between the Gambia and the interior. "Far be it from me to decry any effort towards the opening up of the interior for trade or to the furnishing of facilities for the transport of goods and commerce (or to assert that the increase of trade is impossible, or even improbable, but such increase is, I think, a very measurable quantity, and that is all I contend for); but where these operations are costly, and where the maintenance of their efficacy involves serious expenditure of men and money, I fear the return would not be much more substantial than that of the scheme known as the South Sea Bubble."[2]

In 1874 the Gold Coast and Lagos were separated from Sierra Leone, but the Gambia still remained under the control of the Governor of the last mentioned Colony,[3] towards whose salary it

---

[1] *Annual Report for* 1881; *Ordinances of the Gambia,* 1883–1885, pp. 196–201.

[2] *Correspondence respecting the recent expedition to the upper Gambia* (1881).

[3] *State Papers,* LXVI, 948.

was required to contribute the sum of £500.[1] The instructions of 1866 had laid it down that the Governor of the British West African Settlements should visit the outlying settlements at least once in every year.[2] In 1884 the Gambia administration contributed £1900 towards the purchase of a yacht to facilitate these visits, but no Governor of Sierra Leone ever visited the Gambia during the three years 1884, 1885, and 1886.[3]

In 1882 the Gambia had been entirely free from debt,[4] but in 1884 the disturbed state of the upper river brought about a very serious falling off in revenue. During that and the three following years it fell by about 30 per cent—from £20,000 to £13,000. In his anxiety to effect every possible economy the Administrator decided to stop the annual subsidy to the British and African Steamship Company. This action called forth a protest not only from the local merchants but also from the Liverpool and Manchester Chambers of Commerce. The home Government took the matter up and eventually the shipping company agreed to continue the monthly service on being exempted from port dues.[5]

One result of the protests of the two chambers of commerce was to bring to light the effect of the dependence of the Gambia upon Sierra Leone. In January 1887 in consequence of representations on the part of the Manchester Chamber of Commerce Sir Samuel Rowe was instructed to proceed to the Gambia to consider the difficulties there and the best means of promoting the increase and development of the country.[6] On his arrival he found that other events in Baddibu were to bring the question of the future of the Gambia into still further prominence. In order to explain those events it is necessary to go back a few years.

When Maba died in 1867, his nephew Momodu N'Dare Ba succeeded to his position. Maba had left an infant son, named Said Matti. According to one story Momodu N'Dare Ba was only put in to act as regent for this son. Momodu himself, however, denied this. He had none of the masterful character of his uncle and very speedily found his authority disputed in Baddibu. In 1868 the

---

[1] *Correspondence respecting the affairs of the Gambia* (1887), p. 85.
[2] Hertslet, *Map of Africa*, p. 18.
[3] *Correspondence respecting the affairs of the Gambia* (1887), pp. 76, 85.
[4] *Annual Report for* 1882.
[5] *Correspondence respecting the affairs of the Gambia* (1887); *Further correspondence relating to the affairs of the Gambia* (1887).
[6] *The Times*, 18 January 1887.

people of Sabach revolted,[1] but by 1873 Momodu had sufficiently gained the upper hand in the district for it to be deemed politic by the Colonial Government to recognise him as the *de facto* ruler of the district. Accordingly in that year he was granted the subsidy, which had formerly been paid to the dethroned "king" of Kataba, in consideration of his guaranteeing protection to British subjects trading in Baddibu, Jokadu, Sabach, Salum and Nyani.[2] He was thus treated as capable of exercising control in regions beyond the limits of Baddibu, where his claims were very shadowy indeed. This recognition gave him a very considerable idea of his own importance. In 1875 he demanded the cession of that portion of the Ceded Mile, which lies between Jurunku and N'Jawarra Creeks, in recognition of his benevolent attitude towards British traders. The acting Administrator was in favour of acceding to the request, but Lord Carnarvon was not prepared to assent in view of the negotiations which were then being carried on with France.[3] In 1877 Momodu N'Dare Ba learnt that he was not omnipotent. One of his lieutenants, named Bairam Sisi, rebelled against him and plunged Baddibu into a civil war, which lasted for several years. As usual, the warfare was not of a very sanguinary nature, but its wearisome indecisiveness destroyed all sense of reasonable certainty and security. Neither trade nor agriculture could possibly thrive in such a state of apparently hopeless instability. The result of the fighting was that Bairam Sisi was forced to retreat into the Salum country, where he built a stockade at Kau-ur overlooking a very important river port.[4] Thereafter hostilities came more or less to an end, largely owing to the spirit of discontent with the unsettled and uncertain state of affairs, which had begun to manifest itself amongst the rank and file of both parties.[5]

In 1884 Said Matti, Maba's son, reached man's estate and at once proceeded to claim his father's chieftainship. Both Momodu N'Dare Ba and Bairam Sisi joined forces to oppose him, but Said Matti had gathered a large following and was soon able to drive Momodu N'Dare Ba to the banks of N'Jawarra Creek.[6] In 1885 Bairam Sisi

---

[1] *Annual Report for* 1868.
[2] *Ordinances of the Gambia*, 1875, p. 541.
[3] *Correspondence respecting...the proposed exchange with France* (1876), pp. 34, 40.
[4] *Correspondence respecting the affairs of the Gambia* (1887), p. 86.
[5] *Annual Report for* 1882.
[6] *Annual Report for* 1886.

left Kau-ur and with the aid of the "king" of Sine Salum swept through Baddibu, pillaging and plundering as he went. Crowds of refugees fled from Baddibu to Bathurst and trade and agriculture on the north bank of the river came to a standstill. A deputation of Bathurst merchants begged the Administrator to intervene in the war, but he was unable to leave Bathurst and had no European officer whom he could spare to send in his place. Sergeant G. J. Thomas of the Police[1] was therefore sent to interview the belligerent leaders. They each of them announced that this was going to be a fight to the finish and that Bathurst traders would be well advised to keep clear of Baddibu until it was finished.[2]

The war continued throughout that year and the next. During that time Said Matti distinctly had the best of matters. Momodu N'Dare Ba was left with only a single stockaded town, but Bairam Sisi managed to retain a hold on a number of scattered towns extending from Sami in Niumi up to Kau-ur in Salum. The Administrator, Mr (afterwards Sir) Gilbert Carter, made many attempts to arrange a peace and had a number of personal interviews with the rival leaders. At one period in 1886 he seemed to be upon the point of success. By that date Momodu N'Dare Ba had ceased to count and the only disputes to be settled were those between the two other belligerents. Negotiations eventually reached a stage at which Bairam Sisi was perfectly willing to recognise Said Matti's overlordship subject to certain terms, to which Said Matti was prepared to agree, but Said Matti wanted the subsidy, which had been hitherto enjoyed by his uncle. If he could have had that, he would have signed a treaty on the spot, but Mr Carter had no power to grant the subsidy. The matter had to be referred through the Governor of Sierra Leone to England.[3] During the delay thus caused the war dragged on for another twelve months.

At length on 8 February 1887 Mr Carter was able to arrange a peace. Said Matti agreed to recognise Bairam Sisi's lordship over the towns, which he then held, and Bairam Sisi agreed to accept Said Matti's overlordship. All future disputes between the two were to be referred to the arbitration of the Colonial Government. Momodu N'Dare Ba's life was to be spared and suitable provision

[1] Promoted to be Manager of British Kombo, 1889; took part in the Toniataba and Sankandi expeditions, 1892 and 1901; retired 1903; died 1935.

[2] *Correspondence relating to the affairs of the Gambia* (1887), pp. 19, 20.

[3] *Ibid.* p. 86.

was to be made by Said Matti for him and his family. Both parties undertook to protect British subjects trading in their territories and to refrain from demanding tribute in the Ceded Mile. Finally, Said Matti was given a subsidy of £100 a year.[1]

It was soon made apparent how much value could be attached to any document, which was signed by Said Matti. Very shortly afterwards he invaded Sine Salum in revenge for the assistance, which the ruling chief had given to Bairam Sisi. The French authorities warned him that he would have to take the consequences, if he did not immediately withdraw. But, like his father some twenty years before, he took no heed of the warning. In May 1887 the French sent a column to co-operate with the chief of Sine Salum. Said Matti was completely routed at Ker Maba and fled to the Gambia, closely followed by the French troops. He took refuge at Albreda, where on 11 May he surrendered unconditionally to Sir Samuel Rowe, who had him conveyed to Bathurst. The French column, which had pursued him, thereupon withdrew.[2]

Said Matti's defeat at once plunged Baddibu into a fresh civil war, which threatened to spread to Sine Salum. In the circumstances the French decided to hoist their flag in a number of Said Matti's towns, including some which were on the actual banks of the Gambia. They also deposed two of Bairam Sisi's chiefs at Sanjal and Sabach and put in their own nominees in their places. Various chiefs in French territory were also authorised to collect "customs" and tribute in Baddibu.[3]

In the circumstances Sir Samuel Rowe decided to take steps to prevent similar events occurring on the opposite bank of the river. In September 1887 he proceeded to Foni. He found that the Jolas were thoroughly weary of the constant depredations of Fodi Kabba and were only too anxious to place their country under British protection. On 15 September he met at Kansala the "kings" of sixteen Jola towns, who begged him to accept the sovereignty of their country and to place it under British protection. They entered into a treaty whereby they engaged not to cede their country to any other power except Great Britain or to enter into any treaty or

---

[1] *Ibid.* pp. 87 *seq.*

[2] *Annual Report for* 1887; *The Times,* 12 May 1887.

[3] Hansard, *Parliamentary Debates,* ccxvi, 561; cccxvii, 1149 and cccxix, 544; *Annual Register for* 1887, p. 353; *The Times,* 7, 12 May and 3 November 1887; *Further Correspondence relating to the affairs of the Gambia* (1892), pp. 3, 4.

arrangement with any other country except through and with the consent of the British Government. Before he left Kansala, Sir Samuel Rowe was urgently requested to hoist the British flag. Two days later he entered into a like treaty with the chief and almami (priest) of Bintang. On 19 September he met a number of chiefs of Central Kiang at Kwinella. They also made a similar treaty and begged him to hoist the British flag in their principal towns. On 14 October 1888, Mansa Koto, the independent chief of Battelling, signed a treaty accepting the provisions of the Central Kiang treaty. All these treaties were signed by Marabout and Soninki chiefs alike, who were all of them thoroughly weary of the disturbances caused by Fodi Kabba.[1]

The act of the French in hoisting their flag on the north bank of the river was not allowed to pass without notice. Questions were asked in the House of Commons and the Government announced that, though Baddibu was not under British protection, it was in a recognised British sphere of influence, where chiefs had entered into agreements with the British Government, and that the French Government had been requested to withdraw.[2] The matter was one capable of amicable settlement between the two respective governments, but it had to be considered along with a number of other boundary questions in other parts of Africa. Consequently it was not completely adjusted until two more years had elapsed.

The boundaries of the Gambia were finally settled by an Anglo-French Convention of 10 August 1889. In the absence of any geographical features, which could provide a natural boundary, those boundaries had necessarily to be determined with a ruler and compasses. The boundary started on the north bank of the river at Jinnak Creek; it proceeded thence in a straight line due east to a point distant ten kilometres from the river; thence it followed the course of the river at the distance of ten kilometres up to and beyond Yabutenda. On the south bank the boundary started at the mouth of the River San Pedro (Allahi River) and followed that river up to the point of its intersection with the parallel 13° 10′ North; thence it proceeded along that parallel due east for a distance of about sixty miles; after that it turned at right angles due north and proceeded to a point within ten kilometres of the river; thence it followed the course of the river at a distance of ten kilometres up to and beyond

[1] Hertslet, *Map of Africa*, pp. 18–20.
[2] Hansard, *op. cit.* cccxvi, 561.

Yabutenda. One or two slight modifications have been made to those boundaries since the Convention of 1889.

Whilst the negotiations leading up to the settlement of the international boundary were still proceeding, an equally important event in the history of the Gambia had taken place. The occurrences, which have been described in this chapter, had shown the necessity for the separation of the country from Sierra Leone. On 28 November 1888 letters patent were issued under the Great Seal erecting the Gambia into a separate colony.

XXXII: The Colony and Protectorate, 1888–1914

One of the earliest tasks, which was undertaken after the separation of the Gambia from Sierra Leone, was the delimitation of the international boundary. A joint Anglo-French Boundary Commission arrived in the country in 1891 and proceeded at once with its work. They very soon encountered considerable obstruction from Fodi Silla of Gunjur and from Fodi Kabba. Three gunboats had consequently to be stationed in the river near to where the Commission was at work. Fodi Kabba himself proved elusive and retired to the Casamance soon after the arrival of the Commission in Bintang Creek, but his lieutenant, Franzwoi, gave a good deal of trouble. Porters and other persons attached to the Commission were waylaid and wounded by his followers. It was therefore decided to make a demonstration by bombarding Kansala. After that Franzwoi sent messengers to disclaim any complicity in the previous outrages and to express his friendliness to the Commission. In contrast to their reception in the lower parts of the river, when the Commission proceeded to the upper parts they were treated with the greatest possible friendliness and received every possible assistance from Musa Molloh and the chiefs of Kantora, Wuli, Sandu, Karantaba and Kunting.

No sooner had the Commission and its attendant gunboats left the Bintang Creek than Fodi Kabba returned and proceeded to raid the Jolas in Foni. A message was sent to him stating that the British Government refused to recognise his authority in any way in Foni and that he was to remove to the French side of the boundary. As Fodi Kabba took no notice of this message, it was decided to take stronger measures against him. Troops were sent from Sierra Leone and on 2 January 1892 a joint naval and military force attacked Fodi Kabba's stockaded town at Marige. The assault was made at night and, though the town was taken and destroyed, Fodi Kabba managed to make his escape on horseback in the dark and thereafter took refuge in French territory. After his defeat the Administrator summoned all the chiefs of western Jarra and eastern Kiang to a meeting at Tendeba. With one exception all appeared and expressed themselves tired of Fodi Kabba and ready to acknowledge the British Government.

The exception was one of Fodi Kabba's men, Suleman Santu, the chief of Toniataba. A party of a dozen men of the First West India Regiment was sent under Major Madden to summon him to appear before the Administrator. The detachment arrived to find the gates of the stockaded town closed against them. Major Madden tried to break down one of the gates with a wooden beam. Suddenly a number of musket muzzles were projected through a double row of loopholes, which had hitherto been masked. Some of those muzzles were within two or three yards of the officer's back. Before Major Madden could realise what was happening, Lance-Corporal W. J. Gordon shouted "Look out, Sir!" pushed the officer aside, and threw himself between him and the muskets. Gordon was badly wounded in the lungs and the party had to retire. For his bravery and devotion, which in all probability saved Major Madden's life, Gordon was subsequently awarded the Victoria Cross—the third of the three Africans to receive that coveted distinction and the second from the Gambia.

It was clear that Suleman Santu required strong measures to be taken against him. Accordingly a punitive expedition comprising contingents from H.M.S. *Alecto* and *Swallow* and the First West India Regiment were sent to deal with him. The operations were successful. Toniataba was taken by storm and destroyed, Suleman Santu being killed in the attack. Thereafter the area was divided into two districts, which were placed in charge of two chiefs who had been deposed by Fodi Kabba some eight years previously. In May 1892 the chiefs of Eastern Kiang and Western Jarra entered into treaties, whereby they agreed to acknowledge British sovereignty, to demand only such "customs" and duties as the Administrator might fix, to deliver up criminals and to repel invasion.[1]

After these troubles it was decided to keep one company of the West India Regiment in the Gambia until such time as the country should become more settled. There was comparatively little disturbance until Fodi Silla once more took up a defiant attitude. Though this chief had caused some trouble in 1892, he had adopted a more submissive attitude after the arrival of British gunboats in

---

[1] *Further Correspondence relating to the affairs of the Gambia* (1892); *London Gazette*, 9 December 1892; Laird Clowes, *The Royal Navy*, vii, 402–406.

the river and had been recognised as chief of his district and had also been granted a subsidy. Two years later, however, he reverted to his old ways. Traders were stopped in his district and robbed and no redress could be obtained. He was requested to meet the Administrator so as to discuss matters in a friendly manner, but declined to do so. It was therefore decided in February, 1894, to send an expedition against his four principal towns, Brikama, Gunjur, Sukuta and Busumballa. The force comprised sailors and marines from H.M.S. *Raleigh, Satellite, Magpie, Widgeon* and *Alecto* and men from the First West India Regiment. The expedition was divided into two parties, one of which proceeded by land from Bathurst to attack Sukuta and the other by water to attack Brikama. The first party took Bakotti with comparative ease, but the other party found two strong stockades between it and its objective. It was found impossible to reach Brikama and the party retired to its boats, which they found left high and dry by the low tide. Whilst the party was waiting for the tide to rise, it was attacked by a strong body of the enemy. In the ensuing fight three officers of the Royal Navy and ten ratings were killed and over forty of the column were wounded. After this disastrous start the expedition was reorganised. This time a landing was made at Gunjur. Fodi Silla was routed and his remaining strongholds were destroyed. The chief himself fled with a few followers to Foni, but the Jolas refused to allow him to enter their country. Fodi Silla was therefore forced to take refuge in French territory. He and his followers were disarmed by the French and he himself was deported to St Louis, where he eventually died. Thereafter foreign Kombo was annexed by the British Government.[1]

After the disappearance of Fodi Silla the only disturber of the peace, who was left, was Fodi Kabba. After the destruction of Toniataba Fodi Kabba kept away from British territory, but he continued to foment trouble in the Gambia between the malcontents and the chiefs who had been installed by the British Government. Although for a long time neither he nor any of his followers indulged in any active forms of hostility, they carried on a furtive, but well organised and by no means unsuccessful, traffic in slaves from Foni. There were no actual raids, but the victims—chiefly women working in rice fields—were kidnapped and conveyed by certain recognised

[1] Laird Clowes, *op. cit.* VII, 426, 427; Hertslet, *Map of Africa*, p. 20; Ordinance of 26 February 1894.

"underground railways" to the banks of the Gambia, where they were ferried over to Baddibu and bartered for cattle, guns and ammunition. Others of his followers entered British territory, committed extensive robberies and fled to French territory before they could be captured. These troubles went on for nearly ten years. During that time the chiefs and people, who had accepted British authority, exhibited a remarkable self-restraint. Though many of these outrages went unpunished, they abstained from attempting reprisals and thus plunging the country into its former state of anarchy and embroiling the British with the French authorities. Credit for this was largely due to the educational propaganda of Mr F. C. Sitwell, the Travelling Commissioner on the south bank of the river, who persuaded them to have the confidence to wait for the British Government to put things right.

Matters came to a head in 1900. There had been a long-standing quarrel in Kiang between the Soninkis of Jataba and the Marabouts of Sankandi over the ownership of a rice field. In 1899 the dispute had been referred to Mr Sitwell, who had given his award, but the people of Sankandi, who were all of them strong supporters of Fodi Kabba, refused to abide by it. In 1900 Mr Sitwell, accompanied by Mr Silva, went to Battelling to investigate the matter. He summoned the leading men of Sankandi to appear before him at Battelling, but they declined to do so. Thereupon Messrs Sitwell and Silva proceeded personally to Sankandi, accompanied by a small police escort and a small band of retainers under Mansa Koto, the chief of Battelling. When they arrived at Sankandi, they told the people to come and discuss the matter outside the town. The Sankandi people said they would not discuss the matter except at the recognised village meeting place, namely, the bantaba tree in the centre of the village. Messrs Sitwell and Silva therefore entered the village, but neither the chief, Dari Bana Dabo, nor any of his followers put in an appearance. Sitwell suddenly caught sight of the chief in the distance and tried to arrest him. The chief called for help and a heavy fire was immediately opened by his followers on the Europeans and their escort. Sitwell and Silva were killed and Mansa Koto was mortally wounded. Six of the constables were also killed. Sergeant Joseph Cox, the commander of the escort, was last seen standing beside Sitwell's dead body and emptying his few remaining rounds of ammunition at close range into the enemy. At least four of them fell before he fell—not the least of the many examples of that remarkable loyalty and devotion, which true leadership has so often inspired in the African soldier.

This disaster had very serious results for the time being. The news of it spread very quickly amongst the natives. Fodi Kabba and his friends took speedy advantage of it to foment further discord. Messengers travelled round the country saying "the Sankandi people had killed two white men and the chief, and the English had done nothing and now every man could do as he liked". Government chiefs found great difficulty in exercising any authority over the more turbulent amongst their people and it became unsafe for the Travelling Commissioners to tour the more disturbed districts. The troubles were not confined to the south bank of the river but spread to the north bank, and in particular to Baddibu, where the Marabout element was still strong and where Fodi Kabba had many allies. The West India Regiment had been withdrawn in 1895 and no troops had been sent to replace them. Owing to the South African War and the Ashanti campaign it was found impossible to send any troops to deal with the situation until the beginning of 1901. During the six months of waiting a very dangerous spirit spread.

When troops were available, it was decided not only to punish the people of Sankandi, but also to deal with Fodi Kabba, who was the real instigator of the whole trouble. As Fodi Kabba was still in French territory and was causing a certain amount of trouble there, the French authorities were invited to co-operate. Musa Molloh, who had consistently shown himself well disposed towards the British, was also invited to assist. The British force, which was detailed for the expedition, comprised half a battalion of the Third West India Regiment from Sierra Leone, half a battalion of the Second Central African Regiment, which was returning from Somaliland by way of Gibraltar, and H.M.S. *Forte*, *Dwarf* and *Thrush*. In order to secure as much secrecy as possible, the carriers were recruited in Sierra Leone, the arrival at Bathurst of the different contingents was arranged to synchronise, and the whole force proceeded to the scene of operations without disembarking at Bathurst. The command of the expedition was given to Lieutenant-Colonel H. E. Brake of the Central African Regiment.

The British programme went through without a hitch. The main body proceeded to Tendeba. Two companies of the West India Regiment proceeded up the Bintang Creek in the *Dwarf* and the colonial steamer *Mansa Kila Ba* so as to prevent the people of Sankandi from retreating across that creek. Musa Molloh's irregular troops assembled in Jarra to prevent a retreat in that direction. The main body disembarked at Tendeba on 11 January 1901, and marched straight to Sankandi, which was surrounded in the early hours of the morning. The inhabitants hoisted a white flag, but opened a heavy fire as soon as one of the companies advanced. The subsequent fighting was short. The enemy inflicted a few casualties but did not put up a very determined resistance. The place was taken and destroyed. Three of the ringleaders were made prisoners and three others were subsequently handed over by the people of Kwinella.

Immediately after this the main body re-embarked at Tendeba and crossed over to Baddibu to deal in the first instance with the people of Salikeni, where in the previous year the Travelling Commissioner and the local chief had had to beat a hasty retreat before a large armed party. After a night march through mangrove swamps the troops arrived at Salikeni before daybreak and at once surrounded the place. The inhabitants were taken completely by surprise and handed over the ringleaders without striking a blow. Other parties proceeded to the disaffected villages of the Saba and Nokunda and disarmed the malcontents there. As there had been several manifestations of disloyalty in other parts of the Protectorate, the next six weeks were occupied in marching detachments of troops through every district except Fuladu. In the majority of the districts they met with a most friendly reception and there was no opposition or trouble in the few areas, where the spirit of lawlessness had been rife amongst a small but very demonstrative minority of the people. Fines were imposed upon certain towns, which had given trouble during the previous months, and were collected without any difficulty.

In March the second part of the operations began. The brunt of this fell upon the French, who were to attack Fodi Kabba's stronghold at Medina, whilst the British troops guarded the international frontier. Musa Molloh was once more to co-operate by advancing from the east. Again the operations went entirely according to plan. The French column under Lieutenant-Colonel Privé made a forced march from Zinguinchor to Medina. Either Fodi Kabba believed that his stronghold was impregnable or else he realised that he was at last brought to bay. "Almost unmolested the French column formed up and the artillery was placed in position, the Spahis riding right round the town without a single shot being fired at them. Fodi Kabba, with a considerable following, seated himself under a cotton tree outside the town to watch the proceedings of the French. He had closed all the gates of the outer walls, and stationed men at each with orders to cut down any person endeavouring to leave the town. His wives, forty in number, were locked up in a room over the inner powder magazine. The guns opened fire against the east wall at midday, and the first shells proved that the mud wall was no protection. Fodi Kabba thereupon withdrew towards the gate, but it is doubtful whether he reached it alive, as his body was found just inside with a bullet through the brain." Shortly afterwards the powder magazine blew up and the women above it all perished. The place was then taken by storm. Fodi Kabba was close on seventy when he fell. He died, no doubt, as he would have wished to die and his last stand cannot but call forth a feeling of admiration. None the less he was in life nothing more nor less than a very powerful bandit, who for close on half a century had brought untold misery upon many of the people of the Gambia. The verdict of history must be that the world was well rid of him.

Dari Bana Dabo and two others of the ringleaders of the Sankandi affair were handed by the French to the British authorities. They were brought to trial in the Supreme Court, where they were assigned legal aid. They were convicted upon the clearest possible evidence forthcoming from reliable witnesses, sentenced to death and executed. Six other persons, who were known to have been ringleaders in the recent disorders in Kiang and Baddibu, were deported to Sierra Leone.[1]

Thereafter, except in a single instance, there was no serious outbreak of lawlessness in the Protectorate. In 1904 the chief and people of Wappai in Foni refused to surrender a murderer. A detachment of the West African Frontier Force was sent to deal with them. The chief and people fled to French territory and their village was destroyed.[2] Otherwise the downfall of Fodi Kabba marks the close of opposition to British rule. That opposition had at all times come from a very small minority, who were opposed to any kind of order and good government because it imposed a restraint upon their

---

[1] *Correspondence relating to the Gambia expedition*, 1901.
[2] *Annual Report for* 1904. The Gambia Company of the West African Frontier Force was raised in 1903.

power to raid and pillage their weaker neighbours with impunity, The vast majority of the people of the Protectorate were thoroughly war weary and only too glad to welcome a government, which would guarantee some security for themselves and their property.

So far in this chapter the proper sequence of events has been interrupted so as to trace the stamping out of the last relics of the Soninki-Marabout war. Though the Sankandi murders caused a very serious temporary setback to the work of the civil administration in the Protectorate, it must not be supposed that this side of the work of the government had been neglected or that considerable progress had not already been made. The best evidence of that progress is to be found in Blue Book statistics. In 1887, just before the separation of the Gambia from Sierra Leone, the annual revenue of the former place had been barely £13,000. In 1890, the second full year after that separation, it exceeded £30,000 and it first topped £50,000 in 1902. When it is remembered that the major portion of this revenue was derived from the export tax on groundnuts cultivated by the people of the Protectorate, it will be realised how far peace and good order had superseded the former internecine warfare and had brought increased prosperity to the inhabitants.

The real work may be said to have begun in 1891, when the Administrator, Mr (afterwards Sir) R. B. Llewellyn, made a very extensive tour of the whole Protectorate. In those early days a certain amount of difficulty was experienced on the north bank of the river owing to the fact that parts of Baddibu and Salum had for the previous four years been controlled by chiefs, who had been appointed by the French and who were many of them resident on the French side of the boundary, but who none the less exacted rents and "customs" on the British side of that boundary. The tricolour was actually seen in 1891 by the members of the Boundary Commission flying on the banks of the river close to Devil's Point. The fact that the international boundary had not yet been delimited added to the difficulty. It was quite understandable that the international convention wanted a good deal of explanation to the native mind. Mr Llewellyn described the situation in the following words:

At Suwarrakunda the people seemed glad, but were afraid to say much until they heard from the Commandant at Nioro. To use their own words—" If Your Excellency sees a woman with her husband, and you like her for wife, you are to drive away her husband before you get her for wife", and the town of Suwarrakunda wants to be informed that the English governor has driven away her French husband.[1]

Fortunately the French authorities actively assisted in explaining the change, which was with very few exceptions accepted very willingly.

The extension of British rule from an area of just under seventy square miles, which contained a population of only 14,000, to an area of over 4000 square miles, which contained a population of over 150,000, naturally brought with it an infinity of new administrative problems. It would be quite impossible to deal with a tithe of those problems here, but some reference should be made to two of the more important ones.

When administration was confined to the Colony proper, traders, who went beyond the limits of British jurisdiction, had to make their own bargains as to the terms upon which they might trade in the territories of local chiefs. From time immemorial those chiefs had exacted "customs" not only from European traders, but also from native traders from the interior. From time to time attempts had been made to fix tariffs for these customs. As early as 1792, for instance, the alkali of Juffure had agreed upon such a fixed scale with the captain of a visiting man-of-war,[2] but native cupidity and keen competition between commercial rivals had usually led to the early breakdown of this and other like tariff agreements. The general uncertainty as to the rate of customs naturally hampered trade. On several occasions attempts were made to place the matter upon a more satisfactory basis. In 1854 Colonel O'Connor made an agreement with the "king" of Barra, whereby traders' passes were issued by the Colonial Secretary to approved persons on payment of a prescribed fee, which was to be handed over to the "king".[3] Colonel D'Arcy made a similar arrangement with Baddibu.[4] But these agreements were not popular inasmuch as the commuted payments went straight into the pockets of the "kings" instead of being as theretofore partly distributed amongst the underchiefs. Moreover the Soninki-Marabout war rendered both agreements more or less nugatory. After 1889, however, the Colonial Government was no

---

[1] *Further Correspondence relating to the affairs of the Gambia* (1892), pp. 3–6.

[2] Mungo Park to Lord Camden, 26 April 1805, Egerton MSS. 3009, f. 40.

[3] Hertslet, *Treaties*, xii, 62.

[4] *Ordinances of the Gambia*, 1875, p. 531; Hertslet, *Treaties*, xii, 82.

longer in the position of having to effect such arrangements by negotiation with local chiefs, but was able to put an end to a very unsatisfactory system by abolishing "customs" and making the trader take out a licence on payment of a fee, which went into general revenue. The innovation was not made until the Travelling Commissioners had had the opportunity to tour the country and explain to the people the object and the necessity of the change, which naturally aroused the opposition of certain vested interests. The Protectorate Trade Licences Ordinance was passed in 1895. It worked smoothly from the start, as experience showed the natives that they benefited indirectly thereby far more than they had done when the trader was at the mercy of the exactions of a few chiefs.

The most serious problem in the new Protectorate was, however, that of slavery. Here it is hardly necessary to mention the fact that slavery and slave trading had existed amongst the natives themselves long before the advent of any European. As in other lands where slavery has at one time existed, the first step to be taken was to abolish the traffic and the second, which has generally proved in practice by far the more difficult, to abolish the status. The raids of Maba, Fodi Silla and Fodi Kabba had made the traffic thoroughly unpopular and there was very little difficulty in persuading the chiefs to suppress it. The status could not, however, be abolished by a mere stroke of the pen. Greatly to be desired as the goal was, it was felt that it could only be reached very gradually. Domestic slavery had been for so long a time one of the foundations of native society that its immediate abolition was neither desirable nor even practicable. As evidence of the strength of native popular feeling in regard to any proposal for the abolition of the institution it may be mentioned that, when in 1862 the Soninkis were really cornered by the Marabouts at Essau, they had the greatest possible hesitation in allowing their herdsmen and their womenfolk to take refuge on British soil, because they feared that the result would be the emancipation of all their slaves.[1] Furthermore, to the Marabout the enslavement of the Soninki unbeliever was more or less an act of faith. The ultimate end could therefore only be obtained by educating public opinion up to it and by the gradual abolition of some of the principal features of the institution.

The task of education fell upon the Travelling Commissioners, who in the course of their tours of the Protectorate explained to the

[1] Colonel D'Arcy to Duke of Newcastle, 22 May 1862.

people the reasons and the objects of the change. In 1894 a Slave Trade Abolition Ordinance was passed. It declared that all slave trading was illegal, and therefore that all slaves who were imported into the Protectorate after that date were free. It did not abolish the status, but enacted that slaves could ransom themselves, the ransom being fixed at £10 for an adult and £5 for a child. Its most far-reaching provision was that which declared a slave to be free on the death of his master. Finally the Governor was given a discretionary power to emancipate either an individual or else a district. The Ordinance, which was repealed and replaced by another with the like title in 1906, did not enact a general emancipation forthwith, but by enacting that a slave was no longer a transferable chattel and that he automatically became free upon the death of his master it made complete abolition only a question of time. The provisions of the Ordinance may be open to criticism but it has to be remembered that the absolute prohibition of the institution would have been useless until there was a free labour market for the freedman. With the close of the internal wars in the Protectorate the revival of agriculture created a new economic structure, which permitted the slave to become a free producer or else a wage-earner. The result was to give the institution of slavery a far more shrewd blow than ever could have been inflicted by mere legislation. The Affirmation of the Abolition of Slavery Ordinance of 1930 has consequently been more than the mere expression of a pious hope. To-day slavery is so far dead in the Protectorate that in native eyes the public imputation, whether true or untrue, of slave ancestry to any person is regarded as a very grave slander likely to provoke a breach of the peace and therefore punishable as a serious criminal offence.

As already seen, the work of carrying out these reforms in the Protectorate fell very largely upon the Travelling Commissioners. The appointment of these officers was in fact the most important and far reaching of all the innovations brought about on the declaration of the Protectorate. In 1893 Messrs J. H. Ozanne and F. C. Sitwell were appointed the first Travelling Commissioners. What they and their successors managed to achieve is best told in the words of the annual report for 1903.

It would be almost impossible for anyone visiting it today to realise the condition of affairs that existed in 1893....Practically nothing was then known of the Protectorate and consequently the instructions given to these two officers were somewhat vague. Their orders were to visit all towns, to get acquainted with the principal chiefs etc. and to report their experiences at head quarters. No reliable maps of the country were to be obtained, with the result that many villages claimed by the French were found to be almost within a stone's throw of the river, while those said to be English were situated twelve to fifteen miles inland. Each chief was a law to himself and did pretty well what he liked in his own district. Slave owners with their wretched property were to be seen passing from town to town. Farmers did not dare venture to their farms without taking their bundouks, or large dane guns, with them, and women going to the rice field were liable to be kidnapped.

Foni, generally known as the "Jola Country", was brought under the Protectorate system a year later. Here it was not deemed advisable for the Commissioner to travel unless accompanied by a small escort, and reports frequently reached head quarters of the robbing and murder of traders passing through the district. Today a very different state of affairs exists, the Commissioner being able to march through his district with no more formidable weapon than a walking stick, his only possible enemies being the bees that abound there.

Throughout the Protectorate native courts, presided over by chiefs, assisted by the principal headmen, have been established in the districts and are conducted in an orderly and impartial manner. A yard tax law, in which there is no penal clause, has been enforced and is readily complied with. The sanitary conditions of the towns have been well looked after. Streets have been opened up and the main roads, which were nothing more than mere bush paths, are now of a uniform width of eighteen feet, their total mileage being estimated at 1121 miles. Numerous streams, swamps and creeks, which formerly had to be waded through, are now crossed by well built bridges varying in length from 150 to 600 feet....

In the upper river the progress has been still more noticeable.... A trip to this district was formerly regarded as a formidable undertaking. Merchants, who had been resident in the Colony ten or twelve years, had never visited it, and in one instance at least a merchant, who for fifteen years had had a trader there, had never seen him. At the present time a journey to the upper river is a matter of almost every day occurrence. Well built houses occupied by Europeans now take the place of cane huts at the landing places. In the trading season launches and lighters are to be seen busily moving from port to port and an air of prosperity prevails....

The credit of the rapid progress of the Protectorate may be fairly said to be due to Sir R. Llewellyn, who inaugurated the system, to Sir George Denton, especially as regards the upper river, and to the Commissioners, amongst whom Mr Ozanne and Mr Sitwell must receive first mention. The former, after nine years' service, died of blackwater fever and the latter was killed two years previously while attempting to arrest a native, who had disputed the authority of his chief.

Since the establishment of the Protectorate there have been twelve Travelling Commissioners appointed to it. Three of these have died while on duty, two have been killed in the performance of their duties, one has been invalided and one has resigned.

In the first instance one of the Commissioners was placed in charge of the north bank and the other in charge of the south bank of the river. Their original instructions limited their touring to the districts below MacCarthy Island, but in 1900 their operations were extended to Sandu, Wuli, and Kantora, where they had a very friendly reception from the start.[1] Fuladu was, however, left alone for the time being. As mentioned in Chapter xxx, this district had been from 1881 under the nominal rule of Bakari Dembel, though Musa Molloh was the real force to be reckoned with. In 1891 Bakari Dembel had inflicted a fine upon Musa Molloh for his refusal to co-operate in an expedition against some Fulas in French territory. Musa Molloh had replied by leading a force to attack his overlord in Jimara. Bakari Dembel had promptly fled and in 1892 Musa Molloh had proclaimed himself ruler of all Fuladu. Before he had made himself "king" he had trouble with his half-brother, Dikori Kumba, who had allied himself with Fodi Kabba. In deference to the wishes expressed to him by Sir Samuel Rowe in 1887 Musa Molloh had hitherto abstained from carrying war into the regions claimed by Fodi Kabba, but on Musa's assumption of the kingship Dikori Kumba had once more proceeded to attack him. As he had in 1883 placed his territory under French protection, and as he had assisted the French in their operations against Momodu Lamin in 1885, Musa Molloh now invoked the assistance of the protecting power. A French force under the command of Lieutenant Bertrandon was sent to help him. Fodi Kabba had just been defeated at Marige and Toniataba and was not in a position to render Dikori Kumba any material aid. Dikori Kumba was easily routed and was himself killed.

[1] *Annual Report for 1903.*

Thus in 1892 Musa Molloh became supreme throughout British and French Fuladu.[1]

As Musa Molloh's kingdom lay on both sides of the international boundary and as he himself lived on the French side of that boundary, it was felt that the time was not yet ripe for intervention in the government of British Fuladu. Musa Molloh himself had always been well disposed towards the British, but he was a warrior chief of an exceedingly autocratic disposition and it was felt that any attempt at interference in the British portion of his territory would be open to grave misunderstanding and would be strongly resented. It was therefore decided that nothing should be done in British Fuladu until after his death. However, Musa Molloh's autocratic ways brought him into trouble with the French with the result that he entered into negotiations with the British authorities. On 7 June 1901 he concluded an agreement with the Governor, Sir George Denton, whereby, in return for the grant of an annual subsidy of £500 he agreed to place that portion of his kingdom, which lay in British territory, under British protection. In 1903 the French authorities summoned him to St Louis to answer certain charges of tyrannical conduct, which were alleged against him. His answer to the summons was to remove himself with a large following into British territory, where he settled peaceably upon the land assigned to him.[2]

This agreement with Musa Molloh enabled the Colonial Government to take a step, which hitherto had not been possible in its entirety, namely, to apply a general scheme for the administration of the whole of the Gambia with the exception of St Mary's Island. That scheme has been described in a number of ordinances as "the protectorate system". For convenience the general scheme, which was nominally in force throughout all the parts of the Gambia which belonged to Great Britain prior to 1888, may be called "the colonial system". The principal feature of this latter scheme was the reproduction of English laws and English institutions upon African soil. It had grown up in a haphazard way and certain modifications,

[1] *Further Correspondence relating to the affairs of the Gambia* (1892), pp. 74–76; Legrand, "Le Fouladou", *La Géographie*, xxvi, 250.

[2] *Annual Report for* 1903; Legrand, *op. cit.* After the European War Musa Molloh's arbitrary conduct resulted in his deportation to Sierra Leone. He was allowed to return in 1923, but was not allowed any part or share in the administration of Fuladu. Thereafter he gave no further trouble up to the time of his death.

additions and alterations had been made from time to time to meet local requirements, but its predominant features were essentially replicas of laws and institutions in England. The colonial system was deemed to be suited to the needs and the requirements of the town of Bathurst, where the population was entirely non-indigenous and comprised very heterogeneous races, none of which had any common laws, customs, institutions or tribal organisation.

Before 1889 the Colonial Government had been called upon to administer beyond St Mary's Island only some sixty square miles of territory and a population of barely 10,000. No clear-cut scheme had ever been evolved for the administration of these outlying areas, but there had been a general tendency to adopt the colonial system. MacCarthy Island had a garrison up to 1866 and a large portion of the civil population comprised the same elements as were to be found in Bathurst. For these the colonial system was regarded as suitable, but there was already a Mandingo village on the island, when the British Government first occupied it, and it continued and increased in size after that occupation. Though no legislation was ever passed to deal with this village, instructions were given to the officers in charge at MacCarthy Island to allow the inhabitants to manage their own affairs in their own way under their own alkali.[1] It was found in practice that these instructions worked remarkably well and with the minimum of friction.

A similar policy was carried out in regard to the Ceded Mile. There was a small garrison at Fort Bullen up to 1870, a settlement of liberated Africans and discharged soldiers and a Wesleyan mission close to that fort at Berwick Town, and a small settlement of European and other traders at Albreda and the adjacent village of Juffure. Police constables maintained law and order at Berwick Town and Albreda and brought offenders before local justices of the peace, who were recruited from the resident officials and merchants and who administered law according to English legal principles.[2] But outside of these small areas no attempt at all was made by the Colonial Government to administer the Ceded Mile.[3] As Essau, the

---

[1] Lt.-Gov. Rendall to Rufus Coffin, 20 October 1830; Lt.-Gov. Rendall to John Grant, 1 January 1833.

[2] *Annual Report for* 1863; Colonel O'Connor to Sir E. B. Lytton, 20 September 1858; Colonel D'Arcy to Duke of Newcastle, 20 June 1863.

[3] *Report on the condition of the British Settlements on the West Coast of Africa* (1865), p. 9.

home of one of the seven ruling families of Niumi, lay within a mile of the river, any such attempt would have been impolitic. Later on, when the Marabouts got possession of all the principal villages within the Ceded Mile, such action became even more difficult. All that could be done to counteract Marabout influence was to settle a colony of Soninki fugitives from Sine Salum under their own chief at Banta Killing, near Albreda, but beyond renaming the village Fitzgerald Town that chief and his followers were left to their own devices.[1] After 1870 the rusting guns on Fort Bullen and two obsolete cannon, which had been mounted behind Albreda and Berwick Town as a protection from attacks from inland,[2] were virtually the only outward and visible signs of the British claim to sovereignty over the Ceded Mile.

A somewhat different course had been taken in British Kombo. The primary object of the acquisition of this district in 1840 had been for the purpose of locating liberated Africans.[3] Even before that date the "king" of Kombo had given away several large tracts of land to members of the early colonial families.[4] In 1853 Colonel O'Connor had settled a number of pensioners from the West India Regiments in the district.[5] Colonel D'Arcy had followed Colonel O'Connor's example and insisted upon military service as an incident of the tenure of any land, which might be allotted to a newcomer.[6] In 1862 a Kombo Militia Ordinance was passed, which provided for the raising of a volunteer reserve force, the members of which were to receive a free grant of land at Hamilton Town conditional upon the performance of twelve days' annual training and answering the call to the colours in time of emergency.[7] All these settlers lived in villages bearing such names as Newcastle, Hamilton Town and Albert Town and belonged to non-indigenous races.

But side by side with these settlers there lived a number of Mandingos and other indigenous people, who were already in the district at the time of its annexation. In 1840 the only indigenous settlement of any consequence was that of Bakau near Cape St Mary. In subsequent years a number of Soninki refugees came over

---

[1] *Proceedings of the Select Committee on Africa (West Coast)* (1865), pp. 431, 432.   [2] Colonel D'Arcy to Duke of Newcastle, 24 November 1862.

[3] Huntley, *Seven Years' Service on the Slave Coast of Western Africa*, pp. 200. 201.   [4] Colonel D'Arcy to Duke of Newcastle, 25 August 1862.

[5] Colonel O'Connor to Sir William Molesworth, 24 September 1855.

[6] Colonel D'Arcy to Duke of Newcastle, 24 April 1861.

[7] *Annual Report for* 1862.

the border and built villages. In addition to them a number of members of different African tribes settled *en bloc* in various parts of British Kombo. In 1857 a number of Serahulis, who had been mercenaries in the service of Demba Sonko of Barra and had quarrelled with him, were at their request given land at Sera Jobe Kunda.[1] Again in 1863 a band of Soninki refugees from Sine Salum were settled in different parts of British Kombo.[2] All these people had their own tribal organisation and were left to a very large extent to manage their own affairs along the lines of that organisation. At the same time this admixture of indigenous and non-indigenous races required that there should be in some respects a uniform system of administration which could be applied to both classes of the population.

In 1850 the "king" of the Kombo formally renounced all rights to any "customs" or rents in British Kombo.[3] Thereafter the Colonial Government undertook the execution of a few minor public works such as the construction of roads and the erection of bridges over swamps. It was therefore felt that the time had come to make the inhabitants of the district contribute to this expenditure by the payment of a small tax and also to make them responsible for the upkeep of their roads.[4] Accordingly in 1862 a Kombo Land Revenue Ordinance and a Kombo Roads Ordinance were passed. The former imposed the precursor of the yard tax, which is levied at the present time in the Protectorate. It imposed a small tax on dwelling-houses and cultivated land in the Kombo. The latter ordinance, which was repealed in 1916, made provision for compulsory labour for the upkeep of roads. As there was neither a recognised headman of the non-indigenous population, nor a chief who was the recognised chief of all the indigenous population, it became necessary to appoint a special officer to put these laws into force. Up to 1862 the officer in command of the troops at Cape St Mary had been in charge of the civil administration of British Kombo, but the arrangement had not proved entirely satisfactory. Accordingly in that year a civil officer was appointed with the title of Manager[5] and British Kombo remained under his supervision until the abolition of the post in 1903.[6]

[1] Colonel O'Connor to H. Labouchere, 14 May 1857.
[2] Colonel D'Arcy to Duke of Newcastle, 11 September 1863.
[3] *Ordinances of the Gambia*, 1875, p. 522.
[4] Colonel D'Arcy to Duke of Newcastle, 24 March 1860.
[5] *Annual Report for* 1862; Colonel D'Arcy to Duke of Newcastle, 24 August 1861 and 24 July 1862.   [6] *Annual Report for* 1903.

When in 1889 the Colonial Government found itself confronted with the task of governing 150,000 instead of 14,000 people, it was very obvious that the colonial system was not suited to the needs and requirements of the 136,000, who then came for the first time under British administration. It was further evident that it was not suited to the needs of many of the remaining 14,000, who lived in the outlying portions of the colony proper and who had never before been brought in actual fact under effective British administration. At the same time it was equally clear that no cast-iron system could be introduced forthwith in the place of the colonial system. The protectorate system, which was introduced in its place, had the great merit of elasticity.

Legal recognition was first given to the protectorate system by the passing in 1894 of a Protectorate Ordinance. That law has since been repealed and replaced by a number of ordinances each successively bearing the same title and its provisions have also been implemented by other legislation, but its main principles still hold good. It provided for the division of the Protectorate for administrative purposes into districts under the charge of chiefs and subchiefs, who were to be under the supervision of the Travelling Commissioners and whose administrative, executive and magisterial powers were outlined in the Ordinance. It also enacted that native laws and customs existing in the Protectorate should, where not repugnant to natural justice, nor incompatible with the principles of the laws of England or with any local law applicable to the Protectorate, continue and remain in full force and effect, and should be taken cognisance of and enforced in Colonial and Protectorate courts alike.

This Ordinance was applicable only to those territories, which did not form part of the colony. It was, however, obvious that its provisions were equally suitable to some of the outlying parts of the colony proper. The only difficulty in regard to its application to such districts would have been the absence of the class of chiefs, which formed the basis of the protectorate system. That difficulty could only arise, where there was a considerable population of non-indigenous races, who had no form of tribal organisation. The problem was in actual fact solved by the force of economic circumstances. The story can be found in the District Meeting Books of the Wesleyan Mission, whose labours in the Protectorate lay very largely amongst the non-indigenous population. Writing in 1876 of Mac-Carthy Island the Superintendent reported that "the troops have been withdrawn and the younger and more intelligent portion of the inhabitants have either removed to Bathurst or are endeavouring to earn a rather precarious living at one or other of the many trading ports in the river ".[1] There was the same story to be told of Berwick Town and of Albreda. In 1868 another writer recorded that a general exodus had already begun of the younger generation to Bathurst from the Kombo[2] and in 1880 the Superintendent of the Wesleyan Mission reported that in nearly all the villages, which had been founded by Colonels O'Connor and D'Arcy, there were left scarcely a dozen, and very often less than a dozen, English-speaking Africans.[3] In the course of the next decade these exotic elements were further reduced to such negligible numbers that no reason existed for excepting any outlying district from the general operation of the protectorate system.

In the years following 1894 a number of ordinances were passed so as to bring various of these outlying districts under the protectorate system. Soon after the declaration of the protectorate it had been found necessary to exercise more or less direct control by placing a Mandingo agent in charge of Brefet and Baijana in Foni, where the Jolas lived in small and scattered villages, had no recognised chief and had not proved very tractable. In 1895 these two small districts were brought under the protectorate system. MacCarthy Island was placed under the same system in 1896, as was the Ceded Mile in the following year. After 1897 the only parts of the Gambia, outside of St Mary's Island, which had not been brought legally under the protectorate system, were the Kombo, Fuladu and the districts above MacCarthy Island. The agreement, which was made in 1901 with Musa Molloh, paved the way for a more universal application of the system. In 1902 a second Protectorate Ordinance was passed to amend the protectorate system and to make its application more clear. By that ordinance the whole of the Gambia, with the exception of St Mary's Island, was placed under the protectorate system.

---

[1] Minutes of the Annual Meeting of the Gambia District, 1 February 1876.
[2] Horton, *West African Countries and Peoples*, p. 79.
[3] Minutes of the Annual Meeting of the Gambia District, 19 January 1880.

XXXIII: Recent years, 1914–1938

As in all other parts of the world, the one event, which stands out most prominently in the recent history of the Gambia, is the European War of 1914–1918. Fortunately the Gambia was spared by reason of its geographical position from being a theatre of war, but, in common with all the rest of the world, its fortunes were affected by that war. Moreover, the Gambia made its contribution towards the final victory.

At the outbreak of the war the only troops in the Gambia were a company of the West African Frontier Force about 130 strong. Of these the signallers were sent, in September 1914, to take part in the Cameroons campaign. Half the company followed in January 1915, and the remaining half in September of that year, leaving the police to garrison the colony. In 1917 the whole of the company was sent to German East Africa and in the course of the next twelve months two drafts followed as reinforcements. In all over 400 natives of the Gambia served in the Frontier Force in the two theatres of war. Of this number, six African non-commissioned officers and privates were awarded the Distinguished Conduct Medal for conspicuous gallantry in the field. The details of the two campaigns and of the part played therein by the Gambia Company hardly come within the scope of this book, but they should not be forgotten. Both campaigns were trying and arduous, and thirty-seven of the number laid down their lives. The warfare revealed the loyalty and fine soldierly qualities of all the Africans who served in the campaigns. Of the many tributes, which have been paid to these men by the officers under whom they served, the most expressive is perhaps that of Brigadier-General F. G. H. Cunliffe:

They have been called upon to take part in a great struggle, the rights and wrongs of which they can scarcely be expected dimly to perceive. They have been brought through the, to them, extremely novel experience of facing an enemy armed with modern weapons and led by highly trained officers. Their rations have been scanty, their barefoot marches long and trying, and their fighting at times extremely arduous. Yet they have not been found wanting in discipline, devotion to their officers, or personal courage.

On 19 September 1914 what Sir Edward Cameron justly described as "a very loyal and large hearted Council", which was composed of officials and non-officials, Europeans and Africans, met to pass the following resolution:

This Council, on behalf of the local Government and the inhabitants of all classes of the Colony and Protectorate, European and Native, official and unofficial, including the chiefs and people of the different tribes and districts of the Protectorate, whose keen and loyal interest in the present conflict has been manifested in various ways, desires to express its unswerving allegiance to the Throne and Government of His Majesty the King.

The Colony having in recent years of continued quiet prosperity under British rule amassed a substantial surplus fund free from liability, this Council, subject to the consent of the Secretary of State for the Colonies, hereby undertakes to provide a sum of £10,000 to be defrayed from the surplus aforesaid, as a contribution to the National Relief Fund inaugurated by His Royal Highness the Prince of Wales for the relief of persons in the British Isles, who are dependents of men serving their country at the front, or who may be suffering poverty and distress from unemployment or otherwise as a result of the existing state of war.

In 1917 and 1919 the Colonial Government contributed sums of £10,000 and £16,000 respectively to the imperial funds for war purposes. Between 1916 and 1918 the Government also contributed £8000 to the Red Cross Fund. In 1918 it also contributed the sum of £1000 to His Majesty King George the Fifth's Fund for Merchant Sailors, "upon whose splendid courage and endeavour the prosperity of the country in war time had largely depended". In addition private citizens contributed generously to the many philanthropic funds, which were raised during the war. Perusal of those subscription lists discloses more than one story of the mite cast into the treasury by some very humble person as a very sincere token of loyalty and devotion to the British Crown.

During the war the Gambia experienced the same difficulties and inconveniences as did other colonies, but it did not suffer any hardship or material check to its prosperity. At the beginning of the war there was a big drop in revenue owing to the inability to sell the groundnut crop, which was due to the uncertainty of the price, the difficulty in obtaining shipping and other causes. But after the first year, although shipping continued to be a great difficulty, things began to go back to a more or less normal condition and by 1917 the revenue had returned to its pre-war figures. One effect of the war was to alter the ultimate destination of a large portion of the colony's exports. In 1914 the French had taken 78 per cent of the groundnut crop and Great Britain only 9 per cent. During the war four English firms entered the business and in 1919 Great Britain took 91 per cent and France only 2½ per cent of the groundnut crop.[1] Though since the last-mentioned year the relative proportions of these exports have varied considerably from year to year, Great Britain now receives a far larger share of the Gambia's exports than she did before the war.[2]

Like other countries the Gambia has been affected by many of the aftermaths of the war. One of these, which was more or less peculiar to the Gambia, but which none the less affected the country very seriously, was due to the depreciation of the franc. As mentioned on a previous page, one result of the annual visits of the "strange farmer" from French territory and of the participation of a number of French firms in the groundnut trade had been to make the five-franc piece the most popular medium of purchase. This coin had in 1843 been made legal tender at the rate of 3s. 10½d. sterling.[3] In 1868 the Administrator reported that it had entirely superseded barter in the river trade.[4] When in 1880 it was decided to demonetise the Spanish dollar, it was found that the five-franc piece formed 85 per cent of the total coinage then in circulation in the Colony. The further fact also came to light that the coin passed current at the rate of 4s. except in payments to the Colonial Government, which were required to be at the legal rate of 3s. 10½d. At that date a suggestion was made to demonetise the five-franc piece as well as the dollar. The English merchants in Bathurst thought that little or no inconvenience would result from this course, but the French merchants were strongly opposed to demonetisation. They urged that many natives came from French territory to the Gambia and that if this, their only coin, were demonetised, they would cease to come to Bathurst for their goods. In the end the Legislative Council decided that it was immaterial whether or not the coin was de-

---

[1] *Annual Report for* 1919.
[2] A full account of the Gambia's part in the war has been contributed by Sir Edward Cameron to Lucas, *The Empire at War*.
[3] Chalmers, *History of Currency in the British Colonies*, pp. 210, 219, 220.
[4] *Annual Report for* 1868.

monetised. In these circumstances and in view of the fact that at that date four-fifths of the exports from the Colony went to France, it was deemed inexpedient to take any further action, so long as the Latin Union continued to limit the issue of five-franc pieces.[1]

After the war the franc dropped a long way below par. As long as coins of any kind were scarce in West Africa and trade was booming, the five-franc piece still remained popular with the native and kept its market value. When, however, in 1920 trade began to decline and the exchange value of the franc dropped to an alarming extent in Europe, the situation arose that the five-franc piece, which then had a market value of 2s. and even less, was still being accepted in the Gambia as legal tender at the rate of 3s. 10½d. As was only to be expected, five-franc pieces flowed into the country and accumulated in the banks and the mercantile houses to such an alarming extent that in 1922 the Colonial Government had no alternative but to demonetise them and to take them over at their fictitious legal value. This operation cost the Government £187,000, or a whole year's revenue. The cost of redemption was met by a loan from the West African Currency Board, which was paid off by instalments.

Despite this very necessary, but very costly, measure and despite subsequent trade slumps the Gambia has proved financially sound. It has managed to balance its budget in years when larger West African colonies were unable to do so and holds to-day the almost unique distinction of having investments well in excess of its liabilities.

So many things have contributed towards this prosperity that it is not really possible to single out any one measure or innovation which has made a more outstanding contribution than others. The wealth of the country has continued to be largely dependent on the groundnut crop, though other crops are also grown and exported. Until 1924 there was no Agricultural Department in the country. Since its inception that department has set about the protection and improvement of the groundnut crop as well as the more extended cultivation of food and other economic crops. When the department started work, there was ample room for improvement in the quality of the nuts exported, as they were obtaining an inferior price because of the amount of foreign matter shipped with them. Careful arrangements were made with various types of groundnut to ascertain that

[1] Chalmers, *op. cit.* p. 220.

which was most suited to the locality and at the same time was likely to give a good yield. A number of agricultural stations were opened in the Protectorate, where field experiments were carried out under circumstances in which they could be watched by the local farmer. Steps were also taken to introduce rotary screens for the purpose of cleaning the nuts at the time of purchase and thus ensuring that they were shipped clean. The immediate effect of this last introduction was to improve the price of the nuts. Previously there had been a trade discount of 30s. per ton for diseased nuts, sand and other foreign matter. After the introduction of the rotary screen this discount was reduced to 2s. 6d. per ton. In addition to this benefit the experiments of the Agricultural Department resulted in the improvement of the general quality of the individual nut by reducing its fatty acid content and yet at the same time increasing its weight.

Work on the groundnut crop has not prevented the Agricultural Department from giving attention to other crops and in particular to food crops. At the time when the department came into being there was room for much to be done in this respect. The high prices, which prevailed for many years, led the native farmer to concentrate upon his groundnut crop and to neglect his food crops, relying upon the proceeds of sale of his groundnut crop to purchase sufficient foodstuffs to meet his requirements until the next harvest. In December 1893 there was a disastrous rain, which seriously affected the seed-nuts and diminished the crops for the next three years. In order to remedy matters the Colonial Government imported in 1896 a quantity of seed-nuts from the Senegal, which they issued to the farmers on credit. The result was that there was a record export in 1898. Thereafter in its anxiety to maintain and to improve the quality of the nuts the Government from time to time bought further supplies of seed-nuts, which were issued to the natives on credit. From 1909 onwards the Government definitely undertook the task of distributing seed-nuts in this manner annually. As long as high prices were maintained the plan proved more or less successful in its working. But when prices began to fall, the grower not only could not repay the amounts, which he owed to the Government for advances on seed-nuts, but also lacked sufficient money to pay for the foodstuffs, which he himself had neglected to grow. The result was the creation of a vicious circle. The Government had to step in and purchase rice, which was issued to the farmers so as to

feed them during the seven months of drought, and also to re-
purchase seed-nuts from the merchants for issue on credit to the
same farmers in the hope that at the end of the harvest they would
be able to repay both debts and also have something left over for
their further personal requirements. The only result was that the
farmers became more and more heavily indebted to the Government
and that finally in 1925 debts amounting to £33,000 had to be
written off. The only solutions of the impasse were to put an end to
both systems of credit, to make other arrangements for the supply
of seed-nuts and to stimulate the increased cultivation of food crops.
In 1932 advances of rice and seed-nuts were discontinued. The
passing in the following year of the Native Authority Ordinance enabled the native authorities in each district to make a rule, whereby
the owner of each groundnut farm was required after the winnowing
of each season's crop to deposit five bushels of seed-nuts in the village
store. Of the amount so deposited four bushels are returned to the
depositor at the beginning of the next planting season, the remaining
bushel being placed in the village reserve. The scheme has met with
the full co-operation of the chiefs and people and has resulted in an
adequate supply of seed-nuts being available at the beginning of
each planting season. At the same time as the result of an educational campaign and of experience the farmer has learnt to grow a
more ample supply of foodstuffs.

This reform, which has resulted in a considerable gain in morale,
is one result of the introduction of the protectorate system, or, as it
is commonly known to-day, of indirect rule. That system is now the
subject of a number of ordinances, which have as their object the
development of local self-government under the advice and supervision of the commissioners. The principal of these are the Native
Authority Ordinance, 1933, the Native Tribunals Ordinance, 1933,
and the Protectorate Ordinance, 1935. The last mentioned, which
has replaced an ordinance of 1913 bearing the same title, gives the
general outline of the protectorate system. The other two deal in
greater detail with particular matters relating to that system.

At the present time the Protectorate is divided into four Pro-
vinces, namely, North Bank, South Bank, MacCarthy Island, and
Upper River. Each province is administered by a Commissioner and
is subdivided into a number of districts. Each district is administered
by a chief known as the Seyfu.[1] Under the Seyfu are a number of

---

[1] *Sc.* the French "chef".

underchiefs, each of whom bears the title of Alkali[1] and administers a village or group of villages. Each Seyfu and Alkali has under him a number of attendants, who from the distinctive emblem worn by them are known as badge messengers and are entrusted with the execution of the chief's orders and act as a local constabulary. In passing it may be observed that these three administrative grades are not the creation of the protecting power but existed long before the advent of British rule. All that has been done is to define and develop their respective powers and authorities.

Each chief is charged with the maintenance of the peace in the area committed to his charge as well as with the prevention of crime and the execution of sentences and orders of courts of law. The Protectorate Ordinance bestows upon him and those acting under him the powers and protection which are requisite for the carrying out of these duties. The Commissioner has the general superintendence of all the districts within his province and the chiefs are guided by his advice as to the order and general management of their respective areas and the carrying into effect of all laws made applicable to the Protectorate.

The Native Authority Ordinance of 1933 provides for the establishment and constitution of Native Authorities in the Protectorate and makes provision for the continuance of existing chiefs as such authorities. It defines in greater detail and also enlarges the duties and the powers of the chiefs in their executive capacity. One of its most important provisions is that which confers certain limited powers of legislation upon the Native Authority by enabling them, subject in some cases to the approval of the Commissioner and in others to that of the Governor, to make orders or pass rules dealing with a variety of matters, which are specified in the Ordinance, in regard to persons subject to their jurisdiction.

Until 1933 provision was made by the successive Protectorate Ordinances for the Commissioner to preside, when necessary, in Native Tribunals. This was altered in that year by the Native Tribunals Ordinance. To-day the Commissioner has a separate court, which has a jurisdiction concurrent with that of any Native Tribunal in his Province but which is also empowered to deal with cases in which one of the parties is not subject to the jurisdiction of the Native Tribunal, and cases which are not cognisable by those tribunals. The Ordinance of 1933 prescribes the constitution of the

---

[1] *Sc.* the Portuguese "alcaide".

Native Tribunals and defines their civil and criminal jurisdictions. Their proceedings are usually presided over by the Seyfu and are subject to review by the Commissioner. Provision is also made for the transfer in certain circumstances of a case from the Native Tribunal to the Commissioner.

From the foregoing it will be seen that the administration of the Protectorate hinges largely upon the chiefs. Of these the Alkali is chosen by the people of the village subject to confirmation of the Commissioner. After appointment the Alkali is bound by tradition and custom to listen to the advice of "the good people" of the village. He acts in many respects as the representative of his village in its dealings with the Government and personifies the village community. It is, for instance, he who allots to those, who need it, unoccupied land, which belongs to the village as a community. Although he is not by virtue of his office armed with any judicial powers, his aid is frequently invoked as an arbitrator in disputes which cannot be settled by the friends or the relatives of the parties. Much naturally depends in such cases upon the individual, but by virtue of his standing the Alkali is very frequently able to compose differences to the satisfaction of the parties and thus to prevent the dispute reaching the point of actual litigation.

The title of Seyfu is a modern one, but his position is largely the heritage of the Mansa or "king" of former times. Many of the old kingly powers were destroyed as the result of the Soninki-Marabout wars and others had necessarily to pass away on the advent of British control. None the less the Seyfu still has much of the standing and the authority of the Mansa. This is more especially the case when the Seyfu comes of one of the old ruling families. Though the civil wars of the nineteenth century wiped out a number of these families, it is still the policy of the Government as far as possible to appoint a Seyfu from one of the families of hereditary rulers, as it is recognised that a great deal of a chief's utility and prestige depends upon the authority inherent in the post. It is now the usual custom to ascertain the wishes of the people of a district in regard to the appointment of a new Seyfu. When the Commissioner has ascertained which of the candidates has the best claim or is the most likely to command respect or obedience in the district, he forwards his recommendation to the Governor, who makes the final selection. This again is not an innovation but an adaptation of an old custom to modern requirements. Though the kingship was as a rule confined in the past to one family or set of families, there was no rule of primogeniture or other immutable rule of descent. Even in cases in which the final choice was known from the start to be a foregone conclusion the new Mansa none the less had to go through the formality of election.

From the foregoing it will be realised that the present policy of the Government is to obtain the co-operation of the natives of the Protectorate in the management of their own affairs along the lines of their tribal organisation. The process of evolution must necessarily be gradual. One example has already been given of the beneficial effect of bringing about an important economic reform through the medium and with the full co-operation of the native authority. Others could also be cited, which whilst possibly not individually in themselves of any very great importance have collectively contributed very materially towards the general benefit of the people of the Protectorate.

It is unfortunately not possible within the limits of this chapter to describe at all adequately the work which has been done during this century by other Government departments, but the very important work, which has been done by the Medical Department, should not be allowed to pass entirely without notice. It is not possible here to do full justice to that work and one is uttering a mere commonplace when one says that since the creation of a West African Medical Service in 1902 a medical revolution has taken place, which has materially aided the economic development of all the West African colonies. All credit and due recognition must be given to research workers in institutes and laboratories in other West African colonies and in England, but it is not out of place to record the debt, which those workers will readily acknowledge that they owe to the work of the medical practitioner on the spot. It is due to the discovery of a Government medical officer in the Gambia that the Colony has gained the somewhat unenviable, but by no means unique distinction of having given its name to a human parasite. In 1901 Dr R. M. Forde, the Principal Medical Officer of the Colony, discovered in the blood of a European patient a trypanosome, which was subsequently named *Trypanosoma gambiense*. Further research disclosed the fact that this trypanosome was the cause of sleeping sickness and that it was carried by a species of tsetse fly, known as *Glossina palpalis*, the distribution of which was limited to open water. Dr Forde's discovery has therefore very materially aided the medical world in its campaign against a very terrible scourge.

Mention of the *Trypanosoma gambiense* and its evil ways indicates but one of the numerous diseases, which the medical authorities have to combat in the Gambia as well as in other parts of West Africa. In addition to disease they have also to combat the ignorance and superstition, which has prevailed for so many centuries in this as in other parts of Africa and which has led in the past to an alarming rate of infant mortality and to a general neglect of many matters vitally affecting public health. The campaign against these things has not been confined to work in hospitals and dispensaries, but has extended beyond these institutions in the form of propaganda and other work, of which such things as "Health Weeks" and "Baby Weeks" are only one example. A civil hospital was erected in Bathurst in 1854. Since that date it has been enlarged and improved. Much has also been done of recent years to provide for the needs of the people of the Protectorate, as for example in the opening of dispensaries in the Protectorate, which, it may be mentioned, treat a number of patients from French as well as British territory, two Maternity and Infant Welfare Clinics, and lastly, but by no means least, by the erection in 1938 of a well-equipped hospital at Bansang.

Some mention must also be made in this chapter of the recent activities of the various missionary societies, which both now and in the past have very materially assisted the Government in its work for the welfare of the native population.

The history of the Church of England in the Gambia dates back to 1821, when at the request of Sir Charles MacCarthy the Church Missionary Society sent out Robert Hughes as chaplain to the garrison. Unfortunately the chaplain and his wife both died within less than six months of arrival. Thereafter further deaths and invalidings very materially interfered with the continuity of the work. During the all too frequent vacancies in the post of chaplain the duty was supplied by one of the members of the Wesleyan Mission. The result of these many casualties was that for many years there was no really settled Anglican congregation as far as the bulk of the people were concerned.[1]

Though communion plate and church furniture were obtained as early as 1819,[2] the Church of England was for many years without a proper place of worship. In 1836 the Government allowed them

[1] Rev. G. W. Nicol in *Annual Report for* 1871.
[2] S. Lushington to H. Goulburn, 30 November 1819.

the use of the former officers' mess for services on Sundays, the building being used on week-days as a garrison school. In 1844 a local subscription was raised for the erection of a church, but the plan came to nothing as Lord Stanley could not see his way to sanction a grant in aid.[1] In 1869 a church school was opened. Two years later another school was opened for Sereres, which was supported by voluntary subscriptions from the Bishop of Sierra Leone and others. In 1900 the Government required the premises, which were then being used as a church, for other purposes and the Church of England was given a fresh site on MacCarthy Square. A building to accommodate 400 people was started in 1900 and was consecrated by Bishop Taylor Smith in 1901.

In 1855 the Anglican Church in the West Indies started a mission to the Susus on the banks of the Rio Pongas. That mission and the church at Bathurst were originally in the diocese of Sierra Leone, which was created in 1852. As the work of that diocese increased, it became necessary to subdivide it into other dioceses. In 1935 the Right Reverend John Charles Sydney Daly was consecrated the first Bishop of the Gambia and Rio Pongas.

Mention has already been made on previous pages of the work of the Wesleyan and Roman Catholic Missions. Upon these two missions and the Church of England with the help of grants in aid from the Government has fallen the bulk of the educational work in the Gambia. At the present time there are six elementary schools (including one Mohammedan school) in Bathurst. There are also four secondary schools in Bathurst, two for boys and two for girls, which are maintained by the Wesleyan and Roman Catholic Missions. In addition a Teacher Training School was opened in Bathurst in 1930 and there is a Manual Training Centre under the supervision of the Public Works Department. In the Protectorate it has been felt that more can be done to improve conditions amongst the people by a central school for the training of the sons and relatives of chiefs than by setting up a number of smaller schools, which would only have a local effect. With this object a boarding school, known as the Armitage School, has been opened at Georgetown, MacCarthy Island. In addition the Methodist Mission maintains two, the Roman Catholic Mission one, and the Anglican Mission one small school in the Protectorate.

[1] T. L. Ingram to Lord Stanley, 14 March 1844; Lord Stanley to T. L. Ingram, 27 September 1844.

Of other recent events in the Gambia there can be no doubt that the inauguration by the Deutsche Luft Hansa Aktiengesellschaft of a transatlantic air service will have a very important effect upon the future of the Gambia. The Company commenced operating their service at the beginning of 1934 and in the latter part of that year entered into an agreement with the Gambia Government for the carriage of airmail between Bathurst and the United Kingdom. At the present time the ports of call are Berlin, Stuttgart, Marseilles, Las Palmas, Bathurst and Port Natal for Buenos Aires. The Company has a landing ground at Jeshwang near Bathurst and keeps a catapulting ship regularly stationed at Bathurst. There is now a flight schedule, which brings Bathurst within twenty hours of both Berlin and Port Natal, but both these distances have been covered more than once in considerably less time.

The official visit of His Royal Highness the Prince of Wales to Bathurst in 1924 was a source of great gratification to the people of the Gambia inasmuch as it afforded them the opportunity of demonstrating their sense of intense loyalty to the British Crown and to the Empire of which His Majesty the King is the supreme head and symbol. Still further gratification was felt in 1933 when the honour of knighthood was conferred upon the Honourable Samuel John Forster, the doyen of the local bar and the senior unofficial member of the Legislative Council, in recognition of his many public services in the Gambia.

If in this concluding chapter one does not enter in any greater detail into all the activities, both official and unofficial, which have been going on in the Gambia during the last quarter of a century, it is not because one is unaware of them or seeks to belittle them. They have of recent years been innumerable and the mere record of them would fill many pages of this book. Many of the previous chapters have had much to say of battle, murder and sudden death, but the story of more recent years and, one would also believe, of the years to come must be largely gleaned from statistics and Blue Books. It may be lacking in drama and pageantry, but it is in reality a far more attractive story—a story of peace and steady progress, which has been carried out through the unassuming and unostentatious labours of many people of very different races and languages, of very different callings and walks in life, and of very different creeds and beliefs, who have none the less been united, consciously and at times subconsciously, in the furtherance of the common purpose of the promotion of the welfare of the people of the Gambia. As these pages have shown, the country has gone through many vicissitudes of fortune, but in all the course of its years it has had those, "who were not wanting to the state in their virtue, but made unto it an honourable contribution". It has behind it a long tradition of loyalty and public spirit, of which it may well be proud and which, one would fain believe, will be carried on far into the unknown future.

Index

32-2

CPSIA information can be obtained
at www.ICGtesting.com
Printed in the USA
BVOW08s1036061116

467065BV00002B/78/P